BLISS DIVINE

A Book of Spiritual Essays
On the Lofty Purpose of Human Life
And the Means to Its Achievement

SWAMI SIVANANDA

Published By

THE DIVINE LIFE SOCIETY
P.O. SHIVANANDANAGAR—249 192
Distt. Tehri-Garhwal, U.P., Himalayas, India

Price] 1997 [Rs. 180/-

First Edition: 1964 Second Edition: 1965 Third Edition: 1967 Fourth Edition: 1991

Fifth Edition: 1997
(6,000 Copies)

ISBN 81-7052-004-5

Published by Swami Krishnananda for The Divine Life Society,
Shivanandanagar, and printed by him at the Yoga-Vedanta
Forest Academy Press, P.O. Shivanandanagar,
Distt. Tehri-Garhwal, U.P., Himalayas, India

H.H. SWAMI SIVANANDAJI MAHARAJ

DEDICATED TO
THE PROMOTION OF
A HAPPY NEW CIVILISATION AND CULTURE
BUILT ON THE BLISSFUL ATMAN
THAT PERVADES ALL

PUBLISHERS' NOTE

This is the age of scepticism and materialism. Wealth tempts people like a deceptive mirage. It hardens the heart of man and causes pride in him and makes him forget God.

Materialistic civilisation has made man insincere and untruthful. Rudderless, the ship of human civilisation is heading fast towards the rock of self-aggrandisement, hatred, aimless living, and eventually, self-destruction.

The present world is full of fear, suspicion, crimes, conflicts, quarrels and struggles. The philosophy of flesh substitutes licence for discipline and self-indulgence for self-sacrifice. The real ideal of religion is forgotten, the spirit of religion is lost, and only a poor external structure remains.

Scientists have conquered the air and the atom. Sputniks circle around the world. But alas! Men have not realised the mysteries of the Atman, their inner Self. They have conquered nature. and outer space, but they have not conquered their arch enemy, mind.

Mere intelligence, without morality and spirituality, is not helpful. It is dangerous. It will lead to disaster.

Today, in the world convulsed by wars and revolutions, there is a great necessity to revive the moral and spiritual value of ancient Indian culture and its everlasting idealism. If the human mind is to be weaned from materialism, if humanity is to be brought together, the only way is the practice of Yoga and Vedanta.

Yoga and Vedanta are basically the same. Vedanta is the sublime philosophy that gives a directive to the Yoga way of life.

Unconscious movement is called natural evolution. Conscious evolution is Yoga or the practice of religion.

Religion is not a matter of belonging to a church or of professing a creed. It is a matter of evolving a deeper insight and understanding and expressing it through life.

It is this insight and this understanding which the great Master Sivananda seeks to impart in the pages of BLISS DIVINE.

BLISS DIVINE is an immortal work, a legacy for ages to

come. It is a spiritual classic. It is a Bible for the Christians, a Bhagavad-Gita for the Hindus, a Koran for the Muslims, a Zend-Avesta for the Parsis. It sums up the teachings of all scriptures of all ages.

Not only that; it offers comfort and consolation, enlightenment and elucidation, in a manner which makes a direct appeal to the modern mind. No line is vague. No explanation is hidden.

Optimism is the keynote of the book. Its pages abound in constructive suggestions for a fuller, happier life, right now, here on earth.

Each essay is self-contained and can be read apart from the rest of the book. The author has prefaced the book with a beautiful introduction, unsurpassed for depth of meaning and lucidity of presentation.

Shivanandanagar,
1st March 1974. —THE DIVINE LIFE SOCIETY

A WORD ABOUT "BLISS DIVINE"

This valuable and excellent anthology of a sage's Wisdom Teachings is in the nature of a devout disciple's votive offering at the feet of his spiritual preceptor or Guru. This book comprises an act of Guruseva and dedication. By this work the compiler, my Guru-Bandhu SRI ANANTHANARAYANAN, fulfilled an ardent wish of the holy Master SWAMI SIVANANDAJI MAHARAJ for such a collection and as such he has given concrete form to a pure Sankalpa of a saint who sought to serve mankind by helping it see light in the midst of darkness and guide it along the Path of Goodness. Unable to fulfil Gurudev's desire during His lifetime due to His sudden and unexpected demise, Sri Ananthanarayanan laboured hard night and day to posthumously offer this work at the altar of his Master's sacred and hallowed memory. This embodies an earnest and unsparing labour of Love.

The worthy compiler's association with Swami Sivanandaji was over a period of more than a decade. Sri Ananthanarayanan was an officer in the Planning Commission in the Central Government at Delhi when he first visited Rishikesh to meet the Sage of Ananda Kutir. He was enthused by Gurudev's idea of Jnana Yajna and inspired by His personality of indubitable spiritual eminence. He was charmed by the saint's spontaneous and motiveless love. Back at Delhi, he set to work and brought out a beautiful little collection of Gurudev's teachings under the caption "Pearls on the Shore of Wisdom". Perhaps this first booklet actually anticipated and proved a precursor to this present "BLISS DIVINE". Eminently qualified for this work more than anyone else, due to his high academic attainment, Ananthanarayanan has been happily endowed by providence with keen intelligence and literary ability. Hence the high quality of this present volume which is being acclaimed by numerous readers as the best publication so far brought out by the Divine Life Society. Born at Kodaikanal in 1927, Ananthanarayanan grew up as an idealistic youth with a sensitive disposition appreciative of higher values in life. It was natural, therefore, that he found scant satisfaction in his secular college education even when he secured a triple First-class in the B.Sc. examination in 1946 at the young age of 19. Going on to pass a higher degree examination, he took a Master of Arts degree in Economics, but felt that the entire period of his education was "wasted" since he saw no substantial benefit therefrom in the shape of inner spiritual evolution or uplift of his higher being.

This discontent made him turn to spiritual literature and he avidly absorbed the wise and lofty teachings of Swami Vivekananda, Mahatma Gandhi, Swami Rama Tirtha and other luminaries of recent times. Inevitably he soon came into contact with Swami Sivananda's spiritual teachings which were at that time flooding this land like the very waters of Life to the seeking souls everywhere. He felt now that Gurudev's writings were showing him the path. At last the right path had been shown to him in clear and unambiguous terms in a most practical manner and inspiringly too. This drew him to Swamiji when he got appointed at Delhi and thus came near to Rishikesh. Gurudev showered gifts of books upon Ananthanarayananji and won his heart for His divine mission of Dissemination of Spiritual Knowledge. Not much later the power and the influence of His sublime teachings decided the future course of this ardent young seeker. He resolved his step and unhesitatingly threw to the winds all prospects of worldly prosperity and advancement, and renouncing his covetable post in the Central Government, turned his back to secular life and joined Swami Sivananda. Since that day he has done and is still doing yeoman service to the great Guru's holy Mission with deep sincerity and earnestness.

Through this present volume "BLISS DIVINE" Sri Ananthanarayanan has presented to modern India a rare compendium of spiritual wisdom and brought to the educated classes a comprehensive yet choicest collection of Sianandaji's teachings to present-day humanity. The essence of our country's culture and ideals is contained in this beautiful compilation of his. He has put us all into a deep debt of gratitude which we can only repay by making this "BLISS DIVINE" our life's Guide and Companion! May God bless him and may Gurudev's Grace be with him always!

Swami Chidananda

ॐ

Shivanandanagar, *President*

Vijaya Dasami,

5-10-1965. THE DIVINE LIFE SOCIETY

CONTENTS

INTRODUCTION

The Atman

Bliss is the essential nature of man. The central fact of man's being is his inherent divinity.

Man's essential nature is divine, the awareness of which he has lost because of his animal propensities and the veil of ignorance. Man, in his ignorance, identifies himself with the body, mind, Prana, and the senses. Transcending these, he becomes one with Brahman or the Absolute who is pure bliss.

Brahman or the Absolute is the fullest reality, the completest consciousness. That beyond which there is nothing, that which is the innermost Self of all is Atman or Brahman. The Atman is the common Consciousness in all beings. A thief, a prostitute, a scavenger, a king, a rogue, a saint, a dog, a cat, a rat—all have the same common Atman.

There is apparent, fictitious difference in bodies and minds only. There are differences in colours and opinions. But, the Atman is the same in all.

If you are very rich, you can have a steamer, a train. an airship of your own for your own selfish interests. But. you cannot have an Atman of your own. The Atman is common to all. It is not an individual's sole registered property.

The Atman is the one amidst the many. It is constant amidst the forms which come and go. It is the pure, absolute, essential Consciousness of all the conscious beings.

The source of all life, the source of all knowledge is the Atman, thy innermost Self. This Atman or Supreme Soul is transcendent, inexpressible, uninferable, unthinkable, indescribable, the ever-peaceful, all-blissful.

There is no difference between the Atman and bliss. The Atman is bliss itself. God, perfection, peace, immortality, bliss are one. The goal of life is to attain perfection, immortality or God. The nearer one approaches the Truth, the happier one becomes. For, the essential nature of Truth is positive, absolute bliss.

There is no bliss in the finite. Bliss is only in the Infinite. Eternal bliss can be had only from the eternal Self.

To know the Self is to enjoy eternal bliss and everlasting peace. Self-realisation bestows eternal existence, absolute knowledge, and perennial bliss.

None can be saved without Self-realisation. The quest for the Absolute should be undertaken even sacrificing the dearest object, even life, even courting all pain.

Study philosophical books as much as you like, deliver lectures and lectures throughout your global tour, remain in a Himalayan cave for one hundred years, practise Pranayama for fifty years, you cannot attain emancipation without the realisation of the oneness of the Self.

What Moksha Implies

Oneness of Self or oneness of Existence is Reality, and the realisation of this Reality is Moksha.

Moksha is the breaking down of the barriers that constitute separate existence. Moksha is the absolute state of Being, where the unity of all-pervading and all-permeating consciousness is realised with certainty, like that of an orange which we see in our palm.

Moksha is not an attainment of liberation from an actual state of bondage, but is the realisation of the liberation which already exists. It is freedom from the false notion of bondage.

The individual soul feels itself to be in bondage on account of ignorance caused by the power of Avidya. When the false belief caused by delusion is removed by Knowledge of Atman, the state of Moksha is realised then and there, in this very life. It is not to follow after death.

The cause of delusion is the desire in man. The desires generate the thought-waves, and the thought-waves veil the real nature of the Soul which is blissful, immortal, and eternal. When the desires are annihilated, Knowledge of Brahman dawns on the individual.

Knowledge of Brahman is not an action. You cannot reach Brahman even as you cannot reach yourself except by knowing yourself. Knowledge of Brahman is absolute and direct. It is intuitive experience.

Reason and Intuition

Intuition dawns like a flash. It does not grow bit by bit. The immediate knowledge through intuition unites the individual soul with the Supreme Soul. Intuition merges the subject and the object of knowledge, together with the process of knowing, into the Absolute where there is no duality. In intuition, time becomes eternity, space becomes infinity.

Intuitive knowledge alone is the highest knowledge. It is the imperishable, infinite knowledge of Truth. Sense-knowledge is a knowledge of appearance, and not of Truth.

Sensing is false knowledge and intuition is right knowledge. You can attain Atma-Jnana or Knowledge of the Self through intuition and intuition alone.

Without developing intuition, the intellectual man remains imperfect. Intellect has not got that power to get into the inner chamber of Truth. Intellect functions in the realm of duality, but is powerless in the realm of non-duality.

Mind and intellect are finite instruments. Reason is finite. It cannot penetrate the Infinite. Intuition alone can penetrate the Infinite.

The scientific attempts to prove the Infinite are futile. The only scientific method here is the intuitional.

Meditation leads to intuition. Meditation is the key to unfold the divinity or Atman hidden in all names and forms.

The Meditational Process

There is no knowledge without meditation. The aspirant churns his own soul. Truth becomes manifest.

Through regular meditation, you gradually grow in spirituality. The divine flame grows brighter and brighter.

Meditation gradually offers you the eternal light and intuition. By constant practice of concentration and meditation, the mind becomes as transparent and pure as a crystal. The din of the strife for things mundane becomes smaller and smaller as one recedes inside.

There are laws on the new plane. The music is different. The notes are very sweet. There is a perpetual pervading of something better.

The lustre of spiritual awakening changes the perspective and one seeks devotedly that which will bring him real lasting joy and peace in the long run. Therefore, the seeking of material and immediate advantages becomes less urgent.

Meditation leads you more and more inward, from the gross to the subtle, from the subtle to the subtler, from the subtler to the subtlest, the Supreme Spirit.

Going beyond the consciousness of the body by meditating on the Lord, one attains the universal lordship. All his desires are satisfied.

Meditation is the only right royal way for attaining immortality and eternal bliss. Peace and bliss are not to be found in books, churches, or monasteries. It is realised when Knowledge of Atman dawns.

Why do you read many books? It is of no use. The great book is within your heart. Open the pages of this inexhaustible book, the source of all knowledge. You will know everything.

Close your eyes. Withdraw your senses. Still the mind. Silence the bubbling thoughts. Make the mind waveless. Merge deep into the Atman or the Self, the Supreme Soul, the Light of lights, the Sun of suns. All knowledge will be revealed to you. All doubts will now vanish. All mental torments will disappear. All hot discussions, heated debates will terminate. Peace and Jnana alone will remain.

All names and forms vanish in deep meditation. There is consciousness of infinite space. This also disappears. There is a state of nothingness. Suddenly dawns illumination, Nirvikalpa Samadhi.

The Bliss of Samadhi

Nirvikalpa Samadhi is the realisation of the highest value. During Nirvikalpa Samadhi, the Reality is intuited in all its wholeness. It is the experience of oneness with the Absolute. You have Brahmic superconsciousness, in place of the stilled Jiva-consciousness.

Experience of fullness is called Samadhi. It is freedom from misery. It is bliss absolute.

Samadhi is not the abolition of personality. It is the completion of personality. In that state of supreme illumination, you feel the oneness of subject and object. You see nothing else, hear nothing else, know nothing else.

The knowledge simply illumines. It does not require you to do something after that illumination.

To know is to be. Knowing and being cannot be separated. Chit and Sat are one and the same. Where absolute knowledge and absolute existence prevail, there is also absolute bliss.

The bliss of Self-realisation cannot be described in words. Tranquillity which nothing can touch, supreme peace without a ruffle, light and bliss unalloyed—such is the glimpse of Self-realisation.

Sensual pleasure is nothing when compared with the bliss of meditation and Samadhi. Rise from the sense-life. Awake and realise that you are the pure, immortal Atman. Behold the one Atman in all beings and attain immortality and bliss eternal.

Hear all about Atman or Soul. Then understand the Atman. Then reflect on the Atman. Then meditate on the Atman. Then realise the Atman. *Tat Tvam Asi.* That Thou Art.

Thou art Atman! Atman art Thou. Realise this and be free. Nothing can hinder thee from the realisation of thy essential nature.

Self-realisation is not an invention. It is only discovery of the Self. It is knowing one's Self. It is awareness.

Self-realisation is nothing to be attained afresh. You need not reach or attain the Atman or the Self. You are, indeed, the Atman or Supreme Self. Only, you will have to open your inner eyes.

The Vedanta philosophy summons the individual to his own freedom, glory, and dignity. Know this source of freedom, the root of bliss, and be free.

Bliss is, indeed, thy essential nature. Bliss is your birthright. You are a glorious heir to bliss infinite. Realise this bliss right now, in this very second.

Look not outside for light, peace, joy, and bliss, but look

within. Moksha or salvation is neither in heaven nor in Mt. Kailas. The inexhaustible, supreme divine treasure, the Atmic pearl, is locked up in the chambers of your own heart, in the casket of silence. Discover the true Reality in the very heart of your own subjectivity, in the very depth of your own being.

Maya and Mind

There is no duality in Reality. All modification is illusory. Multiplicity is an illusion.

Maya projects multiplicity. Maya creates division, division between the individual soul and the Supreme Soul.

Maya is a tremendous, delusive power of God. Maya is the material stuff of this world. Maya is the source of the physical universe. This world of names and forms is a false show kept up by the jugglery of Maya.

Just as a stick burning at one end, when waved round quickly, produces an illusion of a circle of fire, Alata Chakra, so is it with the multiplicity of the world. Maya deludes us.

Maya havocs through the mind. The things that we perceive all round us are only mind in form or substance.

The world is a product of the mind. The whole world is an expansion of the mind. The entire universe arises and exists in the mind.

Nothing of the world is outside the mind. Earth, mountains, and rivers—all are fragments of the mind, appearing as it were to exist outside

The world does not exist by itself. It is not seen without the aid of the mind. It disappears when the mind ceases to function.

It is imagination alone that assumes the forms of time, space, and motion. Space and time have no independent status apart from Brahman or the Self, which is Awareness.

There is no space without time, and there is no time without space. Space and time go together. Space and time are interdependent. They are unreal.

Time and space are mental creations. Time and space are mental projections, unreal as dreams. However real they may seem to be, they are not ultimately real. Timeless, spaceless Brahman is the only Reality.

Brahman alone is. It is Brahman alone that shines as the world of variegated objects, like waves differentiating the water into many kinds of foam, bubbles, etc. Brahman appears as the world when cognised through the mind and the senses.

Matter and Spirit

This whole universe is the body of God. This entire world is God or Virat Svarupa. This world is not a world of dead matter, but a living Presence. This world is a manifestation of the Spirit.

The fundamental error of all ages is the belief that the spiritual world and the material are separate. Spirit and matter are neither different nor separable.

Matter is Spirit cognised through the senses. Matter is spirit in manifestation. Matter is Spirit in motion. Matter is power of the Lord. Matter is dynamic aspect of the static Lord. The world is an expression of Brahman, the Absolute.

This world is a shadow of Brahman. It is an overflow of the bliss of Brahman. It is an emanation of God. It is a manifestation of God. It is a reflection of God. The world is charged with the splendour, glory, and grandeur of God.

God is the one light that shines in various forms. He is the one voice that speaks in various languages. He is the one life that thrills through every atom in the universe.

God fills everywhere. God is equally and fully contained in all things.

The world is a play of God. God, the warp and the woof, is blended with the world.

As there is no difference between gold and ornaments, so there is no difference between God and the universe. God is the relisher. He Himself is the relish.

The world is not different from God. God is within and without everything. There is no place where God is not. Everything is God, and there is nothing but God.

Is the World Unreal?

In reality, there is no world. It is a mere appearance, like the snake in the rope. All names and forms are unreal like the shadow, like water in the mirage, blueness in the sky.

The unreality of the world is the truth in the ultimate analysis. But, in relative existence, one cannot deny it. It is quite real from the empirical standpoint.

This world is not absolutely unreal, because you experience it, you feel it. It is not absolutely real also, because it vanishes when you attain wisdom.

This world is unreal: for whom? and when? For a liberated sage alone, this world is unreal. It is a solid reality for a worldly man. When you wake up alone, the dream becomes unreal. When you are dreaming, the dream is quite real to you.

This world is unreal. But in what sense? Is it as unreal as the horn of a hare or a barren woman's son or the lotus in the sky? No. It is not as much solid or reality as Brahman is. When compared with Brahman, it is unreal. It is mere appearance.

Creation is the appearance of the Lord, who is one, as many. Atman, who is one and immutable by nature, seems to have assumed innumerable forms. Brahman or the Absolute manifests Itself as the universe through forms.

The Riddle of Evil

This world is God's revelation of Himself. His bliss or joy assumes all these forms.

All life is alike. The universal heart beats in the minutest life. The Lord breathes in all life.

Just as one thread penetrates all flowers in a garland, so also, one Self penetrates all these living beings. Behold this one Self in all. Serve all. Love all. Be kind to all. Give up the idea of diversity.

The world is neither good nor bad. The mind creates good and evil. Thinking makes it so.

To the good, the world is full of good; but to the bad, the world is full of evil.

The evil is not in the world. It is in the mind. Man sees only the reflection of his mind. If you become perfect, the world will appear good.

Behold the Lord always, in everything. You will see no evil. You will see good everywhere. You will find peace.

Unity of Existence

One Soul abides in all. There is one humanity. There is one brotherhood. There is one Atmahood. None is high. None is low. All are equal. Vain are the distinctions. Man-made barriers should be ruthlessly broken down. Then alone there will be peace in this world.

There is only one caste, the caste of humanity. There is only one religion, the religion of love. There is only one commandment, the commandment of truthfulness. There is only one law, the law of cause and effect. There is only one God, the omnipresent, omnipotent, omniscient Lord. There is only one language, the language of the heart or the language of silence.

All life is one. The world is one home. All are members of one human family. All creation is an organic whole. No man is independent of that whole. Man makes himself miserable by separating himself from others. Separation is death. Unity is eternal life. Cultivate cosmic love. Include all. Embrace all. Recognise the worth of others. Destroy all barriers, racial, religious and natural prejudices that separate man from man. Recognise the non-dual principles, the immortal essence within all creatures. Protect animals. Let all life be sacred. Then this world will be a paradise of beauty, a heaven of peace and tranquillity.

When one Atman dwells in all living beings, then why do you hate others? Why do you sneer and frown at others? Why do you use harsh words? Why do you try to rule and domineer over others? Why do you exploit others? Why are you intolerant? Is this not the height of your folly? Is this not sheer ignorance?

Learn to live as members of a single family. Champion the ideal of one humanity. Live in peace in one world. All are children of God. The whole world is one family of God. Feel this. Realise this. Be happy.

Behold the One-in-all and all-in-One. Feel: "I am the all" and "I am in all". Feel: "All bodies are mine. The whole world is my body, my sweet home". Feel: "I work in all hands. I eat in all mouths". Feel: "I am the immortal Self in all". Repeat these formulae mentally several times daily. Repeat Om mentally and feel oneness of life or unity of consciousness when you play football or tennis, when you drink and eat, when you talk and sing, when you sit and walk, when you bathe and dress, when you write a letter, when you do work in the office, when you answer calls of nature. Spiritualise every movement, action, thought, and feeling. Transmute them into Yoga.

Yoga and the Practice of Religion

Yoga is a conscious and sustained attempt towards self-perfection. The goal of Yoga is to calm the mind so that it may mirror without distortion the Atman that is behind the mind.

Restrain the senses. Control the mind. Meditate regularly. Be a Yogi, be a Yogi, be a Yogi. Live the Yogic life and spread the great doctrine.

You have forgotten to look within, to gaze within, to introspect, concentrate and meditate, and so you are ignorant, you are lost in darkness.

Introspect. Look within. Try to remove your defects. This is the real Sadhana. This is the most difficult Sadhana. You will have to do it at any cost. Intellectual development is nothing. It is more easy.

Sit at the Central Library, Baroda or Imperial Library, Calcutta for three to six years with a dictionary by your side. You can develop your intellect. But removal of defects needs a great deal of struggle for many years. Many vicious habits will have to be rent asunder.

There are big Mandalesvars who can deliver lectures for a week on one Sloka of the Gita or the Upanishads. They command respect, and yet they are disliked by the public, because they still have great defects. They have not done much introspection. They have not done drastic Sadhana to remove their defects. They have developed only their intellect. What a great pity!

True religion begins where intellect ends. An impure heart, a conceited intellect, cannot understand the spirit of religion.

Religion is a manifestation of the eternal glow of the Spirit within man. The main purpose of religion is the unfoldment of the divinity within man.

Prayer and meditation are the chief pillars of religion. A life of selfless service and sacrifice, with regular prayer and meditation, is the highest religion.

Practice of religion is the practice of righteousness, goodness, justice, truth, love, and purity. The righteous man is the truly religious man.

The ringing notes of religion are: Be good. Do good. Be pure. Be kind. Be compassionate. Serve all. Love all. See God in all.

The practice of these precepts alone will awaken man to the consciousness of the unity of existence and the realisation of the Divine Spirit within and without.

Religion is life. Life is sacrifice. One may meticulously perform religious devotion, and yet be very irreligious at heart and conduct. Religion should be a living experience in the life of man.

Religion is living, not speaking or showing. Real religion is the religion of the heart. The heart must be purified first.

The Path of Selfless Service

Practise the religion of the heart. Build on the edifice of love.

Selfless service purifies the heart and opens it for the receipt of divine light. Plunge in selfless service.

Cheer up a man who is in distress. Encourage a man when he is dispirited. Wipe the tears of the afflicted. Remove the sorrow in a man by kind, loving words. Make a man smile when he is in despair.

Be a lamp to those who have lost their way. Be a doctor and nurse to the ailing patients. Be a boat and bridge to those who want to reach the other shore of fearlessness and immortality.

Do your duty to the best of your ability and leave the rest to God. Do all your actions detachedly in a spirit of dedication to the Divine. Then actions will not bind you. Your heart will be purified.

Spiritualise all your activities. Let your eyes look with kindness, your tongue speak with sweetness, your hand touch with softness. Be thou as compassionate as Buddha, as pure as Bhishma, as truthful as Harischaṇdra, as brave as Bhima.

Feed your mind with thoughts of God, your heart with purity, and your hands with selfless service. Remain soaked in the remembrance of God with one-pointed mind.

The Goal of Life

God has a Master-plan. We have our parts to play.

Play out your part well in the worldly play. But, do not fetter yourself. Keep your mind steady on the lotus-feet of the Lord. You will swim in the ocean of divine bliss.

Have no attachment for this mortal body of flesh and bone. Cast it off like a slough anywhere, just as the snake throws away its skin. Make up your mind to give up the body at any moment. Become absolutely fearless.

As long as there is the least Deha-Adhyasa, identification with the body, so long you cannot expect Self-realisation. Exhibit undaunted spirit, intrepidity, and manliness. Make a strong resolve: "I will die or realise".

Birth and death, bondage and freedom, pleasure and pain, gain and loss, are mental creations. Transcend the pairs of opposites. You were never born. You will never die. Thou art the immortal Self always, O Prem! Thou art ever free in the three periods of time. It is the physical body that goes and comes.

Recognise, O Prem, that you are the living Truth. Realise that you are always inseparable from the one essence that is the substratum of all these illusory names and forms, these false shadowy appearances. Get yourself firmly established in the Brahman, the Light of lights. Nothing can disturb you now. You have become invulnerable. Feel this. Feel this through intuition when you enter into deep Samadhi or supreme silence, my child!

The god of death will tremble before you now. By your command the sun shines, the fire burns, and the wind blows. By your command Indra, Prajapati, Agni, and Varuna do their respective functions. Thou art beyond time, space, and causation.

You must not be afraid of Maya now. She is under your perfect control now. Stand firm like the yonder rock. Be adamantine. Move about in the world now like a lion and lift up the young, struggling souls out of the mire of Samsara. Disseminate Knowledge of the Self. Share it with others. Be catholic, liberal, universal, all-inclusive. Love all. Be kind to all. Expand thy heart. Have space in thy heart for all, even for that man who is planning to poison you, who is drawing the dagger to cut your throat. Become a practical Vedantin. Become a Kriya-Advaitin.

Rely on your own Self, your own inner spiritual strength. Stand on your own feet. Do not depend on money, friends, or anyone. When the friends are put to the test, they will desert you. Lord Buddha never trusted even his disciples. When he was seriously ailing, he himself jumped like a frog to drink water from the river. Be not bound to anybody, any place, or thing. Do not desire to possess. Possessions bring pain. Become absolutely free by identifying with the inner Self, thy Inner Ruler, immortal. Challenge the whole world now.

Stand up, O Prem! Follow me. Enjoy the bliss of Atman. The river of Atmic joy is flowing all around. There is a deluge of Bliss of Self. Drink this nectar to your heart's content. Care not for the world. Go thy own way. Let others hoard up wealth and become multi-millionaires and mill-owners. They are misers only. Let others become barristers, high court judges, and ministers. They are still ignorant men. Mind not a bit. The wealth of the three worlds is nothing, mere straw, before the spiritual wealth, the wealth of Atma-Jnana. The joy of the three worlds is a mere drop when compared to the ocean of bliss of the Self. The knowledge of all secular sciences is mere husk when compared to the Knowledge of the Self. Here are the priceless treasures of Atman for thee. Here is the inexhaustible wealth of Brahma-Jnana. Enjoy these riches. No dacoit or robber can rob thee of this imperishable wealth of Tattva-Jnana. No insolvency, no failure of bank, no bankruptcy here. Take possession of this spiritual treasure, the splendour of Brahman, and enjoy for ever and ever. Thou art now a real King of kings, Shah of shahs. Emperor of emperors. Indra and Brahma will be jealous of thee now, O Prem! Go and distribute this imperishable wealth of Knowledge of Self far and wide. Glory unto thee! Peace be with thee for ever and ever!

Bliss Divine

1. AHIMSA

In the regeneration and divinisation of man, the first step is to eliminate the beastly nature. The predominant trait in beasts is cruelty. Therefore wise sages prescribed Ahimsa. This is a most effective master-method to counteract and eradicate completely the brutal, cruel Pasu-Svabhava in man.

Practice of Ahimsa develops love. Ahimsa is another name for truth or love. Ahimsa is universal love. It is pure love. It is divine Prem. Where there is love, there is Ahimsa. Where there is Ahimsa, there is love and selfless service. They all go together.

The one message of all saints, prophets of all times and climes, is the message of love, of Ahimsa, of selfless service. Ahimsa is the noblest and best of traits that are found expressed in the daily life and activities of perfected souls. Ahimsa is the one means, not only to attain Salvation, but also to enjoy uninterrupted peace and bliss. Man attains peace by injuring no living creature.

There is one religion—the religion of love, of peace. There is one message, the message of Ahimsa. Ahimsa is a supreme duty of man.

Ahimsa, or refraining from causing pain to any living creature, is a distinctive quality emphasised by Indian ethics. Ahimsa or non-violence has been the central doctrine of Indian culture from the earliest days of its history. Ahimsa is a great spiritual force.

Meaning of Ahimsa

Ahimsa or non-injury, of course, implies non-killing. But, non-injury is not merely non-killing. In its comprehensive meaning, Ahimsa or non-injury means entire abstinence from causing any pain or harm whatsoever to any living creature, either by thought, word or deed. Non-injury needs a harmless mind, mouth and hand.

Ahimsa is not mere negative non-injuring. It is positive, cosmic love. It is development of the mental attitude in which hatred is replaced by love. Ahimsa is true sacrifice. Ahimsa is forgiveness. Ahimsa is Sakti. Ahimsa is true strength.

Subtle Forms of Ahimsa

Only the ordinary people think that Ahimsa is not to hurt any living being physically. This is but the gross form of Ahimsa. The vow of Ahimsa is broken even by showing contempt towards another man, by entertaining unreasonable dislike for or prejudice towards anybody, by frowning at another man, by hating another man, by abusing another man, by speaking ill of others, by backbiting or vilifying, by harbouring thoughts of hatred, by uttering lies, or by ruining another man in any way whatsoever.

All harsh and rude speech is Himsa. Using harsh words to beggars, servants or inferiors is Himsa. Wounding the feelings of others by gesture, expression, tone of voice and unkind words is also Himsa. Slighting or showing deliberate discourtesy to a person before others is wanton Himsa. To approve of another's harsh actions is indirect Himsa. To fail to relieve another's pain or even to neglect to go to the person in distress is a sort of Himsa. It is the sin of omission. Avoid strictly all forms of harshness, direct or indirect, positive or negative, immediate or delayed. Practise Ahimsa in its purest form and become divine. Ahimsa and divinity are one.

Ahimsa, A Quality of the Strong

If you practise Ahimsa, you should put up with insults, rebukes, criticisms and assaults also. You should never retaliate nor wish to offend anybody even under extreme provocation. You should not entertain any evil thought against anybody. You should not curse. You should not harbour anger. You should be prepared to lose joyfully even your life in the cause of Truth. The Ultimate Truth can be attained only through Ahimsa.

Ahimsa is the acme of bravery. Ahimsa is not possible without fearlessness. Non-violence cannot be practised by weak persons. Ahimsa cannot practised by a man who is terribly afraid of death and has no power of endurance and resistance. It is a shield, not of the effeminate, but of the potent. Ahimsa is a quality of the behaviour of the strong. It is weapon of the strong. When a man beats you with a stick, you should not entertain any thought of retaliation or any unkind feeling towards the tormentor. Ahimsa is the perfection of forgiveness.

Remember the actions of great sages of yore. Jayadeva, the author of Gita-Govinda, gave large and rich presents to his enemies who cut off his hands, and got Mukti for them by sincere prayers. He said, "O my Lord! Thou hast given Mukti to Thy enemies Ravana and Kamsa. Why canst Thou not give Mukti to my enemies now?". A saint or a sage possesses a magnanimous heart.

Pavahari Baba carried the bag of vessels and followed the thief and said, "O Thief Narayana! I never knew that You visited my cottage. Pray accept these things". The thief was quite astonished. He left off his evil habit from that very second and became a disciple of Pavahari Baba.

Remembering the noble actions of saints like Jayadeva and Pavahari Baba, you will have to follow their principles and ideals.

Gradational Practice of Ahimsa

When thoughts of revenge and hatred arise in the mind, try to control the physical body and speech first. Do not utter evil and harsh words. Do not censure. Do not try to injure others. If you succeed in this by practice for some months, the thoughts of revenge, having no scope for manifesting outside, will die by themselves. It is extremely difficult to control such thoughts from the very beginning without having recourse to control of body and speech first.

First control your physical body. When a man beats you, keep quiet. Suppress your feelings. Follow the instructions of Jesus Christ and his Sermon On The Mount. Says Jesus: "If a man beats you on one cheek, turn to him the other cheek also. If a man takes your coat, give him your shirt also". This is very difficult in the beginning. The old Samskaras of revenge, 'tooth for tooth', 'tit for tat', 'eye for eye', and 'paying in the same coin' will all force you to retaliate. But you will have to wait coolly. Reflect and meditate. Do Vichara. The mind will become calm. The opponent who was very furious will also become calm, because he does not get any opposition from your side. He gets astonished and terrified also, because you stand like a sage. By and by, you will gain immense strength. Keep the ideal before you. Try to get at it, though with faltering steps at first. Have a clear-cut mental image of Ahimsa and its immeasurable advantages.

After controlling the body, control your speech. Make a strong determination, "I will not speak any harsh word to anybody from today". You may fail a hundred times. What does it matter? You will slowly gain strength. Check the impulse of speech. Observe Mouna. Practise Kshama or forgiveness. Say within yourself, "He is a baby soul. He is ignorant. So he has done it. Let me excuse him this time. What do I gain by abusing him in return? To err is human;

to forgive is divine". Slowly give up Abhimana. Abhimana is the root cause of human sufferings.

Finally go to the thoughts and check the thought of injuring. Never *think* also of injuring anyone. One Self dwells in all. All are manifestations of the One God. By injuring another, you but injure your own Self. By serving another, you serve your own Self. Love all. Serve all. Hate none. Insult none. Injure none in thought, word and deed. Try to behold your own Self in all beings. This will promote Ahimsa.

Benefits of the Practice of Ahimsa

If you are established in Ahimsa, you have attained all virtues. Ahimsa is the pivot. All virtues revolve round Ahimsa. Just as all footprints get accommodated in those of the elephant, so also do all religions and ethical rules become merged in the great vow of Ahimsa.

Ahimsa is soul-force. Hate melts in the presence of love. Hate dissolves in the presence of Ahimsa. There is no power greater than Ahimsa. The practice of Ahimsa develops will-power to a considerable degree. The practice of Ahimsa will make you fearless. He who practises Ahimsa with real faith can move the whole world, can tame wild animals, can win the hearts of all, and can subdue his enemies. He can do and undo things. The force of Ahimsa is infinitely more wonderful and subtle than that of electricity or magnetism.

The law of Ahimsa is as much exact and precise as the law of gravitation or cohesion. You must know the way to apply it intelligently with scientific accuracy. If you are able to apply it with exactitude and precision, you can work wonders. You can command the elements and Nature also.

The Power of Ahimsa

The power of Ahimsa is greater than the power of the intellect. It is easy to develop the intellect, but it is difficult to develop the heart. The practice of Ahimsa develops the heart in a wonderful manner.

He who practises Ahimsa develops a strong will-power. In his presence, enmity ceases. In his presence, cobra and frog, cow and tiger, mongoose and cobra, cat and rat, wolf and lamb, will all live together in terms of intimate friendship. In his presence, all hostilities are given up. The term 'hostilities are given up' means that all beings—men, animals, birds and poisonous creatures—would approach the practitioner without fear and would do no harm to him. Their hostile nature disappears in them in his presence. The rat and the cat, the snake and the mongoose, and other beings that are enemies to each other by nature, give up their hostile feelings in the presence of the Yogi who is established in Ahimsa. Lions and tigers can never do any harm to such a Yogi. Such a Yogi can give definite orders to lions and tigers. They will obey. This is Bhuta Siddhi obtainable by the practice of Ahimsa. The practice of Ahimsa will culminate eventually in realisation of unity and oneness of life, or Advaitic consciousness.

Limitations to the Practice of Ahimsa

Absolute Ahimsa is impossible. It is not possible to the most conscientious Sannyasin. To practise that, you must avoid killing countless creatures, walking, sitting, eating, breathing, sleeping and drinking. You cannot find a single non-injurer in the world. You have to destroy life in order to live. It is physically impossible for you to obey the law of non-destruction of life, because the phagocytes of your blood also are destroying millions of dangerous intrusive spirilla, bacteria and germs.

According to one school of thought, if by the murder of a dacoit thousands of lives can be saved, it is not considered as Himsa. Ahimsa and Himsa are relative terms. Some say that one can defend himself with instruments and use a little violence when he is in danger; and this also is not considered to be Himsa. English people generally shoot their dear horses and dogs when the animals are in acute agony, and when there is no way of relieving their sufferings. They wish that the soul should be immediately freed from the physical body. Motive is the chief factor. It underlies everything.

A Sannyasin should not defend himself and use violence even when his life is in jeopardy. To an ordinary man, Ahimsa should be the aim; but he will not fall from this principle if, out of sheer necessity and with no selfish aim, he has recourse to Himsa occasionally. One should not give leniency to the mind in this respect. If you are lenient, the mind will always take the best advantage of this and will goad you to do acts of violence. *Give a rogue an inch, he will take an ell:* the mind at once adopts this policy, if you give a long rope for its movement.

Ahimsa is never a policy. It is a sublime virtue. It is the fundamental quality of seekers of Truth. No Self-realisation is possible without Ahimsa. It is through the practice of Ahimsa alone that you can cognise and reach the Supreme Self or Brahman. Those with whom Ahimsa is a policy may fail many a time. They will be tempted to do violent acts also. On the contrary, those who strictly adhere to the vow of Ahimsa as a sacred creed or fundamental canon of Yoga can never be duped into violence.

A Universal Vow

Ahimsa is a Mahavratam or great universal vow. It should be practised by all people of all countries. It does not concern the Hindus or Indians alone. Whoever wishes to realise the Truth must practise Ahimsa. You may encounter any amount of difficulties; you may sustain any amount of losses; but you must not give up the practice of Ahimsa. Trials and difficulties are bound to come in your way to test your strength. You should stand adamant. Then alone will your efforts be crowned with sanguine success.

There is a hidden power in Ahimsa which protects the practitioners. The invisible hand of God gives protection. There is no fear. What can pistols and swords do?

Even now there are people who do not give the least pain to flies or ants. They carry sugar and rice for distribution to the ants in their holes. They do not use lights at night for fear of killing the small insects. They are very careful in walking in the streets, as they do not want to trample down small insects. Blessed are these men. They will soon see God as they have soft hearts.

2. ANGER

A Bengalee used one word, *Sala* or *Badmash*, in anger against a Sikh, when they were crossing the Ganga in a boat. The Sikh became very furious, caught hold of the neck of the Bengalee, and threw him into the Ganga. The Bengalee died. How mentally weak was the Sikh, though he was physically very strong! A little sound, a single word, upset his mind and threw him out of balance. He became a slave of anger.

Anger makes everybody its slave and victim. It breaks the friendship of even very intimate friends. It induces wives to quarrel with their husbands and makes them file suits. It excites all. It holds sway more or less over the whole world and over the Devatas also.

Anger destroys reason and makes man do things which cannot be dreamt of. An angry person can even kill the worshipful and vilify the pious with rude expressions. The angry man cannot decide what to speak and what not to utter. There is no sin that cannot be committed by him. Under the influence of anger, man abuses, insults and even murders his father, brother, wife, Guru or king and repents afterwards.

Anger is very powerful. It can destroy all Tapas. It subdued Devatas. It conquered Yajnavalkya. It is the enemy of peace. It is the foe of knowledge. It makes the Jiva senseless. It makes him do all Adharmas. It makes him perfectly blind. It makes him its slave.

A Sign of Weakness

Anger is a strong emotion, excited by a real or a fancied injury, and involving a desire for retaliation. Anger arises from an idea of evil having been inflicted or threatened.

Anger resides in the astral body, but it percolates into the physical body just as water percolates through the pores to the outer surface of an earthen pot. The blood boils. The eyes are blood-shot. There is great heat in the body. Limbs tremble. Lips quiver. Fists are clenched. And the man stammers and fumbles for words in great fury.

The fire you kindle for your enemy burns yourself. Anger acts as a boomerang, because it injures the man who becomes angry. It comes back to the angry man and does harm to him.

Anger is a sign of mental weakness. It always begins in folly or weakness, and ends in repentance or remorse. If you control anger, you will have limitless energy in your reserve. Anger, when controlled, will be transmuted into a spiritual power which can move the whole world.

How Anger Is Caused

It was Arjuna who asked Sri Krishna: "But what impels man to commit sin, O Krishna, in spite of himself and driven as it were by force?". The blessed Lord said: "It is desire; it is wrath, which springs from passion. Know that it is our enemy here, a monster of greed and sin".

The cause of sin or wrong action in this world is desire. Anger is only a modification or form of desire. Anger is desire itself.

You think of objects of senses. Attachment to these objects develops. From attachment, desire is born. When a desire arises, it generates Rajas and urges the man to work in order to possess the object of desire. When the desire is not gratified and when someone stands in the way of its fulfilment, the man becomes angry. The desire gets transformed into anger. Just as milk is changed into curd, so also, desire becomes changed into anger.

The root cause of anger is ignorance and egoism. Anger arises when one is insulted, abused, criticised, when his defects are pointed out. Anger comes when someone stands in the way of gratifying one's desire. Anger manifests from loving one's own opinion, from desiring to be honoured, from imagining that one is wiser than and superior to all others.

Anger arises in him who thinks of his enemy. Even if you have forgotten the feeling of annoyance, it lurks in the mind in a dormant form. The effect is there for sometime. If you renew a number of times the same kind of thought of jealousy, envy or hatred about the same person, the effect lasts longer. Repetition of angry feeling intensifies hatred. Mere ill-feeling develops into intense malice by repetition of anger.

Too much loss of semen is the chief cause of irritability and anger. A passionate man is more angry than others. A man who has wasted his seminal energy becomes irritated soon for little things even. A Brahmachari, who has preserved his Veerya, always keeps a balanced mind. He has a cool brain at all times.

Passion is the root, and anger the stem. You will have to destroy the root, passion, first. Then the stem, anger, will die by itself.

Forms of Anger

Irritation, frowning, resentment, indignation, rage, fury, wrath are all varieties of anger, classified according to the degree of intensity. Anger is a sudden sentiment of displeasure. It is sharp, sudden and brief. Resentment is persistent. It is continued anger. It is the bitter brooding over injuries. Wrath is a heightened sentiment of anger. Rage drives one beyond the bounds of prudence or discretion. Fury is stronger still and sweeps one away into uncontrollable violence.

Irritability is a mild form, a subtle form, of anger. Still subtler is displeasure. It is pride mixed with anger. With a sharp word or a grunt, you dismiss the 'nuisance'. These are all forms of anger.

Anger and Righteous Indignation

Anger is personal and usually selfish. It is aroused by real or supposed wrong to oneself. Indignation is impersonal and unselfish displeasure at unworthy acts. Pure indignation is not followed by regret and needs no repentance. It is also more self-controlled than anger. Anger is commonly a sin. Indignation is often a duty. We speak of "righteous indignation".

If a man wants to correct another man, and manifests slight anger unselfishly as a force to check and improve him, then it is called 'righteous indignation' or 'spiritual anger'. Suppose a man molests a woman and tries to outrage her modesty, and a bystander becomes angry with the criminal, it is called righteous indignation or noble anger. This is not bad. Only when the anger is the outcome of greed, of selfish motives, it is bad. Sometimes a religious teacher has to manifest a little anger outwardly to correct his disciples. This is not bad. He has to do it. But he should be cool within, and hot and impetuous without. He should not allow the anger in his Antahkarana for a long time. It should pass off the next moment even as a wave subsides in the sea.

A good man's anger lasts for a second, a middling man's for three hours, a base man's for a day and a night, and a great sinner's until death.

Ill-effects of Anger

Anger spoils the brain, nervous system and blood. when a wave of anger arises in the mind, Prana begins to vibrate rapidly. You are agitated and excited. Blood becomes hot. Many poisonous ingredients are formed in the blood. When the blood is agitated, the semen also is affected.

Even three minutes of violent hot temper may produce such deleterious effects in the nervous system that it will take weeks or months for repair of the injury. In the light of modern psychology, rheumatism, heart disease, and nervous disease are all due to anger.

Once a child sucked the breasts of his mother when she was in a fit of violent fury, and died immediately on account of poisoning by virulent chemical products that were thrown into the blood of the mother when she was in great excitement. Many such cases have been recorded. Such are the disastrous effects of anger.

When anger is on the throne, reason takes to its heels. He who is influenced by anger is like one intoxicated with a strong liquor. He loses his memory, his understanding becomes clouded and his intellect gets perverted.

Anger clouds understanding. When the mind is violently agitated, you cannot understand a passage of a book clearly. You cannot think properly and clearly. You cannot write a letter with a cool mind. When the lamp is flickering through wind, you do not see the objects clearly. Even so, when the Buddhi is flickering or agitated by anger, chaos arises in the Buddhi and you are not able to see and understand things properly.

All evil qualities and actions proceed from anger. If you can eradicate anger, all bad qualities will die by themselves. Anger begets injustice, rashness, persecution, jealousy, taking possession of others' property, killing, harsh words and cruelty. An angry man loses his normal consciousness for the time being. He falls a prey to anger.

A man who is a slave to anger may have washed himself well, anointed himself well, dressed his hair, and put on white garments; yet he is ugly, being overcome by anger. There are symptoms on the face to indicate the presence of anger in the mind. If you have an easily irritable mind, you will not be able to do your daily duties and business in an efficient manner. If you get anger, you will lose the battle of life.

Methods to Control Anger

Anger is a manifestation of Sakti. It is very difficult to fight against it directly. First try to reduce its force or Vega, its frequency and duration. Endeavour to attenuate or thin out this formidable modification or Vritti. Do not allow it to assume the form of a big wave in the surface of the conscious mind. Nip it in the bud when it is in the form of irritability in the subconscious mind. Divert the mind now. Entertain divine thoughts. Do rigorous Japa or Kirtan. Repeat some prayer or Slokas of the Bhagavad Gita, the Ramayana, or the Upanishads. Develop gradually the opposite positive divine virtues such as patience, love and forgiveness. The anger will gradually die by itself.

Food has a great deal to do with irritability. Take Sattvic food such as milk, fruits, Moong-ki-dal, curd, spinach, barley, ground-nuts and buttermilk. Do not take carrots, onion, garlic, cauliflower, Masoor-ki-dal and drumstick. Give up hot curry and chutney, meat, alcohol and smoking. Smoking, meat-eating and drinking of liquors make the heart very irritable. Therefore they should be completely abandoned. Tobacco brings diseases of the heart. It gives rise to 'tobacco-heart' which gets easily irritated.

Whenever there is likelihood of a burst of anger during a conversation or debate, stop your speech. Do not argue. Do not enter into heated debates and discussions. Always try to speak sweet and soft words. The words must be soft and the arguments hard; but if the words are hard, it will bring discord. Speak sweetly. Speak little. Be mild. Be gentle. Be soft. Cultivate mildness, gentleness and softness again and again.

Control anger by pure reason. Why do you feel offended when a man calls you a dog or a donkey? Have you developed now four legs and tail like a dog? What is this abuse? Is it not mere vibration in the ether?

When you become angry with your servant when he fails to supply your usual milk on a day, raise a question within yourself: "Why should I be a slave to milk?". Then the wave of anger will at once naturally subside. It will not arise on other occasions also, if you are careful and thoughtful. It takes forty muscles to frown and only fifteen to smile. Why do you make the extra effort?

If you find it difficult to control anger, leave the place at once.

Take a long walk. Drink cold water. Repeat *Om Santi* a hundred and eight times. Do Japa of your Ishta Mantra or count from one to thirty. The anger will subside.

Self-restraint and Serenity

Good and bad are both in man. The human being is a mixture of both. All creatures contain forces of virtue and evil. It is the restraint of the evil and the active exercise of the good that raises man above other creatures. Anger makes the evil break out into harmful action. Self-restraint keeps the evil in check and affords scope for the exercise of virtues. Thus, when anger is controlled, evil is controlled. Good prevails. Anger is the outlet or channel through which emerge harshness, cruelty, pain and harm, vengeance, violence, war and destruction. When anger is overcome, your understanding becomes clear, and discrimination is active. You are enabled to choose between right and wrong. You proceed without confusion upon the straight, narrow path of moral rectitude.

Do not cause pain or suffering to any living being from greed, selfishness, irritability or annoyance. Give up anger or ill-will. Give up the spirit of fighting. Try your level best to keep a serene mind always.

Be serene and tranquil under all circumstances. The divine light will descend on a calm mind only. An aspirant with a calm mind only can enter into deep meditation and Nirvikalpa Samadhi. He only can practise Nishkamya Karma Yoga.

Cultivate this virtue, serenity or Sama, again and again through constant and strenuous endeavour. Serenity is like a rock; waves of irritation may dash on it, but cannot affect it. Meditate daily on the ever-tranquil Atman or the Eternal which is unchanging. You will attain this sublime virtue gradually.

It is easy to do evil for evil, to do good for good; but it is difficult and sublime to do good for evil. The downward path to evil is very easy, but the upward path to good is very difficult, thorny and precipitous. Those who are endowed with strength and wisdom in order to do good for evil are, indeed, blessed people. They are veritable gods on earth.

3. AVATARA

When Lord Jesus was born, the angels sang a beautiful song in praise of the Lord and, in so doing, revealed the purpose of His descent:

Glory to God in the highest,
And on earth peace, goodwill toward men.

Lord Jesus had come into this world of men in order to re-establish the true and the highest glory of God—peace on earth, and goodwill in the hearts of men towards all fellow-beings.

Law Governing the Lord's Descent

The law governing the Lord's descent upon earth is the same all times, everywhere. There is descent of God for the ascent of man. The aim of every Avatara is to save the world from some great danger, to destroy the wicked and protect the virtuous. Says Lord Krishna: "Whenever there is decay of righteousness, then I myself come forth. For the protection of the good, for the destruction of the evil-doers, for the sake of firmly establishing righteousness, I am born from age to age".

When unrighteousness grows and righteousness is on the wane, when the forces of undivine seem to be stronger than the divine forces, when world of God or Commandments of His Messengers is forgotten or disobeyed, when religious fanaticism follows the letter of the scriptures killing their spirit, it is then that Lord incarnates Himself on earth, to save man, to save righteousness. He takes human form when He comes down on the physical plane. He is called an Avatara.

Difference Between a Jivanmukta and an Avatara

A simple Jivanmukta is like a star that glitters at night. He throws a little light only. Somehow or the other, he has crossed to the other shore through some Tapas and Sadhana. He cannot elevate a large number of people. Just as the waters of a small spring can quench the thirst of a few pilgrims only, so also, this Kevala-jnani can bring peace to a few persons only. Whereas, an Avatara is a mighty person. He is like a big Manasarovar lake. He removes the veil of ignorance of thousands of men and women, and takes them to the land of eternal rest, bliss and sublime.

The Avataras are one with the Supreme. They are not parts like the individual souls. Avataras or Incarnations are rays of the Lord. When the work of Loka-sangraha is over, they disappear from the world.

Kinds of Avataras

Avataras are of various kinds. There are Purna-avataras, with full Kalas or rays. There are Amsa-avataras or partial incarnations. There are Lila-avataras.

Lord Krishna was a Purna-avatara. Sri Sankaracharya was an Amsa-avatara. Mastya, Kurma, Varaha, Narasimha, Vamana, Rama and others were Lila-avataras.

Krishna and Rama were the Avataras of Lord Vishnu. Dakshinamurthy was an incarnation of Lord Siva. Dattatreya was the Avatara of the Trimurtis—Brahma, Vishnu and Siva are three aspects of God. Brahma is the creative aspect; Vishnu is the preservative aspect; and Siva is the destructive aspect. There is no polytheism in the Hindu religion. Siva, Vishnu, Brahma and Sakti are different aspects of the one Lord.

The Ten Avataras of Vishnu

The Bhagavata Purana is a chronicle of the various Avataras of Lord Vishnu. There are ten Avataras of Lord Vishnu. There are: Matsya (the Fish), Kurma (Tortoise), Varaha (the Boar), Narasimha (the Man-loin), Vamana (the Dwarf), Parasurama (Rama with the Axe), Ramachandra (the hero of the Ramayana), Sri Krishna, Buddha (the prince-ascetic, Founder of Buddhism) and Kalki (the Hero on a white Horse who is to come at the end of the Kali Yuga).

The object of the Mastya Avatara was to save Vaivasvata Manu from destruction by a deluge. The object of the Kurma Avatara was to enable the world to recover some precious things which were lost in the deluge. The tortoise gave its back for keeping the churning-rod when the gods and the Asuras churned the Ocean of milk. The purpose of the Varaha Avatara was to rescue, from the waters, the earth which had been dragged down by a demon named Hiranyaksha. The purpose of Narasimha Avatara, half-lion and half-man, was to free the world from the oppression of

Hiranyakasipu, a demon, the father of Bhakta Prahlada. The object of Vamana Avatara was to restore the power of the gods which had been eclipsed by the penance and devotion of King Bali. The object of Parasurama Avatara was to deliver the country from the oppression of the Kshatriya rulers. Parasurama destroyed the Kshatriya race twenty one times. The object of Rama Avatara was to destroy the wicked Ravana. The object of Sri Krishna Avatara was to destroy Kamsa and other demons, to deliver His wonderful message of the Gita, and to become the centre of the Bhakti Schools of India. The object of Buddha Avatara was to prohibit animal sacrifices. The object of Kalki Avatara, who will appear before the end of the Kali Yuga, is the destruction of the wicked and the re-establishment of virtue.

Degree of the Lord's Manifestation in Different Avataras

The Rishis of yore have expounded the doctrine that Lord of the universe exists in sixteen expanding Kalas or digits of manifestation, that one digit of His life manifestation in the vegetable kingdom, two in the animal, and from five to eight in the human, according as we pass from the savage at one end of the scale to the highest evolved state at the other. The Lord's manifestation in His Avataras ranges from nine to sixteen digits or rays. The full or Purna Avataras are those in whom all sixteen rays are present. Lord Krishna was a Purna-Avatara, with sixteen rays. Lord Rama was an Avatara of fourteen rays. Theosophists also make mention of seven rays, and so on, when they describe the stage of spiritual development of their Masters and Adepts.

The Divine Form of an Avatara

Some people say: "How can we take Krishna as the Lord or Bhagavan? He took birth and died. He is only a man". This is a false statement. This is the utterance of an ignorant child. Lord Krishna only manifested himself, for the time being, to do Loka-sangraha work, to effect the solidarity or well-being of humanity, and then disappeared. Lord Krishna is Lord Hari Himself. There is no doubt of this.

Lord Rama is the Supreme Soul, the Antaryamin, the protector of all beings. He is omniscient, omnipotent and omnipresent. He is Lord Hari. He was never born. He never died. Lord Hari simply manifested in the form of Rama to do Loka-sangraha and then vanished.

Lord Rama and Lord Krishna had no physical bodies. Their bodies were not made of five elements. They had divine forms. They had Chinmaya bodies, though to all appearance, it looked like flesh. They had no real birth and death like human beings. They appeared and disappeared, just as a Yogi does. Their bodies were not left in this world. There is no destruction for their bodies.

Just as a tailor who makes coats for others can make a coat for himself also, God who has created bodies for others, can create a body for Himself as well. There is no difficulty. He is omnipotent and omniscient. As He has control over Maya, He is fully conscious of His divine nature though He assumes a form. Still He is infinite and unconditioned.

Sometimes, the king visits the jail and enters the cell of a prisoner to see how matters are getting on in the prison. He does this for the good of the prisoners. He is quite independent, and yet, out of his own free will, he himself enters the cell. Even so, an Avatara puts on a body out of His own free will for the ascent of man. He is quite independent and has absolute control over Maya, like the king; while the Jiva is a slave of Avidya, so long as he has no Self-realisation.

Contact with Avataras

Some people want to have contact with Avataras without being endowed with proper qualifications. Even if an Avatara appears before you, you will not be able to find Him out. You have not got the eyes to see Him as such. You will take Him for an ordinary man only. How many were able to detect the divinity of Lord Krishna? Did Jarasandha, Sisupala and Duryodhana recognise Him as the Avatara of Lord Hari? Very few people, like Bhishma, recognised Lord Krishna as the Avatara. That is the reason why the Lord says: "The foolish disregard Me, when clad in human semblance, ignorant of My supreme nature, the great Lord of beings".

It is only a saint who can understand a saint. Only a Jesus can understand a Jesus. How can a patient know the merits of a doctor?

A neophyte or beginner in the spiritual path should prepare himself gradually. He must get spiritual instructions from various Upa-gurus and follow them strictly. He should make himself fit to approach a Brahma-nishtha Guru. To practise meditation, and to see the Lord in meditation.

If you are endowed with the Four Means of Salvation, if you have burning Vairagya like that of Lord Buddha or Raja Bharthrihari, if you possess forgiveness and patience like the Avanti Brahmin of Ujjain, if you have devotion to the preceptor like Trotaka or Padmapada, you can contact Avataras and sages now, in this very second.

Can you serve like Florence Nightingale? Can you obey like a soldier in the battle-field? Can you be generous like Ranti Deva? Can you spend sleepless nights in devotion to the lord, like Mira? Can you do Tapas like Dhruva? Can you stick to your convictions like Mansoor and Shams Tabriez? Can you be fearless like the sage who met Alexander, the Great, on the banks of the Indus?

If you say *Yes,* you will have Self-realisation this very second. You will contact Avataras and full-blown Yogis this very second. First deserve, and then desire.

God-realisation through Worship of Avataras

You can attain God-realisation through worship of Avataras like Lord Krishna and Lord Rama. Many have already attained God-realisation in this manner. Tukaram, Ramdas, Surdas, Mira Bai and Tulasidas have seen God face to face. Their powerful writings bespeak their high spiritual attainments.

Worship Lord Rama or Lord Krishna at all times, with all your heart and with all your mind. Glorify Him in your heart. He will soon reveal Himself to you and you will feel His Presence. You will attain immortality and eternal bliss.

God reveals Himself to His devotees in a variety of ways. He assumes the very form which the devotee has chosen for his worship. If you worship Him as Lord Hari with four hands, He will come to you as Hari. If you adore Him as Siva He will give you Darshan as Siva. If you worship Him as Mother Durga or Kali, He will come to you as Durga or Kali. If you worship Him as Lord Rama, Lord Krishna or Lord Dattatreya, He will come to you as Rama, Krishna or Dattatreya. If you worship as Christ or Allah, He will come to you as Christ or Allah.

All are aspects of one Isvara or Lord. Under whatever name and form, it is Isvara who is adored. Worship goes to the Indweller, the Lord in the form. It is ignorance to think that one form is superior to another. All forms are one and the same. All are adoring the same Lord. The differences are only differences of names due to differences in the worshippers, but not in the object of adoration.

The real Jesus or Krishna is in your own heart. He lives there for ever. He is your Indweller. He is your partner always. There is no friend like the Indweller. Resort to Him. Take refuge in Him. Realise Him and be free.

4. BHAGAVATA PURANA

The Puranas hold a unique place in the history of religious literature of the Hindus. They contain a mine of knowledge and information on all philosophical and religious topics. Srutis and Smritis cannot be easily understood by the common people. So the all-merciful Vedavyasa composed the eighteen Puranas for the benefit of mankind and explained in an easy way the subtle truths and deep problems of the Srutis. They are indeed an encyclopaedia of Hindu religion and ethics. The task of the Puranas is to popularise the Vedic truths by means of narratives, stories and anecdotes. The Puranas contain fables, fairy tales, philosophy, religion, myth and legend.

The Origin of the Bhagavata Purana

Sri Vyasa was meditating on the sacred banks of the Sarasvati. His heart was in a disturbed condition. He has no satisfaction and peace. He reflected within Himself: "I have observed strict Brahmacharya. I have paid due regard to the study of the Vedas and to the worship of preceptors and sacred fires. I have obeyed the commands of my preceptors. I have explained the meaning of the Vedas in the form of Mahabharata wherefrom Dharmas and other things can be clearly understood even by women, Sudras and others. Still I think that my work is not fully done".

At this juncture, Narada appeared before Vyasa and said : "You have fully known all that is knowable. You have written the excellent Maha Bharata which contains everything. How is it you feel uneasy and dissatisfied?".

Sri Vyasa replied: "I quite agree with what you say. Still I have no satisfaction. I want to know the cause of it from you. You are born of Brahma and you possess infinite knowledge".

Narada said: "O great Muni! Thou hast treated of Dharma and other things but thou hast not recited the glory of Vasudeva. For this reason, I think, the Lord is not satisfied. Therefore, O blessed one, write about the various glorious deeds of Lord Krishna so that all people may obtain the final emancipation by knowing them. This universe is also an aspect of Bhagavan, because its creation, preservation and dissolution proceed from Him. Thou knowest all this thyself but thou hast shown to others only a portion of this truth. Therefore, O sage, sing the glory of the omnipresent Hari, by knowing which even the wise reach the end of their quest. The wise know this alone and no other to be the remedy for the miseries of beings that are repeatedly tossed into Samsara". Thereupon Sri Vyasa wrote Srimad Bhagavata consisting of eighteen thousand verses, three hundred and thirty-five sections and twelve chapters. The book is named Bhagavata because it speaks of the glory of Bhagavan or Vishnu. It is one of the most authoritative of Hindu scriptures. It is a work of great repute in India. It exercises a direct and powerful influence on the opinions and feelings of the people. It contains the essence of all the Puranas.

Avataras of the Lord

The Bhagavata Purana is a chronicle of the various Avataras of Lord Vishnu. The aim of every Avatara is to save the world from some great danger, to destroy the wicked and protect the virtuous. The ten important Avataras are: Matsya (the Fish), Kurma (the Tortoise), Varaha (the Boar), Narasimha (the Man-lion), Vamana (the Dwarf), Parasurama (Rama with axe, the destroyer of the Kshatriya race), Ramachandra (the hero of Ramayana—the son of Dasaratha and consort of Sita—who killed Ravana, the ten-headed Rakshasa or monster), Sri Krishna (the consort of Rukmini and teacher of the Gita), Buddha (the prince-ascetic, founder of Buddhism) and Kalki (the hero on a white horse who is to come at the end of the Kali-Yuga).

The object of the Mastya Avatara was to save Vaivasvata Manu from destruction by a deluge and that of Kurma Avatara was to enable the world to recover some precious things which were lost in the deluge. The Tortoise gave its back for keeping the churning rod when the gods and Asuras churned the ocean of milk. The purpose of Varaha (Boar) Avatara was to rescue, from the waters, the earth which had been dragged down by a demon named Hiranyaksha and that of Narasimha Avatara, half-lion and half-man, was to free the world from the oppression of Hiranyakasipu, a demon, the father of Bhakta Prahlada. The Vamana Avatara was taken by the Lord to restore the power of gods which had been eclipsed by the penance and devotion of king Bali and Parasurama Avatara to deliver the country from the oppression of the Kshatriya rulers. Parasurama destroyed the kshatriya race twenty-one times. In Rama Avatara the

Lord destroyed the wicked Ravana. The object of Sri Krishna Avatara was to destroy Kamsa and other demons, to deliver His wonderful message of the Gita, and to become the centre of the Bhakti cult. The object of Buddha Avatara was to prohibit animal sacrifices. The object of the Kalki Avatara is the destruction of the wicked and the re-establishment of virtue.

The Unique Nature of the Bhagavata Purana

In the Bhagavata Purana alone the history of the universe is systematically dealt with. Lord Krishna is the central figure of this unique book. It is an authoritative book on devotion. The Bhagavata teaches devotion that is associated with Jnana (Bhaktiyukta-Jnana). It does not divorce knowledge from Bhakti. It teaches that Jnana is extremely help to the perfect attainment of Bhakti. In the Bhagavata the ambrosia of Bhakti is mixed with the elixir of Jnana.

The teachings given by Lord Krishna to Uddhava on the eve of His departure from this world are wonderful. These are contained in the eleventh Skandha (chapter). Sri Krishna clears all doubts of Uddhava, His friend, foremost disciple and the chief of the Yadavas. He gives instructions on a variety of subjects, but the one ringing note is: "See Me in everything. Surrender yourself to Me. Do all actions for My sake. Cut off all sorts of attachments. Have perfect unswerving devotion to Me. Sing My glories".

The Bhagavata Purana prescribes various kinds of meditation to suit different types of aspirants. A beginner is asked to meditate on the Virat Purusha. He must think that the whole universe is the body of the Lord. This is given in the second Skandha. In the same Skandha and in the third also, meditation on the form of the Lord in the heart, and on His various limbs, beginning from the feet, is described. In the eleventh Skandha meditation on the lotus of the heart with three layers, Agni as the first, Surya as the second and Moon as the third, one over the other, is prescribed. In the same Skandha one is asked to meditate on the form of Lord Krishna first, and then to fix the mind on ether or the supreme cause, and finally to merge it in the Para Brahman. The Bhagavata Dharma as taught by the nine sages to king Nimi in the beginning of this Skandha is thrilling and soul stirring. The tenth Skandha contains all the Lilas of the Lord. The youthful sports and pastimes, the fun and frolic of the divine child, Kumara Lilas, Brindavan Lilas, Madhura Lilas,

Dvaraka Lilas, Kurukshetra Lilas and Prabhasa Lilas are described in this Skandha. It contains ninety sections. It is in this chapter we find the outpourings of the heart or expressions of rapturous love of the human soul when it is freed from the impurities of the mind. When the impurities of the mind are removed and the heart thoroughly purified, the human soul is naturally drawn or attracted towards the Lord and is finally absorbed in Him. The truths hidden in the tenth Skandha cannot be understood by those whose hearts are filled with worldliness.

Bhagavata Saptahams are held all throughout India, in which the whole Bhagavata is recited within seven days. This provides a good occasion for listening to and understanding the whole of the Bhagavata. The Bhagavata is the solace of life. It is unique in its beauty and charm, in its diction and philosophy. A study of this book inspires devotion, instils knowledge and creates real Vairagya. The glories of Lord Vasudeva are vividly described in this book.

5. BHAKTI

Bhakti is resting on God. Bhakti is flow of devotion like the flow of a river. Bhakti is continuity of devotion, just as there is continuity in the flow of oil from one vessel to another vessel. Bhakti is attraction of the Jiva to the Lord, just as there is attraction of the needle to the magnet.

Bhakti is love for love's sake. The devotee wants God and God alone. There is no selfish expectation here. There is no fear also. Is the son afraid of his father who is Sessions Judge? Is the wife afraid of her husband? So also, a devotee entertains the least fear of God. The fear of retribution vanishes in him. He feels, believes, conceives and imagines that his Ishtam is an ocean of love or Prema.

Bhakti transmutes man into Divinity. It intoxicates the devotee with divine Prema. It gives him eternal satisfaction. It makes him perfect. It weans the mind from the sensual objects. It makes him rejoice in God.

Emotional excitement is not devotion to God. Devotion is pure love. Fanaticism is not devotion. It is frenzy. It is mere excitement.

Bhakti is not emotionalism, but is the tuning of the will as well as the intellect towards the Divine. It is supreme love of God. It blossoms afterwards into Jnana. It leads to immortality or God-realisation.

Bhakti is the direct approach to the ideal through the heart. Love is natural to everybody.

Bhakti Is Open to All

Bhakti can be practised under all conditions and by all alike. Learning, austere penance, study of the Vedas, and brilliant intellect are not needed for the attainment of Bhakti or devotion. What is wanted is constant and living remembrance of God, coupled with faith. That is the reason why the path of Bhakti is available for everyone.

Nishada was born in a low caste; Sabari was a rustic woman; Dhruva was an uneducated boy; Vidura and Sudama were very poor; Vibhishana was an ugly Rakshasa; Hanuman was a monkey; Jatayu was a bird; Gajendra was an elephant; the Gopis of

Brindavan were not initiated into Vedic rites; but all these attained God-realisation on account of their devotion and self-surrender.

The Easiest Approach to God

Bhakti is easier than any other way of approach to God. In Jnana and Yoga, there is the risk of a fall. In the path of devotion, there is no risk as the devotee receives full support and help from God.

Those who tread the path of Jnana and Yoga are liable to become proud of their powers and wisdom. Bhaktas are humble. Humility is the foundation of Bhakti Yoga.

Jnana Yoga is the Yoga of wisdom. It is the path of analysis and rejection. It is the path of endless negation. This is a very difficult path.

Raja Yoga also is difficult. It is like stilling the waves of the ocean. You will have to still all the thought-waves. Karma Yoga also is difficult. It is like climbing to the highest peak. You need tremendous will-power. Bhakti Yoga alone is easy. The Lord is stretching His hands to lift you up from the mire of Samsara. You will have to grasp His hand firmly. But, one thing is absolutely essential here. You should not have any other thought than that of God and God alone.

One-pointedness in Devotion

The child thinks of the mother and mother alone. A passionate husband thinks of his wife and wife alone. A greedy man thinks of his money and money alone. Even so, the devotee should entertain in his heart the picture of his Ishtam and Ishtam alone. Then he can have Darshan of God easily.

Objects are enemies of God. Sons, wife, property, cattle, houses, friends and relatives are enemies of God. You must cherish perfect indifference to these objects.

You must not think of the body and its wants too much. Thoughts of body, thoughts of food, thoughts of wife and children make you forget God. You cannot have thoughts of God if you have thoughts of Anatma things.

If the devotee loves God sometimes and his wife, son, money, house, cattle, and property also at other times. It is Vyabhicharini Bhakti. The love is divided. A small portion of the mind is given to God. The remaining portion is given to family and possessions.

The lord becomes the slave of a Bhakta only when the latter has made absolute, ungrudging self-surrender. The Lord is very cruel and puts His devotees to severe tests and trails. He did not hear the words of Draupadi so long as she kept up her own strength and traces of egoism. When she carried aloud with perfect sincerity and total resignation, "Dvarakanath, my beloved! Come to my rescue," then He ran to the scene, and she had abundant cloth and her modesty was saved.

Generally the Aspirant, consciously or unconsciously, wittingly or unwittingly, keeps up some desires for his gratification. He does not wish to part completely with his desires. Therefore the self-surrender does not become perfect and unreserved. So the grace of the Lord does not descend. Even if there is an atom of desire or egoism, there is no possibility of divine grace.

Devotion and Desire

Desire obstructs the growth of devotion. Devotion to the Lord increases in intensity when mundane desires are renounced.

Renunciation is the very essence of devotional love. Divine love has no element of desire in it.

Devotion cannot co-exist with desire of any kind, not even the desire for Liberation. The devotee wants God and God alone, and His service.

The devotee loves God and serves Him and His creation. He does not strive consciously for Mukti, but God confers Mukti on His devotee unsolicited.

How to Cultivate Devotion

People put a question: "How can we love God whom we have not seen?".

Live in the company of saints. Hear the Lilas of God. Study the sacred scriptures. Worship Him first in His several forms as manifested in the world. Worship any image or picture of the Lord or the Guru. Recite His Name. Sing His glories. Stay for one year in Ayodhya or Brindavan, Chitrakuta or Pandharpur, Benares or Ananda Kutir. You will develop love for God.

Every act must be done that awakens the emotion of Bhakti. Keep the Puja room clean. Decorate the room. Burn the incense. Light a lamp. Keep a clean seat. Bathe. Wear clean clothes. Apply

Vibhuti or Bhasma and Kumkum on the forehead. Wear Rudraksha or Tulasi Mala. All these produce a benign influence on the mind and elevate the mind. They generate piety. They help to create the necessary Bhava or feeling to invoke the Deity that you want to worship. The mind will be easily concentrated.

Practice of right conduct, Satsanga, Japa, Smarana, Kirtan, prayer, worship, service of saints, residence in places of pilgrimage, service of the poor and the sick with divine Bhava, observance of Varnasrama duties, offering the presence of the Lord in all beings, prostrations before the image and saints, renunciation of earthly enjoyments and wealth, charity, austerities and vows, practice of Ahimsa, Satyam and Brahmacharya—all these will help you to develop Bhakti.

Bhavas in Bhakti Yoga

There are six kinds of Bhavas in Bhakti. In Santa Bhava, the devotee is Santa or peaceful. He does not jump and dance. He is not highly emotional. His heart is filled with love and joy. Bhishma was a Santa Bhakta.

Sri Hanuman was a Dasya Bhakta. He had Dasya Bhava. He served Lord Rama whole-heartedly. He pleased his Master in all possible ways. He found joy and bliss in the service of his Master.

In Sakhya Bhava, God is a friend of the devotee. Arjuna had this Bhava towards Lord Krishna. The devotee moves with the Lord on equal terms. Arjuna and Krishna used to sit, eat, talk and walk together as intimate friends.

In Vatsalya Bhava, the devotee looks upon God as his child. Yasoda had this Bhava with Lord Krishna. There is no fear in this Bhava, because God is your pet child. The devotee serves, feeds, and looks upon God as a mother does in the case of her child.

The fifth Bhava is Sakhya Bhava. This is also known as Gopi Bhava. The Gopis united Radha and Krishna when they separated. They identified themselves with Radha and Krishna and enjoyed the bliss resulting from their union.

The last is Madhurya Bhava or Kanta Bhava. This is the highest form of Bhakti. This was the relation between Radha and Krishna. This is Atma-samarpana. The lover and the beloved become one. The devotee and God feel one with each other and still maintain a separateness in order to enjoy the bliss of the play of love between them. This is oneness in separation and separation in oneness. The relationship is that of husband and wife. Jayadeva, Mira and Andal had this Bhava.

Apara Bhakti and Para Bhakti

Bhakti is of two kinds, Apara Bhakti and Para Bhakti. Apara Bhakti is lower Bhakti. In Apara Bhakti, the devotee is a neophyte. He observes rituals and ceremonies. He has no expanded heart. He is a sectarian. He dislikes other kinds of Bhaktas who worship other Devatas.

A devotee of Para Bhakti type is all-embracing and all-inclusive. He has cosmic love or Visvaprema. The whole world is Brindavan for him. He does not visit temples for worship. He sees the Lord in everything. He feels that the world is a manifestation of the Lord, and all movements and actions are His Lila. He has no Ghrina or dislike for faecal matter or dirt, for the Chandala, the scavenger, the cobbler, the beggar, the prostitute or the thief. He says, "I see everywhere my sweet Lord. It is Hari who is playing the part of the prostitute, the thief, the dacoit, the scavenger!" He has an all-embracing, all-inclusive, exalted mental state. This cannot be adequately described in words. It has to be felt. Mira, Gouranga, Hafiz, Tulsidas, Kabir, Ramdas—all enjoyed this state.

Namdev said to the dog: "O Vittala, my dear, in the form of a dog, do not run away with the dry bread. It will affect your soft throat. Pray, let me apply ghee to the bread". He ran with ghee in a cup to the dog. Sri Ramakrishna Paramahamsa prostrated before an outcaste girl: "O Mother Kali! I see Thee in this girl". Eknath, a Maharashtrian Bhakta, gave his ring voluntarily to the thief when the latter entered the house: "O thief! Take this ring also. Your duty is to steal things. Thou art Krishna. Keep up this Lila". Have you understood the sublime state of these exalted Bhaktas who have a new angle of vision? A day will come to you also. Exert. Struggle.

Para Bhakti and Jnana

Para Bhakti is Jnana only. Para Bhakti and Jnana are one. Sri Sankara, a Kevala-advaita-jnani, was a great Bhakta of Lord Hari, Hara and Devi. Sri Ramakrishna Paramahamsa worshipped Kali and got Jnana through Swami Totapuri, his Advaita Guru. Appayya

Dikshitar, famous Jnani of South India, was a devout Bhakta of Lord Siva.

Para Bhakti and Jnana are one. The only slight difference is: A Bhakta uses his emotion; a Jnani uses his will and intellect. Bhakti begins with love, and Jnana with thinking and self-analysis. The end of both is the same, union with the Divine.

A devotee contracts. A Vedantin expands. The former contracts and enters the Lord through self-surrender. The latter expands and becomes one with Brahman through assertion and identification.

The fruit of Bhakti is Jnana. Jnana intensifies Bhakti. Even Jnanis like Sankara, Madhusudana, and Suka Deva took to Bhakti after Realisation to enjoy the sweetness of loving relationship with God.

Knowledge or wisdom will dawn by itself when you practise Bhakti Yoga. Bhakti is the pleasant, smooth, direct road to God. Bhakti is sweet in the beginning, in the middle, and in the end. It gives the highest, undecaying bliss.

Kindle love divine in thy heart, for this is the immediate way to the Kingdom of God.

Pray to the Lord. Sing His glory. Recite His Name. Become a channel of His grace.

Seek His will. Do His will. Surrender to His will. You will become one with the cosmic will.

Surrender unto the Lord. He will become your charioteer on the field of life. He will drive your chariot well. You will reach the destination, the Abode of Immortal Bliss.

6. BRAHMACHARYA

Brahmacharya is a divine word. It is the sum and substance of Yoga.

Brahmacharya is the Achara or conduct by which you attain or reach Brahman. It is life in the Absolute. It is movement towards God or Atman.

Brahmacharya is purity in thought, word and deed. It is celibacy and continence.

Brahmacharya is not mere bachelorhood. Strict abstinence is not merely from sexual intercourse, but also from auto-erotic manifestations, from masturbation, from homo-sexual acts, and from all perverse sexual practices. It must further involve a permanent abstention from indulgence in erotic imagination and voluptuous reverie.

In a narrow sense, Brahmacharya is celibacy. In a broad sense, it is absolute control of all senses. The door of Nirvana or perfection is complete Brahmacharya.

Brahmacharya is to the Yogi what electricity is to an electric bulb. Without Brahmacharya, no spiritual progress is possible.

There cannot be any language without vowels. You cannot draw a picture without a canvas. So also you cannot have health and spiritual life without Brahmacharya.

A true Brahmachari will not feel any difference in touching a woman, a piece of paper, a log of wood, or a piece of stone. A true Brahmachari only can cultivate Bhakti. A true Brahmachari only can practise Yoga. A true Brahmachari only can acquire Jnana.

Brahmacharya is meant for both men and women. Bhishma, Hanuman, Lakshmana, Mirabai, Sulabha and Gargi were all Brahmacharins.

The Vital Energy

One of the students of Dhanvantari approached his teacher after finishing his full course of Ayurveda and asked him, "O Bhagavan, kindly let me know the secret of health now". Dhanvantari replied: "This seminal energy is verily Atman. The secret of health lies in the preservation of this vital force. He who wastes this energy cannot have physical, mental, moral and spiritual development".

Veerya is God in motion. Veerya is dynamic will. Veerya is soul-force. Veerya is the essence of life, thought, intelligence and consciousness.

The vital energy, Veerya, which supports your life, which is the Prana of Pranas, which shines in your sparkling eyes, which beams in your shining cheeks, is a great treasure for you. It is the quintessence of blood.

From food, chyle is manufactured. Out of chyle comes blood; out of blood comes flesh; out of flesh comes fat; out of fat comes marrow; out of marrow comes semen. Semen is the last essence. It is the Essence of essences.

Just as sugar is all-pervading in the sugar-cane, butter in milk, so also, semen is pervading the whole body. It exists in a subtle form throughout the body. It is withdrawn and elaborated into gross form in the sexual organs under the influence of the sexual will and sexual excitement.

Sexual Excitement and Its Evil Consequences

When a man is excited by passion, the Prana is set in motion. The vital air or Prana moves the internal sap or semen. The semen is put into motion. It falls downwards, just as the clouds burst into the rain water; just as the fruits, flowers and leaves of the tree drop down by the force of the blowing winds.

If the Veerya is lost, Prana gets unsteady. Prana is agitated. Man becomes nervous. Then the mind also cannot work properly. The man becomes fickle-minded. There is mental weakness.

Bad memory, premature old age, impotence, various sorts of eye-diseases and various nervous diseases are attributable to the heavy loss of this vital fluid.

When once lost, Veerya can never, never be recouped in your lifetime by your taking any amount of Badam, nervine tonics, milk, cream, cheese, Chyavanaprash, or Makaradhvaja.

Indulgence in the sexual act is exhausting to the female system and a drain upon the vitality as in man. The nervous strain it imposes is very great indeed. Their systems being more delicate and highstrung, females are often more affected than men.

Need for Brahmacharya

How can you expect to be strong and healthy, if the energy that is acquired through various means, with great difficulty, is wasted daily? It is impossible to be strong and healthy unless males and females, boys and girls, try their level best to keep up Brahmacharya or the vow of celibacy.

Pure air, pure water, wholesome food, physical exercise, outdoor games like tennis—all contribute to the maintenance of good health, strength and a high standard of vigour and vitality. There are, indeed, many ways to gain health and strength. These ways are, doubtless, indispensably requisite. But, Brahmacharya is the most important of all. It is the only specific that keeps up the true manliness.

Benefits of the Practice of Brahmacharya

The practice of celibacy is not attended with any danger or disease, or undesirable results such as the various sorts of 'complex' wrongly attributed by the Western psychologists. They have no practical knowledge of the subject on hand. They have a wrong and ill-founded imagination that the ungratified sex-energy assumes the various forms of 'complex' such as touch-phobia. The complex is due to some other causes. It is a morbid state of mind due to excessive jealousy, hatred, anger, worry and depression brought about by various causes.

On the contrary, even a little of self-restraint or a little practice of continence is an ideal 'pick-me-up'. It gives inner strength and peace of mind. It invigorates the mind and nerves. It helps to conserve physical and mental energy. It augments memory, will-force and brain-power. It bestows tremendous strength, vigour and vitality. It renovates the system or constitution, rebuilds the cells and tissues, energises digestion, and gives power to face the difficulties in the daily battle of life. One who has perfect control over sexual energy attains powers unobtainable by any other means.

If a man leads a life of celibacy even in his house-holder's life and has copulation occasionally for the sake of progeny only, he can bring forth healthy, intelligent, strong, beautiful, self-sacrificing sons. The ascetics and saviours of ancient India, when married, used to follow this excellent rule very carefully for this purpose, and also used to teach by example and practice how to lead a life of a Brahmacharin even as a householder.

The Importance of Right Diet

Diet plays a prominent part in keeping up Brahmacharya. There are different compartments in the brain and each food produces its own effect on each compartment and on the general system. A confection of sparrow produces aphrodisiac effect. It directly stimulates the reproductive organs. Garlic, onions, meat, fish and eggs stimulate the passion.

Give proper attention to food. Have moderation in diet. Take Sattvic food such as milk, fruits and wheat. Occasional fasting checks passion, calms the emotions, controls the Indriyas, and helps Brahmacharya.

Theory and Practice

People talk of Brahmacharya; but practical men are rare, indeed. A life of continence is really beset with difficulties.

It is easy to tame a tiger or a lion or an elephant. It is easy to play with a cobra. It is easy to walk over the fire. It is easy to uproot the Himalayas. It is easy to get victory in the battlefield. But, it is difficult to eradicate *lust.*

You need not despair even a bit, however. Have faith in God, in His Name and in His grace. You are bound to succeed if you have faith in Him.

Mere human effort alone will not suffice. The divine grace is needed. Lust cannot be completely uprooted from the mind except by the grace of the Lord. God helps those who help themselves.

Lack of spiritual Sadhana is the main cause for all sexual attractions. Mere theoretical abstention from sensuality will not bring you good results. You must mercilessly cut off all formalities in social life and lead a pious life. Leniency to internal lower tendencies will land you in the region of suffering. Excuse will not be of use in this respect. You must be sincere in your purpose for the sublime life of spirituality. Half-heartedness will leave you in your old state of misery.

How to Get Established in Celibacy

Do not think of women. Do not look at women. Looking at the opposite sex will create a desire to talk to them. Talking will create a desire to touch them. Eventually you will have an impure mind and will fall a victim. Therefore never look at the opposite sex. Never talk intimately with them. Do not be familiar with them.

Lustful look, lustful thinking, wet-dreams are all failures or breaks in celibacy. Be chaste in your look. Be chaste in your thought. Be chaste in your talk. See mother in all women. Cultivate sublime, divine thoughts. Repeat the Lord's Name and meditate regularly. You will be established in celibacy.

There are four processes in the practice of Brahmacharya. First *control* the sex-impulse and sex-Vasana. Then practise *conservation* of sex-energy. Shut out all holes through which energy leaks. Then *divert* the conserved energy into the proper spiritual channels through Japa, Kirtan, selfless service, Pranayama, study, vigilance, self-analysis, introspection and Vichara. Then have *conversion* or sublimation of the sex-energy. Let it be converted into Ojas or Brahmatejas through constant meditation or Brahma-Chintana.

Danger of Reaction

You will have to be very careful of reaction. The senses that are put under restraint for some months, or for one or two years, become rebellious if you are not always vigilant and careful. They revolt and drag you out when opportunities arise. Some people, who observe Brahmacharya for one or two years, become more passionate and waste the energy considerably in the end. Some become incorrigible, moral wrecks also.

You must not labour under the delusion that you have eradicated lust completely by adjusting the diet a bit, by practising Pranayama, and by doing a little Japa, and that you have nothing more to do. Temptation or Mara may overcome you at any moment. Eternal vigilance and rigorous Sadhana are very essential.

You may be able to stop copulation for months and years, but there should not be any sexual craving or attraction for ladies. Evil thoughts also should not arise when you look at a lady, when you are in the company of ladies.

The state of mental Brahmacharya must be kept up even amidst temptations and sickness. Then only you are safe. The senses begin to revolt during times of ailment and also when you come in contact with sense-objects.

You cannot attain perfect Brahmacharya by limited effort. Just as a machine-gun is necessary to kill a powerful enemy, so also, constant, rigorous and powerful Sadhana is necessary to annihilate this powerful enemy, lust. You must not be puffed up with pride for your little achievement in celibacy. If you are put to test, you will hopelessly fail. You must be ever conscious of your shortcomings and you must constantly strive to get rid of them. The highest effort is necessary. Then only you will have sanguine success in this direction.

7. BRAHMAN

Brahman is a great mystery; and yet He is the simple, easy truth.

Brahman is the Soul of our soul. He is our very Self. He is the inner ruler. He is the indwelling one.

Brahman is the governor of the world. He is the Supreme Self. He is the Lord. He is changeless. He is the cosmic being. He is the Self of the universe. He is the great goal of knowledge. He is the supreme refuge.

The word *Brahman* is derived from the root *Brimh*, which means to swell, to grow great, to pervade all space, to be complete and perfect.

There is an abiding reality in the midst of change. That abiding reality is Brahman, or the Absolute. Brahman is the warp and woof of the web of this universe.

The vast ocean has only one taste of salt. Even so, the whole world has only one flavour, the flavour of Atman.

All musical notations, whether they be played on a drum or on any stringed instrument, are no more than mere vibration of sound. Similarly, whatever is seen or felt during sleeping or waking is none other than consciousness; and consciousness is Atman or Brahman.

Brahman is infinite intelligence. He is a mass of bliss-consciousness. His name is Sat-Chit-Ananda. His abode is pure consciousness. His language is silence. Be silent. He speaks. Speak. He is dumb. You cannot get hold of Him.

Ocean can be compared to ocean alone. Akasa can be compared to Akasa alone. Even so, Brahman or the Absolute can be compared to Brahman alone.

An answer in words regarding the Absolute is delusion. The Absolute is beyond speech and mind.

Brahman Transcends Time, Space and Causation

Brahman cannot be proved. It exists before the act of proving. It is the basis of proof. It is self-proved.

Brahman or the Absolute is the cause of all, but Himself is causeless. He is the origin of the entire creation.

Brahman or the Eternal is beyond time, space and causation. Time is caused by the succession of events. This is mental creation.

How can there be time in Eternity? Space is the distance between two objects. How can there be space when you feel and behold the Self everywhere? In this world, everything has a cause. The seed is the cause for the tree and so on. How can there be a cause for Brahman which is the causeless Cause, which is self-existent, which is not an effect of anything?

The Neti-neti Doctrine

Brahman cannot be really described. It can only be described by 'Neti, Neti', 'not this, not this'. That which is neither like this nor like that is Brahman or the Eternal.

You can sublate or negate all names and forms through the 'Neti, Neti' doctrine, but you cannot eliminate Brahman or the Absolute, the substratum. What is left behind or Sesha after negation or sublation is Brahman or the Eternal.

There is nothing in this world but the Self, the Atman. All is Brahman alone. 'I', 'thou', 'he', 'this', 'here', 'there', 'now', 'then', have all no real meaning.

Atman Is the Essence of All

Atman or the Self is not elsewhere. It is your own innermost Self.

Smaller than the small, greater than the great, is the Atman that dwells in the heart. It is the Soul of the ant. It is the Soul of the elephant. It is the Soul of the universe. It is Over-soul too. It is the Soul of the sinner and also of the saint. It is the Soul of the soul; it is the Supreme Soul. It is the Supreme Purusha. It is Chaitanya.

The knower and the known are one. God and I are one in knowledge. The Jiva and Brahman are one in essence. The Soul of a cat and a rat is one. The essence in the sun and the moon is one. There is only one homogeneous essence in all forms. That essence is the Absolute or the Immortal. That essence is Atman, Brahman, or the Infinite.

Brahman is formless. Consciousness is formless. Bliss is formless. Peace is formless.

The Substratum behind Names and Forms

In the manifested world of names and forms, colour, shape, size and sounds are necessary to differentiate objects; but Brahman is one homogeneous essence of bliss, peace and wisdom. He is partless and indivisible. He is the same everywhere. He is infinite and motionless; and so He is colourless, formless and shapeless.

Brahman is formless in the midst of all forms. He is bodiless in the midst of all bodies. He is nameless in the midst of all names.

The canvas is the substratum. Various pictures are drawn on the canvas. Pictures are nothing but colours. There are no pictures independent of the canvas. There are no pictures separate from the cinema screen.

Brahman or the Eternal is the substratum. Names and forms are drawn on the canvas of Brahman. There are not independent of Brahman.

There is cloth in front of you. A cloth is nothing but threads. Cloth is only a mere name. There is no cloth independent of thread. If you remove the threads, the cloth disappears. Thread is nothing but cotton. If you burn the threads, all are reduced to ash. Cloth, thread, cotton and ash exist. Existence is the Sat aspect of Brahman. They all shine. This is the Chit aspect of Brahman. You love a cloth, thread and cotton. This is the Ananda or bliss aspect of Brahman. Sat-chit-ananda is the only reality. Cloth, thread and cotton are false appearances. Names and forms are illusory.

Brahman or the Absolute is one, perfect and all pervading. He circulates in all names and forms. He is all-comprehensive. He contains within Himself this entire universe. He is the inner light or pure consciousness.

The Nature of Pure Consciousness

Pure consciousness is pure awareness. There is neither thinking nor perception here. There is neither 'within' nor 'without' here. It is a homogeneous essence of wisdom-bliss. The awareness of Tom and John cannot be different. It is one.

There is difference only in objects which exist in space. In pure awareness, there is neither space nor time. Pure consciousness is infinite, unchanging, beyond cause and effect, beyond good and evil. It is desireless, and so, perfect, pure and free. Pure consciousness exists forever.

Pure consciousness is neither physical nor mental consciousness.

It is absolute consciousness on which depend physical and mental consciousness.

There is no thinking in pure consciousness. You can hardly conceive of this. There is no play of senses in pure consciousness. There is neither seeing nor hearing. There is no perception here. It is a mass of wisdom. It is Bhuma or the Infinite wherein there is neither seer nor knower. It is just the Thing-in-itself. It is pure self-awareness beyond the reach of sense, mind and intellect. The ego-sense is absolutely dead here. Brahmic consciousness shines by itself, in its own pristine glory.

Turiya or the Fourth State

There are three states of consciousness. They are waking, dreaming and deep sleep states. There is common supreme consciousness that connects the three states of consciousness, that is the basis of these three states. That is the reason why the man who wakes up remembers the bliss of deep sleep. That connecting, permanent, eternal consciousness is Brahman or Turiya or the Fourth, which is pure or absolute consciousness. Otherwise, he who sleeps, he who dreams, and he who wakes up will be different individuals.

Waking state vanishes during dreaming state. When you wake up, there is no dreaming state. During the deep sleep, there is neither the waking nor the dreaming state. Hence, these states are illusory. Sat or Brahman always exists. The one connecting state of all these three states, viz., Turiya, ever exists as the substratum of these three. Turiya state is the only reality. It is the silent witness of the three states. It is distinct from the three states. Turiya is Brahman or the Absolute.

Mind and Brahman

The Absolute is always the witnessing subject. It can never become the object of perception. If Atman becomes the object of perception, it will become a finite object. Atman is always the knower or the experiencer or the witness.

Mind can only know the external objects. How can mind know the knower? You cannot jump on your shoulders. Fire cannot burn itself.

Brahman is the cause. Mind is an effect. Brahman is infinite.

Mind is finite. How can the effect know its cause? How can a part know the whole? How can the finite know the infinite?

Book-learning and Realisation

You cannot know Brahman or the Absolute through the finite instrument, intellect. The intellect draws its power and light from its source, Brahman, the Supreme Soul. Intellect can only know the nature and attributes, colour, form, etc., of sense-objects. But, it cannot know the knower. Intellectual understanding of the nature of Brahman, mere study of Upanishads or theoretical knowledge of Brahman, cannot give you Self-realisation or Freedom. The intellect and senses must cease functioning. The ego must merge in the ocean of bliss. The individual soul must fuse in the Supreme Soul. Then alone the aspirant attains Salvation.

Brahman or the Absolute cannot be reached just as one reaches a village. The village is outside oneself; but Brahman is omnipresent. He is everywhere. He is your own innermost Self or Atman. The mind melts in Brahman. The individual soul becomes one with the Supreme Soul or the Absolute, just as the drop becomes one with the ocean.

Identity of Jiva and Brahman

The individual soul and the Supreme Soul are essentially one and the same. This is the fundamental teaching of Vedanta. This conception is not easy to grasp at first sight. Maya, the veiling power of God, hides the real nature of the Supreme Self and makes a fragment of It appear as the individual soul, Jiva. But this condition is not real. No real change has taken place. It is only phenomenal. This is a great mystery.

A spark is only fire. A wave or bubble is only water. A ring or bracelet is only gold. The prince is only future king. Even so, Jiva or individual is only Para Brahman or the Absolute.

You are really a mass of Wisdom. But you think and feel, "I am ignorant; I do not know". This is due to your Avidya. You are really Beauty of beauties. You give beauty to all forms. You illumine the sun, the moon and the stars, but you are attracted by a little colour. You have become a slave of physical form. What a sad, deplorable state! You are really an Emperor of emperors, but you have become a beggar on account of various desires. You are really the Infinite, but you feel, "I am five feet, five inches", through identification with the body. You are really beyond time. You are Eternity, but you say, "I am thirty years old". You are really Deathless. Lord Yama is terribly afraid of you. He runs here and there to carry out your behest. But you are afraid of death. Rise above all limitations and realise: "I am Infinite Brahman".

Fill your mind with thoughts of Brahman. Think on Brahman. Reflect on Brahman. Meditate on Brahman. Be solely devoted to Brahman, Brahma-parayana. Take refuge in Brahman. Ever converse on Brahman with aspirants. Merge yourself in Brahman. Get established in Brahman. Let your mind and Prana be absorbed in Brahman. This is Brahmabhyasa or Jnanabhyasa or Brahma-chintana or Vedantic Sadhana.

8. BUDDHISM

Buddhism was founded by Gautama Sakya Muni, the rebel child of Hinduism. It sprang up directly from Hinduism. Buddha never thought of founding a new religion. He made no new discovery. He was proclaiming only the ancient and pure form of religion which had prevailed among the Hindus.

The pure and noble religion of the Vedas and the Upanishads had degenerated into dead forms, unmeaning rites and ceremonies. The Brahmins claimed honour merely by their birth. They neglected the study of the Vedas and the practice of virtue. The Brahmins were treated with undue leniency, and the Sudras with undue severity. In order that flesh-eating might have the sanction of religion, animals were slaughtered and sacrificed in Yajnas. Such was the state of society at the time when Buddha appeared. His tender and loving heart could not bear the shedding of so much innocent blood in the sacred name of religion.

Buddha declared that merit, and not birth, determined the position of a man in society. The persecuted Sudras joined him in large numbers. He directed his energy and time in removing the distinction of caste and stopping all sacrifices in which animals were slaughtered. If Buddha had been born in a period when these evils did not exist, he would have made little impression. There would have been no occasion for his reform. But, as he lived in a period in which the above two evils existed, he naturally attracted a large number of followers and unconsciously became the founder of a new faith.

Buddhism Is Not Agnosticism

Buddha came to the world to show the path of righteousness, to destroy the path of error and to break down sorrow. Buddhism is not agnosticism or atheism. Buddhism is not nihilism. Buddha did not deny God. He only said: "Do not bother about questions like 'Is there God?', 'Do I exist?', 'Is the world real or not?'. Do not waste your time and energy in useless discussions. Become a practical religious man. Purify your heart. Control the mind. Lead a virtuous life. You will attain Nirvana or emancipation or eternal bliss".

To accuse Buddha as an atheist or agnostic is simply foolish. Buddha found no use in metaphysical wrangling. He declined to enter into metaphysics. Is there God or no God? Is life eternal or non-eternal? These questions were set aside as not requiring an answer for the attainment of Nirvana. The immediate great problem for Buddha was suffering and annihilation of suffering. He asked his followers not to bother about the transcendental questions. He set aside all those things which did not help towards the attainment of the goal. He thought it wise to give his followers a way, and not a creed. He thought that speculation about the nature of the ultimate reality was an unnecessary drag on the path of truth and spiritual attainment. The vital and fundamental thing is not to discuss about the ultimate truth, but to tread the path which takes man out of the world of pain and suffering into the supreme abode of eternal bliss and immortality. The nature of the ultimate truth is beyond the reach of mind and speech. If Buddha refused to define the nature of the Absolute, or if he contented himself with negative definitions, it is only to show that the Absolute or the Ultimate is above all definitions.

Way of Self-reliance

Buddhism is the religion of earnest, undaunted effort. Buddha demands from you faith in your own Self, in your own latent forces. Without this faith, nothing can be achieved. The first words of Buddha, after his Enlightenment, were: "Wide open are the gates of Immortality. Ye that have ears to hears, release your faith".

Buddha did not want his followers to believe in his words, but to understand them and take them for starting their own investigations and experience. He proclaimed that the experience was open only to one who trod the path of virtue, piety and self-discipline. He said to the Kalamas: "Accept not what you hear by report. Accept not tradition, because it is old and has been handed down through many generations. Do not hastily conclude that it must be so. Do not accept a statement on the ground that it is found in our books, or on the supposition that it is acceptable, or because it is the saying of your teacher or priests. Whatsoever according to your own experience, and after thorough investigation, agrees with your reason and is conducive to your welfare as well as to the good of other living beings, that accept as true, and mould your life in accordance with that".

This is the view of free-thinkers and rationalists also. But, this will not help the aspirants to attain the goal. Intellect is finite. It has its own limitations. The Upanishads boldly declare that one can attain Self-realisation through the help of a wonderful teacher, a Brahma-srotri and Brahmanishtha who has theoretical knowledge of the scriptures and who has direct knowledge of the ultimate truth or Brahman also.

Lord Buddha, the Apostle of Ahimsa and Love

Buddha was the greatest benevolent man or humanitarian which the world has ever produced. He is one without a second. Benevolence and humanitarianism are the keynotes of all religious movements of the world; but, the benevolence and humanitarian spirit and work of Lord Buddha stand unrivalled in the religious history of the world.

Buddha abandoned his kingdom and went about begging his bread through the streets of India, and preached for the good of men and animals. He had a heart as wide as the sky or the ocean. He did not want heaven. He did not want money or throne. What an exalted selfless Yogi he was! He was the only man who was ever ready to give up his life for animals to stop a sacrifice. He once said to a king: "If the sacrifice of a lamb helps you to go to heaven, sacrificing a man will help you better. Therefore, sacrifice me". He has left an indelible impression on this world by his extraordinary sacrifice, great renunciation and purity of life.

Many Rishis and prophets have preached the doctrine of love and Ahimsa, but there has never been, in the entire history of the world's ethical thought, a greater affirmation of the principle of Ahimsa and love than has been done by Lord Buddha. No one has disseminated so widely the doctrine of Ahimsa and universal love as Lord Buddha. No one has practised these two fundamental virtues of love and Ahimsa as Buddha. No one has possessed such a tender, kind and merciful heart as Buddha. Hence he is enshrined even now in the hearts of millions of people. His heart throbbed severely and melted when he saw a little suffering in an ant or a worm or a dog. He gave up his body as food for a hungry ferocious animal in his previous birth. Several acts of kindness done in several births made him a Buddha in his last birth.

Not a single drop of blood has ever been shed in the name of Buddhism. Religious persecution is unknown to Buddhism. At the present day, it is estimated that more than one-third of the population of the world is Buddhist. Buddhism spread by the spirit of strong grace. The history of Buddhism does not relate any great wars as having been waged, or countries vanquished, in its name. It has always adopted peaceful ways of disseminating its teachings. Tolerance and serenity characterise the Buddhistic faith.

The Noble Eightfold Path

The gospel of Buddha is simple and yet wonderfully profound. Buddha analysed all experiences and the world-process as it appears to all of us, with a scientific frame of mind. He finds out that everything is mutable, changing and impermanent or transitory. There is suffering, disharmony, discord and discontent everywhere in life, on account of the impermanence or transitoriness of things around. This universal experience of sorrow or Duhkha is the starting point in Buddha's thought. Buddha did not preach pessimism. He was wonderfully optimistic. He emphatically asserts that there is a way out of sorrow, and a haven of eternal bliss, within the reach of every man.

The four cardinal truths or principles which Buddha preached are: that there is suffering in the world; that the cause of suffering is Tanha or craving; that the extinction of craving leads to cessation of suffering; and that this extinction of craving can be achieved by the Noble Eightfold Path.

The Noble Eightfold Path consists of the practice of right belief; right understanding or right views; right aspiration; right speech, right conduct or right action; right living or right means of livelihood; right exertion; right mindfulness or attentiveness; and right concentration or meditation.

These are the eight steps in the Way of Life presented by Lord Buddha which annihilate suffering of all kinds and lead to the attainment of Nirvana or emancipation. The Noble Eightfold Path destroys lust, anger, greed, malice and other evils, and purifies the heart. Then dawns Bodhi or Enlightenment which bestows perfect everlasting peace, eternal bliss and immortality.

Nirvana—Its Meaning

The religion of Buddha is a pathway to the Nirvanic beatitude. It is a way and not a creed. It is a scheme of spiritual development and not a set of doctrines.

The world 'Nirvana' literally means 'going out'. It signifies a spiritual experience full of peace and bliss, which is characterised by the 'going out' from the heart of the three fires of lust, ill-will and dullness.

Nirvana is not utter annihilation. Nirvana is total extinction of all that is base in us.

The present-day world needs very badly the teachings of Lord Buddha. Everywhere we see preparations for the destruction of the human race and its culture. Fear of the atomic bomb is causing restlessness everywhere. Scientists and dictators have neither rest nor peace. There is mistrust amongst the leaders of the nations. Malice, hatred and prejudice have grown to such a large extent that the very structure of human civilisation seems to be crumbling. The one great ambition of every nation is to possess more atomic bombs. Scientists are working day and night in the laboratories to release as much atomic energy as possible to destroy people. What a horrible state of affairs! It is really shocking. The only way by which the world can be saved lies in a return to the great principles of Ahimsa and Maitri inculcated by Lord Buddha and Maharshi Patanjali. Hatred can never be cured by hatred. It can only be cured by love. This is a lesson which the world has to learn again and again. Take a solemn vow now to meet hatred with love, and malice with goodwill. This is the best way to pay our homage to the great sage Lord Buddha, the apostle of love and Ahimsa, the saviour of the world, the Avatara of Lord Vishnu.

9. CHARITY

Charity is the disposition to think favourably of others and do them good. Charity is universal love. It is liberality to the poor. It is benevolence. That which is given to relieve the needy is charity.

In a general sense, charity means love, benevolence and goodwill. In a theological sense, it is universal goodwill to men and supreme love to God.

True charity is the desire to be useful to others without thought of recompense or reward. Charity is love in action.

Charity begins at home, but it should go abroad. The whole world is your home. You are a citizen of the world. Cultivate a generous feeling for the welfare of the whole world.

It is a sin to hoard money. All wealth belongs to the Lord. He who lives only as a trustee of his property and spends his money in charity thinks that the property really belongs to the Lord and lives happily. He attains Moksha or eternal peace.

The water of the Ganga cannot decrease if thirsty people drink it. So also, your wealth cannot decrease if you do charity.

Give one-tenth of your income, or six Paise per rupee, in charity. Give cheerfully, quickly, and without hesitation. Defer not charities till death. Do charity daily.

Prayer takes you half-way to God, fasting to the door of His Supreme Abode, and charity procures you admission.

What Is Charity

Every good act is charity. Giving water to the thirsty is charity. An encouraging word to a man in distress is charity. Giving a little medicine to the poor, sick man is charity. Removing a thorn or a glass-piece on the road is charity.

To be kind and loving is charity. To forget and forgive some harm done to you is charity. A kind word said to a suffering man is charity.

Charity is not confined to giving in terms of dollars, rupees, or shillings. Think well towards suffering people. Pray for their welfare. This will accomplish more good than much money.

Kinds of Charity

The best form of charity is Vidya-dana, imparting wisdom. If you give food to a poor man, he again wants food when he becomes hungry. Whereas wisdom removes ignorance, the cause for taking a body, and destroys *in toto* all sorts of miseries and suffering for ever.

The second best form of charity is giving medicine to the sick. The third best form of charity is Anna-dana or giving food to the hungry.

Do discriminate charity in the beginning. Later on, practise indiscriminate charity. When you feel that every being is a manifestation of the Lord, it is difficult to discriminate who is good and who is bad.

Give to the poor, the sick, the helpless and the forlorn. Give to the orphans, the decrepit, the blind, the helpless widows. Give to the Sadhus, Sannyasins, religious and social institutions. Thank the man who gives you an opportunity to serve him by doing charity. Give with the right mental attitude, and realise God through charitable acts. Glory to those who do charity with the right spirit.

The Glory of a Silent Gift

Some people do charity and are anxious to see their names published in the newspapers with their photos. This is a Tamasic form of charity. This is no charity at all. That charity which advertises ceases to be charity. It is only pride and ostentation.

You should not advertise your charity and charitable nature. There must not be any exaltation in your heart when people praise you for your charitable nature. Charity must be spontaneous and unrestrained. Giving must become habitual. You must experience extreme joy in giving. You must not think: "I have done a very charitable act. I will enjoy happiness in heaven. I will be born as a rich man in the next birth. The charitable act will wash away my sin. There is no charitable man like me in my town or district. People know that I am a very charitable man". Bragging is mean and deplorable.

Do charity silently. Do not advertise. Do not boast. What your right hand does, the left hand should not know.

It is easy to fight in the battle, but it is difficult to give a gift silently, without manifesting pride and self-glorification and without expressing to others.

Mean-minded Charity

Prof. XYZ, M.A., Ph.D., gave a blanket in charity to a poor man. He afterwards thought, "I ought not to have given him a blanket". His heart was in a state of agitation and agony. He wanted to get the blanket back from the poor man. If you do such a kind of charity, you will not derive any benefit. You will not get purity of heart. Many worldly-minded people perform charitable acts of this description only. This world abound in such charitable persons.

All are very generous for themselves. Many will take first-class milk or tea, and offer second-class milk to their friends, and third-class milk to strangers. They will eat first-calss fruits and offer rotten ones to strangers, neighbours and servants. They will wait for three days for getting a good opportunity to use the old preparations of food, and then throw them to their servants with a painful heart. They do not like to part with these decaying things also. You will find such heart-rending instances in almost all the houses of rich persons. How crooked are such people! What a small, constricted heart they have! Their lot is, indeed, not only pitiable, but also highly deplorable. They do not know what they are exactly doing.

Always give the best things, best food, best fruits, best milk, best clothes to friends, neighbours, strangers, guests and servants. You will derive immense joy, strength and happiness. Put this into practice and realise the benefits yourself.

The Tragic Plight of Miserly People

The majority of householders are absolutely selfish in these days. Money is their blood. You will find cheerlessness and ugliness in their face. Worry, greed, passion, jealousy, hatred, depression, and all other evil qualities stick to the man who has the miserly nature in him, and they consume the very core of his heart.

If a miserly man keeps fifty thousand rupees, he will not enjoy the money, but crave for a lakh more. A millionaire will be craving to become a multimillionaire. Such persons will not give even a pie in charity.

They are first-class misers. They hoard money in some way or the other. Their money goes away in medical bills. Their sons squander their money in drinking, gambling, licentious living. The die of broken heart on account of bank failures, failures in speculations. Their final fate is bankruptcy, starvation here; torture in hell hereafter. Pitiable and deplorable is their lot. They have not eaten good food even one day. They have not worn good clothes even one day. They are mere caretakers of money.

Some officers retire from service and live on the banks of the Ganga, Narmada and Yamuna. They do a little Japa and meditation, and study Yoga-Vasishtha and the Upanishads, and imagine that they are Jivanmuktas. They entertain intense Moha for their children. They remit their pension to their sons and grandchildren. They will not spend even a pie in charity. They are the embodiment of miserliness. They are hopeless, self-deluded souls! A miser cannot dream of Self-realisation even in a thousand births. Lord Jesus says, "It is easier for a camel to go through the eye of a needle than for a rich man to enter into the Kingdom of God".

Miserliness is a great curse. It is an enemy of oneness and a friend of selfishness.

Miserly persons are quite unfit for the spiritual path. Their very company is highly dangerous for spiritual-minded persons. They poison the whole atmosphere on account of their corrupted, contracted heart.

You should have a very large heart. You should throw money like stones to the poor people. Only then can you develop Advaitic feeling, Samadhi and cosmic love.

How to Do Charity

Share with others what you have. Keep a few pies in your pocket always and distribute them in charity daily to poor people. Practise this at once.

In sharing, there is joy and peace. Sharing generates cosmic love and destroys greed. Sharing removes selfishness and creates selflessness. Sharing purifies the heart. Sharing develops oneness.

Share with others whatever you possess, physical, mental, or spiritual. This is a real Yajna. You will expand. You will experience oneness and unity of life. This will lead you to Advaitic realisation.

You should be thirsty to do charitable acts daily. You should not lose any opportunity. You should create opportunities. There is no Yoga or Yajna greater than Sattvic charity of the spontaneous type. Karna, Raja Bhoja did countless charitable acts. So they still live in our hearts.

Charity should be given with faith. Charity should never be given without faith. Charity should be given in plenty. Charity should be given with modesty. Charity should be given with sympathy.

The food you are able to give a guest may be meagre fare, but if you offer it with love, it acquires great power, nutrition and taste. If you serve your guest with rich dishes and proudly say, "All right, now that you have come, go and fill your belly", the food turns into poison. Whether he is a relation, friend, or beggar, whatever be the quality of the food you give, give it with love and affection. Hospitality is the essence of food.

Charity Purifies the Heart

Sins can be destroyed by charity. Lord Jesus says, "Charity covereth a multitude of sins". Charity is a great purifier of heart. In the Gita you will find: "Yajna, charity and austerity are the purifiers of the intelligent".

If one can destroy one's miserly nature, a great portion of Sadhana is over. One has then achieved something substantial.

Develop this Udara Vritti. Then you can become a King of kings. If you give, the whole wealth of the world is yours. Money will come to you. This is the immutable inexorable, unrelenting law of nature. Therefore, give. Give. You make a living by what you get, but you make a life by what you give. Always give, give, give. This is the secret of abundance and divine life.

Many have achieved power, popularity, peace and happiness only through a generous heart. Miserly persons can never dream to have all these and get success in life.

If you want wealth and children, do plenty of charity. If you want to become wise, serve old men and Mahatmas. If you want to get rid of sins, do Havan.

See God everywhere. Share with all. The major portion must be given to others. Destroy the ingrained miserliness. Your heart will expand. You will have a broad outlook on life. You will have a new, wide vision. You can feel the help you get from the Indweller of the heart. You can experience an indescribable thrill of divine ecstasy and spiritual bliss. This will give you tremendous inner strength.

O man! Give plenty in charity. You will enjoy peace, plenty and prosperity here. You will go to heaven hereafter. You will attain purity of heart, and Moksha too.

10. CHRISTIANITY

Christianity derives its name from Christ. Christianity speaks of a Personal God. There is not much deep philosophy or Yoga Sadhana in Christianity. There is reason for this. Jesus had to deal with the illiterate fishermen of Galilee. He gave them only moral precepts and showed them the way of righteous living.

Christianity is based chiefly on Judaism and partly on Buddhism. The doctrines of the Christian religion are all taken from Judaism. Jesus never professed to abolish Judaism and set up a new religion of his own. He says, "Think not I am come to destroy the Law or the Prophets. I am not come to destroy but to fulfil. For verily I say unto you: 'Till heaven and earth pass, one jot or one title shall in nowise pass from the law, till all be fulfilled.' Whosoever, therefore, shall break one of these least commandments and shall teach men so, he shall be called the least in the Kingdom of Heaven; but whosoever shall do and teach them, the same shall be called great in the Kingdom of Heaven".

Christianity faith sprang from the wisdom of India and overspread the old trunk of Judaism. Buddhism prevailed in Palestine when Christ was born. Christ himself came in contact with it through John the Baptist. There is a striking resemblance between Buddhism and Christianity in their precepts, in their forms and ceremonies, in the architectural style of their temples, and even in the accounts of the lives their founders.

The dogmas or metaphysical doctrines of Christianity are the same as those of Judaism but its moral precepts are much higher and nobler than those of the Jewish prophets. Christianity owes to Buddhism that higher morality which distinguishes it from Judaism. The moral precepts and teachings of Buddhism have much in common with those of Christianity. Christ himself taught no dogmas.

The teaching of Jesus which is chiefly ethical is embodied in the Sermon on the Mount, the Lord's Prayer and certain parables known as the parables of the Good Samaritan, the Prodigal Son and the Sheep and the Goats.

Philosophy and Teachings

Christianity is essentially a radiant way of life, a way of happy and victorious living in this world. Jesus astonished people by his insight when discussing religion with the religious leaders of his day. For three years he explained his claim as the "Only Son of God" and taught people about the nature of his "Father" God, and the true paths of human life in the shape of Sermon on the Mount, etc. Jesus Christ was called "The Great Exemplar". He explained the real nature of God, man and the world he lived in. He taught people to change their way of looking at things. He told them that if they would change their outlook on life from its materialistic to its spiritualistic aspect, they would realise that the world they were living in was God's Kingdom.

He has left no written records of his important teachings. He delivered all his teachings orally. Neither he, nor his followers ever wrote down even a single word which was spoken by him, in his lifetime.

His words have been misunderstood, wrongly annotated, mutilated, deformed and transformed and yet they have survived almost two thousand years and as they were very powerful and came from the heart of a realised Yogi.

Here is the gist of Jesus's teachings: God is Spirit. He is Omnipresent. He loves His creatures with infinite love. He is the Father of all. God is immanent in the world. He is transcendental also. He sent His son Jesus Christ unto the world to show them the way to attain immortality.

The theological doctrine of Jesus is belief in the Fatherhood of God and brotherhood of man. In God-head there are three Persons, viz., Father, Son and the Holy Ghost or Spirit. This is the Trinity of Christianity. All men are brothers, because they are all members of the family of God. If the teaching of Christ is carried out there will be no war.

Here is a gist of his "Sermon on the Mount":

Blessed are the poor in spirit; for theirs is the Kingdom of Heaven.

Blessed are they that mourn; for they shall be comforted.

Blessed are the meek; for they shall inherit the earth.

Blessed are they that hunger and thirst after righteousness; for they shall be filled.

Blessed are the merciful; for they shall obtain mercy.

Blessed are the pure in heart; for they shall see God.

Blessed are the peacemakers; for they shall be called the sons of God.

Inward purity, meekness, forgiveness, returning good for evil—these are the distinctive features of Christianity. Man does not live by bread alone, but by every word that proceedeth out of the mouth of God.

Jesus laid great stress on love of God, love of fellow-men and of Law. Faith in God is the central teaching of Jesus.

11. CIVILISATION

What is civilisation? Are you really civilised now? When you suffer from phthisis or asthma, septicaemia or malaria, doctors give you various sorts of injections. Can you call this civilisation? You can hear songs sung in Paris or Constantinople at the beach at Triplicane, Madras. Is this civilisation? The germs of phthisis and pyorrhoea are broadcast by motor-cars, railways and soda-water shops. Millions of people are packed up in insanitary houses in lanes and gullies. Life has become entirely dependent. Freedom is unknown. When the switch fails, there is no light in the house. There is no water in the tap when you want it very badly. We never heard of blood-pressure some fifteen years ago. Now, ninety per cent of the people suffer this terrible malady.

The Panorama of City Life

The dust raised by the running of motor-cars and lorries in the roads and streets enters the eyes, nose, lungs, trachea and stomach; and produces various sorts of diseases of the eyes, lungs, stomach, etc. This is due to modern civilisation. Man wants money and money alone. He dies for money. He does not want religion. He says: "I want not only bread, but bread with butter and jam". To eat this buttered-bread, he has to swallow the dust of the roads and the smoke of the chimneys of the factories, and spend all his earnings in the treatment of pyorrhoea, blood-pressure, asthma and phthisis.

People take their food at 9 a.m. and immediately run to catch the first train to attend offices and courts at 10 a.m. There is no rest. The whole stomach and the intestines are shaken violently. Dyspepsia and a host of stomach troubles result. This is due to modern civilisation.

People have learnt intelligent ways to cheat others. They utilise mesmerism and hypnotism to rob others and to molest ladies. They have discovered various kinds of palatable dishes to satisfy the tongue. This is modern civilisation.

Hotels have become centres of Mayaic play. You will have all sorts of comforts—hot water tap, cold water tap, etc. There is dancing, band-playing during meals. There are all kinds of materials to excite all your senses to their climax, to make you forget God and Truth completely. There is beauty competition among males and females through votes. A Rich man presides. Males vote for the most beautiful woman. Females vote for the most handsome man. They get prizes too. The woman who gets the first prize is invited to dinners by rich men. She is ruined miserably here and there. This is modern civilisation.

One rich engineer says, "In my life, I have used thirty cars". One rich doctor says, "I have twenty servants in my house". One barrister says, "I have gone to Europe and America ten times". A big business-man says, "I have five hundred bungalows in different places. I cannot take food with Kheer and Rasogolla. I get fruits from Bombay and Calcutta". A fashionable judge says, "I have two hundred suits and three hundred shirts". Nobody says, "I have performed twenty-four lakhs of Gayatri Japa. I have studied Yoga-Vasishtha ten times, Gita a hundred times, Ramayana fifty times. I have fasted throughout Dusserah. I have meditated for twelve hours on Sunday. I do Pranayama for three hours daily, Asanas for two hours, Mantra-writing for two hours". This is modern civilisation.

To wear spectacles at the age of ten, to wear ring-watch, to buy a car by borrowing money, to wear fashionable dinner-uniform and Ellwood hat, health boots, to have a French crop or bobbed hair, to smoke *Three Castles* cigarettes or *Navy Cut* or *Manila* cigars, to constrict the neck with stiff collars, to take the food at tables with spoons, forks and table-knives, to walk along the sea-beach with their wives in clasped hands, to have newspaper in their pocket, to have a trimmed or Kaiser moustache at the middle of the upper lip, to take meat and brandy, to play bridge, to gamble, to dance in ball-rooms, to borrow money, to go to talkies and in short, to lead a life of dissipation.... this is modern civilisation!

Fashion and Passion

People are dying for fashion. Gents and ladies have become slaves of fashion. If there is a slight error in the cutting of a gown or uniform, there are damage-suits in courts in London and Paris against tailors. You can see the multifarious fashions in the evening. Fashion consists in half-nudity. They will call this scientific, hygienic ventilation of the exposed parts. Half the chest, half the arms, half the legs must be exposed. This is fashion. They have full control of their hairs. This is their Siddhi or psychic power. They can cut it and dress it in any way they like in a hair dressing saloon. Fashion increases and excites passion.

The whole world can be clothed out of the cuttings of the vain, fashionable people. Money is wasted enormously in fashion. If this money that is wasted in fashion is utilised in virtuous actions, in charity and service of society, man will be transmuted into Divinity. He will be in the enjoyment of eternal peace and bliss. What do you see now instead in fashionable people? Restlessness, anxiety, worry, fear, depression and pallor of face. They may be dressed in silken gowns, or dinner suits in up-to-date fashion and style with stiff double collar ties and bows. But, you see in their faces cheerlessness and ugliness. The canker of worry, greed, passion, and hatred has eaten the very core of their hearts.

Why do ladies and gents put on fashionable dress? They want to appear as big people in the eyes of others. They think they will get respect and honour by putting on fashionable dress. The wife wants to appear beautiful in the eyes of her husband. She wants to attract him. The husband puts on fashionable dress to attract his wife. The sister of ill-fame wants to get more customers by putting on fashionable dress. This is all delusion. Can a fashionable dress give real beauty? This is all artificial decoration. Temporary, false glittering! Decaying, false beauty! If you possess good virtues such as mercy, sympathy, love, devotion and forbearance, you will be respected and really honoured. This will give everlasting beauty even though one is clad in rags. How simple was Mahatma Gandhi in his dress!! He had a loin cloth only. How simple was Ramana Maharshi! He had a Kowpeen only.

Baneful Effect of Artificial Living

Life has become very artificial. There is physical, mental and moral degeneration. You do not find robust, sinewy, stalwart, healthy people. Longevity is unknown. People are short-lived. You see puny, stunted creatures with poor physique, dilapidated frame and sickly appearance. They cannot walk even a furlong. They want a rickshaw. Children beget children. People die like moths. They have become weaklings. They have become effeminate and impotent. How strong and healthy our forefathers were! They had a very long life. They could walk forty miles a day. They could swim across a big river during floods at the age of seventy. They could split fuel. They could carry heavy weights. They were strong and sinewy. They were living on simple fare. Even now, look at the Gurkha and Maharashtra labourers. They live on ordinary bread, salt and two chillies. Look at the tremendous work turned out by them! Look at their health and marvellous strength! Now, every one of you want *Ovaltine,* vitamin extracts, *Allenbury Rusks,* and oat-meal. The wife wants an exclusive servant and a cook. You want a servant to put on your shoes. The child wants an Ayah.

Science had added many comforts to man. Electricity does all sorts of work. It pumps water. It lifts us to the top storey. It cooks food. It carries us to London and Paris. Science has made our travel and communication easy and quick. There are some advantages. But the disadvantages outweigh the advantages. It has made living very costly and luxurious. Man is more restless now. A luxury of today becomes a want of tomorrow. Every man and woman want a pocket radio, a torch, a wrist-watch, a car, a household cinema. The standard of living has become very high. Clerks and officers do not hesitate to tell lies and take bribes to make both ends meet. The cinema and fashion are devouring all their earnings.

Sense-gratification has become the goal of life. Intelligent people devise intelligent methods to take bribes and to earn money by various dishonest means. There is corruption everywhere. Honesty and candidness have taken to their heels. Double-dealing, crookedness, cheating and chicanery, have taken possession of all. All these are the products of luxurious living, consequent upon scientific inventions and Western civilisation.

A doctor or pleader, even if he is starving, must maintain a car. Otherwise he cannot get patients or clients. His wife wants silk saris, face powder, rouge, lipstick and scents. Seats have to be reserved for picture-houses. Where to go for money? He has to tap the poor people. He fills up a bottle with water and coloured tinctures, and charges heavily. He extorts money by charging too much for injection and visits. Mercy, sympathy, and honesty have fled away from his heart. When the mind is filled with greed, passion and dishonesty, conscience is destroyed.

In this age of the so-called modern civilisation, greed, passion and selfishness are increasing day by day—nay, hour by hour. Man has lost his manliness. The son drags his father to the courts for division of property. The wife divorces her husband and marries another if he happens to be more rich, more beautiful and younger. The younger brother poisons his elder brother to take possession of the estate. You see cruelty, dishonesty, injustice and atrocity everywhere. No one keeps his promise. The father has no faith in the son. The wife has no faith in the husband and the husband has no faith in the wife.

Life Divorced from God and Religion

This is Kali-Yuga. Dharma has become a decrepit. He is somewhere in a decrepit hospital. People are acting according to their own whims and fancies. There is no check. Every man is a Guru. He does not care for any religious instruction. Passion is swaying everyone. Discrimination, right thinking and Vichara have taken to their heels. Eating, drinking and procreation are the goal of life. Moksha has become a non-entity and a visionary dream. Evil habits of all sorts have cropped up in all.

A friend greets another friend not with the Names of God, *Jai Sri Krishna* or *Jai Ramji Ki,* but with a packet of cigarettes and a peg of whisky. He says, "Come along, Mr. Naidu. Have a smoke. Have a drink of gin-squash".

Money—The Modern Curse

Money is, doubtless, necessary for man; but, money is not the goal of life. One should not worship mammon. The dollar cannot give peace and bliss. There are buildings in America one hundred and twenty-three storeys high. Each room in each storey is air-conditioned, and has up-to-date electric equipments. But tell me, brother, who is superior? He who lives in a hundred and twenty-three storeyed building in America with plenty of aeroplanes and cars, with plenty of money, rolling in dollars, with plenty of cares, worries, anxieties, with plenty of blood-pressure and other diseases with a small constricted heart, with plenty of ignorance and its modifications such as lust, greed and wrath? Or, he who lives in a small grass-hut on the banks of the Ganga, in Rishikesh, Himalayas, with plenty of health, with a large magnanimous heart, with plenty of divine qualities, with plenty of divine bliss, perennial joy and peace, with plenty of knowledge of the Self, without any money, cares, worries and anxieties?

What is wanted is a spacious or large loving heart with high sublime thinking. You may live in a small thatched cottage. It does not matter much.

The other day, an Englishman, a military officer of Meerut, came to this Ashram. He was very much attracted by the quiet and calm atmosphere of Ananda Kutir. I told him that he could have the same quietude in some of the silent corners of England, in some parts of the hills. He replied, "No, there also aeroplanes ever move about above the heads. Quietude is unknown to England".

A Scene of Chaos and Bewilderment

You yourself have made your life complex and intricate. You have entangled yourself in this quagmire of Samsara. You have multiplied your wants and desires. Every day you are forging an additional link to the chain of bondage. Simplicity has vanished. Luxurious habits and ways of living are embraced. No wonder there is unemployment everywhere. People are dying of starvation. There is depression in trade. There is unrest everywhere. Divorce courts are also multiplying. One nation is afraid of another nation. One nation suspects that the other nations are preparing for a big war. Life has thus become a matter of uncertainty. It has become a mass of confusion, chaos and bewilderment. It has become stormy and boisterous. It is full of under-currents, cross-currents, subterranean currents, and mixed currents.

The Way of Escape

Now then, is there no way of escape from these troubles and difficulties? There is only one way. Lead a life of dispassion, self-control, purity, selfless service and cosmic love. Develop the habit of taking the right point of view, right thinking, right feeling, right acting with the right mental attitude or Bhava. Practise devotion and meditation.

To move in Rolls-Royce is not real civilisation. To have sky-scrapers is not civilisation. To have helicopters is not civilisation. To have abundant wealth is not civilisation. To have titles and honours is not civilisation. To be honest, humble and pious is civilisation. To be saintly and compassionate is civilisation. To be endowed with devotion and wisdom is civilisation. To have the spirit of service and sacrifice is civilisation.

We will have to get back to nature and natural living. We will have to adopt the simple living and high thinking of our forefathers. Lead a simple, natural life. Wear simple clothing. Walk daily. Give up cinemas and novel-reading. Eat simple food. Lead a hard, laborious life. Be self-reliant. Do not engage servants. Reduce your wants. Be honest in your dealings. Earn at the sweat of your brow. Control the Indriyas and mind. Develop noble qualities. Take recourse to the company of wise men. Remember God. Sing His Name. Feel His presence. Speak truth. Learn to discriminate. Learn how to lead a divine life while remaining in the world. Serve society with Atma-bhava. Then the whole question is solved. You have regained your Godhead. You have regained your lost paradise. All miseries will come to an end. You will have success in every walk of life and undertaking. Keep this master-key with you and open the chambers of elysian bliss.

12. CONCENTRATION

If you focus the rays of the sun through a lens, they can burn cotton or a piece of paper; but, the scattered rays cannot do this act. If you want to talk to a man at a distance, you make a funnel of your hand and speak. The sound-waves are collected at one point and then directed towards the man. He can hear your speech very clearly. The water is converted into steam and the steam is concentrated at a point. The railway engine moves. All these are instances of concentrated waves. Even so, if you collect dissipated rays of the mind and focus them at a point, you will have wonderful concentration. The concentrated mind will serve as a potent searchlight to find out the treasures of the soul and attain the supreme wealth of Atman, eternal bliss, immortality and perennial joy.

Real Raja Yoga starts from concentration. Concentration merges in meditation. Concentration is a portion of meditation.

Meditation follows concentration. Samadhi follows meditation. The Jivanmukti state follows the attainment of Nirvikalpa Samadhi which is free from all thoughts of duality. Jivanmukti leads to emancipation from the wheel of birth and death. Therefore, concentration is the first and foremost thing a Sadhaka or aspirant should acquire in the spiritual path.

You are born to concentrate the mind on God after collecting the mental rays that are dissipated on various objects. That is your important duty. You forget the duty on account of Moha for family, children, money, power, position, respect, name and fame.

Concentration of the mind on God after purification can give you real happiness and knowledge. You are born for this purpose only. You are carried away to external objects through attachment and infatuated love.

What Is Concentration?

Once a Sanskrit scholar approached Kabir and asked him, "O Kabir, what are you doing now?" Kabir replied, "O Pundit, I am detaching the mind from worldly objects and attaching it to the lotus-feet of the Lord". This is concentration.

Concentration or Dharana is centering the mind on one single thought. Vedantins try to fix the mind on the Atman. This is their

Dharana. Hatha Yogins and Raja Yogins concentrate their mind on the six Chakras. Bhaktas concentrate on their Ishta Devata. Concentration is a great necessity for all aspirants.

During concentration, the various rays of the mind are collected and focussed on the object of concentration. There will be no tossing of the mind. One idea occupies the mind. The whole energy of the mind is concentrated on that one idea. The senses become still. They do not function. When there is deep concentration, there is no consciousness of the body and surroundings.

When you study a book with profound interest, you do not hear if a man shouts and calls you by your name. You do not see a person when he stands in front of you. You do not smell the sweet fragrance of flowers that are placed on the table by your side. This is concentration or one-pointedness of mind. The mind is fixed firmly on one thing. You must have such a deep concentration when you think of God or the Atman.

Everybody possesses some ability to concentrate. Everybody does concentrate to a certain extent when he reads a book, when he writes a letter, when he plays tennis, and in fact, when he does any kind of work. But, for spiritual purposes, concentration should be developed to an infinite degree.

There is great concentration when you play cards or chess, but the mind is not filled with pure and divine thoughts. The mental contents are of an undesirable nature. You can hardly experience the divine thrill, ecstasy, and elevation when the mind is filled with impure thoughts. Every object has its own mental associations. You will have to fill up the mind with sublime, spiritual thoughts. Then only the mind will be expurgated of all worldly thoughts. The picture of Lord Jesus or Buddha or Lord Krishna is associated with sublime, soul-stirring ideas; chess and cards are associated with ideas of gambling, cheating and so forth.

Objects of Concentration

Sit on any comfortable pose. Place a picture of your Ishta Devata in front of you. Look at the picture with a steady gaze. Then close your eyes and visualise the picture in the centre of your heart or in the space between the eyebrows.

When the picture fades out in your mental vision, open the eyes and gaze at the picture again. Close your eyes after a few seconds and repeat the process.

It is easy to concentrate the mind on external objects. The mind has a natural tendency to go outwards. In the beginning stage of practice, you can concentrate on a black dot on the wall, a candle flame, a bright star, the moon, or any other object that is pleasing to the mind.

The mind should be trained to concentrate on gross objects in the beginning; and later on, you can successfully concentrate on subtle objects and abstract ideas.

There is no concentration without something to rest the mind upon. Concentrate on anything that appeals to you as good or anything which the mind likes best. It is very difficult to fix the mind, in the beginning, on any object which the mind dislikes.

Practise various sorts of concentration. This will train or discipline your mind wonderfully. Now concentrate on the Himalayas, a very great object. Then concentrate on a mustard or a pin-point. Now concentrate on a distant object. Then concentrate on a near object. Now concentrate on a colour, sound, touch, smell or taste. Then concentrate on the 'tik-tik' of a watch. Now concentrate on the virtue 'mercy'. Then concentrate on the virtue 'patience'. Now concentrate on the Sloka, *"Jyotishamapi Tat Jyotih....."* Then concentrate on *"Satyam Jnanam Anantam"*. Now concentrate on the image of Lord Siva. Then concentrate on the *"Aham Brahmasmi"* Mahavakya.

An Uphill Task for the Beginner

For a neophyte, the practice of concentration is disgusting and tiring in the beginning. He has to cut new grooves in the mind and brain. After some months, he will get great interest in concentration. He will enjoy a new kind of happiness, the concentration-Ananda. He will become restless if he fails to enjoy this new kind of happiness even for one day.

The vital point in concentration is to bring the mind to the same point or object again by limiting its movements in a small circle in the beginning. That is the main aim. A time will come when the mind will stick to one point alone. This is the fruit of your constant and protracted Sadhana. The joy is indescribable now.

Concentration will increase by lessening the number of thoughts. Certainly, it is an uphill work to reduce the number of thoughts. Just as you will have to take back with care your cloth that is fallen on a thorny plant by removing the thorns one by one slowly, so also, you will have to collect back with care and exertion the dissipated rays of the mind that are thrown over the sensual objects for very many years. In the beginning, it will tax you much. The task will be very unpleasant.

A Mental Process, Not a Muscular Exercise

Concentration is purely a mental process. It needs an inward turning of the mind. It is not a muscular exercise. There should be no undue strain on the brain. You should not fight and wrestle with the mind violently.

When you concentrate on any object, avoid tension anywhere in the body or mind. Think gently of the object in a continuous manner. Do not allow the mind to wander away.

How to Increase Your Power of Concentration

Concentration can be done only if you are free from all distractions. A man whose mind filled with passion and all sorts of fantastic desires can hardly concentrate on any object even for a second. His mind will be jumping like an old monkey. Japa of any Mantra and Pranayama will steady the mind, remove tossing, and increase the power of concentration.

Too much physical exertion, too much talking, too much eating, too much mixing with ladies and undesirable persons, too much walking, will cause distraction of mind. Those who practise concentration must abandon these things.

Whatever work you do, do with perfect concentration. Never leave the work without finishing it completely.

When you sit for prayers and meditation, never think of your office work. When you work in the office, never think of the child who is sick or of any other household work. When you take bath, do not think of games. When you sit for meals, do not think of the work that is pending in the office. You must train yourself to attend to the work on hand with perfect one-pointedness.

Celibacy, Pranayama, reduction of wants and activities, renunciation of objects, solitude, silence, discipline of the senses, annihilation of lust and greed, control of anger, non-mixing with undesirable persons, giving up of the newspaper habit and visiting cinemas, all these pave a long way in increasing the power of concentration.

You must try to be always cheerful and peaceful. Then only you will have concentration of mind. The practice of friendship with equals, compassion towards inferiors or distressed persons, complacency towards superiors or virtuous persons, and indifference towards sinners or wicked persons will produce cheerfulness or serenity and destroy hatred, jealousy, and dislike.

You should have real and intense thirst for God-realisation. Then all obstacles will be obviated. Concentration will be quite easy for you then. Mere emotional bubbling for the time being out of sheer curiosity, or for attainting psychic powers, cannot bring any tangible result.

Concentration and Pranayama

The practice of concentration and the practice of Pranayama are interdependent. If you practise Pranayama, you will get concentration. Natural Pranayama follows practice of concentration. A Hatha Yogi practises Pranayama and then controls mind. He rises upwards from below. A Raja Yogi practises concentration and thus controls his Prana. He comes downwards from above. They both meet on a common platform in the end. There are different practices according to the different capacities, tastes, and temperaments. To some, the practice of Pranayama will be easy to start with; to others, the practice of concentration will be easier. The latter had already practised Pranayama in their previous births. Therefore they take up, in this birth, the higher limb of Yoga, *i.e.,* concentration.

Importance of an Ethical Basis

Purify the mind first through the practice of right conduct and then take to the practice of concentration. Concentration without purity of mind is of no avail.

Some foolish, impatient students take to concentration at once without in any manner undergoing any preliminary training in ethics. This is a serious blunder.

There are some occultists who have concentration. But, they

have no good character. That is the reason why they do not make any progress in the spiritual line.

Concentration—The Master-key to Success

Those who practise concentration evolve quickly. They can do any work with scientific accuracy and great efficiency. What others do in six hours can be done, by one who has concentration, within half an hour. What others read in six hours can be read, by one who does concentration, within half an hour. Concentration purifies and calms the surging emotions, strengthens the current of thought, and clarifies the ideas.

Concentration helps a man in his material progress also. He will have a very good out-turn of work in his office or business house. He who practises concentration will possess very clear mental vision. What was cloudy and hazy before becomes clear and definite now. What was difficult before becomes easy now. And what was complex, bewildering, and confusing before comes easily within the mental grasp. You can achieve anything through concentration. Nothing is impossible to a man who practises regular concentration.

It helps the scientists and professors to do great research work. It helps the doctor and the lawyer to do much work and earn more money. It develops will-power and memory; it sharpens and brightens the intellect. Concentration bestows serenity or calmness of mind, inner spiritual strength, patience, great capacity to turn out tremendous work, alacrity, acumen, agility, beautiful complexion, sweet voice, brilliant eyes, powerful voice and speech, power to influence others and attract people, cheerfulness, joy, bliss of soul, supreme peace. It removes restlessness, agitation of mind, laziness. It makes you fearless and unattached. It helps you to attain God-realisation.

The more is the mind fixed on God the more is the strength you will acquire. More concentration means more energy. Concentration opens the inner chambers of love or the realm of eternity. Concentration is a source of spiritual strength.

Be slow and steady in concentration. By practice of concentration, you will become superhuman.

Those who practise concentration off and on will have a steady mind only occasionally. Sometimes the mind will begin to wander and will be quite unfit for application. You must have a mind that will obey you at all times sincerely and carry out all your commands in the best possible manner at any time. Steady and systematic practice of Raja Yoga will make the mind very obedient and faithful. You will be successful in every attempt. You will never meet with failure.

13. CONFUCIANISM

Confucius was born in 551 B.C. in the feudal State of Lu, a portion of what is now the province of Shangtung on north eastern seaboard of China. Confucius and Lao-Tze, founder of Taoism, were contemporaries. They were Sages and Philosophers. They are not regarded as Saviours.

Confucianism is not a religion in the customary sense. It has neither priesthood nor any monastic order. It existed in China long before the time of Confucius. In one of his recorded sayings he speaks of himself as a "transmitter" and not a "maker" or originator. He did not give a new religion to the world or a new ethical code. What he gave to the world was only a powerful restatement of the fundamental principles of human morality or ethics. He issued a new and improved edition of the old one. The moral code he framed was most admirable. It contained grand ethical truths.

Confucius devoted himself to the improvement of Society. He ever thought of the well-being of the Society. He tried his level best to contribute much to social welfare. 'The Analects' or collection of sayings treats mainly of social welfare, human peace and harmony in Society. He strained his every nerve in giving moral training to people. He laid very great emphasis on cultivation of ethical virtues. He tried to remove the disturbing elements in Society. He had a strong conviction that if superiors and elders had a blameless character, others would follow them and there would be love and universal peace everywhere. As this social thought ever occupied his mind, he had no time to discuss on God and life after death. Moreover, he did not find it necessary also to dwell on these subjects.

Many of the sayings of Confucius are admirable. He says: "The love or virtue should be like the love of beauty—from an inward constraint. Have sufficient self-control even to judge of others in comparison with yourself, and to act towards them as you would wish them to act to you". This is what one may call the 'doctrine of humanity', and there is nothing beyond this.

"The way to become a superior man is to set one's affection on what is right and to love learning, which is the source of knowledge and virtue, with which nothing else can be compared. When righteousness is pursued with sincerity and a mind free from self-deception, the heart becomes rectified.

"Upto a particular stage the individual is busy only with his own improvement; but the cultivation of the person influences primarily those around him, and ultimately the whole empire. Everyone, therefore, should carefully cultivate his person, having due regard for others besides himself. Each man must guard his words and watch his conduct. He must fly all that is base and disquieting, and must take benevolence as his dwelling place, righteousness as his road, propriety as his garment, wisdom as his lamp, and faithfulness as his charm. Dignity, reverence, loyalty and faithfulness make up the qualities of a cultivated man. His dignity separates him from the crowd; being reverent, he is beloved; being loyal, he is submitted to; and being faithful, he is trusted".

The various sayings of Confucius presented the attributes of the superior man. Confucius asked his disciples to admire the superior man and to emulate him. He said that every human being cherishes the aspiration to become a superior man—superior to his fellows, superior to this own past and present self.

Confucius speaks of the superior or the ideal man thus: "The superior man is catholic and not a partisan. He does what is proper to the position in which he is. He does not wish to go beyond it. He finds himself no position in which he is not himself.

"The scholar considers honesty and good faith to be his coat of mail and helmet, propriety, and righteousness to be his shield, and buckler. He walks along, bearing over his head benevolence; he dwells holding righteousness in his arms before him. The government may be violently oppressive, but he does not change his course—such is the way in which he maintains himself".

Teachings

His teaching was largely concerned with the problem of good government. He said: "The Ruler himself should be virtuous, just, honest, and dutiful". "A virtuous ruler is like the Pole-star which, by keeping its place, makes all other stars revolve round it. As is the Ruler, so will be the subjects".

What was Confucius' idea of virtue? His word for it was 'Zen'. The proper understanding of this ethical doctrine chiefly depends on the implication of Zen. There is no single English equivalent of

Zen in all its shades of meaning. The essence of all his teachings may be summed up under this one word 'Zen'. The nearest equivalent to this difficult word is 'social virtue'. All those virtues which help to maintain social harmony and peace like benevolence, charity, magnanimity, sincerity, respectfulness, altruism, diligence, loving kindness, and goodness are included in Zen. A chief disciple of Confucius said: "The single principle that ran throughout the teachings of my Master is loyalty to oneself and charity to one's neighbour".

Confucius said: "A virtuous man has three awes:- (1) awe for Heaven's decree, (2) awe for great men, and (3) awe for saints' words. When worshipping God, one must feel as if He were visibly present".

The teaching of Confucius is that the entire world and every being are constantly changing and that the most essential aspect for human life is the present Reality.

Confucius held that Society was made up of five relationships, *viz.,* those of husband and wife, of parent and child, of elder and younger brother or generally of elders and youngsters, of Ruler and Minister or subject, and of friend and friend. A country would be well governed when all the parties performed their parts aright in these relationships. Confucius said: "There was Tao (a way or road of righteousness) only when fathers were fathers, when sons were sons, when Rulers were Rulers and when ministers were ministers".

Confucius laid great stress on the cultivation of character, purity of heart and conduct. He exhorted the people to develop a good character first which is a priceless jewel and which is the best of all virtues.

The nature of man, according to Confucius, is fundamentally good inclined towards goodness. Perfection of goodness can be found in sages and saints. Every man should attempt to reach the ideal by leading a virtuous life, by possessing a very noble character, and by doing his duty unselfishly with sincerity and truthfulness. He who is endowed with a good character and divine virtue is a princely type of man. The princely man sticks to virtue, and the inferior man clings to material comfort. The princely man is just while the inferior man expects rewards and favours. The princely man is dignified, noble, magnanimous, and humble while the inferior man is mean, proud, crooked, and arrogant.

In the "Great Learning" Confucius revealed the process, step by step, by which self-development is attained and by which it flows over into the common life to serve the state and bless mankind. The order of development which Confucius set forth is as follows:

Investigation of phenomena,
Learning,
Sincerity,
Rectitude of purpose,
Self-development,
Family-discipline
Local self-government, and
Universal self-government.

"The ancients", "he said, when they wished to exemplify illustrious virtue throughout the empire, first ordered well their states. Desiring to maintain well their states, they first regulated their families. Wishing to regulate their families they first rectified their purposes. Wishing to rectify their purposes they first sought to think sincerely. Wishing to think sincerely, they first extended their knowledge as widely as possible. This they did by investigation of things.

"By investigation of things, their knowledge became extensive; their knowledge being extensive, their thoughts became sincere; their thoughts being sincere, their purposes were rectified; their purposes being rectified, they cultivated themselves; they being cultivated, their families were regulated; their families being regulated, their states were rightly governed; their states being rightly governed, the empire was thereby tranquil and prosperous".

Conclusion

Confucius has rendered immortal the sixth century B.C. He was a born ruler of men. He would have shone as one of the world's greatest monarchs, if circumstances had been favourable. He had a highly developed moral sense and a profound realisation of the supreme importance of morals in human life. His greatness has been universally recognised for many centuries. He is held in the highest reverence by hundreds of millions of the world's inhabitants.

Glory to Confucius, the great moralist, statesman, and social reformer of China.

14. CONSCIENCE

Conscience is the light of the soul that is burning within the chambers of your heart. It is the little spark of celestial fire which makes known to you the presence of the Indweller, the author of the divine laws of truth and holiness. It raises the voice of protest whenever anything is thought of or done contrary to the interest of its Master.

Conscience is the voice of the Self which says 'yes' or 'no' when you are involved in a moral struggle. It is a call from within to do an act or to avoid it. Conscience is the internal monitor.

Conscience is a form of truth. It is the knowledge of our own acts and feelings as right or wrong. It is a sensitive balance to weigh actions. It is the faculty or principle by which we distinguish right from wrong. It is a guiding voice from within. Sense of duty is conscience. Scrupulousness is conscience. Conscience is like silent teacher.

Conscience is a moral faculty. It is a delicate instrument or sense that tells you then and there what is right and what is wrong. It is the inner voice without sound, that shows you the path of virtue and godliness. It is indeed very, very delicate. It is very easy to stifle it. It is so very clear that it is impossible to mistake it.

Conscience is above reasoning and discussion. It is a sudden, dictatory command to plunge deep into the depths of virtue, or to rise high above the level of vice. The positive elements which adorn conscience are truth, courage, and justice.

Conscience is the consciousness of the moral goodness or badness of one's own conduct or motives, together with a feeling of obligation to do right or be good.

Conscience is a needle that points steadily to the Pole Star of God's Eternal Justice.

Conscience is your preceptor. It dictates to you: "Do this action. It is right". It warns you also. "This is wrong. Do not do this act".

Conscience is a great ledger-book. All your offences are written and registered in this ledger. It is a terrible witness.

Conscience is the best Minister of Justice. It threatens, promises, rewards, and punishes, and keeps all under its control. If conscience stings you once, it is an admonition; if twice, it is a condemnation. To act against conscience is to act against reason and Divine Law.

How Conscience Operates

When you do a wrong action, the conscience pricks you. You experience pin-pricks. It says to you in a clear, small, shrill voice, "Do not do this wrong action, my friend. It will bring misery to you". A conscientious man at once ceases to act further, and becomes wise.

Conscience warns you like a teacher or a friend, before it punishes as a judge. It tells you to do the right.

Cowardice asks: "is it safe?" Avarice asks: "Is there any gain in it?" Vanity asks: "Can I become famous?" Lust asks: "Is there pleasure?" But Conscience asks: "Is it right?" Conscience prompts you to choose the right instead of wrong, and tells you that you ought to do the right.

The first impulse of conscience is apt to be right.

If there are pin-pricks and twists in the conscience, if there is a sense of shame, depression in the heart, know you have done a wrong action. If there is exhilaration, cheerfulness, feel you have done a virtuous action.

When Conscience Can Be Relied Upon

Do not mistake the promptings of the lower mind for the voice of the soul. That mind which tends towards luxury and evil is the lower or Rajasa-tamasic mind. It is the impure mind, instinctive mind, or desire-mind. Voice from the instinctive mind will mislead you. This lower mind is the cause for one's downfall.

The higher mind which tends towards virtue is the Sattvic mind or Suddha Manas. This higher mind elevates man. It guides him. It acts as a true preceptor. You should try to hear the voice of the Sattvic mind. Annihilate Rajas and Tamas by increasing Sattva. You will be quite safe.

Conscience can act freely and fully only when one has abandoned self-interest in everything that he does.

The conscience of Mukherji will not allow him to do one thing, but the conscience of Chatterji may allow him to do that very thing. Therefore you cannot rely on conscience entirely, until you have cleared your mind and feeling from personal prejudice and predilections.

How Conscience Is Stifled and Destroyed

Conscience is obscured through human sin and weakness. The faint inner voice of the spirit is stifled by the rumbling of emotional conflicts, base impulses, and dictates of the flesh. It is awakened and sharpened to new clearness through purity of conduct and practice of ethical virtues.

Through misuse, conscience becomes blunt. Through abuse or misuse, it is even destroyed. Through wickedness, it becomes perverted. Uttering falsehood and taking bribes destroy the conscience altogether.

In the world, people think of one thing, say another thing, and do another thing. This is horrible. This is nothing but crookedness. You must carefully watch your thoughts, speeches, and actions. The little gain that you get by telling lies is no gain at all. You pollute your conscience, and infect your subconscious mind. The habit of telling lies is carried to your next birth also, and you undergo suffering from birth to birth.

You have become insincere on account of intoxication from selfishness and greed. You do not know what you are exactly doing. You have a clouded understanding. Your conscience will prick you severely at one time. Your heart will bleed when you come to your senses. Your heart must bleed through repentance with a contrite heart. Then only can you purify yourself.

The habit of taking bribes is very common. If you ask anybody working in any office, "What is your salary, Mr. Jayadev?", he will say, "Well, my salary is only Rs. 50/-, but my income is about Rs. 75/-". This income is nothing but bribe. People are ignorant. Even the so-called educated people have no idea of the law of action and reaction, Samskaras and their force. If you take bribe, you will be punished for this wrong action, and the Samskara of taking bribes will force you to take bribes even in the next birth. You will be a dishonest man even in the next birth. Your thoughts and actions are registered in the subconscious mind. You carry your dishonesty from birth to birth, and undergo enormous sufferings.

Reduce your wants and live honestly within your means. You will have a clean conscience. You will be ever free from anxieties and worries. you will have a peaceful death. I suppose you now understand the gravity of the law. Become an honest man and be true from this very second you read these lines. Never, never join those offices which are amenable to corruption and temptations. You will be corrupted.

The Best Professions

Never wish to become a police officer. The whole play of Maya is here. You will become a slayer of Atman. You cannot have peace of mind even for a second.

Advocates kill their conscience and soul by twisting truth and uttering deliberate falsehood.

The doctor's profession is noble, indeed; but, on account of greed, doctors become worldly-minded. The greedy doctors fills up a bottle with water and coloured tinctures and charges heavily. He extorts money by charging too much for injections and visits. Mercy, sympathy and honesty have fled from his heart. When the mind is filled with greed, passion and dishonesty, conscience is destroyed.

In business, there is much corruption. From morning till night, you will be telling lies only. God is very far from a business-man.

The educational line is very good. There are very few chances of taking bribes or committing sins. You can lead a quiet life.

The agricultural profession will make you quite independent. You will be free from the distractions of a modern city. You can lead a very peaceful life.

Therefore, become a teacher or a professor, or an agriculturist. You can remain virtuous.

The Subtle Mechanism of Conscience

A virtuous man alone can use the instrument of conscience. He alone can clearly hear the inner voice of the soul. In a wicked man, this faculty becomes dead. The sensitive nature of conscience is destroyed by sin or corruption. Hence he is not able to discriminate right from wrong.

If you do wrong actions and sinful deeds and treat them lightly today, you will not hesitate to do serious crimes the next day. If you allow one sin to enter and dwell in your conscience, you certainly pave the way for the entry of a thousand sins. Your conscience will become blunt. It will lose its sensitiveness. The habit of doing evil deeds will pervade the whole body like the poison of the scorpion and the cobra.

If an honest man begins to take bribe for the first time, he shudders. His conscience quivers and trembles. He feels a lot of uneasiness. If he repeats it again several times, his conscience becomes blunt. He does not feel any uneasiness at all. If a chaste man begins to visit for the first time a house of ill-fame, his conscience pricks; his conscience shudders. If he frequently visits, his conscience becomes blunt. He will not feel anything. The inner mechanism of conscience is very subtle. Keep it sensitive by doing virtuous deeds only.

How to Cultivate a Pure Conscience

Keep the conscience always bright and sharp by adhering to truth, Dharma, and virtue. It will be your constant, elevating companion.

Virtuous acts, charity, benevolence, nobility, generosity, acts of mercy, and practice of truthfulness, Brahmacharya and Ahimsa sharpen the conscience.

Food plays an important role in the development of a pure conscience. Sattvic food helps man to have a clean conscience. Animal food makes the conscience impure. It produces a hard crust on the surface of the conscience and blunts it totally.

The Clear Conscience and the Guilty Conscience

A man of clear conscience is ever pure, joyful, and cheerful. A man of guilty conscience is morose, cheerless.

A man of pure and clean conscience sleeps happily, and wakes up happily, and moves about happily in this world. He attains happiness in this world and in the next world. A man of guilty conscience is ever restless and unhappy in this world and in the next world also.

A man of guilty conscience is dead even while living. A man of pure conscience is a veritable god on this earth.

Health of the Soul

A clean conscience discerns evil quickly and shuns it. A good conscience bestows on you ease, serenity, joy and happiness. It prevents calamities, troubles, afflictions and miseries.

That noble man who has a clean and pure conscience is not afraid of anybody in this world. He is not afraid of death even.

A good, clear conscience is the temple of God. It is the paradise of bliss. It helps the aspirant to reach the goal quickly.

What good health is the body, so is good conscience to the soul. There is inward satisfaction of conscience when a good action is done, when virtue is practised, when you lead a virtuous life.

The most natural beauty in the world is honesty and moral truth. Be beautiful within. Have a clean conscience. Be virtuous. Physical beauty fades.

Conscience or the voice of wisdom speaketh in all Lord's creation, but the little, finite, impure human intellect does not comprehend it. Purify your mind, O arrogant self-willed man! Tune your mind-radio by brushing it, and hear His voice and become wise. The voice of the Soul will lead thee to safety, truth, peace, and immortal bliss.

15. CREATION

The universe is a mystery. No one can say how it came to be.

You will find in the Rig-Veda: "Who knows here, who can here state whence came all this multifarious universe? Even the Devas are posterior to its creation; who then knows whence this came out?".

Some hold that the universe was created out of nothing by a fiat of God and that it will again lapse into nothing at the period of deluge. This dogma of creation *ex nihilo* is not endorsed by scientists. They say emphatically that what exists now should have existed always and will continue to exist always in some form or the other. In Sankhya philosophy also you will find: "That which is cannot come out of that which is not". The Gita also states: "There can be no existence out of non-existence, nor can the existent cease to be. The truth about both has been perceived by seers".

Something cannot come out of nothing. Something can come out of something only.

The grass comes out of the earth and is absorbed into the earth. Even so, this universe comes out of Brahman, rests in Brahman, and dissolves in Brahman.

The Cause of This Universe

In the beginning, Brahman who is one without a second, alone exists. When darkness was rolling over darkness, there was existence alone.

In Brahman, there was a Spandana or vibration before the world was projected. This is the Sankalpa of Brahman. He thought or willed: *"Ekoham Bahu Syam:* I am one; may I become many". This vibration corresponds to the bulging of the seed within the ground when it is soaked with water. Then the whole world was projected.

When an ordinary, meagre juggler can bring forth mangoes, fruits, money, sweetmeats, an imaginary palace, etc., through Indrajala or Sammohana-vidya, can He—the omnipotent, omniscient Ruler—not create this insignificant world for His own play? When a mortal king adorns his palace with furniture, pictures, curios, garden, fountain, etc., can He not furnish this world with beautiful landscape, brilliant sun, moon and stars, mighty rivers and oceans?

Nature of the Creative Process

This visible world is God's jugglery. This world is not chaos. It is an organised, divine institution. The world is a shadow of God.

Brahman creates this unthinkable universe through His illusive power of Maya for His own Lila or sporting. The phenomenon of this universe is due to the power called Maya, by which the Absolute, without undergoing any change in or by Itself, appears as an ever-changing succession of phenomena conditioned by time and space.

Brahman has projected this universe without being affected in any way. The Absolute is not affected by the world-process that is going on within It, just as the rains from a cloud do not wet the sky. The one Brahman, through His Sakti, can put on all these countless names and forms and appear as many. There is no change in Himself. The world is mere appearance.

Brahman does not require any instruments or hands for making these forms. He is Chaitanya, self-luminous intelligence. By mere willing, He can bring forth countless worlds.

Just as the potentiality of a seed brings forth a tree, so also, the Svabhava or potentiality of Brahman brings forth this universe. Projection co-exists with existence.

God and the Universe

This whole universe is the body of God. This entire world is God or Virat-Svarupa.

This world is not a world of dead matter, but a living Presence. Brahman or the Absolute manifests Itself as the universe through forms.

Creation is a joyous self-expression of the One.

A king played the part of a beggar for his own sporting. A sage played the part of a fool for his own sporting. Even so, this world is a sport or Lila of Brahman.

Brahman appears as the world. It is Brahman alone that shines as the world of variegated objects. Brahman Himself appears as stone, tree, stars, etc. The One Consciousness alone appears as the universe of plurality.

Just as one man alone becomes many in dream, so also the one God exists as many.

The whole universe is Brahman only in essence. All this is Brahman only, appearing in Brahman and through Brahman.

Earth, food, fire and sun are forms of Brahman. East, west, north and south are parts of the Lord. The sky, heaven, ocean are portions of Brahman.

Breath is a part of Brahman. Sight is a part of Brahman. Hearing is a part of Brahman. Mind is a part of Brahman. This life is Brahman. Brahman or Truth is the essence in which the universe has its being, from which it is born, and in which it dissolves at the end of each world-cycle.

An effect does not exist apart from its cause. A pot does not exist apart from clay. This universe does not exist apart from Brahman. It has no independent existence. It is one with Brahman.

If you have a candle light, and from it you light a thousand other candles, is not the first light in all the other candles? So it is with God. Creating all things, He is in all by spirit, breath and being.

The world is charged with the splendour, glory and grandeur of God. Just as sugar-cane juice pervades the sugar-cane, just as salt pervades the water when a lump of salt is dissolved in it, just as butter pervades milk, so also, Brahman pervades all the objects, animate or inanimate.

Brahman is one. Manifestation is many. One has become many.

As from a blazing fire, sparks all similar to one another, come forth in thousands, so also, from the one imperishable Brahman proceed all breathing animals, all worlds, all the gods, and all beings.

Evolution of the Elements

By dint of His will, the Lord, the undecaying substratum or reality of the universe, gave the first impetus to Nature to shake off her state of primal equipoise and to be gradually and successfully evolved into those categories and elements which were necessary for the formation of the present universe.

The first evolute is Akasa. Why should Akasa be the first evolute? Because, without space, nothing can exist. Prana acted on Akasa. There was Spandana or vibration. Wherever there is vibration, there must be motion. Motion is the quality of air. Therefore, air came out of Akasa. Motion produced heat. Therefore, fire was born of Vayu or air. When there is heat, water is produced. On a hot day, the body perspires. Hence, water was born of fire. Wherever there is water, there is food. Earth is Annam or food. Therefore, earth was born of water.

The subtler the element, the more powerful it is. Water is more powerful than earth, because it is more subtle than earth. Water removes away earth. Fire is more powerful than water, because it is more subtle than water. Fire dries up all water. Air is more powerful than fire, because it is more subtle than fire. Air blows up fire. Ether or Akasa is more powerful than air, because it is more subtle than air. Air rests in Akasa. Akasa is the support for air. Air is born of Akasa, fire is born of air, water is born of fire, earth is born of water. During cosmic Pralaya, earth is reduced or involved into water, water into fire, fire into air, and air into Akasa.

The whole world, the gross bodies of the four kinds of beings, *viz.,* Udbhija or the seed-born, Svedaja or those born of sweat, oviparous or those born of egg, and viviparous or those born of placenta, and all objects of enjoyment are formed out of the five elements.

The Doctrine of Ajati-vada

As people with gross minds cannot grasp the theory of Ajati-vada or non-creation, this kind of Srishti-krama is given. If you study the doctrine of Ajati-vada, propounded by Gaudapada in his Karika, you will find that this world does not exist in the past, present and future. This doctrine can be understood only by high-class aspirants who lead a life of seclusion and meditation.

If you remain in Allahabad for six months, you forget all about your native place which is Madras. There is no Madras for you while you live in Allahabad, and there is no Allahabad for you while you live in Madras. This world is a mere collection of Samskaras created by the mind.

If you can consciously destroy the mind by Sadhana and Samadhi, the world vanishes. It is all Brahman only. You shut yourself in a room for a fortnight, give up reading newspapers, engage yourself in deep meditation, and see whether there is world or not.

World Is Mental Creation

It is only the waking state that brings before us this creation. This universe is nothing but a mode of the mind, self-evolved from Brahman, the cause of the universe.

The motion or vibration of Prana moves the mind. The movement of the mind generates the universe. The mind manifests itself as the external world. Names and forms arise owing to Vikshepa Sakti, one of the powers of Maya. The Vikshepa force operates both in the Jagrat and in the Svapna states. The whole world is projected on account of this power only. In sleep, it disappears.

In the deep sleep state you have no experience of the world, because there is no mind. This clearly shows that there will be world only if there is mind and that the mind alone creates this world.

World is mental creation. There is no world in sleep. There is no world in Samadhi. There is no world for a sage. That is the reason why the Srutis declare that this world is *Manomatra Jagat, Manah-Kalpita Jagat.*

This ever-agitated Manas, having come into existence out of the ineffable Brahman, creates the world according to its own Sankalpa or thoughts. This legerdemain of the universe springs out of the Sankalpa of Manas. It is through the Sankalpa of your Manas that the universe appears to be and it is this Sankalpa that is asked to be given up by you if you wish to soar to the One Reality beyond the universe.

With the growth of a paltry Sankalpa, there will arise the universe; with the extinction of the former, the latter will also disappear. With the annihilation of Sankalpa, all conception of differences between the seer and the seen will vanish, and then the Reality of Brahman will begin to shine uninterruptedly. Then the shadow of all the universe, movable and fixed, will be found absorbed in It in a non-dual state.

When the mind ceases to think, the world vanishes, and there is bliss indescribable. When the mind begins to think, immediately the world reappears, and there is suffering.

With the contemplation of 'I', all the train of ideas of the universe will set in; otherwise all the universe will vanish as instantaneously as darkness before the sun. Mind and 'I' are one. Destroy the 'I'; then the mind is destroyed. If the mind, which is the instrument of knowledge, perception and activity, vanishes, with it disappears this subjective world also.

The Cosmic Drama

This phenomenal universe is but an outcome of the Divine Will, seeming to be real through the workings of the mind.

Before you write out a drama, you have a vivid mental picture of the whole drama in your mind. Then you write it out in succession in four acts. When it is staged, it is acted in succession, part by part. Similarly, the universe and its movements are a vivid mental picture in the Cosmic Mind, in the mind of Isvara.

There is neither 'past' nor 'future' for Him. Everything is 'present' for Him. There is neither 'near' nor 'far' for Him. Every place is 'here'. Every time is 'now'. The events come out in succession on the stage of the long world-drama as Time rolls on.

Atoms rotate continuously. Old becomes new and new becomes old. In reality, there is no such thing as old; there is no such thing as new. The Jivas with individual minds are witnessing the events in succession. But the Isvara knows all events at one sweep. He is all-knowing. He is all-understanding also. He knows every detail of His creation.

This vast sense-universe shines as Atma-sankalpa. The Cosmic Mind creates the Maya. Individual minds receive things under delusion.

Why Has God Created This World?

The answers to the question, "Why has God created the world?", are very unsatisfactory. For His own glorification? We cannot attribute to Him so much vanity. By love of mankind? How may He love a thing before it exists and how may it be called love to create millions for misery and eternal pain? The creation of the world is a moral necessity. It is to give fruits for enjoyment to the souls and to help them attain God-realisation. God's desire for His creation is to provide all that is needed to bring His creation into an awareness of Himself.

The question, "Why has God created the world?", is an Ati-prasna or transcendental question. The finite mind cannot give a proper answer. The reason can give answers only to worldly questions. The question itself is wrong.

What is the cause for Avidya, Maya, and Samsara? This is an Ati-prasna. In enquiring the cause, you abuse your innate mental organ of causality to penetrate into a region for which it is not made and where it is no more available. You are here in ignorance, pain and misery. You know the way out of them. The question of a cause for them is senseless.

A finite mind that is gross and conditioned by time, space and causation cannot comprehend the why and how of the universe, a question that is transcendental. The question has never been answered by anybody, by any Sastra, by any sage or Acharya. Do not rack your mind on this point. You can never get a solution for this problem. It is Mouja of Brahman to create this universe. It is His Lila-vilasa. It is His Maya. It is His Svabhava.

You simply waste your energy and time by entering into hot discussions regarding the question, "Why has God created this world? Is the world real or unreal?". It would matter nothing to you whether the world be real or not. You will not gain anything substantial by entering into such controversies. You will have to dive deep into the chamber of your heart by withdrawing the mind and the outgoing senses to rest in the Supreme Self. Give up, therefore, these useless discussions and proceed straightaway in the quest of the Self and Its realisation. Instead of counting the number of the leaves in a tree, try to eat the fruits directly. Try to enjoy the eternal bliss of the Self by realisation. This is wisdom.

God Only Is: the World Is Not

There is only the eternal Brahman in truth. Nothing else really exists. Only Brahman, the absolute, undifferentiated mass of Satchidananda, exists.

Creation is a dream. Waking also is a dream. The body is a dream.

The whole world is an utter untruth. This world is utterly non-existent. Sensual enjoyments are like fondling the son of a barren woman in dream.

Heaven, Moksha and world are mere words only, just like the son of a barren woman.

Everything is a great delusion. There is neither dream nor deep sleep, neither heaven nor emancipation. The truth is that everything is the Peace and Bliss of Eternity.

Nothing here is ever born; nothing here ever dies. The subject of instruction, and the purpose, of all teachings is only a play of words or sounds.

The infinite which is both inside and outside appears as this world through space and time.

Brahman appears as the world. World is mere appearance. It is like snake in the rope, like water in the mirage, like blueness in the sky.

The snake appears because of the ignorance of the rope; when the rope is known, the snake disappears. The world appears because of the ignorance of the Self; it does not appear when there is Knowledge of Atman.

When one forgets Himself, Brahman appears to him as the universe. When one is established in one's own Self, the universe appears as the Brahman.

Know the Truth

If you attain Knowledge of the Self, the meaning of life will cease to be a mystery. You will clearly understand the why and how of this universe. The purpose and progress in the scheme of things will become clear to you. All transcendental things will be known to you like the apple in the palm of your hand.

Withdraw. Meditate. Dive deep into the recesses of your heart. You will have awareness of a Reality, very different from empirical reality, a timeless, spaceless, changeless Reality. You will feel and experience that whatever is outside of this only true Reality is mere appearance, is Maya, is a dream.

Know the Truth, the Absolute. You are saved. You are liberated. You are enlightened. You are free.

You can know Brahman only by becoming Brahman. To become Brahman is to identify yourself with the divine element—the Supreme Soul—which constitutes your essential nature. The Knower of Brahman becomes Brahman. The river joins the ocean and becomes one with the ocean. The drop mixes with the sea and becomes one with the sea.

16. DEATH

Great scientists, the inventors of many marvellous things, mighty emperors who have done stupendous work, inspired poets, wonderful artists, many Brahmas, Rishis, Yogins, have come and gone. You are all extremely anxious to know what has become of them. Do they still exist? What is there at the other side of death? Have they become non-existent or have they dwindled into an airy nothing? Such questions do arise spontaneously in the hearts of all. The same question arises today as it arose thousands of years ago. No one can stop it, because it is inseparably connected with our nature.

The idea of death has ever been the strongest motive power of religion and religious life. Death stirs a man to search for immortality.

Man is afraid of death. Man does not want to die. He wants to live forever. This is the starting point of philosophy. Philosophy enquires and investigates. It boldly proclaims, "O man, do not be afraid of death. There is an immortal abode. That is Brahman. That is your own Atman that dwells in the chambers of your heart. Purify your heart and meditate on this pure, immortal, changeless Self. You will attain immortality".

You cannot die, because you were never born. You are immortal Atman. Birth and death are two false scenes in the unreal drama of Maya. They concern the physical sheath only, a false product formed by the combination of the five elements. The ideas of birth and death are mere superstition.

Every soul is a circle. The circumference of this circle is nowhere, but its centre is in the body. Death means the change of this centre from body to body. Why, then, should you be afraid of death?

What Is Death?

Death is separation of the soul from the physical body. The entrance of a soul into a body is called birth. The soul's departure from the body is called death. A body is dead if the soul is absent.

Death is a door opening from one aspect of life to another. Death is cessation of bodily or physical activity, of physical and organic function, of physical consciousness. Death is a transition from one state of being to another, a change of the form of consciousness to another plane, astral or mental. Ice becomes water, and water becomes steam, vapour and invisible gas, according to the degree of vibration. So is life in the physical, astral and mental planes.

Death does not end your personality and self-consciousness. It merely opens the door to a higher form of life. Death is only the gateway to a fuller life.

Death is not extinction of personality. It is merely the cessation of an important individuality. It is only a change of form. Life flows on to achieve its conquest of the universe, life flows on till it merges in the Eternal.

Death is not the end of life. It is an aspect of life. It is a natural incident in the course of life. It is necessary for your evolution.

Death is not the opposite of life. It is only a phase of life. Life flows on ceaselessly. The fruit perishes, but the seed is full of life. The seed dies, but a huge tree grows out of the seed. The tree perishes, but it becomes coal which has a rich life. Water disappears, but it becomes the invisible steam which contains the seed of a new life. The stone disappears, but it becomes lime which is full of new life. The physical sheath only is thrown, but life persists.

Dissolution of the body is no more than sleep. Just as man sleeps and wakes up, so is death and birth. Death is like sleep. Birth is like waking up. Death brings promotion to new, better life. A man of discrimination and wisdom is not afraid of death. He knows that death is the gate of life. Death, to him, is no longer a skeleton bearing a sword to cut the thread of life, but rather an angel who has a golden key to unlock for him the door to a far wider, fuller and happier existence.

Birth follows death, just as waking follows sleep. You will again resume the work that was left off by you in your previous life. Therefore do not be afraid of death.

Birth and death are jugglery of Maya. He who is born begins to die. He who dies begins to live. Life is death and death is life. Birth and death are merely doors of entry and exit on the stage of this world.

Just as you move from one house to another house, the soul passes from one body to another to gain experience. Just as a man, casting off worn out garments, takes new ones, so the dweller in this body casting off worn-out bodies, enters into others which are new.

O man, do not be afraid of death at all. Death is Maya's illusory phenomenon. Death is dissolution of the elements. Thou art immortal, Amara.

Signs of Death

It is very difficult to find out the real signs of death. Stoppage of the heart-beat, stoppage of the pulse or breathing are not the actual signs of death. Stoppage of the heart-beat, pulse and respiration, cadaveric rigidity of the limbs, clammy sweat on the body, absence of warmth in the body, are the popular signs of death. The doctor tries to find out whether there is corneal reflex in the eye. He tries to bend the leg. These signs are not the real signs of death, because there have been several cases where there were cessation of breathing and beating of heart, and yet, the persons revived after some time.

Hatha Yogins are put in a box and buried underneath the earth for forty days. Afterwards they are taken out, and they revive. Respiration may stop for a long time. In cases of suspended animation, respiration stops for two days. Many cases have been recorded. The heart-beat may stop for many hours, even for days, and then it can be recovered. Hence it is extremely difficult to say what would be the actual or the final sign of death. The decomposition and putrefaction of the body may be the only final sign of death.

No one should be buried immediately after death, before decomposition sets in. One may think that a man is dead, whereas he may be in a state of trance, catalepsy, ecstasy, or Samadhi. Trance, Samadhi, catalepsy, and ecstasy are states which resembles death. The outward signs are similar.

Persons suffering from heart-failure should not be buried immediately, as breathing might commence once again after a particular time. Burial should take place only after the body begins to putrefy.

Soul's Journey after Death

When a man dies, he carries with him the permanent Linga

Sarira which is made up of the five Jnana Indriyas, the five Karma Indriyas, the five Pranas, mind, Buddhi, Chitta, and Ahankara, and the changing Karmasraya which determines the formation of the next life.

The soul contracts and withdraws all the senses. The Physical senses become dimmer and dimmer, just as the flame in a lamp becomes dimmer and dimmer when the oil gets exhausted. The subtle body or Sukshma Sarira passes out of the physical body like a mist.

The soul, accompanied by the chief vital air or *Mukhya Prana*, the sense-organs, and the mind, and taking with itself Avidya, good and evil actions, and the impressions left by its previous existences, leaves its former body and obtains a new body. When it passes from one body to another, it is enveloped by the subtle parts of the elements which are the seeds of the new body.

The soul has a vision of the body to come. Just as a leech or a caterpillar takes hold of another object before it leaves its hold of one object, The soul visualises the body to come before it leaves the present body.

Dissolution of the Elements at Death

This physical body is composed of the five great elements or the Mahabhutas, viz., earth, water, fire, air, and ether. The Devas or gods are endowed with a divine or luminous body. The fire Tattva is predominant in them. In man, the earth Tattva is preponderating. In the case of acquatic animals, the element of water predominates. In the case of birds, the element of air predominates.

Hardness of the body is due to the portion of earth; the fluidity is due to the portion of water; The warmth that you feel in the body is due to fire; moving to and fro and such other activities are due to air; space is due to Akasa or ether. Jivatma or the individual soul is different from the five elements.

After death, these elements are dissolved. They reach their primordial sources in the inexhaustible storehouse of nature. The element of earth goes and joins its store of Prithvi Tattva. The other elements also go back to their sources.

The respective functions of the organs are blended with the presiding gods. Sight goes to the sun from where it had its power of vision, speech goes to fire, life-breath to air, the ear into the quarters, the body into the earth, hairs into annual herbs, hairs of the head into trees, and blood and semen into waters.

Death Pangs

There is no pain at the time of death. Ignorant people have created much horror and terror regarding death. In the Garuda Purana and the Atma Purana, it is described that the pangs of death are tantamount to the pain caused by the stings of 72,000 scorpions. This is mentioned only to induce fear in the hearers and readers, and force them to work for Moksha. In spiritualism, there is the unanimous report from the enlightened spirits that there is not even a bit of pain during death. They clearly describe their experiences at death and state that they are relieved of a great burden by the dropping of this physical body, and that they enjoy perfect composure at the time of separation from the Physical body. Maya creates vain fear in the onlookers by inducing convulsive twitchings in the body. That is her nature and habit. Do not be afraid of death pangs. You are immortal, Amara.

Prayer for the Dead

The departed souls remain in a state of swoon or unconsciousness immediately after death. They cannot feel that they are detached from their previous gross material bodies. Prayers, Kirtan, and good thoughts from relatives and friends can give real solace to the departed souls. They create a potent vibration and an awakening in their stupefied condition of mind, and bring back their veiled consciousness. The souls begin to realise that they are not really in their gross material bodies.

Then they endeavour to cross the borderland, a narrow river of ether, which is known as Vaitarani to the Hindus, as Chinnat-bridge to the Parsis, and Sirat to the Mohammedans.

When the departed souls are sinking peacefully and when they are ready to have a glorious awakening in heaven, they are aroused into vivid remembrance of the mundane life by weeping and wailing of their friends and relatives. The thoughts of the mourning people produce similar vibrations in their minds and bring about acute pain and discomfort. And the uncontrolled grief of their relatives drags them down from their astral planes. This may seriously retard them on their way to the heaven-world. This produces serious injury to them.

Last Thought-forms

The last thought of a man governs his future destiny. It determines his future birth.

The last thought of a licentious man will be the thought of his woman. The last thought of an inveterate drunkard will be that of his peg of liquor. The last thought of a greedy money-lender will be that of his money. The last thought of a fighting soldier will be that of shooting his enemy. The last thought of a mother who is intensely attached to her only son will be that of her son only.

Raja Bharata nursed a deer out of mercy and became attached to it. His last thought was the thought of that deer. Hence he had to take the birth of a deer.

Man always desires to die a peaceful death with his mind fixed on God. That is the reason why Gita, Bhagavata, Vishnu Sahasranama, and other holy scriptures are recited at the death-bed of the sick man; even though he may not be able to speak, he may hear what is read out to him. This will help the sick man in forgetting the body-idea or his ailment and think of the Lord. When his memory fails, these sacred sentences of the scriptures will remind him of his real nature.

It is very difficult to keep up God-consciousness at the time of death when diseases torment the body, when consciousness fades away. But, for that man who has disciplined his mind all throughout his life who has tried to fix the mind on the Lord through constant practice, the last thought will be thought of God only. It cannot come by a stray practice in a day or two, in a week or month. It is a life-long endeavour and struggle.

Interval between Death and Rebirth

People wish to know the exact period that lapses between the time of leaving the body and being born again. Does the soul take a new body in one year? Does it take ten years? How long does one live upon the subtler planes before reappearing on the earth plane? These are some of the questions.

In main, two factors decide this issue, *viz.*, the nature of the individual Karma, and the last impression before death. It may vary from hundreds of years to a few months even. Those that work out some of their Karmas in other planes in subtler regions take a considerable time before entering a fresh body. The interval is very long, for a year of the earth-period passes off as a single day on the celestial plane. There is an instance cited where, seeing the amazement and admiration of foreign tourists at the imposing ruins of certain ancient monuments, a saint present in the vicinity remarked that some of these very people had fashioned the monuments centuries ago.

Sometimes, a very sensual individual with strong craving, or one with intense attachment, is reborn quickly. Also in cases where life is cut short by a violent death, or by a sudden unexpected accident, the Jiva resumes the thread very soon. Usually, in such cases of immediate rebirth, the Jiva often remembers many of the events of its previous life. It recognises its former relatives and friends, and identifies old home and familiar objects.

This sometimes leads to very queer developments. There are some instances where a murdered person, being reborn, has declared the manner of his death and revealed the identity the killer. A reincarnated individual had, at times, unerringly gone and uncovered the treasure that had been hidden away by him.

In the vast majority, this memory is not present. This is really a blessing conferred by the all-wise Being. Such recollection would greatly complicate our present lives. The past is veiled to you until such time as it is good and helpful to remember it. When you attain perfection and reach the end of a cycle, all will be revealed and you will see a whole rosary of lives threaded upon the one personality.

But such cases of immediate rebirth are not common. Generally, for an average individual, the interval between death and rebirth happens to be a considerable period measured in terms of earth-time. Persons who have done much good Karma spend a great deal of time on the Daivic plane before being born again. Great souls, spiritually advanced persons, wait for a long time before reincarnating.

In the intervening period between death and new birth, the departed spirit, especially if the person is physically and spiritually developed, can frequently materialise upon the earth plane if necessity arises. It takes human form, talks, and can even make itself felt by tangible touch. It is possible to photograph such an apparition.

Such materialised form is different from the astral body which is not visible to normal vision. It is an exact counterpart, a subtle 'double' to the physical body, and forms the vehicle in which the departed soul journeys after death.

Astral consciousness, however, cannot guarantee you freedom from birth and death. Occultism and spiritualism can never give ultimate emancipation; nor can they reveal the full secret of the beyond. Spiritual realisation and knowledge of the Self alone will reveal the mystery of life and death and the life beyond death.

Be Not Afraid of Death

Death is painful to worldly man. A Yogi or a sage, or even a real aspirant, has no fear of death. A desireless man never weeps when he dies. A full-blown Jnani never dies. His Prana never departs.

Your highest duty is to prepare for a peaceful life here-after. Conquer the fear of death. Conquest of the fear of death, conquest of death, is the highest utility of all spiritual Sadhana. The one aim of all Yoga Sadhana is to meet death fearlessly and joyfully.

Man is afraid of death. In old age, he tries to think of God. If he remembers God even from his boyhood, he will reap a rich spiritual harvest in old age.

Bhishma had death at his command. Savitri brought back Satyavan, her husband, to life through her power of chastity. Markandeya conquered death through worship of Lord Siva. You also can conquer death through devotion, knowledge, and the power of Brahmacharya.

17. DEVI

Devi or Maheswari or Parasakti is the Supreme Sakti, or power of the Supreme Being. When Vishnu and Mahadeva destroyed various Asuras, the power of Devi was behind them. Devi took Brahma, Vishnu, and Rudra and gave them necessary Sakti to proceed with the work of creation, preservation and destruction.

Devi is the creatrix of the universe. She is the Universal Mother. Durga, Kali, Bhagavati, Bhavani, Ambal, Ambica, Jagadamba, Kamesvari, Ganga, Uma, Chandi, Chamundi, Lalita, Gauri, Kundalini, Tara, Rajesvari, Tripura-sundari, etc., are all Her forms. She is worshipped, during the nine days of Dusserah as Durga, Lakshmi and Sarasvati.

Devi is the Mother of all. The pious and the wicked, the rich and the poor, the saint and the sinner—all are Her children.

Devi or Sakti is the Mother of Nature. She is Nature itself. The whole world is Her body. Mountains are Her bones. Rivers are Her veins. Ocean is Her bladder. Sun, moon are Her eyes. Wind is Her breath. Agni is Her mouth. She runs this world show.

Manifestation of Sakti

Sakti is symbolically female; but it is, in reality, neither male nor female. It is only a force which manifests itself in various forms.

The five elements and their combinations are the external manifestations of the Mother. Intelligence, discrimination, psychic power, and will are Her internal manifestations. Humanity is Her visible form.

She lies dormant in the Muladhara Chakra in the form of the serpentine power or coiled-up energy known as the Kundalini Sakti. She is at the centre of the life of the universe. She is the primal force of life that underlies all existence. She vitalises the body through the Sushumna Nadi and the nerves. She nourishes the body with chyle and blood. She vitalises the universe through Her energy. She is the energy in the sun, the fragrance in the flowers, the beauty in the landscape, the Gayatri or the Blessed Mother in the Vedas, colour in the rainbow, intelligence in the mind, potency in the homoeopathic pills, power in the Makaradhvaja and gold-oxide, will and Vichara Sakti in sages, devotion in Bhaktas, Samyama and

Samadhi in Yogins. Vidya, Santi, lust, anger, greed, egoism, pride are all Her forms. Her manifestations are countless.

Siva and Sakti

The Supreme Lord is represented as Siva, and His power is represented as His wife—Sakti, Durga, or Kali. Mother Durga is the energy aspect of the Lord. Without Durga, Siva has no expression; and without Siva, Durga has no existence. Siva is the soul of Durga. Durga is identical with Siva. Lord Siva is only a silent witness. He is motionless, absolutely changeless. He is not affected by the cosmic play. Durga does everything.

Siva is omnipotent, impersonal, inactive. He is pure consciousness. Sakti is dynamic. The power or active aspect of the immanent God is Sakti. Sakti is the embodiment of power.

Siva and Sakti are related as Prakasa and Vimarsa. Sakti or Vimarsa is the power that is latent in the pure consciousness. Vimarsa gives rise to the world of distinctions. In other words, Sakti is the very possibility of the Absolute's appearing as many, of God's causing this universe. God creates this world through Srishti-Sakti, preserves through Sthiti-sakti and destroys through Samhara-sakti.

There is no difference between God and His Sakti, just as there is no difference between fire and its burning power. Sakti is inherent in God. Just as you cannot separate heat from fire, so also you cannot separate Sakti from God, the possessor of Sakti. Sakti is Brahman Itself. Siva and Sakti are one. Siva is always with Sakti. They are inseparable. Worship of Durga or Parvati or Kali is worship of Lord Siva.

Matter, Energy and Spirit

Mother is the creative aspect of the Absolute. She is symbolised as Cosmic Energy. Energy is the physical ultimate of all forms of matter, and the sustaining force of the spirit. Energy and spirit are inseparable. They are essentially one.

Matter is reducible to energy. The Prasnopanishad says that Rayi and Prana—matter and energy—constitute the whole of creation. Matter is the outward index of the inward Power that is expressed by God. The Power that originates and sustains the universe is not the Jada Sakti or the electrical energy which is the ultimate reality of the scientists, but Chaitanya Sakti, the Power of the immutable consciousness of Brahman. In fact, it is not a Power which is *of* Brahman, but a Power which *is* Brahman.

The Divine Mother

Sakti may be termed as that by which we live and have our being in this universe. In this world, all the wants of the child are provided by the mother. The child's growth, development and sustenance are looked after by the mother. Even so, all the necessaries of life and its activities in this world, and the energy needed for it, depend upon Sakti or the Universal Mother. The human mother is a manifestation of the Universal Mother. All women are forms of the Divine Mother.

You are more free with your mother than with anybody else. You open your heart more freely to your mother than to your father. There is no God greater that the mother. It is the mother who protects you, nourishes you, consoles you, cheers you and nurses you. She is your first Guru. The first syllable which almost every quadruped or human being utters is the beloved name of the mother, *Ma.* She sacrifices her all for the sake of her children.

A child is more familiar with the mother than with the father, because the former is very kind, loving, tender and affectionate, and looks after the wants of the child. Whenever the child wants anything, it runs with outstretched hands to the mother, rather than to the father. If she hears the cry of the child, she leaves her domestic work and runs immediately to attend to the child. In the spiritual field also, the aspirant or the devotee—the spiritual child—has more intimate relationship with Mother Durga than with the Father Siva. Lord Siva is quite indifferent to the external world. He is a Tyagi and a Virakta. He wears the garlands of the skulls of His devotees, rubs the whole body with Vibhuti or holy ash, and remains in the crematorium in an intoxicated state. He is absorbed in contemplation of the Self. He remains in a state of Nirvikalpa Samadhi. He has handed over the power of attorney to His consort, Durga. It is Mother Durga only who looks after the affairs of the world. Lord Siva gazes at Durga, His Sakti. She engages Herself in creation, preservation and destruction.

Durga—Lakshmi—Sarasvati

The Divine Mother is everywhere triple. She is endowed with the three Gunas, *viz.,* Sattva, Rajas and Tamas. She manifests as Will or Iccha-sakti, Action or Kriya-sakti, and Knowledge or Jnana-Sakti. She is Brahma-sakti (Sarasvati) in conjunction with Brahma, Vishnu-sakti (Lakshmi) in conjunction with Lord Vishnu, Siva-sakti (Mahakali or Durga) in conjunction with Lord Siva.

Sarasvati is cosmic intelligence, cosmic consciousness, cosmic knowledge. Lakshmi does not mean mere material wealth like gold, cattle, etc. All kinds of prosperity, glory, magnificence, joy, exaltation, or greatness come under Lakshmi. Appaya Dikshitar calls even the final Liberation as Moksha-samrajya-lakshmi. Mahakali is the transformative power of Divinity, the power that dissolves multiplicity in unity.

The Devi assumes many aspects according to the tasks to be performed by Her—sometimes sweet and tender, and at others, terrible and devouring. But She is always kind and gracious to Her devotees. Arjuna, the Pandava hero, worshipped the Goddess before starting the fight against the evil-minded Kauravas. Sri Rama worshipped Durga at the time of the fight with Ravana, to invoke Her aid in the war. He fought and won through Her grace.

The Navaratri and Its Spiritual Significance

During Navaratri or The Nine Nights, the whole of India adores the Mother and worships Her with great devotion. Dusserah, Durga Puja and Navaratri are one and the same. On the first three nights, Durga or the destructive aspect of the Mother is worshipped. On the succeeding three nights, it is the creative aspect or Lakshmi that is adored. And on the last three nights, the knowledge aspect or Sarasvati is invoked. The tenth is the Vijaya Dasami day or the Day of Victory.

There is a special significance in this arrangement. When the Devi is worshipped by a devotee in this order, as Durga, She first destroys the evil propensities that lurk in his mind. Then, as Lakshmi, She implants therein the Daivi Sampat or the divine qualities conducive to spiritual unfoldment. Then as Sarasvati, She bestows true knowledge on him.

The tenth day commemorates the victory of knowledge over nescience, of goodness over evil. It is the day on which boys are put in the school. Aspirants are initiated on this day. On this memorable Vijaya Dasami day, the carpenter, the tailor, the mason, the artist, the songster, the typist and all technical workers do Puja for their instruments and implements. This is Ayudha Puja. They behold and recognise the Sakti or Power behind these instruments, and worship the Devi for their success, prosperity and peace.

Worship of the Divine Mother

Worship of Devi or the Universal Mother gives not only prosperity, but liberation from all bondages. It leads to the attainment of Knowledge of the Self. The story of the Kenopanishad, known as the Yaksha-prasna supports this view. Uma taught the Truth to the Devas.

Sakti is all. She can do anything. She can make or mar. She can mend or end. For the sake of the continuance of Her divine play here, She Herself, as Avidya Maya, has veiled the Truth from you and bound you to this Samsara. When She is propitiated through the practice of sincere devotion and unconditional self-surrender, She, as Vidya Maya, removes the veil and enables you to perceive the Truth.

No one can free himself from the thraldom of mind and matter without the Mother's grace. The fetters of Maya are too hard to break. If you worship Her as the great Mother, you can very easily go beyond Prakriti through Her benign grace and blessings. She will remove all obstacles in the path and lead you safely into the illimitable domain of eternal bliss and make you absolutely free.

May Parasakti or Devi—the Universal Mother Jagadamba—bless you all with wisdom, peace and immortal bliss.

18. DISCIPLE

A disciple is he who follows the instructions of the Guru to the letter and spirit, and who propagates the teachings of the Guru to less evolved souls in the path till the end of his life.

A true disciple is concerned only with the divine nature of the Guru. The Guru's action as man is not the disciple's concern. He is totally oblivious of it. To him, the Guru is Guru even if he acts unconventionally. Always remember that the nature of a saint is unfathomable. Judge him not. Measure not his divine nature with the inadequate yardstick of your ignorance. Criticise not your Guru's action which is done on universal vision.

True discipleship opens the vision. It kindles the spiritual fire. It awakens the dormant faculties. It is most necessary in one's journey along the spiritual path. Guru and disciple become one. The Guru blesses, guides and inspires the disciple. He transmits his spiritual power to him. He transforms and spiritualises him..

Who Is Qualified to Approach the Guru?

To approach a Guru, you must be a proper Adhikari. Correct understanding, non-attachment to worldly objects, serenity of mind, restraint of the senses, absence of base passions, faith in the Guru, and devotion to God are the necessary equipments with which the aspirant has to approach the Guru.

The Guru will impart spiritual instructions only to that aspirant who thirsts for liberation, who duly obeys the injunctions of the Shastras, who has subdued his passions and senses, who has a calm mind, and who possesses virtuous qualities like mercy, cosmic love, patience, humility, endurance, forbearance, etc. Initiation into the mysteries of Brahman will fructify only when the disciple's mind becomes desireless, and will produce Jnana in it.

Guru-Seva

Aspirants should direct their whole attention in the beginning towards the removal of selfishness by protracted service to the Guru. Serve your Guru with divine Bhava. The cancer of individuality will be dissolved.

The captain of a ship is ever alert. A fisherman is ever alert. A surgeon in the operation theatre is ever alert. Even so, a thirsting hungry disciple should be ever alert in the service of Guru.

Live to serve the Guru. You must watch for opportunities. Do not wait for invitation. Volunteer yourself for the Guru's service.

Serve your Guru humbly, willingly, unquestioningly, unassumingly, ungrudgingly, untiringly and lovingly. The more your energy you spend in serving your Guru, the more the divine energy will flow into you.

He who serves the Guru serves the whole world. Serve the Guru without selfish ends. Scrutinise your inner motives while doing service to the Guru. Service must be done to the Guru without expectation of name, fame, power, wealth, etc.

Obedience to the Guru

Obedience to the Guru is better than reverence. Obedience is precious virtue, because if you try to develop the virtue of obedience, the ego, the arch-enemy on the path of Self-realisation, slowly gets rooted out.

Only the disciple who obeys his Guru can have command over his lower self. Obedience should be very practical, whole-hearted, and actively persevering. True obedience to Guru neither procrastinates nor questions. A hypocritical disciple obeys his Guru from fear. The true disciple obeys his Guru with pure love, for love's sake.

Learn how to obey. Then alone you can command. Learn how to be a disciple. Then alone you can become a Guru.

Give up the delusive notion that to submit to the preceptor, to obey him, and to carry out his instructions is slavish mentality. The ignorant man thinks that it is beneath his dignity and against his freedom to submit to another man's command. This is a grave blunder. If you reflect carefully, you will see that your individual freedom is, in reality, an absolutely abject slavery to your own ego and vanity. It is the vagaries of the sensual mind. He who attains victory over the mind and the ego is the truly free man. He is the hero. It is to attain this victory that man submits to the higher spiritualised personality of the Guru. By this submission, he vanquishes his lower ego and realises the bliss of infinite consciousness.

Happy-go-lucky Disciples

The spiritual path is not like writing a thesis for the Master of Arts degree. It is quite a different line altogether. The help of a teacher is necessary at every moment. Young aspirants become self-sufficient, arrogant and self-assertive in these days. They do not care to carry out the orders of a Guru. They do not wish to have a Guru. They want independence from the very beginning. They think they are in the Turiya Avastha when they do not know even the A-B-C of spirituality or truth. They mistake licentiousness of "having their own ways and sweet will" for freedom. This is a serious, lamentable mistake. This is the reason why they do not grow. They lose their faith in the efficacy of Sadhana and in the existence of God. They wander about in a happy-go-lucky manner, without any aim, from Kashmir to Gangotri, and from Gangotri to Ramesvaram, talking some nonsense on the way, something from Vichara Sagara, something from Panchadasi, and posing as Jivanmuktas.

Surrender and Grace

If you want to drink water at the tap, you will have to bend yourself. Even so, if you want to drink the spiritual nectar of immortality which flows from the holy lips of the Guru, you will have to be an embodiment of humility and meekness.

The lower nature of the mind must be thoroughly regenerated. The aspirant says to his preceptor: "I want to practise Yoga. I want to enter into Nirvikalpa Samadhi. I want to sit at your feet. I have surrendered myself to you". But he does not want to change his lower nature and habits, old character, behaviour and conduct.

One's individual ego, preconceived notions, pet ideas and prejudices, and selfish interests should be given up. All these stand in the way of carrying out the teachings and instructions of one's Guru.

Lay bare to your Guru the secrets of your heart. The more you do so, the greater the Guru's sympathy, which means an accession of strength to you in the struggle against sin and temptation.

The aspirant, before he desires the grace of the Master, should deserve it. The supply of divine grace comes only when there is a real thirst in the aspirant, when he is fit to receive it.

The Guru's grace descends upon those who feel utterly humble and faithful to him. Faith is confidence and trust in the Guru. Faith is firm conviction of the truth of what is declared by the preceptor by way either of testimony or authority, without any other evidence or proof. The disciple who has faith in the Guru argues not, thinks not, reasons not, and cogitates not. He simply obeys, obeys and obeys.

The disciple's self-surrender to the Guru and the Guru's grace are interrelated. Surrender draws down the Guru's grace, and the grace of the Guru makes the surrender complete.

The Guru's grace works in the form of Sadhana in the aspirant. If an aspirant sticks to the path tenaciously, this is the grace of the Guru. If he resists when temptation assails him, this is the grace of the Guru. If people receive him with love and reverence, this is the grace of the Guru. If he gets all bodily wants, this is the grace of the Guru. If he gets encouragement and strength when he is in despair and despondency, this is the grace of the Guru. If he gets over the body-consciousness and rests in his own Ananda Svarupa, this is the grace of the Guru. Feel his grace at every step, and be sincere and truthful to him.

How the Guru Teaches

The Guru teaches through personal example. The day-to-day conduct of the Guru is a living ideal to the disciple who is observant. The life of the Guru is a living sermon to the sincere disciple. By constant contact, the disciple imbibes the virtues of his Guru. He is moulded gradually. Study the Chhandogya Upanishad. You will find that Indra stayed with Prajapati for a period of a hundred and one years and served him whole-heartedly.

The Guru alone knows the spiritual needs of his disciples. He will give Upadesa according to the disciple's temperament and evolution. This Upadesa should be kept a secret. Discussion among disciples will lead to criticism of the Guru and slackness in Sadhana. There will be no spiritual progress. Follow the Guru's Upadesa to the very letter. Remember it is meant for you only. The other disciples have received Guru-upadesa, too. Let them follow it. Do not impose the Upadesa you have received on others.

The student can imbibe or draw from his teacher in proportion to his degree of faith. When the Guru comes to the aspirant to give spiritual instructions, if the aspirant does not pay any attention, if he is self-sufficient and heedless, if he bolts the door of his heart, he is not benefited.

How the Guru Tests

The Sadguru communicates the secret knowledge of the Upanishads to his trusted disciples only after repeated entreaty and severe testing. Sometimes, the Guru may even tempt his disciple, but the later should overcome the temptation by firm faith in the Guru.

In days of yore, the tests were very severe. Once Gorakhnath asked some of his students to climb up a small tree and throw themselves, head downwards, on a very sharp trident or Trisula. Many faithless students kept quiet. But one faithful student at once climbed up the tree with lightning speed and hurled himself downwards. He was protected by the invisible hand of Gorakhnath. He had immediate Self-realisation.

Once Guru Govind Singh tested his students. He said, "My dear disciples! If you have real devotion towards me, let six of you come forward and give me their heads. Then we can have success in our attempt". Two faithful disciples offered their heads. Guru Govind Singh took them inside the camp and cut off the heads of two goats instead.

The Guru tests the students in various ways. Some students misunderstand him and lose their faith in him. Hence they are not benefited.

Four Classes of Disciples

The best disciple is like petrol or aviation spirit. Even from a great distance, he will instantly react to the spark of the Guru's Upadesa.

The second class disciple is like camphor. A touch awakens his inner spirit and kindles the fire of spirituality in him.

The third class of disciple is like coal. The Guru has to take great pains in order to awaken the spirit in him.

The fourth class of disciple is like a plantain stem. No efforts will be of any avail over him. Whatever the Guru may do, he remains cold and inert.

Two things are necessary for a beautifully finished idol or image.

One is a perfect, faultless, good piece of marble; the second is the expert sculptor. The piece of marble should but unconditionally remain in the hands of the sculptor in order to be carved and chiselled into the fine image. So too, the disciple has but to cleanse himself, purify himself, and make himself a perfectly faultless piece of marble, and placing himself under the expert guidance of his Master, allow to be carved out and chiselled into the image of God.

19. DREAM

Chuang Tze, a Chinese philosopher, once dreamt that he was a butterfly. On waking, he said to himself, "Now, am I a man dreaming that I am a butterfly, or am I a butterfly that thinks, 'I am Chuang?' "

When you dream, you see the events of fifty years within an hour. You actually feel that fifty years have passed. Which is correct, the time of one hour of waking consciousness or the fifty years of dreaming consciousness? Both are correct.

Pascal is right when he asserts that if the same dream comes to us every night, we should be just as much occupied by it as by the things which we see every day. To quote his words: "If an artisan were certain that he would dream every night for fully twelve hours that he was a king, I believe that he would be just as happy as a king who dreams every night for twelve hours that he is an artisan".

A Change in Consciousness

Just as a large fish swims alternately to both the banks of the river, the right and the left one, or to the eastern and the western, so glides the Purusha between both the boundaries, the boundary of dream and the boundary of the waking state.

Consciousness changes. This change in consciousness brings about either the waking or the dream experience. The objects do not change in themselves. There is only change in the mind.

Waking, Dreaming and Deep Sleep

Dream is called Sandhya or the intermediate state, because it is midway between waking and the deep sleep state, between Jagrat and Sushupti.

The dream world is separate from the waking one. Deep sleep is separate from both the dream world and the world in the waking state.

The sun is the source and the temporary resting place of its rays. The rays emanate from the sun and spread in all directions at the time of sunrise. They enter into the sun at sunset, lose themselves there, and come out again at the next sunrise. Even so, the states of wakefulness and dream come out from the state of deep sleep and re-enter it and lose themselves there to follow the same course again.

As soon as you wake up, the dream becomes unreal. The waking state does not exist in the dream. Both the dream and the waking states are not present in deep sleep. Deep sleep is not present in the dream and the waking states. Therefore, all the three states are unreal. They are caused by the three qualities, Sattva, Rajas and Tamas. Brahman or the Absolute is the silent witness of the three states. It transcends the three qualities also. It is pure bliss and pure consciousness. It is Existence Absolute.

The Mind in Dream

The mind is ever rotating like a wheel. It plays with the five senses of perception and gets experiences in the waking state. It receives the different sense impressions through the avenue of the senses. The impressions are lodged in the causal body. Ajnana or the causal body is like a black sheet of cloth. In it are contained the Samskaras of all your previous births.

During dream, the mind creates various kinds of objects out of the impressions produced by the experience of the waking state. Sometimes, the experiences of the previous births which are lodged in the causal body flash out during the dreaming state.

The mind is the perceiver and the mind itself is the perceived in dream. The dream objects are not independent of the mind. They have no separate existence apart from the mind. So long as the dream lasts, the dream creatures will remain, just as the milkman remains so long as the milking goes on. Whereas, in the Jagrat state, the object exists independent of the mind. The objects of the waking experiences are common to us all, while those of dreams are the property of the dreamer.

The mind creates the bee, flower, mountain, horses, rivers, etc., in the dream, without the help of any external means. It creates various curious, fantastic mixtures. You may witness in the dream that your living father is dead, that you are flying in the air. You may see in the dream a lion with the head of an elephant, a cow with the head of a dog. The desires that are not satisfied during the waking state are gratified in dream. Dream is a mysterious phenomenon. It is more interesting than the waking state.

Desires are the rulers of all experiences in waking and also in dream. Waking is physical functioning of desires; dream is mental functioning of desires. The senses are moved by desires in waking; the mind is moved by desires in dreaming. In waking, the mind experiences through the senses; in dream, the mind alone experiences.

The dreamer creates the world of his own in the dreaming state. Mind alone works independently in this state. The senses are withdrawn into the mind. The senses are at rest. The mind is then like a furious elephant let loose.

Just as a man withdraws himself from the outside world, closes the door and windows of his room, and works within the room, so also, the mind withdraws itself from the outside world and plays in the dream world with the Vasanas and Samskaras and enjoys objects made up of fine or subtle ideas which are the products of desire. Dream is a mere play of the mind only.

Just as pictures are painted on the canvas, so also, the impressions of the waking state are painted on the canvas mind. The pictures on the canvas seem to possess various dimensions though it is all on a plane surface only. Even so, though the dream-experiences are really states of the mind only, the experiencer experiences internality and externality in the dream world. He feels, while dreaming, that the dream world is quite real.

The dreamer only *appears* to be doing things in dream, but actually there is no activity. The scripture, in describing our doings in dreams, qualifies them by an 'as it were': "As it were rejoicing together with women, or laughing as it were,...". Ordinary people also describe dreams in the same manner: "I ascended, as it were, the summit of a mountain.... I saw a tree, as it were". Therefore, the dreaming self has no activity in dreams.

Dreams and Karma

The dreamer is not affected by any result whatever of the good and the evil he sees in the dream state. Because in dream the dreamer does not actually do what is holy or evil, he is not chained by either; for, good or evil actions and their consequences are not imputed to the mere spectator of them.

No one regards himself a sinner on account of the sins committed in dreams. Nor do people who have heard of them condemn or shun the person on that account. Hence he is not touched by them.

Dreams Are Created by the Lord

The dream objects are created by the Lord as fruition of the minor works of the Jiva. In order to reward the soul for very minor Karmas, the Lord creates the dreams.

The Universal Soul is the creator of dreams and not the individual soul; for, had it been possible for the latter to shape his dreams, he would never have dreamt a bad dream, but would always have dreamt only propitious ones.

Prophetic Dreams

Many riddles of life are solved through hints from dreams. Through dreams one may receive proper advice for self-correction. Through dreams one may know how to act in a particular situation. Saints and sages appear in dreams during times of difficulty and point out the way.

Works of genius like poems, etc., are found in dreams. Remedies for diseases are prescribed in dreams. Some times the exact object seen in dreams is seen afterwards in the waking state.

Dreams, an Index of One's Moral Condition

Dreams, though of a strange and illusory nature, are a good index of the high or the low spiritual and moral condition of the dreamer. He who has a pure heart and an untainted character will never get impure dreams. An aspirant who is ever meditating will dream of his Sadhana and his object of meditation. He will do worship of the Lord and recite His Name and Mantra even in dream through the force of Samskara. Brahma-jnanins or sages have no dreams.

Dreams reveal to us that aspect of our nature which transcends rational knowledge. That in the most rational and moral man there is an aspect of his being which is absurd and immoral, one knows only through the study of one's dreams. All our pride of rationality and morality melts into nothingness as soon as we reflect upon our dreams.

Subjective Reality, Objective Reality and Absolute Reality

Waking experience is a perception. Dream experience is a memory. As perception precedes memory, waking precedes dream. Whereas waking experience is independent of dream experience and its effects, dream experience is the result of the impressions of waking experience.

There is a kind of order or system in the waking experiences, at least more than in dream. Every day, the same persons and things become the objects of waking experience. There is a definite remembrance of previous day's experiences and of survival and continuity of personality in waking experience. The consciousness of this continuity, regularity and unity is absent in dream. Dream is not well ordered, while waking is comparatively systematic.

Dream is less real than waking, in as much as the direct contact with the external world of waking experience is absent in dream. Though there is an external world in dream also, its value is less than that of the world in waking. Though the form of the dream world agrees with that of the waking world, in quality, the dream world is lower than the waking world.

Space, time, motion and objects, with the distinction of subject and object, are common to both waking and dreaming. Even the reality they present at the time of their being experienced is of a similar nature. But, the difference lies in the degree of reality manifested by them. The Jiva feels that it is in a higher order of truth in waking than in dreaming.

That the waking world has relative reality does not prove that it is real in the absolute sense. From the standpoint of the highest reality, waking experience also is unreal. As dream is transcended in the state of waking, the world of waking too, is transcended in the state of Self-realisation.

Dream is apparent reality. Waking is relative reality. Turiya or Brahman is absolute reality.

Waking is the reality behind dream. Turiya is the reality behind waking.

From the point of view of Turiya,.both waking and dreaming are unreal. But, waking, taken by itself in relation to dream experience, has greater reality than dream. To a certain extent, as Turiya is to waking, so waking is to dream.

Dream is no dream to the dreamer. Only by one who is awake, dream is known to be a dream. Similarly, waking appears to be real to one who is still in the waking state. Only to one who is in Turiya, waking is devoid of reality. Waking is Deerghasvapna, a long dream, as contrasted with the ordinary dream which is short.

There are degrees of reality in the experiences of the individual. The three main degrees are subjective, objective and absolute. Dream experience is subjective. Waking experience is objective. The realisation of Atman or Brahman is experience of the absolute reality. The individual is the subjective being in comparison with the objective world. The subject and the object have equal reality, though both these are negated in the Absolute.

Waking—A Long Dream

In both states, waking and dreaming, objects are *perceived,* are associated with the subject-object relationship. This is the similarity between the two. The only difference between the two states is that the objects in dream are perceived in the space within the body, whereas in the waking condition, they are seen in the space outside the body. The fact of their 'being seen' and their consequent illusoriness, are common to both states.

The perception of an object is unreal, because objects are creations of the mind. An object has got a particular form, because the mind believes it to be so. In fact, objects of both the dreaming and the waking states are unreal.

Anything that has got a form is unreal. Forms are special modes of cognition and perception. They are not ultimate. In waking, there are physical forms; in dreaming, there are mental forms. Anyhow, all are forms only, limited in space and time. A form lasts only so long as that particular mental condition lasts. When there is a different mental condition, the forms of experience also change. This is why the form of the world vanishes when Self-realisation is attained.

Dream relations are contradicted by waking relations. Waking relations are contradicted by superconsciousness, which is uncontradicted. Non-contradiction is the test of reality.

The unreal world appears as real, whereas it is in reality a long dream arisen in our mind. As in dream, so in the waking state, the objects seen are unsubstantial, though the two conditions differ by the one being internal and subtle, and the other external, gross and long. This world is nothing but a long dream.

When, at sixty years age, you take a retrospective view of your life in college, it is all a dream to you. Is it not so? The future also will turn out to be so.

The past is a dream. The future is a dream. The solid present is also a dream. The fact that in Self-realisation there is absolute cessation of phenomenal experience shows that all phenomena are unreal.

Objections Refuted

It may be said that objects in the waking state serve some definite purpose and those of dream do not serve a purpose. This argument is incorrect, because the objects used as means to some end or purpose in the waking state are contradicted in the dream state. A man in the waking state eats and drinks and appeases his hunger and is free from thirst. But, when he goes to sleep, he finds himself in dream again afflicted with hunger and thirst as if he has not taken food and drink for days together. And the contrary also happens and is found to be true. The utility and objective worth of things, etc., in waking are cancelled in the dream state, even as the conditions and experiences in dream are invalidated in waking. Objects act as means to ends only in a particular condition, and not in all conditions. Things are real only in their realms, and not always. That which is not always real is an appearance, is unreal; for, reality is everlasting. As the objects of the waking state do not work in dream, they are unreal. As the objects of the dream do not work in the waking state, they are unreal. Hence, everything is unreal.

It may be contended that objects of dream are queer, fantastic and unnatural. And hence, waking cannot be like dream. But the experiences in dream, however grotesque or abnormal, are not abnormal to the dreamer. They appear fantastic only in a different state, viz., in waking. One cannot say what is really fantastic, and what is normal and real. The mind gives values to objects, and its conception of normality and abnormality changes according to the state in which it is. The dreamer has his own conception of space, time and causation, even as the waking one has his own notions. One state is absurd when compared to the other. This shows that both states are illogical, and therefore, absurd from the highest standpoint.

It may be said that objects seen in waking are not mere mental imaginations, because the objects of waking experience are seen by other people also, whether or not one's mind cognises them. But, it is seen in the dream state also, objects of experience are open to the perception of other people, though the people as well as the objects are all subjective imaginations.

It may be said that in waking we perceive through the sense-organs and not merely through ideas. But it is seen, that in dream also, we perceive through the sense-organs belonging to the dream state, which are not less real than those of the waking state. As dream is unreal, waking also must be unreal.

The Dreamless Atman

There is one pure Consciousness or Atman in all beings which is infinite, eternal, all-pervading, self-existent, self-luminous and self-contained; which is partless, timeless, spaceless, birthless and deathless. This is the real 'I'. This 'I' never wakes, dreams or sleeps. It is always the seer or the silent witness of the three states of waking, dreaming and sleeping. It is the Turiya or the fourth state. It is the state that transcends the three states.

It is the false or relative 'I' called Ahankara or ego or Jiva that wakes up, dreams and sleeps. The waker, the dreamer and the sleeper are all changing personalities and unreal.

The real Self, the real 'I', never wakes up, dreams and sleeps. From the viewpoint of the absolute truth or Paramarthika Satta, no one wakes up, dreams and sleeps.

Wake Up and Realise

Learn to be the witness of your thoughts in the waking state. You can be conscious in the dream state that you are dreaming. You can alter, stop or create your own thoughts in the dream state independently. You will be able to keep awake in the dream state. If the thoughts of the waking state are controlled, you can control the dream thoughts also.

Do not allow the mind to run into the sensual grooves. Fortify yourself by developing the intellect through enquiry of Brahman, reflection and contemplation. The intellect will serve the purpose of a strong fortress. It will not allow the sense-impressions to be lodged in the causal body. It will not allow the impressions of the causal body to come out. It will serve a double purpose.

Brahman alone is really existent. Jiva, world are false. Kill this illusory egoism. The world is unreal when compared to Brahman. It is a solid reality for a passionate worldly man, even as dreams are real to the childish. The world does not exist for a Jnani or a Mukta.

You dream that you are a king. You enjoy various kinds of royal pleasures. As soon as you wake up, everything vanishes. But you do not feel for the loss, because you know that the dream creatures are all false. When you know the real Tattva, Brahman, the waking consciousness also will become quite false like a dream. Even in the waking consciousness if you are well established in the idea that the world is a false illusion, you will not get any pain.

Wake up and realise, my child!

20. EDUCATION

Education is the root. Culture is the flower. Wisdom is the fruit.

Education is to effect the culture of man's higher nature. Real education is education of man as man. Education should stimulate intellectual virility and make the students pious, sincere, bold and self-controlled. There must be man-making and character-building education that will give full development to the latent powers of children in their ethical, intellectual, aesthetic, physical and spiritual life.

Education is development of the whole man. Head, heart and hand—all three must be trained by artistic, scientific and practical education. The body, mind, intellect and spirit must have harmonious development. Only then will evolution be quick.

Education must be best calculated to promote plain living and high thinking. Education should enable the student to fit himself to his environments, and help him equip himself for the battle of life and the attainment of Self-realisation.

Education should teach the pupils to love God and man. Education should instruct the students to be truthful, moral, fearless, humble and merciful. Education should teach the students to practise right conduct, right thinking, right living, right action, self-sacrifice, and attain knowledge of the Self. That which develops character, initiative and a spirit of service to God and humanity is real education.

Ultimately, the aim of real education is drawing out the dormant divinity lying hidden within each human being. Spiritual enlightenment is the fruit of the real, inner education. The supreme state of blessedness or superconscious Samadhi is the culmination of all true education and culture.

You cannot have the right type of man by merely stuffing him with lectures. What is wanted is rigid and rigorous spiritual discipline in schools and colleges. Ideal souls are the product of ideal institutions which impart ideal education. The great responsibility of training children to grow into ideal men and women lies with the professors, teachers and parents.

Relationship between Teacher and Student

In ancient India, there was a very intimate relationship between the student and the teacher. It should be revived now. The relationship between the teacher and the student should be like that of a loving father and a devoted son. It should not be of a commercial nature. The teacher and the student should understand each other well. There should be a deep and profound spiritual bond between them.

The teacher should be a friendly guide of the student and never a superior, domineering master. The student should respect and love the teacher, rather than fear and hate him. It is a primary responsibility of the teacher to win the respect and love of the student. Only then will his teaching be effective.

A great, onerous duty rests with the teachers and professors of schools and colleges in training the students properly. They themselves should be strictly moral and pure. They should be endowed with ethical perfection. Their dealings with the students and others should be strictly ethical. Only then can they train the students in the right path. Before taking to the profession of a teacher, every teacher should feel the high responsibility of his position. Mere intellectual achievement in the art of delivering dry lectures alone will not adorn a professor.

The teachers and professors should be religious or spiritual-minded. They should practise spiritual Sadhana and regular meditation. They should lead the spiritual life. Teachers must be worthy ideals to be emulated by the students. The students should draw inspiration from the personal lives of their teachers.

Teachers must be imbued with a spirit of self-dedication in the great task of raising the citizens of tomorrow. They must be spiritual heroes with a missionary zeal. The State must provide the teachers with adequate means to keep themselves completely free from pecuniary difficulties.

The principals and professors of colleges, and the headmasters of high schools must be guided by learned and realised Sannyasins and Yogins. Then only real education can be imparted to students. If students who are equipped with real education come out of the universities every year, we will have a glorious new India, and a new era of peace, plenty and prosperity.

Studentship under Rishis

If you compare the present system of education with our ancient

Gurukula system, there is a wide gulf between the two. Mark the difference between the secular education in universities and spiritual teachings of seers. Note how the Rishis had given instructions to their students when they had finished their course of study: "Speak truth. Do your duty. Do not neglect the study of the Vedas. Do not swerve from Truth. Do not swerve from duty. Do not neglect your welfare. Do not neglect your prosperity. Do not neglect the learning and teaching of the Vedas. Do not neglect the duties towards God and forefathers. May the mother be thy God. May the father be thy God. May the preceptor be thy God. May the guest be thy God. Do such actions as are blameless; not others. Those that are good works, they should be performed by thee; none else".

Every student in the Gurukula had a knowledge of Pranayama, Mantra, Yoga, Asana, the code of morals, the Gita, Ramayana, Mahabharata and the Upanishads. Every student possessed humility, self-restraint, obedience, spirit of service and self-sacrifice, good demeanour, politeness, courteous nature, and last but not the least, a desire for acquiring Atma-Jnana.

Every student in the Gurukula was pure. Every student had perfect moral training. This was the predominating feature of ancient culture.

Students of the Present Day

The college students of the present day do not possess any of these virtues at all. Self-control is a thing unknown to them. Luxurious living and self-indulgence begin from their very boyhood. Arrogance, impertinence, disobedience are deep-rooted in them. They have become confirmed atheists and rank materialists. Many are ashamed to say that they believe in God. They have no knowledge of Brahmacharya and self-control. Fashionable dress, undesirable food, bad company, frequent attendance at theatres and cinemas, applying Western manners and customs have rendered them weak and passionate.

Our college students have become creatures of vile imitation. They imitate the West in smoking; putting on pants, hats, boots, neckties, collars; cropping of hair; applying scents to handkerchiefs, etc. But they have not imbibed various other virtuous qualities such as self-sacrifice, patriotism, spirit of service, punctuality, perseverance, tolerance, scholarly erudition, etc., that are the admirable, characteristic features in the Westerners. The condition of some of the boys belonging to some aristocratic families is highly lamentable and hopeless. They get monthly season-tickets for the cinema and spend their time in playing cards, leading a morbid unholy life when they are young. Religion and philosophy produce nausea and mental dyspepsia in them. They dislike religious-minded students. They are slaves to fashion and style.

Fashion, style, epicureanism, gluttony, luxury have occupied the minds of our college students. It is very pitiable to hear the life-history of some of the college students. Indeed, it has been detected that the health of the students has deteriorated throughout India. Moreover, the vices and bad practices which are ruining their health are on the increase. There is no ethical culture in modern schools and colleges. Modern civilisation has enfeebled our boys and girls. They lead an artificial life. The cinema has become a curse.

Professors of some colleges insist on the students putting on fashionable dress. They even dislike students who wear clean but simple clothing. A great pity! Cleanliness is one thing, and fashion is another thing. The so-called fashion takes root in worldliness and sensuality.

Call for a Spiritual Basis

Education must be based on a sound philosophy of life. If there is no right understanding of the ultimate aim of human life, if there is no clear idea of what man is meant to become through the process of life, no scheme of education will be satisfying and beneficial.

Education is training for life, in which ethics has the most dominant role. Education of the intellect, without moral discipline, is injurious to human progress. Intelligence without character is a source of danger, both to the individual concerned and to his fellow-men. Development of the body and the intellect alone, without moral discipline, will produce selfish men and women who will have no feeling or sympathy for the poor, or reverence for the elders and the wise, or respect for life. Education must help to form a strong, pure and beautiful character. There is nothing in our present system of education that will teach our young boys and girls how to form a stable character.

No boy or girl can be counted as properly educated, unless he or she gets a sound sense of spiritual evaluation. The young men and women in the universities must be given a sound training in practical spiritual life, which is vital, fundamental and essential, and which they hopelessly lack at present. If spiritual training is excluded in schools and colleges, there will be irreligiousness and Godlessness among the future citizens.

Our present-day schools and colleges give secular education. There is neither ethical discipline nor spiritual instruction. Many of the students go through their academic education without a proper aim or ideal before them. Even if they have an aim, it is the worthless aim of getting a job to earn the daily bread! They learn something in order to eke out their livelihood. They study only to get emoluments. That is the reason why they turn out to be spiritual bankrupts in the end. Laxity of moral conduct in our younger generation is due to the absence of spiritual and moral education in the present curriculum. Educate the boys without religion and you make them wonderful rogues.

Secular State Is No Godless State

The secular state is not necessarily a Godless state. All the same, if they have a basis against introducing the teachings of a particular religion, it does not mean that broad-based religious teachings should be excluded from the curriculum. Religion should be the foundation for education. Do not mix bigotry with religion. If religion is cut off from education, you will die spiritually.

Morality cannot take the place of religion, but morality is an essential part of religion.

Common prayers, brief meditation, and recitation of universal hymns should be conducted at the beginning and at the close of the day's studies. Short passages from scriptures, which convey broadbased, universal spiritual teaching, should be read by the students every day. Stories which illustrate different virtues should be expounded. The incidents in the noble lives of saints, sages and prophets have a great moral significance. The students will breathe an atmosphere of sublime teachings and noble sentiments. The foundations of divine virtue will be deeply and firmly laid in their hearts. They will become good citizens of the land.

Need for Reorientation of Our Educational System

India's educational ideals are in a ferment today. Our schools and colleges have become shops of profit and loss. Our graduates run after money, power, comforts, honours and titles. The mind of the youth is corrupted by much undesirable literature.

Education has lost its value today. It is now becoming fragmentary. It is not integral, rich and full. The different intellectual sciences which are taught in the universities of today are a feeble apology for the integral education which is necessary for the attainment of Perfection. Degrees like 'Master of Arts' mean nothing. It is the wisdom that matters. Sri Sankara graduated himself, not at some foreign academy or university, but in the lore of Govindapada and his predecessors Vyasa, Vasishtha, Suka and Parasara.

The present system of education in India needs a thorough, drastic overhauling immediately. The ancient Gurukula system should be revived and adequately revised according to the needs of the time, so that the students might be able to derive the maximum benefit from it.

Education makes or mars civilization. Universities are really the custodians of the character, culture and civilisation of nation. Universities should not be mere cramming institutions. Universities must be sanctuaries of light and wisdom.

Much more can be achieved through proper education than by force of law. So long as the inner man is not educated, law will remain a dead letter. If the inner man is educated, then not only shall we be rendering a great service to the man himself and the nation, but also to the entire world at large.

21. ETHICS

Ethics is the science of morality. Morality is virtuous life. In a limited sense, it means sexual purity.

Without ethical perfection, there is no spiritual progress. Without spiritual progress, there is no emancipation.

All aspirants commit mistakes in jumping to Samadhi and Dhyana all at once as soon as they leave their houses without caring a bit for ethical perfection. The mind remains in the same condition although they have practised meditation for fifteen years. They have the same jealousy, hatred, idea of superiority, pride, egoism, etc. No meditation or Samadhi comes by itself when one has no ethical perfection.

Life without ethics is living death. A man who has no regard for ethics is more death-masked than the one actually dead. An ethical man is far better and nobler than one who is otherwise religious and possesses occult powers.

Ethics and Religion

Ethics and morality are the basis of spiritual life. Without ethics, philosophy is mere wishful thinking and religion quite meaningless. Spirituality, devoid of moral principles, is deceit. Spirituality, religion and ethics are synonymous terms. It is erroneous to separate them.

Morality is religion in practice; religion is morality in principle. Religion gives us ultimate data upon which ethical science may be built. There is no true and abiding morality that is not founded on religious fervour.

Morality without religion is a tree without roots, a house built on sand, a stream without any spring to feed it. Morality, without religion, has no roots. It becomes a thing of custom, changeable or transient, and optional. Put morality on its proper and right basis, namely, the love of God. Morality without God is like a rudderless boat.

Ethics—Eastern and Western

All religions have taught ethical precepts such as: "Do not kill. Do not injure others. Love your neighbour as yourself". But they have not given the reason. Western ethics does not speak a word on Atman or Soul.

The ethics of Western philosophers is superficial. Their ethics is mere surface ethics. It speaks of a little social service, altruism, humanitarianism, philanthropy. It treats a little of 'good and evil', of 'right and wrong', of 'conduct and behaviour'. But the ethics of Hindus is subtle, sublime and profound. Hindu ethics is based on the sublime philosophy of Vedanta, which propounds the doctrine of oneness of life and unity of consciousness.

Atman or Self is one. One life vibrates in all beings. Life is common in animals, birds and human beings. Existence is common. There is one common consciousness. If you hurt any other creature, you hurt yourself. If you serve another man, you serve yourself. By serving others, you purify your heart, and purification of heart leads to descent of divine light and final emancipation or Mukti. This is Hindu ethics. This is the basic metaphysical truth that underlies Hindu ethical codes.

Western ethics does not sufficiently treat of absolute self-control and Brahmacharya, cultivation of divine virtues, and eradication of vices. There is neither Tapas nor asceticism nor control of the senses. Eastern ethics is profound. Eastern ethics gives paramount importance to Dama or perfect restraint of all the senses. There is intense asceticism. There is perfect control of the outgoing senses.

Western ethics may make one a dry philosopher, but not a sage or a Yogi. Eastern ethics makes one a dynamic sage or a dynamic Yogi. It transforms man into Divinity.

The Guides of Right Conduct

The guides of right conduct are the Dharma Shastras or the scriptures, the examples of saints, the Inner Self or Conscience, and established usage.

Undeveloped persons cannot think for themselves. Selfishness clouds understanding. Therefore, if a man has got even a tinge of selfishness, he cannot detect what is right and what is wrong. A very pure, subtle, sharp intellect is needed for this purpose. Hence rules of conduct have been laid down by great sages or seers like Lord Manu, sage Yajnavalkya.

As you have got neither the power nor the time to think of the moral principles and rules given in the scriptures, you can get the moral precepts or instructions from sages and saints and follow them to the very letter.

The Universality of Ethics

Every religion has its ethics. The Sermon on the Mount by Lord Jesus and the Ten Commandments contain ethical teachings for the uplift of man. The Noble Eightfold Path of Lord Buddha is the essence of ethics. The Yama, Niyama of Patanjali Maharshi constitute ethics. Manu Smriti, Yajnavalkya Smriti and Parasara Smriti contain the code of conduct for man. The three kinds of austerity of the Gita are nothing but ethics.

Basic principles of morality are everywhere the same, because it all comes from God. The laws or the great commandments issue directly from God, the Most High.

Universality is the very root of all morality. Without universality, morality will die.

Do not do any act which brings no good to others or which will make you repent later on or ashamed. Do such acts which are praiseworthy and which bring good to you and to others. This is a brief description of right conduct. Moral precepts have been made to free one another from all injuries.

Why should a man lead a moral life? Why should he do this and not that? Because man will be no better than an animal if he does not lead a moral life. The aim of morality is to raise man to the level of Divinity by transforming his brutal nature.

Kinds of Morality

We have human morality, family morality, social morality, national morality, professional morality. A doctor has his own professional ethics. He should not divulge to others the secrets of his patients. He should be kind and sympathetic towards his patients. He should not give injections of water and charge highly as for best medicines. Although the guardian of the patient did not pay the fees of his last visit, he should go voluntarily and attend the case. He should treat the poor cases freely.

An advocate also has his own ethics. He should not coach up false witnesses. He should not take up the weak cases only for the sake of fees. He should argue freely for the poor people. There is ethics for a business man also. He should not expect much profit. He should do much charity. He should not speak falsehood even in his business.

Ethics Is a Relative Science

Ethics is a relative science. Right and wrong, Dharma and Adharma, are relative terms. It is very difficult to define these terms precisely. What is good for one man may not be good for another. What is good at one time may not be so at another time or on another occasion. Ethics is relative to the man and his surroundings.

Morality is a changing and relative term. That passionate man who molests his legally married wife frequently to gratify his passion is more immoral than the man who visits the house of his sister of ill-fame once in six months. That man who dwells constantly on immoral thoughts is most immoral man. Do you clearly note the subtle difference now? To kill an enemy is right for a Kshatriya king. A Brahmin or a Sannyasin should not kill anybody even for protecting himself during times of danger. He should practise strict forbearance and forgiveness. To speak an untruth to save the life of a Mahatma or one's Guru, who has been unjustly charged by the unjust officer of a state, is right. Untruth has become a truth in this particular case. To speak a truth which brings harm to many is untruth only. To kill a dacoit who murders the wayfarers daily is Ahimsa only. Himsa becomes Ahimsa under certain circumstances.

Forgiveness or Kshama befits an ascetic or a Sannyasin who leads the life of Nivritti Marga or renunciation. It cannot befit a ruler. The ruler may forgive one who has injured him, but he cannot forgive one who has done the greatest harm to the public.

Dharma-sankata

Sometimes one is puzzled as to what to do under certain circumstances. There is conflict of duty. One has to choose between alternatives both of which go against Dharma. Sometimes you will have to choose the lesser evil and you must be prepared to undergo the results of that Karma. One man's father was in a dying condition. He had no food. He was dying of starvation. The father would die if he was not given any food. Food could only be had by stealing. What is the Dharma of the son at this critical juncture? To save the life of his father is his Dharma. He stole some food and saved the life of his father. He must suffer for the evil act of stealing.

The Importance of Motive

It is the motive that counts in the performance of an action. Right and wrong are to be determined, not by the objective consequences, but by the nature of the subjective intention of the agent. God looks to the motive of the doer.

Lord Rama fought with Ravana. Ravana also engaged himself in battle. But the motives of both were different, though the action was the same.

Sri Rama fought in order to establish Dharma and protect the people from the trouble and havoc of wicked Ravana. He had no selfish interests. But Ravana had evil motive.

A Karma Yogi works in the society intensely, with more zeal than a worldly man. The action is the same, but the motives are different in each person, The Karma Yogi marches forward towards the Goal or *summum bonum,* but the worldly man entangles himself through his impure motive of self-interest.

The inner motives of a man form the seed and root of all his life's activities. If the inner motive is pure, all the subsequent consequences are pure and good. Else, only evil and unhappiness will accrue.

You must have purification of the motive. There must be an internal resolve or attitude of the will to be free from all impure feelings of pride, self-esteem, etc., in the discharge of duties. Only then you will have purity of motive.

Moral living starts through dedication to ideal principles and maxims. A man of right conduct has ideal principles and mottoes. He strictly follows them, removes his weaknesses and defects, develops good conduct, and becomes thus an ethically perfect man. First you must have righteous principles and then you will not fail to do virtuous actions.

The Active Practice of Virtue

Virtue survives only when it is kept in the perpetual practice. Virtue will develop and survive only when practised positively and actively. The mind and will must be exercised and disciplined through deliberate acts of self-denial and self-sacrifice in everyday life.

Rigidly observe truth and purity in your thoughts, speech, actions, in your inner motive and general conduct. Be loving, tolerant and charitable in your opinion of men and things, in your dealings with others.

In every sphere, the individual should strive to adhere to these qualities and to manifest them. Thus, this ideal is to be practised between parents and children, elders and youngsters, teacher and pupil, friend and friend, Guru and disciple, leader and follower, subject and ruler, nation and nation.

God-realisation, the Highest Duty of Man

All duties—domestic, social and the like—are only relative. The ultimate and chief duty of every human being is the attainment of Truth, God-realisation. The discharge of all duties is, in reality, to qualify man to do this highest duty.

All ethics have, as their aim, the realisation of the Self. Ethics leads to restraint of the lower self and thereby the mind is calmed. Through calmness of the mind, discrimination dawns, and one knows the Self in a short time.

One cannot attain to perfection by mere goodness and practice of virtue. He has to meditate intensely on the ideal with the help of purity acquired through virtue. Virtue and morality act as auxiliaries to meditation and final mergence of the individual in the Supreme.

Virtue Is the Gateway to Bliss

Ethics gives a sustaining stamina to life. A character without ethics is like a saltless dish. There can be no high civility, no courtesy, no politeness, no elegant manners, without a profound moral sense.

Practice of ethics will help you to live in harmony with your neighbours, friends, your own family members, fellow-beings, and all other people. It will confer on you lasting happiness and final liberation by invoking God's grace. Your heart will be purified. Your conscience will be cleansed.

There is no greater comfort than a righteous, virtuous life guided by a clear conscience. Acts of kindness, charitable services, and compassion for the distressed are the paths of righteousness.

Righteousness is essential. Do not leave the path of righteousness for any gain. Do not leave the path of morality even if your life is in danger.

The path of truth is narrow and precipitous, but its principles are as precise and exact as the law of gravitation. Do not leave the path, for it leads to immortality.

You must obey the laws, or the rules of conduct. The rules are given to you for your own betterment and spiritual uplift.

To stick to Sadachara is difficult, no doubt. Mockery, misunderstanding and persecution will have to be faced. Therefore, the cultivation of forbearance, meekness of spirit, calm endurance and spirit of forgiveness are of great importance. Uphold virtue at any cost; for its sake, bear any calumny. Return good for evil.

There is no religion higher than virtue. Virtue brings peace. Virtue is greater than life and prosperity. Virtue is the gateway to bliss. Therefore be virtuous always. Let virtue be your mainstay.

Consult the Shastras and Mahatmas whenever you are in doubt. Build up your character. Grow. Evolve. Keep up your ideal always before your mind. Stick to Sadachara or right conduct. Practise it. You will soon attain eternal bliss and immortality.

22. FEAR

Fear is an instinct common in every man. Fear is universal. It can happen at any place. It can come at any time.

The king is afraid of his enemy. The Pundit is afraid of his opponent. A beautiful lady is afraid of old age. A lawyer is afraid of the judge, and his clients. The wife is afraid of her husband. The student is afraid of the teacher. The police inspector is afraid of the superintendent. The frog is afraid of the snake. The cobra is afraid of the mongoose. No one is absolutely free from some sort of fear.

What Is Fear?

Fear is painful emotion excited by danger. It is apprehension of danger or pain. Fear is an emotion excited by threatening evil or impending pain, accompanied by a desire to avoid or escape it and to provide for one's security.

There are various degrees in fear. They are simply fright, timidity, shyness, alarm, terror and terrible fear. When there is terrible fear, the whole body perspires; urine and faecal matter are ejected involuntarily. The mind becomes like a log of wood. Sometimes shock and immediate collapse take place, and the man dies of sudden heart-failure.

Fear assumes various forms. The Gurkha soldier is not afraid of knife or bullet; but he is afraid of scorpions. A hunter is not afraid of tigers in the forest, but is afraid of surgeon's knife. The man of the frontier is not afraid of knife; he can even allow the surgeon to open his intestines without chloroform; but he is terribly afraid of snakes. Some are afraid of ghosts. Some are afraid of diseases. The vast majority of persons are afraid of public criticism.

Normal Fear and Imaginary Fear

Fear is of two kinds, viz., normal fear and imaginary fear. The percentage of normal fear will be only five. Imaginary fear will come to ninety per cent.

Normal fear is healthy. It paves the way for one's progress. It preserves life. A headmaster is afraid of the inspector of schools. He takes a very keen interest in training the boys. All the boys get success in the examination. An engine-driver of the railways is afraid of his superior officer. He is very careful in the discharge of his duties. No collision occurs. A physician is afraid of getting a bad reputation. He takes great care of his patient. He makes researches. He saves many lives. He becomes a famous physician also.

Imaginary fears cause diseases, deplete all energies in man, and produce all sorts of feverish excitement, low vitality, uneasiness, discomfort, disharmony, etc. When there is an epidemic of cholera or typhoid, fear is the predisposing cause. Man is terribly afraid of cholera, worries himself, and imagines that the germs have entered his body. Imagination does serious havoc. He becomes a victim to the actual disease itself!

Illustrations of Imaginary Fear

A student prepares himself day and night for the ensuing examination. He has passed creditably in all the class-examinations. But he develops a kind of imaginary fear—examination fear—as soon as he enters the examination hall, becomes nervous, and gets confused. His hands tremble. He is not able to write. He fails in the examination.

Sri R.S. Banerjee was sleeping in a room in his friend's house at Dehra Dun. He and his friends were talking, on that night, about the mischievous actions done by evil spirits. These thoughts went deep into his subconscious mind. He dreamt that the room in which he was sleeping was a haunted room and some evil spirit had done some mischief on him. From that day he began to lose his health gradually. This was due to some kind of imaginary fear.

Every man has some imaginary fear. Some develop on imaginary fear that they will lose their job. Some imagine and think, "What will become of my fate if my wife dies now? I have to look after nine children". Some have the imaginary fear: "What can I do if my business fails?" or "What will become of Hinduism if the whole of India becomes Pakistan? If communism pervades the whole of India?". There is no end to such imaginary fears.

Phobias

Peculiar, private, irrational, unnatural fears are called phobias. Phobia is an unnatural form of fear. Phobias have no objective reality. There is nothing to frighten people. There is no threatening situation in their environment which should cause fear in them, and yet they cannot free themselves from fears and negative feelings.

Some are afraid of rats. This is rat-phobia. Some are afraid of thunder. Some are afraid of walking in the dark. Some are afraid of seeing great multitudes of people. This is plurophobia. Some Brahmacharins are afraid of seeing a bevy of ladies. Some are afraid to remain alone. Some are afraid to sleep in a room without lamp. Some are afraid of closed spaces such as tunnels, etc. This is claustrophobia. Some are afraid of open spaces. This is agoraphobia. Though the doctor has definitely said that there is nothing organically wrong with some patients, they still think that they have some heart trouble or kidney disease or liver complaint. These are all phobias of the body.

Some are afraid of anything and everything.

The Americans are afraid of the Russians. The Russians are afraid of the Americans. The frontier people of India are afraid of the tribal people. Phobias are endless.

The causes of phobias are nervousness, stupidity in a mild or intense form, and lack of right thinking and right understanding.

A Word to Parents and Teachers

The origin of most neurotic fears can be traced to childhood. The seeds of fear may lie dormant in childhood in the subconscious mind. They sprout forth after some time during some period of crisis or stress.

The minds of children are very impressionable. They are very plastic. Mothers and teachers should be very careful when they deal with children. They should not tell them anything that will frighten them. On the contrary, they should tell them stories of chivalrous persons which will make them bold and courageous. Even during the period of pregnancy, mothers should read inspiring books like the Ramayana, the Bhagavata and the Mahabharata, if they wish to bring forth intelligent and brave children.

Mothers, fathers and teachers should have at least an elementary knowledge of psychology. Then alone can they mould the children properly.

Ill Effects of Fear

Fear is the beginning of all evil. From fear proceeds misfortune. The fears of a coward expose him to dangers.

Constant fear saps your vitality, shakes confidence, and destroys your ability. It makes you powerless. It is an enemy of your success.

What paralysis is to the physical body, so is fear to the mind. It paralyses the mind and makes you powerless. Fear is the most destructive emotion. It breaks down the nervous system and undermines your health. It creates worry, and renders happiness and peace of mind impossible.

Fear, in all its different phases, is the greatest enemy of man. It has destroyed the happiness and efficiency of man. It has made more men cowards, more people failures. Fear kills effort and stultifies endeavour. Poverty and failure are due to thoughts of fear.

Fear is a great human curse. Fear blights many lives, makes people unhappy, and unsuccessful. Fear is a negative thought. Fear is your worst enemy.

Cause of Fear

Raga or attachment is the long-standing associate of fear. Attachment is the cause of fear. You are attached to a fountain-pen, walking-stick, book, watch, towel, cloth. Fear slowly creeps in. There is fear of losing them.

Wherever there is Raga, there is fear. Fear and Raga co-exist. Man is attached to his wife. The body of his wife is his greatest pleasure-centre. So there is fear for him, fear of losing her, fear of her death, fear of her running away with another man, fear of her divorcing him, fear of her being displeased with him, etc. As he is attached to his children, house and property, he has fear of losing his house, property and children. He is drowned in sorrow and gets terrible shock if these objects are destroyed or lost.

Attachment to objects causes fear. Attachment to name and fame causes fear. Attachment to money and women causes fear. Any attachment is the womb of terrible fear. One who possesses, fears. He does not fear who has renounced everything, who perceives the Atman in all.

If there is no Raga, there is no fear. The first link in the chain of Raga is man's attachment to his body. All kinds of Raga start from this Raga to the physical body. Clinging to life and body or love of earthly life is the main cause for all fears.

Worse than in waking, many undergo drastic, alarming

abnormality in sleep. This is all due to loading the mind with stray thoughts while retiring. One should never go to bed in a state of worry or fear, nor with a heavy heart, nor when he broods over an impending evil. Before retiring, everyone must evacuate all such thoughts and meditate upon God till he is released from them. He must have perfect peace in mind and soul. If he is unable to meditate upon God, let him loudly recite some hymn or poem till he sinks in the bed. He is sure to have peaceful, deep sleep.

Drowning waves of fear may at times rush down upon us. We may lose mental balance for a while. We may be over-sensitive and agitated. A chain of evil happenings appear before us one after another in quick succession. Memory of the past gallops with winged speed. Imagination soars, and we picture disaster after disaster awaiting us. Yet, under all these circumstances, we must lay our fullest faith in God, take refuge in Him, and fully believe that He alone can deliver us.

Conquest of Fear

Overcoming in this way will not suffice. This must be brought into practice. We must first face only those which we are afraid of. If a man is afraid of facing an audience, it must be the first and foremost duty he should do until he is free from stage-fear and nervousness. If one trembles to approach his superior, or any other person who he thinks is endowed with superior powers, that must be taken up as his first duty every day till he gains sufficient moral strength. If you are afraid of something, look at it in the face. Fear will vanish.

Sit for a while. Reflect well. Introspect. All imaginary fear will take to their heels. They will dwindle into an airy nothing. Mind deceives you through imaginary fears. Learn to discriminate, cogitate, reflect and meditate. The mind will lurk like a thief. You will feel now that you were duped all these years by this mischievous mind and that fear is a non-entity, a big zero.

Put the seeds of courage in your heart. Allow courage to grow. Fear will die by itself. The positive always overcomes the negative. This is an immutable psychological law. This is the Pratipaksha-bhavana method of Raja Yogins. Try this method again and again. You are bound to succeed.

Develop your will-power. Cultivate courage and fortitude.

Develop mental power of endurance, firmness in meeting danger, and power of resistance. Be courageous and patient in sharp pains, on the occasion of loss of children or property, and in protracted illness. Have courage and manly character. Remember the saints and their virtuous deeds. Live in the company of sages and Yogins. Meditate on the fearless Atman. You will develop courage, a manly character, and other virtues. All phobias will disappear.

God bestows perfect security on His devotees and removes all sorts of fears. He transforms the sense of insecurity and fear into one of confidence and faith. He saves him from panic and despair. Take refuge in the Lord, in His Name and grace. All fears will vanish completely. He will instil strength, fortitude, courage, presence of mind, etc., in you.

Abandon attachment through practice of non-attachment or Vairagya, and attachment to the lotus feet of the Lord. All fears will vanish. Always entertain the thought: "All objects are illusory, perishable, and pain-giving". You will have no attachment. Even if there is attachment, it will be mild. You can drive it away with slight thinking and discrimination. Renunciation of everything and cultivation of Brahma-bhava is the best remedy to overcome all fears.

An Error of the Psychologists

Psychologists are of the opinion that there cannot be absolute fearlessness, and that only determined effort can be made to conquer fear. This is incorrect. Psychologists have no transcendental experience. A perfect sage who has Knowledge of Brahman is absolutely fearless. The Upanishads declare in a thundering voice. "The Knower of fearless Brahman himself becomes absolutely fearless".

There can be fear only where there is duality. If one feels that there is a second object besides himself, at once fear is generated. He is afraid of the other man. How can there be fear for one who experiences non-duality? The perfect sage who is established in non-duality is the most courageous of men. The courage of a soldier in the battle-field, or of a dacoit, is only Tamasic courage. It is not courage at all. It is only brutal ferocity born of hatred or jealousy. That Sattvic courage born of Wisdom of the Self alone is real courage.

You should not have any dualism in the mind. You must always develop cosmic love and universal brotherhood. When there is love and brotherhood, there is no enmity. There is no superiority or inferiority of power. Of course, this is a partial stage. The final stage is feeling the oneness of all. All are Brahman. All merge in Brahman. There is Brahman alone pervading throughout the universe. There is no second thing in His creation at all. This knowledge entirely uproots fear and brings one into eternal peace.

23. FREEDOM

Freedom is man's birthright. Freedom is Sat-chit-ananda. Freedom is immortality. Freedom is knowledge, peace and bliss. Consciously or unconsciously, wittingly or unwittingly, all are attempting for this freedom. Nations are fighting in the battle-field for getting freedom. A robber robs for getting freedom from want—though his movement may be crooked and circuitous. Every movement of your foot is towards freedom or Sat-chit-ananda.

Everybody wants independence. A small cook working in a coffee hotel collects money, purchases vessels and opens a coffee hotel. He wants independence. He does not want to serve under anybody. A paid servant working in a cloth shop wants independence. He collects money and opens a cloth shop of his own. A professor wants independence. He wishes to become a principal. A disciple wants independence. He starts an Ashram of his own and becomes a Guru. There is an innate urge in everyone to become independent, not to serve under another.

Everybody wishes to be independent. Everybody wants to be a ruler. Everyone desires others to be guided by his wishes; no one likes to be guided by the wishes of others. Everybody, in his heart of hearts, really desires to rule over all others if only he could; nobody wishes to have a rival.

The real cause is that there is in you the immortal, self-effulgent Soul or Atman, which is one without a second, which has no rival, which is the inner ruler, which is the support for the whole universe. In reality, you are this Atman. That is the reason why you have such a feeling and desire.

In every heart, there is desire for freedom, this all-consuming passion for liberty. Freedom is the birthright of man. Freedom is the very nature of Brahman or the Eternal Soul. Brahman is Nitya-mukta, eternally free. The desire for freedom is there even in the lowliest of God's creatures. Freedom is an attribute of the soul. It is born with you. No force, no known human device, can suppress that desire. Freedom's flame is ever burning bright. Freedom or Moksha is the ultimate goal of man. Freedom is liberation from the thraldom of mind and matter.

Freedom—True and False

Loose life is not perfect freedom. Eating anywhere from anybody's hands, sleeping anywhere you like, talking anything you like: these are not freedom. You have become a slave of body, senses, mind, creature-comforts, food and fashion.

Liberty of speech is not freedom. Liberty of thought is not freedom. To move about aimlessly is not freedom. To do just as one likes is not freedom. To be in a nude state is not freedom. To be a king or monarch is not freedom. To have Svarajya is not freedom. To have plenty is not freedom. To have a comfortable living is not freedom. To possess immense wealth is not freedom. To conquer nations is not freedom. To shirk responsibility is not freedom. To renounce the world is not freedom.

Material independence will not give you perfect happiness, cannot give you perfection. Bread and jam cannot give you real happiness. These little things of the world cannot give you eternal joy.

Real Freedom

Real Svarajya is not merely political or economic, though political and economic freedom is essential for the welfare of a people. Real Svarajya is lordship over oneself. It is Atma-Svarajya. It is immortality. It is perfection. It is attainable only by slow and painful stages.

From time, pass into eternity. This is freedom or emancipation. Still the mind. Herein lies freedom and bliss eternal.

Real freedom is freedom from birth and death. Real freedom is freedom from the trammels of flesh and mind. Real freedom is freedom from the bonds of Karma. Real freedom is freedom from attachment to body, etc. Real freedom is freedom from egoism and desires. Real freedom is freedom from thoughts and likes-dislikes. Real freedom is freedom from lust, anger, greed, etc. Real freedom is identification with the Supreme Self. Real freedom is merging in the Absolute.

Freedom is in detachment. Freedom is in desirelessness. Freedom is in mindlessness. Eradication and extinction of desires lead to the sublime state of supreme bliss and perfect freedom.

Cause of Bondage

You have created your own bondage through your desires, attachments, egoism and cravings; and you cry for emancipation.

Attachment is the most powerful weapon of Maya for binding the Jivas to the Samsaric wheel of births and deaths. You would never come into this world if you had no attachment for anything. The first attachment starts with the physical body. Then all other attachments crop up. The identification of the Self with the body is extended to those who are connected with the body, such as, wife, son, house, father, mother, sister, etc., and cares increase a hundredfold. You will have to take care of all these people. You will have to take care of the toys of your son also, because the toys are connected with your son. There is absolutely no end for these cares and worries. Man creates for himself all these cares. No one is to blame. Just as the silkworm and the spider create a web for their own destruction, out of their own saliva, so also man creates these cares and worries for his own destruction out of his own ignorance.

The Play of Mind

Mind is the cause of the bondage and salvation of man. The mind has two aspects: one is discriminative, and the other is imaginative. Mind, in its aspect of discrimination, releases itself from the bondage and attains Moksha. In its aspect of imagination, it binds itself to the world.

It is the mind which binds a man to this world. Where there is no mind, there is no bondage. Mind imagines, through indiscrimination and ignorance, that the soul has been confined and located in this body, and hence it perceives the soul to be in bondage. Mind exactly identifies itself with the Jivatman and feels itself to be 'I', and hence thinks, "I am in bondage". The egoistic mind is the root of bondage. The non-egoistic mind is the root of Moksha.

When there is no 'I' or egoism, there is liberation. When there is 'I' or egoism, there is bondage, or birth and death. It is bondage when the mind is attached to any object or any sense-organ. It is liberation when the mind is not attached to any object or any sense-organ. It is bondage when the mind desires or grieves over anything, rejects or accepts anything, feels angry or happy at anything. It is liberation when the mind does not desire or reject or accept, or feel happy or angry. Emancipation is release from the bondage of the ego and its desires, of the ego and its propensities, its cravings for the sensuous.

Eradication of the Mind's Disease

The sovereign specific presented by the wise sages for the eradication of the mind's disease can be had easily through the mind alone. The intelligent cleanse a dirty cloth with the dirty earth only. A murderous Agni-astra or fire-missile is counteracted by Varuna-astra, another missile only. The venom of serpent-bite is removed by its antidote of an edible poison. So also is the case with the Jiva. Having developed discrimination, destroy the delusions of the heterogeneous mind through the one-pointed Manas, like an iron severing another iron.

Arsenic, when purified and administered in proper doses, is a blessing. It removes many diseases. It improves the blood. When it is not purified properly and given in over-doses, it brings about many ill effects. Even so, when the mind is rendered pure and Nirvishaya, it leads on to Moksha. When it is impure, and Vishayasakta or fond of sensual objects, it leads on to bondage.

On this side is matter. On the other side is pure Spirit or Atman or Brahman. Mind forms a bridge between the two. Cross the bridge. Control the mind. You will attain Brahman. You will gain liberation. You will be free from the trammels of births and deaths. The differentiations such as 'I', 'you', 'he' will vanish. All tribulations, annoyances, miseries, grief, will cease.

He is a real potentate and Maharaja who has conquered the mind. He can do anything. He can move about wherever he likes. He is as free as the atmospheric air. His happiness, freedom and peace are unbounded. The freedom and joy of such a Yogi cannot be imagined by the poor, petty-minded worldlings. Attachment and luxury have enfeebled them.

A Sad Mistake

Know your real, divine nature. Come out of this earthly rut. You are lions, not sheep. You are real emperors, not beggars. You are children of God, not weaklings tied to this perishable earth.

You think of your body, food, wife, son, friend, etc., but you do not turn your mind inward to find out what lies within yourself. You think that your body—this bundle of flesh and bones—is real, and on this basis, you build the whole citadel of life's ambition and activities. You have mistaken the shadow for the substance. You are contented with superficial things. Though you are endowed with the power of thought, you do not wish to utilise this power in quest of the Immortal Self. You have abandoned the precious jewel of Atman, and caught hold of a broken glass-piece. Is this not a foolish act?

Why do you bleat like a lamb? Assert. Recognise and realise your Brahmic nature. I will tell you a small story. Just hearken with rapt attention. There was once a lion-cub, left by its dying mother among some sheep. The sheep took care of the lion-cub. The lion-cub soon grew into a big lion, and bleated *ba-a-a* when the sheep bleated *ba-a-a*.

One day, another lion came and heard the sheep-lion bleating aloud with the other sheep. He was struck with amazement. He asked the sheep-lion, "Brother! What is the matter with you? Why are you here in such an abject state?". The sheep-lion replied, "I am a sheep. I am happy here amidst my brothers and sisters". "Nonsense", roared the other lion, "Come along with me. I will show you. You are under a false delusion". He took the sheep-lion to the side of a river and showed him his reflection in the water. He said to the sheep-lion: "Look at your reflection now. You are a lion. I am a lion". The sheep-lion looked at the reflection and then said in joy, "What a terrible mistake I have committed! I am certainly a lion, indeed. I am not a sheep at all". He made a terrible roar and went along with the other lion.

Brother! You are also bleating like the sheep-lion. You have forgotten your real, divine nature. Suzerainty is quite natural to you. Suzerainty is an attribute of Atman. On account of ignorance, you have mistaken the body for Atman, and you try to have no rivals in the physical body, in business, in office, in college, in games, in dominions, and in any field of activity. You can have absolute suzerainty only by realising the Atman. Atma-Svarajya only can make you absolutely independent. Atma-Svarajya only can make you the supreme ruler or absolute monarch of the whole universe. Therefore realise this wonderful Atman, and become a veritable, mighty potentate of the three worlds.

24. GANGA

The Ganga is the most sacred river of India. The origin of the Ganga is ascribed to celestial glory. Lord Krishna says in the Gita: "I am the Ganga among rivers".

For a Hindu, the word Ganga has its own sacred association. Every Hindu thirsts for a dip in the Ganga, and for a drop of its water at the time of his death. Aspirants and mendicants build their huts on the banks of the Ganga for practising penance and meditation. Bhishma spoke very highly of the glory of the Ganga in his parting instructions to the Pandavas from his bed of arrows.

In the Satya Yuga, all places were sacred. In the Treta Yuga, Pushkara was considered the most holy place. In the Dvapara Yuga, Kurukshetra was regarded as the most sacred place. In Kali Yuga, the Ganga has that glory. Devi Bhagavata says: "He who utters the name of Ganga even from hundreds of miles afar is freed from sins and attains the abode of Lord Hari".

The Ganga Bath

Thousands of pilgrims visit Hardwar and Rishikesh every year and take a dip in the sacred river. They have immense faith in the glory of Mother Ganga. They believe that all their sins are washed away if they take a dip in the sacred waters of the Ganga. Really they are washed off. A dip in the Ganga instantly purifies. There is no doubt about this. Even confirmed atheists and rationalists come to Hardwar for a refreshing bath in the Ganga.

Wherever a pious Hindu goes to take his bath, he invokes first the Ganga and feels Her presence in the water before he takes a plunge in the river. If he lives in a place far away from the Ganga, he intensely yearns to see Her some day and bless his being by bathing in the holy waters. When he is blessed to have a Ganga bath, he carries some water to his house and carefully saves it in a vessel so that he may use it for purposes of purification.

Ganga—A Form of the Supreme Being

Ganga is the form of Vishnu. She came out of the Supreme Being. Her sight is soul-stirring and elevating. She flows in the valleys and lives by the side of Parvati, daughter of Himavan. How magnificent she is when she flows in the valley of Rishikesh! She has a blue colour like that of the ocean. The water is extremely clear and sweet. Rich people from the plains get water from Rishikesh. It is taken in big copper vessels to far-off places in India.

To have a look at the Ganga in Rishikesh is soul-elevating. To sit for a few minutes on a block of stone by the side of the Ganga is a blessing. To stay for some months in Rishikesh on the banks of the Ganga and do Anushthana or Purascharana is great Tapas which will take the aspirant to the abode of Lord Hari. To live for ever on the banks of the Ganga and spend the life in meditation is Sivanandam.

Mother Ganga bestows seen and unseen powers on those crave for Her grace. Sit alone on the banks of the Ganga. Concentrate. Meditate. Realise how spiritual vibrations accelerate your inner heart, even overriding your guilty conscience. Where has the supreme joy that fills you now all over, come from all on a sudden! How she does instantaneously withdraw your mind and conscience from the physical world to the regions of immortality, only to suckle you with bliss and blessedness!

Purity of the Ganga Water

The water of the Ganga is extremely pure and sanctifying. No germs can flourish in this. This has been tested by various scientists in the laboratory. Rich in minerals this water cures almost all kinds of diseases.

The Ganga is saturated with antiseptic minerals. Even in the West, doctors prescribe Ganga water for rubbing in the treatment of diseases of the skin. Ganga is not merely a river. It is a sacred Tirtha. It is possessed of mysterious powers which are not found in any other river of the world. Even scientists have admitted the efficacy of the Ganga water.

Dr. F.C. Harrison of McGill University, Canada writes: "A peculiar fact which has never been satisfactorily explained is the quick death, in three or five hours, of the cholera vibrio in the waters of the Ganga. When one remembers sewage by numerous corpses of natives, often cholera casualties, and by the bathing of thousands of natives, it seems remarkable that the belief of the Hindus, that the water of this river is pure and cannot be defiled and that they can safely drink it and bathe in it, should be confirmed by means of modern bacteriological research".

A well-known French physician, Dr. D. Herelle, made similar

investigations into the mystery of the Ganga. He observed some of the floating corpses of men dead of dysentery and cholera, and was surprised to find "that only a few feet below the bodies where one would expect to find millions of these dysentery and cholera germs, there were no germs at all". He then grew germs from patients having the disease, and to these cultures added water from the Ganga. When he incubated the mixture for a period, much to his surprise, the germs were completely destroyed.

A British physician, Dr. C.E. Nelson, F.R.C.S., tells us of another striking fact. He says that "ships leaving Calcutta for England take their water from the Hooghly river which is one of the mouths of the filthy Ganga and this Ganga water will remain fresh all the way to England. On the other hand, ships leaving England for India find that the water they take on in London will not stay fresh till they reach Bombay, the nearest Indian port, which is a week closer to England than Calcutta. They must replenish their water-supply at Port Said, Suez or at Aden on the Read Sea". It is no wonder that the Indian people should hold that the Ganga is very sacred and possessed of mysterious powers.

A Silent Teacher

The Ganga starts from Gangotri in Himalayas. She encounters many obstacles on her way, but she finally reaches the goal—the ocean. Similarly, the Sadhaka should never give up his struggle, however insurmountable the obstacles in the path may appear to be. All difficulties and obstacles will be removed through the grace of the Lord if he is sincere in his Yogic practices, and he will reach the goal.

The Ganga gives you always cool, pure water. It does not expect anything from you in return. The sun sheds its light on all without anticipating any reward. Derive lessons from them. Always give, give. Ask nothing in return. Expect nothing in return. Do not expect even appreciation, approbation, or recognition.

A rogue and a saint can drink the water of the Ganga. The sun sheds its light on the wicked and the virtuous. The mango tree gives its fruits both for the caretaker and the man who cuts its branches. Develop equal vision like the Ganga, the sun and the mango tree.

I love Ganga and the Himalayas. Ganga is my Mother Divine. Himalayas is my Father Divine. They inspire and guide me. I take bath in Ganga. I swim in Ganga. I adore Ganga. I feed the fishes of Ganga.

I wave light to Mother Ganga. I pray to Ganga. I do salutations to Ganga. I sing the glory of Ganga. I write about the grandeur and glory of Ganga.

Ganga has nourished me. Ganga has comforted me. Ganga has taught me the truths of the Upanishads.

O friend! Follow the lines of Mother Ganga. Be pure. Be adaptable. Be tolerant. Be forgiving. Be sweet. Pour out your love on all. Share what you have—physical, moral, mental and spiritual—with the whole of humanity. The more you give the more you get. Give without any selfish motive, without expecting any reward. Embrace all. Cultivate equal vision.

All glory be unto Mother Ganga, the giver of life, light and love. Worship Her with faith, devotion and piety. Adore Her with flowers of purity, love, self-restraint and equal vision. Sing Her Names. Attain Brahman through Her grace. May Mother Ganga bless you all! May She help you to live on Her banks and practise Yoga and Tapas.

25. GITA

Mahatma Gandhi once visited one of the biggest libraries in London and asked the librarian, "What spiritual book was issued frequently?". The librarian replied, "It was Gita". The greatest gift, the best blessing, that India has conferred upon the world, upon all humanity, is this sublime yet eminently practical, universal gospel of the Srimad Bhagavad Gita. The great thinkers and philosophers of the Occident have vied with one another in paying their devout tribute at the shrine of the Gita. Wilhelm von Humbolt, the famous occidental scholar, says: "The Bhagavad Gita is the deepest and sublimest production the world possesses". Emerson, the great sage of America, had a copy of the Gita always on his table.

The Gita is the voice of God. It is the song of ancient wisdom. It is a great text-book of spiritual culture. It is a book of eternity. It has been my constant companion of life. It is a gospel for the whole world.

The Song Celestial

Srimad Bhagavad Gita is a dialogue between Lord Krishna and Arjuna narrated in the Bhishma Parva of the Mahabharata. It comprises eighteen chapters of seven hundred and one Sanskrit verses. Considerable matter is condensed and compressed within these Slokas. In the midst of the battle-field of Kurukshetra, Lord Krishna, during the course of His most interesting and instructive talk with Arjuna, revealed the profound, sublime and soul-stirring spiritual truths, and expounded to Arjuna the rare secrets of Yoga, Vedanta, Bhakti and Karma. All the teachings of Lord Krishna were subsequently recorded as the Song Celestial or the Srimad Bhagavad Gita by Sri Bhagavan Vyasa for the benefit of the humanity at large.

There are countless commentaries on the Gita at the present day. A volume can be written for each Sloka. A busy man with Karmic tendencies will be benefited by 'Gita Rahasya', the commentary of Sri Bal Gangadhar Tilak; a man of devotion by studying Sridhara's commentary; and a man of reason by Sri Sankara's commentary.

Need for a Teacher

As the Gita contains subtle and profound teachings, you should study it under a qualified teacher, a Brahma-nishtha Guru, with great faith, single-minded devotion and purity. Then only the truths of the Gita will be revealed unto you like the Amalaka fruit in the hand. Good commentaries like Swami Madhusudana's Gita, Sri Swami Sankarananda's Gita, Sri Sankara's commentary, etc., written by realised sages, will be of immense help to you.

Lord Krishna speaks from different levels of consciousness. Therefore, the help of a teacher is necessary if you wish to know the right significance of the Slokas. You cannot rightly comprehend the meaning of the verses of the Gita without the help of a teacher. Otherwise, you will be like the man who brought a horse before one who asked for 'Saindhava' when he was taking his food. 'Saindhava' means 'salt' as well as a horse'.

A Scripture for All

Gita is a universal gospel which appeals to all, irrespective of age, race, or religion. It has a universality which embraces every aspect of human action, which suits and elevates every stage of human development. That is the reason why tributes have been paid to the Gita by eminent scholars of the world.

The Bhagavad Gita deals with Yoga. And Yoga is neither Eastern nor Western; it is of the world, of humanity in general. Yoga is the science of right living. It has nothing to do with any religious belief, traditional faith, colour, vocation, or clime.

Krishna is not merely a Hindu god; He is the representative of the Inner Reality which is in all without difference. He gave His Gita not merely to Arjuna, but through Arjuna, to the whole world at large. The problems that faced Arjuna face mankind in general. The Gita is the answer to the universal question of life as a whole.

To live means to fight, for all life is a battle wherein the forces of good and evil, the divine and the demoniacal, purity and passion, are ceaselessly at war. The battle of Mahabharata is still raging within you. Ignorance or Avidya is Dhritarashtra. The individual soul is Arjuna. The Indweller who dwells in your heart is Lord Krishna, the Charioteer. The body is your chariot. Indriyas are the horses. Mind, egoism, senses, Samskaras, Vasanas, cravings, Raga-dvesha, lust, jealousy, greed, pride, hypocrisy are your dire enemies.

The Gita symbolises the solution of this eternal struggle between the spiritual and the material in every human being. It does not exclude any being from receiving its message and becoming blessed. It is entirely non-sectarian, and is pre-eminently a practical gospel. It has a workable message for you, for me, and for every man and woman living their ordinary life in the busy, everyday world.

A Practical Guide to Regulate Daily Life and Conduct

The Gita embodies in itself a solution, more than an exposition or a revelation. It embodies in itself a solution to the immediately pressing problems of man, and carries a wonderful message of encouragement, hope, cheer and consolation. It is a direct appeal to divinise the entire nature of man.

The Gita is at once a rousing and inspiring gospel that throws a flood of light upon the most vexing problems of life, lights up with bright rays of hope and assurance the dark corners of gloom, despondency and despair, raising the reader at once from weakness to strength, from diffidence to robust confidence in his own infinite powers and imperishable nature.

It has the heartening message, that to realise his immortal nature, man is not required to become a recluse breaking off from family and friends and holding far from the society; that union with the Divine Self may be achieved and maintained even in the midst of worldly work and activities. The obstacles to this blissful union lie within us, and not in external environment. This is the central lesson of this unique and blessed book.

The Gita gives you practical lessons to regulate your daily life and conduct. It tells you to resist Adharma, to develop the divine virtues which will help to attain God-consciousness. The message of the Gita is the message of sacrifice, love and duty. Love all. Share what you have with others. Do your duties well. Rise above petty likes and dislikes. Keep open the portals of your heart by removing selfishness, greed, lust, so that the Supreme Lord Himself may come and dwell therein. These are the lessons of the Gita.

The Gita does not ask man to do anything which will be impossible for anyone of average capacity to do. The Lord says: "I do not want you to undertake gigantic processes. I want Bhava; I want the heart. Whatever is easily possible for you, find out, and do that. I shall fulfil it; fulfilment is in my hands". The Gita gives man a positive promise of Salvation and makes him fearless. Therein lies the supreme value of the Gita.

Harmony in the Gita

Srimad Bhagavad Gita formulates the theory of the three Margas or paths, viz., the Jnana Marga, the Bhakti Marga, and the Karma Marga. According to the teaching of the Gita, there is no conflict between the three. The Gita wonderfully harmonises the philosophies of action, devotion and knowledge.

Love is knowledge in diffusive expression. Knowledge is love in concentrated essence. Service is love expressed through action. Love, knowledge and service are equally necessary in the complete setting up of divine life. Heart, head and hand must be harmoniously developed. Then only you will attain perfection.

You should have the head of Sri Sankara, the heart of Lord Buddha, and the hand of Sri Janaka. The three horses of this body-chariot—action, emotion and intellect—should work in perfect harmony. Then only this body-chariot will move smoothly and you can reach the destination safely and quickly. Then only you can rejoice in the Self within. Then only you can sing the song of Soham. Then only you can be in tune with the Infinite. Then only you can hear the soundless voice of the Soul and enjoy the sweet internal music of the Atman.

Precept and Practice

Some thoughtless people begin to entertain doubt and say, "How can the Gita be taught to Arjuna in the battlefield in such a short time? It could not be". This is wrong. It was all a revelation to Arjuna. Lord Krishna gave Arjuna the divine eye of intuition. The omniscient, omnipotent Lord can do anything. His grace can make the dumb man eloquent, and the cripple a climber of mountains.

Gita-Jayanti or the Birthday of Srimad Bhagavad Gita is celebrated throughout India by all admirers and lovers of this unique book on the eleventh day of the bright half of the *Marga Sirsha* month according to the Hindu almanac. It was the day on which, over five thousand years ago, Lord Krishna taught to His disciple Arjuna, the Celestial Song.

A Treasure-trove of Wisdom

The Gita is the cream of the Vedas. It is the quintessence of the

Upanishads. It is the crest-jewel of the Mahabharata. It is a book that comes under the category of the Prasthanatraya, the authoritative books of the Hindu religion.

You will find a solution here for all your doubts. The more you study with devotion and faith, the more you will get deeper knowledge, penetrative insight, and clear right thinking. Ask. You shall be given. Seek. You shall find. Knock. It shall be open to you. This is the unopposed quality of this scripture. You obtain access, at one stroke, to the entire range of wisdom, human and divine.

The Lord, in His Immanence as Krishna, gave His Song Divine replete with the profoundest wisdom. And what branch of knowledge will it not include! What Yoga will it not embrace! Truly it is said: *Sarvashastramayee Gita.* The Gita is an embodiment of all sciences, scriptures, and knowledge. Its word is law.

Gita is like the Lake of Manasarovar for the Paramahamsas and thirsting aspirants to sport in. It is the ocean of bliss in which the seekers of Truth swim with joy and ecstasy. If the philosopher's stone touches piece of iron only at one point, the whole of it is transformed into gold. Even so, if you live in the spirit of one verse even of the Gita, you will doubtless be transmuted into Divinity.

Worship the Srimad Bhagavad Gita as a holy scripture. Study a chapter from it daily. But, stop not with that. Live in the spirit of the teachings of the Gita. Mere talk and lecture will not help you in any way. You may know the whole of the Gita by heart; you may deliver lectures on the Gita for hours together; and yet, you may not have a ray of the wisdom of the Gita. What is wanted is regular practice of the teachings of the Gita. Become intensely practical. Let the Gita guide your thoughts, prompt your speech, and rule your actions. Then your whole attitude towards life will be gradually changed. You will become a God-man with God-vision. You will no more be perturbed by success or failure, pleasure or pain, loss or gain. You will attain courage, strength, peace and bliss in this very life, right where you are.

26. GOD

Who is God? What is God? Is there a God? Where is God? How to realise God? Man wants an answer to these eternal questions. Certainly there is God. God exists. He is the only reality. God is your creator, saviour and redeemer. He is all-pervading. He dwells in your heart. He is always near you. He is nearer to you than your jugular vein or nose. He loves you. He can talk to you. You cannot find God by the intellect. But, you can find Him by feeling, meditation, experience and realisation.

Who Is God?

The Petromax does not talk, but it shines and sheds light all round. The jessamine does not speak, but it wafts its fragrance everywhere. The lighthouse sounds no drum, but sends its friendly light to the mariner. The Unseen beats no gong, but Its omnipresence is felt by the dispassionate and discriminating sage.

Behind all names and forms is the one nameless, formless Essence. Behind all governors is the one Supreme Governor of governors. Behind all lights is the one Light of lights. Behind all sounds, there is the soundless Supreme Silence. Behind all teachers is the one Supreme Guru of Gurus.

Behind all these perishable objects is the one imperishable Absolute. Behind all these motions is the one motionless Infinite. Behind time, minutes, and days is the one timeless Eternity. Behind hatred, riots and wars is the one hidden Love.

God is the totality of all that exists, both animate and inanimate, sentient and insentient. He is free from ills and limitations. He is omnipotent, omniscient and omnipresent. He has no beginning, middle, or end. He is the indweller in all beings. He controls from within.

God is all in all. God is the only reality in this universe. The existence of things is by the light of God.

God is ever living. All depend on Him. He is not depending on any. He is the Truth.

God is the end or goal of all Yoga Sadhanas. He is the centre towards which all things strive. He is the highest purpose or highest good of the world. You have the urge of hunger. There is food to appease the hunger. You have the urge of thirst. There is water to quench the thirst. There is the urge to be always happy. There must be something to satisfy this urge. This something is God, an embodiment of happiness. God, Immortality, Freedom, Perfection, Peace, Bliss, Love are synonymous terms.

What Is God?

What is God? It is hard to tell. But, when I look at the Ganga, I know it is God. When I see the jessamine, I know it is God. When I behold the blue sky, I know it is God. When I hear the chirping of birds, I know it is God. When I taste honey, I know it is God.

The Supreme is indefinable, though scholars give intellectual accounts of It which are not absolutely true.

Every man has his own conception of God. The God of a military man wears a helmet. The God of a China-man has a flat nose and a pipe for smoking opium. The God of a Hindu has marks on his forehead, and wears a rosary and a garland of flowers. The God of a Christian wears a Cross. For some, God has wings. A buffalo will think that God is a very big buffalo.

Such an anthropomorphic conception of God is obviously puerile. The greatest and most important thing in all the world is to get a right concept of God, because your belief about God governs your entire life.

Is There a God?

God is beyond human imagination, but he is a living reality. Brahman is no metaphysical abstraction. It is the fullest and the most real being.

The existence of God cannot be proved by scientific experimentation. The Absolute baffles the mind of even the greatest scholar. It eludes the grasp of even the mightiest intellect. It is experienced as pure consciousness, where intellect dies, scholarship perishes, and the entire being itself is completely lost in It. All is lost, and all is found.

You want laboratory proofs? Very fine, indeed! You wish to limit the illimitable, all-pervading God in your test-tube, blow-pipe, and chemicals. God is the source for your chemicals. He is the substratum for your atoms, electrons and molecules. Without Him, no atom or electron will move. He is the inner ruler.

It is God who lends power to our senses, perception to our mind, discernment to our intellect, strength to our limbs. It is through His will that we live and die. But man vainly imagines that he is the actor and the enjoyer. man is a mere nothing before the almighty, governing Power that directs the movement in the universe.

God's will expresses itself everywhere as law. The laws of gravitation, cohesion, relativity, cause and effect, the laws of electricity, chemistry, physics, all the psychic laws, are expressions of God's will.

As we explain everything within nature by the law of cause and effect, so also, nature as a whole must be explained. It must have some cause. This cause must be different from the effect. It must be some supernatural entity, i.e., God.

Nature is not a mere chance collection events, a mere jumble of accidents, but an orderly affair. The planets move regularly in their orbits; seeds grow into trees regularly; the seasons succeed each other in order. Now, nature is Jada, insentient. It cannot order itself. It requires the existence of an intelligent being—God—who is responsible for it. Even Einstein, the scientist, was strongly convinced of the creation of the universe by a Supreme Intelligence.

Though you do not see the stars in the daytime, yet they do exist. Though you cannot see the sun during a cloudy day, yet it does exist. Even so, though you cannot see God with these physical eyes, yet He does exist. If you get the divine eye or the eye of intuition by the practice of meditation, you will behold Him.

God is self-proved. He does not want any proof, because He is the basis for the act or process of proving.

Where Is God?

Where is God? There is nowhere where He is not. Just as one thread penetrates all the flowers in a garland, so also, one Self penetrates all these living beings. He is hidden in all beings and forms, like oil in seed, butter in milk, mind in brain, Prana in the body, foetus in the womb, sun behind the clouds, fire in wood, vapour in the atmosphere, salt in water, scent in flowers, sound in the gramophone records, gold in quartz, microbes in blood.

God dwells in all beings as life and consciousness. God is in the roar of a lion, the song of a bird, and the cry of a babe. Feel His presence everywhere.

See God in the wings, of a butterfly, in the letters Alpha and Omega, in the cough of a patient, in the murmur of a brook, in the sound of a bell. Behold the wonder of the Lord's face in every object of this world.

Every breath that flows in the nose, every beat that throbs in the heart, every artery that pulsates in the body, every thought that arises in the mind, speaks to you that God is near.

Every flower that wafts fragrance, every fruit that attracts you, every gentle breeze that blows, every river that smoothly flows, speaks of God and His mercy.

The vast ocean with its powerful waves, the mighty Himalayas with its glaciers, the bright sun and stars in the wide sky, the lofty tree with its branches, the cool springs in the hills and dales, tell you of His omnipotence.

The music of the sweet singers, the lectures of the powerful orators, the poems of the reputed poets, the inventions of the able scientists, the operations of the dexterous surgeons, the utterances of the hole saints, the thoughts of the Bhagavad Gita, the revelations of the Upanishads, speak of God and His wisdom.

Everything is God. Good is God. Misfortune is God. Greet Him in everything and rest peacefully in bliss.

God pervades the entire universe. He walks in the garb of a beggar. He moans in pain in the guise of the sick. He wanders in the forest clad in rags. Open your eyes. See Him in all. Serve all. Love all.

Feel the Divine Presence everywhere—in every form, in every thought, in every feeling and in every sentiment in every movement, in every emotion.

God, seen through the senses, is matter. God, seen through the intellect, is mind. God, seen through the spirit, is Atman or the Self.

Thou art indwelt by the Lord. He is the inner ruler, Antaryamin, guarding and controlling your life. He is in you and you are in Him. He is quite close to you. He is not very far, but is nearer to you than you are to yourself. You were thinking in the beginning that He could be found only in Mount Kailas, Ramesvaram, Mecca, Jerusalem, sky or heaven. You had very vague ideas. This body is His moving temple. The sanctum sanctorum is the chamber of your own heart. Close your eyes. Withdraw your Indriyas from the sensual objects. Search Him in thy heart with one-pointed mind, devotion and pure love. You will surely find Him. He is waiting there with outstretched arms to embrace you. If you cannot find Him there, you cannot find Him anywhere else.

How to Realise God?

God is a question of supply and demand. If you really yearn for His Darshan, He will reveal Himself to you in an instant.

You need neither art nor science, neither study nor erudition for God-realisation, but faith, purity and devotion.

Combine all the love you cherish towards all worldly objects—wife, son, wealth, property, relatives, friends—and then apply this combined love towards God. You will realise in this very second.

To serve God and Mammon at the same time is impossible. You cannot enjoy the bliss of the Self and the sensual pleasure in one and the same cup. You cannot have light and darkness at the same time.

The Lord demands your whole heart.

Reduce yourself into zero before God. Only then will God completely take care of and guide you. Only then surrender becomes complete.

Forget your own interests, your own longings, your own desires. You will attain the bliss of the Supreme Self.

Crucify, sacrifice the lower self, if you wish to have union with God.

Empty your egoism. You will be filled with God. Lose your personality. You will find the Divine Life. You will realise God.

27. GURU

The Guru is God Himself manifesting in a personal form to guide the aspirant. Grace of God takes the form of the Guru. To see the Guru is to see God. The Guru is united with God. He inspires devotion in others. His presence purifies all.

The Guru is verily a link between the individual and the Immortal. He is a being who has raised himself from *this* into *That,* and thus has free and unhampered access into both the realms. He stands, as it were, upon the threshold of immortality; and, bending down he raises the struggling individuals with his one hand, and with the other lifts them up into the *imperium* of everlasting joy and infinite Truth-Consciousness.

The Sadguru

To be a Guru, one must have a command from God.

Mere study of books cannot make one a Guru. One who has studied the Vedas, and who has direct knowledge of the Atman through Anubhava, can alone be enrolled as a Guru. A Jivanmukta or liberated sage is the real Guru or spiritual preceptor. He is the Sadguru. He is identical with Brahman or the Supreme Self. He is a Knower of Brahman.

A Sadguru is endowed with countless Siddhis. He possesses all divine Aiswarya, all the wealth of the Lord.

Possession of Siddhis, however, is not the test to declare the greatness of a sage or to prove that he has attained Self-realisation. Sadgurus generally do not exhibit any miracle or Siddhi. Sometimes, however, they may do so in order to convince the aspirants of the existence of super-physical things, give them encouragement, and instil faith in their hearts.

The Sadguru is Brahman Himself. He is an ocean of bliss, knowledge, and mercy. He is the captain of your soul. He is the fountain of joy. He removes all your troubles, sorrows, and obstacles. He shows you the right divine path. He tears your veil of ignorance. He makes you immortal and divine. He transmutes your lower, diabolical nature. He gives you the rope of knowledge, and takes you up when you are drowning in this ocean of Samsara. Do not consider him to be only a man. If you take him as a man, you are a beast. Worship your Guru and bow to him with reverence.

Guru is God. A word from him is a word from God. He need not teach anything. Even his presence or company is elevating, inspiring, and stirring. His very company is self-illumination. Living in his company is spiritual education. Read the Granth-saheb. You will come to know the greatness of the Guru.

Man can learn only from man, and hence God teaches through a human body. In your Guru, you have your human ideal of perfection. He is the pattern into which you wish to mould yourself. Your mind will readily be convinced that such a great soul is fit to be worshipped and revered.

Guru is the Moksha-dvara. He is the gateway to the transcendental Truth-Consciousness. But, it is the aspirant who has to enter through it. The Guru is a help, but the actual task of practical Sadhana falls on the aspirant himself.

The Need for a Guru

For a beginner in the spiritual path, a Guru is necessary. To light a candle, you need a burning candle. Even so, an illumined soul alone can enlighten another soul.

Some do meditation for some years independently. Later on, they actually feel the necessity of a Guru. They come across some obstacles in the way. They are unable to know how to obviate these impediments or stumbling blocks. Then they begin to search for a Master.

Only the man who has already been to Badrinath will be able to tell you the road. In the case of the spiritual path, it is still more difficult to find your way. The mind will mislead you very often. The Guru will be able to remove pitfalls and obstacles, and lead you along the right path. He will tell you: "This road leads you to Moksha; this one leads to bondage". Without this guidance, you might want to go to Badrinath, but find yourself in Delhi!

The scriptures are like a forest. There are ambiguous passages. There are passages which are apparently contradictory. There are passages which have esoteric meanings, diverse significance, and hidden explanations. There are cross-references. You are in need of a Guru or Preceptor who will explain to you the right meaning, who will remove doubts and ambiguities, who will place before you the essence of the teachings.

GURU

A Guru is absolutely necessary for every aspirant in the spiritual path. It is only the Guru who will find out your defects. The nature of egoism is such that you will not be able to find out your own defects. Just as a man cannot see his back, so also he cannot see his own errors. He must live under a Guru for the eradication of his evil qualities and defects.

The aspirant who is under the guidance of a Master or Guru is safe from being led astray. Satsanga or association with the Guru is an armour and fortress to guard you against all temptations and unfavourable forces of the material world.

Cases of those who had attained perfection without study under any Guru should not be cited as authority against the necessity of a Guru; for, such great men are the anomalies of spiritual life, and not the common normality. They come into existence as spiritual masters as a result of the intense service, study and meditation practised in previous births. They had already studied under the Guru. The present birth is only its continuative spiritual effect. Hence, the importance of the Guru is not lessened thereby.

Some teachers mislead their aspirants. They say unto all: "Think for yourself. Do not surrender yourself to any Guru". When one says, "Do not follow any Guru!", he intends to be the listeners' Guru himself. Do not approach such pseudo-Gurus. Do not hear their lectures.

All great ones had their teachers. All the sages, saints, prophets, world-teachers, incarnations, great men, have had their own Gurus, however great they might have been. Svetaketu learnt the nature of Truth from Uddalaka, Maitreyi from Yajnavalkya, Bhrigu from Varuna, Narada from Sanatkumara, Nachiketas from Yama, Indra from Prajapati; and several others humbly went to wise ones, observed strict Brahmacharya, practised rigorous discipline, and learnt Brahma-vidya from them.

Lord Krishna sat at the feet of His Guru Sandeepani. Lord Rama had Guru Vasishtha who gave Him Upadesha. Lord Jesus sought John to be baptised by him on the banks of the river Jordan. Even Devas have Brihaspati as their Guru. Even the greatest among the divine beings sat at the feet of Guru Dakshinamurti.

A neophyte must have a personal Guru first. He cannot have God as Guru to begin with. He must have a pure mind. He must have ethical perfection. He must be intensely virtuous. He must be above body-consciousness. Then alone can he have God as Guru.

How to Choose Your Guru

If you find peace in the presence of a Mahatma, if you are inspired by his speeches, if he is able to clear your doubts, if he is free from greed, anger and lust, if he is selfless, loving, and I-less, you can take him as your Guru. He who is able to clear your doubts, he who is sympathetic in your Sadhana, he who does not disturb your beliefs but helps you on from where you are, he in whose very presence you feel spiritually elevated—he is your Guru. Once you choose your Guru, implicitly follow him. God will guide you through the Guru.

Do not use your reason too much in the selection of your Guru. You will fail if you do so. If you fail to get a first-class Guru, try to follow the instructions of the Sadhu who is treading the path for some years, who has purity and other virtuous qualities, and who has some knowledge of the scriptures. Just as a student of the Intermediate class will be able to teach a student of Third Form when a professor with M.A. qualification is not available, just as a sub-assistant surgeon will be able to attend on a patient when the civil surgeon is not available, this second-class type of Guru will be able to help you.

If you are not able to find out even this second-class type of Guru, you can follow the teachings contained in the books written by realised saints like Sri Sankara, Dattatreya, and others. You can keep a photo of such a realised Guru, if available, and worship the same with faith and devotion. Gradually you will get inspiration, and the Guru may appear in a dream and initiate and inspire you at the proper time. For a sincere Sadhaka, help comes in a mysterious manner. When the time is ripe, the Guru and the disciple are brought together by the Lord in a mysterious way.

Mysterious Help from the Lord

Just see how the Lord has helped the devotees in the following instances. Eknath heard an Akasavani, a voice from the sky. It said, “See Janardan Pant at Deva Giri. He will put you in the proper path and guide you”. Eknath acted accordingly and found his Guru. Tukaram received his Mantra, *Rama Krishna Hari,* in his dream.

He repeated this Mantra and had Darshan of Lord Krishna. Lord Krishna directed Namdev to get his higher initiation from a Sannyasin at Mallikarjuna. Queen Chudalai assumed the form of Kumbha Muni, appeared before her husband Sikhidhwaja in the forest, and initiated him in the mysteries of Kaivalya. Madhura Kavi saw a light in the firmament for three days consecutively. It guided him and took him to his Guru Nammalvar who was sitting in Samadhi underneath a tamarind tree near Tinnevelly. Vilvamangal was very much attracted to Chintamani, the dancing woman. The latter became his Guru. Tulasidas received instructions from an invisible being to see Hanuman and, through Hanuman, to get Darshan of Sri Rama.

Competent disciples are never in want of a competent Guru. Realised souls are not rare. Ordinary ignorant-minded persons cannot easily recognise them. Only a few persons, who are pure and embodiments of all virtuous qualities, can understand realised souls, and they only will be benefited in their company.

So long as there is a world, there are Gurus and Vedas to guide the struggling souls in the path of Self-realisation. The number of realised souls may be less in the Iron Age when compared with the Satya Yuga, but they are always present to help the aspirants. Let each man take the path according to his capacity, temperament and understanding. His Sadguru will meet him along that path.

Siksha Gurus and Diksha Guru

Man has a twofold duty here on earth—to preserve his life, and to realise his Self. To preserve his life, he has to learn to work for his daily bread. To realise his Self, he has to serve, love, and meditate. The Guru who teaches him the knowledge of worldly arts is the Siksha Guru. The Guru who shows him the path of Realisation is the Diksha Guru. Siksha Gurus can be many—as many as the things he wishes to learn. The Diksha Guru can be only one—the one who leads him to Moksha.

Stick to One Guru

Do not dig here and there shallow pits for getting water. The pits will dry up soon. Dig a very deep pit in one place. Centralise all your efforts here. You will get good water that can supply you throughout the year. Even so, try to imbibe thoroughly the spiritual teachings from one preceptor alone. Drink deep from one man. Sit at his feet for some years. There is no use of wandering from one man to another man, out of curiosity, losing faith in a short time. Do not have the ever-changing mind of a prostitute. Follow the spiritual instructions of one man only. If you go to several people and follow the instructions of many persons, you will be bewildered. You will be in a dilemma.

From a doctor, you get a prescription. From two doctors, you get consultation. From three doctors, you get your own cremation. Even so, if you have many Gurus, you will be bewildered. You will be at a loss to know what to do. One Guru will tell you: "Do Soham Japa". Another will tell you: "Do Japa of *Sri Ram*". A third Guru will tell you: "Hear Anahat sounds". You will be puzzled. Stick to one Guru and follow his instructions.

Listen to all, but follow one. Respect all, but adore one. Gather knowledge from all, but adopt the teachings of one Master. Then you will have rapid spiritual progress.

Guru-Parampara

Spiritual knowledge is a matter of Guru-parampara. It is handed down from Guru to disciple. Gaudapadacharya imparted Self-knowledge to his disciple Govindacharya; Govindacharya to his disciple Sankaracharya; Sankaracharya to his disciple Suresvaracharya. Matsyendranath imparted knowledge to his disciple Gorakhnath; Gorakhnath to Nivrittinath; Nivrittinath to Jnanadeva. Totapuri imparted knowledge to Sri Ramakrishna, and Ramakrishna to Swami Vivekananda. It was Ashtavakra who moulded the life of Raja Janaka. It was Gorakhnath who shaped the spiritual destiny of Raja Bhartrihari. It was Lord Krishna who made Arjuna and Uddhava get themselves established in the spiritual path when their minds were in an unsettled state.

Initiation—Its Meaning

A Bhakta will be initiated by a Bhakta saint in the path of devotion. A Jnani will initiate a student of Vedanta in the Mahavakyas. A Hatha Yogi or a Raja Yogi can initiate another in his particular path. But, a sage of perfect realisation, a Purna-jnani or Purna-yogi, can give initiation in any particular path. A sage or saint like Sri Sankara or Madhusudana Sarasvati can initiate a Sadhaka in any particular path for which the aspirant is fit. The Guru will find out by close study of the aspirant his tastes, temperaments, and capacity, and decide for him the most suitable path. If his heart is impure, the teacher will prescribe selfless service for a number of years. Then the Guru will find out for what particular path the student is fit and initiate him in that.

Initiation does not mean reciting a Mantra into another's ears. If Rama is influenced by the thoughts of Krishna, the former has got initiation already from the latter. If an aspirant treads the path of truth after studying the books written by a saint, and imbibes his teachings, that saint has already become his Guru.

Sakti-sanchar

Just as you can give an orange to a man, so also, spiritual power can be transmitted by one to another. This method of transmitting spiritual powers is termed Sakti-sanchar. In Sakti-sanchar, a certain spiritual vibration of the Sadguru is actually transferred to the mind of the disciple.

Spiritual power is transmitted by the Guru to the proper disciple whom he considers fit for Sakti-sanchar. The Guru can transform the disciple by a look, a touch, a thought or a word, or mere willing.

Sakti-sanchar comes through Parampara. It is a hidden mystic science. It is handed down from Guru to disciple.

Lord Jesus, through touch, transmitted his spiritual power to some of his disciples. A disciple of Samartha Ramdas transmitted his power to that dancing girl's daughter who was very passionate towards him. The disciple gazed at her and gave her Samadhi. Her passion vanished. She became very religious and spiritual. Lord Krishna touched the blind eyes of Surdas. The inner eye of Surdas was opened. He had Bhava Samadhi. Lord Gouranga, through his touch, produced divine intoxication in many people and converted them to his side. Atheists even danced in ecstasy in the streets by his touch and sang songs of Hari.

The disciple should not rest satisfied with the transmission of power from the Guru. He will have to struggle hard in Sadhana for further perfection and attainments. Sri Ramakrishna Paramahamsa touched Swami Vivekananda. Swami Vivekananda had superconscious experience. He struggled hard for seven years more, even after the touch, for attaining perfection.

Grace and Self-effort

Realisation cannot come to you as a miracle done by your Guru. Lord Buddha, Lord Jesus, Rama Tirtha have all done Sadhana. Lord Krishna asks Arjuna to develop Vairagya and Abhyasa. He did not say to him, "I will give you Mukti now". Therefore, abandon the wrong notion that your Guru will give you Samadhi and Mukti. Strive, purify, meditate and realise.

Guru-kripa—grace of a Guru—is very necessary. That does not mean that the disciple should sit idle. He must do rigid Purushartha, spiritual practices. The whole work must be done by the student. Nowadays, people want a drop of water from the Kamandalu of a Sannyasin and desire to enter into Samadhi immediately. They are not prepared to undergo any Sadhana for purification and Self-realisation. They want a magic pill to push them into Samadhi. If you have got such delusion, give it up immediately.

The Guru and the Shastras can show you the path and remove your doubts. Anubhava of the Aparoksha kind or direct intuitive knowledge is left for your own experience. A hungry man will have to eat for himself. He who has a severe itching will have to scratch for himself.

No doubt, the Guru's blessing can do everything. But how can one have his blessings? By pleasing the Guru. A Guru can be pleased with his disciple only if the latter carries out his spiritual instructions implicitly. Carefully follow, therefore, the instructions of the Guru. Act up to his instructions. Then only will you deserve his blessings, and then alone his blessings can do everything.

28. HAPPINESS

Man wants happiness. He shuns pain. He moves heaven and earth to get the happiness he wants from sensual objects, and lo, gets himself entangled in the inextricable meshes of Maya. Poor man! He does not know that these objects are perishable and evanescent, finite and conditioned in time, space and causation. And what is more, he fails to get the desired happiness from them.

Sensual pleasure is tantalising. There is enchantment so long as man does not possess the objects. The moment he is in possession of the object, the charm vanishes. He finds that he is in entanglement.

The bachelor thinks of his marriage, day and night. He thinks he is in imprisonment after the marriage is over. He is not able to satisfy the extravagant wants of his wife. He wants to run away from the house to forests. The rich but childless man thinks he will be more happy by getting a son; he worries himself day and night to get a son, goes on pilgrimage to Ramesvaram and Kasi, and performs various religious ceremonies. But when he gets a child, he feels miserable; the child suffers from epileptic fits and his money is given away to doctors. Even then, there is no cure. This is Mayaic jugglery. The whole world is fraught with temptation.

A Spectacle of Sorrow

A worldly man is always drowned in sorrow. He is ever struggling to get something, some money, some power, some position and so on. He is always anxious as to whether or not he would get it. Even when he is in actual possession of the thing he so passionately longed for, he is very anxious lest he should lose it.

A rich man has great wealth, but he has no children. And so he is pained at heart. A poor man has fourteen children, but has nothing to eat, and so he is miserable. One man has wealth and children, but his son is a vagabond, and so he is worried. One man has riches and good sons, but his wife is very quarrelsome. No one is happy in this world.

The sessions judge is very discontented. He thirsts to become a high court judge. The minister is also discontented. He longs to become the premier. A millionaire is discontented; he yearns to become a Croropati. The husband is discontented; his wife is black and thin; he wants to marry another wife with good complexion. The wife is discontented; she wants to divorce and marry a rich, young husband. A lean man is discontented; he wants to put on fat and gulps cod-liver oil. A fat man is discontented; he wants to reduce his fat and takes anti-fat pills. No man is contented in this world.

A doctor thinks that the advocate is very happy. The advocate thinks that the business-man is more happy. The business-man thinks that the judge is more happy. The judge thinks that the professor is more happy. No one is happy in this world.

An emperor is not happy. A dictator is not happy. A president of a state is not happy. God Indra is not happy.

Who is happy then? A sage is happy. A Yogi is happy. He who has controlled his mind is happy.

Happiness comes from peace of mind. Peace of mind comes from a state of mind wherein there are no desires, no Moha, no Vishaya, no thoughts of objects. You should forget all ideas of pleasure before you enter the domain of peace.

Pleasure Is Mixed with Pain

You cannot have pleasure without pain. Wherever there is pleasure, there is pain. You vainly seek pleasure in gold, in women, in this mundane existence. You cannot have absolute happiness in a relative physical plane of pairs of opposites. The pairs of opposites rotate in their turn. Death follows life. Night follows day. Light follows darkness. Pain follows pleasure.

One anna of pleasure is mixed with fifteen annas of pain. Pleasure that is mixed with pain, fear, and worry is no pleasure at all. If you carefully begin to analyse this one anna of pleasure also, it will dwindle into an airy nothing. You will find that it is a mere play of the mind.

Pleasure and pain are relative terms only. They are not two entities. They are obverse and reverse sides of the same coin. The difference is not in kind, but in degree only.

Pleasure and pain are two names for one thing. They are two aspects of one thing. For a worldly man without philosophical knowledge, they appear as two different entities.

Pleasure and Pain Lie in the Mind

What is pleasure for you is pain for another man. What is pleasure for you now is pain after some time. The first two cups of milk give you pleasure. The third cup induces disgust, nausea, and retching. Milk does not give pleasure during fever. Therefore, pleasure is not in the objects, but in the imagination or inclination of the mind.

Pleasure and pain, beauty and ugliness, are all false imaginations of the mind. Mind is a false, illusory product. Conceptions of the mind also must, therefore, be false.

Pleasure and pain are in the mind only. It is subjective. Things, when longed for, are pleasant; but are bitter if not longed for. Desires are the cause for pleasures.

You can convert pleasure into pain and pain into pleasure by thinking, by Bhavana, by imagination. Many vegetarian students who have gone to England to prosecute their studies have become inveterate meat-eaters. Meat was very repulsive to them when they were in India. Mere sight used to induce vomiting. How is it they are able to relish meat with avidity, cupidity, and stupidity now? By simple change in thinking.

Ignorant persons attribute their pleasures to external objects. That is a serious blunder, indeed. Really, there is no pleasure in objects. There is neither pleasure nor pain in objects. It is all mental creation, mental perception, mental jugglery. It is only the mental attitude or a certain kind of mental behaviour towards objects that brings joy or grief, pleasure or pain. Maya has her powerful seat in the imagination of the mind.

When you are in acute agony, a cup of coffee, milk or tea does not give you any pleasure. When you are in acute agony, the whole world which appeared to you to be full of bliss while in good health, appears quite dreary. The world loses all its charms while you are seriously ailing. A real thing must give pleasure for everybody at all times. Is it not?

Pleasure Is the Cause of Pain

The cause of pain is pleasure. The man who is addicted to taking tea, and is in the habit of taking fruits and milk after meals, feels very miserable when he cannot get tea, or fruits and milk, in a certain place. When the wife dies, the husband is drowned in sorrow, not because of the loss of his loving partner in life, but because he cannot get sexual pleasure now.

The cause of pain is pleasure. The cause of death is love for sensual life. Give up all sensual pleasures, if you do not want pain. Give up sensual life, if you do not want death.

Enjoyment cannot bring satisfaction of desire. On the contrary, it aggravates and intensifies desires and makes the mind more restless through sense hankering or Trishna, just as the pouring of ghee or oil aggravates fire. The fewer the wants, the greater the happiness.

Many rich persons, in spite of their immense wealth and possession of two or three wives, are extremely miserable and unhappy. I have come in contact with several rich landlords. They are all discontented, restless, peevish, and very miserable. It is evident, therefore, that happiness does not lie either in money, objects, or woman.

The Source of Happiness

There is no happiness at all in any of the objects of the world. There is not an iota of happiness in objects, because they are insentient. Even the sensual pleasure is a reflection of the Atmic bliss only. It is sheer ignorance to think that we derive any pleasure from the sense-objects or from the mind.

When there is a desire in the mind, the mind is filled with Rajas. It is in an agitated condition. It is restless and unpeaceful. It will be restless till the desired object is attained. When the object is attained and enjoyed, when the desire is gratified, the mind moves towards the Inner Soul. It ceases functioning. It is filled with Sattva. All thoughts subside for a split second; the mind rests in the Soul within. The Soul's bliss is reflected in the intellect. But the ignorant man thinks that he is getting the happiness from the object; just as the dog which is biting a dry bone imagines that it is getting the pleasure from the bone, that the blood is oozing from the bone, whereas in reality, the blood comes from its own palate.

Real Happiness Is Within

Real happiness is within you. It is in the Atman. It is subjective. It manifests when the mind is concentrated. When the Indriyas are withdrawn from the objects outside, when the mind is one-pointed, when there is Vasana-kshaya and Manonasa, when you become desireless and thoughtless, Atmic bliss begins to dawn, spiritual Ananda begins to thrill.

The musk is in the navel of the deer, but it runs here and there to smell it. The chain is in the neck of the damsel, but she runs hither and thither in search of it. The precious diamond is within you, but you run after the broken glass-pieces in vain. Even so, the ocean of bliss is within you; the fountain of joy is within you; and yet, you run here and there in search of it. The Sun of suns is ever shining in you, but your blind eyes cannot behold it. The eternal sound is ringing within you, but your deaf ears cannot here it.

Go wherever you may, to Gulmarg or Pahalgam in Kashmir, to Darjeeling or Simla, to Vienna or the Alps. It is all the same. You will not find any real rest. The charming scenery may soothe the retina for a second. Raga, Dvesha, Jealousy, passion, and greed are everywhere. You will find the same earth, the same sky, the same air, and the same water. And you carry with you the same mind. Imagination and change of place have deceived not a few. O man! Be contented. Live where you may, but discipline the mind and the senses. Meditate on the Inner Self, the Antaratman, ceaselessly. Here you will find the everlasting peace. Mind will stop deceiving you now.

Raja Bhartrihari, Raja Gopichand, Lord Buddha deserted kingdom and all pleasurable objects, palaces, music, children, wife, etc., to attain Atmic bliss which is everlasting. They attained immortality. They are not fools. Had there been real happiness in objects, they would have stuck to this world. The difficulty is that the worldly men with gross Vyavaharic Buddhi are not able to understand or comprehend a supersensual spiritual bliss that exists beyond the senses, mind, and intellect.

Sensual Pleasure and Spiritual Bliss

Spiritual bliss is the highest bliss. Spiritual bliss is bliss of one's own Soul. It is transcendental bliss. It is independent of objects. It is continuous, uniform, and eternal. It is enjoyed by the sage only.

Sensual pleasure comes out of emotion. But bliss of the Soul is self-delight. It is the innate nature of the Atman. Pleasure is temporary and fleeting. Bliss is eternal and everlasting. Pleasure is mixed with pain. Bliss is unalloyed happiness. Pleasure depends upon nerves, mind, and objects. Bliss is independent and self-existent. There is effort in attaining sensual pleasures, but there is no striving in experiencing the bliss of the Soul. The drop joins the ocean. The Jiva floats in the ocean of bliss.

Purify the mind by Japa, Satsanga, charity, control of mind, self-restraint, selfless service, study of the Gita, the Upanishads and the Yoga-Vasishtha, practice of Yama and Niyama, Pranayama, Vairagya and Tyaga. You will then get a proper instrument for meditation, a calm, sharp, subtle, one-pointed mind. Start meditation with the help of this instrument for three hours in the morning and three hours at night. Then a new kind of indescribable Ananda will dawn in you. You will be convinced of a supersensuous spiritual bliss. You will have to feel this spiritual Ananda yourself. You will have to enjoy it yourself. You will have to eat it yourself. Can you explain the sexual happiness to a boy of twelve? Can you explain the happiness of sugar-candy to a boy who has not tasted the same? No, you cannot. The boy himself must eat sugarcandy. He must, when he has grown up, taste the carnal pleasure.

Worldly men think they are quite happy because they get a few ginger biscuits, some money, and a woman. O, if they would just taste the nectar of immortality, what should be the intensity of happiness they should feel!

The body is an abode of misery and disease. Wealth brings a lot of trouble in acquiring and keeping safe. Sorrow springs from every connection. Women are a perpetual source of vexation. Alas! People prefer this path of misery to that of spiritual enjoyment.

Enough, enough of your tea and coffee, enough of soda and lemonade, enough of father, mother, son, daughter, brother, sister and relations. You have had countless fathers and mothers, wives and children in the past. You came alone. You will go alone. None will follow you save your own actions. Realise God. All miseries will come to an end.

Though surrounded by pleasurable or painful objects to disturb your equilibrium of mind, remain immovable as a rock, receiving all things with equanimity. Be always cheerful. Laugh and smile. How can a mind that is gloomy and dull think of God? Try to be happy always. Happiness is your very nature. This is termed cheerfulness. This spirit of cheerfulness must be cultivated by all aspirants.

Keep the mind in a state of moderation or happy, golden mean. Never let it run to excesses. People die of shock from extreme depression as well as from extreme joy. Do not allow Uddharsha to crop up in the mind. It is excessive merriment. Mind always runs to extremes, either to extreme depression or extreme joy. Extremes meet. Extremes bring about reaction. Mind can never be calm in excessive joy. Let the mind be cheerful, but calm.

This world is a mere appearance. Mind and the senses are deceiving you every moment. You have mistaken pain for pleasure. There is not even an iota of happiness in this sense-universe. Abandon these selfish struggles and schemes for amassing wealth. March directly to that wire-puller who is moving these toys of fleshy human bodies, who is keeping up this big show, who is behind this show. In Him only you will find lasting happiness and perennial joy. Merge in Him by practising daily meditation and Japa.

29. HEALTH

The whole universe from the mightiest sun to the tiniest atom is controlled by law. There is perfect order everywhere. The sun performs its duties quite regularly. It rises at the proper time and sets at the proper time. The stars and planets revolve in an orderly manner. They are governed by laws.

There are laws in the mental plane. There are laws of physics, of astronomy, of mathematics. There are laws of hygiene and health which govern our own being.

In the vast universe, man only breaks and violates all rules and laws. He is the single example of lawlessness and discord. He wilfully disregards the laws of health, leads a life of dissipation, and then wonders why he suffers from disease and disharmony. He deliberately ignores the rules of hygiene and right living and then weeps when he is ailing from an incurable dire malady.

Every human being is the author of his own health or disease. Disease is the result of disobedience to the immutable laws of health that govern life.

The laws of health are the laws of nature. These should not be violated with impunity. Those who neglect these laws become victims to incurable diseases and drag a cheerless existence.

Health, the First Requisite

Life without good health is a miserable condition even if one is the lord of the whole earth. What is the use of wealth and possessions, if a man cannot eat well on account of disease of the stomach, if he cannot walk on account of rheumatism or paralysis, if he cannot see the beautiful scenery of nature on account of cataract or defective vision?

The first wealth is health. It is the greatest of all possessions. It is the basis of all virtues. Without health, life is not life. It is only a state of languor, suffering, and half-death. The difficulties and troubles that people suffer arise from ill health. He who has good health has hope. He who has hope has everything.

The first requisite in life is good health. Good health is a valuable asset for one and all. You should have physical as well as mental health. If you do not possess good health, you cannot prosper in any walk of life.

Even for spiritual pursuits, good health is the prerequisite. Without good health, you cannot penetrate into the hidden depths of the vast ocean of life within and attain the final beatitude of life. Without good health, you cannot wage war with the turbulent senses and boisterous mind.

Without good health, you cannot achieve anything. Without good health, you cannot perform any service or Nishkama Karma Yoga. Without good health, you cannot pray and meditate. Without good health, you cannot do any Asanas and Pranayama. That is the reason why scriptures declare that this body is a boat to cross this ocean of Samsara, an instrument for doing virtuous deeds and attaining Moksha.

The instrument must be kept clean, strong, and healthy. This body is a horse for you to take you to the goal. If the horse tumbles down, you cannot reach the destination. If this instrument breaks down, you will not reach the goal of Atma-sakshatkara.

Health Is a Positive State

Health is that state in which a man sleeps well, digests his food well, is quite at ease, is free from any kind of disease or uneasiness. When you are in a state of perfect health, all the organs, viz., the heart, lungs, brain, kidneys, liver, intestines, work in perfect harmony and concord and discharge their functions satisfactorily. The pulse-rate and the rate of respiration are in perfect order. The bodily temperature is normal.

A healthy man smiles and laughs. He is cheerful and happy. He discharges his daily duties with ease and comfort. A healthy man is capable of doing work for a long time without getting fatigued. His bowels move very freely every day. He possesses the highest kind of mental and physical efficiency.

Health is a positive state. It is not simply negation of disease. A healthy man can turn out more physical and mental work. He can practise good meditation for a long time. Health is a gift from Mother Nature who is the power behind life. Health is your birthright, but not disease. It is as natural to be well as to be born.

How to Be Healthy

Be sober and temperate. You will be healthy. Bask in the sun. Live in the open air. Sleep in the open air. The sun and the open air are your good doctors. Let your food be simple. Never eat too much. Take sufficient exercise. If you do not keep well, fast till you are well again.

Become your own physician. Assist nature, but do not force nature. Allow nature to heal you. Nature is the best healing agent. Medicines and doctors only help nature in its recuperative work. An injudicious doctor who disturbs nature's work does more harm than good.

By drinking pure water, by eating pure and wholesome food, by observing the laws of health and hygiene, by taking regular exercise and cold baths in the morning, by practising Japa and meditation, by right living, right thinking, right action, right conduct, by observing Brahmacharya, by living in the open air and sunshine for some time daily, you can have wonderful health, vigour, and vitality.

A healthy man need not be necessarily strong, and a strong man need not be healthy. A very strong man may suffer from diseases. A healthy and strong man becomes a centre of great attraction. He radiates health and strength to all persons with whom he comes in contact.

Health and Diet

The secret of being healthy and happy at all times is to be a little hungry all the time. Do not overload the stomach.

Overeating is the chief cause of most diseases. The vast majority of persons dig their graves through their teeth. No rest is given to the stomach. Though we boast ourselves to be civilised men, yet, when the question of food comes, we make many imperceptible blunders. Man generally eats twice as much as his system needs. It hinders elimination, assimilation, and growth. All the organs are over-worked and get diseased quickly. Hence, avoid overeating and observe perfect moderation in diet.

The right kind of food is most important. Half the illnesses of the nation are due to an ill-balanced diet. There is no mystery about diet. It can be learnt very easily. A correct diet is a fundamental factor in the maintenance of perfect health and a high standard of vitality. Good food is not expensive. A well-balanced diet is not costly. It is knowledge of dietetics that we hopelessly lack.

Diet is a vital factor in one's life. Have a good knowledge of diet and nutrition. You can save doctors' bills. You can build a healthy constitution.

Eat moderately what you know by experience is agreeable to you and what is digestible. Simple diet is the best.

Physical Health and Mental Health

There is intimate connection between the mind and the body. Whatever you hold in your mind will be produced in the physical body. Any ill-feeling or bitterness towards another person will at once affect the body and produce some kind of disease in the body. Intense passion, hatred, long-standing bitter jealousy, corroding anxiety, fits of hot temper, actually destroy the cells of the body and induce diseases of the heart, liver, kidneys, spleen, and stomach. Worry has caused new deadly diseases like blood-pressure, heart-trouble, nervous breakdown, etc.

All diseases take their origin in the mind. The pains that afflict the physical body are called secondary diseases, whilst the Vasanas that affect the mind are termed mental or primary diseases. If bad thoughts are destroyed, all bodily diseases will vanish.

Treat the mind first. Mental health is more important than physical health.

Removal of hatred through cosmic love, service, friendship, mercy, sympathy and compassion; removal of greed through disinterested service, generous acts, and charity; removal of pride through humility—these will help you a great deal in the achievement of good mental health.

You must be always cheerful. You must cultivate this virtue again and again. Laughter and cheerfulness increase the circulation of blood. They are blood-tonics.

Be courageous. Be cheerful. Be kind. Be tolerant. Pray. Sing. Meditate on the Lord. Do Japa, Pranayama, and Asanas. You will have wonderful physical and mental health. You will have always a calm and poised mind.

When you have controlled the mind, you have perfect control over the body. The body is only a shadow of the mind. It is the mould prepared by the mind for its expression. The body becomes your slave when you have conquered the mind.

Ill-health Is a Myth

Be not a victim to imaginary ills and diseases. Even if you have disease, thinking of the disease constantly will intensify it. As you think, so you become. Feel always, "I am healthy in body and mind".

Ill-health is a myth. It does not exist beyond the range of the physical and mental sheaths. The body and the mind alone are subject to diseases. The Atman, your true Self, is beyond these, and therefore eternally free from diseases and death.

Atman or the Self that resides in the chambers of your heart is the storehouse for health, strength, vigour and vitality. It cannot be affected by germs, microbes, bacilli, cholera, pyorrhoea, plague, etc. Weakness, depression, uneasiness, feeling out of sorts, morbidity have no place there. Germs and diseases take to their heels if anyone simply remembers the Atman or one's own Self.

During illness, detach yourself from the body. Connect the mind with the Buddhi and soul. Again and again assert: "I am the bodiless, diseaseless, all-pervading, immortal Soul or Atman". The disease will take to its heels.

The Tragedy of the Times

The vast majority do not avail of this rare panacea, though they have very often heard of this from saints and spiritual books. This is due to their deep-rooted ignorance and lack of faith. People are immersed in worldliness. They are engrossed in passion and Samsaric activities. They have no time to think of this inner, real, unfailing remedy. They have neither leisure nor interest to do introspection and self-analysis.

The world is now flooded with multifarious injections and tonics. People are carried away by pompous advertisements. Money is wasted enormously in paying doctors' bills. They immediately run to find relief in outside objects and from physical doctors, who despite their qualifications and degrees, are still ignorant of many things, who are still groping in darkness, who are yet not able to diagnose when there is a complication, who have no real genuine specifics to cure diseases like asthma, malaria, lumbago, phthisis, cerebro-spinal-meningitis, typhoid, diabetes, blood-pressure, etc., who are still only experimenting on the patients.

In olden days, an ordinary Vaidya would cure a disease with some, bazaar drugs worth about two pies. In these days of modern civilisation and scientific advancement, allopathic medical treatment has become very costly. Poor people cannot afford to have this. The patient has to get his blood, urine, faeces, and sputum examined. He has to visit the Saptarishis of the medical profession. He has to go to a bacteriologist first for this purpose and has to jingle something on the table. The bacteriologist directs the patient to go to a dentist to remove the tartar and treat his pyorrhoea which is believed to be the root cause for all diseases. He has to pay for this Rs. 10/. Then he has to go to the radiologist for taking a skiagraph. He has to pay him Rs. 25/. Sometimes he has to pay a board of doctors for expert diagnosis. He finds no real relief even after spending so much money.

Vedanta for Health

The best medicine or tonic for any complaint, physical or mental, is constant thinking: "I am the Spirit, the Atman which is independent of the body and the mind, which is Anamaya, diseaseless". Repeat this formula mentally several times daily. Meditate on the meaning. Chronic incurable diseases that are declared to be hopeless by boards of eminent doctors can be cured by this method. This is an unfailing infallible divine remedy. Sometimes you will have to wait patiently for results.

Auto-suggestion is only an offshoot of Vedanta. The formula of this school—*By the Grace of God, I am becoming better and better, day by day, in every way*—is only a Vedantic assertion and affirmation.

People say, "One apple a day keeps the doctor away". This is costly. This is doubtful. I say, "Live in the spirit of the Vedantic formulae. This alone can keep the doctors away. This is dead cheap. This is a sure sovereign specific and a sheet-anchor and a cure-all. This is a potent, easily available medicine that lies at your command, that is very close to you, that is within easy access or approach. Doctors' bills and money can be saved. This will give you Self-realisation as well". Believe me. Give up doubting. I assure you, my dear brother! Thou art not this perishable body. Thou art the immortal, all-pervading Soul. *Tat Tvam Asi:* Thou art That. Rejoice in the Satchidananda Atman within and become a Jivanmukta in this very birth

30. HINDUISM

Hinduism is the religion of the Hindus. It is the oldest of all living religions. Hinduism is not a man-made religion. It was not founded by any single person. It is not based on a set of dogmas preached by a particular set of teachers. It was not started as a system, like Islam or Christianity. It is the product of the seers of the Vedas. It was developed from age to age by the teachings of Avataras, Rishis, Vedas, the Upanishads, the Gita, and the Itihasas. It will exist as long as the world lasts. There is a peculiar, mysterious spiritual force that is ingrained in the heart of every Hindu.

Hinduism is also known by the names Sanatana Dharma and Vaidika Dharma. Sanatana Dharma means the eternal religion, the Ancient Law. Vaidika Dharma means the religion of the Vedas.

Hinduism is as old as the world itself. Hinduism is the mother of all religions. Lord Buddha, who was born and bred up in the Hindu religion, made some changes here and there and brought forth a new religion, Buddhism, to suit the temperament and stage of evolution of the people who lived in his time. Buddhism is only an offshoot of Hinduism. Lord Jesus, who made Tapas in Kashmir and Banaras, imbibed the teachings and principles of Hinduism and brought forth a religion to suit the fishermen of Palestine. Mahavira made some changes here and there, and brought forth a religion, Jainism, which is only an offshoot of Buddhism. Zoroastrianism and Christianity and all 'isms are all really offshoots of Hinduism only.

A Religion of Freedom

Hinduism allows absolute freedom to the rational mind of man. Hinduism never demands any undue restraint upon the freedom of human reason, the freedom of thought, feeling and will of man.

Hinduism is a religion of freedom. It allows the widest freedom in matters of faith and worship. It allows absolute freedom to the human reason and heart with regard to questions such as the nature of God, soul, creation, form of worship, and goal of life. It does not force anybody to accept particular dogmas or forms of worship. It allows everybody to reflect, investigate, enquire, and cogitate. Hence, all sorts of religious faiths, various forms of worship or

Sadhana, diverse kinds of rituals and customs, have found their honourable place side by side within Hinduism, and are cultured and developed in harmonious relationship with one another.

Hinduism, unlike other religions, does not dogmatically assert that the final emancipation is possible only through its means and not through any other. It is only a means to an end, and all means which will ultimately lead to the end are equally approved.

The religious hospitality of Hinduism is proverbial. Hinduism is extremely catholic and liberal. This is the fundamental feature of Hinduism. Hinduism pays respects to all religions. It does not revile any other religion. It accepts and honours truth, wherever it may come from and whatever garb it may put on.

The Hindu Scriptures

The Sruti and the Smriti are the two authoritative sources of Hinduism. 'Sruti' literally means 'what is heard', and 'Smriti' means 'what is remembered'. Sruti is revelation; Smriti is tradition. What is revealed is Sruti. Upanishad is a Sruti. What is remembered is Smriti. Bhagavad-Gita is a Smriti.

Sruti is direct experience. Great Rishis heard the eternal truths of religion and left a record of them for the benefit of posterity. These records constitute the Vedas. Hence, Sruti is primary authority. Smriti is a recollection of that experience. Hence, it is secondary authority. The Smritis or Dharma Shastras are founded on the Sruti. They also are books written by sages, but they are not the final authority. If there is anything in a Smriti which contradicts the Sruti, the Smriti is to be rejected. Bhagavad-Gita also is a Smriti. So is Mahabharata, too.

The Vedas and the Upanishads

Srutis are called the Vedas or the Amnaya. These are direct intuitional revelations and are held to be Apaurusheya or entirely superhuman, without any author in particular.

The Vedas are eternal truths revealed by God to the great ancient Rishis of India. The word 'Rishi' means 'a seer'. He is the seer of thought. The thought was not his own. The Rishis saw the truths or heard them. Therefore the Vedas are called Sruti or what are heard. The Rishi did not write. He did not create it out of his mind. He was the seer of the thought which existed already. He was only the spiritual discoverer of the thought.

The Rishi is not the inventor of the Veda. He is only a medium or agent to transmit to people the intuitional experiences which he received. The truths of the Vedas are revelations. All the other religions of the world trace their authority to having been delivered by special Messengers of God to certain persons, but the Vedas do not owe their authority to anyone. They are themselves the authority as they are eternal, as they are the knowledge of the Lord

The Vedas are the oldest books in the library of man. The Vedas are the ultimate source to which all religious knowledge can be traced. Religion is of divine origin. It was revealed by God to man in the earliest times. It is embodied in the Vedas.

The Upanishads are the concluding portions of the Vedas, or the end of the Vedas. The teaching based on them is called Vedanta. The Upanishads are the gist, the goal of the Vedas. They form the very foundation of Hinduism.

The most important Upanishads are Isa, Kena, Katha, Prasna, Mundaka, Mandukya, Aitareya, Taittiriya, Chhandogya, Brihadaranyaka, Kaushitaki and Svetasvatara. These are supremely authoritative.

The different philosophers of India belonging to different schools such as Advaita, Qualified Monism or Visishtadvaita, Dualism, Pure Monism, Bhedabheda, etc., have acknowledged the supreme authority of the Upanishads. They have given their own interpretations, but they have obeyed the authority. They have built their philosophy on the foundation of the Upanishads.

The philosophy of the Upanishads is sublime, profound, lofty, and soul-stirring. The Upanishads reveal the most subtle spiritual truths. Even the Western scholars have paid their tribute to the seers of the Upanishads. They have been amazed at the lofty heights scaled by the Upanishads. Schopenhauer studied the Upanishads and meditated on the thoughts of the Upanishads just before going to bed. He said: "The Upanishads are the solace of my life, and they will be solace to me after my death also".

The teachings of the Rishis of yore do not pertain to Hindus alone. They are of an all-embracing, universal nature. They are meant for the people of the whole world. The Gita and the Upanishads are books for the people of the whole world.

Hindu Mythology

In every religion, there are three parts, viz., philosophy, mythology and ritual. Philosophy is the essence of religion. It sets forth its basic principles or fundamental doctrines or tenets, the goal and the means of attaining it. Mythology explains and illustrates philosophy by means of legendary lives of great men or of supernatural beings. Ritual gives a still more concrete form to philosophy so that everyone may understand it. Ritual consists of forms and ceremonies.

Mythology is a part of every religion. Mythology is concretised philosophy. Mythology is the science which investigates myths or fables or legends founded on remote events, especially those made in the early period of a people's existence. Mythology inspires the readers through precepts and laudable examples, and goads them to attain perfection or the highest ideal. The abstract teachings and subtle ideas are made highly interesting through the garb of stories, parables, legends, allegories, and narratives. The sublime and abstract philosophical ideas and ideals of Hinduism are taken straight to the heart of the masses through impressive stories.

Mythology is slightly mixed up with a little history. It is difficult to make a fine distinction between history and mythology.

There are great truths behind the ancient mythology of Hinduism. You cannot ignore a thing simply because it has a garb of mythology. Do not argue. Shut up your mouth. Keep your intellect at a respectable distance when you study mythology. Intellect is a hindrance. It will delude you. Give up arrogance, vanity. Cultivate love for imagery. Sit like a child and open your heart freely. You will comprehend the great truths revealed by mythology. You will penetrate into the hearts of the Rishis and sages who wrote the mythology. You will really enjoy mythology now.

You study geography through maps. There is no real country or town in a map, but it helps you to know a great deal about the different countries. Similar is the case with myths. You can grasp the subtle, philosophical truths through myths only. The object of myth and legend is merely to lure the mind to the truths of the religion.

By studying mythology, you will get several objective lessons for moulding your character and leading an ideal, divine life. The lives of Sri Rama, Sri Krishna, Bhishma, Nala, Harischandra, Lakshmana, Bharata, Hanuman, Yudhishthira, Arjuna, Sita, Savitri, Damayanti, Radha, are sources of great spiritual inspiration for moulding your life, conduct, and character. When you are in a dilemma as to what to do during puzzling situations, when there is conflict of duties, you will get the exact solutions through study of mythology.

Puranas contain various myths. Religion is taught in a very easy and interesting way through these Puranas. Even to this day, the Puranas are popular. The Puranas contain the history of remote times. They also give a description of the regions of the universe not visible to the ordinary physical eye. They are very interesting to read and are full of information of all kinds. Children hear the stories from their grandmothers. Pundits and Purohits hold Kathas in temples, on the banks of rivers, and in other important places. Agriculturists, labourers, and bazaar people hear the stories. Thus the minds of the people are saturated with Hindu ideas and ideals, and lifted to great spiritual heights.

Emphasis on Practice

Hinduism provides spiritual food. Yoga is eminently practical. In no religion will you find such a variety of Yoga practised, and such sublime unique philosophy expounded.

Hinduism provides spiritual food and Yoga Sadhana for all sorts of people to suit their temperaments, capacities, tastes, stages of spiritual development, and conditions of life. It prescribes Yoga Sadhana even for a scavenger or a cobbler to attain God-realisation, while doing his ordinary avocation in the world. Hindu Yoga and Vedanta teachers lay great stress on self-restraint, Tapas, renunciation and practical Sadhana, which is best calculated to control the mind and the senses and unfold the Divinity within or attain Self-realisation.

Religion is the practical aspect of philosophy. Philosophy is the rational aspect of religion. The philosophy of Hinduism is not armchair philosophy. It is not meant for intellectual curiosity and vain discussion. Hindu philosophy is a way of life. The philosopher of Hinduism seriously reflects after hearing the Srutis, does Atma-Vichara, constantly meditates, and then attains Self-realisation or Atma-sakshatkara. Moksha is his goal. He attempts to attain Jivanmukti now and here.

Hindu Sects

A foreigner is struck with astonishment when he hears about the diverse sects and creeds of Hinduism. But, these varieties are really an ornament to Hinduism. They, certainly, are not its defects. There are various types of mind and temperament. So, there should be various faiths also. This is natural. This is the cardinal tenet of Hinduism. There is room in Hinduism for all types of souls—from the highest to the lowest—for their growth and evolution.

The term Hinduism is most elastic. It includes a number of sects and cults, allied, but different in many important points. Hinduism has, within its fold, various schools of Vedanta, Saivism, Saktism, Vaishnavism, etc. It has various cults and creeds. It is more a league of religions than a single religion with a definite creed. It is a fellowship of faiths. It is a federation of philosophies. It accommodates all types of men. It prescribes spiritual food for everybody, according to his qualification and growth. This is the beauty of this magnanimous religion. This is the glory of Hinduism. Hence there is no conflict among the various cults and creeds. Lord Krishna says in the Gita: "Howsoever men approach Me, even so do I welcome them, for the path men take from every side is Mine". All diversities are organised and united in the body of Hinduism

Sanatana Dharmists, Arya Samajists, Deva Samajists, Jains, Sikhs, and Brahmo Samajists are all Hindus only. Despite all the differences of metaphysical doctrines, modes of religious disciplines, and forms of ritualistic practices and social habits prevalent in the Hindu society, there is an essential uniformity in the conception of religion, and in the outlook on life and the world, among all sections of Hindus.

Reasons for Survival of the Hindu Religion

Mohammedan emperors ruled India for seven hundred years. The British ruled India for two hundred years. Some joined Islam through force. The number of Mohammedans in undivided India was nine crores. The number of Christians in India is more than a crore. The Mohammedan emperors and the British were not able to convert the whole of India. Still the glory of Hinduism persists. The culture of Hinduism prevails. Nothing can shake its greatness and root.

Hinduism is neither asceticism nor illusionism, neither polytheism nor pantheism. It is a synthesis of all types of religious experiences. It is a whole and complete view of life. It is characterised by wide toleration, deep humanity, and high spiritual purpose. It is free from fanaticism. That is the reason why it has survived the attacks of the followers of other great religions of the world.

Hinduism is extremely catholic, liberal, tolerant, and elastic. No religion is so very elastic and tolerant like Hinduism. Hinduism is very stern and rigid regarding the fundamentals. It is very elastic in readjusting to the externals and non-essentials. That is the reason why it has succeeded in living through millennia.

The foundation of Hinduism has been laid on the bedrock of spiritual truths. The entire structure of Hindu life is built on eternal truths, the findings of the Hindu Rishis or seers. That is the reason why this structure has lasted through scores of centuries.

Hinduism stands unrivalled in the depth and grandeur of its philosophy. Its ethical teachings are lofty, unique, and sublime. It is highly flexible and adapted to every human need. It is a perfect religion by itself. It is not in need of anything from any other religion. No other religion has produced so many great saints, great patriots, great warriors, great Pativratas. The more you know of the Hindu religion, the more you will honour and love it. The more you study it, the more it will enlighten you and satisfy your heart.

31. IDOLATRY

A piece of ordinary white paper or coloured paper has no value. You throw it away. But, if there is the stamp or picture of the king or emperor on the paper—if it is a currency note—you keep it safe in your money-purse or trunk. Even so, an ordinary piece of stone has no value for you. You throw it away. But, if you behold the stone Murti of Lord Krishna at Pandharpur or any other Murti in shrines, you bow your head with folded hands, because there is the stamp of the Lord on the stone.

A flag is only a small piece of painted cloth, but for a soldier, it stands for something that he holds very dear. He is prepared to give up his life in defending his flag. Similarly, the image is very dear to a devotee. It speaks to him in its own language of devotion. Just as the flag arouses martial valour in the soldier, so also, the image arouses devotion in the devotee.

Just as the child develops the maternal Bhava of the future caressing, nursing, protecting mother by playing with its imaginary toy-child made up of rags and suckling the child in an imaginary manner, so also, the devotee develops the feeling of devotion by worshipping the Pratima and concentrating on it.

The Idol—A Symbol of God

The Pratima or idol is only a symbol of the Divine. A devotee does not behold therein a block of stone or a mass of metal. It is an emblem of God for him. It is precious, as it bears the mark of his Lord, as it stands for something which he holds holy and eternal.

When you worship an image, you do not say, "This image has come from Jaipur. It was brought by Prabhu Singh. Its weight is fifty pounds. It is made of white marble. It has cost me rupees five hundred". You superimpose all the attributes of the Lord on the image and pray, "O Antaryamin! You are all-pervading; you are omnipotent, omniscient, all-merciful. You are the source for everything. You are self-existent. You are Sat-chit-ananda. You are eternal, unchanging. You are the Life of my life, Soul of my soul! Give me light and knowledge! Let me dwell in Thee for ever". When your devotion and meditation become intense and deep, you do not see the stone image. You behold the Lord only, who is Chaitanya.

A Medium for Establishing Communion with God

Idols are not the idle fancies of sculptors, but, shining channels through which the heart of the devotee is attracted to, and flows, towards God. Even as you can catch the sound waves of people all over the world through the radio receiving-set, it is possible to commune with the all-pervading Lord through the medium of an idol. The idol remains an idol, but the worship goes to the Lord.

There are others who would glibly say, "Oh, God is all-pervading, formless Being. How can He be confined to this idol?" Are these people ever conscious of His omnipresence? Do they always see Him and Him alone in everything? No. It is their ego that prevents them from bowing to the idols of God, and with that motive, puts this lame excuse forward!

A Prop for the Spiritual Neophyte

Image-worshp is very necessary for beginners. It is not possible for all to fix the mind on the Absolute or the Infinite. To behold God everywhere and to practise the presence of God is not possible for the ordinary man. A concrete form is necessary for the vast majority for practising concentration. The mind wants a prop to lean upon. It cannot have conception of Absolute in the initial stages.

The Idol is a support for the neophyte. It is a prop of his spiritual childhood. It is a reminder of God. The material image calls up the mental idea.

Everyone, an Idol-worshipper

Idol-worship is not peculiar to Hinduism. Christians worship the Cross. They have the image of the Cross in their mind. The Mohammedans keep the image of Kaaba stone when they kneel and do prayers. The people of the whole world—save a few Yogis and Vedantins—are all worshippers of idols. They keep some image or the other in the mind.

The mental image also is a form of idol. The difference is not one of kind, but only one of degree. All worshippers, however intellectual they may be, generate a form in the mind and make the mind dwell on that image.

Everyone is an idol-worshipper. Pictures, drawing, etc., are only forms of Pratima. A gross mind needs a concrete symbol as a prop or Alambana; a subtle mind requires an abstract symbol. Even a

Vedantin has the symbol OM for fixing the wandering mind. It is not only the pictures or images in stone and wood that are idols. Dialectics and leaders also become idols. So, why condemn idolatry?

When Idols Become Alive

The God in you has the power to awaken the latent divinity in the idol. Regular worship, Puja, and other modes of demonstrating our inner feeling of recognition of divinity in the idol unveils the divinity latent in it. This is truly a wonder and a miracle. The picture comes to life. The idol speaks. It will answer your questions and solve your problems.

For a devotee the image is a mass of Chaitanya or consciousness. The devotee beholds actually the Lord in the idol. He draws inspiration from the image. The image guides him. It talks to him. It assumes human form to help him in a variety of ways.

The image of Lord Siva in the temple at Madurai, in South India, helped the fuel-cutter and the old woman. The image in the temple at Tirupati assumed human form and gave witness in the court to help His devotees. The idols in the temples of Tirupati, Pandharpur, Palani, Kathirkama, etc., are powerful deities. They are Pratyaksha Devatas. They grant boons to the devotees, cure their ailments and give Darshan. Wonderful Lilas are associated with these deities.

For a Bhakta or a sage, there is no such thing as Jada or insentient matter. Everything is Vasudeva or Chaitanya: *Vasudevah Sarvam Iti*. Narsi Mehta was put to the test by a Raja. The Raja said: "O Narsi, if you are a sincere devotee of Lord Krishna, if as you say the idol is Lord Krishna Himself, let this idol move". According to the prayer of Narsi Mehta, the idol moved. The sacred bull Nandi before Siva's idol took the food offered by Tulasidas. The Murti played with Mira Bai. It was full of life and Chaitanya for her.

Vedanta and Idol-worship

A pseudo-Vedantin feels himself ashamed to bow or prostrate before an idol in the temple. He feels that his Advaita will evaporate if he prostrates. Study the lives of the reputed Tamil saints, Appar, Sundarar, Sambandhar, etc. They had the highest Advaitic realisation. They saw Lord Siva everywhere. And yet, they visited all temples of Siva, prostrated before the idol, and sang hymns which are on record now. The sixty-three Nayanar saints swept the floor of the temple, collected flowers, made garlands for the Lord and put on lights in the temple. They were illiterate, but attained the highest realisation.

Tulasidas had cosmic consciousness. He communed with the all-pervading, formless Lord. And yet, his passion for Lord Rama with bow in His hand did not vanish.

Tukaram also had the same cosmic experience as that of Tulasidas. He sings in his Abhanga, "I see my Lord all-pervading, just as sweetness pervades the sugar-cane". And yet, he always speaks of his Lord Vitthala of Pandharpur with His hands on the hips.

Mira also realised her identity with the all-pervading Krishna, and yet, she was not tired of repeating again and again, "My Giridhar Nagar".

Image-worship is not contrary to the view of Vedanta. It is rather a help. When one advances in meditation, the form melts in the formless, and he becomes one with the formless essence.

Steps on the Spiritual Ladder

There is nothing wrong in worshipping an idol in the beginning. The worshipper must superimpose God and His attributes on the idol. He must think of the Antaratman that is hidden in the idol. Gradually he begins to feel that the Lord he worships is in the idol, in the hearts of all creatures, and in all the names and forms of this universe. He begins to feel His presence everywhere.

Idolatry is only the beginning of religion. Certainly it is not its end. The same Hindu scriptures which prescribe idol-worship for beginners speak of meditation on the Infinite or the Absolute, contemplation on the significance of the *"Tat Tvam Asi"* Mahavakya, for advanced aspirants.

The Hindus know that the images, crosses and crescents are simply so many symbols to fix the mind in the beginning for developing concentration, so many concrete pegs to hang their spiritual ideas and convictions on. The symbol is not necessary for everyone. It is not compulsory in Hinduism. It is not needed for an advanced Yogi or sage. A symbol is like the slate which is useful for a boy of the first standard. Those who are not in need of it have no right to say that it is wrong. If they say that it is wrong, they only betray their ignorance.

Each marks a stage of progress. The human soul makes different kinds of attempts to grasp and realise the Infinite or the Absolute according to his strength, degree of evolution. He soars higher and higher, gathers more and more strength and eventually merges himself in the Supreme and attains oneness or identity.

32. INDIA

India is the sacred land which has given birth to countless sages, Rishis, Yogins, saints, and prophets. India is the land that has produced many Acharyas or spiritual preceptors like Sri Sankara, Sri Ramanuja; many saints like Kabir, Ramdas, Tukaram, Gouranga Mahaprabhu; many Yogins like Jnana Dev, Dattatreya, Sadasiva Brahman; many prophets like Buddha and Guru Nanak. Buddha is our flesh and blood.

India is proud of Guru Govind Singh and Shivaji. India is proud of King Bhoja and Vikramaditya. India is proud of Sankara and Kabir. India is proud of Kalidas and Valmiki. Krishna, Rama and all Avataras were born in India. How sacred is India! How sublime is India! The dust of Brindavan and Ayodhya, the land trodden by the sacred feet of Krishna and Rama, still purifies the heart of countless people. Even Jesus, during the missing period of his life, lived in Kashmir and learnt Yoga from the Indian Yogins.

India is the sacred land with several holy rivers and powerful spiritual vibrations. It is a land peculiarly suitable for divine contemplation and Yogic practices. The hoary Himalayas attract the people of the whole world.

How charming is the Himalayan scenery! How sweet is Mother Ganga! How soothing and elevating are their vibrations! How soul-stirring is the company of the Yogins! How beautiful and lovely is Rishikesh, with Yogins, Ganga, and Himalayas!

India is a spiritual country. Religion governs all the departments of Hindu life. The Hindu must realise the freedom of the soul in every department of life. Religion affords the greatest scope to him for the culture of true freedom.

It is in India alone that every man knows something of philosophy. The cowherd who tends the cattle, the peasant who ploughs the fields, the boatman who pulls at his oar, sings songs replete with philosophical truths. Even the barber repeats *Om Namah Sivaya, Sivoham* before he takes up the razor. The Paramahamsa Sannyasins, the itinerant monks of Hinduism, have disseminated the highest of Vedanta from door to door. In exchange for a handful of rice, they have distributed from door to door, through religious songs, the priceless gems of Hindu religion and philosophy.

History of Indian Civilisation

Indian civilisation has had a long history. It has influenced the history of the world at every stage.

Hindus have had a culture, civilisation, and religion millennia older than those of any other country or people. When the ancestors of the Westerners were completely uncivilised savages, India was full of sages, saints, Yogins, seers, and Maharshis with Self-realisation, and the highest culture and civilisation. Hindu culture and Hindu civilisation were at their zenith in days of yore. The Greeks and the Romans imitated the Hindus, and absorbed Hindu thoughts.

The Ramayana and the Mahabharata tell us clearly about the ancient India, about her people, her customs, her ways of living, her arts, her civilisation and culture, her manufactures. Even today, our domestic, social, and national ideals are copied from the noble characters in the Ramayana and the Mahabharata. The great national heroes stand even today as beacon-lights to guide and inspire the people of the whole world. If you read these two books, you will come to know how great India once was, and you will be inspired to make her great once more. No other country has produced so many great men, great teachers, great Yogins, great seers, great Rishis, great prophets, great Acharyas, great kings, great heroes, great statesmen, great patriots, and great benefactors as India. Each and every province of the country has produced intellectual giants, poets, and saints. Even now India abounds in sages and great souls. The more you know of India and Hinduism, the more you will honour and love it and the more thankful to the Lord you will be that you were born in India as a Hindu.

Spirituality—The Bedrock of Indian Culture

England is famous for coal and iron, America for dollars, Italy for sculptural works; but India is famous for its religious devotion, Yogins, and saints. The history of India is a history of religion. Its social code and regulations are founded upon religion. Minus its Yoga, religion and its regulations, India will not be what it has been for millennia. India cannot be India without the Gita and the Upanishads.

The culture of India is built round the central idea of Dharma or righteousness. India is the land of Dharma. Her breath is Dharma.

Her life and light is Dharma. She moves and has her being in Dharma. Dharma protects India and she shall protect Dharma.

The solid foundation of Indian culture has enabled it to withstand the rigours of political strifes and alien invasions. Temporary periods of political bondage have not sullied the soul of India. The passage of time has not diminished the glory of Indian culture. The civilisations of ancient Egypt, Assyria, Babylon, Greece, and Rome have faded out; but the ancient civilisation of India lives through ages.

Self-restraint and mastery over the senses have been the keynote of India's culture from the earliest period of her history. The goal of India is Self-realisation through renunciation and knowledge. The national ideals of India are renunciation and service. The ideal of renunciation and detachment is the one factor that has kept intact the virility of Bharatavarsha as a nation.

India is a garden rich with the fragrance of the flowers of tolerance, virtue, love, and goodness cultured out of the seeds of the recognition of universal brotherhood and oneness of mankind. Unity of mankind and universality of religion are the prerogatives of the Indian tradition.

India is the most tolerant country in the world. She has a very expansive heart. She includes all nations in the embrace of her love. For more than eight centuries, she was oppressed by some greedy men. And yet, she served them and made them happy and rich. She is ever rich, liberal, and catholic. She nourishes the whole world. Her resources are inexhaustible.

Indian culture is not a dead culture. It has an undying vitality. It can be revitalised age after age to suit the needs of changing times. There is a fundamental vitality which has enabled India to carry on through all these millennia in spite of her weaknesses.

India and the West

To India, Brahman is the only reality. Its nature is Sat-chit-ananda. To the West, matter is the only reality. To have plenty of dollars is freedom. To have abundant atom bombs and aeroplanes is freedom. To India, Self-realisation is the goal. To the West, power and dominion is the goal. To India, self-restraint gives happiness. To the West, self-indulgence gives pleasure. To India, renunciation bestows joy. To the West, possession gives joy. To

India, the practice of Ahimsa is the ideal. To the West, 'kill and conquer' is the ideal.

In the West, he who has many wants is the most civilised man. A Westerner calls a man who has few wants a barbarian. A Yogi or a devotee of the East is a savage in the eyes of a Westerner. The Westerners have not realised the axiomatic, great truth that "the fewer the desires, the greater the happiness". This is, indeed, a great pity.

Western culture is for the self-aggrandisement of the Westerners; Eastern culture is for the whole world. Western culture turns the mind outwards; Eastern culture turns the mind inwards. Western culture thickens egoism and strengthens the personality; Eastern culture annihilates egoism and individuality, and leads to universality. Western culture brings bondage; Eastern culture leads to salvation. Western culture makes a man materialistic and Asuric; Eastern culture makes a man divine.

The West is material. The East is spiritual. Science is the offspring of the material force, and Yoga is the child of the spiritual force.

India will not be able to rival the West in physical science, but in the spiritual field, she will certainly be unparalleled. She will always guide the entire universe in spiritual matters, in Yoga, Vedanta, etc. She will ever be the world's preceptor. India will always lead the world in spirituality. She does not stand in any need of spiritual enlightenment from others.

India's Contribution to the World

India has given much to the world in the form of mental and spiritual culture. The Indian Rishis of yore rejoiced in spiritual wisdom, communed with God, and enlightened the world with divine knowledge. The spiritual literature of India, given by her Rishis, will ever continue to retain their infinite brilliance through ages to come.

The teachings of India's ancient seers are, indeed, the most universal. The works of Yoga belong to the entire world. They are also practical to the core.

Numerous persons are turning from a war-torn and sullied

atmosphere to India and her ancient, divine wisdom which is found in the Gita, the Upanishads, and the Advaita Vedanta philosophy.

India, due to her glorious heritage, can show the right road to all, and lead all to prosperity, peace, and perpetual bliss. Let India lead the countries which are spiritually bankrupt. She alone can undertake this gigantic task. India alone can lead the world towards better understanding, harmony, fraternity, and peace.

The Future of India

India's mission is different from that of others. The mission of India is the achievement of spiritual greatness, but not political eminence and military power.

Military glories are not the criterion of a nation's progress. India has never sought them at the cost of other people's freedom. India has never attached importance to wealth and power, from the beginning of her history.

India is always a land of seers, sages, Yogins, and Munis. If she imitates the West, she will lose her spiritual glory. For everything Indian should have a spiritual basis. Her conquest is through Ahimsa, love, and wisdom. She should ever maintain her ancient culture, ancient wisdom, and Yogic attainments. She cannot become glorious through building of more aeroplanes and warships. She should produce more Yogins, and victors over self. The governors of India should consult the saints on important matters of administration. They should accord them a high place of honour. Then and then alone will the India Government be righteous, divine, and peaceful.

India has attained freedom now, but her problems of poverty, ignorance, and economic crises remain still unsolved. There is the great need for cleansing the public life and ridding it of those excrescences which are poisoning the springs of national life in India at its very source. Let all live the Gita-life.

Those in India who imitates the West have lost their soul. This is a great pity, indeed.

The future destiny of India depends on her spiritual strength rather than upon her material wealth. Atman or the Spirit is the rock-foundation of wisdom, prosperity, strength, and peace. Be ever a beacon-light of the spiritual essence of Bharatavarsha's culture. Live the exemplary personal and social life of the ideal Hindu.

India will rise. India must rise. It is a glorious land of Rishis and sages. It is a Punyabhumi with Ganga and Yamuna. It is the best of all lands.

33. ISLAM

Islam is the name given by Mohammed, the Prophet of Arabia to the religion which he founded. Islam is an Arabic word which means peace. It means submission to the will of God. It moans surrender, acceptance of the revelation and commands of God. The personal name of God is Allah. The aim of Mohammed's preaching was the establishment of the religion of one God, Allah. Islam is a religion of universal brotherhood. Firm unswerving belief in one God is the essence of true religion according to Islamic faith. It makes no distinction between caste and caste and creed and creed.

"There is no God but Allah and Mohammed is the Messenger of Allah". This is the fundamental teaching of the Prophet of Islam. This is the doctrine of Islam. The religion of Islam is expressed shortly in this short formula. Mohammed preached the unity of God. He taught the love of God, respect for parents and the aged, reverence to women and a noble standard of life. Alms-giving or charity was a religious duty. He said: "Every good act is charity. Your smiling in your brother's face is charity. Putting a wanderer in the right path is charity".

The beauty of this religion is marred by the un-Islamic behaviour of some of the followers of Islam. It is clearly said in Koran: "No man is a true believer unless he desireth for his brother that which he desires for himself. God will not be affectionate to that man who is not affectionate to God's creatures. He is the most favoured of God, from whom the greatest good comes to His creatures. The best of men is he from whom good accrueth to humanity. All God's creatures are his family. He is most beloved by God, who trieth to do more good to God's creatures. Feed the hungry and visit the sick and free the captive if he is unjustly confined. Assist any person oppressed whether he is Muslim or non-Muslim. Love your fellow-being first".

Prophet Mohammed taught to the people more of ethics than deep philosophy, as they had no proper culture.

A Muslim believes in God, His Angels, His books and His messengers, the Last day, the Resurrection from the dead, Predestination by God, good and evil, the Judgment, the Balance, Paradise and Hell-fire, the divine inspiration of Mohammed, the origin of the Koran as divine inspiration, and the future state. He is ready to enter into the religious war (Jihad) when so ordered by the divine as a religious duty.

The first principle of Islam is "God has sent messengers to mankind through the ages to teach them that all messengers and all holy books are true", thereby emphasising the universality of faith.

Teachings

The five cardinal tenets of Islam are: (1) Oneness of God and the revelation of God's will to man through a series of prophets, the last of the series being Mohammed, (2) Prayer, (3) Fasting, (4) Alms-giving or charity, and (5) Haj (pilgrimage to Mecca). These are the five pillars of Islam

Prayer, fasting, Zakat or charity and pilgrimage to Mecca are rather the four duties or observances incumbent upon every Mohammedan. Haj is compulsory only for those who can afford to travel to Mecca.

The sacred book of the Muslims is the Koran. This book deals with many different subjects, doctrines, morals, legal enactments, matters of State, manners and matters of private import. They have been collected into chapters. To the Muslim it is the word of God eternal and uncreated conveyed to the Prophet in Arabic by the angel Gabriel.

Koran says: "Any man may attain liberation by his faith and good actions. The flesh and blood of the animals that are sacrificed shall never reach God, but your purity shall reach God. The flesh and blood of the animals you kill, shall not bring salvation for you. Kill this ego. Serve the suffering humanity. Sacrifice your money, time, and energy in the service of the poor, the oppressed. This will give you salvation or freedom".

In Koran the brotherhood of man and the equality of woman with man socially, economically, and spiritually are emphasised. Man is a member of a great fraternity. Woman is the counterpart of man.

Selflessness and service are the ideals which a Muslim is enjoined to follow. The essence of Islam is the service of the suffering humanity. The sacred Koran says: "Woe to those who pray, who are unmindful of their prayers, who make a show and refuse help to the needy".

The Prophet of Islam also was a great lover of the doctrine of Ahimsa. Injuring people in any way or destroying any living creature is reprehensible. He taught that men would be specially judged on the day of judgment with regard to their cruel treatment of dumb creatures.

Prophet has enjoined on his followers full and broad toleration of the views and beliefs of people other than their own. Koran says: "Let there be no compulsion in religion".

There is no asceticism in Islam. The rigorous austere practices which cause torture to human body are strictly prohibited. What is wanted is a contrite heart, sincere repentance and serious continuous effort to avoid evil and practise virtue.

The great Muslim fast is that of Ramzan. It is a fast for one month. Eating and drinking are forbidden during the day, but are allowed at night.

Jihad is exerting oneself for the cause of religion. It is not taking part in war against unbelievers. Islam strictly prohibits application of force for its observance. There is no compulsion in religion.

Islam teaches that the followers of it should acquire the manifold attributes of Allah. No one can be a Muslim and none can attain Allah without acknowledging the essential truths of all religions.

Allah is the Protector of the universe. Allah is all-merciful. Allah is the Supreme Judge who dispenses justice in accordance with the merits and demerits of the person. Allah is Rahim. Rahim is one who shows compassion and beneficence for virtuous actions and noble virtues.

There is no such thing in Islam that a Muslim should fight in order that religion should live. Islam forbids fighting. Islam says: "You shall not take up arms except in the cause of self-defence". In every sentence of the Koran those who are tyrants have been told: "If you tyrannise over people, if you are cruel to them, you shall be punished".

Islam is a religion of peace. It is submission to the will of God. A true Mussalman must be tolerant. Islam teaches that every religion is true. Islam teaches that God has sent Prophets and religious teachers to mankind to bring them to the path of goodness, to teach them the noble things of life, to be kind, to be noble, to be merciful, to be good, and to be Just. Islam teaches to regard not only human beings with kindness and tolerance, but also to treat animals with kindness.

Prayers

On Fridays, the Sabbath of Muslims' special prayers known as the. Salat-i-Juma are offered at noon instead of the usual Salat-i-Zuhr. A sermon is delivered on the occasion.

The compulsory prayers (Salat) offered five times a day must be offered in congregation under the leadership of an Imam (religious leader).

Salat-i-Fajr is the morning prayer; Salat-i-Zuhr is noon prayer; Salat-i-Asr is evening prayer; Salat-i-Maghrib is sunset prayer; Salat-i-Asha is night prayer.

Conclusion

The philosophical side of Islam is very noble. It teaches that all is from God, that there is no beauty in the world that is not His beauty, that there is no love in heart of man, that is not a breath of His love.

Sufism

Sufism is liberal Mohammedanism with a colouring of Vedanta. Sufism is Islamic in origin. Sufism is the religion of love with Madhurya Bhava, with the concepts of the lover and the Beloved.

The Mohammedans think that Sufism is indigenous to Islam. Other broad-minded scholars have traced an Indian Origin for the movement. Indian mysticism and oriental Christian mysticism have affected the later development of Sufism. Indian Sufism is a blend of Persian Sufism and Hindu mysticism.

Sufistic Saints

Lal Shahbaz, Mansoor, Shamas Tabriez, Sachal, Rohal, Dalpat, Shah Inayet, Shah Latif, Bulleh Shah, Haifiz, Rumi, and Jami were all Sufistic mystics.

The Sufistic saints are as liberal and catholic as the Vedantic Sannyasins. They are mystic saints. They are devotional. Their utterances or sayings have a wonderful directness, freshness, spontaneous loveliness, and charm.

The Sufi mystic sees the Lord in all. He experiences cosmic vision. He beholds his Beloved everywhere and in all objects. He has no sense of possession. He is free from egoism, lust, greed, anger, and pride. He is perfectly passionless and enjoys perfect peace and poise. His state is beyond description. He is like the Jivanmukta or liberated sage. He calls the heart as the palace of the

Beloved. He does not care for dogmas or doctrines, creeds or sects. He has attained Para Bhakti or the supreme devotion.

Doctrines

Asceticism is an essential feature of Sufism. The Sufi consecrates all his acts, physical, mental, and spiritual to the will of God. Unity of God, brotherhood of man and self-surrender to the Lord are the most vital doctrines of Sufism. In Sufism God has form. The Sufis recognise His formless aspect too.

Sufism combines ecstasy and service of man. A Sufi wants to remain in the world and serve the humanity, but to be above worldliness.

The Sufi language of ecstasy describes the divine experience in a variety of ways such as sweetness, intoxication, perfume, sleep and death. Wine is a symbol of divine intoxication.

In Sufism, Beauty leads to Love and Love to Bliss. All duality melts. The lover and the Beloved become one. The Sufis strive to attain Absolute Beauty, Absolute Love and Absolute Bliss.

For a Sufi, music is a means to ecstasy. Music plays a very important part in Sufi religious exercise. Sufis worship beauty.

Sadhana

Concentration, meditation, obedience to a Guru, poverty, discipline, fasts, penances, Japa or recitation of the sacred word (Zikr), the use of rosary, rhythmic and controlled breathing, prayer, universal love, non-injury, detachment, introspection, dispassion, purity of heart, and self-control are the means to attain God or the Beloved through divine grace.

The Sufi aspirant looks in a mirror and concentrates on the Trikuti or the space between the two eyebrows in his own reflection in the mirror.

It is very difficult to practise the Bhava of the lover and the Beloved. This sort of Sufistic Sadhana proves dangerous in the case of unregenerate, passionate practitioners and leads to corruption. They mistake the intoxication caused by the drinking of wine for Divine Intoxication and indulge themselves in drinking and sensuality. The aspirant should remain under the strict guidance of a Guru during his Sadhana period.

34. JAINISM

Introduction

"Jain" or more properly speaking "Jaina" means a follower of Jina, which is applied to those persons who have conquered the lower nature, passion, hatred, etc. The word 'Jain' comes from the word 'Jina' which means a conqueror. 'Jina' comes from the root 'Ji'—'to conquer'. It means conquering the passions. It does not mean conquering nations. The passions are considered as enemies of the soul. They taint the natural qualities of the soul, obscure right belief, cause false knowledge and wrong conduct. Lust, anger, pride, and greed are considered as the major passions.

The Jain theory is based on reason. It is based on right faith, right knowledge, right conduct, tempered with mercy. Jainism is not a theistic system in the sense of the belief in the existence of a God as the Creator and the Ruler of the world. The highest being in the Jain philosophy is a person and not a Being without attributes like the Brahman of the Vedanta.

The chief point in the Jaina creed is the reverence paid to holy men who have raised themselves to divine perfection through long discipline. The Jina or the 'conquering saint', who has conquered all worldly desires, is with Jains what the Buddha or the perfectly enlightened saint is with Buddhists. He is also called Jinesvara (chief of the Jinas), Arhata (the Venerable), Tirthankara (the saint who has made the passage for the world), Sarvajna (omniscient), and Bhagavan (holy one). 'Tirtha' literally means a ford, a means of crossing over. It metaphorically denotes a spiritual guide or philosophy which enables one to cross over the ocean of recurring births in this world. 'Kara' means 'one who makes'. The word Tirthankara means a 'Jain Holy Teacher'.

According to the belief of the Jains, only the omniscient are able to give a right code of rules of life. These teachers or Tirthankaras are not creators or rulers of the world. They are pure divine souls who have attained perfection. They never again take human birth.

Mahavira is not the founder of Jainism. He revived the Jain doctrines. He was more a reformer than the founder of the faith. He was the first active propagator. He was the twenty-fourth Tirthankara. He is claimed to have been omniscient. 'Maha' means 'great' and 'Vira' means 'a hero'. Parasvanath was the twenty-third. The first of these twenty-four was named Rishabha Dev.

Time is divided into cycles. In each half cycle, twenty-four Tirthankaras at long intervals preach anew the doctrines.

Time with Jainas proceeds in two eternally recurring cycles of immense duration, defying all human calculation: (1) The Utsarpini or ascending cycle. (2) Avasarpini or descending cycle. Each of these has six stages.

The idols which represent the Tirthankaras are like that of Buddha in a meditative posture. Jainism is a representative of Buddhistic ideas. It has much in common with Buddhism. It is a near relative of Buddhism, if not its actual descendant.

There are two classes of Jainas, *viz.*, Sravakas (those who engage in secular occupations), and Yatis (monks or ascetics or Sadhus who shave their heads and live in Mathas or monasteries). The monks abandon all worldly connections. They take lifelong vows of absolute renunciation. They take five vows. They are divided into two principal sects, *viz.*, the Svetambaras (clothed in white garments) and the Digambaras (skyclad or naked).

Jain Philosophy

The Jain philosophy bases its doctrine on the absolute necessity of conquering the lower nature for the realisation of Truth.

The Jains do not accept the authority of the Vedas.

Jainism divides the whole universe into two main divisions *viz.*, sentient beings (Chetana, also called Jiva or soul) and non-sentient things (Jada, also called Ajiva or non-soul). Soul is that element which thinks, knows, and feels. It is the divine element in the living being. The true nature of the soul is right knowledge, right faith, and right conduct. The soul is undergoing evolution and involution, so long as it is subject to transmigration. Whatever is not soul is non-soul (Ajiva).

The combination of the Jiva and the Ajiva causes all diversities in this universe. Their interaction or interplay is the cause of the world-process or evolution. When the soul is stripped of all its Ajiva bondage, it becomes pure and attains its ultimate Mukti.

There are five gateways of Knowledge. The first is the senses. There is only one sense, the sense of touch in the lowest form of life. There are two, three, four and five senses in higher forms of life. The second source is study. The third is Avadhi or the psychic faculty through which more subtle things are known. The fourth is mind, knowing by which the mental processes of others are known. The fifth is Absolute Knowledge.

The Jain canon is divided into two parts, *viz.*, (1) Sruta Dharma, i.e., philosophy, and (2) Charitra Dharma, i.e., ethics. The Sruta Dharma enquires into the nature of nine principles, six kinds of living beings and the four states of existence. The first four principles are: Soul (Jiva), non-soul (Ajiva), merit on account of which man is happy, and demerit on account of which man suffers from misery. The fifth is the state which brings in merit and demerit. The sixth is Samvara which stops the inflow of foreign energies. The seventh is destruction of actions. The eighth is bondage of soul with actions. The ninth is total and permanent freedom of soul from all actions.

Dharma is that which keeps the soul from falling downwards. The bonds which keep it attached to the universe are those of Karma, virtuous and evil actions.

The four states of existence are Devas (celestial beings), Manushyas (human beings), Tiryanch (infra-human, vegetables, animals, birds, etc.), and Naraka (the lowest state of existence that of being a denizen of hell).

Living beings are of six kinds *viz.*, the one-organed (having body only); the two-organed (having body and taste); the three-organed (having body, taste, and smell); the four-organed (having body, taste, smell, and sight); and the five-organed (having body, taste, smell, sight, and hearing); and animals and human beings (having body, taste, smell, sight, hearing, and touch).

Jiva-Ajiva (Soul, Non-soul)

That which knows is soul. That which does not know is non-soul. Jiva and Ajiva have no origin. They have been in existence in the past. They exist now. They will exist in future also. We cannot say when the combination of the two has taken place. They have been found intermingled from time immemorial. Jivas and Ajivas are innumerable. Souls are infinite. Each soul retains its individuality. Each soul has to take births and rebirths till it destroys all its Karmas. Through right knowledge, right perception, right conduct, and self-control or penance, the bonds of accumulated Karmas can be loosened and annihilated.

Jiva (soul): Jivas, the living beings or souls are classified under two headings: (1) Siddha or liberated, and (2) Samsari or worldly beings.

The Jain philosophy teaches that each soul is a separate individuality, uncreated and eternal in existence. The soul evolves from the lower to the higher condition through the law of Karma, or cause and effect. It takes fresh bodies after death so long as the Karmas or forces generated in previous lives have not been fully worked out. Eventually it unfolds its absolute purity by breaking the bonds of Karma and attains perfection, Nirvana, or Mukti. The individuality is not merged into anything. It is not annihilated also. The perfected soul is neither masculine, feminine, nor neuter. Every soul is potentially omniscient. Consciousness is the very nature of the soul. Soul is a pure embodiment of knowledge. The soul has infinite potentialities. It has infinite capacity for removing Karma-bondages.

Ajiva (non-soul): There are five main sub-divisions, *viz.*, Dharmastikaya (that substance which helps soul and matter to move), Adharmastikaya (that substance which helps the soul and matter to rest), Akasasti or the space (that substance which gives shelter to the living and non-living), Kala (time), and Pudgala (matter).

God

God in the sense of, an extra cosmic personal Creator has no place in the Jain philosophy. But there is a subtle essence underlying all substances, conscious and unconscious, which becomes the cause of all modifications. This is termed God. The Jain idea of Godhood is the perfected soul (Siddha), the liberated soul (Mukta). The Jains worship these liberated souls (Tirthankaras), who have destroyed all Karmas and attained salvation, as their God. They accept those enlightened souls only, who have abandoned all worldly connections, who lead the life of true Sadhus and who have controlled all selfish desires, as their spiritual teachers. They accept that only as the true religion which is promulgated by them.

Tirthankaras

The Jain Tirthankara is free from faults. He is true God. He is the knower of all things and the revealer of Dharma. He is free from the 18 kinds of blemishes, *viz.,* hunger, thirst, senility, disease, birth, death, fear, pride, attachment, aversion, infatuation, worry, conceit, hatred, uneasiness, sweat, sleep, and surprise.

World

Jainism has two ways of looking at things, one called Dravyarthi Kanaya and the other Paryayarthi Kanaya According to the former the world is without beginning and end, but according to the latter there is creation and destruction at every moment. The Jains affirm that, being formed of eternal atoms, the universe has existed and will exist eternally.

There are six real substances which constitute the world. These six are space, time, matter, souls, Dharmastikaya (fulcrum of motion), and Adharmastikaya (fulcrum of stability, or rest). Space serves as a receptacle for the other substances. It is infinite. Time is real. It is beginningless and endless. Material objects consist of atoms. There is no extra cosmic creator or ruler of the world. There is nothing in the world save substance. There are many kinds of substances. Existence cannot be separated from substance.

Doctrine of Karma

The doctrine of Karma occupies a very prominent place in the Jain philosophy. A student of Jain Karma philosophy can trace any effect to a particular Karma. Those who by right faith, right knowledge, and right conduct destroy all Karmas, attain perfection. They become divine and are called Jinas. Those Jinas who, in every age, preach the law and establish the order, are called Tirthankaras.

The Jain doctrines are summed up in the maxim *'Ahimsa Paramo Dharmah'*. Ahimsa is the foundational tenet of Jainism. Jainism always tends to protect and advance the interests of all kinds of living beings. The universal principles of Jainism are Ahimsa, Satyam, Asteya, Brahmacharya, and Aparigraha.

Right faith, right knowledge, and right conduct constitute the triple jewels, the path to Nirvana.

According to the Jain philosophy all evils are due to Raga and Dvesha (attachment and hatred). All the rules of conduct are based on Daya (mercy). Daya has four forms: (1) performing a kind act without expectation of a return, (2) rejoicing at the prosperity of others, (3) sympathy with distressed people and relieving their afflictions, and (4) pity for the criminal.

Jainism preaches universal brotherhood and equality of all beings. It enjoins on all its followers the practice of the greatest self-control. The individual by his own efforts liberates all his latent qualities which are obscured by foreign elements. The state of purity or perfection is attained only in the human life through the triple jewels, *viz.*, right faith, right knowledge, and right conduct. The liberated soul goes to the abode Siddhakshetra which is at the top of this world.

35. JAPA

The Power of the Lord's Name

There is a Sakti in every word. If you utter the word 'excreta' or 'urine' when your friend is taking his meals, he may at once vomit his food. If you think of 'Garam Pakoda', 'hot Pakoda', your tongue will get salivation. When anyone suddenly shouts 'Scorpion! Scorpion!', 'Snake! Snake!', you at once apprehend the scorpion or the snake and jump in fright. When anyone calls you a 'donkey' or an 'ass', you are annoyed and you show anger.

When such is the power of the names of the ordinary things of this world, what tremendous power should there be in the Name of God! God is the completion or the fullness of existence. Hence, the Name which denotes Him, too, is full and perfect. Therefore, the power of the Name of God is incalculable, for it is the height or the zenith of power. The Name of God can achieve anything. There is nothing impossible for it. It is the means to the realisation of God Himself. Even as the name of a thing in this world generates the consciousness of that thing in the mind, the Name of God generates God-consciousness in the purified mind and becomes the direct cause of the realisation of the Highest Perfection or God.

The Name of God, chanted correctly or incorrectly, knowingly or unknowingly, carefully or carelessly, is sure to give the desired result. Just as burning quality is natural to and inherent in fire, so also, the power of destroying sins with their very root and branch, and bringing the aspirant into blissful union with the Lord through Bhava-samadhi, is natural to and inherent in the Name of God.

The glory of the Name of God cannot be established through reasoning and intellect. It can be experienced or realised only through devotion, faith, and constant repetition of the Name.

Pingala was a Ganika or prostitute. She obtained a parrot, as a lovely present from a thief. The parrot was trained to utter the Name 'Sri Rama, Sri Rama'. Pingala knew nothing of Rama-Nama. She heard the sound *Rama, Rama* through the mouth of the parrot. It was very melodious and charming. Pingala was very much attracted. She fixed her mind on the Rama-Nama uttered by the parrot, and mysteriously entered into Bhava-samadhi, union with Rama.

Ajamila was a righteous Brahmin in the beginning. He fell in love with a low-caste girl and committed many atrocious crimes. It was at the time of death that he uttered the name of his son Narayana, and there came the messengers of Lord Narayana Himself to his rescue, and Ajamila was released from this world for ever.

The greatest of sinners can attain God-realisation through the blessings of the Name. Nothing is impossible to be achieved through God's Name. The Lord's Name is all-powerful.

Benefits of Japa

Repetition of any Mantra or Name of the Lord is known as Japa. Japa is an important Anga of Yoga. It is a spiritual food for the hungry soul. Japa is the rod in the hands of the blind Sadhakas to plod on the road to Realisation. Japa is the philosopher's stone or divine elixir that makes one God-like. In this iron age, Nama-smarana or Japa is the easiest, quickest, safest, and surest way to reach God and attain immortality and perennial joy.

Japa purifies the heart. Japa steadies the mind. Japa destroys birth and death. Japa burns sins. Japa scorches Samskaras. Japa annihilates attachment. Japa induces Vairagya. Japa roots out all desires. Japa makes one fearless. Japa removes delusion. Japa gives supreme peace. Japa develops Prem. Japa unites the devotee with the Lord. Japa gives health, wealth, strength, and long life. Japa brings God-consciousness. Japa awakens the Kundalini. Japa bestows eternal bliss.

Japa gives a nice, refreshing, exhilarating spiritual bath. It wonderfully washes the subtle body or astral body.

Mantra Yoga—An Exact Science

A Mantra is divinity encased within a sound-structure. It is divine power or Daivi Sakti manifesting in a sound-body.

The sacred Mantra or the Divine Name is a vital symbol of the Supreme Divinity directly revealed in the innermost depths of divine communion to the sages of Self-realisation in the hoary Vedic and Upanishadic times. These symbols are in the nature of unfailing keys to gain access into the transcendental realms of absolute experience.

Mantra Yoga is an exact science. A Mantra, in the Hindu religion, has the following six parts. It has got a Rishi who had Self-realisation for the first time through this Mantra, and who gave this Mantra to the world. He is the seer for this Mantra. Sage Visvamitra is the Rishi for Gayatri. Secondly, the Mantra has a metre, which governs the inflection of the voice. Thirdly, the Mantra has a particular Devata or supernatural being, higher or lower. as its informing power. This Devata is the presiding deity of the Mantra. Fourthly, the Mantra has got a Bija or seed. The seed is a significant word, or series of words, which gives a special power to the Mantra. The Bija is the essence of the Mantra. Fifthly, every Mantra has got a Sakti. The Sakti is the energy of the form of the Mantra, i.e., of the vibration-forms set up by its sounds. These carry the man to the Devata that is worshipped. Lastly, the Mantra has a Kilaka—pillar or pin. This plugs the Mantra-Chaitanya that is hidden in the Mantra. As soon as the plug is removed by constant and prolonged repetition of the Name, the Chaitanya that is hidden is revealed. The devotee gets Darshan of the Ishta Devata.

Sound and Image

Sounds are vibrations. They give rise to definite forms. Each sound produces a form in the invisible world, and combinations of sound create complicated shapes.

The repetition of a Mantra has a mysterious power of bringing about the manifestation of the Divinity, just as the splitting of an atom manifests the tremendous forces latent in it. When a particular Mantra appropriated to a particular God is properly recited, the vibrations so set up create in the higher planes a special form which that God ensouls for the time being. The repetition of the Panchakshara Mantra—*Om Namah Sivaya*—produces the form of Lord Siva. The repetition of *Om Namo Narayanaya,* the Ashtakshara Mantra of Vishnu, produces the form of Vishnu.

Potencies of Different Mantras

Mantras are in the form of praise and appeal to the deities, craving for help and mercy. Some Mantras control and command the evil spirits. By constant repetition of the Mantra, the Sadhaka imbibes the virtues and powers of the deity that presides over the Mantra.

Repetition of the Surya Mantra bestows health, long life, vigour, vitality, Tejas or brilliance. It removes all diseases of the body and the eye. No enemy can do any harm.

Repetition of the Sarasvati-Mantra—*Om Sri Sarasvatyai Namah*—will bestow on you wisdom and intelligence, and make you a learned person. You will get inspiration and compose poems. You will become a great scholar.

Repetition of *Om Sri Mahalakshmyai Namah* will confer on you wealth and remove poverty.

The Ganesh-Mantra will remove any obstacle in any undertaking. It bestows wisdom on you, as also Siddhi, wealth, etc.

The Maha Mrityunjaya Mantra will save you from accidents, incurable diseases, and calamities, and bestow on you long life and immortality. It is a Moksha-Mantra, too. Those who do Japa of this Mantra daily will enjoy good health and long life, and attain Moksha in the end.

Repetition of the Subrahmanya-Mantra—*Om Sri Saravanabhavaya Namah*—will give you success in any undertaking and make you glorious. It will drive off evil influences and evil spirits.

Repetition of the Sri Hanuman-Mantra—*Om Sri Hanumate Namah*—will bestow victory and strength.

Repetition of the Gayatri, or the Pranava, or Om Namah Sivaya, or Om Namo Narayanaya, or Om Namo Bhagavate Vasudevaya, one and a quarter lakh times, with Bhava, faith, and devotion, will confer on you Mantra-Siddhi.

Om, Soham, Sivoham, Aham Brahmasmi are Mokshamantras. They will help you to attain Self-realisation.

Om Sri Ramaya Namah, Om Namo Bhagavate Vasudevaya are Saguna-mantras which will enable you to attain Saguna realisation first, and then Nirguna realisation.

You can attain God-realisation by doing Japa of any Mantra. All Mantras have equal potency or power.

Rogue Ratnakara became sage Valmiki by repeating 'Mara, Mara', the inverted form of Rama. Tukaram, the Maharashtra saint, had direct Darsana of Lord Krishna several times, by repeating simply 'Vitthal, Vitthal', the Name of Lord Krishna's deity at Pandharpur. Dhruva, that wonderful boy of devotion, repeated *Om*

Namo Bhagavate Vasudevaya, the Dvadasakshara Mantra of Lord Krishna, and had his Darsana. Prahlada uttered 'Narayana, Narayana', and saw Hari face to face. Ramdas, the spiritual preceptor of Sivaji, repeated thirteen crore times the Rama Mantra "Sri Ram, Jaya Ram, Jaya Jaya Ram", standing in water in the Godavari. He became a great saint. The reputed Swami Vidyaranya, author of the Panchadasi, had direct Darsana of Mother Gayatri through Japa of the Gayatri Mantra.

Mantra-Diksha or Initiation into the Divine Name

It is better if you get your Mantra from your Guru. This has a tremendous effect on the disciple. The Guru imparts his Sakti along with the Mantra. The Mantra-Chaitanya, the power hidden in the Mantra, is easily awakened.

If you cannot get a Guru, you can select any Mantra according to your own liking and taste, and repeat it daily, with Sraddha and Bhava. This also has a great purificatory effect. You will attain realisation of God.

It is better to stick to one Mantra alone. If you love Krishna, love Him alone till the end. See Lord Krishna in Rama, Siva, Durga, Gayatri and everyone. To love Lord Krishna for three months, Rama for another three months, Sakti for six months, Hanuman for sometime, Lord Siva for some time, is not good.

Practical Aids to Japa

The most effective time for Japa is early dawn and dusk, when Sattva is predominant.

Face the north or the east when sitting. This exercises a subtle influence and enhances the efficacy of the Japa. By facing the north, you will be in communion with the Rishis of the Himalayas and will be mysteriously benefited by their spiritual currents. A spiritual neophyte should observe this rule.

Sit on Kusa-grass seat, or deer skin, or rug. Spread a sheet of cloth over it. This conserves body-electricity.

Have a steady pose. This helps to make the mind also steady, and aids concentration.

Do some prayer before starting the Japa. Invoking the aid of the Ishta Devata with appropriate prayer induces proper Sattvika Bhava.

Now start the Japa, pronouncing each letter of the Mantra correctly and distinctly. Do not repeat the Mantra too fast or too slow. Increase the speed only when the mind wanders. Do not do the Japa in a hurried manner, as a contractor tries to finish his work in a hurried way. It is not the number of Japa, but purity, concentration, Bhava and feeling, and one-pointedness of mind that help the aspirant in the attainment of God-consciousness.

Do the Japa with feeling. You must have the same flow of love and respect in your heart at the time of thinking of or remembering His Name as you naturally may have in your heart at the time when you really see Him.

Using a Mala helps alertness, and acts as an incentive to carry on the Japa continuously; but, it is not necessary for an advanced aspirant.

Variety in Japa is necessary to sustain interest, avoid fatigue and counteract monotony. Repeat aloud for a time, then hum the Mantra, and repeat mentally sometimes.

Do not beg to God any worldly objects while doing Japa. Feel that your heart is being purified and the mind is becoming steady by the power of the Mantra, with the grace of God.

Keep your Guru Mantra a secret. Never disclose it to anyone.

After Japa is over, do not immediately leave the place, mix with everyone, or plunge into worldly activity. Sit very quietly for about ten minutes at least, humming some prayer, remembering the Lord or reflecting upon His infinite love. Then, after devout prostration, leave the place and commence your routine duties. Spiritual vibrations will be intact.

Likhita Japa

Write down daily in a notebook your Ishta Mantra or Guru-Mantra for half an hour. When you write the Mantra, observe Mouna. Write the Mantra clearly in ink. On Sundays and holidays, write this for one hour. This is Likhita Japa. You can develop a wonderful power of concentration. Incalculable spiritual benefits are derived from Likhita Japa.

In Mantra writing, there is no restriction about any particular script. It may be written in any language.

Japa Sadhana while at Work

Regularity in Japa Sadhana is most essential. Sit in the same place, and at the same time. Japa must become habitual.

Carry on the current of Japa mentally even at other times, in whatever works you may be engaged. Give your hands alone to work, but give the mind to God—do mental Japa—, like the typist or the harmonium-player who types or plays and talks to you, or like the lady who knits clothes and talks and jokes with her comrades while she is walking along the road.

You can do Japa even in the latrine. But do it there mentally. Ladies can do Japa mentally even during their monthly periods. There are no restrictions of any kind in Mantra Japa for those who do it with Nishkama-bhava, for the attainment of Moksha. Restrictions or Vidhis come only when people repeat any Mantra with Sakama-bhava, to get fruits such as wealth, Svarga, son, and so on.

Remember the Name of the Lord with every incoming and outgoing breath. Form a strong habit of repeating the Name of the Lord. Even in dream you must be doing Japa. Then only it will be easy for you to remember Him at the time of death.

36. JESUS

Two thousand years ago, Divinity incarnated upon this planet to show to all humanity the glorious path to everlasting life by actually living the divine life upon this earth. Jesus was not an ordinary human being. He was the divine power and love incarnated upon this globe for a special, divine purpose. His advent was in the nature of a fulfilment of the divine plan for this world process. This will be seen from the very manner of his birth and its background.

The Manner of the Christ's Birth and Its Significance

The time and the manner of the birth of Jesus reveals a deep spiritual law. Jesus Christ was not born in a grand palace. He was not born to very wealthy or learned parents. Also, he was not born in the full blaze of daylight, with the knowledge of all men. Jesus Christ was born in a simple, lowly place—a corner of a stable. He was born to humble and poor parents who had nothing to boast about except their own spotless character and holiness. Also, he was in darkness, in the obscure hour of midnight when no one even knew about it, except a few divinely blessed people.

The above point of deep significance tells you that the spiritual awakening comes to the seeker who is perfectly humble and 'meek' and 'poor in spirit'. The quality of true humility is one of the indispensable fundamentals. Then come simplicity, holiness, and the renunciation of all desire for worldly wealth and pride of learning. Thirdly, even as Christ was born unknown to the world and in the obscurity of darkness, the advent of the Christ-spirit takes place in the inwardness of man when there is total self-effacement, self-abnegation.

This is the birth into divine life. It was the secret of this birth that, centuries ago, the Lord Jesus sweetly explained to the good Nicodemus. The good man did not quite understand what precisely Christ meant when he taught that a man must be born again if he is to attain the Kingdom of God. "How can this be?", Nicodemus asked. Then it was that Christ explained that this birth was inward, not of the body, but in the Spirit. Such inner spiritual birth is essential if the Supreme is to be attained, if true bliss is to be experienced.

The Simplicity and Power of Lord Jesus' Utterances

The way in which Jesus lived and taught was simple, yet sublime. His mode of teaching was something extraordinary. Jesus was no academic scholar. He could lay claim to neither degrees nor doctorates. He was not a Pundit or a savant. He had not attained proficiency or mastery in any practical art or science. He did neither indulge in high-flown oratory nor deliver learned pulpit sermons. When he spoke, he spoke but shortly, and his brief words were few. His sayings were short, pithy, and almost aphoristic. But, his words were vibrant with an extraordinary power that was not of this world. The words of Jesus were vital and aflame. They burnt themselves into the depths of the very consciousness of his hearers.

And the reason?

When Jesus spoke, his blessed words came from the depths of a limitless love and an infinite divine compassion that thrilled and thrilled again with an all consuming, powerful desire to do good to men, to serve, to help and to save. This compassion to purify, to raise, and to save mankind verily constitutes the Sacred Heart of Jesus, the Christ. This love enlivened his words with a divine force, which made them to be permanently enshrined in the hearts of the fortunate hearers.

Christianity

There is not much of intricate philosophy or Yoga Sadhana in Christianity. There is reason for this. Jesus had to deal with the illiterate fishermen of Galilee. He gave them only moral precepts and showed them the way of righteous living. Leaving aside all abstruse philosophical theory and subtle intellectual researches, Jesus told man how he must do. To do this, he clothed even the highest truths of spiritual life with simple stories and parables, which even the common man in the street could easily grasp and comprehend. Couched in the form of simple parables, the deepest wisdom of spiritual life became expressed before man, through the sweet and blessed words of Divine Jesus.

Jesus explained the real nature of God, man, and the world he lived in. He taught people to change their way of looking at things. He told them that if they would change their outlook on life from its materialistic to its spiritualistic aspect, they would realise that the world they were living in was God's Kingdom.

Jesus has left no written records of his important teachings. He delivered all his teachings orally. Neither he, nor his followers, ever wrote down even a single word which was spoken by him, in his lifetime. The words of Jesus were not collected till some generations after they were uttered.

His words have been misunderstood, wrongly annotated; mutilated, deformed and transformed; and yet, they have survived almost two thousand years as they were very powerful and came from the heart of a realised Yogi.

The Voice of Jesus

The voice of Jesus is verily the voice of the Eternal Being. Through him is expressed the call of the Infinite to the finite, of the Cosmic Being to the individual, the call of God to man. His divine voice is the same, therefore, as the voice of the Vedas and the Upanishads, the voice of the Koran and the Zend-Avesta, the Dhammapada, and all such sacred scriptures of the great religions of the world. Fundamentally, the gospel that he preached is at one with the gospel expounded through these holy books. It is the way of denying the flesh and asserting the Spirit. It is the way of crucifying the lower self to bring about a glorious resurrection of the Spirit, and the final ascension unto the Infinitude, and the transcendence unto the Divine. It is no other than the Upanishadic path of rejecting the Preyas and accepting the Sreyas, the negation of the Anatman and the living of the life in the Atman.

Jesus declares: "Ye cannot serve both God and Mammon". In other words, his teaching implies: Detach; attach. Detach yourself from the material objects of this transient world. Attach yourself to the eternal spiritual treasure of Atman. Christ thus teaches us the great way of going beyond all sin and sorrow.

The Life of Jesus

Jesus is the embodiment of all his teachings. In Jesus we see perfect holiness, goodness, kindness, mercy, gentleness and justice. He said: "I am the Truth, the Way and the Life". He is the embodiment of all that is best, sublimest and most beautiful. He is the most perfect type and ideal of humanity. He is a philosopher, prophet, teacher, reformer. He always practised what he taught.

An almost supernal, spotless purity rested like a divine mantle upon the sublime personality of Jesus, the Christ. His life was a wonderful combination of Jnana, Bhakti and Karma. An ideal, integral development of head, heart and hand has rendered his life a model for mankind to emulate for all eternity. Christ was ever conscious of his inseparable identity with the Supreme Self. Yet, deep devotion and love for the personal God constantly found expression in him in the form of prayers, praises and glorification. And, in his actual day-to-day life, Jesus was the very personification of the spirit of Karma Yoga. His entire life was a continuous ministry unto the afflicted. His feet moved but to reach where aid was needed. If his hand moved, it was but to help the troubled and the oppressed. His tongue spoke only to utter soft, honeyed words of compassion, consolation, inspiration and enlightenment. With the very glances of his luminous Yogic eyes, Jesus awakened, elevated and transformed those whom he gazed upon. He felt, thought, talked and acted for the good of others. Amidst this all, he dwelt in the unbroken awareness of the assertion: "I and my Father are one". His life was like that of a sage in Sahaja Samadhi.

The life of Jesus displays a silent yet supreme heroism in the face of the most determined opposition, persecution and misunderstanding. And he has set an example how a true seeker repulses the temptations on the spiritual path. Long before the outward drama of crucifixion, Jesus had voluntarily crucified himself spiritually by annihilating the lower self and living a purely divine life.

Jesus was God Himself. The Holy Scripture reminds us of this fact again and again. Yet, why did he have to endure so much of persecution and suffering? Could he not have overwhelmed his foes by a mere exercise of his divine will? Yes. But the supreme incarnation of love that Lord Jesus was, he had willed it that his own life would be an example for people to emulate. Therefore he behaved like any other human being; and while so doing, fully demonstrated in his own brief but eventful life the great Sermon that he gave on the Mount.

Jesus and the Modern Man

True, Lord Jesus bled on the Cross for the redemption of his people. Today, from his eternal seat in the Kingdom of God, his divine compassionate heart bleeds even more profusely. For, the people of his time were ignorant of the Law and they erred; but the people of the modern world have the resplendent light of Lord Jesus' life and teachings illumining the path of righteousness, and yet, the wantonly walk the path of darkness, ignorance, sin, selfishness, sensuousness and misery. If his merciful heart bled for the ignorant sinners, how much more would it not bleed for the sins of those who err, ignoring His light!

Is this the way in which you would like humanity to show its gratitude to the Saviour? No, a thousand times no. It is never too late to mend. Study the Gospels again. Meditate on the resplendent, spiritually glowing, divine form of Lord Jesus. How sweet, how compassionate, how gentle and loving he was! And yet, he showed no leniency towards himself. He turned resolutely away from Satan—not that he could ever be tempted, but to set an example before us.

Trials and temptations come but to be overcome by the brave. Tests and trying situations come to strengthen your mind and to purify your heart. They are, as it were, the wise men that discover the Jesus in you. To succumb to these trials is weakness. To fast, to pray, to discriminate and to overcome these obstacles with the help of the grace of the Lord is spiritual heroism. When the victory is achieved, to feel, to realise and to proclaim that it was the Lord's grace that enabled you to attain victory is real meekness. Meekness is virtue; weakness is sin. Learn this great lesson from the life of Lord Jesus.

Study the Sermon on the Mount again and again. Meditate upon it. Choose the Lord's instructions one after the other, month after month, and endeavour diligently to put them into practice. Thus will you grow into a worthy child of Lord Jesus. Thus will you reincarnate Lord Jesus in your own heart. There are many today who truly and sincerely follow the teachings of the Saviour. In their hearts has Jesus reincarnated, to guide you, to lead you to the Kingdom of God, where he has his supreme seat. May you all walk the path that Jesus laid out! May you all be living embodiments of the Sermon on the Mount! May you realise the Kingdom of God within you here and now!

37. JIVANMUKTA

A Jivanmukta is a liberated sage. He is released even while living. He lives in the world, but he is not of the world. He always revels in the eternal bliss of the Supreme Self. He is Isvara Himself. He is a God on earth.

The Jivanmukta or full-blown Jnani is full of pure love, compassion, mercy, exquisite gentleness, and hidden power and strength. Love and lustre shine through his brilliant eyes.

The Jivanmukta has not a bit of selfish interest in him and is absolutely free from worries, difficulties, troubles, tribulations, sorrows and anxieties under all circumstances. Even when pains and the rest attaching themselves to his body exhibit themselves on his face, his mind never writhes under them and their antithesis. He is not a slave of his moods; he is ever cheerful and peaceful. His higher excellences have been perfectly unfolded; all divine attributes are fully awakened in him. Every one of his weaknesses and limitations is burnt *in toto.* He shines in his own pristine glory, in his own essential nature of divine consciousness. He radiates peace and joy everywhere.

The true greatness of a realised Yogi is indescribable. His eyes are serene and steady, his actions perfect and holy, his speech sweet and short, inspiring and impressive. His gait is magnanimous, his touch purifying; his looks are merciful, gestures illuminating. He is omniscient; he has intuitive transcendental knowledge and clear insight into the very heart of all things and beings. You will experience a deep sense of peace and harmony, great elevation and inspiration, in his presence.

Signs of a Jivanmukta

The Jivanmukta or liberated sage is absolutely free from egoism, doubt, fear and grief. These are the four important signs that indicate that one has attained perfection.

The Jivanmukta has perfect contentment, unruffled peace of mind, deep abiding joy and bliss, possession of super-sensual spiritual knowledge and ability to clear any kind of doubt of aspirants. Doubts vanish when one remains in his company.

The Jivanmukta does not care even for the wants of body. He is not afraid of death. He has no longing to live also. Maya or Prakriti is his obedient and sweet nurse. She attends upon him carefully. Bodily wants come by themselves. Prakriti arranges everything for him before-hand. This is her look-out.

Balanced mind, equal vision, indifference to pairs of opposites like pleasure and pain, censure and praise, heat and cold, success and failures—these are the marks of a Jivanmukta. Jivanmuktas are not frightened or astonished at any unusual occurrence in nature. They will never be disconcerted even should the sun grow cold, or the moon turn hot, or the fire begin to burn with its flame downwards, or the course of the river begin to rise upwards. The Jivanmukta is not perturbed under any condition. He is undistracted amidst distractions.

The Double-Consciousness of a Jivanmukta

A man who stands in water up to his neck has a twofold experience. His head is exposed to the sun. He experiences both heat and cold. Such is the experience of a Jivanmukta. He has double consciousness. He enjoys the bliss of Brahman. He also has the experience of this world. He is like a man who knows two languages.

Just as the pot in which asafoetida or onion is kept emits a certain amount of smell even when it is cleaned several times, so also, a small trace of ignorance still remains in the mind of a Jnani even. The Jivanmukta has a consciousness of the body in the form of a Samskara. That is the reason why he eats and drinks. Though the instinctive mind with low desires is destroyed, the Sattvic mind does not perish in the Jivanmukta. How will he be able to do Vyavahara or worldly dealings without an instrument, viz., the mind?

Difference between a Worldly Man and a Liberated Sage

The phenomenal universe does not vanish from the vision of the Jivanmukta. The Jivanmukta sees the world as a dream within himself. Just as the mirage appears even after the illusory nature of the water is understood, so also, the world appears for the Jivanmukta even after he has attained Self-realisation, even after he has clearly understood the illusory nature of the world. But, just as the man who has understood the nature of the mirage will not run after the mirage for drinking water, so also, the Jivanmukta will not run after sensual objects like the worldly-minded people, though the world appears to him. That is the difference between a worldly man and a liberated sage.

When he is absorbed in Brahman, the Glory of glories, the Soul of souls, the Jivanmukta will not be able to work. But, when he comes down from his full Brahmic consciousness owing to the force of Prarabdha and Vikshepa Sakti, he will pour forth his love at the cry of a suffering soul. So radiant and compassionate is he. He is the ocean of mercy and love and peace, a Buddha or Jesus.

Cosmic Vision

The Jivanmukta beholds the one Reality or God everywhere and in all things. For his there is no distinction between a rogue and a saint, gold and stone, honour and dishonour. He actually feels that all is himself only, that snakes, scorpions, tigers, bears and lions are as much part of himself as his own eyes, nose, ears, hands and feet. He is one with the flower, ether, sun, ocean, mountain and sky. He has cosmic vision and cosmic feelings.

Samadhi Jnani and Vyavahara Jnani

The way of living of Jivanmuktas or sages differs. One sage lives in a princely style. Bhagiratha lived this kind of life. Another sage lives in a beggarly manner. One sage is always in a meditative mood. He never works. He never talks. He lives always in seclusion. Jada Bharata lived this kind of life. Another sage lives in a busy crowded city. He plunges himself in service. He talks with the people. He delivers lectures, holds religious classes, writes books, etc. Sri Sankara led this kind of life. This is due to Prarabdha. Every sage has his own Prarabdha. If all sages have the same kind of living and the same kind of Prarabdha, this world will be like a prison. Variety in manifestation is the nature of Prakriti.

The Jnani who has desire for worldly activities or Vyavahara and works in the world is a Vyavahara Jnani. The Jnani who withdraws himself completely from the universe is a Samadhi Jnani.

Knowledge is the same in those two types of Jnanis. But the Samadhi Jnani enjoys more Ananda than the Vyavahara Jnani. The Samadhi Jnani is one who is ever absorbed in Brahman. He does not see names and forms. The world has entirely vanished for him.

He is quite unable to work. He is a Muzub. He is a Paramahamsa. Food has to be thrust forcibly in the case of a Samadhi Jnani.

A Vyavahara Jnani will experience pain when his finger is cut, but a Samadhi Jnani will not experience pain even a bit even if his leg is amputated. The case of Shams Tabriez of Multan would serve as an example to justify the truth of the above statement. When he was skinned out, he laughed and uttered *Analhaq, Analhaq.* 'Analhaq' means 'I am He', and corresponds to the Hindu 'Soham'.

A Vyavahara Jnani sees names and forms. A Vyavahara Jnani knows that this is Vishta, this is Chandana; this is a fool, this is an intelligent man; this is an Adhikari, this is a rogue, this is an honest man. But, he is not affected in his feelings. He is neither exalted when he gets success nor depressed when he fails. He neither loves an honest man nor hates the rogue. In this sense, he has Sama Drishti or equal vision.

The desire for work in the case of the Vyavahara Jnani is due to his Prarabdha. He uses his body and mind as his instruments just as a carpenter used his tools. While working, he has not lost his Brahmic consciousness even for a second. He is settled always in the Chaitanya Svarupa or pure consciousness.

The Vyavahara Jnani sees the whole world within himself. He sees nothing outside, just as you do. He sees through his Divya Drishti or Jnana Chakshus, and not through the physical eyes. A Jnani with the help of the powerful lens, the eye of Atman, sees the whole world with all the details of creation. He sees the astral body, the causal body with its Samskaras, the Pranic aura, psychic aura, magnetic aura, etc., of a man. It is very difficult for a worldly man with practical Buddhi to mentally visualise how a Jnani sees the physical universe while he is working.

How the Jivanmukta Lives and Works

A Jivanmukta is not a whimsical man. He is not bound by the rules of Sastra or society. And yet, he will not deviate from Dharma. All that he does will be in strict accordance with the scriptures or sacred books. He spontaneously does only what is good. An expert dancer never makes a false step. So is a Jivanmukta when he works.

The sage works without effort, without agency, without egoism, attachment and desire. Like a child, his conduct is neither good nor evil.

The Jivanmukta acts only like a child. The sense of right and wrong will be natural in him independently of scriptural teachings. He has destroyed all egoism. He is above Karma, and Karmas cannot touch him. He may, for the instruction of the world, perform works or refrain from forbidden acts.

The Jivanmukta does not care for public criticism. He keeps a cool mind even when he is assaulted. He blesses those who persecute him. He beholds only his own Self everywhere.

His mark or characteristic is an internal mental state. It cannot be perceived or detected by others. The Lord uses him for His divine work.

Physical Nudity and Mental Nudity

A Brahma Jnani or Jivanmukta need not be a genius. He need not be an eloquent speaker, orator, lecturer, or professor. But he is calm, serene and tranquil. He is taciturn and silent. His silence is superior eloquence. He has divine wisdom and intuitive knowledge. In his presence, all doubts are cleared.

Householders make wrong judgments in deciding the nature of a Jivanmukta. They take into consideration only the external conditions of a Jivanmukta. Even educated people commit mistakes in this regard.

A Sadhu may be physically nude. He may not keep anything with him. He may use his hands as the begging bowl and live underneath a tree. He may live in a forest. Yet, he may be the greatest scoundrel; he may be the most worldly-minded man with internal and external attachments. He may dance in joy when he gets an eight-anna piece for his opium-smoking. His mind may be full of distractions and disturbances. Whereas, a man may live in the bustle of a town or city. He may lead the life of a big Babu. He may wear fashionable dress. He may eat dainties. Yet he may not have the least attachment and craving for anything. Sri Ramanuja lived amidst luxuries. There had been instances of realised persons who had elephants, horses and all royal paraphernalia without being affected in the least by these external objects. They had always Jana Nishtha and Svarupa Sthiti amidst multifarious activities. This is integral development. This is the gist of the Bhagavad-Gita. This is the central teaching of Lord Krishna.

What is wanted is mental nudity. Jnana is purely an internal state. The external marks are no sure criterion.

The ways of a Jnani are mysterious. Only a Jivanmukta can know a Jivanmukta. The description given of a Jnani in the Bhagavad-Gita and various other books is quite inadequate, incomplete and imperfect. His state can never be imagined by the limited mind and can never be described by the finite speech. He shines in his own pristine glory.

He will sometimes appear like a Sarvajna, all-knower. He will sometimes appear like an Ajnani, ignorant man. He knows when to act like a Brahmanishtha, and when to behave like a fool. Do not judge him. If you approach him with the proper Bhava, with faith, devotion and spiritual thirst, he will impart the highest knowledge to you. If you approach him with a bad motive, he will behave like a mad man, and you will be deceived. Great will be your loss then.

A Blessing to the World

A Jivanmukta is sustainer of the world. He is a source of perpetual inspiration. He is an embodiment through which divine grace is transmitted to the unregenerated men.

Like flowers that bloom to scent and purify the air around, great souls like Sadasiva Brahman, Yajnavalkya, spring up in the world to gladden men's heart and to lead them to immortality and perfection.

The Jivanmukta is a power-house of spiritual energy. He radiates his spiritual currents to the different corners of the world. Sit before him. Your doubts will be cleared by themselves. You will feel a peculiar thrill of joy and peace in his presence.

The Jivanmukta, like unto holy waters, purifies others by mere sight, touch, and the utterances of his name. Sometimes he remains unnoticed. Sometimes he becomes known to those who desire welfare. He eats food offered to him by pious devotees and burns up their past and future evils or impurities.

A Jivanmukta or a saint is the ultimate source of Knowledge of the soul. Satsanga with a Jivanmukta even for a minute is much better than rulership of a kingdom. His very presence is thrilling and inspiring. Seek his company and evolve. Serve him with faith and devotion.

The Sage Lives for Ever

The sage lives for ever. He has attained life everlasting. Cravings torture him not. Sins stain him not. Birth and death touch him not. Pains and tribulations torment him not.

A Jivanmukta may give up his body in any place, at any time. Just as the falling leaves and fruits of a tree will not affect the tree itself, so also, the dropping of the body will not affect the Atman, which survives like the tree. His Pranas do not depart elsewhere for transmigration. They are absorbed in Brahman after the exhaustion of his Prarabdha, the results of past actions that have already begun to bear fruit. He is freed from further births.

The Jivanmukta is freed from the trammels of mind and matter. He is absolutely free, perfect, independent. He is absolutely free from hatred, lust, cares, worries and anxieties. Everybody will surely like this state of beatitude or final emancipation. It is the final goal of life. It is the end of all human aspirations

The state of Jivanmukti is the be-all and end-all of existence. There is fullness in this state. All desires are burnt. It is a state of plenum of absolute satisfaction. There is no gain greater than this, no bliss greater than this, no wisdom greater this.

There, at the summit of the Hill of Eternal Bliss, you can see now the Jivanmukta or a full-blown Yogi. He has climbed the stupendous heights through intense and constant struggle. He did severe, rigorous spiritual Sadhana. He did profound Nididhyasana or meditation. He spent sleepless nights. He kept long vigils on several halting stages. He persevered with patience and diligence. He has surmounted many obstacles. He conquered despair, gloom and depression. He is a beacon-light to the world now. Remember that he was also rotting in those days in the quagmire of Samsara, like yourself. You can also ascend to that summit if only you will.

38. JUDAISM

Introduction

Judaism constitutes the religious doctrines and rites of the Jews as enjoined in the laws of Moses. Judaism is based on Zoroastrianism. It has given rise to two great religions of the world, i.e., Christianity and Mohammedanism. The Mohammedans admit that their religion is founded on Judaism. The Koran also is very clear on this point.

Zoroastrian conception of Ahura Mazda as the Supreme Being is perfectly identical with the idea of Elohim (God) Jehovah which we find in the books of Old Testament.

Abraham, the Prophet, was the first man who has revealed God to all humanity. He is the Founder of the Hebrew race. Hebrew is one of the descendants of Jacob, as Israelite, a Jew. Isaac had two sons, viz., Essan and Jacob and their descendants are the Christians and Jews respectively. Abraham had two sons (one from Sarah and one from Hagar, the Egyptian woman), viz., Isaac and Ismael who are the fathers of Jews and Mohammedans respectively.

Old and New Testament

The Old Testament contains the sacred writings of the ancient Jewish race. The newer portion is known as the New Testament which was begun after the coming of Jesus Christ, more than nineteen hundred years ago. Long before Jesus came to this world, the Jews wrote and studied their sacred books. These were written in their Hebrew tongue. The old Hebrew books were translated into Greek about two hundred years before the Christian era.

The books of the Jews were arranged into three main divisions. The first was called "The Law". It dealt with the laws of the world. These books are now the first part of the Bible, viz., Genesis, Exodus, Leviticus, Numbers and Deuteronomy. The second class was that of the Prophets. It included Joshua, Isaiah and Jeremiah. Psalms and Proverbs constituted third class. The Old Testament contains 39 books.

The New Testament contains 27 books. The first four books are Gospels which describe the life of Christ on this earth. The next book tells us of the Acts of the Apostles, particularly of the important Apostle Paul. The twenty-one shorter books give out the ideas underlying the Christian faith of the early Christians. The last book is the book of Revelations. It gives a description of the series of visions, viz., the lamb of God and the heavenly city. The author is John, the favourite Apostle of Jesus. All these books were written in Greek, which was the language of educated men at the beginning of the Christian era.

Jewish Sects

The Law was set forth as a complete system by which men should live. By the Law was understood in a special sense the Pentateuch. Every word of Pentateuch was considered as inspired and an immediate revelation of Moses.

(a) There was a need for explanation of the Law. The Scribes were the interpreters of the Law. They explained and applied the rules of the Torah to special cases. The Scribes were recognised as the legislators and the judges of Israel. Their decisions had the force of Law. The first Scribes were priests.

(b) The fraternity of the Pharisees were the popular or nationalist party. They believed in the doctrine of immortality, resurrection of the body, the existence of angels and spirits. As religious teachers, they upheld the authority of oral tradition as of equal validity with the written Law. They were inclined to fatalism in the question of the freedom of the will. The Zealots represented one extreme side of the Pharisaic movement.

(c) Sadducus were aristocratic priests. They held to the letter of the Mosaic revelation. They denied the authority of the oral tradition as interpreted by the Pharisees. They taught complete freedom of the will in moral action. They had no belief in angels or spirits. They did not accept the doctrine of immortality as a deduction from the Pentateuch.

(d) The Essenes followed celibacy, isolation, silence, ceremonial ablutions and abstinence from animal food. They practised asceticism. They did worship of the sun and the angels. They believed in the dualistic theory of good and evil and the symbolism of light. They abstained from sacrifices and temple worship.

Torah

The Prophets of Israel were the great religious leaders who brought great progress in Behraic thought. Rabbis also were authoritative teachers. They worked very hard in the field of Torah. They produced the massive Talmudic literature. They were the representatives of Pharisiasm. Talmud is indispensable for a knowledge of Hebraic thought.

The Torah was given in ten words. Each word became a voice. Every voice was divided into 70 voices all of which shone and glittered before the eyes of all Israel. Torah denotes the divine revelation to Israel on Mount Senai as embodied in the five Books of Moses. The Torah (Law) as given to Moses consists of 613 commandments which are the essence of the divine and terrestrial mysteries. Torah indicates a way of life rather than a form of belief.

Moses received the Torah (Law, direction, instruction) on Senai and handed it down to Joshua, Joshua to the elders, the elders to the prophets and the prophets handed it down to the men of the Great Synagogue, a synod of zealous men created by Ezra, the Scribe in the fifth century B.C. The function of the synagogue was to study and teach Torah. The Synagogue was a church, a school and a court of justice. It was a house of instruction. The unity of God, the Incorporeality of God, and the Holiness of God are the main features of Judaism.

God gave His ten commandments to Moses on the Mount Senai. The Lord called unto him out of the mountain and said: "Thus shall thou say to the house of Jacob and tell the children of Israel".

The Ten Commandments

(i) I am the Lord Thy God, which have brought thee out of the land of Egypt, out of the house of bondage.

(ii) Thou shalt have no other gods before me. Thou shalt not make unto thee any graven image, or any likeness of anything that is in heaven above, or that is in the earth beneath, or that is in the water under the earth; thou shalt not bow down thyself to them, nor serve them; for I the Lord thy God am a jealous God, visiting the iniquity of the fathers upon the children unto the third and fourth generation of them that hate me and shewing mercy unto thousands of them that love me and keep my commandments.

(iii) Thou shalt not take the name of the Lord thy God in vain; for the Lord will not hold him guiltless that taketh his name in vain.

(iv) Remember the Sabbath-day, to keep it holy. Six days shalt thou labour and do all thy work; but the seventh day is the Sabbath of the Lord thy God; in it thou shalt not do any work, thou, nor thy son, nor thy daughter, nor thy man-servant, nor thy maid-servant, nor thy cattle, nor thy stranger that is within thy gates: for in six days the Lord made heaven and earth, the sea, and all that in them is, and rested the seventh day; wherefore the Lord blessed the Sabbath-day and hallowed it.

(v) Honour thy father and thy mother; that thy days may be long upon the land which the Lord thy God giveth thee.

(vi) Thou shalt not kill.

(vii) Thou shalt not commit adultery.

(viii) Thou shalt not bear false witness against thy neighbour.

(x) Thou shalt not covet thy neighbour's house, thou shalt not covet thy neighbour's wife, nor his man-servant, nor his maid-servant, nor his ox, nor his ass, nor anything that is thy neighbour's.

Mosaic Cosmogony

This is the Mosaic account of Cosmogony. On the first day heaven and earth were created; on the second, firmament and waters; on the third, dry land, grass, the birds and fruit trees; on the fourth, lights, the sun, the moon, the stars; on the fifth, moving creatures, winged fowls, great whales; on the sixth living creatures, cattle, creepers, beasts, man. In Genesis, the Creation ends with the creation of man. God created Adam on the sixth day and gave him the charge of the animals. Adam had three children viz., Cain, Abel and Sheth. Cain killed Abel. The descendants of Cain were drowned in the flood. The descendants of the Sheth are all the humanity of the world. The Lord took Adam and put him into the garden of Eden to till it and to keep it.

Tenets of Judaism

The Jews believe in resurrection, in angels, and in the existence of two powers, viz., God and the Devil or Satan.

The Jews believe that everyman's actions will be weighed on the day of Judgment in a balance. Men will have to pass after their resurrection along the bridge of Hell.

The unity of God is the cardinal principle of the religion of the Hebrews. God is bodiless. This is also a doctrine of great importance. God is ever pure and holy. This is third important attribute of God. He is the Creator of the entire world. He is the Father of all His creatures. He is just and merciful. He is without iniquity.

The Jewish saints have spoken much about the efficacy and power of repentance. Happy is the man who repents. The gates of repentance never close. Repentance prolongs a man's life. The tears of true repentance are not shed in vain. Even the most righteous shall not attain to so high a place in heaven as truly repentant. Repent one day sincerely with a contrite heart before you die. After repentance you should not repeat the same wicked act. Even an hour spent in repentance with a contrite heart in this world is preferable to a whole life in the world to come. The end and aim of all wisdom is repentance.

39. KARMA

Karma is a Sanskrit term that signifies action or deed. Any physical or mental action is Karma. Thinking is mental Karma. Karma is the sum total of our acts, both in the present life and in the preceding births.

Karma means not only action, but also the result of an action. The consequence of an action is really not a separate thing. It is a part of the action, and cannot be divided from it.

The Law of Karma means the law of causation. Wherever there is a cause, there an effect must be produced. A seed is a cause for the tree, which is the effect. The tree produces seeds, and becomes the cause for the seeds. The cause is found in the effect and the effect is found in the cause. The effect is similar to the cause. This is the universal chain of cause and effect which has no end.

No link in the chain is unnecessary. This world runs on this fundamental, vital law. This law is inexorable and immutable. This grand law operates everywhere in the physical and mental planes. No phenomenon can escape from the operation of this mighty law. All other laws of nature are subordinate to this fundamental law.

No event can occur without having a positive, definite cause at the back of it. The breaking of a war, the rise of a comet, the occurrence of an earthquake or a volcanic eruption, the breaking of an epidemic, thunder, lightning, floods, diseases in the body, fortune, misfortune, all have got definite causes behind them.

The grand law of causation includes the law of action and reaction, the law of compensation and the law of retribution. All these laws come under one general, all-embracing heading, viz., the Doctrine of Karma.

The Law of Action and Reaction

If there is an action, there must be a reaction. The reaction will be of equal force and of similar nature. Every thought, desire, imagination, sentiment causes reaction. Virtue brings its own reward; vice brings its own punishment. This is the working of the law of reaction.

God neither punishes the wicked nor rewards the virtuous. It is their own Karmas that bring reward and punishment. It is the law of action and reaction that brings the fruits. No one is to be blamed.

The law operates everywhere with unceasing precision and scientific accuracy. The law of action and reaction operates both in the physical and mental planes.

The Law of Compensation

The law of compensation operates everywhere in nature's phenomena. The seed breaks and a big tree comes out of the seed. There is no loss in the breaking of the seed. There comes out a tree in accordance with the law of compensation. Fuel burns. Fuel is destroyed. But there is heat, in accordance with the law of compensation. Many articles are cooked in the fire on account of the heat.

If there is extreme heat in Vijayawada, there is extreme cold in Mt. Kailas or Uttarkashi in the Himalayas. This is the law of compensation. If there are ten scoundrels in a place, there are two Sattvic souls to bring compensation. If there is flood-tide at Puri, there is an ebb-tide at Waltair. This is the law of compensation. If there is day in India, there is night in America. Peace follows a war and *vice versa.* This is the law of compensation. The law of compensation operates in the mental place also.

The law of compensation keeps up the balance and establishes peace, concord, equilibrium, harmony and justice in nature. Think deep. Cogitate. Reflect. You will see that this law of compensation is operating everywhere in the phenomena of nature beautifully. It is inexorable and immutable. No one can defy this relentless and irresistible law. If you do an evil act, you will reap a bad fruit in compensation.

If you take an individual life as an isolated event that beings with the birth of the physical body and terminates with its death, you cannot find any correct explanation or solution for the affairs of life. You will be groping in darkness and despair. Your present life is nothing, when compared with the whole soul-life. It is momentary. It is a mere fragment. Whenever you want to find out the cause or antecedent of anything, you will have to go deep into the affairs of the eternal soul-life. Then alone there will be perfect balance of cause and effect, antecedent and consequence. You will have to judge from a broad view of the eternal soul-life. The law of compensation embraces a wide range of the whole soul-life. Life does not end with the disintegration of this physical body alone.

There is reincarnation. There had been countless previous lives also. You will have to take into consideration the widest view of the life of the soul. Then the line is quite clear. Then you will find a perfect, satisfactory solution for all the intricate and complicated affairs of life. Then there will be no room for grumbling or lamentation or misapprehension.

The Law of Retribution

Every wrong action or crime brings its own punishment in accordance with the law of retribution. The law of causation, the law of action and reaction, the law of compensation and the law of retribution—all operate together. He who robs another man, robs himself first. He who hurts another man hurts himself first. He who cheats another man cheats himself first.

Remember that God is neither partial nor unjust. Remember that God is not responsible for the wealth of a man or the poverty of another. You suffer on account of your own wicked actions.

There is nothing chaotic or capricious in this world. Things do not happen in this universe by accident or chance in a disorderly manner. They happen in regular succession. They follow each other in a regular order. There is a certain definite connection between what is being done now by you and what will happen in the future. Sow always the seeds which will bring pleasant fruits and which will make you happy herein and hereafter.

How Karma Is Fashioned

Man is threefold in his nature. He consists of Ichha, Jnana and Kriya. Ichha is desire or feeling. Jnana is knowing. Kriya is willing. These three fashion his Karma. He knows objects like chair, tree, etc. He feels joy and sorrow. He wills—to do this, or not to do that.

Behind the action, there are desire and thought. A desire for an object arises in the mind. Then you think how to get it. Then you exert to possess it. Desire, thought and action always go together. They are the three threads, as it were, that are twisted into the cord of Karma.

Desire produces Karma. You work and exert to acquire the objects of your desire. Karma produces its fruits as pain or pleasure. You will have to take births after births to reap the fruits of your Karmas. This is the Law of Karma.

Sanchita, Prarabdha and Kriyamana

Karma is of three kinds, viz., Sanchita or the accumulated works, Prarabdha or the fructifying works and Kriyamana or the current works.

Sanchita is all the accumulated Karmas of the past. Part of it is seen in the character of man, in his tendencies and aptitudes, capacities, inclinations and desires.

Prarabdha is that portion of the past Karma which is responsible for the present body. It is ripe for reaping. It cannot be avoided or changed. It is only exhausted by being experienced. You pay your past debts.

Kriyamana is that Karma which is now being done for the future. It is also called Agami or Vartamana.

In Vedantic literature, there is a beautiful analogy. The bow-man has already sent an arrow; it has left his hands. He cannot recall it. He is about to shoot another arrow. The bundle of arrows in the quiver on his back is the Sanchita. The arrow he has shot is Prarabdha. And the arrow which he is about to shoot from his bow is Agami. Of these, he has perfect control over the Sanchita and Agami, but he must surely work out his Prarabdha. The past which has begun to take effect he has to experience.

Prarabdha cannot be prevented even by Isvara or the Lord. Even Nala, Rama and Yudhishthira who had great powers and wisdom had to undergo this Prarabdha. Nala did not want to go to the forest. and yet he was forced to go. His Karma compelled him. Lord Rama alone was to be installed as the King of Ayodhya. He was forced to enter the forest. Gandhiji wanted to live for one hundred and twenty years; he did not like himself to be shot down. And yet, Prarabdha Karma brought about this event.

Destiny and Self-effort

Even if the Law of Karma is inexorable, there is the scope for divine grace. Grace comes through penitence, austerity and devotion. Penitence does not alter the Law of Karma. It is an act that has its fruit like any other act.

What one has to reap cannot be altered by the individual; but, its recurrence can certainly be checked by self-effort.

Self-effort is Purushartha. Destiny is Prarabdha. Prarabdha is only Purushartha which is done in previous births. The self-effort of today becomes the destiny of tomorrow. Self-effort and destiny are one and the same. Prarabdha and Purushartha are one. They are two names which indicate only one thing. Just as the present becomes the past and the future becomes the present, just as there is only the present, so also, there is only Purushartha. When God works through man, it is Purushartha. Grace becomes Purushartha.

Rainfall, etc., are not under human control. Yet, a farmer ploughs his fields; he exercises Purushartha or self-effort. The crop may fail due to lack of rain. Still, man does not lose heart. He performs sacrifices for getting rain and reaps a good harvest. Similarly, Yoga-practice is self-effort to neutralise evil Prarabdha which obstructs Atma-Sakshatkara. If Prarabdha is powerful, Yoga is more powerful than Prarabdha.

Every soul is like a husbandman who has got a plot of land. The acreage, the nature of the soil, the conditions of weather are all predetermined. But the husbandman is quite at liberty to till the earth, manure it and get good crops, or to allow it to remain as a waste land.

Prarabdha concerns the past only. The future is in your hands. You can change your destiny. You have a free will to act.

Have a new angle of vision. Arm yourself with discrimination, cheerfulness, discernment, alacrity and undaunted spirit. A glorious brilliant future is awaiting you. Let the past be buried. You can work miracles. You can do wonders. Do not give up hope. You can destroy the harmful effects of unfavourable planets through your will-force. You can command the elements and nature. You can neutralise the effect of the evil influences and the antagonistic dark forces that may operate against you. You can change the unfavourable circumstances into best possible ones. You can nullify destiny.

Destiny is your own creation. You have created your destiny through thoughts and actions. You can undo the same by right thinking and right action. Even if there is an evil or a dark antagonistic force to attack you, you can diminish its force by resolutely turning your mind away from it. Thus you can disarm destiny.

Do not say: "Karma, Karma. My Karma has brought me like

this". Exert. Exert. Do Purushartha. Do Tapas. Concentrate. Purify. Meditate. Do not become a fatalist. Do not yield to inertia. Do not bleat like a lamb. Roar *Om, Om, Om* like a lion of Vedanta. See how Markandeya who was destined to die at his sixteenth year became a *Chiranjivi,* an immortal boy of sixteen years, on account of his Tapas. Also note how Savitri brought back to life by her Tapas her dead husband, how Benjamin Franklin and the late Sri T. Muthuswami Aiyer of the Madras High Court elevated themselves. Remember, friends, that man is a master of his destiny. Visvamitra Rishi, who was a Kshatriya Raja, became a Brahmarshi like Vasishtha and even created a third world for Trisanku by his power of Tapas. Rogue Ratnakar became the sage Valmiki through Tapas. Rogues Jagai and Madai of Bengal became highly developed saints. They became the disciples of Lord Gouranga-Nityananda. What others have done, you can also do. There is no doubt of this.

How Destiny Is Built Up

Thought is Karma. Thinking is the real Karma. Thought moulds your character. Thought materialises and becomes an action. If you allow the mind to dwell on good, elevating thoughts, you will develop a noble character; you will do naturally good and laudable actions. If you entertain evil thoughts, you will develop a base character. This is the immutable law of nature. Therefore, you can deliberately shape your character by cultivating sublime thoughts.

You sow an action and reap a habit. You sow a habit and reap a character. You sow a character and reap your destiny. Hence, destiny is your own make-up. You have built it. You can undo it by entertaining noble thoughts and doing virtuous actions and changing your mode of thinking.

The impressions of small and big acts coalesce together and form tendencies. The tendencies develop into character. Character produces will. If a man has a strong character, he has a strong will. Karma produces character, and character in turn produces will. People of gigantic will have developed their will through Karma done in countless births. It is not in one birth that a man develops a mighty will. He does various good actions in several births. The potencies of these actions collect together and in one birth the struggling man bursts out as a giant like Buddha, Jesus and Sankara. No action goes in vain. Nothing is lost. Patient, indefatigable effort is needed. You will have to watch every thought, word and action.

Man's will is ever free. Through selfishness his will has become impure. He can render his will pure, strong and dynamic by getting rid of his base desires and likes and dislikes.

Man Is Master of His Destiny

You are *not* a creature of environment or circumstance. You are the master of your own fate. You are the architect of your own fortune. You are responsible for what you suffer. You are responsible for your present state. If you are unhappy, it has been your own making. If you are miserable, it has also been your own making. Every action bears a fruit sooner or later. A virtuous action produces pleasure as its effect. An evil deed causes pain.

Charity in your past life gives you riches in the present life. Service of humanity in your past life makes you a famous leader in the present life. Strong thoughts of your past life make your character in the present life. Tendencies of your past life become your capacities in the present life. Virtuous deeds of your past life give you good environments in the present life. Experiences of your past life make your conscience in this present life. Selfless actions of your past life give you discrimination, dispassion, aspiration in this present life, through the Lord's grace.

If you oppress a man, you will suffer oppression in another life and reap the fruit of the seed you have sown in this life. If you injure the eye of a man, your eye will be injured in another life. If you break the leg of a man, your leg will be broken in another life. If you feed the poor, you will have plenty of food in another life. If you build rest-houses, you will have many houses in another life. Action and reaction are equal and opposite. There is no power on this earth which can stop the actions from yielding their fruits. Such is the Law of Karma. Such is the law of birth and death. Such is the circle through which you must pass on your way.

Three Kinds of Action

Actions are of three kinds, viz., good, bad and mixed. Good Karmas make you a god or angel in heaven. Bad Karmas throw you in lower wombs. Mixed actions give you a human birth. If you rob a man and feed the poor, it is a mixed action. If you earn money by unlawful means and build a temple or a hospital, this is a mixed action. If you get money by cheating a man and construct an Ashram for Sannyasins, this is also a mixed action.

Every work is a mixture of good and evil. There can be neither absolute good work nor absolute bad work in this world. This physical universe is a relative place. If you do some action, it will do some good in one corner, and some evil in another corner. You must try to do such actions that can bring the maximum of good and the minimum of evil.

Veracity of the Law of Karma

The Doctrine of Karma forms an integral part of Vedanta. The Law of Karma is one of the fundamental doctrines not only in Hinduism, but also in Buddhism and Jainism.

As a man sows, so shall he reap. This is the Law of Karma. It expounds the riddle of life and the riddle of the universe. It brings solace, satisfaction and comfort to one and all. It is a self-evident truth. Fortunately, the Westerners have also begun now to acknowledge its importance and veracity. The Americans have now full belief in this doctrine. Every sensible man will have to accept it. There is no other go.

A close study of this law gives encouragement to the hopeless man, to the desperate and the ailing. Destiny is created by man's thoughts, habits and character. There is every chance for his correction and improvement by changing his thoughts and habits. The scoundrel can become a saint; the prostitute can become a chaste lady; a beggar can become a king. The mighty law provides for all this.

The Doctrine of Karma only can explain the mysterious problem of good and evil in this world. The Doctrine of Karma only can bring solace, contentment, peace and strength to the afflicted and the desperate. It solves our difficulties and problems of life. It gives encouragement to the hopeless and the forlorn. It pushes a man to right thinking, right speech and right action. It brings a brilliant future for that man who lives according to this universal law. If all people understand this law correctly and discharge their daily duties carefully, they would rise to sublime heights in the ladder of spirituality. They will be moral and virtuous and have a happy, peaceful, contented life. They can bear the burden of Samsara with patience, endurance and strength of mind. There will not be any room for complaint when they see the inequalities in birth, fortune, intelligence, capacities, etc. There will be heaven on earth. All will rejoice even in suffering. Greed, jealousy, hatred, anger, passion will vanish. Virtue will reign everywhere. We will have a glorious Satya Yuga now with peace and plenty everywhere. Blessed is the man who understands and lives in the Law, for he will soon attain God-consciousness and become one with the Law-giver! Then the Law will no longer operate on him.

40. KRISHNA

The auspicious hour came. The star Rohini was shining. It was Vijaya Muhurta. The elements were extremely pleasant. Winds were blowing auspiciously. The stars were shining with lustre. The lakes were filled with lotuses. Lord Krishna incarnated at midnight on this earth. The gods played divine music. The Kinnaras and Gandharvas sang. Siddhas and Charanas praised. The Vidyadharas danced along with the Apsarasas, sages and Devas. There was a rain of flowers from the heavens in joy.

Vishnu incarnated with lotus eyes, with four hands armed with conch, disc, mace and lotus, with the mark Srivatsa adorning the chest. Vasudeva saw this marvel of a divine child.

Vasudeva praised Him: "Thou art known to me already as the Supreme Being. Thou art an embodiment of knowledge and bliss. Thou art seated in the hearts of all beings. Thou art the witness of the minds of all. Thou art beyond Maya and Avidya".

Devaki beheld marks of Vishnu on her son and praised Him: "Thou art beginningless, Omnipresent, self-luminous, attributeless, changeless and actionless. Thou art the source and place of dissolution, for everything. Kindly do not show me this form with four hands. Let me see You as an ordinary child. Withdraw this divine, transcendental form. We are afraid of Kamsa".

The Lord said: "Let both of you often meditate with love on Me as a son and as the Supreme Being, and you will obtain eternal bliss and immortality".

The Lord assumed the form of a handsome baby through the power of His own Maya.

The Purna Avatara

Lord Krishna was the highest incarnation of the great Vishnu. He was the Purna Avatara. He had all the sixteen Kalas or rays of the Lord. He was a noble scion of the illustrious Yadava dynasty. He was the world-teacher. He was the one Lord of love. He was the lover of men. His enchanting form, with flute in hand, holds the heart of India captive in chains even today.

The object of Sri Krishna's Avatara was three-fold—to destroy the wicked demons, to take the leading part in the great war fought on the battlefield of Kurukshetra where He delivered His wonderful message of the Gita, and to become the centre of a marvellous development of the Bhakti Schools of India.

The purpose of the Krishna-avatara was not only to destroy Adharma, but also to reveal to the world the magnificence of God. Sri Krishna was the symbol of the Absolute, the representation of the mighty Sovereign of the universe. In His well-adjusted, symmetrical conduct of life is portrayed the majestic perfection of God.

Sri Krishna's life is the Bhagavad-Gita in action. In Him are found the supreme knowledge and the supreme power blending to form the God-man of all times. In Him the highest Vidya and Vinaya coexist, as inseparable virtues of the Great Hero of the world.

Sri Krishna was a perfect Master. He was a Karma Yogi, Bhakta, Raja Yogi and Jnana Yogi. He preached Karma, Upasana, Yoga and Jnana. Lord Sri Krishna drove the chariot in the battle-field, and danced with the Gopis in the shady retreats of Vrindavana, and taught Yoga and Jnana to Uddhava and Arjuna. The four Yogas are blended in His Gita or the Immortal Song.

Lord Krishna was great in knowledge, great in emotion, great in action, altogether. The scriptures have not recorded any life more full, more intense, more sublime, more grand than His.

The Bhagavad-Gita contains the teachings of Sri Krishna to Arjuna. It is a wonderful book for constant study. Aspirants study this book with great care daily. The first six chapters deal with Karma Yoga and represent the 'Tat' Pada of the "Tat Tvam Asi" Mahavakya. The next six chapters deal with Bhakti Yoga and represent the 'Tvam' Pada. The last six chapters deal with Jnana Yoga and represent the 'Asi' Pada.

Student Days with Sage Sandipani

Sri Krishna received His instructions from Sandipani, a sage of Avantipur. He lived with His teacher like an ordinary student. He was meek, humble and obedient. He led a laborious life. He gathered fuel from the woods for His preceptor's household. He inspired His class-mates with love.

Sri Krishna had wonderful retentive memory. He mastered the sixty-four arts in sixty-four days.

The Lord's Life of Selfless Action

Krishna was a man of action. He was a history-maker and righter of wrongs. He stood for justice and righteousness. His policy was to defend the oppressed from the oppressor.

Lord Krishna was the greatest Karma Yogi of all time. He held up the torch of wisdom. He was an embodiment of wisdom and selfless action.

He was all love for the cowherd boys, cows and Gopis. He was the friend and benefactor of the poor and the helpless. He was extremely kind and merciful towards the meek and the humble.

Krishna was the thunderbolt to the wrestlers assembled in the arena of Kamsa, and yet, He had the softest heart among men. He was Yama unto Kamsa, a Cupid unto Gopis, the object of constant meditation for Yogins and devotees, the form of bliss and beatitude to the sages, and a child to His parents. He was Cupid unto Cupid Himself.

Lord Krishna was an embodiment of humility, though He was the Lord of the universe. He became the charioteer of Arjuna. He accepted the duty of washing the feet of the visitors voluntarily at the time of the Rajasuya Yajna performed by Yudhishthira.

A Great Statesman

Sri Krishna was a great statesman. The world has not witnessed a great statesman than Sri Krishna. He was a champion of liberty and a peace-maker. He had wonderful foresight, and held extremely liberal views. Even when He was a boy, He taught people the essentials and the true significance of religion when He rose against the popular worship of Indra for getting rains.

Krishna was a king-maker. He was the founder of the city of Dvaraka. He was the towering genius of His age. He was a great historical figure.

He was appointed as peace-maker to stop the civil war that was to be fought between the Kauravas and the Pandavas. Yudhishthira sent Krishna to negotiate with the Kauravas. Krishna made a long and wise exhortation to Duryodhana. The thrilling and soul-stirring speech delivered by Sri Krishna before the court of Dhritarashtra proves that He was the greatest statesman. He said to Duryodhana: "O Prince of the Bharata race! Make peace with the wise, brave and righteous Pandavas. Peace alone brings happiness to friends, relations and the whole world. He who does not act according to the wise instructions of his friends meets with destruction and sorrow".

Sri Krishna's political insight and wise statesmanship were admired by the ablest rulers of His time. His wise counsel was sought by kings and rulers.

Lord of the Yogins

You can count even the stars and the particles of sand on the seashore, but it is not possible to count the marvellous and heroic deeds and glorious actions of Sri Krishna, the Lord of the three worlds.

When He was a child, He did countless miracles. He showed Visvarupa to His mother, Yasoda, in His mouth while He yawned. He uprooted the Yamala Arjuna trees. He danced on the Kaliya serpent. He raised the Govardhana Hills on His little finger to protect Gokula from the heavy rains caused by Indra.

He multiplied Himself into various forms, when Brahma kept the Gopas and calves away from Krishna's view. He multiplied Himself and appeared in countless forms in the Rasa-lila. Can a human being do this? It is only a Yogesvara who can perform these great miracles.

Krishna gave eyesight to the blind Vilvamangal. He gave unlimited clothes to Draupadi. He gave cosmic vision to Arjuna.

Who can describe the glory of Lord Krishna, Lord of the Yogins and the Supreme Lord of the three worlds, the Soul of the universe? Durvasa and his countless disciples were satisfied when Lord Krishna ate a small particle of vegetable. This itself clearly proves that Lord Krishna is the one Soul that dwell in all beings.

The sage Narada wished to find out how Krishna could lead a happy, married life with His sixteen thousand wives. He visited their mansions, and found Krishna in every one of their homes engaged in a variety of duties. What a great marvel! Narada was stunned. Does this not prove that Krishna is the Lord of Yogins and is Lord Hari Himself?

Krishna is the Lord of all beings. He is, in fact, the husband of all women in this world. The real husband is the Lord only. It is to demonstrate this to the world that Lord Krishna incarnated Himself as the son of Devaki and Vasudeva.

An Embodiment of Love and Mercy

Lord Krishna is styled as one who steals butter, because He used to eat stealthily the butter in the houses of the Gopis on account of His extreme love for them. This stealing of butter was a sort of sport or Lila when He was a boy, to instil delight in the hearts of the Gopis who were His devotees. The Gopis liked this immensely. They were eagerly expecting Krishna to come and eat their butter. Krishna really steals or captivates the hearts of His devotees, makes them forget the world, draws their minds towards His blessed feet, and makes them enjoy everlasting peace and bliss.

Krishna had the Bhava of mother even for Putana who came to kill Him, and gave her salvation. He gave salvation even to His bitterest enemies, Kamsa and Sisupala who insulted Him openly in the Rajasuya Yajna. Then, what to speak of those who are highly devoted to Him?

The Lord's Teachings

Sri Krishna was the friend of Arjuna and Uddhava. His immortal teachings to Arjuna and Uddhava on Yoga, Bhakti and Jnana are unique. They even now stir the hearts of the readers and goad them towards the spiritual path, and instil peace into their hearts.

Arjuna had various kinds of doubts. Lord Krishna cleared his doubts one by one. He pushed Arjuna up in the ladder of Yoga from one rung to another rung. Ultimately Arjuna placed his step in the highest rung of the ladder, attained Knowledge of the Self, and then exclaimed in joy, "O my Lord! My delusion is destroyed. I have attained Knowledge through Thy grace. I am firm now. My doubts have vanished now *in toto*. I will act according to Thy word".

Sri Krishna asked man to consider himself a doll in the hands of God. He asked man to think himself a soldier, God as his great general, his worldly acts as duties under orders. He asked him to act on the faith and belief that whatever he does is the work of God. He asked man to act, but act only with devotion to God without desire for fruits.

The teachings given by Lord Krishna to Uddhava on the eve of His departure from this world are wonderful. He gives instructions on a variety of subjects. But the one ringing note is: "See Me in everything. Surrender yourself to me. Do all actions for My sake. Cut off all sorts of attachments. Have perfect unswerving devotion to Me. Sing My glories".

Call of the Flute

The flute is the symbol of the Pranava. It is this flute that attracted the devoted Gopis, the maidens of Vraja, to meet their beloved Lord on the banks of the sacred Yamuna. The sound of this divine flute thrilled the heart with rapturous delight, and instilled new life and joy. It produced God-intoxication in all beings and infused life even in insentient objects. The sweetness of the music was unsurpassed. He who heard once the music of Krishna's flute cared not for the nectar of heaven or the bliss of Moksha.

The Lord's flute and its music had stirred the souls of the Gopis. They lost all control over themselves. The world was nothing to them. They felt irresistibly drawn towards Sri Krishna. They had neither shame nor fear in leaving their homes. There was a soul-awakening in them. Their mind was not of this world. Their husbands and brothers stopped them in vain. Who can resist the torrent of divine love for the Lord?

The love that the Gopis bore towards Krishna was a divine love. It was the union of souls. It is no union of sex. It is the aspiration of the Jivatman to merge in the Paramatman. It is the blending of the individual soul with the Supreme Soul.

The Gopis were the sages of Dandaka forest in their previous births. At that time, they wished to embrace Lord Rama. They were promised satisfaction in the later Avatara. They got blended into the Paramatman in the Krishna-avatara.

Krishna has preached Prem through His flute. Radha asked Krishna: "O my dear! Why do You love the flute more than me? What virtuous actions has it done so that it can remain in close contact with Your lips? Kindly explain to me, my Lord, the secret of this. I am eager to hear". Sri Krishna said: "This flute is very dear to Me. It has got some wonderful virtues. It has emptied off its egoism. It has made its inner hollow quite void and I can bring out any kind of tune, Raga or Ragini, to My pleasure and sweet will. If you also behave towards Me in exactly the same manner as this flute, if you remove your egoism completely and make perfect self-surrender, then I shall also love you in the same manner as I love this flute".

This body also is the flute of Lord Krishna in the macrocosm. If you can destroy your egoism and make total self-surrender, unreserved Atma-nivedana to the Lord, He will play on this body-flute nicely and bring out melodious tunes. Your will will become merged in His will. He will work unhampered through your instruments, body, mind and Indriyas. You can rest very peacefully then without cares, worries and anxieties.

O my dear children of Immortality! Lord Krishna is still roaming about in the gullies of Vrindavana. Just as Lord Dattatreya is still moving about with His astral body in the reputed Girnar Hills and gives Darsana even now to His sincere Bhaktas, just as Sri Jnana Dev is still moving about with his astral body in Alandi, near Poona, and gives Darsana even now to His sincere devotees, so also, Lord Krishna is still moving about in Vrindavana and gives Darsana to His sincere Bhaktas. You can find Him in the Seva Kunja in the Kunja gullies if you really want Him. He is the Brij Raj, the unprecedented Monarch of the three worlds. He is waiting with outstretched hands to embrace you with His warm love in His sweet bosom as He did with Mira, Surdas and others in days of yore. Purify your mind. Destroy your evil Vasanas and egoism. Hear once more the flute of the Bansiwala, Bankibehari of Vrindavana, His immortal song of the Gita, and allow Him to play in this body-flute of yours. Lose not this rare opportunity. It is very difficult to get this human body.

41. KUNDALINI

Behind all activity, there is a static background. Behind energy, there is consciousness. Behind Sakti, there is Siva.

Sakti itself has two polar aspects, static and dynamic. You cannot have Sakti in a dynamic form without at the same time having it in a static form, much like the poles of a magnet.

The Cosmic Sakti manifests in the human body as Kundalini and Prana. Kundalini is the static support for the moving Pranic forces.

Man is a microcosm or Kshudra Brahmanda. Whatever exists in the outer universe exists in him. All things seen in the universe, mountains, rivers, Bhutas, etc., exist in the body also. All the Tattvas and Lokas are within the body and so are the supreme Siva-Sakti.

In the human body, Siva resides in the Sahasrara Chakra at the crown of the head. Kundalini resides in the Muladhara Chakra, at the base of the spinal column. 'Muladhara' means 'root-support.' Kundalini is the power which is the static of the whole body and all its moving Pranic forces.

The Nature of Kundalini

Kundalini is the primordial energy that lies in the basal Muladhara Chakra in a dormant, potential state. It is the cosmic power in the individual bodies. It is an electric, fiery occult power, the mighty pristine force underlying all organic and inorganic matter. 'Kundala' means 'coiled.' Her form is like a coiled serpent. Hence the name Kundalini.

Kundalini is not a material force like electricity or magnetism. It is a spiritual potential Sakti. In reality, it has no form. The gross intellect and mind have to follow a particular form in the beginning stage. From this gross form, one can easily understand the subtle formless Kundalini.

Kundalini is also called Bhujangini or the Serpent Power, on account its spiral-like working in the body of the Yogi developing the power in himself. When it is awakened, it makes a hissing sound like that of a serpent beaten with a stick, and proceeds to rise upwards through the Brahma Nadi within the Sushumna.

In Kundalini Yoga, the creating and sustaining Sakti of the whole body is actually and truly united with Lord Siva. The Yogi goads

Her to introduce him to Her Lord. The rousing of the Kundalini Sakti and Her union with Lord Siva in the Sahasrara effects the state of Samadhi and spiritual Anubhava. The Yogic student drinks the nectar of immortality.

Kundalini Yoga is an exact science. This is also known as Laya Yoga.

Nadis and Chakras

A detailed knowledge of the Nadis and the Chakras is of paramount importance for all students of Kundalini Yoga.

The physical body is shaped in accordance with the nature of the astral body. The physical body is something like water. It is the gross form. The astral body corresponds to steam or vapour. It is the subtle form. In the same way, the astral body or Sukshma Sarira is within the gross or physical body. The gross body cannot do anything without the astral body. Every gross centre of the body has its astral centre.

Nadis are psychic nerves or astral tubes for carrying Prana. They are made up of astral matter that carry psychic currents. It is through these subtle passages that the vital force moves or flows. Since the Nadis are made up of subtle matter, they cannot be seen by naked physical eyes, and you cannot make any test-tube experiment in the physical plane. These Yoga Nadis are not the ordinary nerves, arteries and veins that are known to the Vaidya Sastra. Yoga Nadis are quite different from these.

The body is filled with innumerable Nadis that cannot be counted. As the leaf of the Asvattha tree is covered with minute fibres, so also, this body is permeated with thousands of Nadis.

All the Nadis of the body spring from the Kanda. Kanda means a bulb. Kanda is the root of all the Nadis. Two fingers above the anus and two fingers below the organ of generation is the Kanda. It is like the bird's egg in shape and of four fingers' breadth in extent. Seventy-two thousand Nadis come out of the Kanda.

Kanda is a centre of the astral body. Corresponding to this centre, you have *cauda equina* in the gross physical body.

Of all the Nadis that spring from Kanda, Ida, Pingala and Sushumna are the most important. And Sushumna is the chief. Sushumna extends from the Muladhara Chakra to Brahmarandhra.

It is the highest and most sought by the Yogins. Other Nadis are subordinate to this.

Western anatomy admits that there is a central canal in the spinal cord, called *canalis centralis,* and that the cord is made up of grey and white brain-matter. The spinal cord itself is dropped or suspended in the hollow of the spinal column. In the same way, the Sushumna is dropped within the spinal canal and has subtle sections. It is of red colour like fire.

Within this Sushumna, there is a Nadi by name Vajra, which is lustrous as the sun, with Rajasic qualities. Again, within this Vajra Nadi, there is another Nadi, called Chitra. It is of Sattvic nature and of pale colour. Here, within this Chitra, there is a very fine, minute canal. This canal is known as Brahma Nadi through which Kundalini, when awakened, passes from the Muladhara to the Sahasrara Chakra. In this Nadi exists all the six Chakras or lotuses.

Chakras are plexuses or centres of Sukshma Prana in the Sushumna Nadi. All the functions of the body are under the control of these centres. Chakras are subtle centres of vital energy. These are the centres of Chaitanya or consciousness. The Chakras are in the astral body even after the disintegration of the physical organism at death.

These Chakras or subtle centres have corresponding centres in the spinal cord and the nerve-plexuses in the gross physical body. For example, Anahata Chakra has its corresponding centre in the physical body at the Cardiac Plexus. Each Chakra has control and function over a particular centre in the gross body.

The gross nerves and plexuses have close relationship with the subtle ones. Since the physical centres have close relationship with the astral centres, the vibrations that are produced in the physical centres by prescribed methods have the desired effects in the astral centres.

The first attempt on the part of the Kundalini Yogi is the purification of Nadis which will lead to the opening of the Sushumna which generally remains closed up in all worldly-minded people.

How Kundalini Can Be Awakened

Before awakening the Kundalini, you must have Deha Suddhi,

Nadi Suddhi, Mana Suddhi, Buddhi Suddhi, Bhuta Suddhi and Adhara Suddhi. Deha Suddhi is purity of body. Nadi Suddhi is purification of the astral tubes. Mana Suddhi is purity of mind. Buddhi Suddhi is purity of intellect. Bhuta Suddhi is purification of the elements. Adhara Suddhi is purification of the Adhara. If there is Suddhi or purification, Siddhi or perfection will come by itself. Siddhi is not possible without Suddhi.

One should become perfectly desireless and should be full of Vairagya before attempting to awaken the Kundalini. If a man with a lot of impurities in the mind awakens the Sakti by sheer force through Asanas, Pranayamas and Mudras, he will break his legs and stumble down. He will not be able to ascend the Yogic ladder. This is the chief reason for people going out of the way or getting some bodily infirmities. There is nothing wrong in the Yoga. People must have purity first; then a thorough knowledge of the Sadhana, a proper guide and a steady, gradual practice. When Kundalini is awakened, there are many temptations on the way, and a Sadhaka without purity will not have the strength to resist.

A Guru is essential. For the practice of Bhakti Yoga and Vedanta, you do not require a Guru by your side. After learning the Srutis for some time from a Guru, you will have to reflect and meditate alone, in entire seclusion, whereas in Kundalini Yoga, you will have to understand thoroughly the location of the Nadis, Chakras, and the detailed technique of the several Yogic Kriyas. These are all the difficult processes. You will have to sit at the Guru's feet for a pretty long time.

Kundalini can be awakened by Pranayama, Asanas and Mudras by Hatha Yogis; by concentration and training of the mind by Raja Yogis; by devotion and perfect self-surrender by Bhaktas; by analytical will by the Jnanis; by Mantras by Tantrikas; and by the grace of the Guru through touch, sight, or mere Sankalpa.

For a selected few, any one of the above methods is quite sufficient to awaken the Kundalini. Many will have to combine different methods.

The Awakening of the Kundalini

As soon as Kundalini is awakened, it pierces the Muladhara Chakra. The aspirant sings and makes peculiar sounds when the Kundalini is awakened. He experiences various sorts of visions and

Divya Gandha. He develops psychic powers. He sees a brilliant Jyotis as if ten thousand suns shine at the same time in the Muladhara.

After Kundalini is awakened, mind, Prana, Jiva, and Kundalini move together in the upward ascent. Prana passes upwards through the Brahma Nadi along with mind and Agni. The Yogi is freed from physical consciousness. You are shut out from the external objective world.

Experiences on the Awakening of the Kundalini Sakti

During meditation, you behold divine visions, experience divine smell, divine taste, divine touch, hear divine Anahata sounds. You receive instructions from God. These indicate that the Kundalini Sakti has been awakened. When there is throbbing in the Muladhara, when hairs stand on their roots, when Uddiyana, Jalandhara and Mula Bandha come involuntarily, know that Kundalini has awakened.

When the breath stops without any effort, when Kevala Kumbhaka comes by itself without any exertion, know that Kundalini Sakti has become active. When you feel currents of Prana rising up to the Sahasrara, when you experience bliss, when you repeat Om automatically, when there are no thoughts of the world in the mind, know that Kundalini Sakti has awakened.

When in your meditation, the eyes become fixed on Trikuti, the middle of the eyebrows, when the Sambhavi Mudra operates, know that Kundalini has become active. When you feel vibrations of Prana in different parts inside your body, when you experience jerks like the shocks of electricity, know that Kundalini become active. During meditation when you feel as if there is no body, when your eye-lids become closed and do not open in spite of your exertion, when electric-like currents flow up and down the nerves, know that Kundalini has awakened.

When you meditate, when you get inspiration and insight, when the nature unfolds its secrets to you, all doubts disappear, you understand clearly the meaning of the Vedic texts, know that Kundalini has become active. When your body becomes light like air, when you have a balanced mind in perturbed conditions, when you possess inexhaustible energy for work, know that Kundalini has become active.

When you get divine intoxication, when you develop power of oration, know that Kundalini has awakened. When you involuntarily perform different Asanas or poses of Yoga without the least pain or fatigue, know that Kundalini has become active. When you compose beautiful sublime hymns and poetry involuntarily, know that Kundalini has become active.

The Upward Ascent of the Kundalini Sakti

When the Kundalini is awakened, it does not directly proceed all at once to the Sahasrara Chakra. You will have to take it from one Chakra to another.

There are six Chakras in the Sushumna. These are the Muladhara, Svadhishthana, Manipura, Anahata, Visuddha and Ajna. Above all these there is the Sahasrara, the chief of all the centres. All the Chakras are intimately connected with the Sahasrara Chakra. Hence it is not included in as one among the six Chakras.

The Muladhara Chakra is at the base of the spinal column. Svadhishthana is at the root of the genitals. Manipura is at the navel. Anahata is in the heart. Visuddha is in the throat. Ajna is in the Trikuti, the space between the two eyebrows.

The seven Chakras correspond to the seven Lokas. The five Chakras from Muladhara to Visuddha are the centres of the five elements. Ajna is the seat of the mind.

If the Yogic student pierces the Muladhara, he has conquered the earth. Earth cannot affect him. If he crosses the Svadhishthana, he has conquered the element water. He is in touch with Bhuvarloka. If he has crossed the Manipura, he has conquered the fire. Fire cannot affect him. He is in touch with Svarga-loka. If he has crossed the Anahata Chakra, he has conquered the element air. Air cannot affect him. He is in touch with Mahar-loka. If he has crossed the Visuddha Chakra, he has conquered the element ether. Ether cannot affect him. He is in touch with Jana-loka. If he has crossed the Ajna Chakra, he is in touch with Tapo-loka. Then he enters the Satya-loka.

There are four routes to Sahasrara for the Kundalini Sakti to pass. The longest route runs from Muladhara to Sahasrara along the back. The Yogi who takes the Kundalini along this path is very powerful. This is the most difficult route. In Sri Sankaracharya, the Kundalini passed along this route. The shortest route is from the

Ajna Chakra to Sahasrara. The third is from the heart to Sahasrara. The fourth route runs from Muladhara to Sahasrara in front.

If the Yogi concentrates on the Ajna Chakra, the lower Chakras are automatically opened and conquered.

The Kundalini current rises through the spine and sometimes crawls like an ant. Sometimes, when the Yogi is pure, it jumps like a monkey and reaches the Sahasrara. Sometimes it rises like a bird that hops from one branch to another. Sometimes the spiritual current rises up like a snake and moves in a zig-zag manner. Sometimes the Yogi swims happily like a fish in the ocean of divine bliss.

The Yogic practitioner will get help from within when he moves from Chakra to Chakra. A mysterious power, a mysterious voice, will guide him at every step. He should have perfect, unshakable faith in the Divine Mother. It is She who guides the Sadhaka. It is She who takes Her child from Chakra to Chakra. She invisibly renders him all assistance. Without Her grace, you cannot move an inch in your ascent in the Sushumna.

Kundalini does not stay for a long time in the Sahasrara. The duration of stay depends upon the purity, degree of Sadhana, and inner spiritual strength of the Yogic practitioner. Many students stay in the lower Chakras only. They are carried away by the happiness they get in the lower Chakras and so they do not attempt further to reach the Sahasrara on account of the false satisfaction and content.

The Yogi is tempted in the lower Chakras or resting places. He should shun all Siddhis. Siddhis are obstacles in his path. If he begins to play with the Siddhis he will miss the goal and get downfall.

It is easy to awaken the Kundalini, but it is very difficult to take it up to the navel, to the Ajna Chakra, and thence to the Sahasrara in the head. It demands a great deal of patience and persistence on the part of the practitioner. There is a great deal of difficulty in piercing the Manipura Chakra. The Yogi has to exert a lot in this centre.

The body will exist even after Kundalini has reached the Sahasrara Chakra, but the Yogi will have no body-consciousness. It is only when Kaivalya is attained that the body becomes lifeless.

You will certainly live even after the Kundalini is taken to the Sahasrara. But remember that even after it is taken to the Sahasrara, it may drop down to the Muladhara at any moment! Only when you are firmly established in Samadhi, when you have attained Kaivalya, the Kundalini cannot and does not drop down.

A Misinterpretation

Awakening of the Kundalini Sakti, its union with Siva, enjoying the nectar, and other functions of the Kundalini Yoga that are described in the Yoga Shastras are misrepresented and taken in a literal sense by many. They think that they are Siva and that ladies are Sakti, and that mere sexual union is the aim of Kundalini Yoga. It is mere ignorance. They are utterly wrong. This sort of union is not at all Kundalini Yoga.

Some foolish young boys practise one or two Asanas, Mudras, and a little Pranayama too, for a few days, in any way they like, and imagine that the Kundalini has gone up to their neck. They pose as big Yogis. They are pitiable, self-deluded souls.

Yogic Kriyas and Inner Purification

Some Yoga students ask me: "How long should one practise Sirshasana or Paschimottanasana or Kumbhaka or Maha Mudra to awaken the Kundalini? Nothing is mentioned about this point in any treatise on Yoga".

A student starts his Sadhana from the point or stage where he left in his previous birth. So it all depends upon the degree of purity, stage of evolution, the amount of purification of the Nadis and the Pranayama Kosa, and above all, the degree of Vairagya and yearning for liberation.

Mere Yogic Kriyas alone will not help you much. Purification of the heart is very necessary.

Do self-analysis and eradicate your faults and evil habits. Rectify your defects like selfishness, pride, jealousy, hatred, etc. Develop your heart. Share what you have with others. Do selfless service. Then alone you will get purity of mind.

In these days, aspirants neglect these things and jump at once to do Yogic Kriyas for getting Siddhis. It is a serious Himalayan blunder. They have the hopeless downfall sooner or later.

My advice is: Never care for Siddhis or quick awakening of the Kundalini. Have devotion to God. Have perfect trust in Him. Have the spirit of service to humanity. The Kundalini will awaken by itself.

Awakening of Kundalini is not so easy as you may imagine. It is extremely difficult. When all desires die out, when the mind becomes absolutely pure, when all the senses are subdued, when you attain one-pointedness of mind to a considerable degree, when all the ideas of egoism and mine-ness melt away, the Kundalini will awaken by itself. Then alone, awakening of the Kundalini is also beneficial.

Premature awakening is not desirable. The aspirant, even though he would have awakened the Kundalini by some means, will not be benefited at all if he has not developed the necessary qualifications. It is not possible for him to feel, and manifest, all the benefits of awakening the Kundalini.

The fruit that is allowed to ripen in the tree itself will be very sweet. But this takes a long time. First-class timber comes out from the slowest growing trees. Even so, that aspirant who does vigorous Sadhana for a long time with patience, perseverance and zeal, who sticks to the spiritual practices tenaciously despite various sorts of obstacles in the path, who admits his faults and weaknesses and tries to remove them by suitable methods, will be able to awaken his Kundalini and will become a dynamic and perfect Yogi.

O emotional, enthusiastic young aspirants! Do not take the movements of rheumatic winds in the back from chronic lumbago for ascent of Kundalini. Do your Sadhana with patience, perseverance, till you get Samadhi. Master every stage in Yoga. Do not take up any higher courses before you completely master the lower steps.

Be not troubled. Be not anxious, my dear friends and brothers! A glorious day is waiting to dawn on you. You will shine with full powers, nay, you will become God Himself. Laugh at all troubles and obstacles and keep your eye on the Kundalini Sakti all the twenty-four hours. Do all you can in order to rouse Her up. If purification is ordained, purify you must. What other alternative is there? Therefore, do purify yourself.

42. LIFE

Life is God in expression. Life is joy. Life is flooding of the bliss of the Spirit.

Life is a conscious stream. Life is vibrant in every atom. There is life in everything. There is no such thing as inanimate matter. Life is involved in a piece of stone. Matter is vibrant with life. This has been conclusively proved by modern scientists.

Life is a voyage in the infinite ocean of time, where scenes are perpetually changing. Life is a journey from impurity to purity, from hatred to cosmic love, from death to immortality, from imperfection to perfection, from slavery to freedom, from diversity to unity, from ignorance to eternal wisdom, from pain to eternal bliss, from weakness to infinite strength. Life is a great opportunity provided by the Lord for His children to evolve into Himself.

Life is service and sacrifice. Life is love. Life is relationship. Life is poetry, but not prose. Life is art and imagination, but no science. Life is worship.

We are here as passing pilgrims. Our destination is God. Our quest is for the lost inheritance, the forgotten heritage. The great central aim in life is the coming into a conscious realisation of our oneness with God. Life has no meaning as a separate life. It has meaning only when it becomes full or the whole, when the individual soul joins the Supreme Soul.

The Goal of Life

The true goal of life is to get back to the source from which we came. Just as the rivers flow restlessly till they join the ocean, the ultimate source from which they got their supply of water, just as fire leaps and burns furiously till it merges in its own origin, so too, we would be restless here till we obtain His grace and become one with Him.

The sole object of life is the attainment of Self-realisation or absolute freedom. The aim of man's life is to unfold and manifest the Godhead which is eternally existent within him. The purpose of life is to lose all sense of distinctive personality and be dissolved in the Lord. The attainment of the Infinite Life is the supreme purpose of finite life.

Life in Matter and Life in the Spirit

Life in the Spirit is the only real, eternal life. The modern life of rush and hurry, with fear, insecurity, illness and friction is not real life. A life or material luxury, of wealth and power, is not the end of life. Such a life does not produce peace of mind and serenity of soul.

Sensuous life is not worth living. Sensual pleasure is like honey that is mixed with virulent poison. One anna of sensual pleasure is mixed with fifteen annas of pain. Sensual enjoyment is attended with various defects, sins, pains, attachments, bad habits and mental restlessness. Indulgence in sensual pleasures destroys devotion to God, and weakens the capacity of the mind to enquire into the Reality. Sensuality destroys life, lustre, strength, vitality, memory, wealth, fame, holiness and devotion to the Supreme. It drags a man down to the abyss of hell.

Mundane life is full of sorrows, pains and bondage. It is full of defects, weaknesses and limitations. It is full of hatred, jealousy, selfishness, treachery, cares, worries, anxieties, diseases and death, meanness, crookedness, deceit, double-dealing, cut-throat competition, impurities and darkness, fights, quarrels, strife and war, disappointment, despair and dejection, cruelty, exploitation, agitation, restlessness. All objects are coated with a little imaginary pleasure. It is like a thin electro-gold-plating. In reality, life here is all tinsel and shadow. Behind the sugar-coating, there is bitter quinine. Behind the electro-gold-plating, it is all brass. Behind the so-called pleasures, there are pain, misery and suffering. Life here is full of fears, attachments and tribulations.

Mundane life is all unreal. It is illusory and transitory. It is trifling and worthless. Its end is only dust. There is nothing but tall talk, gossiping, eating and sleeping. All is illusory; all is painful. All is transitory; all is fleeting. Mundane experience has no value, no reality. God alone is real.

Any number of zeroes have no value, unless you add 1 before them. Similarly, even if you do not lead a spiritual life, if you have no spiritual wealth, if you have no Self-realisation. You will have to live in the Soul. You will have to add the Atman to the life here. That is the reason why Lord Jesus says: "Seek ye first the Kingdom of God and His righteousness, and all these things shall be added unto you".

Life in the Eternal is abundant life. It is rich, inner spiritual life. This life is free from sorrow and pain. It is full, perfect and independent. It is full of wisdom and eternal bliss. It is all-pervading, changeless. There is perfect Tushti and Pushti.

Embrace the life of the Soul. You will be made pure and free. The chief beauty of life is the sacrifice of one's dearest interest at the altar of Truth. To live means pursuing the Truth, and surmounting all obstacles with courage. The greatest joy of life is devotion to God, and meditation on God in one's own heart. Spiritual life gives a meaning to human life and imparts glory to it.

The Struggle of Life

To live is to fight for ideal. Life is fight for fullness and perfection. Life is a battle for attaining supreme independence. Life is struggle and resistance. Life is a series of conquests. Man evolves, grows, expands, gains various experiences through struggle. Life and society cannot exist without struggle or fighting. If you want to continue your existence, struggle is imperative. You will cease to exist the moment you cease to struggle.

Fight bravely with the internal foes on the battle-ground of your heart. Even a little victory in the inner battle with your mind and senses will develop your will-power, and give more assurance and courage. The harder the struggle, the more glorious the triumph. Self-realisation demands very great struggle.

Live for God. Boldly face all the difficulties and tribulations of this petty, earthly life. Be a man. With courage, struggle for the Great Attainment. Climbing a mountain, crossing a channel, bombing a city, or blasting a fort—these are not the true acts of heroism and real courage. Controlling your mind and senses, and overcoming anger, passion and egoism by attaining self-mastery—these constitute the real heroism in man. How long will you be a slave of passion and the senses? Assert your real divine nature, and your mastery over your lower nature and lower self. This is your most important duty.

Life Is a School

This does not mean, however, that we should ignore the life in the physical plane of matter. Matter is expression of God for His own Lila. Matter and spirit are inseparable like head and fire, cold and ice, flower and fragrance. Brahman and Maya are inseparable and one. A life in the physical plane is a definite preparation for the eternal life in Brahman. Life is a great school for learning many useful lessons, and for the development of character and divine virtues. Life is a school in which every sorrow, every pain, every heart-break brings a precious lesson. Life on earth is the means of self-perfection.

The world is your best teacher. This world is your best Guru. There is a lesson in everything. There is a lesson in each experience. The world is the best training ground for the development of various divine virtues, such as mercy, forgiveness, tolerance, universal love, generosity, nobility, courage, magnanimity, patience, strong will, etc. The world is an arena for fighting with the diabolical nature, and for expressing divinity from within. The central teaching of the Gita and the Yoga Vasishtha is that one should realise his Self by remaining in the world. Be in the world, but be out of the world. Behave like the water on the lotus-leaf. Give up the lower Asuric nature which consists of selfishness, lust, anger, greed, hatred and jealousy. Assert the divine nature. Live a life of mental renunciation and self-sacrifice.

Sure Ways for Success in Life and God-realisation

Have a simple and unassuming manner of life. Live not to eat, but eat to live. Bear no envy. Commit no slander. Speak no falsehood. Practise no deceit. Harbour no malice. You will be ever joyful, happy and peaceful.

Righteousness is the rule of life. Lead a virtuous life. Strictly adhere to Dharma. Human life is not human without virtues.

The salt of life is selfless service. The bread of life is universal love. Life is not fully lived, life has not been fully realised, if you do not serve and love the entire humanity. The secret of true life is in the love of God and the service of humanity. Live to help others. The divine power will stream through you as life-giving force.

Study the lives of saints and draw inspiration from them. Cultivate a melting heart, the giving hand, the kindly speech, the life of service, equal vision, and impartial attitude. Your life will, indeed, be blessed.

Serve, love, give, purify, meditate. Your journey will take you into a new realm of infinite bliss. You will discover shining treasures. You will rediscover God. You will be strong, you will be healthy, you will be free, you will be nice, you will be happy, you will be peaceful. You will inspire and bless all whose lives you touch.

Make life a perpetual joy. Derive joy from Satya. Derive joy from Tapas. Derive joy from Daya. Derive joy from Dana.

Lead a simple life. Lead a regulated life. Lead a hard life. Take hold of each day as if it were the last day, and utilise every second in prayer, meditation and service. Let your life become a continuous sacrifice to God.

Live in the present. Forget the past. Give up hopes of the future.

Understand well the meaning of life, and then start the quest. Life is thy greatest gift. Utilise every second profitably. Success often comes to those who dare and act. It seldom comes to the timid.

Unity of Life

See life as a whole. Have a comprehensive view of life. All life is one. All life proceeds from Brahman or the Absolute, which is the one and only Reality. The Lord breathes in all life. All is one. The world is one home. All are members of one human family. All creation is an organic whole. No man is independent of that whole. Man makes himself miserable, by separating himself from others. Separation is death. Unity is eternal life. Cultivate cosmic love. Include all. Embrace all. Recognise the worth of others. Destroy all barriers that separate man from man. Recognise the non-dual principle, the immortal essence, within all creatures. Protect animals. Let all life be sacred. Then this world will be a paradise of beauty, a heaven of peace and tranquillity.

Smile with the flower and the green grass. Play with the butterflies, birds and deer. Shake hands with the shrubs, ferns and twigs of trees. Talk to the rainbow, wind, stars and the sun. Converse with the running brooks and the waves of the sea. Speak with the walking-stick. Develop friendship with your neighbours, dogs, cats, cows, human beings, trees, flowers, etc. Then you will have a wide, perfect, rich, full life. You will realise oneness or unity of life. This can be hardly described in words. You will have to feel yourself.

43. LOVE

Love is the Law of life. To love is to fulfil the Law. And to fulfil the Law means eternal peace and everlasting happiness.

This world has come out of love. It exists in love. It finally dissolves in love. Love is the motive-power of the universe.

Love is life. Love is joy. Love is warmth. Love is the golden tie which binds heart to heart, soul to soul.

Love is constructive and creative. Love binds and builds. Love is the principle of regeneration. Love is an actual substance you can use with confidence. Love is a positive, concrete thing. He who applies the law of love with scientific precision can work wonders. The law of love is a far greater science than any modern science. The law of love prevails among saints and good men.

To live is to love. To love is to live. You live that you may learn to love. You love that you may learn to live in the Eternal. A life without faith, love and devotion is a dreary waste. It is real death.

There is no virtue higher than love; there is no treasure higher than love; there is no knowledge higher than love, there is no Dharma higher than love; there is no religion higher than love; because love is Truth; love is God. God is an embodiment of love. In every inch of His creation, you can verily understand His love.

Love is the immediate way to Truth or the Kingdom of God. It is the life-principle of creation. It is the highest expression of soul-force. It is the sum total of all the duties of religion. It is the magic wand in the hand of a devotee by which he conquers the whole world. It was the driving force behind Mira, Radha, Tukaram, Tulasidas, Gouranga, Jesus and the God-intoxicated Sufis, Mansoor and Shams Tabriez.

Passion and Pure Love

Love of body or skin is passion. Love of God is Prem or devotion. It is pure love. It is love for love's sake.

To love anyone for attaining some selfish gain is selfish love. It binds you to this earth. To love all beings with Narayana Bhava as manifestations of the Lord is pure love. It is divine love. It leads to liberation.

A husband loves his wife not for the sake of his wife, but loves her for the sake of his own self. He is selfish. He expects sensual pleasure from her. If leprosy or smallpox destroys her beauty, his love for her ceases.

There is physical passion in this love. There is deep selfishness. The love is mercenary.

In mercenary love, there cannot be any real happiness between the two, the lover and the beloved. If the husband is in a dying condition, the wife takes the bank pass-book and walks to her mother's house quietly. If the husband loses his job for sometime, the wife shows wry faces, speaks harsh words, and does not serve him properly with any love. This is selfish love. There is no real affection from the core of the heart. There is no element of sacrifice. So there are always quarrels, fighting and Asanti in the house. Husbands and wives are not really united. There is always a tug-of-war. They pull on anyhow, dragging a dreary, cheerless existence.

Even our sisters of ill-fame show for some time abundant love, sweet smile and honeyed words towards their customers so long as they can extract money. Can you call this love and real happiness? Just tell me frankly. There are cunningness, diplomacy, crookedness and hypocrisy here.

In every earthly love, there is hollowness, a jarring note, a hidden doubt and a flaw. But true, pure love is rich, profound, full and flawless. It is eternal, unchanging, infinite.

Selfish passion seeks gratification through others. But pure, divine love seeks to make the beloved happy, and to derive happiness from the happiness of the latter. Love is sacrifice. To love is to share and serve.

Service Is Love in Expression

Love vibrates in the form of service, charity, generosity and benevolence.

Daya is active benevolence. It is the positive expression of love. Ahimsa is the negative expression of love.

Passive goodness alone is not sufficient. Active goodness or positive goodness is very essential for one's spiritual advancement. The aspirant should be ever doing actions.

The spirit of service must be ingrained in you. The spirit of service must be innate or inherent in you. There should not be a mere show. All service is empty if there is no love, affection, sincerity and Bhava. If you serve with Bhava and love, God is behind you.

Sankara, Jesus, Buddha and Mohammed served. Janaka and Samartha Ramdas served. Serve, love, give. He who practises these instructions can live through hard times and bad days enlightened by heavenly ray.

Make others truly happy as you strive to make yourself happy. Speak a helpful word. Give a cheering smile. Do a kind act. Serve a little. Wipe the tears of one who is in distress. Render smooth a rough place in another's path. You will feel great joy.

Cosmic Love or Visva-prema

Worship the poor, the down-trodden and the oppressed. These are your gods. These are your first gods.

Love all. You will reap the benefit of more than a million Yajnas or sacrifices, austerities and Vratas. Regard your neighbour's happiness as your own happiness, and regard your neighbour's pain as your own pain.

Man is one. God is one. Love is one. Law is one. Realisation is one. We are all the fruits of one tree and the leaves of one branch. There is no stranger, no alien in this world. Everyone is God in the process of evolution.

Identify yourself with everything that lives. Live at peace with friend and foe.

All men are limbs of one body. All creation is the family of God. Love all God's creation. Love even the leaf; love the animals; love the birds; love the plants; love everything. This is the way to a knowledge of the mystery underlying them all.

I follow the religion of love. I am a true Christian, a true Mussalman, a true Hindu, a true Buddhist, a true Sikh and a true Parsi.

True religion does not consist in ritualistic observances, baths and pilgrimages, but in loving all. Cosmic love is all-embracing and all-inclusive. In pure love, no one is shut out from its warm embrace. It is wide enough to include the humblest of us, from the tiny ant to the mighty elephant, from the condemned prisoner to the mighty emperor, from the worst scoundrel to the most reputed saint on the surface of this earth. It is hatred that separates man from man, nation from nation, and country from country. It is pride and egoism that divide a man from another man. Hatred, pride and egoism are mental creations. They are the products of ignorance only. They cannot stand before pure love.

The Need of the Hour

Hatred breeds hatred. Love begets love. Fear breeds fear. This is the immutable psychological law. It is the natural right of love, the power of God, to prevail upon this earth, conquering all the forces of hate and evil.

In love lies the salvation of all beings. Love is the hope of this dark and lonesome world. This world needs leaders filled with sympathy, co-operation, love, sacrifice, compassion and tolerance. In the cultivation of this cosmic love is individual spiritual progress, the welfare of the community, and the peace of the whole world. Set to work, therefore and spread this gospel of cosmic love throughout the whole world.

Visit every Mohalla, every house. Do Kirtan. Conduct mass-prayer. Spread the message of love, unity, goodwill, service, sacrifice, co-operation and sympathy. Let the spiritual message of oneness and the divine call to unity, friendship, amicable co-operation, reach the hearts of all and awaken love and brotherhood in the bosom of humanity. Let all the world be circled with a heart of love.

Love—The Goal of Life

The saints, seers and prophets of the world have spoken of love as the end and aim or goal of life. The Rasa-lila of Sri Krishna is full of Prem and divine mysteries. The stripping of clothes of the Gopis means the destruction of egoism. Lord Krishna has preached love through His flute. Lord Buddha was an ocean of love. He gave up his body to appease the hunger of a cub of a tiger. Raja Sibi gave, from his own breast, an equivalent weight of the pigeon's flesh to satisfy the appetite of the hawk. What a noble soul! Lord Rama lived a life of love and showed love in every inch of his activity. My dear children of Love, draw inspiration from their teachings. Tread the path of love, commune with God, and reach the eternal abode of love. This is your highest duty. You have taken this body to achieve Love, which alone is the goal of life.

Live in love. Breathe in love. Sing in love. Eat in love. Drink in love. Talk in love. Pray in love. Meditate in love. Think in love. Move in love. Die in love. Purify your thoughts, speech and action in the fire of love. Bathe and plunge in the sacred ocean of love. Take the honey of love and become an embodiment of love.

Feel that this body is a moving temple of God. Feel that all beings are images of God. Feel that this world is indwelt by the Lord. Feel that the one power of God works through all hands, sees through all eyes, hears through all ears. You will become a changed being. You will enjoy the highest peace and bliss.

44. MAHABHARATA

The Mahabharata was composed by Sri Vyasa (Krishna Dvaipayana) who was the grandfather of the heroes of this epic. He taught this epic to his son Suka and his disciples Vaisampayana and others. King Janamejaya, son of Parikshit, the grandson of the heroes of the epic, performed a great sacrifice. The epic was recited by Vaisampayana to Janamejaya at the command of Vyasa. Later on, Sauti recited the Mahabharata, as was done by Vaisampayana to Janamejaya, to Saunaka and others, during the sacrifice performed by Saunaka in Naimisaranya, which is near Sitapur in Uttar Pradesh (India).

Contents of Mahabharata

Mahabharata contains the essence of all scriptures. It is an encyclopaedia of ethics, knowledge, politics, religion, philosophy and Dharma. The great author has said in the first chapter, addressing Brahma (Creator) regarding the contents of his proposed work: "Sire, the secrets of the Vedas established by me elsewhere, the teachings of the Upanishads, details of the Vedic rituals, the subtle teachings of the Itihasas and Puranas, knowledge of the triple indications—past, present and future—of time, definite specifications of old age, death, fear and diseases, the particulars of the duties prescribed to the different Asramas, details of the classification of the four Varnas, directions for maintaining austerities and celibacy, particulars of the influences and movements of the planets, the sun, the moon and the earth, the spiritual teachings of the Vedas, logic, medical science, rules of charity, the Pasupata religion, details of celestial and human life, descriptions of sacred rivers, countries and places, the science of war, the style of the science of language and speech, the way of conducting worldly life—all these are included in this work. There is nothing more to be written, existing in the world". Concluding, the author has said: "What is said here, you find elsewhere; what is not here, is nowhere else". The Mahabharata contains one hundred thousand verses.

It contains eighteen Parvas or sections, viz., Adi Parva, Sabha Parva, Vana Parva, Virata Parva, Udyoga Parva, Bhishma Parva, Drona Parva, Karna Parva, Salya Parva, Sauptika Parva, Stri Parva, Santi Parva, Anusasana Parva, Asvamedha Parva, Asramavasika

Parva, Mausala Parva, Mahaprasthanika Parva and Svargarohanika Parva. Each Parva contains many sub-Parvas or subsections.

Synopsis of Mahabharata

Mahabharata is the history of the Great War of India between the Pandavas and the Kauravas. The two brothers Dhritarashtra and Pandu were born through sage Vyasa after the death of Vichitravirya. Dhritarashtra being blind, Pandu succeeded to the throne but he entrusted the kingdom to his elder brother and himself proceeded to the forest where his five sons Yudhishthira, etc., were born and were called the Pandavas. Dhritarashtra also had one hundred children in Gandhari, Duryodhana and others, who were called the Kauravas. Pandu died during the infancy of his sons and Dhritarashtra continued to rule the kingdom with the help of their grand uncle Bhishma who had pledged himself to lifelong celibacy. The Pandava and Kaurava princes were brought up together and also educated and trained alike through Dronacharya. Both sets of princes considered themselves entitled to the kingdom and looked upon the other with hostility, and their feelings and relations grew strained from day to day. On account of persecution from Kauravas, the Pandavas left their home and suffered much hardship and pain, but on their marriage with the daughter of Drupada, king Dhritarashtra sent for the Pandavas and made over half the kingdom to them. The Pandavas improved their country and established their capital at Indraprastha and then performed the horse-sacrifice with great pomp. The Kauravas were also invited there but on seeing the good fortune of the Pandavas and being offended by jokes made at them, they were overcome with jealousy and resentment and returned home with feelings of enmity and revenge. They then conspired against the Pandavas and invited them to gamble and thereby they won all their wealth, kingdom and their persons and also insulted and ill-treated their wife, Draupadi, in the presence of all. In the end, it was settled that the Pandavas should go out in exile to the forest for twelve years and pass another year in secrecy and on return from the exile be entitled to get back their lost kingdom. The Pandavas did all this, but on their return the Kauravas refused to return the kingdom. This gave rise to the family war in which all Kauravas and the two armies were annihilated and the Pandavas alone survived and got the victory.

The Pandavas were assisted by Sri Krishna and other relations, Drupada, Virata etc., and their forces numbered seven battalions (Akshauhinis). The Kauravas were also assisted by their relations and friends and their forces numbered eleven battalions. The Pandavas were successful on account of their righteous cause and divine grace.

The Mahabharata, the most renowned epic of India, is the only book of its kind in the whole world. It is also called the fifth Veda. It contains countless stories besides the main episode—the Mahabharata—which teach moral lessons or illustrate some characteristics of the ancients of India. It contains the history of political, social and religious life. The stories, songs, nursery tales, anecdotes, parables, the discourses and sayings contained in this epic are marvelous and highly instructive. It contains the brilliant records of mighty heroes, warriors of great prowess, deep thinkers, profound philosophers, sages and ascetics, and devoted wives of chastity.

The Bhishma Parva of Mahabharata contains the sacred gospel Srimad Bhagavad Gita, a dialogue between Lord Sri Krishna and Arjuna. The Gita is the kernel of the Mahabharata. Since Yoga is given such prominence here, there can be no doubt that the rest of the Mahabharata which mentions Yoga directly and allegorically, is a treatise on Yoga.

It is very interesting to remember the opening and closing lines of this great epic. It begins with: "Vyasa sang of the ineffable greatness and splendour of Lord Vasudeva, who is the source and support for everything, who is eternal, unchanging, self-luminous, who is the Indweller in all beings, and of the truthfulness and righteousness of the Pandavas". It ends with: "With raised hands, I shout at the top of my voice, but alas, no one hears my words which can give them Supreme Peace, Joy and Eternal Bliss. One can attain wealth and all objects of desire through Dharma (righteousness, duty). Why do people not practise Dharma? One should not abandon Dharma out of passion or fear or covetousness or for the sake of preserving one's life. This is the Bharata Gayatri. Meditate on this daily, O man, when you retire to sleep and when you rise from your bed every morning. You will attain everything. You will attain glory, fame, prosperity, long life, eternal bliss, ever-lasting peace and immortality".

Characters of Mahabharata

Each and every character described in the epic has left an immortal name behind, which teaches moral lessons. The noble and heroic grandsire Bhishma—who controlled his death and who was unconquerable in war even by the gods—still inspires us with the spirit of self-sacrifice, undaunted courage and purity. Yudhishthira is still a model of justice and righteousness. He is an inspiring example, even now, for the rulers of kingdoms and states. He was an embodiment of justice, patience, steadiness, purity, truthfulness and forbearance. Remembrance of his very name generates a thrill in our hearts and goads us to tread the path of truth and virtue. Karna still lives in our hearts on account of his extreme munificence and liberality. Karna's name has become proverbial. People even now say, whenever they come across a very generous man: "He is like Karna in gifts". Even now, we admire Arjuna as a perfect man and worship Lord Krishna as our Protector and Saviour. Whenever we are in trouble and distress we pray to Him: "O Lord! Save us just as you saved Draupadi and Gajendra in days of yore".

The lustre and high renown of these brilliant personages of Mahabharata have not suffered a diminution, in spite of the ravages of cruel time. Their character was untainted and sublime. Hence their deeds also were admirable, laudable and sublime. Determination has ever been the key to success in the lives of great men of all countries. Heroes would not move an inch from the path of their duty when they are called upon to perform it. One is struck with amazement and becomes tongue-tied when he reads of the marvellous strength of Bhima, of the wonderful skill in archery and bowman-ship of Arjuna, of the dexterity of Sahadeva in the use of swords, of the profound knowledge of Nakula in astronomy, and of the extreme righteous conduct and justice of Yudhishthira in all matters. The deeds of heroism done by Bhishma, Karna, Drona, Parasurama, Jayadratha, Dhrishtadyumna, Asvatthama and many others are superhuman. These heroes did severe Tapas and obtained rare boons from the Lord. That is the reason why they did marvellous heroic deeds which baffle description.

Draupadi, Savitri, Kunti, Madri, Damayanti and Gandhari were highly devoted to their husbands. They were bold and fearless when they were under extreme difficulties, hardships, sufferings and privations. They were pious. They bore the sufferings through the force of their chastity and moral strength. They were ideal wives and ideal mothers. That is the reason why they have left an immortal name behind them.

The sufferings of the Pandavas and Draupadi, Nala and Damayanti, Savitri and Satyavan, clearly explain to us the fact or hard truth that the goal of life or perfection, can only be attained through pain and suffering. Pain is the means through which man is moulded, disciplined and strengthened. Just as impure gold is turned into pure gold by melting it in the crucible, so also the impure and imperfect weak man is rendered pure, perfect and strong, by being melted in the crucible of pain and suffering.

The blind Dhritarashtra represents Avidya or ignorance; Yudhishthira represents Dharma; Duryodhana Adharma; Draupadi Maya; Bhishma dispassion; Dussasana evil quality; Sakuni jealousy and treachery; Arjuna the individual soul; and Lord Krishna the Supreme Soul. Kurukshetra is the Antahkarana.

Teachings

The message of Mahabharata is the message of Truth and Righteousness. The great epic produces a moral awakening in the readers and exhorts them to tread the path of Satya and Dharma. It urges them strongly to do good deeds, practise Dharma, cultivate dispassion by realising the illusory nature of this universe and its vain glories and sensual pleasures, and attain Eternal Bliss and Immortality. It induces people to do what Yudhishthira did and abandon what Duryodhana did. Stick to Dharma tenaciously. You will attain everlasting happiness and Moksha, the *summum bonum* of life. This is the final purport or central teaching of Mahabharata.

May the teachings of this illustrious and ancient epic guide you in every walk of your life. May you stick to Dharma. May the great characters of the Mahabharata inspire you. May you imbibe the righteousness of Yudhishthira, the purity of Bhishma, the courage of Arjuna, and the liberality of Karna. Glory to Sri Bhagavan Vyasa, the grandsire of the heroes, the author of the Mahabharata, a *Chiranjivi* and an Avatara of Lord Hari. May His blessings be upon you all!

45. MAN

The baby mews. The child jumps, dances, and plays with toys. The schoolboy walks with his books. The grown-up boy gets degrees. The adolescent twists his moustache, fights and quarrels, and runs after women. He tries to get name and fame. He hoards wealth. He begets children. Then he grows old, wears spectacles, puts on a dental set. He totters with a stick. Finally he passes away with a hiccup.

A drop of water sprinkled on a heated iron piece produces a hissing sound and is immediately vapourised. Man makes a little noise during the short period called his life and disappears in a moment.

What is man? What can he become? What is mind? What is the best state? A study of these things is really profitable.

Body, Mind and Soul

To the Westerner, man is merely a physical creature, endowed with a mind and possessing a soul. To the Hindu, man is essentially a soul, expressing himself through mind, which has the body as its counterpart to function upon the physical plane.

Man is a soul having a body. Man is essentially a spiritual being. Man lives, because he is a spirit or soul in essence. Man's innermost essence is Atmna or the Divine Spirit. Man's true nature is God. Physical body and intellect depend on the soul within, about which man knows little or nothing. Realising the Spirit, man achieves security, certainty, perfection, freedom, independence, immortality and bliss eternal.

All men are by nature, equal. One Atman dwells equally in all beings. By the nature of consciousness, all men are alike; but, by the nature of mind and life, they are wide apart.

The electricity that passes through several bulbs is one and the same. But, that is seen in different ways due to different kinds of bulbs. So, men are different owing to different kinds of mind and temperament.

Man is the trinity of body, mind and soul. Consciousness is veiled by mind and matter. Therefore he is not able to realise his essential, divine nature. Unless man is liberated from the bondage of mind and matter, he cannot have Knowledge of the Self or Atman.

Immortality of the Soul

Man is not this body. Man is not his senses, or even his mind. These are his Upadhis or vehicles. Body and mind are subject to change, decay and death; whereas the real man, the Immortal Self or Atman, is ever abiding, never ending, eternal, unborn, perfect and ancient.

You have a body, but you are not the body. You have a mind, but you are not the mind. Body and mind are your instruments, like the tools of a carpenter. This body is an instrument or servant of the soul, and not its prison.

Know that the body is the temple of the radiant Spirit or self-effulgent Atman or Soul within, which controls and moves all the faculties of the mind and the body. Know that you are breathing the breath of the Spirit, but not a physical breath.

Death does not end all. Death does not mean total annihilation. Death does not end the chain of sequence. The working agent, the soul in the body, does not and cannot die with body. Man's soul is immortal. Just as the man lays aside the overcoat, so also he lays aside the physical body at death.

The body is the slough of the soul. The soul is the mover of the body-chariot. When the body is destroyed, the spirit continues living. You still have your thoughts, memory, will-power and subtle body.

Man's Downfall

Man is a bundle of desires, cravings, emotions, appetites and thoughts. He is a conglomeration of desire, will and action. He becomes extinct if the fire of the desire is extinguished. He thinks and then acts. Thinking is the real action. He acts to obtain his objects of desire. He may sit quiet with closed eyes, but this is not inaction. His mind may be working and planning. Wherever there is desire, wherever there is action, there is imperfection. A desire is the outcome of imperfection aand finitude.

Man is finite and imperfect. He is full of limitations. He depends upon objects for his happiness and stay. He ever keeps his relationship with objects outside. He is swayed and impelled by desires. He becomes a slave of desires and objects.

Desires dominate man and he turns his face away from God. He has forgotten his essential, divine nature. He thinks he is a separate individual. He separated himself from the absolute on account of ignorance and egoism. So he feels miserable. He forgot his original, divine, infinite nature.

If man kills his egoism and sense of separateness, if he annihilates desires and cravings, if he identifies with the Infinite, all limitations, imperfections, and miseries will end. He will attain immortality and eternal bliss.

Man—A Many-levelled Being

Man is a many-levelled being, and has various sheaths, organism, and so he is definitely characterised by the possession of certain physiological functions such as circulation of blood, digestion, respiration, excretion, etc. He is also definitely characterised by the possession of certain psychological functions such as thinking, perception, memory, imagination, etc. He sees, thinks, tastes, smells, and feels. Philosophically speaking, he is the image of God, nay, he is God Himself. He lost his divine glory by tasting the fruit of the forbidden tree. He can regain his lost divinity by mental discipline and the practice of concentration.

Man has a many-levelled being, and has various sheaths which conceal his real personality. He may identify himself with the gross physical body, and look to its needs as an animal does; or he may identify himself with the self-conscious reason; or he may feel his oneness with his real Self which is the eternal witness of both. Man's vital aims, however valuable they may be in their own place, cannot take control of the spiritual being for a long time without complete disorder to one's personality. In the modern man, self-conscious intellect, with all its natural limitation, takes the highest place; and suicidal scepticism is the result.

Man is a mixture of three ingredients, *viz.*, human element, brutal instinct, and divine ray. He is endowed with a finite intellect, a perishable body, a little knowledge, and a little power. This makes him distinctly human. Lust, anger, hatred belong to his brutal nature. The reflection of cosmic intelligence is at the back of his intellect. So he is an image of God. When the brutal instincts die, when his ignorance is rent asunder, when he is able to bear insult and injury, he becomes one with the Divine.

Man is the highest manifestation of life on this earth. He is the image of the Lord. He is the ray of the Lord. God made man after His own Self. In essence, man is united with Lord. He thinks, feels, and knows. He can discriminate, reflect, and meditate. He can attain the highest Knowledge of the Self. Therefore he is superior to other beings, though eating, sleep, fear, and coition are common.

Evolution

Man was but animal yesterday. He is man today. His destiny is to become Brahman or the Absolute as the result of a gradual process of self-perfection.

The mineral becomes the plant with life. The plant becomes the animal with a higher development of life. The animal becomes a man with life and thought.

The stone sleeps. The plant breaths. The animals moves. Man is conscious. The sage is superconscious.

A human being is rational. An animal is instinctive. A sage is intuitive.

Of all the animals creations of God, man alone can realise God. He alone is endowed with discrimination, intelligence, discernment, reasoning, and judgement. Intellect is the greatest gift of God to man. Man is a poor being physically; but, his dignity consists of thought, discrimination, reasoning, and enquiry.

Man evolves himself according to his thoughts and actions. Man is changed by every thought he thinks, and by every action he does.

From the Bombay junction, a train goes to Delhi direct; another goes to Madras; another goes to Nagpur. Even so, this body is a junction. You can go to heaven, Brahma-loka, or Brahman, if you do virtuous deeds. You will go downwards to lower animal births if you do vicious deeds. You can remain as a man if you do ordinary mixed deeds. Man himself—and he alone—is responsible for all that is good or bad in his life. He can attain perfection and freedom through a long process of evolution and persistent self-effort. He is born again and again, and learns from his earthly lives how to attain perfection, and becomes united with God.

If the wick with the lamp is very small, the light is also will be small. If the wick is very big, the light also will be powerful. Similarly, if the Jiva is pure, if he practises meditation, the manifestation or expression of the Self will be powerful. He will radiate a big light. If he is unregenerate and impure, he will be like a burnt-up charcoal. The greater the wick, the greater the light. Likewise, the purer the soul, the greater the expression.

The Spiritual Man

To every man I say: "Regenerate yourself. Strive to attain perfection and freedom". Turn Godwards. Turn towards the Divine Light. You have taken birth to manifest the Light of Brahman through the flesh.

A moral life will lead you to the mighty temple of wisdom. There is only one sacred temple in this universe, and that is the heart of a moral and spiritual man. The heart of a good and pious man is the shrine or temple of God in this world. Therefore, be righteous. Practise virtue.

A moral man alone is really beautiful. A man of good actions, and good, pleasant and sweet speech has no equal. Even Devas and Brahma adore him. He who is truthful, gentle, humble virtuous, and honest is the best type of man.

He who has no ethical virtues is like a wild flower without fragrance. A man without virtuous qualities is a dead man while living. He is a disgraceful specimen to the world. He is shunned by society. A sensuous man is no better than a beast. Most people are no better than animals. They are excommunicated from the Kingdom of Peace and Bliss Eternal. Therefore, develop virtuous qualities at once. Charity, gratefulness, knowledge of sciptures, nobility of character, self-restraint, and courage make a man glorious and celebrated.

God and Man

Man is God in disguise who puts on a garb in fun, but quickly forgets his true identity. Desires drags him down. Discrimination lifts him up.

Man evolved is God. God involved is man. God in bondage is man, and man free from bondage is God. A deluded, ignorant man is worldly. A perfect man is God.

God became man. Man will become God again. God plus desire

is man. Man minus desire is God. The most impious of man can, by earnestly devoting themselves to God, reach the highest bliss.

Truth is not outside you. It is within you. It dwells in the cave of your heart. You are a truth of God, a work of God, a will of God. You are unfettered, free, eternally free. You are Nitya-mukta Atman. Roar OM. Come out of the cage of flesh and roam about freely.

46. MARRIAGE

Marriage is entry into the second Ashrama. The life of the householder begins. Now he takes up his duties as man and pays his debts by sacrifice, by study, and by procreating children. The bridegroom tells the bride, "I take your hand for good fortune. I seize your hand so that we may have a good progeny, that you may live with me, your husband, till you become old. The one God, represented as Bharga, Aryaman, Savitru, and Purandhi, has given you to me for doing the duties of a householder. Give birth to heroes, and worshipping the one God, bring about our happiness".

Again, during the Garbhadanam which sanctifies the creative act, the husband prays fervently from the core of his heart that a child may be conceived. He repeats sacred Mantras during the Ritusanti ceremony or nuptials. The new child is conceived amidst the vibration of Mantras. Good impressions are impressed in the brain cells of the embryo. For a real Hindu who is endowed with pure intellect and right understanding, the sexual union is not for the sake of mere enjoyment. He utlises the divine, creative, vital energy for the formation of a human body.

The Hindu Ideal of Marriage

Marriage is a sacrament for Hindu. The wife is his partner of life. She is his Ardhangini. He cannot do any religous ritual without her. She stands by his left side when he performs any religious performance. The husband and the wife keep Rama and Sita as their ideal.

What a wife is to a Hindu husband is well illustrated by a verse in the Ramayana where Sri Rama, referring to Sita, says: "In counsel, she is my counsellor; in action, she is my servant; in religious performances, she is my partner; in tolerance, she is like the earth; in affection, she is like unto my mother; in bed, she is like the celestial Rambha; and in play, she is my companion. Such indeed, O Lakshmana, is my beloved...". This is the Hindu ideal of a wife.

Of all the Ashramas, the Grihasthasrama is the most important, because it supports all the others. As all creatures live supported by the air, so the other orders exist supported by the householder. As all streams and rivers flow to rest in the ocean, so all the Ashramas flow to rest in the householder. The Grihastha is the very heart of Aryan life. Everything depends on him.

Duties of a Householder

The householder should lead the life of an ideal Grihastha. He should perform the Pancha-mahayajna or fivefold sacrifice prescribed in the Hindu scriptures. He should practise self-restraint, mercy, tolerance, non-injury, truthfulness, moderation in everything.

A householder should earn money by honest means and distribute it in the proper manner. He should spend one-tenth of his income in charity. He should enjoy sensual pleasures within the limits of the moral law.

Householders have got a very responsible duty in training their children. If they want to shirk this responsibility, they ought to have checked their itching sensation caused by lust, and should have stopped procreation by becoming Naishthika Brahmacharins. Serious punishment is awaiting them in the other world if they leave their children untrained in this world. They themselves should lead an ideal life. Then alone, their children can copy them. If they have wrong evil habits, their children will try to imitate them. Children have got the power of imitation.

When the householder sees that his sons are able to bear the burden of his duties, when his grandsons are around him, the time has come for his wife and himself to retire from the world and spend their time in study and meditation.

Sex and Divorce

In the West, babies are born and brought up in nursery hospitals and maternity homes. They do not know the health-giving, affectionate, tender, and soul-expanding caresses of their mothers. They do not know what it is to sleep in the warm embrace of a loving mother. Brought up in the atmosphere of bargain and economics, they develop, even in their teens, the unceasing devotion to the dollar and the sovereign, and afterwards give a lifelong worship to mammon.

The social atmosphere in the West is overcharged with sex. Too early marriages may be very rare in the West, but not too early sex-indulgence. Western philosophers permit pre-marital indulgence. They advocate it. These unions are common in the West. A large number of children are conceived before the unions of the parents are legalised. The parties try each other. As the Germans say, "One does not buy even a penny pipe without trying it". The halfway experiments produce disastrous results. There cannot be real love between the parties. Marriage becomes a business contract, but not a sacrament. Hence there are countless divorces.

In India, too, women have now gained the right to divorce. What a shame! They are following the footsteps of Western women. This is vile imitation. This is the work of some fashionable, westernised women. In this holy land of Aryavarta, in this sacred Bharatavarsha where Sita, Radha, Damayanti, Savitri led the ideal life of chastity and Dharma, some vain, ignorant, so-called educated women who smoke publicly, who play cards publicly with men in the club, who have lost their feminine grace, motherly virtues and Satee-dharma, wish to have new privileges which are not conducive to their happiness, elevation, and salvation. They are doomed to destruction.

The Ideal Married Life

Great Rishis of yore were married, but they did not lead the life of passion and lust. Their life of Grihasthashrama was a life of Dharma only. If it is not possible for you to emulate them to the very letter, you will have to keep their lives before you as landmarks, as the ideal for emulating, and you must tread the path of Truth. Grihasthashrama is not a life of lust and loose living. It is a strict life of selfless service, of Dharma pure and simple, of charity, goodness, kindness, self-help, and all that is good and all that is helpful to humanity. If you can live such a life, the life of a Grihastha is as good as the life of a Sannyasin.

Married life, if lived in a perfect ideal manner, is no bar to the attainment of Mukti. A good woman is to man what banks are to the river. She is the rhythm which leads him to Truth. Her love is God's grace.

The main object of marriage being the procreation of a son, marrying several wives should not be resorted to by those who are desirous of mental, physical, and spiritual well-being. Excessive indulgence and waste of energy should be avoided at all costs.

Early Marriages and Over-population

Early marriages form a menace to society. It is, indeed, an evil. Bengal and Madras are filled with young widows. Young boys, who have no idea of this world and this life, are married when they are eight or ten years of age. We see children begetting children. There are child mothers. A boy of about eighteen has three children. What a horrible state of affairs! There is physical and mental degeneration. There is no longevity. All are short-lived. Frequent child-bearing destroys the health of women and brings in a host of ailments.

A clerk who gets a salary of rupees fifty has six children at the age of thirty. Every two years there is an addition. He never thinks, "How shall I maintain such a big family? How shall I educate my sons and daughters? How shall I arrange for the marriage of my daughters?" At the heat of sexual of excitement, he repeats the same ignoble act agaïn and again. He has not a bit of self-control. He is an absolute slave to passion. Like rabbits, he procreates and brings forth numberless children to swell up the number of beggars in the world. Even animals have got self-control. Lions visit their partners only once in all their lives or once in a year. It is only man with his boasted intellect that breaks the rules of health and has become a criminal in this direction. He will have to pay a heavy penalty in the near future for violating the laws of nature.

The population of the world is increasing by leaps and bounds. People are trying to have birth-control methods, using pessaries, french letters, rubber goods, injection and application of protargol jellies. These are foolish attempts. No one has succeeded till now. Even a single spermatozoa has got tremendous power of movements. Further, the seminal energy is wasted. There is conservation and transmutation of this energy into Ojas by the practice of celibacy. People are wasting their money in these useless contraceptives. The whole world is under a tremendous sexual intoxication. The so-called educated persons are no exceptions to this rule. All are deluded and move in the world with perverted intellects. Poor miserable specimens of humanity! My sympathies are with them. May God elevate them from this quagmire and open their eyes towards spiritual realms.

Self-restraint and celibacy are the only effective natural methods in birth-control.

Marriage—A Lifelong Bondage

It is very difficult to live the life of a housholder. The householder's life is prescribed to one who cannot control his passions. One without passions should revert to the path of Nivritti.

Wife is only a luxury. It is not an absolute necessity. Every househloder is weeping after marriage. He says: "My son ailing from typhoid. My second daughter is to be married. I have debts to clear. My wife is worrying me to purchase a gold necklace. My eldest son-in-law died recently".

Marriage is a curse and a lifelong imprisonment. It is the greatest bondage. The bachelor who was once free is now tied to the yoke, and his hands and feet are chained. This is the experience of all married people, invariable as it were. They weep after marriage.

A Common Spectacle in Married Homes

Quarrels arise daily in the house between the husband and the wife on account of misunderstanding and difference of opinion. The wife thinks that the husband should obey and please her in all respects. The husband thinks that the wife should obey and please him in all respects. Is this possible? No. And so they quarrel every hour. It may not come to regular fists and blows at all times, but they will not speak for some hours in the day. Sometimes there will be boxing and cane-beating also, if the husband is short-tempered and lacks self-control. If the wife is like Mrs. Socrates or Jijabai, the table will be turned. There will be thunder and rain on the husband's head. Sometimes, the wife, when she becomes angry, refuses to cook the food, and lies down in the bed drawing a blanket over her body and head under the pretext of severe stomach-ache. The poor husband runs to the hotel to take his meals in order to catch the pilot train to go to his office. Sometimes, the wife goes to her mother's house without informing the husband. The poor, shameless, weak-willed husband runs to his mother-in-law's house to bring her back with fresh glowing, golden promises and entreaties.

But still, if you ask a householder, "Which is better, a householder's life or a life of a Brahmachari?", surely he will say,

"A householder's life is a thousand times better than the life of a celibate". He will vehemently fight with all his clumsy arguments to support this view.

People have neither discrimination nor dispassion nor subtle, sharp intellect. Hence they are not able to know things in their true light. Their intellects are clouded, perverted, turbid, intoxicated, and veiled by passion, delusion, infatuation, and ignorance. Hence they do not know what they are exactly doing.

When they are swayed by passion, husbands and wives forget all about their quarrels which occured in the morning. They think that their life is a blessed one. They utter pleasantly some flowery speech for the time being, though there is no real union and love in the core of their heart.

Religion at Home

Some have taken Sannyasa on account of the bad behaviour of their wives and their hindrance in their Yogic practices at home. If their wives had allowed them to continue their practices and helped them, they would have remained in the Grihashtha Ashrama. It is the duty of intelligent girls to co-operate with their husbands in leading a religious life at home. Then only both husband and wife can lead a life of peace and happiness at home.

The husband also should not interfere with the religious practices of his wife. He should help her in all possible ways in her spiritual evolution and purity of life. It is the duty of the husband to train his wife in the religious line. She must do some Japa, Kirtan. She must study religious books such as the Ramayana, the Bhagavata, and the Mahabharata. She must take recourse to occasional fasting. He must take her to places of pilgrimage, and attend discourses and Kathas conducted by Mahatmas. Then only the house will be a blessed place. The scritptures declare: "Without religion, a house is a burial ground though it is a place".

O Ram! Treat your wife like a Devi. She is the queen or Lakshmi of the house. Where a woman is honoured, there are wealth, prosperity, success, and peace. O Lila! Become a Pativrata. Do not quarrel with your husband. Become like Savitri, Anusuya, or Sita.

May you all lead a life of purity, with devotion, and attain the supreme blessedness in this very life. May there be temperamental, psychological, and spiritual unity between the husband and the wife! May the husband help the wife and *vice versa* in religious and Yogic practices! May God-realisation be your watchword! May purity be your maxim! May Dharma be your guide!

47. MAYA

That which truly is not, but appears to be, is Maya. That which causes infatuation or Moha is Maya.

Maya is an appearance. It is a semblance. It is the illusory power of God.

Maya is the illusory power of God. She is the creatrix of this universe. She projects this world for His Lila. Mind, intellect, body, and senses are her forms. She is the energy or mother-aspect of the Lord.

Just as heat is inseparable from fire, coldness from ice, Maya is inseparable from Brahman. It is dependent on Brahman.

Maya has countless potencies. Solidity of stone is a power of Maya. Fluidity of water is another power of Maya. Fire is a third burning power of Maya. Air is the moving power of Maya. Ether is void or space power of Maya.

The Great Illusion

By the force of this Maya, the whole world appears in the place of the Supreme Being. Maya creates this world without affecting Brahman in the least. The power of bringing about impossibilities is peculiar to Maya.

Maya is the mother of infinite riddles. Maya envelops Brahman and makes It appear otherwise than It is. It splits the infinite Brahman, which is without name and form and without quality, into the finite centres of experience, investing them with names and forms and qualities.

Maya exists as the cause of perception of the manifoldness of the universe, but in truth, it has no reality. It is also an appearance like the appearances which it causes. It cannot be said to exist, nor can it be said not to exist. It is the false cause of the seeming appearances. One cannot say what exactly it is. It is inscrutable or indeterminate.

Maya is neither true nor false. It is truly false and falsely true. It is neither real nor unreal. It is not real like Brahman, because it disappears when one gets Knowledge. It is not unreal like a barren woman's son or the horn of a hare. because its presence is felt.

This Maya is a sort of jugglery. You are astonished so long as the juggler is not seen. As soon as the juggler is known, the results are known to be unreal; the wonder ceases at once. When you realise Brahman, the wonder of Maya's working vanishes. You come to know that what inspired wonder is unreal.

When the mesmerist hypnotises the whole audience, all people believe that the man is ascending the rope in the air. All people see that the mesmerist devours a big sword and cuts the body of a lad in the box. Even so, you are all hypnotised by Maya and Avidya and you take this unreal world as a solid reality. De-hynoptise yourself by getting Knowledge of Brahman. Then alone you will understand the grand jugglery of Maya.

Manifestations of Maya

Maya is the greatest artist and the greatest juggler. The worldlings can hardly detect her tricks. She deludes the passionate and the uncautious. She hides the real, and makes the unreal appear as real. She makes the impermanent appear as permanent, the impure appear as pure, pain appear as pleasure, Anatman appear as Atman.

You know that you will die, and yet you think you will live for ever. This is Maya. You know that the world is full of miseries, and yet you take delight in the perishable objects and will not leave them. This is Maya. You know that the body of a woman is made up of all sorts of impurities, flesh, bone, urine and faecal matter, and yet you rejoice in embracing her. This is Maya.

Maya causes false glittering and entraps the deluded Jivas. She does a little electroplating work. Man is entrapped. He is caught in the wheel of birth and death.

Behind Maya's sugar-coating, there is the bitter quinine. Behind the garden of sensual pleasures, there is the vale of tears. Behind the smile of a woman, there is hatred, deception, cunningness, insincerity. Behind the scarlet-lips, there are phlegm and disease-causing germs. Behind the rosy cheeks, there is raw flesh. Behind the buoyant youth, there is the old age with tottering steps. Behind beauty, there is ugliness. Behind the charm of this universe, there are death, diseases, snake-bites, scorpion-sting, censure, dishonour, earthquake, cyclone, war and atom bombs. Do not be duped by this tempting Maya.

Maya binds you in a variety of ways. It is difficult to find out her secret workings. A man abandons the world. He takes Sannyasa and develops an Ashram. He slowly gets attached to the Ashram and to his disciples. He develops institutional egoism, Sannyasa Abhimana, and pride of Tyaga and learning.

A man in the street smiles, pays respects, and touches your feet. You get attached to him. A man serves you, praises you, and gives you some presents. You get attached to him.

Another man speaks kind words, gives you good food, and comfortable house. You get attached to him and the house itself.

Smile, affection, comfort, name, fame, kind words, wife, children, house, property, respect, honour, power, prestige, position, titles, heaven are all Maya's tempting baits to ensnare the deluded souls. Beware of Maya's charms.

O ignorant man! Do not fall into the meshes of Maya. The whole world is a net of Maya to entrap the ignorant, deluded souls. Be careful, be on the alert, beware! The entire universe is Avidya's false glittering. It is full of snares and temptations. Colour, sound, and touch are Maya's tempting baits. Women, money, and power are her allurements. Sweetmeats, flowers, and gold are Maya's charms.

The Lord's Maya is mysterious. She assumes various subtle foms and deludes man in diverse ways. When you give passion, you see that anger remains. When you control anger, greed is with you still. When greed is controlled, pride clings to you tenaciously. When you renounce tea and coffee you cling to milk and fruits. When you control the tongue, the eye is waiting to harass you. When you abandon old friends, new friends cling to you. When you give up one kind of work, another kind of work is waiting for you.

At every step, Maya puts a veil. Do not think that you will have to break only one veil at the last stage of Sadhana. Maya puts countless veils: attachment, cravings, desire, likes and dislikes, infatuation, pride, jealousy, hatred, greed, sexual instincts, impulses and urges, the five Koshas, running after Siddhis, false contentment in Sadhana, clouded understanding, grossness of intellect, are all forms of her veil. If you are a little careless and non-vigilant, she puts veil after veil. You have to encounter countless veils all of which have to be torn down.

Vidya Maya and Avidya Maya

Maya binds the Jiva through Avidya or ignorance and frees him through Vidya or knowledge. She is both Avidya and Vidya. Avidya Maya takes you down the path of bondage and is characterised by lust, anger, greed, pride, hatred, etc. The Vidya Maya takes you on the path of liberation and is characterised by discrimination, dispassion, devotion.

Maya and Mind

Maya is manifest in the human individual as mind. Mind alone is Maya. Maya is only mind. Control of mind is control of Maya. Control of Maya is control of mind. Maya plays through mind. Maya havocs through mind.

Maya plays havoc through the imagination of the mind. Woman is not beautiful, but the imagination is beautiful. Sugar is not sweet, but the imagination is sweet. Food is not palatable, but the imagination is palatable. Man is not weak, but the imagination is weak. Understand the nature of Maya and mind and become wise. Curb this imagination of the mind by right thinking, and rest in Brahman wherein there is neither imagination nor thought.

If there is mind, there will be this universe. There is no functioning of mind during deep-sleep. So there is no world. The more you think of the objects, the more this world will appear to you as real. The conception of the reality of the universe will increase if you think of sense-objects often and often.

If the mind runs towards the sensual objects wildly, Maya takes a stronghold of the man. Maya havocs through the mind. This lower impulsive mind drags you down in all kinds of petty sensual enjoyments and deludes in a variety of ways. Maya, through her power, raises millions of Sankalpas in the mind. The Jiva becomes a pray to the Sankalpas.

This lower Manas cannot approach those who have a strong power of discrimination between the real and the unreal. Maya is very easy to be detected, and the Self very easy to be realised, by men who possess discrimination and strong determination. Through these powers, *viz.*, Viveka and will, Maya can be controlled.

The 'Why' of Maya

The why of Maya, the why of man, the why of the universe, the riddle of existence and the riddle of the universe, are problems that are beyond the reach of the finite intellect of man. The human intellect is utterly incapable of solving these questions and the more it attempts them the more does it become muddled. These problems can be understood only after the attainment of Brahma-jnana or divine wisdom. The answers are locked up in the Absolute and the doors are shut up for the relative mind and intellect. No words can adequately describe the origin of Maya. He who attains Atma-jnana, having overcoming Maya, will alone know what Maya is, how it arises and is destroyed.

The why of Maya can be understood only when you attain Knowledge of Brahman. Do not rack your brain now to know the why of Maya. You cannot find an answer in any of the scriptures. The why is itself a logical absurdity. You can have a why only for worldly matters where Buddhi functions. There can be no why for questions of the transcendental plane where a gross and finite intellect, conditioned by time and space, cannot reach.

Everyone who had endeavoured to account for the empirical world has been confronted by ignorance at every step, and has been obliged to confess that human wit could go only so far and no further. All seers of truth, all Acharyas, all prophets, all philosophers, all metaphysicians, and all theologians have entirely failed.

So please do not rack your brain any longer as to the origin of this Maya. But, enquire into the means of its destruction. If it is destroyed, then will you be able to know how it arose, whence it arose, what its nature is, and how it perishes. If you get an injection of a dose Jnana, then you will not be drowned in the ocean of baneful rebirths. The terrific Maya really is not.

Maya—A Negative Existence

Absence of light is darnkness. Darkness is not real entity. Darkness has a negative existence. So Maya has a negative existence. When light is brought, darkness vanishes. Similarly, when Knowledge comes, Maya disappears.

The veil hides the beauty. The pot hides the clay. The ring hides the gold. The elephant hides the wood. The sweetmeat hides the sugar. The cloth hides the thread. The nail hides the iron. Avidya hides the Eternal. Forms hide Brahman. Behind Maya's veil hides Brahman. Break the veil. Behold the Light of lights.

The journey of life in the path of illumination is long and weary. It demands sincere, earnest, practical efforts with dauntless and indefatigable energy. Give up vain discussions. Proceed quickly on the path. Eat the fruit.

A man whose clothes are caught by fire will immediately run towards water. He will never enquire, at the heat of the moment when he is in acute distress, how the fire came, how his clothes were burnt up. Even so, when you are caught up in this terrible Samsaric wheel of births and deaths with various kinds of miseries, afflictions, pains and tribulations, you must try your level best to get rid of Maya. There are ways to destroy Maya. After this destruction, you will know the why and the nature of Maya.

Wake up from the slumber of ignorance. Develop dispassion, discrimination, and enquire "Who am I?" You will free yourself from Maya's clutches. You will attain the eternal bliss of Brahman.

Persevere. Plod on. March courageously. Be regular in your Sadhana. Practise eternal vigilance and introspection. Pray. Do Japa. Worship and meditate. Maya can never, never approach you. You will have ever the grace of the Lord. All the veils will be torn.

48. MEDITATION

Leading a virtuous life is not, by itself, sufficient for God-realisation. Concentration of mind is absolutely necessary.

A good, virtuous life only prepares the mind as a fit instrument for concentration and meditation. It is concentration and meditation that eventually lead to Self-realisation.

Without the help of meditation, you cannot attain Knowledge of the Self. Without its aid, you cannot grow into the divine state. Without it, you cannot liberate yourself from the trammels of the mind and attain immortality.

Meditation is the only royal road to the attainment of salvation or Moksha. It is a mysterious ladder which reaches from earth to heaven, from error to truth, from darkness to light, from pain to bliss, from restlessness to abiding peace, from ignorance to knowledge. From mortality to immortality.

What Is Meditation?

Meditation is keeping up of an unceasing flow of God-consciousness. All worldly thoughts are shut out from the mind. The mind is filled or saturated with divine thoughts, divine glory, and divine presence.

Meditation is the seventh rung or step in the ladder of Yoga. Yogins call this 'Dhyana'. Jnanins term this 'Nididhyasana'. Bhaktas style this 'Bhajana'.

Forget the body. Forget the surroundings. Forgetting is the highest Sadhana. It helps meditation a great deal. It makes the approach to God easier. By remembering God, you can forget all these things.

Lord Jesus says, "Empty thyself and I shall fill thee". This corresponds to the teaching of Patanjali Maharshi: "Yoga is annihilation of all mental functions". This emptying process or making the mind blank is, no doubt, a trying discipline. But, continued practice of an intense type will bring success. There is no doubt in this.

In a big city, there is much bustle and sound at 8 p.m. At 9 O'clock, there is not so much bustle and sound. At 10 p.m., it is still more reduced; and at 11 p.m., it is much less. At 1 a.m., there is peace everywhere. Even so, in the beginning of Yogic practices, there are countless Vrittis in the mind. There is much agitation and tossing in the mind. Gradually, the thought-wave subsides. In the end, all mental modifications are controlled. The Yogi enjoys perfect peace.

How to Practice Meditation

Sit in a lonely place on Padma, Siddha, or Sukha Asana. Free yourself from all passions, emotions, and impulses. Subjugate the senses. Withdraw the mind from objects. Now the mind will be calm, one-pointed, pure and subtle. With the help of this trained instrument, disciplined mind, contemplate on that one Infinite Self. Do not think of anything else. Do not allow any worldly thought to enter the mind. Do not allow the mind to think of any physical or mental enjoyment. When it indulges in these thoughts, give it a good hammering. Then it will move towards God. Just as the Ganga flows continuously towards the sea, thoughts of God should flow continuously towards the Lord. Just as oil, when poured from one vessel to another, flows in an unbroken, continuous stream, just as the harmonious sound produced from the ringing of bells falls upon the ear in a continuous stream, so also, the mind should 'flow' towards God in one continuous stream.

You must have a mental image of God or Brahman—concrete or abstract—before you begin to meditate. When you are a neophyte in meditation, start repeating some sublime Slokas, Stotras, or hymns for ten minutes as soon as you sit for meditation. This will elevate the mind. The mind can be easily withdrawn from the worldly objects. Then stop this kind of thinking also and fix the mind on one idea only by repeated and strenuous efforts. Then Nishtha will ensue.

When you start a fire, you heap up some straw, pieces of paper, thin pieces of wood. The fire gets extinguished quickly. You blow it again several times through the mouth or the blowpipe. After some time, it becomes a small conflagration. You can hardly extinguish it now even with great efforts. Even so, in the beginning of meditation in neophytes, they fall down from meditation into their old grooves. They will have to lift up their minds again and again, and fix on the Lakshya. When the meditation becomes deep and steady, they get established in God eventually. Then the meditation becomes Sahaja, natural. It becomes habitual.

What Happens during Meditation

In meditation, now grooves are formed in the brain, and the mind moves upwards in the new spiritual grooves. When the mind becomes steady in meditation, the eye-balls also become steady. A Yogi whose mind is calm will have a steady eye. There will be no winking at all. The eyes will be lustrous, red or pure white.

When you enter into very deep, silent meditation, the breath will not come out of the nostrils. There may be occasional, slow movement of the lungs and the abdomen.

In profound and continued meditation, thinking ceases. There is only one idea of "Aham Brahmasmi". When this idea also is given up, Nirvikalpa Samadhi or Sahaja-advaitanishtha ensues. Just as salt melts in water, the Sattvic mind melts in silence in Brahman, its substratum.

Aids to Meditation

For meditation, you must have a calm, clear, pure, subtle, sharp, steady, and one-pointed intellect. Brahman is pure and subtle, and you need a pure and subtle mind to approach Brahman.

If you apply fire to a green wood, it will not burn; if you apply fire to a piece of dried wood, it will at once catch fire and burn. Even so, those who have not purified their minds will not be able to start the fire of meditation. They will be sleeping or dreaming—building castles in the air—when they sit for meditation. But, those who have removed the impurities of their minds by Japa, service, charity, Pranayama, etc., will enter into deep meditation as soos as they sit for meditation. The pure, ripe mind will at once burn with the fire of meditation.

For purposes of meditation, everything must be rendered Sattvic. The place of meditation must be Sattvic. The food must be Sattvic. The wearing apparel must be Sattvic. The company must be Sattvic. Talking must be Sattvic. The sound that you hear must be Sattvic. Thinking must be Sattvic. Study must be Sattvic. Everything must be Sattvic. Then only good progress in Sadhana is possible, particularly with the beginners or neophytes.

Practise meditation in the Brahma Muhurta. This is the best period for meditation. You will have a clear and calm mind in the early morning hours. The mind is like a blank sheet of paper or a clean tablet and comparatively free from worldly Samskaras or impressions at this period. The mind can be moulded very easily at this period in any way you like. You can charge the mind now easily with divine thoughts.

There is a spiritual influence and mysterious silence then. All saints and Yogins practise meditation at this period and send their spiritual vibrations to the whole world. You will be highly benefited by their vibrations if you start your prayer, Japa, and meditation at this period. You need not exert. The meditative state of mind will come of itself.

Practise regular systematic meditation during the same hours daily. You will get the meditative mood easily.

A solitary place with spiritual vibratory conditions, a cool, Sattvic place with temperate climate as at Uttarkashi, Rishikesh, Lakshmanjhula, Kankhal, or Badrinarayan, is indispensably requisite for concentration of mind and meditation, because the brain gets hot during meditation. The banks of the Ganga or Narmada, Himalayan scenery, lovely flower-gardens, sacred temples—these are the places which elevate the mind in concentration and meditation. Have recourse to them.

You can meditate only when the mind is beyond all anxieties. All physical activities should be completely suspended, all attachments should be ruthlessly cut asunder completely for five or six years, if you want to practise Dhyana Yoga, if you want to realise God through concentration of mind. Newspaper-reading, and correspondence with friends and relatives, should be completely stopped, as they cause distraction of mind and strengthen the world-idea. Seclusion for a period of five or six years is indispensable.

Some Useful Hints

In meditation, do not strain the eyes. Do not strain the brain. Do not struggle or wrestle with the mind. It is a serious mistake. Many neophytes commit this grave error. That is the reason why they get easily tired soon.

Make no violent effort to control the mind. But, rather allow it a little freedom for a while, and let it run and exhaust its efforts. The mind will jump now like an untrained monkey first. Gradually, it will slow down. Then you can fix the mind on your Lakshya.

Do not voluntarily and violently drive away intruding thoughts. Gently allow the divine thoughts to flow. Vicious thoughts will, by themselves, vanish.

When you begin to sweep a room that was kept closed for six months, various kinds of dirt come out from the corners of the room. Similarly, during meditation, under pressure of Yoga, through the grace of God, various kinds of impurities float about on the surface of the mind. Bravely remove them one by one suitable methods and counter-virtues.

You must daily increase your Vairagya and Sattvic virtues such as patience, perseverance, mercy, love, forgiveness, purity, etc. Vairagya and good qualities help meditation. Meditation increases the Sattvic qualities.

When you meditate, when you develop divine or Sattvic virtues, a spiritual road is constructed in the mind. If you are not regular in meditation, if your dispassion wanes, if you become careless and non-vigilant, the spiritual road will be washed away by the flood of impure thoughts and evil Vasanas. Therefore, be regular in your meditation. Regularity in meditation is of paramount importance.

Reasons for Failure in Meditation

There is always a complaint amongst the aspirants: "I am meditating for the last twelve years. I have not made any improvement. I have no Realisation". Why is it so? What is the reason? They have not plunged themselves in deep meditation into the innermost recesses of their hearts. They have not properly saturated the mind with thoughts of God. They have not done regular, systematic Sadhana. They have not disciplined the Indriyas perfectly. They have not collected all the outgoing rays of the mind. They have not made the self-determination, "I will realise this very second". They have not given the full hundred per cent of the mind or sixteen annas of the mind—their full mind—to God.

If the meditator has divine thoughts for ten minutes, and then worldly conflicting thoughts for the next ten mintes, he will not succeed in getting at the divine consciousness. You must run after one rabbit only with vigour, strength, and one-pointedness. You are sure to catch it. You must have only divine thoughts at all times. Then you are sure to realise God soon.

You must not be too hasty in longing for the fruits at once, when you take to meditation. A young lady perambulated the Asvattha tree a hundred and eight times for getting an offspring, and then immediately touched her abdomen to see whether there was a child or not. It is simply foolishness. She will have to wait for some months. Even so, if you will meditate for some time regularly, then the mind will be ripened, and eventually you will get Atma-sakshatkara or Self-realisation. Haste makes waste.

Experiences in Meditation

Various persons get various spiritual experiences in meditation. There cannot be a common experience for all. It depends upon the temperament, mode of Sadhana, place of concentration, and various other factors. Some hear melodious sounds in the ears. Some see lights. Some get Ananda or spiritual bliss. Some get both Prakasa and Ananda. During meditation, you may experience that you are rising from your seat. Some experience that they fly in the air.

If you get experiences of glimpses of the Self during intense meditation, if you see a blazing light during meditation, and if you get spiritual visions of angels, archangels, Rishis, Munis, Devatas, and any other extraordinary spiritual experiences, do not fall back in terror. Do not mistake them for phantoms. Do not give up the Sadhana. Plod on. Persevere diligently. Break veil after veil.

Aspirants are eager to get spiritual experiences soon. As soon as they get them, they are afraid. They are awfully alarmed when they go above the body-consciousness. They entertain a passing wonder whether they will come back again or not. Why should they be afraid at all? It does not matter much whether they return to body-consciousness or not. All our attempts are mainly directed towards getting over this body-consciousness. We are used to certain limitations. When these limitations suddenly drop away, we feel that there is no definite base left to stand upon. That is the reason why we are afraid when we go above the body-consciousness. That is a novel experience. Courage is needed. Bravery is an indispensable requisite.

Sometimes, bad spirits will trouble you. They may have ugly fierce faces, with long teeth. Drive them with your strong will. Give the word of command: “Get out”. They will go away. They are vampires. They are elementals. They will not do any harm to the Sadhakas. Your courage will be tested here. If you are timid, you cannot march further. Draw power and courage from the Atman within, the inexhaustible source. You will come across very good spirits also. They will help you a lot in your onward march.

During meditation, some of the visions that you see are your own materialised thoughts, while some others are real, objective visions.

If your general health is sound, if you are cheerful, happy and strong, physically and mentally, if the mind is peaceful and unruffled, if you get Ananda in meditation, and if your will is growing strong, pure and irrestible, think that you are improving in meditation and everything is going all right.

Meditation and Work

He who meditates is not able to work. He who works is not able to meditate. This is not balance. This is not equanimity. The two principles, meditation and action, must be well-balanced. You must be able, if you are ready to follow the divine injuction, to take up whatever work you are given—even a stupendous work—and leave it the next day, with the same quietness with which you took it up and without feeling that the responsibility is yours. You must be able to work hard in the world with tremendous force, and when the work is over, you must be able to shut yourself up in a cave as an absolute recluse for a long time with great peace of mind. That is balance. That is real strength.

Benefits of Meditation

Meditation acts as a powerful tonic. The divine energy freely flows from the feet of the Lord to the different systems of the Sadhakas. The holy vibrations penetrate all the cells of the body and cure the diseases of the body. Those who meditate save doctors' bills.

Meditation helps a lot in checking various emotions and impulses. If you can regulate your emotions and moods, you will not do foolish and wrong actions.

If you wind the watch at night, it will run smoothly for twenty-four hours. Even so, if you meditate for one or two hours in the Brahma Muhurta, you can work very peacefully throughout the day. Nothing can disturb your mind. The whole system will be charged with the spiritual vibrations or divine waves.

Regular meditation opens the avenues of intuitional knowledge, makes the mind calm and steady, awakens an ecstatic feeling, and brings the Yogic student in contact with the source of Supreme Purusha. If there are doubts, they are all cleared by themselves when you march on the path of Dhyana Yoga steadily.

Meditation develops strong and pure thoughts. Mental images are clear-cut and well-defined. Good thoughts are well grounded. Through clarification of ideas, confusion vanishes. You will yourself feel the way to place your foot-steps on the next rung of spiritual ladder. A mysterious inner voice will guide you. Hear this attentively.

The fire of meditation annihilates all foulness due to vice. Then suddenly comes knowledge or divine wisdom which directly leads to Mukti or final emancipation.

Meditate. Meditate. Do not lose even a single minute. Meditation will remove all the miseries of life. That is the only way.

49. MIND

That which separates you from God is mind. The wall that stands between you and God is mind.

Mind is not a gross thing, visible and tangible. Its existence is nowhere seen. Its magnitude cannot be measured. It does not require a space in which to exist. Mind is made up of subtle matter of various grades of density with different rates of vibration.

The mental body varies much in different people. It is composed of coarse or fine matter, according to the needs of the more or less unfolded consciousness connected with it. In the educated, it is active and well-defined, in the undeveloped, it is cloudy and ill-defined.

Functional Aspects of the Mind

Manas, Buddhi, Chitta, and Ahankara are only functional aspects of the mind. When the mind does Sankalpa-vikalpa or will-thought and doubt, it is called mind, when it discriminates and decides, it is Buddhi; when it self-arrogates, it is Ahankara; when it is the storehouse of Samskaras and seat of memory, it is Chitta; also when it does Dharana and Anusandhana.

Mind, Buddhi, and understanding are in the Linga Sarira; but, they operate through corresponding centres in the physical brain. The brain is not mind as the Westerners think. Mind has its seat in the physical brain. It gains experiences of this physical universe through the vibrations of the brain.

Mind, though it is all-pervading throughout the body, has got three places to reside in during the three states. The seat of the mind in deep sleep is the heart. In dream, the seat of the mind is the neck. In the waking state, the seat of the mind is the Ajna Chakra. Just mark what you do in deep thinking. You hold your finger in the chin, turn the neck to the right side, turn the gaze towards the space between the two eyebrows, and then begin to think seriously on the problem in hand.

Mental Aura

The vital sheath is more subtle than the physical body. It overlaps the physical sheath and is more extensive than it. The mental sheath is more subtle than the vital sheath and more extensive.

You have to touch the body of another man to have a physical influence over him. Whereas, you can stand at a distance and by mere 'passes' you can impart your Prana to him, because Prana is more subtle than the body. You can influence a man mentally through thought even though he lives a thousand miles away from you, because mental force is more subtle than Prana.

Mind has got aura, mental aura or psychic aura. Aura is Tejas, brilliance, or halo that emanates from the mind. The aura of those who have developed their minds is extremely effulgent. It can travel along distances and affect in a beneficial manner a large number of persons who come under its influence.

He who has purified his mind becomes a centre of force. All the lesser, impure, weak minds are unconsciously drawn towards the purified, greater mind, because they derive peace, power and strength from the greater, purified mind.

Fluctuation and Imagination

Just as heat is inseparable from fire, so also, fluctuation is inseparable from mind. It makes the mind restless. It is this fluctuation that causes Asanti or absence of peace of mind.

The power of fluctuation is the mind itself. This fluctuating mind alone is the world. The mind becomes no mind if fluctuation disappears. The mind ceases to exist if it becomes destitute of this fluctuation.

Mind havocs through the power of fluctuation. Fluctuation is Mara or Satan. It was this fluctuation that tempted Viswamitra. It is this fluctuation that brings the downfall of a struggling aspirant.

As soon as fluctuation manifests, various sorts of imaginations crop up. Imagination co-exists with fluctuation. Imagination is as much dangerous as fluctuation. Fluctuation moves the mind. Imagination fattens the mind. Mind minus fluctuation and imagination is a regular zero.

Fluctuation and imagination are the two seeds of the mind. Fluctuation is the fuel. Imagination is the fire. The unceasing fire of imagination is kept up by the fuel of fluctuation. If the fuel of fluctuation is withdrawn, the fire of imagination gets extinguished. The mind becomes tranquil. It is withdrawn into its source, the Atman.

Desire and Enjoyment

Desire excites the mind and senses. Just as China-man is drawn hither and thither by his five wives, so also, the mind is tossed hither and thither by the five Indriyas. It is always restless.

Desires are innumerable, insatiable and unconquerable. Enjoyment cannot bring in satisfaction. It is a mistake to think so. Enjoyment fans the desire. It is like pouring ghee in fire. Enjoyment strengthens, increases and aggravates a desire.

You may become old; your hairs may turn grey; but your mind is ever young. The capacity may vanish, but the craving remains even when you have reached advanced senility. Cravings are the real seeds of birth. These craving seeds give rise to Sankalpa and action. The wheel of Samsara is kept revolving by these cravings.

Destruction of Desires

The mind is ease-loving, easy-going and happy-go-lucky. You must check this nature. The desire for ease and comfort is ingrained in the mind. Aspirants should be very cautious and careful. Do not try to fulfil your desires. This is one way of controlling the mind.

You must not give indulgence or leniency to the mind. If you increase your wants even by one article, the articles will begin to swell in number. Luxuries will come one by one.

Whatever object the mind likes much must be given up. Whatever object the mind dwells upon constantly, thinks about very often, must be abandoned. If you like brinjals or apples much, give them up first. You will gain a great deal of peace, will-power and control of mind.

You must not take back those things which you have once renounced. Whenever you give up an object, the desire for that particular object becomes keen and strong for a few days. It agitates your mind. Keep quiet. Stand firm. It gets thinned out and dies eventually. Whenever the mind hisses to get back the objects that are rejected, raise the rod of Viveka. It will lower down its hood. It will keep quiet.

Take everything as it comes, instead of complaining. By this means, one seizes every opportunity. One develops easily, gains a great deal of mental strength and evenness of mind. Irritability vanishes. Power of endurance and patience will develop.

The Wandering Habit of the Mind

The mind in the vast majority of persons has been allowed to run wild and follow its own sweet will and desire. It is ever changing and wandering. It jumps from one object to another. It is fickle. It wants variety. Monotony brings disgust. It is like a spoiled child who is given to much indulgence by its parents, or a badly trained animal. The minds of many of us are like menageries of wild animals, each pursuing the bent of its own nature and going its own way. Restraint on the mind is a thing unknown to the vast majority of persons.

This wandering habit of the mind manifests itself in various ways. A householder's mind wanders to the cinema, theatre, circus, etc. A Sadhu's mind wanders to Varanasi, Brindavan and Nasik. Many Sadhus do not stick to one place during Sadhana. The wandering habit of the mind must be controlled by rendering it chaste and constant by Vichara. The mind must be trained to stick to one place for five years during your meditative life, to one method of Sadhana, to one path of Yoga, to one spiritual objective, and to one guide.

When you take up a book for study, you must finish it before you take up another. When you take up any work, you must devote your whole-hearted attention to that work and finish it before you take up another work. "One thing at a time and that done well is a very good rule as many can tell". This is the Yogi's way of doing. This is a very good rule for success in life.

Do not allow the mind to wander here and there like the strolling street dog. Keep it under your control always. Then alone you can be happy. It must be ever ready to obey you, to carry out your behests. If the mind says to you, "Go eastward", then go westward. If the mind says to you, "Go southward", then march northward. If the mind says to you, "Take a hot cup of tea in winter", then take a cup icy cold water. Swim like fish against the mental current. You will control the mind quite easily.

Mastery of Mind—The Only Gateway to Moksha

True freedom results from the disenthralment of the mind. He is a real potentate and a Maharaja who has conquered the mind. He is the richest man who has conquered desires, passions and the mind. If the mind is under control, it matters little whether you stay in a palace or a cave in the Himalayas, whether you do active Vyavahara or sit in silence.

The mind can be controlled by untiring perseverance and patience equal to that of one engaged in emptying the ocean, drop by drop, with tip of a blade of grass. To tame a lion or a tiger is far more easy than the taming of one's own mind. Tame your own mind first. Then you can tame the minds of others quite easily.

How to Control the Mind

Constantly think of God. You can very easily control the mind. Constant thinking of God thins out the mind.

The mind can very easily think of worldly objects. It is its Svabhava. The mental force can easily flow in old grooves and avenues of mundane thoughts. It finds it extremely difficult to think of God.

The difficulty in weaning the mind from objects and fixing it on God is the same as in making the Ganga flow towards Badrinarayana instead of its natural flow towards Gangasagar. It is like rowing against the current of Yamuna. Still, through strenuous efforts and Thyaga, the mind must be trained to flow towards God, much against its will, if you want to free yourself from birth and death. There is no other go if you want to escape from worldly miseries and tribulations.

Introspect. Have an inner life always. Let a portion of the mind and the hands do their work mechanically. An acrobat girl, while exhibiting her performances, has her attention rivetted on the water-pot she bears on her head although all the time she is dancing to various tunes. So does the truly pious man attend to all his business concerns, but has his mind's eye fixed upon the blissful feet of the Lord. This is balance. This will lead to integral development.

The World—A Projection of the Mind

The whole experience of duality, made up of perceiver and perceived, is pure imagination. There is no world apart from the mind. On destruction of the mind, all is destroyed.

The activity of the mind is the cause of all appearance. On account of ignorance or illusion in the mind, you see the objects, trees, etc., outside and feel as if they are separate from you and real.

So long as there is mind, there are all these distinctions of big and small, high and low, superior and inferior, good and bad, etc. The highest truth is that in which there is no relativity. If you can transcend the mind by constant and profound meditation on the Atman, you will be able to attain the state beyond the pairs of opposites wherein lies supreme peace and the highest knowledge.

Mind and Man

The thinker is different from thought. Mind is as much your property and outside of you as your limbs, the dress you wear, or the building you dwell in. You always say, "My mind", as if mind is one of your instruments, just like your walking-stick or umbrella. Even in cases of delirium or in cases where there is paralysis of the mental functions, where a man loses his memory and other faculties partly or wholly, he remains. The 'I' exists. Therefore, mind is different from 'I'. Mind is your tool or instrument only. You must know how to handle it nicely.

When emotions, moods, sentiments, arise in the mind, separate them, study their nature, dissect and analyse them. Do not identify yourself with them. The real 'I' is entirely distinct from them. It is the Silent Witness. Master your impulses, emotions and moods and rise from the position of a slave to that of a spiritual king who can rule over them with force and power.

You are eternal, all-pervading Atman in reality. You are Pure Consciousness Itself. Mind is a mere beggar. It borrows its light and intelligence from the Inner Ruler, the Atman is self-effulgent, just as the iron rod borrows its heat and effulgence from fire. Mind is non-intelligent, but appears to be intelligent by borrowing light from Brahman, just as water exposed to the sun borrows heat from the sun.

Shake yourself, therefore, from the tyranny of the mind that has oppressed you for so long, domineered over you, and exploited you uptil now. Rise up boldly like a lion. Assert the magnanimity of your real Self and be free.

50. MUSIC

Music is Gandharva Vidya. It is the most ancient of arts. Ravana propitiated Lord Siva through music.

Music is the medium for expressing emotion. Music kindles love and infuses hope. It has countless voices and instruments. Music is in the hearts of all men and women. Music is on their tongues.

Nature's Music

Music is in the winds and the waves. Music is in the nightingale. It is in the cinema-stars and musicians. It is in the concert, orchestra and theatres.

There is music in the running brooks. There is music in the crying of children. There is music in all things, if you have ears.

The Power of Music

Sound is the first manifestation of the absolute. Supercharged with transcendent soul-force, sound is, in all creation, the one powerful principle that widely influences and effectively brings under control all other manifestations. Many examples can be quoted to bear testimony to this claim of sound with reference to both the individual and the cosmos.

We have heard how Tansen was able to make it rain through the Megha Raga, how he lighted the lamp through singing in Dipaka Raga. There are, again, certain accounts relating to the Tibetan Lamas, which tell us how the Lamas drove away and dispersed rain-bearing clouds, or gathered the clouds and made them rain by blowing the horns and the trumpets and beating the drums.

We have also heard how the deer is entrapped by sweet sound, how the cobra is enchanted by sweet music. Raga Punnagavarali charms the cobra. Nada entraps the mind. The mind gets Laya in sweet Nada.

Mark the power of gentle, sweet sounds: *Sa, Ri, Ga, Ma, Pa, Dha, Ni, Sa.* Music has charms to soothe a ferocious tiger. It melts rocks and bends the banyan tree. It enraptures, lulls, and energises. It elevates, inspires, strengthens and invigorates. It vibrates in the memory. It cures incurable diseases.

Music fills the mind with Sattva. Music generates harmony in the heart. Music melts the hardest heart. Music softens the brutal nature of man.

Music comforts, soothes and cheers up people when they are afflicted. It comforts the lonely and the distressed. Music removes worries, cares and anxieties. It makes you forget the world. Man wants music to relax and elevate him.

The devotee sits with his Ektar Tambura to melt his mind in his Lord in silence. Narada Rishi roams about in the three worlds with his Tambura in his hand, singing *Sriman Narayana Narayana.* Music helps the devotee to commune with the Lord. It makes the mind one-pointed quickly. Music brings Bhava Samadhi. Tyagaraja, Purandara Das, Mira and Tukaram have all realised God through music.

Pranava—The source of All Music

Wherefrom has music derived this mighty power? From the supreme music of Brahman, the sacred Pranava. Listen to the vibration of Tambura the Veena: do you hear the majestic Pranava-Nada? All the musical notes are blended beautifully into this Pranava. All the musical notes spring from this Pranava. Music is intended to reverberate this Pranava-Nada in your heart. For, Om or the Pranava is your real name, your real Svarupa. Therefore you love to hear music, which is but the most melodious intonation of your own essential name. When the mind thus gets attracted, and gets unified with one's essential nature, the great power of God stored up there wells up within and heals body and mind.

Bhava Samadhi and Super-intuitional Knowledge

He who does Sangita forgets the body and the world. Sangita removes Dehadhyasa or identification with the body. The Bhakta enters into Bhava Samadhi by singing devotional music. He comes face to face with the greatest storehouse of knowledge and wisdom, Ananda or Supreme Bliss. Therefore he emerges from the Samadhi as a Jnani, and radiates peace, bliss and wisdom all around.

Tukaram was an agricultural peasant. He could not even sign his name. He was always doing Sankirtan of Lord Krishna's Name *Vitthala, Vitthala* with cymbals in his hands. He had Darshana of Lord Krishna in physical form. His inner sight or Divya Drishti was opened by Sankirtan. His inspiring Abhangas are texts for M.A.

students of the Bombay University. Wherefrom did the unlettered Tukaram derive his knowledge? He tapped the fountain of knowledge through Sankirtan. He penetrated into the divine source through Bhava Samadhi that was brought about by deep Sankirtan.

Music Is Spiritual

Music is not an instrument for titillation of the nerves or satisfaction of the senses; it is a Yoga Sadhana which enables you to attain Atma-sakshatkara. It is the foremost duty of all musicians, and institutions interested in the promotion of music, to preserve this grand ideal and this pristine purity that belong to music.

Saint Thyagaraja, Purandara Das and others have repeatedly pointed out; and by their own life of renunciation and devotion they have emphasised that music should be treated as Yoga, and that true music can be tasted only by one who has freed himself from all taints of worldliness, and who practises music as a Sadhana for Self-realisation.

Tyagaraja was a devotee of Lord Rama. Most of his devotional songs are in praise of lord Rama. He had direct Darshan of Lord Rama on several occasions. Purandara Das worshipped Lord Vitthala, and spent forty years in the dissemination of Bhakti all over the land through his songs. He heard the music of the soul inside, and so he gave his thrilling music outside. Mira came face to face with Krishna. She talked with Krishna, her beloved. She drank the Krishnaprema-rasa. She has sung from the core of her heart the music of her soul, the music of her beloved, her unique spiritual experiences. Her language of love is so powerful that even a downright atheist will be moved by her devotional songs. Shyama Sastrigal was a great devotee of Devi. He enjoyed the abundant grace of mother Kamakshi. Muthuswami Dikshitar, the great Nada Jyotis, regarded Lord Subrahmanya Himself as his Supreme Guru, and all his compositions bear the Mudra GURU-GUHA.

Music is Nada Yoga. The various musical notes have their own corresponding Nadis or subtle channels in the Kundalini Chakras; and music vibrates these Nadis, purifies them, and awakens the psychic and spiritual power dormant in them. Purification of Nadis not only ensures peace and happiness of mind, but goes a long way in Yoga Sadhana and helps the aspirant to reach the goal of life very easily.

Influence of Music over Mind and Body

Sweet melody exercises a powerful influence on the mind and physical nature of every living being. Trapped in music, the mysterious mind with its thousand hoods of Vasanas and Vrittis, lies quiescently on the lap of the Sadhaka; and he can make it dance to his tune, control it according to his will, and mould it as he pleases. Mind, the instrument of Satan in man, the magic-wand of Maya, the terror of all spiritual aspirants, is there in the hands of this music Yogi under his perfect control. The wonder of wonders in the case of this music Yoga is that it is not only the mind of the musician which thus controlled, but the minds of all those who listen to the music. They become calm and blissful. That is why great saints like Mira Bai, Tukaram, Kabir Das, Sri Tyagaraja, Purandara Das and others wove their Upadesa into sweet music; with the sweet music, these sublime thoughts would easily get into the heart of the listener, which is at other times zealously guarded by the vicious cobra of worldliness.

The Rishis of yore have invariably written their inspiring works either in the form of poetry or in the form of songs. Our scriptures—the Vedas, Smritis, Puranas, etc.—are all set to music, and are metrical compositions. There is rhythm, metre and melody in them. Sama Veda, especially, is unrivalled in its music.

Music is an aid to treatment of diseases. Sages affirm that many diseases can be cured by the melodious sound of a flute or a violin, a Veena or a Sarangi. They maintain that there is, in music, an extraordinary power over diseases. Harmonious rhythm caused by sweet music has attractive property. It draws out disease. The disease comes out to encounter the music wave. The two blend together and vanish in space.

Music relaxes nervous tension, and makes parts of the body affected by tension to resume their normal functions. In America, doctors are treating patients who are suffering from nervous diseases through music. In ancient Egypt, music was used in temples in healing diseases of the nervous class.

Sangita or Kirtan is the best medicine and tonic when all other systems of medicine have failed to cure a disease. Kirtan will work wonders. Kirtan is the sole refuge and sheet-anchor in the treatment of chronic incurable diseases. Try this unique medicine and realise its marvellous benefits. If anyone is suffering from any disease, do Kirtan near his bed. He will soon be cured of his disease.

Kirtan Bhakti

Kirtan is singing of the Lord's glories. The devotee is thrilled with divine emotion. He loses himself in the love of God. He gets horripilation in the body due to extreme love for God. He weeps in the middle when thinking of the glory of God. His voice becomes choked, and he flies into a state of divine Bhava.

Kirtan is singing God's Name with feeling, love and faith. In Sankirtan, people join together and sing God's Name collectively in a common place. There is accompaniment of musical instruments such as harmonium, violin, cymbals, Mridanga or Khol, etc. Christians sing hymns in the church with piano. This is only Sankirtan. Kirtan is one of the nine modes of Bhakti. Sankirtan is an exact science. One can realise God through Kirtan alone. This is the easiest method for attainment of God-consciousness. Great divine persons like Narada, Valmiki and Suka in ancient times, and Gouranga, Nanak, Tulasidas, Surdas, etc., in comparatively recent times, have all attained perfection through Kirtan Bhakti alone.

The harmonious vibrations produced by the singing of the Names of the Lord help devotees to control their mind easily. They produce a benign influence on their mind. They elevate the mind at once from its old ruts or grooves to magnanimous heights of divine splendour and glory. If one does Sankirtan from the bottom of his heart with full Bhava and Prem, even the trees, birds and animals will be deeply influenced. They will respond. Such is the powerful influence of Sankirtan.

The Psychology behind Kirtan Bhakti

Kirtan is a very effective method of devotion for another reason. Man is an erotic being. He loves and loves. He cannot but love things of the world; but, his love is only passion and is not pure divine love. He wants to hear sweet music, wants to see beautiful objects, and wants to witness a dance. Music melts the heart of even the stone-hearted man. If at all there is anything in this world which can change the heart of a man in a very quick time, that is music and dance. This very method is made use of in Kirtan Bhakti; but, it is directed towards God instead of towards sensual enjoyments.

Man's emotion of erotism is directed towards Divinity, and his love for music and singing is not destroyed; because, sudden destruction of such a sentiment which he holds as very dear will not prove successful in making him perfect. Kirtan is sweet and pleasant, and easily changes the heart.

Kirtan is most suitable method even for householders. This gives pleasure to the mind, and at the same time, purifies the heart. This has a double effect.

Do Sankirtan daily. Disseminate Sankirtan Bhakti far and wide. Develop Visva-prem through Sankirtan. Establish Sankirtan Mandalis everywhere. Bring Vaikuntha on earth—in every house—by doing Sankirtan! Realise your Sat-Chit-Ananda state.

51. OM

Adorations to Om. Salutations to Om. Prostrations to Om. Devotion to Om.

Glory to Om. Victory to Om. Hosanna to Om. Hail to Om.

Om is sacred monosyllable. Om is the mystic letter. Om is the immortal Akshara. In Om, the world rests. In Om, we live and move. In Om, we go to rest. In Om, we find our quest.

Om is the symbol of Brahman. Om is the word of power. Om is the life of all lives. Om is the soul of all souls.

Om is verily Brahman. Om is the Satchidananda. Om is infinity. Om is eternity. Om is immortality.

Om is the source of everything. Om is the womb of all Vedas. Om is the basis for all languages. In Om merge all trinities. From Om proceed all sounds. In Om exist all objects.

Om is the highest Mantra. Om is Soham. Om is *Om Tat Sat.* Om is a lamp unto thy feet and a light unto thy path.

Sound—The First Manifestation of the Absolute

Om is Nada Brahman. Nada is sound. Sound is vibration. Om is the first vibration of sound. Sound is the first manifestation of the Absolute.

We know not anything about the nature of the absolute except that It is. With all their kindness, the scriptures have tried to tell us all about creation, how it proceeded from the Absolute. They say: "Brahman was one and non-dual. It thought, *'Ekoham Bahu Syam'*. That caused a vibration, eventually bringing in sound, and that sound was Om, whence are all other manifestations".

Thus, sound is virtually the comprehensible basis for all creation. Brahman is incomprehensible in Its transcendent aspect. The nearest approach to It is only sound, or we can call sound as Apara Brahman.

Om—The Basis of All Sounds

All the objects are denoted by sounds, and all sounds merge in Omkara. All the collection of speech or words terminate in one sound 'Om'.

The humming of the bees, the sweet melody of the nightingale, the seven tunes in music, the sound of the Mridanga and

Kettledrum, the lute and the flute, the roaring of the lion, the singing of the lover, the neighing of the horses, the hissing of the cobra, the 'hu, hu' sound of the invalids, the crying of the baby, the clapping of the audience when an orator delivers his peroration—all are emanations from Omkara only.

The sound produced in the flowing Ganga, the sound that is heard at a distance and that which proceeds from the bustle of a market, the sound that is produced when the flywheel of an engine is set in motion, the sound that is caused when it rains—it is all 'Om' only. You split any word: you find 'Om' there. Om is all-pervading like Akasa, like Brahman.

Om is the basis of all sounds. Om consists of three letters, A, U, and M. A, U, M cover the whole range of sound-vibrations.

The larynx and the palate are the sounding-boards. When you pronounce A, no part of the tongue or palate is touched. When you pronounce U, the sound rolls from the very root to the end of the sounding-board of the mouth. M is the last sound which produced by closing the two lips. Therefore, all sounds are centred in Om. All languages originate from Om.

The essence of the four Vedas is Om only. He who chants or repeats Om really repeats the sacred books of the whole world. Om is source or womb for all religions and scriptures. *Om, Amen* and *Ahamin* are all one. They present the truth or Brahman, the One Existence. There is no worship without Om.

Om Represents All Trinities

Om is everything. Om is your real name. Om covers all the three fold experiences of man. Om stands for all the phenomenal worlds. From Om this sense-universe has been projected. The world exists in Om and dissolves in Om. A represents the physical plane; U represents the mental plane and astral planes, the world of spirits, all heavens; M represents the deep sleep state and all that is unknown even in your wakeful state and all that is beyond the reach of the intellect. Om represents all. Om is the basis of your life, thought and intelligence.

Every kind of trinity is represented by Om, such as Brahma-Vishnu-Siva, past-present-future, birth-life-death, creation-preservation-destruction, waking-dreaming-deep sleep, being-non-being-becoming, and so on.

All triplets are represented by Om, such as Sarasvati-Lakshmi-Durga, Father-Son-Holy Ghost, Rajas-Sattva-Tamas, body-mind-soul, Sat-Chit-Ananda, omniscience-omnipotence-omnipresence, gross-subtle-causal.

A is Brahman. M is Maya. U is interaction between the two.

Om also represents the *Tat Tvam Asi* Mahavakya. A is Jiva. M is Isvara. U connects, shows the identity of Jiva and Isvara or Brahman.

Om is very, very important. It should be worshipped. It should be chanted loudly. It should be repeated mentally with meaning and Bhava. It should be meditated upon.

The Power of Om-Chanting

A loud sound is produced in chanting Om. Om is repeated with a big sound with three and a half Matras. The Pranava sound is generated in the navel with the sound O, and taken up very slowly to the Brahmarandra on the top of the head with the closing sound M. The vibration of M is prolonged for some time.

There is another kind of chanting Om with eighteen Matras. It very, very long chanting. It takes a long time. The Pranava is Deergha.

The pronunciation of the sacred syllable Om is one which has engaged the attention of all Europeans devoted to Eastern studies. The vibrations set up by this word are so powerful, that if one persists in taking recourse to them, they would bring the largest building to the ground. This seems difficult to believe in until one has tried the practice; but once having tried it, one can easily understand how the above statement may be true and perfectly correct. I have tested the power of the vibrations and can quite believe that the effect would be as stated.

Pronounced as spelt, the chanting of Om will have a certain effect upon the student; but pronounced in its correct method, it arouses and transforms every atom in his physical body, setting up new vibrations and conditions, and awakening the sleeping power of the body.

The chanting of Om drives away all worldly thoughts and removes distraction. It is very powerful. The Pancha Koshas vibrate rhythmically when Om is chanted. Chanting of Om infuses new vigour in the body. Five persons can sit in a circle and then can chant Om in a chorus. It will be beautiful and exhilarating. All can at once feel a new life.

When you feel depressed, chant Om fifty times. You will be filled with new vigour and strength. Chanting of Om is a powerful tonic. You need not pay anything to the doctor. When you chant Om, feel you are the pure, all-pervading light and consciousness.

Those who chant Om will have a powerful, sweet voice, Ekagrata of mind comes quickly by chanting Om. When you take walk in the morning and evening, you can chant Om nicely. Chant Om in a moonlit night. Chant Om when you walk along the seaside or the banks of a river. You can sing Om in a beautiful way also. The rhythmic pronunciation of Om makes the mind serene and one-pointed and induces the spiritual qualifications which ensure Self-realisation.

The Greatest of all Mantras

The Pranava or Om is the greatest of all Mantras. It bestows directly liberation. All Mantras begin with Om. Om is the life or soul of all Mantras. It precedes the Panchakshari and the Ashtakshari. Every hymn begins with Om. Every Upanishad begins with Om. The Gayatri begins with Om. The oblations that are offered to the various gods are preceded by the chanting Om. The Archanas, *viz.,* the Ashtottari, the Trisati, and the Sahasranama are also preceded by the Pranava. The greatness of the Omkara cannot be adequately described by anybody. Even Parvati, Adisesha, and great sages were unable to describe the greatness of Om. Such is the potency or Mahima of Om.

What *Sree Ram* Mantra is for a Vairagya of Ayodhya, what *Hrim* is for a Tantric of Bengal, what the Gayatri is for a Madrasi Brahmin, so is Om or the Pranavaa for a Vedantin or a Sannyasin of Rishikesh.

Om is otherwise known as Omkara, Ekakshara, or Udgitha in the Chhandogya Upanishad. Any man or woman whose mind is sincerely turned towards Brahman, who has mental Sannyasa, and who has Vedantic Samskaras and real taste in Vedanta, can repeat this Mantra.

Those who do Japa of Om daily will get tremendous power. They will have lustre in the eyes and the face.

Meditation on Om

Have the picture of Om in front of you in your meditation room. Concentrate on this picture. Do Trataka also with open eyes, steady gazing without winking till tears flow profusely. Associate the ideas of infinity, eternity immortality, etc., when you think of Om.

Neophytes in the path of Jnana Yoga should do Trataka, gazing on Om with open eyes, in the beginning for about three months. Then they should visualise Om with closed eyes. Visualisation of Om is the calling up of a clear mental image of Om by closing the eyes. They should repeat Om mentally with Bhava and meaning, and make the ears hear the sound also so that they may not run outside to hear other sounds.

Meditate on Om. Retire into your meditation chamber. Sit on Padma, Siddha, or Sukha Asana. Close the eyes. Relax the muscles and nerves completely. Concentrate the gaze on Trikuti, the space between the two eyebrows. Silence the objective or conscious mind. Repeat Om mentally with Suddha-bhavana or Brahma-bhavana.

This Bhavana is a *sine qua non.* You will have to repeat Om with the Bhava or feeling that you are in the infinite, all-pervading, pure intelligence. Mere gramophonic repetition or parrot-like repetition of Om will not bring out the desired result.

When you think of Om, you will have to think of Brahman, the thing signified by the symbol. Association with Om is to become one with the signified. Try to identify yourself with the all-blissful Self when you meditate on Om.

Keep the meaning of Om always at heart. Feel Om. Feel that you are the all-pervading, infinite Light. Feel that you are the pure, perfect, all-knowing, eternally free Brahman. Feel you are absolute consciousness. Feel that you are infinite, unchanging existence. Every atom, every molecule, every nerve, vein and artery should powerfully vibrate with these ideas. Lip-repetition of Om will not produce much benefit. It should be through the heart, head and soul. Your whole soul should feel you are at the subtle, all-pervading intelligence. This feeling should be kept up all twenty-four hours.

Convert a room into a forest. Renounce the idea that you are different from Brahman. Practise regularly, steadily, with interest, faith, zeal, perseverance and enthusiasm. Have congenial company, and light Sattvic food as milk, curd, fruits, nuts, Moong-ki-dal, rice and bread. Practise for three hours in the morning from 4 a.m. to 7 a.m., and three hours at night from 7 p.m. to 10 p.m. Keep up the Brahmic feeling while at work also. You are bound to succeed in three or four years. You will rest in your own Svarupa, in your own Suddha Sat-chit-ananda state. *Nastyatra Samsayah*: there is no doubt of that here.

Remember Om Always

Remember Om. Remember *Soham, Om Soham, Sivoham, Aham Brahma Asmi, Analhaq.* Truth is one. These Mantras remind you of your identity with Supreme Soul. They are Mahavakyas, great sentences of the Upanishads. They blow out this false ego, this illusory 'I', into airy nothing.

Om is your birthright. It is the common heritage of all. It is the common property of all the people of the world. It is the word of power. It brings inspiration and intuition. It elevates the mind to spiritual heights of ineffable splendour and glory.

Om is your spiritual food. Om is your spiritual tonic and vitamin. It is full of divine potencies. It is your constant companion. It is your saviour. It is your joy and life. Live in it day and night. Be absorbed in it.

Live in Om. Meditate on Om. Inhale and exhale on Om. Rest peacefully in Om. Take shelter in Om.

Sing Om rhythmically. Chant Om loudly. Roar Om forcibly. Repeat Om mentally. Draw strength from Om. Get inspiration from Om. Drive energy from Om. Imbibe bliss from Om. All desires vanish. You will attain Self-realisation.

Rely on Om. Reflect on Om. Concentrate on Om. Meditate on Om. Know this sacred syllable Om. You will know everything. You will attain the highest knowledge.

The sacred word Om is the bow. The mind is the Arrow. Brahman is the aim or mark. It is to be hit by one whose thoughts are concentrated. Then he will enter the target. He will become of the same nature as Brahman. Just as the lump of ice becomes one with water of the bucket, so also, he will become one with Brahman.

52. PATANJALA YOGA

The Author

Patanjali Maharshi is the exponent of Yoga philosophy. Patanjali is now regarded as the last of the Avataras of Lord. You will find in Yajnavalkya Smriti that Hiranyagarbha was the original teacher of Yoga. Patanjali Maharshi is only a compiler or explainer of the Yoga precepts, doctrines and tenets taught by Hiranyagarbha.

Yoga Sutras

Patanjali Yoga philosophy is written in Sutras. A 'Sutra' is a terse statement. It is an aphoristic saying. It is pregnant with deep, hidden significance. Rishis of yore have expressed the philosophical ideas and their realisation in the form of Sutras only. It is very difficult to understand the meaning of the Sutras without the help of commentary, a gloss or a teacher who is well-versed in Yoga. A Yogi with full realisation can explain the Sutras beautifully. Literally, Sutra means a thread. Just as various kinds of flowers of different colours are nicely arranged in a string, to make a garland, and just as rows of pearls are beautifully arranged in a string to form a necklace, so also, Yogic ideas are well-arranged in Sutras. They are further grouped into Chapters.

The First Chapter

The first Chapter is Samadhipada. It deals with different kinds of Samadhi. It contains 51 Sutras. Obstacles in meditation, five kinds of Vrittis and their control, three kinds of Vairagya, nature of Isvara, various methods to enter into Samadhi and the way to acquire peace of mind by developing virtues, are described here.

The Second Chapter

This Chapter is called Sadhanapada. It contains 55 Sutras. It treats of Kriya Yoga, viz., Tapas, study and self-surrender to God, the five Klesas (afflictions), the methods to destroy these afflictions which stand in the way of getting Samadhi, Yama and Niyama and their fruits, practice of Asana and Pranayama and their benefits, Pratyahara and its advantages, etc.

The Third Chapter

The third Chapter is Vibhutipada. It contains 56 Sutras. It treats of Dharana, Dhyana and various kinds of Samyama on external objects, mind, internal Chakras, and on several objects, and to acquire various Siddhis.

The Fourth Chapter

The fourth Chapter is called Kaivalyapada and it deals with Kaivalya or Independence. It contains 34 Sutras. It treats of the Independence of a full-blown Yogi who has perfect discrimination between Prakriti and Purusha, and who has separated himself from the three Gunas. It also deals with mind and its nature. Dharmamegha Samadhi also is described here.

What Is Raja Yoga

Raja Yoga is the king of all Yogas. It concerns directly with mind. In this Yoga there is no struggling with either the vital force or the physical body. There are no Hatha Yogic Kriyas. The Yogi sits at ease, watches his mind and silences the bubbling thoughts. He stills the mind and restrains the thought-waves and enters into the thoughtless state or Asamprajnata Samadhi. Hence the name Raja Yoga. Though Raja Yoga is a dualistic philosophy and treats of Prakriti and Purusha, it helps the student in Advaitic Realisation of oneness eventually. Though there is the mention of Purusha, ultimately the Purusha becomes identical with the Highest Self, or Brahman of Upanishads.

Raja Yoga is the royal road to freedom from misery. It treats of the four great principles—misery, its cause, freedom from misery, and the means. The practice of the methods prescribed in Raja Yoga leads to the cessation of all miseries and the attainment of eternal bliss.

Raja Yoga is also called Ashtanga Yoga or Yoga of eight limbs. The eight limbs are Yama, Niyama, Asana, Pranayama, Pratyahara, Dharana, Dhyana and Samadhi.

Yama and Niyama

Yama and Niyama are the most important preliminaries to the practice of meditation. Without acquiring these, if you run to meditation and Samadhi you will only break your legs. But you cannot wait either to perfect yourself in all the Yamas and Niyamas. For, it will take one lifetime to practise even one of the Yamas. Therefore, you will have to go on practising Yama-Niyama, and at the same time, go on with your concentration and meditation, even though you are not fully established in Yama-Niyama.

Yama consists of Satya, Ahimsa, Brahmacharya, Aparigraha and Asteya. Satya means truthfulness in every respect in one's daily life. We hear of only one Harishchandra who was perfectly established in truth. It is so difficult to get established in this virtue. But there are many who are attempting to practise truth in daily life. Love all—this is the practice of Ahimsa. Though you cannot observe perfect Brahmacharya (self-restraint) lead a well-regulated life. Do not lead a luxurious life, reduce your wants—this is the essence of Aparigraha. Asteya is not coveting the wealth of others. Those who wish to attain the Imperishable Absolute should observe these canons uncompromisingly.

Niyama consists of Saucha, Santosha, Tapas, Svadhyaya and Isvarapranidhana. Saucha means internal and external purity. Internal purity—purity of the mind and heart—is more important. Get rid of evil Vrittis. Santosha (contentment) is the greatest asset, greatest treasure. Tapas is austerity. Egolessness and selfless service are the forms of Tapas. Humility and desirelessness are the greatest forms of austerity. Practise these through ceaseless, untiring, selfless service. Practise the three kinds of Tapas mentioned in the Gita. Disciplinary practices like fasting, etc., also come under Tapas. You will get the meditative mood while fasting. Svadhyaya is study of religious books. Recitation of Mantras also is regarded as Svadhyaya. Then you have Isvara-Pranidhana. Surrender to the Lord. "I am Thine, all is Thine, my Lord; Thy Will be done", is the Mantra for self-surrender.

Asana and Pranayama

After Yama and Niyama comes Asana. Patanjali does not pay much attention to Asanas. He prescribes steady and comfortable sitting posture. He only wants that you should assume a comfortable posture in which you can sit for a long time, and not allow sleep to overcome you. In Hatha Yoga only there are various Asanas and Pranayama. These are all later developments. Like Asanas, later on the Ashta-Kumbhakas were developed in Pranayama. I will show you the four easy and important exercises in Pranayama. The first is easy—Sukha Purvaka—Pranayama. You can practise it even lying down in bed. Draw the air through both the nostrils as long as comfortable, retain as long as comfortable and breathe out. The next Pranayama is the Sandhya Pranayama or the Anuloma-Viloma Pranayama. Draw the air through the left nostril, retain and exhale through the right nostril; then draw the air through the right nostril, retain and exhale. These constitute one round of Pranayama. The ratio between Puraka (inhalation), Kumbhaka (retention) and Rechaka (exhalation) is expected to be 1:4:2. But in the beginning, you need not bother yourself about this. When you become an expert, the ratio will come by itself. During retention of breath, particularly, repeat your Ishta Mantra. This is more effective. This will fill you with divine energy. The third is Bhastrika. It is rapid exhalation and inhalation. It is like blowing of the bellows. Even one round of Bhastrika will invigorate you, within a few seconds. Do it in winter. In summer you can do one round; and that, too, in the early morning hours. The fourth is Sitali. Make a tube of your tongue and draw the air through it, retain, and then exhale. In summer Sitali is very good. It will instantly cool your system. It will purify your blood. This is equal to taking a glass of ice-cold water. If you practise all these Pranayamas for a considerable time, Kevala Kumbhaka will come of its own accord. Kevala Kumbhaka is Kumbhaka without Puraka and Rechaka—retention of breath without inhalation and exhalation. The mind becomes quite steady after this Pranayama.

Pratyahara

Pratyahara is abstraction. It is the withdrawal of the Indriyas from the objects. The senses are assimilated in the mind which is rendered pure through the practice of Yama, Niyama and Pranayama. The mind becomes more calm now. He who has mastery over Pratyahara will never complain of Vikshepa or distraction of mind. Pratyahara gives power to the practitioner. When the Indriyas are withdrawn from the objects, then you can fix the mind on a particular point. Pratyahara and Dharana are interdependent.

Dharana, Dhyana and Samadhi

Dharana is the fixing of the mind on something external or internal. The mind can be fixed externally on the picture of Lord Hari. Lord Krishna or Lord Rama or on any other object or point. Internally it can be fixed on any Chakra or any part of the body or on any abstract idea. Having controlled the Prana through Pranayama, and the Indriyas through Pratyahara, you should try to fix the mind on something. Dharana can be done only if you are free from the distractions of mind. After Dharana comes Dhyana. In Dhyana you allow the mind to dwell on the same thought. The Bhagavadgita gives a beautiful description of the process of Dhyana. Study the sixth Chapter. Resort to a secret place of seclusion. Here spread out a seat on a place which is neither too high nor too low. Cloth, deerskin and Kusa grass, one placed over the other, form the ideal combination. Restrain the senses. Still the mind. Keep the body erect, with the head, neck, and trunk in a straight line. Gaze at the Trikuti. Shut out the avenues through which the senses flow outwards; fix the mind on the Lord or the Self seated in the heart; retain the breath at the crown of the head by the practice of Kevala Kumbhaka; and then you will get perfect concentration of the mind. You will enter into Dhyana and Samadhi quickly. The three, viz., Dharana, Dhyana and Samadhi are more internal than the preceding Yama, Niyama, Asana, Pranayama and Pratyahara. The three (Dharana, Dhyana and Samadhi) together constitute Samyama. These three constitute the Antaranga Sadhana of Raja Yoga. The real Raja Yoga commences with Pratyahara. Samyama constitutes the actual practice of Raja Yoga.

Through the practice of Samyama you can enter into the truth about the thing meditated upon. Nirbija (seedless) Samadhi or Asmprajnata Samadhi is the final goal of Raja Yoga. Compared to that, Samyama also is external or indirect. It is also preparatory. There is Alambana or something for the mind to depend upon; whereas in Nirbija Samadhi, there is nothing for the mind to depend upon. It is Niralambana. The practitioner ascends the various rungs of the Yogic ladder, stage by stage and acquires different experiences, knowledge and powers. He feels his absolute freedom and attains Kaivalya, the highest goal of Raja Yoga. The sum total of all knowledge of the three worlds, of all secular science is nothing but mere husk when compared to the Infinite knowledge of a real Yogi who has attained Kaivalya. Glory to such exalted Yogins. May their blessings be upon us all!

53. PEACE

Peace is a divine attribute. It is a quality of the soul. It cannot remain with greedy persons. It fills the pure heart. It deserts the lustful. It runs away from selfish people. It is an ornament of a Paramahamsa.

Peace is a state of quiet. It is freedom from disturbance, anxiety, agitation, riot or violence. It is harmony, silence, calm, repose, rest. Specifically, it is the absence or cessation of war.

Peace is the happy, natural state of man. It is his birthright. War is his disgrace.

Everybody wants peace and is clamouring for peace; but peace does not come easily. Even if it comes, it does not last for a long time.

The Abode of Peace

Peace is not in the heart of the carnal man. Peace is not in the hearts of ministers, advocates, businessmen, dictators, kings and emperors. Peace is in the hearts of Yogins, sages, saints and spiritual men. It is in the heart of a desireless man, who has controlled his senses and the mind. Greed, lust, jealousy, envy, anger, pride and egoism are the enemies of peace. Slay these enemies by the sword of dispassion, discrimination, and non-attachment. You will enjoy perpetual peace.

Peace is not in money, estate, bungalows and possessions. Peace does not dwell in outward things, but within the soul.

Money cannot give you peace. You can purchase many things, but you cannot purchase peace. You can buy soft beds, but you cannot buy sleep. You can buy good food, but you cannot buy good appetite. You can buy good tonics, but you cannot buy good health. You can buy good books, but you cannot buy wisdom.

Withdraw yourself from external objects. Meditate and rest in your soul. You will realise everlasting peace now.

Nothing can bring you peace, but yourself. Nothing can bring you peace, but the victory over your lower self, triumph over your senses and mind, desires and cravings. If you have no peace within yourself, it is vain to seek it in external objects and outward sources.

Inner Peace

Perfect security and full peace cannot be had in this world, because this is a relative plane. All objects are conditioned in time, space and causation. They are perishable. Where then can you look for full security and perfect peace? You can find this in the immortal self. He is an embodiment of peace. He is beyond time, space and causation.

Real, deeper peace is independent of external conditions. Real, abiding peace is stupendous stillness of the Immortal Soul within. If you can rest in this ocean of peace, all the usual noises of the world can hardly affect you. If you enter the silence or the wonderful calm of divine peace by stilling the bubbling mind and restraining the thoughts and withdrawing the outgoing senses, all disturbing noises will die away. Motor-cars may roll on the streets; boys may shout at the pitch of their voices; railway trains may run in front of your house; several mills may be working in your neighbourhood—and yet, all these noises will not disturb you even a bit.

Peace Is Vital for Growth

Peace is the most covetable possession on earth. It is the greatest treasure in all the universe. Peace is the most important and indispensable factor for all the growth and development. It is in the tranquillity and quiet of the night that the seed slowly sprouts from under the soil. The bud opens in the depth of the most silent hours. So also, in a state of peace and love, people evolve, grow in their distinctive culture, and develop perfect civilisation. In peace and calmness, spiritual evolution is also facilitated.

Impact of Politics and Social Reform

The 'peace' that prevails today is the peace of fear and the peace of preparation. Ignoring the sincere advice of wisdom, the great nations of the world are intent upon demonstrating their destructive strength. That way lies war, not peace.

No political 'ism can ever solve the problem and bring about peace. All 'isms are only the different hoods of the hydra-headed monster of selfishness-*cum*-egoism. When autocratic monarchs ruled over the nations, people thought that democracy would shower peace, plenty and prosperity upon earth. They dethroned the kings. Democracy also failed to yield the fruit of peace. Some people tried totalitarianism, socialism, communism—so many 'isms. Each man thought that his solution alone was the best for the world! And each new 'ism created only more problems and more quarrels.

Many are working today for the promotion of world peace, without having peace in themselves. Their loud propaganda, big talk, and lectures cause more confusion, conflict and discord.

All over the world, great conferences are held for bringing about universal brotherhood, and universal religion. It is the vanity of man that goads him to reform society without first reforming himself. Vanity rules the world. When two vain people meet, there is friction and quarrel.

So also in the case of social reform. Self-styled enlightened men started interfering with the customs and manners of people, in an effort to civilise them. The people lost their old moorings, and the reforms could not offer new, sound ones. Masses of people drifted away into chaos. How can blind men lead other blind men? You must acquire the Supreme Knowledge of the Reality. Then, and then alone, can you lead another in the right path.

You can elevate others only if you have elevated yourself. This world can be saved only by those who have already saved themselves. A prisoner cannot liberate other prisoners. One realised sage can do more for the promotion of peace than a thousand missionaries preaching and disputing, day in day out.

Politics has its basis in sociology; sociology has its basis in individual personal development; individual personal development is governed by the philosophy and the religion that each man follows. The philosophy of the East considers man as the unit. Man is asked to perfect himself.

Individual Reformation and Social Transformation

Reform yourself. Society will reform itself. Get worldliness out of your heart. The world will take care of itself. Remove the world out of your mind. The world will be peaceful. That is the only solution. This is not pessimism. This is glorious optimism. This is not escapism. It is the only way to face the situation. If each man tries to work out his own salvation, there will be nobody to create the problems! If each man strives heart and soul to practise religion, to do Sadhana, and to attain God-realisation, he will have very little inclination and very little time to create quarrels. Automatically there will be peace on earth.

The Role of Religion

A Christian thinks, "There will be peace if all people embrace Christianity". A Muslim thinks, "There will be peace if all people embrace Islam". This is an erroneous notion. Why do people in the world fight? Why do Catholics and Protestants fight? Why do Saivites and Vaishnavites fight? Why do brothers fight among themselves? The heart must change. Greed and selfishness must perish. Then alone there will be peace in the world.

People merely talk of religion. They are interested in practising it, in living it. If Christians lived by the Sermon On The Mount, if the Buddhists followed the Noble Eightfold Path, If the Muslims truly followed the teachings of the Prophet, and the Hindus shaped their life in accordance with the teachings of the Lord, of saints and sages, there will be peace everywhere.

Peace, to be lasting and constructive, must be achieved through God. There can be no peace without the Lord or God. God is peace. Root yourself in Peace or God. Now you are fit to radiate peace.

54. PRANAYAMA

Through Prana the gods live, and also do men and beasts. Prana is verily the life of beings. Therefore it is called the universal life or the life of all.

Prana is the universal principle of energy or force. It is vital force. It is all-pervading. It may be either in a static or a dynamic state. It is found in all forms from the highest to the lowest, from the ant to the elephant, from the unicellular amoeba to a man, from the elementary form of plant life to the developed form of animal life.

Prana is force on every plane of being, from the highest to the lowest. Whatever moves or works or has life, is but an expression or manifestation of Prana.

It is Prana that shines in your eyes. It is through the power of Prana the ears hear, the eyes see, the skin feels, the tongue tastes, the nose smells, the brain and the intellect do their functions. The smile in a young lady, the melody in the music, the power in the emphatic words of an orator, the charm in the speech of one's beloved, are all due to Prana. Fire burns through Prana. Wind blows through Prana. Rivers flow through Prana. The aeroplane moves in the air through Prana. The steam engine works through Prana. Trains and motor-cars move through Prana. Radio waves travel through Prana. Prana is electron. Prana is force. Prana is magnetism. Prana is electricity. It is Prana that pumps the blood from the heart into the arteries or blood vessels. It is Prana that does digestion, excretion and secretion.

Prana is expended by thinking, willing, acting, moving, talking, writing, etc. A healthy, strong man has abundance of Prana or nerve-force or vitality.

The Prana is supplied by food, water, air, solar energy, etc. The supply of Prana is taken up by the nerve system. The Prana is absorbed by breathing. The excess of Prana is stored in the brain and nerve centres. When the seminal energy is sublimated or transformed, it supplies abundance of Prana to the system. It is stored up in the brain in the form of Ojas. Ojas is nothing but Prana.

The Yogin stores an abundance of Prana by regular practice of Pranayama just as the storage battery stores electricity. That Yogin who has stored up a large supply of Prana radiates strength and vitality all around. He is a big power-house. Those who come in close contact with him imbibe Prana from him, and get strength, vigour, vitality and exhilaration of spirits. Just as water flows from one vessel to another, Prana actually flows like steady current from a developed Yogin towards weak persons. This can be actually seen by the Yogin who has developed his inner Yogic vision.

Nature of Prana

Behind the physical sheath of Annamaya Kosha which is made of the essence of food, there is the Pranamaya Kosha or the vital sheath which is formed by Prana or energy or the vital airs. This Prana manipulates the physical body. This Prana fills the whole physical sheath.

Prana is the link between the astral and the physical bodies. When the slender thread-like Prana is cut off, The astral body separates from the physical body. Death takes place. The Prana that was working in the physical body is withdrawn into the astral body.

Breath is the external manifestation of Prana, the vital force. Breath is gross. Prana is subtle. By exercising control over the gross breath, you can control the subtle Prana inside.

The aim of Pranayama is the control of Prana. Pranayama begins with the regulation of the breath for having control over the life-currents or inner, vital forces.

Pranayama is an exact science. It is fourth Anga or limb of Astanga Yoga.

Pranayama and Life-span

According to Yoga, man's life is constituted of so many breaths. The number of respirations per minute is fifteen. If you can reduce the number of breaths by the practice of Kumbhaka or retention of breath, or stop the breath through Khechari Mudra, you can increase your span of life.

When the breath is expired, it is Rechaka. When the breath drawn in, it is termed Puraka. When it is suspended, it is called Kumbhaka. Kumbhaka is retention of breath. Kumbhaka increases the period of life. It augments the inner spiritual force, vigour and vitality. If you retain the breath for one minute, this one minute is added to your span of life. Chang Dev lived for one thousand and four hundred years through the practice of Kumbhaka.

Patanjali does not lay much stress on the practice of different kinds of Pranayama. He mentions: "Exhale slowly, then inhale and retain the breath. You will get a steady and calm mind". It was only the Hatha Yogins who developed Pranayama as a science and who have mentioned various exercises to suit different persons.

Pranayama Exercises

Sit on Padmasana or Siddhasana in your meditation room before the picture of your Ishta Devata. Close the right nostril with the right thumb. Draw in the air very, very slowly through the left nostril. Then close the left nostril also with the little and right fingers of the right hand. Retain the air as long as you can comfortably do. Then exhale very, very slowly through the right nostril after removing the thumb. Now half the process is over. Then draw air through the right nostril. Retain the air as before and exhale it very, very slowly through the left nostril. All these six processes constitute one Pranayama. Do twenty in the morning and twenty in the evening. Gradually increase the number.

Have a mental attitude that all the divine qualities, *e.g.*, mercy, love, forgiveness, Shanti, joy, etc., are entering into your system along with inspired air, and all the devilish qualities such as lust, anger, greed, etc., are being thrown out along with the expired air. Repeat *Om* or the Gayatri mentally during Puraka, Kumbhaka and Rechaka.

You must so nicely adjust the Puraka, Kumbhaka and Rechaka that you should not experience the feeling of suffocation or discomfort at any stage of Pranayama. You should never feel the necessity of catching hold of a few normal breaths between any two successive rounds. The duration of Puraka, Kumbhaka and Rechaka must be properly adjusted. Exercise due care and attention. Matters will turn to be successful and easy.

You must not unnecessarily prolong the period of exhalation. If you prolong the time of Rechaka, the following inhalation will be done in a hurried manner, and the rhythm will be disturbed. You must so carefully regulate the Puraka, Kumbhaka and Rechaka that you must be absolutely comfortable and perform not only one Pranayama, but also the full course or required rounds of

Pranayama. Experience and practice will make you all right. Practice makes one perfect. Be steady. Another important factor is that you must have efficient control over the lungs at the end of the Kumbhaka to enable you to do the Rechaka smoothly and in proportion with the Puraka. The ratio between Puraka, Kumbhaka and Rechaka is 1:4:2.

There are many other varieties of Pranayama. Suryabheda and Ujjayi produce heat. Sitkari and Sitali are cooling. Bhastrika preserves normal temperature. Suryabheda destroys the excess of wind; Ujjayi phlegm; Sitkari and Sitali bile; and Bhastrika all the three.

Suryabheda and Ujjayi must be practised during winter. Sitkari and Sitali must be practised in summer. Bhastrika can be practised in all seasons. Those persons whose bodies are hot even in winter can practise Sitali and Sitkari during the winter season.

What Control of Prana Means

Pranayama occupies a very important place in the Hindu religion. Prana is related to mind; and through mind, to will; and through will, to the individual soul, and through this, to the Supreme Soul. If you know how to control the little waves of Prana working through the mind, then the secret of subjugating the universal Prana will be known to you.

If you can control the Prana, you can completely control all the forces of the universe—mental and physical. The Yogin can also control the omnipresent manifesting power out of which all energies take their origin, whether concerning magnetism, electricity, gravitation, cohesion, nerve-currents, vital forces, or thought-vibrations.

The Yogins who becomes an expert in the knowledge of this secret, will have no fear from any power, because he has mastery over all manifestations of power in the universe. What is commonly known as the power of personality is nothing more than the natural capacity of a person to wield his Prana. Some persons are more successful in life, more influential and fascinating than others. It is due to the Power of this Prana. Such people manipulate unconsciously, every day, the same influence which the Yogin uses consciously by command of his will.

Benefits of the Practice of Pranayama

Pranayama, though it concerns the breath, gives good exercise for the various internal organs and the whole body. Pranayama removes all sorts of diseases, improves health, energises digestion, invigorates the nerves, removes passion, and awakens the Kundalini Sakti.

A Pranayama practitioner will have a light body free from disease, very fair complexion, a sweet melodious voice, and pleasant smell from his body. He will have good appetite, cheerfulness, a handsome figure, good strength, courage, enthusiasm, a high standard of health, vigour and vitality, and good concentration of mind.

Pranic Healing

Those who practise Pranayama can impart their Prana for healing morbid diseases. They can also recharge themselves with Prana in no time by Practising Kumbhaka.

If there is a rheumatic patient, gently shampoo his legs with your hands. When you do shampooing, do Kumbhaka and imagine that the Prana is flowing from your hands towards your patient. Connect yourself with Hiranyagarbha or the Cosmic Prana and imagine that the cosmic energy is flowing through your hands towards the patient. The patient will at once feel warmth, relief and strength.

Try once or twice in healing yourself. Your convictions will grow stronger.

You can cure headache, intestinal colic, or any other disease by massage and by your magnetic touch. When you massage the liver, spleen, stomach, or any other portion or organ of the body, you can speak to the cells and give them orders: "O cells! Discharge your functions properly. I command you to do so". They will obey your orders. They, too, have got subconscious intelligence. Repeat your Mantra when you pass your Prana to others. Try a few cases. You will gain competence.

Faith, imagination, attention and interest play a very important part in curing diseases by taking Prana to the diseased areas. When you advance in your concentration and practice, you can cure many diseases by mere touch. In the advanced stages, many diseases are cured by mere will.

You can transmit Prana through space to your friend who is living at a distance. This is known as "absent treatment" also. The Prana travels unseen like the wireless waves and flashes like lightning across space. The Prana that is coloured by the thought of the healer is projected outside. You can recharge yourself with Prana by practising Kumbhaka. This requires long, steady and regular practice.

Never think that you will be depleted of your Prana by distributing it to others. The more you will give, the more it will flow to you from the cosmic source. That is the law of nature. Do not become a niggard.

Popular Fears on Pranayama Practice

You can practise ordinary Pranayama exercises without the help of a Guru. A Guru is necessary if you want to practise Kumbhaka for a long time.

There is no danger in practising Pranayama, Asanas, etc., if you are careful and if you use your commonsense. People are unnecessarily alarmed.

There is danger in everything if your are careless. If you are careless in getting down through the steps of a staircase, you will fall down and break your bones. If you are careless when you walk in the busy parts of a city, you will be crushed by the motor-car. If you are careless when you purchase a ticket at the railway station, you will lose your money purse. If you are careless in dispensing mixtures, you will kill the patients by giving a poison or a wrong medicine, or administering a medicine in overdoses.

Even so, when you practise Pranayama, you will have to be careful about your diet. You should avoid overloading. You should take light, easily digestible, and nutritious food. You should be moderate in copulation. You should not go beyond your capacity in retaining the breath. You should first practise inhalation and exhalation only, without retention of breath, for one or two months. You should inhale very, very slowly. If these rules are observed, there is no danger at all in the practice of Pranayama.

Some Instructions

Correct posture is indispensably requisite for the successful practice of Pranayama. You need not wait, however, for practising

Pranayama till you get full mastery over the Asanas. Practise Asana and, side by side, you can practise Pranayama also. In course of time, you will acquire perfection in both.

The room in which you practise Pranayama must not be damp and ill-ventilated. It must be dry and airy. You can do the practice by the side of a river or a lake, in the corner of a garden, in the open air, when there is no chill or draught of cold air, or on the top or foot of a hill.

In summer, you can have the practice in the cool hours of the morning only. Sit by the side of a river or a lake or the sea, if you can manage. If hot winds blow, stop doing Pranayama. You can do Sitali to cool the body in summer.

Always inhale and exhale very slowly. Do not make any sound. In Pranayamas like Bhastrika, Kapalabhati, Sitali and Sitkari, you can produce a little mild sound or the lowest possible sound.

There should be no strain in any stage of Pranayama. You must experience joy and pleasure in doing the same. You should not feel any undue strain.

Do not perform Pranayama till you are fatigued. Do not take bath immediately after finishing the Yogic exercises. Take rest for half an hour.

During the practice of Pranayama, repeat your Ishta Mantra. This will be pure Yoga.

In ordinary worldly persons, the breathing is irregular. A correct habit of breathing must be established by the regular practice of Pranayama.

Many Yogins of yore, like Sri Jnana Deva, Trailinga Swami, Ramalinga Swami and others had utilised this force, the Prana, in a variety of ways. You can also do so, if you practise Pranayama by proper breathing exercises.

It is Prana that you are breathing rather than the atmospheric air. Realise the occult inner life-powers which underlie the breath. Become a Yogin and radiate joy, light and power all around you.

55. PRAYER

The kitten mews, and the cat runs to it and carries it away. Even so, the devotee cries, and the Lord comes to his rescue.

Prayer is depending on God for help in distress. Prayer is giving an opportunity to God to comfort the devotee. Prayer is lightening the heaviness of your heart by opening it to God. Prayer is expecting God to decide what is best for you when you are in dilemma. From despair, man learns prayer.

A Mystic State

Prayer is not asking. Prayer is communion with God through single-minded devotion.

Prayer is nearness to God. Prayer is tuning the mind with God. Prayer is fixing the mind on God. Prayer is meditation on God. Prayer is surrendering oneself to God completely. Prayer is melting the mind and ego in silence in God. Prayer represents a mystic state when the individual consciousness is absorbed in God.

Prayer is an uplifting of the soul to God. It is an act of love and adoration to Him. Prayer is worship of God. Prayer is glorification of God. Prayer is thanksgiving to God for all His blessings.

Prayer is an invocation, a calling forth of spiritual forces ever flowing through the human heart, mind and soul. Prayer is mighty spiritual force. It is as real as the force of gravity or attraction.

Prayer is the very soul and essence of religion. It is the very core of man's life. No man can live without Prayer.

All Can Pray

The blind, the deaf and the lame, the armless, the puny, the ignorant and the debased, the lowliest and the forlorn—all can pray to God, for Prayer belongs to the heart and its feeling, and to the body.

Prayer does not demand high intelligence or eloquence. God wants your heart when you pray. Even a few words from a humble, pure soul—though illiterate—will appeal to the Lord more than the eloquent flowing words of an orator or Pundit.

The child does not know grammar and pronunciation: it utters some sounds, but the mother understands! The Indian butler of a European officer is not a professor of English: he talks some predicateless sentences, but the officer understands! When others can understand the language of the heart, what to say of Antaryamin? He knows what you wish to say! Even if you make mistakes in your prayers to Him, even if there are mistakes in the Mantras you recite, if you are sincere, if the prayer comes from your heart, He listens to it, because He understands the language of your heart.

Whose Prayer Is Heard?

Prayer should spring from the heart. It should not be lip-homage. Empty prayer is like a sounding brass or tinkling cymbal.

Prayer that comes from a sincere, pure heart is at once heard by the Lord. The prayer of a cunning, crooked, wicked man is never heard.

God ever responds to the appeal of His sincere devotees. It is only the insincere man who says that God is deaf.

God is ever watching for the distress signals of His children. Open your heart to Him without reservations. The response will be instantaneous.

The Practice of Prayer

Thy breath has been given to you by the Lord to be spent in prayer. Kneel down and pray; but, let the prayer not cease when you rise. Prayer should be lifelong, and your life should be one long prayer.

There are no problems that cannot be dissolved by prayer, no sufferings that cannot be allayed by prayer, no difficulties that cannot be surmounted by prayer, and no evil that cannot be overcome by prayer. Prayer is communion with God. Prayer is the miracle by which God's power flows into human veins. Therefore, kneel down and pray.

When within your bosom rage the storms of lust and anger, vanity and viciousness, kneel down and pray. For, the Lord—and He alone—hath power over the elements. In the supplication is thy strength. You will be filled with His blessings, protected by His grace, shielded by His mercy, and spurred on the path of righteousness by His divine will.

Therefore, kneel down and pray. Not for earthly goods, nor for heavenly pleasures, but for His grace. "Thy will be done, my Lord!

I want nothing" shall be thy prayer. For, you know not what is good for you; and you may be asking for trouble, and praying for perdition. Pray for grace. Pray that His righteousness might descend on the soul of all men.

Greet the dawn of the day, and bid adieu to the setting sun, with a prayer of thankfulness; first for a fresh day granted, and last for His grace received. Thus shall your life be blessed, and thus will you radiate His blessings to all around you.

Benefits of Prayer

Prayer is a mighty spiritual force. Prayer is spiritual food for the soul. Prayer is a spiritual tonic.

Prayers are powerful spiritual currents. There is nothing so purifying as prayer. If you pray regularly, your life will be gradually changed and moulded. Prayer must become habitual. You will feel as if you cannot live without prayer, if prayer becomes a habit in you.

Prayer lightens the heart and fills the mind with peace, strength and purity. When the mind becomes pure and Sattvic through the power of prayer, the intellect becomes sharp and keen. Prayer elevates the mind. When you pray, you link yourself with the inexhaustible cosmic power-house of energy—Hiranyagarbha—and thus draw power, energy, light and strength from Him.

Prayer is the trusty companion along the weary path of Moksha. Prayer is the rock to which man can cling when he is drowning in the ocean of Samsara. Prayer frees the devotee from the fear of death. It brings him nearer to God, and makes him feel the divine consciousness and his essential immortal, blissful nature.

Prayer works wonders. Prayer moves mountains. Even when the medical board has pronounced a case to be hopeless, prayer comes to rescue, and the patient is miraculously cured. There have been many instances of this description. You may be aware of this. Healing by prayer is really miraculous and mysterious.

Prayer is an unfailing remedy for all situations. Many a time have I experienced its marvellous potency. You, too, can experience it.

Prayer and Prosper

You cry when your house is burgled. You weep and wail when

your child is dead. You writhe in agony when your limbs are crushed. O Ram! Do you ever weep for God? Cry for Him always. He will avert all calamities. Twine yourself around God for support. You will be free from the injuries of life. Follow the method and reap the harvest. Pray and prosper.

None in this world save you. It is God who likes you the most. Call on Him. He will run to you. Seek His guidance. Praise His glory. Invoke His mercy.

Draupadi prayed fervently. Lord Krishna ran from Dvaraka to relieve her distress. Gajendra prayed ardently; Lord Hari marched with His Disc to protect him. It was the prayer of Mira that converted the bed of nails into a bed of roses, cobra into a flower garland. It was the prayer of Prahlada that rendered cool the burning oil when it was poured on his head. Namadev prayed and Vitthal came out of the image to eat his food. Eknath prayed and Lord Hari showed His form with four hands. Damaji prayed and Lord Krishna played the part of a menial in paying due to the Badshaw. Narada is still praying. What more do you want? Pray fervently right now from this very second. You will attain eternal bliss.

56. PURITY

A Bania once approached a Sadhu for initiation. The Sadhu said, "Wait, I will initiate you after some time". The Bania pressed the Sadhu again and again on several occasions for quick initiation. The Sadhu totally declined and went away. He, however, visited the Bania after a couple of years with his Bhiksha-bowl containing some mud, hair, urine and excreta, and asked the Bania for alms. The Bania brought out nice sweetmeats, Kheer, Halva, etc. He had prepared these nice dishes, as he thought that he would be initiated this time by the Sadhu. The Sadhu said to the Bania, "Put everything into the bowl". The Bania said, "How can I place them, Swamiji, in this dirty bowl! Kindly clean the bowl and bring it to me. I will then place in it all the nice preparations". The Sadhu replied: "When such is the case with this bowl, how can I place the pure Lord in your heart which is filled with various impurities, viz., lust, anger, pride, greed, etc? How can I initiate you now, when your mind is very dirty like this bowl?". The Bania got depressed and went away in shame. He then purified himself through charity, selfless service, etc., and got initiated by the Sadhu later.

Just as the coloured water penetrates freely and nicely into a piece of cloth when it is pure white, so also, the instructions of a sage can penetrate and settle down in the hearts of aspirants only when their minds are calm, when there are no desires for enjoyments, and when the impurities of their minds are destroyed.

Discipline and purification of the mind and the Indriyas are the prerequisites for an aspirant in the path of Truth and Self-realisation. The ground must be well-prepared first. Then initiation will come by itself.

Internal Purity and External Purity

Purity is of two kinds, internal purity and external purity. Freedom from Raga-dvesha, purity intentions, purity of motives, and purity of Bhava constitute internal purity. Purity of body through bath, etc., purity of clothes, purity of surroundings like the house and its neighbourhood, constitute external purity.

External purity generates pure thoughts. Practice of external purity brings disgust for one's own body and the body of others also. You will soon give up Mamata, mineness of body.

Internal purity is more important than external purity. Internal purity makes the mind one-pointed, bestows serenity, cheerfulness, joy, strength, harmony, poise and happiness, instils love, patience and magnanimity.

If you take pure food, you will have a pure mind. If you have purity of mind, you will remember God. If you always remember God, the knots of the heart, viz., ignorance, desire and action, will be rent asunder. You will attain Moksha.

Sadhana without Purity Is a Fruitless Waste

Mental purity through ethical training is, therefore, of paramount importance, if you wish to achieve success in meditation and Samadhi.

To practise meditation or contemplation in a mind perturbed by non-adherence to the moral precepts, is like building a house on a rotten foundation. You may build up the house, but it will surely fall. You may practise meditation for many years, but you will not realise any tangible result or fruit, if you have no ethical training as foundation.

If you want to enthrone God in your heart, you must eradicate all evil modifications in the mind. What do you do when you expect to receive a very high personage in your bungalow? You keep the compound quite clean and remove all the weeds and rubbish. You clean all the rooms and spread nice carpets. Similarly, you will have to remove all the dross of impurities from the mind if you want to have communion with the Lord, if you desire to call upon God earnestly to take His seat in your heart.

It takes a long time to purify the heart. Just as various kinds of dirt and dust are hidden underneath the carpet, so also, various kinds of impurities are hidden in the different corners of the mind.

Mind is such a mischievous imp. It is the Mara that tempted Buddha. It is the Satan that allured Jesus. It is the Kama who disturbed Siva when He was in deep meditation. It is the ghost of lust that spoiled the Tapas of Visvamitra.

You cannot wash the mind with soap and water to get rid of its impurities; but if you eradicate desire and attachment, the mind will be purified itself.

Desires move the senses. Desires can be controlled only if the senses are curbed. Tapas curbs the senses and annihilates desires.

The Nature of Tapas

Tapas is the third Anga of Niyama in Raja Yoga. Tapas is one of the three items of Kriya Yoga. Tapas means austerity or practice of penance.

That which purifies the impure mind is Tapas. That which regenerates the lower, animal nature and generates divine nature is Tapas. That which cleanses the mind and destroys lust, anger, greed, etc., is Tapas. That which produce Brahma-Tejas and destroys Asuric or diabolical nature is Tapas. That which destroys Tamas and Rajas and increases Sattva is Tapas. That which steadies the mind and fixes it on the Eternal is Tapas. That which arrests the outgoing tendencies, extroversion or Bahirmukha Vritti, and produces introversion or Antharmukha Vritti is Tapas. That which destroys the Vasanas, egoism, Raga-dvesha and generates dispassion, discrimination and meditation is Tapas. Tapas is spiritual discipline. Tapas is worship, Sadhana and meditation.

The Gita has given very valuable hints upon the subject of Tapas. A flood of light is thrown upon this subject through the divine words of Lord Krishna addressed to Arjuna. The Gita speaks of a threefold Tapas of body, speech and mind.

Conventionally, eating neem leaves, standing in water, sitting in the hot sun, bearing heat and cold, standing on one leg with raised hands, etc., are considered as Tapas. People speak of such persons as Tapasvins. They say, "Ram Brahmachari is a great Tapasvi. He lives on leaves and has no clothing. He does Panchagni Tapas in hot summer". These are all forms of physical Tapas.

Mental Tapas is more powerful than physical Tapas. He who bears heat and cold does physical Tapas. He increases his power of endurance; but he may not be able to bear insult. He will be easily upset by a harsh or unkind word. He may take revenge and do tit for tat. He has no control over the mind. He has disciplined only his physical body. To keep a balanced mind in all conditions of life, to bear insult, injury and persecutions, to be ever serene, contented and peaceful, to be cheerful in adverse conditions, to have fortitude in meeting danger, to have presence of mind and forbearance, are all forms of mental Tapas.

Philosophically, meditation is the highest form of Tapas. Fixing the wandering mind on God or Brahman is great Tapas. Vichara and Nididhyasana are the highest Tapas.

Vratas or Vows of Austerity

Hindus observe various kinds of Vratas, such as Satyanarayana Vrata in honour of Lord Narayana, Varalakshmi Vrata in honour of Goddess Mother Lakshmi, Anantapadmanabha Vrata, Savitri Vrata, Janmashtami Vrata, Chandrayana Vrata and Pradosha Vrata.

All Vratas aim at purifying the heart, controlling the senses, and cultivating devotion to the Lord. The worldly people are always busy in earning money and doing various kinds of work. At least during days of Vrata, they have opportunities to introspect, to worship, to do Japa and intense meditation, to study holy scriptures and to practise self-analysis.

Each Vrata has its peculiarities. Certain features are common to Vratas of different kinds. The aspirant observes Brahmacharya or sexual continence, fasts or takes milk and fruits or light diet. No fish or meat is taken.

Fasting and Its Purificatory Effects

Fasting is a common feature of most Vratas.

Fasting is commended by all religions and all creeds of thought. A man with a genuine practice of fast at regular intervals has clear-cut thoughts, an expression all his own, an imagination which others cannot excel. His ideal can only be Divinity. His aim in life can only be immortality. The ego stands nowhere before him. His thoughts are sublime and firm. His actions are diligent. There is a transcendental glow in him. He has the Kingdom of God on earth in his own personality. He never wounds the feelings of others. His ideas are rays of light in the darkness of human life in everyday world.

The Ekadasi, the Sabbath day, or Saturday, whichever suits you best, can be observed as a fasting day. Keep it at definite and regular intervals as it suits you.

Purity Is the Passport to the Land of Bliss

Tapascharya is essential. Tapasya is useful. Tapasya is a great help. Understand it truly. Practise it wisely. Intensify it gradually.

Exercise it vigilantly. Give up foolishness. Be discriminate. Give no leniency. Adhere your vows. Be firm and resolute. Aspire fierily. Assert and manifest your mastery over the mind and senses as a true Tapasvin. Shine with spiritual radiance. You will achieve the glorious goal of spiritual life. You will attain immortality and supreme Kaivalya-moksha.

Purity is the path way to the kingdom of God. Without purity, no spiritual progress is possible. Brahman is purity. You will have to attain Brahman, or know Him and become one with Him, only through purity. There is no other way.

Your soul is Nitya Suddha, eternally pure. Through your contact with the mind and senses, you have become impure. Regain your original purity through Japa, Kirtan, prayer, meditation, enquiry of 'Who am I?', the practice of Pranayama, study, Satsanga and Sattvic food.

Purify the intellect. Purify your heart. Purify your speech. Purify your body. Purify your senses. Purify your Prana. Purify, purify, purify.

Purity of heart is the gateway to God. It is antechamber to the presence of the Lord. It is the key by which the doors of intuition that lead to the abode of supreme peace are opened. Therefore, attain purity at all costs. Purity is the passport to the land of eternal bliss.

57. RAMAYANA

The Ramayana of Valmiki is perhaps the most ancient and glorious epic in the world. It is known as the Adikavyam,—the first poem. Ramayana exercises a great moulding power on the life of man. It contains object lessons for husbands and wives, parents and children, brothers and sisters, friends and enemies.

Its Origin

Valmiki once asked Narada, "O Venerable Rishi! Please tell me whether there is a perfect man in this world who is at once virtuous, brave, dutiful, truthful, noble, steadfast in duty, and kind to all beings".

Narada replied, "There is such a one, a prince of Ikshvaku's line named Rama. He is virtuous, brave, gentle, and wise. He is a great hero. He loves his subjects immensely. He is a protector of Dharma. He is firm and steadfast. He is just and liberal. He is well-versed in the Vedas and in the science of arms. He is unique in the possession of virtues and matchless in beauty. He is an obedient son, a kind brother, loving husband, a faithful friend, an ideal king, a merciful enemy, and a lover of all living beings. All people adore him".

Valmiki, reflecting over this flowing description, was walking along the banks of the river Tamasa. He happened to see a pair of Kraunchas (birds) sporting with each other in love. Suddenly the male bird was shot dead by a cruel fowler and the female, seeing her mate rolling on the ground in the agony of pain, screamed out most pitifully her lamentations. The sage felt great pity at the sight of the fallen bird and his grieving spouse and burst forth in the exclamation: "Never, O fowler, shalt thou obtain rest, as thou hast killed a Krauncha in the midst of his love". These words came out spontaneously in the form of a musical verse having four feet of eight syllables each (Anushtup metre).

Then Brahma himself, the Creator of the world, appeared before the poet and said, "Sing Rama's charming story in the same melodious metre. As long as this world endures, as long as the stars shine in heaven, so long shall thy song spread among men". So saying Brahma vanished. He inspired the poet with the knowledge of Sri Rama's whole story, whereupon Valmiki sat down in meditation and saw every event in Sri Rama's story in detail in his

Yogic vision. Then he began to write the Ramayana. The melody of Ramayana was born from a heart of love and pity for the wounded bird. When applied to Ramayana, the verse of Valmiki sung out of pity for the Krauncha, can be interpreted thus: Sri Rama and Sita represent the two Kraunchas. Ravana represents the cruel hunter. Sita was cruelly separated from Rama by the cruel hunter Ravana. There is a slight similarity in these cases. The hunter's cruel act was a forerunner to Valmiki's inspiration to narrate the Ramayana.

Valmiki Ramayana contains 24,000 verses which have been grouped into 500 Chapters and that again into seven Kandas or sections, *viz.,* Bala, Ayodhya, Aranya, Kishkindha, Sundara, Yuddha and the Uttara Kandas. In contains genuine classical Sanskrit poetry. Rama's young sons, Kusa and Lava, were the first reciters to the world, who sang to music this reputed work. They came in the garb of ascetics from the hermitage of their teacher Valmiki, and sang the wonderful poem in the presence of their father Rama and other heroes of the story.

The Ramayana is a marvellous book which contains the essence of all Vedas and all sacred scriptures. It is a treasure for man. It is a reservoir which contains the nectar of Immortality. It delineates the character of a son who kicks off the throne and the pleasures of the senses and the world to fulfil the words of his father and lives in the forest for a period of fourteen years. It depicts the character of a father who sends even his most beloved son in exile in order to keep up his word. It delineates the character of an ideal, chaste wife who is devoted to her husband till the end of her life, shares his adversities, and serves him untiringly in the forest, and who also regards her husband as God. Above all, it also points out the character of a brother, who places brotherly affection above everything else in this world and follows his brother in the forest leaving all pleasures of the palace and leading the way to ward off all dangers. The description of nature in Ramayana is most sublime and beautiful. One can actually feel that the hills, the rivers, the trees, and the birds are really one with human joys and sorrows. The description of battle-scenes is magnificent. The chief characteristic of Ramayana is simplicity. Pathos and tenderness run through the whole poem. Poetry and morality are charmingly united. There is loftiness of moral tone. The Ramayana has a historical basis. It is a book of antiquity. It is not a mere allegoric poem. It is a marvellous inspiring book for all times, that has loomed large for centuries over the destinies of millions of people and will certainly continue to do so for ages to come.

Synopsis of the Seven Kandas

In Bala-Kanda the Incarnation of Sri Rama and his childhood life are described. Rama helps Visvamitra by guarding his sacrifice. He slays ogress Tataka and Subahu. He frees Ahalya from her curse. He breaks the bow of Siva and marries Janaki and annihilates the pride of Parasurama.

In Ayodhya-Kanda preparations are made for installing Rama as heir-apparent. His step-mother Kaikeyi stands in the way and sends him in exile for fourteen years. Rama's brother Lakshmana and wife Sita follow him. Raja Dasaratha (father) becomes very much afflicted at heart on account of his separation from Rama and dies due to grief. Rama, Lakshmana, and Sita are entertained by Guha, a hunter-chief. They cross the Ganga and meet Rishi Bharadvaja. They go to Chitrakuta on the advice of the Rishi. They build a cottage made up of grass and leaves (Parna Kutir) there. Then Bharata (another devoted brother) goes to the forest and insists Rama to return to the country and finally takes Rama's sandals alone. He places the sandals on the throne and rules the kingdom in the name of Sri Rama. Bharata himself lives at Nandigrama.

In Aranya-Kanda, Viradha, a giant, attacks Rama and Lakshmana in the Dandaka forest. Rama kills him. Thereafter, they pay a visit to the Rishis Sarabhanga, Sutikshna, and Atri. Anasuya, wife of Atri, gives an inspiring discourse on the duties of a wife to Sita. Then they meet Rishi Agastya. Rama receives celestial weapons from him. They encounter the giantess Surpanakha in the Panchavati forest. She is disfigured by Lakshmana. Lakshmana cuts her nose and ears. Khara and Trisiras (along with fourteen thousand giants), brothers of Surpanakha, are very much enraged. They fight against Rama. They are slain in the battle.

Surpanakha goes to Lanka and complains to her brother Ravana. Under Ravana's plan, Maricha, uncle of Ravana, assumes the form of a golden deer and appears before Sita, Rama, and Lakshmana. Sita requests Rama to get the deer for her. Rama proceeds to catch the deer and kills it. In the mean time, Ravana carries away Sita in the absence of Rama and Lakshmana. Jatayu, the king of vultures challenges Ravana, but he is mortally wounded. Rama obtains all information about Sita from the dying Jatayu. He is very much afflicted at heart. Subsequently, Rama and Lakshmana kill Kabandha near the lake Pampa. Then they meet the pious Sabari. She offers them roots and fruits with great devotion.

In Kishkindha-Kanda Rama meets Hanuman on the banks of Pampa. They proceed to Mount Rishyamuka and make an alliance with Sugriva. Sugriva kills Vali with the help of Rama. Sugriva is crowned as the king of Kishkindha. Rama consoles Tara, wife of Vali. Thereupon, Hanuman with a party of monkeys proceeds in search of Sita. He takes with him the ring of Rama as token. He makes a vigorous search and is not able to find out Sita. Jambavan (chief of bears) finds out Sampati, brother of Jatayu, in a cave, who gives out facts. Hanuman climbs up the top of a hill by his direction and from there he leaps across the ocean to Lanka.

In Sundara-Kanda Hanuman's exploits are described. During his aerial journey, Mainaka, an island peak, invites Hanuman to rest on its top at the request of the ocean. Afterwards, Simhika, a monstress living in the ocean, drags him down by catching his shadow. Hanuman kills her. Then he gets a distant view of Lanka and enters the city at night. He finds out Sita in the Asoka grove. He gives her Rama's token and message. Hanuman destroys the Asoka grove. The Rakshasas imprison Hanuman. Hanuman frees himself and sets fire to Lanka. He returns back to the place where Rama is staying and gives Sita's gem to Rama. Rama is highly delighted when he receives Sita's token and her message.

In Yuddha-Kanda, Nala (one of the monkey-chiefs) builds a bridge across the ocean by the advice of the ocean. The heroes with a large army of monkeys cross the ocean and reach Lanka. Vibhishana (brother of Ravana) joins them and tells them how to destroy Ravana and his army. Kumbhakarna, Indrajit, and Ravana are killed in battle. During the battle, both the parties of Rama and Ravana use Astras or weapons charged with Mantras. Rama sends an Astra on Ravana's' party. All Rakshasas appear as Rama. They kill one another. Ravana discharges on Rama, Nagastra (arrow that becomes serpents full of poison). The arrows have their mouths like serpents and vomit forth fire all around. The Rama discharges Garudastra. The arrows becomes Garudas and cut off the serpent arrows on all sides. Garudas are the enemies of serpents. Rama uses

Brahmastra to kill Ravana. Sita is rescued. Sita's honour is tested the fire. She comes out more glorious and effulgent than eve Vibhishana is then crowned as king in Lanka. Sri Rama with h party returns to Ayodhya in the flying car called Pushpaka. Rama crowned as Emperor. The people of his kingdom feel extreme happy.

In Uttara-Kanda, Sri Rama's reign is described as Rama-Rajy There is righteousness everywhere. Everywhere there are plen and prosperity. There is neither disease nor sorrow. There a neither dacoits nor thieves. Life and prosperity are quite safe. Th four Varnas duly observe their Dharmas. Sri Rama goes back to H Supreme Abode (Saketa-Puri or Dhama) after a long ar prosperous rule.

The esoteric meaning of Ramayana is this: Ravana represen Ahankara or egoism. His ten heads represent the ten senses. Th city of Lanka is the nine-gated city of the physical body. Vibhishar corresponds to the intellect. Sita is peace. Rama is Jnana (wisdom To kill the ten-headed Ravana is to kill the egoism and curb th senses. To recover Sita is to attain the peace which the Jiv (individual) has lost on account of desires. To attain Jnana is have Darsana of Rama or the Supreme Self.

He who crosses this ocean of Moha and destroys th Rakshasas,—Raga and Dvesha (likes and dislikes),—is a Yogi who is united with Santi or Peace, ever rests in Atman, and enjoy the eternal bliss. Sri Rama stands for the 'Good' (Sattva); Ravan for the 'Evil'. Sri Rama and Ravana fought with each othe Eventually Sri Rama became victorious. The positive alway overcomes the negative. Good always overcomes evil.

58. REINCARNATION

Man can be compared to a plant. He grows and flourishes like a plant and dies in the end, but not completely. The plant also grows and flourishes, and dies in the end. It leaves behind it the seed, which produces a new plant. Man leaves, when dying, his Karma behind—the good and bad actions of his life. The physical body may die and disintegrate, but the impressions of his actions do not die. He has to take birth again to enjoy the fruits of these actions.

The doctrine of reincarnation is as old as the Vedas. It is the foundation of Hinduism, Buddhism, and Jainism. This doctrine is supported by Guru Nanak Dev in Guru Granth Saheb.

The ancient Egyptians believed it. The Greek philosophers made it the corner-stone of thier philosophy. It is the key-note of Plato's philosophy when he says that all knowledge is reminiscence.

Emerson, Plato, Pythagoras had perfect belief in the doctrine of reincarnation. Philosophers like Kant, Schelling, and Schopenhauer have upheld this doctrine. Theologians like Julius Muller, Dorner, and Edward Beecher have maintained it. It is accepted by the majority of mankind at the present day.

Body—A Vehicle for the Soul

The union of the soul with a particular body is known as birth, and its separation therefrom is called death. When the soul leaves its physical sheath, it transmigrates into another body, human, animal, or even vegetable, according to its merits.

Petrol and steam are great forces. But, by themselves, they cannot make the journey with a definite course and a definite destination. They must be harnessed to a machine, a running train or steamer. Even so, the soul must have a body to run its course and reach its destination in God. The body was designed by God to carry the soul in its onward march. A good soul makes a good body, a bad soul a bad body. Body is an indispensable aid to the soul in its progress towards God.

The progress of transmigration continues—we cannot say through how many lives—till the soul, being purged of all its impurities and having acquired a true and full knowledge of the Imperishable Soul by Yoga, attains Mukti or the final emancipation and enjoys perfect, eternal bliss by its union with the Supreme Self or Para Brahman. There is no more transmigration.

Proofs for Rebirth

One of the important arguments for reincarnation has been built by the Hindus on the feeling of instinct. Instinct is the result of past experience.

The baby sucks. The young duck swims. Who taught this? They are the Samskaras or the tendencies of previous births.

Love at first sight is a certain feeling of a previous life altogether. These souls loved before. They remember that, and actually feel as if they had met each other. Such loves are not at all a matter of sex, and are seldom broken off. Lord Buddha told his wife of her kindness to him in a previous birth and several times gave details of the previous lives of other people.

Every child is born with certain tendencies or predilections generated by past conscious actions. No child is born with a vacant mind or a clean blank page of a mind. We have had past lives.

We have got boy geniuses. A boy of five becomes an expert in piano or violin. Sri Jnana Dev wrote his commentary on the Gita when he was fourteen years old. There had been boy mathematicians. There was the boy Bhagavatar in Madras who conducted Kathas when he was eight years old. How could you explain this strange phenomenon? This is not a freak of nature. The theory of transmigration only could explain all these things. If one man gets deep grooves in his mind by learning music or mathematics in this birth, he carries these impressions to the next birth and becomes a prodigy in these sciences even when he is a boy.

Heredity cannot explain all these inequalities and diversities—the cases of geniuses. The parents, brothers and sisters of these prodigies are quite common persons. Tendencies are the result of the past actions. They do not come through heredity. The geniuses have gained their talents in their previous lives.

Man develops tendency and aptitude in several births and becomes a genius in one birth. Buddha gained experiences in several births. He became a Buddha only in his last birth.

In one birth, all virtues cannot be developed. One can cultivate the virtues only by gradual evolution. Saints possess excellence in all virtues. The existence of saints and adepts indicates that there is rebirth.

Why Do We Not Remember Our Past?

An objection is brought against the doctrine of reincarnation. That objection is: "Why do we not remember our past?". Do you remember what you did in your childhood? Will you say you did not exist then, because you cannot remember? Certainly not. If your existence depends upon your memory, then this argument proves that you did not exist as children, because you do not remember your childhood. The details have passed out of your memory, but the knowledge you have acquired through your experience is part and parcel of your being. Those experiences are still in your subconscious mind or Chitta as impressions. Even so, past experience influences your present life.

So far as we are living in a body, we exercise the faculty of memory through the brain. In passing from one incarnation to the other, the soul does not carry the former brain in the new body.

Knowledge of the Past

All the experiences that you have had in various births remain in the form of impressions or residual potencies in the Chitta or subconscious mind. They remain in a very, very subtle form, just as the sound remains in a subtle state in the gramophone record. A Yogin can remember his past lives through concentration on these impressions. He can tell you all about your past lives also through concentration on the Samskaras or impressions that are lodged in your subconscious mind.

Mother Nature has concealed the past from you. It is not desirable to remember the past. Suppose, for a moment, you know the past. You know that you have committed a sinful action in your past life and you are going to suffer for it. You will be thinking of this always. You will worry yourself constantly. You will not have sound sleep. You will not relish your food.

If you remember your past, you may make a bad use of the present. Your inveterate enemy in your past life may be born as your son in this life. If you remember the past, you will draw your sword to kill him. Feelings of enmity will rise in your heart at once.

Real-Life Instances that Prove Rebirth

Here is a challenge to the non-believers of the Hindu theory of transmigration. Recently the little girl Santi Devi gave a vivid description of her past lives in Delhi. There was great sensation in Delhi and Mathura, nay, throughout Uttar Pradesh. There was a great assembly of persons to hear her statements. She recognised her husband and child of her previous birth who are living in Mathura. She pointed out the place where money was kept, and an old well in the house which is covered now. All her statements were duly verified and corroborated by respectable eyewitnesses.

Several cases like this have occurred in Rangoon, Sitapur, and various other places. They are quite common now. In such cases, the Jiva takes immediate rebirth with the old astral body or Linga Sarira. That is the reason why memory of the previous birth comes in. He did not stay in the mental world for a long time to rebuild a new mind and astral body according to his various experiences of the world.

Karma and Rebirth

The doctrine of rebirth is a corollary to the Law of Karma. The differences of disposition that are found between one individual and another must be due to their respective past actions. Past action implies past birth. Further, all your Karmas cannot certainly bear fruit in this life. Therefore, there must be another birth for enjoying the remaining actions. Each soul has a series of births and deaths. Births and deaths will continue till you attain Knowledge of the Imperishable.

Good Karmas lead to incarnation into higher spheres and bad Karmas into lower. By virtue is obtained ascent to higher planes; by vice, descent to the lower. From wisdom results beatitude; and bondage from the reverse. So long as Karmas—whether good or bad—are not exhausted, men do not attain Moksha or the final emancipation even in hundreds of Kalpas. Both good and bad Karmas bind the Jiva tight in their chains. One is a chain of gold; the other is a chain of iron. Moksha cannot be attained by man, so long as Knowledge of the Eternal is not attained.

Christian Theory Contradicted

The purpose of transmigration is betterment and perfection. It prepares the human being for the ultimate realisation which frees him from the cycle of births and deaths.

Man can hardly attain perfection in one life. He has to develop his heart, intellect, and hand. He has to mould his character in a perfect manner. He has to develop various virtuous qualities such as mercy, tolerance, love, forgiveness, equal vision, courage, etc. He has to learn many lessons and experiences in this great world-school. Therefore he has to take many lives. Reincarnation is very true. One small life is a part of the long series that stretches behind you and in front of you. It is quite insignificant. One gains a little experience only. He evolves very little. During the course of one life, man does many evil actions. He does very little good actions. Very few die as good men.

Christians believe that one life determines and settles everything. No opportunity is afforded to the sinner to purify himself in later births. His finite sin, if not somehow purged, precipitates him at death into endless misery. How could this be? How can the everlasting future of man be made to depend on that one, small, little insignificant life? If, in that life, he believes in Christ, he will get eternal peace in heaven; if he is an unbeliever in that life, he will get eternal damnation; he will be thrown for ever in the lake of fire or horrible hell. Is this not the most irrational doctrine? Should he not get his chances for correction and improvement? The doctrine of reincarnation is quite rational. It gives ample chances for man's rectification, growth, and gradual evolution. Vedanta says that there is hope of salvation even for the worst sinner.

The sinner reaps the harvest of his misdeeds for a limited period. After he has been purged of his sins, he is again born as a rational being and is thus given a fresh chance for working out his emancipation with freedom of will to choose the right path or the wrong one, and with knowledge to distinguish the one from the other.

Birth in Lower Yonis

No human being is out and out an incarnation of Lucifer. Certain good qualities, and actions prompted by such good qualities, always outweigh the bad qualities and their actions; and the human being steps into another birth, either low or high, out of the same species for the future evolution of the soul.

Generally, man evolves upwards. Evolution to the higher, and not deterioration to the lower, is generally the law and principle of Nature. But there are exceptions. If a man is endowed with devilish traits and does highly brutal acts, if he behaves worse than an animal, if he acts like a dog or a monkey, he surely does not deserve a human birth in the next life. He will take birth in the womb of animals. He will be born as a dog or a monkey or a donkey. Such cases are however, rare indeed.

Even if man does heinous sins, he can get the maximum punishment while dwelling in this physical body. It is not necessary that he should take the birth of an animal. Man suffers more for his sins while remaining in the body of a man than taking an animal birth. The sufferings of a leper, or a consumptive, a person suffering from syphilis, gonorrhoea are beyond description.

Man learns lessons through bitter and painful experiences in this world. However sinful, cruel, and brutal a man may be, he corrects and educates himself through sufferings, pain, sorrows, troubles and difficulties and diseases, loss of property, poverty, and death of dear and near relations. God moulds and corrects the sinners in a mysterious manner. Sufferings and pain act as useful educative forces. They serve as eye-openers in the case of the evil-doers. They check them from falling back and pull them upwards. The erstwhile sinners begin to do good actions and seek the company of the saints.

Cut the Knot of Births and Deaths

It does not matter much what kind of body we wear. It matters much what our thoughts are. A man of high position may have the thoughts of a beast. When he becomes a prey to lust and anger, he is worse than an animal. A cow is a thousand times better than such a man who is devoid of discrimination, who indulges in vulgar enjoyments, who loses his temper for trifles.

Do not worry yourself as to what birth you will take in the future. Utilise the present life profitably and free yourself from death and birth. Develop devotion to the Lord. Renounce base desires. Be ever intent on doing good to others. Be kind and do good.

Lord Hari is the protector of the three worlds. The responsibility of taking every one of His creation to His immortal abode rests with Him. Let Him take you through any path He likes. Let Him give you Mukti when you are in the body of a man, a beast, or a devil. Let your mind be ever centred on Him. Let it ever cling to His lotus feet like the bee that sticks to a full-blown lotus.

The chains that tie you to this round of births and deaths are your desires. So long as you desire objects of this world, you must come back to this world in order to possess and enjoy them. But, when all your desires for the mundane objects cease, then the chains are broken and you are free. You need not take any more births. You attain Moksha or the final emancipation.

You wander in this Samsara as you think that you are different from the Lord. If you unite yourself with Him through meditation and Yoga, you will obtain immortality and eternal bliss. Cut the bonds of Karma through Knowledge of the Eternal and enjoy the supreme peace of the Atman, thy innermost Self and inner ruler. You will be freed from the round of births and deaths. Freed from sin, freed from passion, you will become a Jivanmukta or liberated sage.

59. RELIGION

Religion is the relationship between the three fundamental principles—God, world and the individual. Religion gives solace to the weary pilgrim in this earth-plane. It explains life's mystery to him. It shows the path to the immortal abode.

Religion is not a denial of life. It is fullness of life. It is life eternal. Man becomes God through discipline, self-restraint, and meditation. That is religion.

Religion consists in doing good to others, in the practice of love, mercy, truthfulness, and purity in all walks of life. Religion is practical philosophy; philosophy is theoretical religion. Philosophy is for ever searching, inquiring, questioning. Religion is sensing, realising, experiencing.

The same type of jacket cannot suit all people. Individual temperaments and traditional backgrounds differ. Hence the need for different religions.

One religion is as good as another. One road or path to the Supreme is as good as any other road or path. Cows have different colours, but the colour of milk is one. There are different kinds of roses, but the scent is one. Religion is one, but many are its forms of practice. Diversity is the order of creation. Religion is no exception to it.

The Essentials of Religion

Religion is not dogma. Religion is not creed. Creed is broken reed. Religion is not theology. It is not merely a belief or emotion. It is not merely a little prayer which one does when he suffers from severe intestinal colic or chronic dysentery. It is pre-eminently a life of goodness and service. Religion is a life of meditation. Religion is life in God. He who is loving, kind, pious and truthful, he who is endowed with faith and devotion, is truly religious.

The essence of religion is not marks on the forehead, not the matted locks and long beard, not standing in hot sun and cold water, not the orange-coloured robe, not the shaven head, not ringing bells, not blowing the conch, not playing the cymbals, but a life of goodness, purity, and service in the midst of mundane temptations.

Religion is living in God. It is not mere discussion about God. Mere intellectual assent cannot make you really religious. Real religion is beyond argument. It can only be lived, both inwardly and outwardly. It is realisation and becoming.

Let not personal bias, force of convention, or the opinion of fanatics and sectarians blind your vision into a narrow view of religion. Do not be prejudiced by observing the religious practices of untutored masses. You must be able to differentiate the essentials from the non-essentials in religion and philosophy, through the power of pure reason and discrimination. Then only you can be happy. The essentials of all religions are one and the same. They all agree. Religions differ only in non-essentials.

The Fruits of a Religious Life

A religious life is the greatest of all blessings. It lifts a man from the mire of worldliness, impurity, and infidelity. Intellect is vain if it is not illuminated by religion. Religion does what philosophy can never do. If you live in accordance with the rules of religion, you will attain wisdom, immortality, everlasting peace, and eternal bliss.

Religion frees one from sorrow and pain. Religion bestows everlasting peace. Religion makes one perfect and free. Religion makes one independent. Religion unites the soul with Brahman. Religion frees one from births and deaths.

Religion is the foundation of society, the source of all goodness and happiness, the basis of the virtue and prosperity of the individual, and through the individuals, of the nation. Civilisation, order, morality—all that elevate man and give peace to the nation—are the fruits of the practice of religion.

Take away religion. Man then lives to no purpose. He stays far, far away from the purposes of his birth. Life becomes a dreary waste here. There is no living without religion. It is only religion that makes existence valuable, and fills the mind with love, devotion, serenity and cheerfulness. No materialistic force can annihilate the religious urge in man, though for a time a certain kind of propaganda may serve as a deterrent.

Religions of the World

Hinduism, Zoroastrianism, Judaism, Buddhism, Christianity, and Mohammedanism are the six great religions of the world. There is no founder for Hinduism. All the other religions have their founders. They are named after the names of the founders. Jainism is only another form of Buddhism. Sikhism is based chiefly on Hinduism, and partly on Islam. Brahmoism is born of Hinduism and Christianity. And so also with other minor religions.

Whenever any important truth of religion was suppressed by the arrogance and selfishness of the priestly class, or forgotten through the ignorance of the people, there appeared a great saint, or prophet, or religious teacher. He emphasised that truth, removed the dross which had concealed or obscured it, and made it shine in its original brilliance, purity, splendour, and glory.

When, in olden times, people forgot all about the Vedic monotheism, there arose Zoroaster. He preached the worship of one God, Ahuramazda, and condemned the worship of Devas.

When the religion of the Vedas degenerated into a blind observance of rites and sacrifice of animals, when the Sudras were treated with contempt by the Brahmins, there appeared the compassionate Buddha, who stopped the killing of animals and raised the status of the Sudras.

When the priests of Judaism became arrogant, there arose Jesus to purify Judaism. When Christianity also degenerated into idolatry and superstition, there appeared Mohammed to preach his monotheism.

In this way, every new religion was only an endeavour to reform the older religion as it then existed, and a protest against its abuses.

The Unity that Underlies All Religions

All prophets are messengers of God. They are great Yogins and realised souls, who have had divine, intuitive perception of God. Their words are infallible and sacred. The Koran or the Zend-Avesta or the Bible is as much a sacred book as the Bhagavad-Gita. All contain the essence of divine wisdom. Ahuramazda, Isvara, Allah, Jehovah are different names for one God.

The ultimate source of religion is God. The fundamental principles which constitute its essence were revealed by God to the Rishis or seers in the beginning of creation. They are found in the Vedas, which are admitted as the oldest religious books or scriptures in the library of mankind.

The fundamentals or essentials of all religions are the same. They are as old as the human race. There never has been, there never shall be, any real invention or discovery in the sphere of religion. There never was a religious founder who had invented a new religion or revealed a new truth. These founders are all transmitters only, but not original makers.

Real religion is one. It is the religion of truth and love. It is the religion of the heart. It is the religion of service, sacrifice, and renunciation. It is the religion of goodness, kindness and tolerance.

Truth is neither Hindu nor Mohammedan, nor Buddhist nor Christian! Truth is one, homogeneous, eternal substance. The follower of the religion of Truth walks on the path of light, peace, wisdom, power, and bliss.

Religious Decadence Its Cause and Cure

Man forgets all about his religion on account of ignorance, or lust for power and greed. He had become irreligious. So he has come down to the level of a brute. He has lost all sense of morality. He does havoc. He creates mischief. He stabs, loots, and burns houses. The law of the jungle prevails.

Many preach Buddhism, but no one gives up desires and Himsa. Many preach Christianity, but no one practises love and forgiveness. Many preach Islam, but no one recognises the brotherhood of man. Many preach Hinduism, but no one realises the Divinity in all. Preaching has become the livelihood of men, while practice has become their object of scorn.

Hence the world is wicked, not for want of truth, nor on account of religions; but, alas, it is wicked for the lack of true followers of these ideals and religions.

What is needed is proper education of the followers of all religions. Place the practical tenets of your own religion before the followers of that religion, and devise ways and means of enabling them to express these tenets in their daily life. Without practice, idealism creates fatalism in man. Unless knowledge alters one's life, it is useless. Selflessness and love are not creeds to be taught, but ideals to be exemplified, demonstrated, and radiated. Therefore, let everyone practise his own religion and strive to attain the goal. Let religion create saints and Yogins, rather than Mandirs, Masjids, and Churches.

60. SADHANA

Sadhana is spiritual movement consciously systematised. Sadhana is the purpose for which we have come to this place.

Abhyasa and Sadhana are synonymous terms. The object of Sadhana is to release life from the limitations with which it is bound.

Sadhana is a lifelong process. Every day, every hour, every minute, is an onward march. Obstacles are innumerable in this great voyage. But, so long as you hold God as thy guide, there is nothing to worry about. You are sure to reach the other shore.

Some people have curiosity for the spiritual line. They have no real thirsting for liberation. They think that they will get certain powers or Siddhis if they do some Yogic practices. When they do not attain the powers, they lose patience and give up the practices, abandon the spiritual path, and pooh-pooh the Yogins and Yoga.

Mere curiosity will not help you to attain any spiritual progress. Curiosity-mongering is more abominable than mischief-mongering. Introspect. Analyse your thoughts and find out whether you have real spiritual hunger or mere curiosity-mongering. Transmute curiosity-mongering into real thirsting for salvation by constant Satsanga, study of good religious books, prayer, Japa, and meditation.

You must have interest and liking in your Sadhana. You must understand well the technique and benefits of Sadhana. You must select a Sadhana that is suitable for you. You must have the ability and capacity to do Sadhana. Then alone you will have joy in doing the Sadhana and full success in it.

Aspiration and Achievement

Good intentions alone will not do. They must be backed up by good actions. You must enter the spiritual path with the best intention of attaining Atma-Jnana, but unless you are vigilant and diligent, unless you do intense and rigorous Sadhana, unless you guard yourself against lust, anger and greed, egoism and selfishness, the good intentions alone will not enable you to achieve success.

Moral purity and spiritual aspiration are the first steps in the seeker's path. Without a strong conviction in moral values, there can surely be no spiritual life, or even a good life.

Stern self-discipline is absolutely essential. Self-discipline does not mean suppression, but taming the brute within. It means humanisation of the animal and spiritualisation of the human.

You will have to break the virgin soil before you sow the seed. The seed breaks itself before it sprouts out as a plant. Destruction precedes construction. This is the immutable law of nature. You will have to destroy your brutal nature first before you develop divine nature.

The spiritual path is rugged, thorny, and precipitous. The thorns must be weeded out with patience and perseverance. Some of the thorns are internal; some are external. Lust, greed, wrath, delusion, vanity, etc., are the internal thorns. Company with the evil-minded persons is the worst of all the external thorns. Therefore, shun ruthlessly evil company.

During the period of Sadhana, do not mix much; do not talk much; do not walk much; do not eat much; do not sleep much. Observe carefully the five 'do-not's. Mixing will cause disturbances in the mind. Talking much will cause distraction of the mind. Walking much causes exhaustion and weakness. Eating much induces laziness and sleepiness.

Dangers of Mixing with Women and Worldlings

During the period of Sadhana, avoid the company of women. You must never mix with young ladies, however strong you may be. Maya works through under-currents so stealthily that you may not be aware of your actual downfall.

Keep the mind fully occupied with spiritual pursuits. Keep yourself at the farthest distance from everything that would stir up your passions. Then only you will be safe.

Do not live with householders. Do not test your spiritual strength and purity when you are a beginner on the spiritual path. Do not rush into evil associations when you are a spiritual neophyte to show that you have the courage to face sin and impurity. It will be a serious mistake. You will be running into a grave danger. You will have a quick downfall. A small fire will be very easily extinguished by a heap of dust.

Mind has a great power of imitation. That is the reason why a spiritual aspirant is prohibited from mixing with householders. His mind will try to imitate the minds of worldlings. Downfall will ensue.

If an aspirant moves with rich people, Zamindars, and Rajas, his mind begins to imitate the luxurious habits of these people and, ere long, he gets an unconscious downfall. Certain bad habits creep in him unconsciously. And he finds it difficult to tear out or remove these bad habits.

An aspirant can live only for a short time in his native place if there is an urgent call. Yogic rules and laws cannot permit him to stay there for a sufficiently long period, however suitable the place may be and whatever may be the degree of Vairagya of the aspirant. The force of impressions is tremendous. Unless all the Samskaras are thoroughly burnt through pure Asamprajnata Samadhi or Nirvikalpa Avastha, it is not safe for one to stay for a long time in one's own native place. He is still within the danger zone.

The Spiritual Path

The spiritual path may, in the beginning, appear to be very hard, thorny, precipitous and slippery. Renunciation of objects gives pain at the outset. If you struggle hard to tread the path, if you once make a strong determination and firm resolve, then it becomes very easy. You get interest and new joy. Your heart expands. You have a broad outlook of life. You have a new, wide vision. You feel the help from the invisible hands of the Indweller of your heart. Your doubts are cleared by themselves by getting answers from within. You can hear the shrill, sweet voice of God. There is an indescribable thrill of divine ecstasy from within. There is deep, abiding, everlasting joy and unruffled peace. There is ineffable, unabating, undiminishing, undecaying spiritual bliss. This gives new strength. The footing in the path becomes firmer and firmer. The Jivanmuktas, Yogins, Nitya-siddhas, Amara-purushas, and Chiranjivis lend their helping hands to the struggling aspirants. The aspirants feel this actually. The feeling of loneliness and of being neglected and forsaken vanishes entirely.

You are backed up at all times by a mighty power that works everywhere in the cosmos. Therefore you have nothing to fear. Take care of the details in Sadhana. The major factor will take care of itself.

Some aspirants leave Sadhana after some time. They expect great fruits quickly. They expect many Siddhis within a short time. When they do not get some, they give up the Sadhana. There are several ranges of consciousness between the ordinary human consciousness and the supra-consciousness of Brahman. Different veils have to be torn down on the way; many lower centres have to be opened up; many hurdles have to be crossed over before the final goal is reached.

Spiritual Progress Is Like a Spiral

You have to plod on and scale many hills. You cannot climb the Everest in one jump. There is no jumping on the spiritual path.

Self-realisation is not like a six-year postgraduate course. It is the result of intense protracted Sadhana.

There is no shortcut in the spiritual path. There is no royal road to the kingdom of immortal bliss. There is no half-measure in the divine path. Strict, hard discipline is wanted. Then alone can you conquer Maya. Only then can you control the mind.

Saints and Yogins will never think that they have controlled the mind. Only the deluded Sadhaka will imagine he has controlled the mind and get a terrible downfall. It is the very nature of life, mind, and Prakriti to be constantly in motion. When there is the idea in the mind that the highest goal is yet to be achieved, you will always move towards it. If you imagine that you have got to the top, you will anyhow have to move, and that movement will be downward. You will have a downfall. Aspire for higher and higher realisation till the breath ceases in the nostril.

Spiritual progress is slow, as the spiritual Sadhana is difficult and laborious. It is like the spiral. In the beginning, greed striving is needed. Gradually, the circle becomes smaller and smaller. So also, the striving becomes less and less. The aspirant gains spiritual strength slowly. He marches faster and faster. Finally, he does not go by furlong after furlong. He proceeds by mile after mile. He gallops and gallops. Therefore, be patient; be persevering; be steady.

Signs of Spiritual Progress

The gradual inward progress is mostly silent and unseen, like the quiet unfolding of a bud into a flower in the hours of the night. Therefore, do not be dejected. Do not depress yourself with the idea that you are not progressing.

Real spiritual progress is really and accurately measured by the peacefulness, serenity, and calmness that you manifest in the waking state. You will have a healthy body and mind, the excretions will be scanty, the voice will be sweet, the face will be brilliant, the eyes will be lustrous. You will be ever calm, tranquil, and poised; you will be ever cheerful, fearless, and contented. You will be dispassionate and discriminative. There will be no attraction for the world. Things that used to upset you before will not upset you now. You will have an unruffled mind. You will have introversion. Things that used to give you pleasure produce disgust or a reverse effect now. You will have a one-pointed, sharp, subtle mind. You will be longing to have more meditation. You will experience lights, visions, divine smell, divine taste. The idea that all forms are forms of the Lord will get stronger and stronger in you. You will feel everywhere the presence of God. You will experience the nearness of God. You will have a very steady Asana. You will develop a burning desire for selfless service.

Watch whether you are stationary in the spiritual path, or retrogressing, or advancing. If your Japa, meditation or Vedantic Vichara thickens your veil and fattens your egoism, it is not then a spiritual Sadhana. Remember this point well. It is only a kind of occult practice. Watch, introspect. Practise self-analysis and kill ruthlessly this formidable egoism. This is important Sadhana. Egoism will lurk like a thief and assume various forms like a chameleon or a Bahurupi or a dramatic actor.

Do not stop Sadhana when you get a few glimpses of realisation. Continue practice till you are fully established in Bhuma, the unconditioned Brahman. This is important. If you stop practice and move about in the world, there is every likelihood of a downfall. The reaction will be tremendous. Examples are not lacking. Numerous persons have been so ruined. A glimpse cannot give you perfect safety. Do not be carried away by name and fame. You can renounce your wife, children, parents, house, friends, and relatives.

It is very, very difficult to renounce the intellectual pleasure, the pleasure from name and fame. I seriously warn you. A man who can draw happiness from the Atman within, will never care a jot for this trivial, paltry affair. The world is a mighty big thing for a worldly man. It is a straw for a Knower of Brahman. It is a mustard, a pin's point, a dot, a bubble, an airy nothing for a Brahma-jnani. Be circumspective. Ignore all these trivial things. Be steady with your practice. Never stop the practice till the final beatitude is reached. Never cease Sadhana till you can constantly dwell in full Brahmic consciousness.

Do not let failures discourage you, but go on doing your best. Do not brood over your past mistakes and failures, as this will only fill your mind with grief, regret, and depression. Do not repeat them in future. Be cautious. Just think of the causes which led to your failures and try to remove them in future. Strengthen yourself with new vigour and virtues. Develop slowly your will-power.

Every temptation that is resisted, every evil thought that is curbed, every desire that is subdued, every bitter word that is withheld, every noble aspiration that is encouraged, every sublime thought that is cultivated, adds to the development of will-force, good character, and attainment of eternal bliss and immortality.

Every bit of Sadhana done is surely recorded without fail in your hidden consciousness. No Sadhana ever goes in vain. Every bit of it is credited immediately towards your evolution. This is the law. Think not negative thoughts, but calmly go on with the Sadhana. Be regularly at it. Without missing a single day, proceed onward with your spiritual practices. Little by little, the power accumulates and it will grow. Ultimately, the cumulative force of all the continuous earnest Sadhana done perseveringly and patiently over a long period of life has its inevitable grand consummation at the supreme moment when it bears fruit in the form of blissful Realisation.

Let the Sadhana be regular, continuous, unbroken, and earnest. Not only regularity, but also continuity in Sadhana and meditation is necessary if you want to attain Self-realisation quickly. A spiritual stream once set going does not dry up, unless the channel-bed is blocked, unless there is stagnation. Be vigilant eternally. Meditate regularly. Annihilate the under-current of Vasanas.

Obstacles to Spiritual Progress

Sometimes the aspirant gets stuck up. He cannot proceed further in his path. Sometimes he is side-tracked through Siddhis. He loses his way and walks in some other direction. He misses the goal. Sometimes he is assailed by temptations and various oppositions. Sometimes he gets false contentment. He thinks he has reached his goal and stops all Sadhana. Sometimes he is careless, lazy, indolent. He cannot do any Sadhana. Therefore, be eternally vigilant, like the captain of a ship, like the surgeon in the operation theatre.

The spiritual path is full of hurdles. If you conquer one obstacle, another obstacle is ready to manifest. If you control the sense of taste, another Indriya is simply waiting to assault you with redoubled force and vigour. If you remove greed, anger is waiting to hurl you down. If you drive egoism through one door, it enters through another door. Great patience, perseverance, vigilance, and undaunted strength are needed.

Be firm, steady, and steadfast. People will mock at you; be silent. People will insult you; be silent. People will spread evil rumours about you; be silent. Stick to the spiritual path. Do not swerve. Seek the truth wherever it may lead you to, and whatever be the cost and sacrifice.

Start Sadhana Now

Act now. Live now. Know now. Realise now. Be happy now.

Every death is a reminder. Every bell that rings says, "The end is near". Every day robs off from you one part of your precious life. Therefore, you should be very earnest in plunging yourself in constant Sadhana.

Never fall a victim to fruitless regret. Today is the best day. Today is the day of your new birth. Start Sadhana now. With folded palms, bid goodbye to past mistakes and faults. You have learnt your lessons. March forward now with new hope, determination, and vigilance.

Waver not. Fear not. Doubt not. Do something substantial in the path of Sadhana instead of wasting your time in idle pursuits and lethargy. You have infinite strength within you. There is a vast reservoir of power within you. Therefore, do not lose heart. Obstacles are stepping-stones to success. They will develop your will. Do not allow yourself to be crushed by them. Defects remind you of perfection. Sin reminds you of virtue. Choose the positive path.

If you think, "I will take a bath when all the waves of the sea subside", this is not possible. The waves will never subside and you will never take a bath. Even so, if you think, "I will start spiritual Sadhana or meditation when all my cares, worries and anxieties cease, when all my sons are fixed up in life, when I have ample leisure after retirement", this is not possible. You will not be able to sit even for half an hour when you become old. You will have no strength to do any rigorous Tapas when you are in advanced senility. You must start vigorous spiritual practices when you are young, whatever your conditions, circumstances and environments may be. Then only you will reap a rich spiritual harvest when you become old. You will enjoy the everlasting peace of the Eternal.

61. SAINTS

A saint is a god on earth. To him, the whole world is mere straw. To him, gold and stone are alike. To him, pleasure and pain are the same.

A saint lives in God. He has realised God. He knows God. He has become God. He speaks of God. He shows the way to God. He is God-intoxicated. He is God Himself. He is one with God.

Saints are God's agents on earth. God reveals Himself in a saint in His full glory, infinite power, wisdom and bliss.

The saints constitute a ladder for the pilgrims to the shrine of God. Wherever saints and sages stay even for a half-second, then and there are sacred places like Varanasi, Prayag, and Brindavan.

A saint is a blessing on the earth. Saints are the living symbols of religion and are the true benefactors of humanity. Throughout history, saints have played a great part in preserving spiritual values in the world.

A saint is a spiritual washerman. He applies the soap of devotion and knowledge, and removes the spots of sin in worldly people. In his presence, man becomes holy.

The moment the mind thinks of a sage, immediately all evil desires, base passions, are brushed aside. Meditation on the lives of saints is equal to holy company. Study of their teachings is equal to holy company.

To think of the lives of saints, to live in their company, to have the good fortune of receiving their blessings, is to draw forth upon yourself a shower of purity, inspiration and divine consciousness.

The Nature of a Saint

A saint is free from I-ness and mine-ness. He is free from lust, anger, and greed. He loves all beings as his own Self. He is endowed with dispassion and mercy. He speaks the truth and serves all. He ever meditates on the Lord. He does not speak ill of others. He has equal vision. He sees Devi or Mother in all women. He is ever joyful and peaceful. He sings the glory of the Lord. He has divine knowledge. He is fearless and generous. He never begs, but gives. He is majestic and lordly. Such a one is rare in the whole world. He is not easily found. He is not born everywhere.

Love is the very breath of a saint. Mercy is his very nature. His heart overflows with compassion. He does not look to the faults of others. He returns good for evil and blesses those who curse him.

The heart of a sage is a flame of love and his whole being thirsts for the uplift of suffering humanity. He forgets himself utterly and lives but for the sake of others.

A saint sees the whole world as the projection of his own soul. A sage sees unity in diversity. He becomes one with the whole world.

A sage is a youth amongst the youth, aged amongst the old, brave amongst the brave, a child amongst children. He feels the pain and suffering among sufferers.

The Life of a Saint

The life of a saint is plain, simple, and attractive. It is full of grace. It is methodical. A saint is ever of good cheer. He knows no ill of life. To him, life is joy. He experiences no trial of misery. He is fearless. No monarch has sway over him.

The life of a saint is always a life of quiet, of indrawn stillness, of solitude and aloofness. He is untouched by the changes of the world. No external happening can shake him off his balance. He is centred in his own Atman or Absolute Consciousness.

A sage is desireless and so he is ever happy. A king possesses everything and so he is happy. But, the happiness of a sage is infinite, because he lives in his own Atman, the ocean of Brahmic Bliss. A king is full of fears and worries. He is afraid that his enemies will conquer him one day and so he is restless and miserable.

The happiness of a liberated sage is not sensual pleasure. It is Atmic Self-bliss. He enjoys the whole world simultaneously as the Self of all objects. His happiness is not in time. It is transcendental bliss.

A sage alone is really wealthy. Multi-millionaires with cravings and desires are beggars. A saint is superior to an emperor, to Indra, the Lord of heaven.

A sage has awakened from the dream of life. He enjoys eternal bliss. To a sage of illumination, the entire world surrenders.

A Sage Need Not Be a Genius

The sage moves among men, but he is unseen by all men; he is taken by them as an ordinary man.

Only a sage can know a sage. He will sometimes appear like a Sarvajna, an all-knower. He will sometimes appear like an Ajnani, an ignorant man. He knows when to act like a Brahmanishtha and when to behave like a fool. Do not judge him. If you approach him with the proper Bhava, with faith, devotion and spiritual thirst, he will impart the highest knowledge to you. If you approach him with a bad motive, he will behave like a madman and you will be deceived. Great will be your loss then.

A Brahma-jnani or liberated sage need not be a genius. He need not be an eloquent speaker, orator, lecturer or professor. But, he is calm, serene, and tranquil. He is taciturn and silent. His silence is superior eloquence. He has equanimity and balanced mind. He has equal vision. He has Samata and Samadrishti. He is a Mouni, Maha Mouni, and Muni. He has divine wisdom and intuitive knowledge. In his presence, all doubts are cleared.

Saints Have No Caste

There is no caste among saints and sages. A sage is like a lion out of the cage, free from shackles of caste, creed, profession, tradition and scripture. Do not look to the caste of saints and sages. You will not be benefited. You cannot imbibe their virtues. In higher religion, there is neither caste nor creed. Cobblers, weavers, and untouchables had become the best saints.

There is no real difference between a Christian mystic and a Hindu saint. Their sayings never clash. The messages of the saints are essentially the same. They have always been a call to men to discover the Wisdom of the Self or Atman.

Sages Differ in Their Conduct

Knowledge is the same in all sages, but their conduct is different. Sri Vasishtha was a Karmakandi; he did Havans and sacrifices. Raja Janaka was a Bhogi; he ruled his dominion; he enjoyed regal pleasures. Sri Dattatreya was a wanderer; he was an Avadhuta, a naked Fakir. Kakabusundhi was a Yogin. Some even marry.

Sages like Dattatreya and Jadabharata roam about happily. They have neither rooms nor clothing. All dualities have become extinct.

They cannot work for the well-being of the world like Raja Janaka and Sri Sankara. But, their mere presence elevates people.

The other type of sage is the benevolent sage—like Raja Janaka and Sri Sankara—who works for the solidarity of the world. He has compassion for all. He writes books, conducts classes, establishes Mutts or Ashrams. You may ask: "Which of the two kinds is superior?". The answer is: "Both are on the same level".

A Sage Is not Selfish

Ignorant people say, "A sage is attempting for his own Self-realisation. He is extremely selfish. He is of no use to society". This is a serious mistake. A sage is the most benevolent superman. He is extremely kind and compassionate. He elevates at once all persons who come in contact with him. Further, he does Sakti-sanchar through his Divya Drishti. He finds out the deserving aspirants and raises them up through Sankalpa Sakti, even while remaining in a cave or Kutir in the distant Himalayas.

A Jnani is not a selfish man as worldly men think. His spiritual vibrations purify the world. His very life is exemplary and elevating. He gives hope and encouragement to others to tread the spiritual path. He is the only real lover of mankind. He feels the presence of God in everyone. He loves his neighbour as himself. A Jnani only does real selfless service as he feels the presence of God in all beings. He is the real altruist and humanitarian.

Do Not Judge a Saint

You cannot apply the worldly yardstick to measure the greatness of the saints. Do not superimpose defects on them on account of your evil eye. You cannot judge their merits.

Brahma-nishthas are like fire. They can consume anything. Their very touch purifies everything. They are beyond good and bad; they are themselves the supreme good. Do not imitate their actions. Their actions are strange and mysterious. They are beyond your intellect. If you commit theft and say, "Did not Krishna steal butter?", you will be hopelessly ruined. Krishna lifted up the Govardhana Hill with His little finger. Can you lift even a big stone with all your strength? Follow the Upadesha of saints and Mahapurushas; you will attain Brahma Jnana here and now.

How to Benefit by the Company of Saints

To benefit from the company of saints, you have to prepare yourself first. Do not go with any preconceived notion or prejudice. Go with an open, receptive mind. Go without expectations. Approach them humbly, respectfully. Assimilate what appeals to you. If some of their teachings do not appeal to you, do not form a hasty opinion. If you do not like them, you need not take them to heart. What may be suitable to another may not be suitable to you. Yet, with regard to broad fundamentals, there can be no difference of opinion.

When you go before a sage, do not ask him questions out of mere inquisitiveness. Sit in his presence humbly. Observe him. Listen to him without prejudice. Ask him only such questions about which you really need clarification. Ask him only pertinent questions. Do not draw him into politics or public bickerings.

Meditate in the presence of a sage. You will get inner light which will clear your doubts.

Saints as Advisers

The very company of sages and saints has a tremendous transforming effect on the lives of true seekers. It lifts them up to heights of sublimity, purity, and spirituality. It does not fail to affect even the rank materialists.

Every school, every college, every boarding house, every jail, every institution, every house should have a saint for the guidance of its members.

Saints and sages only can become real advisers to the kings, because they are selfless and possess the highest wisdom. They only can improve the morality of the masses. They only can show the way to attain eternal bliss and immortality. Shivaji had Swami Ramdas as his adviser. King Dasaratha had Maharshi Vasishtha as his adviser.

Saints are in abundance. You do not want them. You do not wish to approach them. You do not wish to serve them. You do not aspire for higher things. You are perfectly satisfied with some broken shells and glass-pieces. There is no thirst or spiritual hunger in you for achieving higher divine knowledge and inner peace.

Spiritual opportunity is a rare privilege. Do not lose such

opportunities. Take recourse to the company of sages and saints. One moment of company with the Holy builds a ship to cross this ocean of life.

God is the great purifier. A saint also is a great purifier. God incarnates as saints and sages when their need is felt most.

Study the lives of saints. You are inspired at once. Remember their sayings. You are elevated immediately. Walk in their footsteps. You are freed from pain and sorrow.

Seek the company of sages and evolve. Satsanga with sages is unfailing in its results.

62. SAMADHI

Samadhi is union with the Lord. It is superconscious experience. It is Adhyatmic Anubhava.

Samadhi or ecstasy is blissful union. The mind melts in the Eternal or the Atman, like salt in water or camphor in flame. It is a state of pure consciousness.

Samadhi instals you in the Atman. Through Samadhi, the finite self is absorbed in the infinite or absolute consciousness. The unity of the Jivatman and the Paramatman is realised.

The knowledge that you obtain from Samadhi is divine knowledge. It is supersensual, intuitive knowledge where reason, inference, and testimony cannot go.

Samadhi is inner, divine experience which is beyond the reach of speech and mind. The state of Samadhi is beyond all relativity. There is no language or means to give expression to it.

Even in worldly experience, you cannot express the taste of an apple to one who has not tasted it, or the nature of colour to a blind man. The state of Samadhi is all-bliss, joy, and peace. This much only can be said. One has to feel this himself.

In Samadhi, there is neither physical nor mental consciousness. There is only spiritual consciousness. There is only existence or Sat. That is your real Svarupa. When the water dries up in a pool, the reflection of the sun in the water also vanishes. When the mind melts in Brahman, when the mind-lake dries up, the reflected Chaitanya also vanishes. The Jivatman or individual personality goes away. There remains Existence alone.

In Samadhi, there is neither meditation nor meditator. The meditator and the meditated, the thinker and the thought, the worshipper and the worshipped, become one or identical. The mind loses its own consciousness and becomes identical with the object of meditation. The meditator has dissolved his personality in the sea of God, drowned and forgotten there till he becomes simply the instrument of God. When his mouth opens, it speaks God's words without effort or forethought, through direct intuition; and when he raises his hand, God flows again through that to work a miracle.

A Condition of Perfect Awareness

Samadhi is not a condition of inertia, forgetfulness, or

annihilation. It is a state of absolute consciousness which baffles all attempts at description. It is the final goal of all. It is Mukti. It is Moksha.

Samadhi is not a stone-like, inert state as many people imagine. A life in the spirit is not annihilation. When the Self is bound down to its empirical accidents, its activities are not fully exercised; and when the limitations of the empirical existence are transcended, the universal life is intensified and you have enrichment of self. You will have a rich inner life. You will have an expanded cosmic life, and supra-cosmic life, too.

Samadhi is not a state of inertia. It is a condition of perfect awareness. It is not merely an emotional enthusiasm or an exhilarating feeling. It is direct, unique, intuitive experience of Truth or Absolute Consciousness or the Ultimate Reality. It is beyond all feeling, throbbing, and thrill. It is a powerful state of transcendental self-awareness. The aspirant rests in his centre now—the goal of his search—and realises the absolute freedom, independence, and perfection.

The Fourth Dimension

The state of Samadhi is neither waking nor dreaming on account of the absence of Sankalpa or desire. It is not also Sushupti or sleep, because of the absence of inertness there. It is the fourth dimension where there is infinite Brahmic bliss.

Generally, when you have what you call dreamless sleep, it is one of two things: either you do not remember what you dreamt of, or you fell into absolute unconsciousness which is almost death—a state of death. But, there is the possibility of a sleep in which you enter into an absolute silence, immortality, and peace in all parts of your being, and your consciousness merges into Sat-chit-ananda. You can hardly call it sleep, for there is perfect "awareness". In that condition, you can remain for a few minutes, or hours, or days: but these few minutes give you more rest and refreshment than hours of ordinary sleep. You cannot have it by chance. It requires a long training.

Jada Samadhi and Chaitanya Samadhi

There is a popular belief that Samadhi means sitting with a Kowpeen in a state of absolute unconsciousness in the Padmasana or lotus pose, with perfect suspension of breath. The ordinary rung of mankind think that the man who is established in Samadhi should not have consciousness of his surroundings and should be absolutely insensible even if a knife is thrust into his body. Such Samadhis do certainly exist. They are all Jada Samadhis induced by Hatha Yogic Kriyas.

A Hatha Yogin, through the practice of Khechari Mudra, can shut himself up in a box which is then buried underneath the ground for months. Doubtless, this is a difficult Yogic Kriya, but it does not give Atma-jnana.

In Jada Samadhi, the Prana is taken up and fixed in some Chakra. The man is practically dead for the time being. This is something like long, deep sleep. These Samadhis are of no value. The Samskaras and Vasanas are not burnt up *in toto*. There is no perfect awareness during this Samadhi. The man returns from his Samadhi as the same old man with the same bundle of old Samskaras and Vasanas. He has no super-intuitional knowledge. This is a kind of acrobatic feat or internal gymnastics. Such Samadhis cannot give Mukti or liberation. Worldly people are deceived by such feats.

True Samadhi gives supersensual knowledge. The Yogin comes down with new, supersensuous wisdom. This is real, Chaitanya Samadhi. In Chaitanya Samadhi, there is perfect awareness. In Jada Samadhi, the Sadhaka is unconscious.

Chaitanya Samadhi is something entirely different from Jada Samadhi. In it, all doubts, delusion, and the three knots—Avidya. Kama, and Karma—are destroyed by the fire of wisdom. It gives absolute fearlessness and an unruffled state of mind. The state of Samadhi is maintained even during work.

He who is established in Samadhi keeps his mind and body in perfect balance and utilises them in the service of humanity with Atma-Bhava. He is ever fixed in Brahman. He is always in Samadhi. There is no tossing for him under any condition. He stands adamantine on account of his Knowledge of the Self.

Real Samadhi should be kept up as much in action, as in meditation. This is the real test of one's inner strength and realisation. This is real Chaitanya Samadhi. A Samadhi that one enters into in the mountain-caves and forests with closed eyes, but that is broken or shattered during work, is no Samadhi at all.

The Mind in Samadhi

Samadhi means the annihilation or absorption of the mind. The mind does not at all function in Samadhi. It gets absorbed in Brahman. If you can consciously induce a state like deep sleep, it is no longer deep sleep, but it is Samadhi. It is sleepless sleep, wherein the senses and the mind entirely cease their functioning, and the veil of ignorance is destroyed by the fire of knowledge. The aspirant enjoys perfect joy of freedom. He enjoys the supreme silence of the Imperishable.

In Samadhi, there is no mental tension. There is perfect stillness or perfect poise. There is total mental inhibition.

In Samadhi, the purified mind resolves itself in the Atman, its source, and becomes the Atman Itself. It takes the form of the Atman, just as camphor becomes the fire itself. To know Brahman is to become Brahman. The mind becomes the very Brahman when it is purified and brought into the Samadhi state.

When the mind becomes Brahman, this world, which is the creation of the mind, also melts away in Brahman and becomes Brahman Itself.

The Samadhi Experience

There is neither darkness nor void in this experience. It is all light. There is neither sound nor touch nor form here. It is a magnanimous experience of unity or oneness. There is neither time nor causation here. There is only eternity. You become omniscient and omnipotent. You become a Sarva-vid or all-knower. You know everything. You know the whole mystery of creation. You get immortality, higher knowledge, and eternal bliss.

All dualities vanish here. There is neither subject nor object. There is neither Sakara nor Nirakara. There is neither meditation nor Samadhi. There is neither Dvaita nor Advaita. There is neither Vikshepa nor one-pointedness. There is neither meditator nor meditated. There is neither day nor night.

When you are established in the highest Nirvikalpa Samadhi, you have nothing to see, nothing to hear, nothing to smell, nothing to feel. You have no body-consciousness. You have full Brahmic consciousness. There is nothing but the Self. It is a grand experience. You will be struck with awe and wonder.

This experience arises when the ego and the mind are dissolved. It is a state to be attained by one's own effort. It is limitless, divisionless, and infinite, an experience of being and of pure consciousness. When this experience is realised, the mind, desires, actions, and feelings of joy and sorrow vanish into a void.

The Jivahood has gone now. The little 'I' has melted. The differentiating mind that splits up has vanished.

Samadhi Gives Moksha

Samadhi brings Kaivalya or absolute independence. Samadhi gives Moksha. This is the culmination or climax of Yoga. With the advent of the Knowledge of the Self, ignorance vanishes. With the disappearance of the root cause, viz., ignorance, egoism, etc., also disappear.

The Yogin has simultaneous knowledge now. The past and the future are blended into the present. Everything is 'now'. Everything is 'here'. He has transcended time and space.

It is only through Samadhi that one can know the Unknown, see the Unseen, can get access into the Inaccessible. The sum total of all the knowledge of the three worlds, of all secular sciences, is nothing, nothing but mere husk when compared to the infinite knowledge of a sage who has attained the highest state of Samadhi.

One who comes down from Samadhi may live and move about in the same ordinary way as before, and there may not be any strikingly perceptible change in his life and behaviour to the casual beholder. But, all the same, the change in his consciousness is undeniably there. What to say of mere change? There will be positive transformation in the personality.

Who Could Enter into Samadhi?

Samadhi is not an experience that can be attained through a little practice. None can enter into Samadhi until he is himself a greatly purified soul. To attain Samadhi, one should observe strict Brahmacharya, dietetic restrictions, and must have purity of heart. The mind should be perfectly purified. Then only the mechanism or vessel will be fit enough to receive the descent of divine light. It should be sufficiently strong to bear the pressure of sudden expansion of consciousness or cosmic vision, which is above mind, and which covers the whole existence in one sweep.

If you are an Uttama Adhikari, a firstclass aspirant, equipped with the four means or qualifications and endowed with Tivra Vairagya and an intense longing for liberation, and if you have a Brahma-srotri, Brahma-nishtha like Sri Sankara or Lord Krishna to back you up, you will realise the Self in the twinkling of an eye. Within the time taken to squeeze a flower with your fingers, you can realise the Self. Through Ashtavakra, Raja Janaka realised within the twinkling of an eye. Arjuna had Self-realisation in the battlefield within an hour and a half. Mukunda Rai of Maharashtra put a Badshah in Samadhi in a second when he was on horseback. There are so many instances.

Like the man who anxiously seeks a means of escape from the midst of a burning house, the aspirant should have a burning desire to free himself from the fire of Samsara. Then only he will be able to enter into deep meditation and Samadhi.

How to Attain Samadhi

Deep meditation leads to Samadhi or oneness with God. The mind is filled with Atman or God. Mind loses its own consciousness and becomes identified with the object of meditation. Just as a toy made of salt melts in water, even so, the mind melts in Brahman in Nirvikalpa Samadhi. A sudden stroke of mystic illumination puts an end to all the empirical existence altogether, and the very idea or remembrance of such a thing as this world or the narrow individuality of the spirit in this world absolutely leaves the self.

Mark the three processes that take place in the mind during meditation. These are: CONTEMPLATION, FILLING, IDENTIFICATION. Remember these three word-images. Repeat them mentally while doing Sadhana. It will help you a lot really.

Contemplate on the Atman. Fill the mind with Atman. Then the mind becomes identified with Brahman in accordance with what is known as the analogy of wasp and caterpillar. As you think, so you become. Think you are Brahman; Brahman you will become.

Be silent. Know thyself. Know That. Melt the mind in That. Truth is quite pure and simple.

63. SANNYASA

Sannyasa is the life of renunciation. It is, in other words, the Upanishadic life. It is the last of the four Asramas.

Action is for the man of the world, and wisdom is for the Sannyasin who has risen above worldliness. Only the man of renunciation with knowledge attains Brahman, and none else. Without perfect renunciation, it is impossible to pursue the path of Brahma-vidya.

The Sannyasin is dead to the world and his family. He renounces the whole universe at a stretch and has nothing to do with anything except the one Self.

To the Sannyasin, fame and name are equal to the faecal matter of a pig. Therefore, renouncing name and fame, the Sannyasin wanders like a fly.

The Sannyasin has only three duties to perform, Saucha, Bhiksha, and Dhyana. There is no fourth duty for a Sannyasin. Meditation is his duty, meditation is his food, meditation is his life. He lives in meditation, breathes meditation. He is ever intent upon the realisation of the Supreme Brahman.

The Sannyasin lives in the height of wisdom, like a fool, like a child. Blossoming with knowledge, he behaves like an idiot. Absorbed in the Atman, the Sannyasin talks not a single word.

Fitness for Sannyasa

Sannyasa is open to a Brahmachari, a Grihastha, or a Vanaprastha, all alike. One can take Sannyasa either direct from Brahmacharya, or otherwise as he likes.

One should qualify himself with *Sadhana Chatushtaya* before entering into Sannyasa. There should be perfect renunciation born of discrimination. The Vairagya or dispassion should not be mild and half-hearted. It should be a burning flame of disgust for everything that is seen and that is not seen. Nothing but the state of Kaivalya or final liberation is to be the ideal of attainment. There should be no desire for wife, children, and worldly activity. He must be encircled by the fence of dispassion from all sides.

The self-arrogating faculty is to be finally reduced to naught. Love and hatred should be effaced out completely. The aspirant must be above the tricks and bondages of Samsara.

As soon as disgust arises in the mind for all objects of the world, then one should take to Sannyasa without any further hesitation.

If you like seclusion, if you are free from Raga or passion, worldly ambition, Karmic tendencies and attractions of this world, if you are reticent and serene, if you have disciplined yourself while remaining in the world, if you can live on simple food, if you can lead a hard life, if you have a strong constitution, if you are not talkative, if you can remain alone without company and talk, if you have a meditative temperament or reflective nature, if you can bear all the difficulties in the spiritual path, if you can lead a difficult life of an ascetic till the end of your life, if you can bear any amount of insult and injury done to you, then you can take to the path of renunciation. Only then you will be benefited by embracing Sannyasa. You should actually lead the life of a Sannyasin for one or two years in the world itself. Otherwise you will find it extremely difficult to tread the path. For a man of dispassion, discrimination, and strong will, this path is all joy and bliss.

A passionate man should not take Sannyasa. A person who takes Sannyasa even when he is being overpowered by passion, goes to the regions of darkness and gloom. Whose tongue, genital, stomach, and hands are properly disciplined, that man is fit to take Sannyasa.

When women are equipped with the four means of salvation, they are also quite eligible for Sannyasa. They are as efficient as men in the field of spirituality. When one is born with Sannyasa Samskaras, no force on the earth can prevent him or her from taking Sannyasa. Even if you keep a hundred guards to prevent such a person from leaving the house, they cannot check him. The father of the great Buddha guarded him in all possible ways, but his horse scaled the heights of the compound and took him to the forest. It is only the effeminate, impotent, timid men, who are only moustached-ladies, with no good Samskaras and no spiritual asset, who are spiritual bankrupts, that will cling to things mundane and die like worms. They will speak against Sannyasa. He who has understood the glory and freedom of Sannyasa, a real child of Sri Sankara, Sri Dattatreya, Sanaka, Sanandana, Sanatana, and Sanatkumara, cannot remain even for a day in the Pravritti Marga.

Role of Sannyasins in Society

Every religion has a band of anchorites who lead the life of

seclusion and meditation. There are Bhikkus in Buddhism, Fakirs i
Mohammedanism, Sufistic Fakirs in Sufism, Fathers and Reverend
in Christianity. The glory of a religion will be absolutely lost if yo
remove the hermits or Sannyasins or those who lead the life o
renunciation and divine contemplation. It is these people wh
maintain and preserve the religions of the world. It is these peopl
who give solace to the householders when they are in trouble an
distress. They bring hope to the hopeless, joy to the depressed
strength to the weak, and courage to the timid by imparting th
knowledge of the Vedanta and the significance of the "Tat Tvan
Asi" Mahavakya.

Sannyasins live on a few pieces of bread, and in exchange, mov
from door to door and spread the sublime teachings of the Vedanta
and the sublime philosophy of Realisation of Brahman, throughou
the length and breadth of the country. The world is under a grea
debt of gratitude to them. Who can repay the debts to them? Thei
writings still guide us. Study a few Slokas of the Avadhuta Gita
You will at once be raised to the magnificent heights of divin
splendour and glory. You will become a changed man. Depression
weakness, anxiety, and tribulations will vanish at once.

A real Sannyasin is the only mighty potentate on this earth. H
never takes anything. He always gives. It was Sannyasins only wh
did glorious, sublime work in the past. It is Sannyasins only wh
can work wonders in the present and in the future also. It wa
Ramakrishna Paramahamsa, Rama Tirtha, Dayananda, an
Vivekananda who disseminated the sublime teachings of th
scriptures and preserved the Hindu religion. It is only Sannyasin
bold, who have cut off all ties and connections, who are fearless
who are freed from delusion, passion, and selfishness, that can d
real service to the world. A Sannyasin alone can do rea
Loka-sangraha, because he has divine knowledge, he is
whole-timed man! One real Sannyasin can change the destiny of th
whole world! It is one mighty Sankara who established the doctrin
of the Kevala-advaita philosophy. He still lives in our hearts. Hi
name can never be obliterated so long as the world lasts.

Just as there are research scholars or postgraduates in science
psychology, biology, philosophy, so also, there should b
postgraduate Yogins and Sannyasins who will devote their time i
study and meditation, in research over the Atman. Thes

postgraduate Yogins will give to the world their experiences and realisations in the field of religion. They will train students and send them into the world for preaching. It is the duty of householders, Zamindars, and the administration to look after the wants of these Sannyasins. In turn, these Sannyasins will take care of their souls. Thus the wheel of the world will revolve smoothly. There will be peace in the land.

Necessity for Sannyasa

I do not believe those people who say, "We have given colouring to our hearts". This is timidity and hypocrisy. If there is real internal change, the external change is bound to come. You cannot be a sage inside and a rogue outside. The inner nature will not allow you to keep an opposite nature outside. I do not admit that merely an attempt towards eradication of egoism, Sankalpas, and Vasanas does really constitute Sannyasa. The Asramabheda is absolutely necessary. Why did sages like Sankara and Sri Ramakrishna take Sannyasa? Why did Yajnavalkya take Sannyasa even after realisation of Brahman? Where is the necessity for this order at all?

Can you imagine a greater Karma-kandi, a follower of the Pravritti Marga, than the great Mandana Misra? He was the greatest votary of Karma. He argued with Sri Sankaracharya for days together on the point that Sannyasa is not necessary. He wanted to establish that we can attain Mukti or salvation by Karma-marga, and that Nivritti is not absolutely essential. But, at last, Sri Sankara defeated Mandana Misra; and Mandana Misra also became one of the four disciples of Sankara. When such a mighty man became a Sannyasin, are you not convinced that Sannyasa is necessary?

You are not treading the path of the Vedas as Mandana Misra did. He was an ideal householder who knew the four Vedas, who was devoted to his elders, who walked in the footsteps of ideal Grihasthas like Yajnavalkya and others. Even he took Sannyasa!

The Gerua and the Shaven Head

The orange colour, Gerua, of the Sannyasin indicates that he is as pure as fire itself. He shines like the burnt gold, free from all impurities of desires and Vasanas. It denotes purity. It stands for purity. For an aspirant who has taken to the path of Nivritti Marga, it is a help. He will swerve and shrink from evil actions. This cloth will remind him that he is not entitled to worldly enjoyments. Gradually his nature will be moulded. This coloured cloth serves as an external symptom to show that one is a Sannyasin.

A Sannyasin shaves his head completely. This removes in him all beauty. He will not take much care about dressing his hair with scented oils, etc. This shows that he has renounced all external beauties and that he dwells in the Self which is the Beauty of beauties. This Mundana or shaving of the head indicates that he is no more of the world. He should not desire any sensual objects. It is only an external symbol of the mental state of complete dispassion and turning away from the pleasures of the world.

Sannyasa—A Mental State

Sannyasa is Gerua or colouring of the heart, and not of cloth alone. Sannyasa is a mental state only. He is a veritable Sannyasin who is free from passions and egoism and who possesses all the Sattvic qualities, even though he lives with the family, in the world. Chudala was a queen Yogini-Sannyasini, though she was ruling a kingdom. That Sannyasin who lives in the forest, but who is full of passions, is worse than a householder and a worldly-minded fool. Sikhidhvaja was a worldly man, though he lived in the forest naked for many years.

True renunciation is the renunciation of all passions, desires, egoism, and Vasanas. If you have a stainless mind, a mind free from attachment, egoism, and passion, you are a Sannyasin—no matter whether you live in a forest or in the bustle of a city, whether you wear white cloth or an orange-coloured robe, whether you shave the head or keep a long tuft of hair.

Shave the mind. Someone asked Guru Nanak, "O saint, why have you not shaved your head? You are a Sannyasin". Guru Nanak replied, "My dear friend, I have shaved my mind". In fact, the mind should be cleanly shaved. Shaving the mind consists in getting rid of all sorts of attachments, passions, egoism, Moha or infatuation, lust, greed, anger, etc. That is the real shaving. External shaving of the head has no meaning so long as there is internal craving Trishna.

Many have not understood what true renunciation is. Renunciation of physical objects is no renunciation at all. True renunciation lies in the abnegation of the mind. It consists in renouncing all desires and egoism, and not world-existence. The real Tyaga, renunciation, consists in the renunciation of egoism or Ahankara. If you can renounce this Ahankara, you have renounced everything else in the world. If the subtle Ahankara is given up, Dehadhyasa or identification with the body automatically goes away.

Sannyasa and Vedanta

Sannyasa and Vedanta of some kind always go hand in hand. One does not become complete without the other. Wherever there is real Sannyasa, there is practical Vedanta. Wherever there is practical Vedanta, there must be Sannyasa of the highest type. Sannyasa without Vedanta or Para Bhakti becomes fruitless. Vedanta without Sannyasa becomes mere intellectualism. When Sannyasa and Vedanta melt into one, there crops up a sage of supreme wisdom. Sannyasa empties the individual of the ego and the negative phenomena, and Vedanta fills it with positive truth. Sannyasa without Vedanta remains empty, and does not serve its purpose. Even so, Vedanta without Sannyasa becomes essenceless, and loses its meaning. Vedanta cannot be grasped without emptying the ego through Sannyasa, and Sannyasa becomes a waste without getting at the supreme ideal through Vedanta.

Vedanta does not want you to renounce the world. It wants you to change your mental attitude and give up this false, illusory 'I-ness' and 'mine-ness'. The snake-charmer removes only the two poisonous fangs of the cobra. The snake remains the same. It hisses, raises its hood, and shows the teeth. In fact, it does everything as before. The snake-charmer has changed his mental attitude towards the snake. He has a feeling now that it has got no poisonous fangs. Even so, you must remove the two poisonous fangs of the mind, viz., Ahamta and Mamata only. Then you can allow the mind to go wherever it likes. Then you will have always Samadhi only.

You must renounce the Tyaga-abhimana also. The Tyaga-abhimana is very deep-rooted. You must renounce the idea, "I have renounced everything; I am a great Tyagi". This Abhimana of the Sadhus is a greater evil than the Abhimana of the householders, "I am a landlord; I am a Brahmin, etc".

Not by carrying a Danda, not by shaving the head, not by dress, not by egoistic action is liberation to be attained. He who possesses wisdom is a real Sannyasin. Wisdom is the sign of a Sannyasin. The wooden staff does not make a Sannyasin.

He is the real Sannyasin of wisdom who is conscious of his absolute nature even in his dream, just as he is during the waking period. He is the greatest of Brahma-jnanins. He is the greatest of Sannyasins.

64. SATSANGA

If the dust is in the company of the wind, it soars high in the sky. If it is in the company of muddy water, it becomes a dirty mire. If the air is in the company of jasmine, it wafts a sweet aroma. If it is in the company of offal, it disseminates a foul odour. Put the parrot in the company of wicked men. It will start abusing. Put it in the company of Sadhus. It will repeat, "Ram, Renga, Renga". Even so, if one is in the company of a sage, he attains knowledge and soars high in the realm of eternal bliss. If he is in the company of a rogue or a drunkard, he drinks and commits vicious deeds.

Disastrous Effects of Evil Company

The effects of evil company are highly disastrous. The mind is filled with bad ideas by contact with evil companions. A neophyte who keeps company with wicked people or worldlings loses his devotion and develops evil qualities. The little faith in God and scriptures also vanishes. He too comes to the level of a worldly man.

Mind imitates. In the company of the wicked, one develops immorality, licentiousness, vicious habits, voluptuousness, sensuality, hypocrisy, arrogance, etc. Evil company destroys all virtues such as purity, truthfulness, compassion, etc.

The company of those who speak lies, who commit adultery, theft, cheating, double-dealing, who indulge in idle talks, backbiting, talebearing, who have no faith in God and in the scriptures, etc., should be strictly avoided. The company of women, and of those who associate with women, is dangerous.

It is not that the company of worldly men alone is evil or bad company. Hearing of vulgar songs, living in bad localities, gambling houses, liquor shops, the vicinity of brothel houses, cinemas, exciting Tamasic foods, the sight of mating of animals, the study of love novels, talks about women, the sight of nude pictures, dress that excites passion, evil thoughts, the company of those persons who speak ill of saints, who are atheists, who condemn scriptures, who use *cannabis indica*, opium, etc., are all evil company, indeed. In short, anything that causes evil thoughts in the mind constitutes evil company.

Aspirants generally complain: "We are doing Sadhana for the last fifteen years. We have not made any solid spiritual progress". Th obvious answer is that they have not totally shunned evil company

Just as a nursery is to be well-fenced in the beginning fo protection against cows, etc., so also, a neophyte should protec himself very carefully from foreign evil influences. Otherwise he i ruined totally.

Satsanga or Association with the Wise

Shun evil company. Everywhere, at all times, by all means, avoi the company of the wicked. Take recourse to the company of sage and saints who will heal your sores, infuse new life into you rejuvenate you, and show you the way to peace and happiness.

The glory and power of Satsanga or association with the wise i described in detail in the Bhagavata, the Ramayana, and other hol scriptures of the Hindus. Kabir, Tulasidas, Sankara, and Gur Nanak have all written volumes on the glory of Satsanga wit Mahatmas.

Vivekananda attended the Satsanga of Ramakrishn Paramahamsa. Jnana Dev had the Satsanga of Nivrittinath Gorakhnath attended the Satsanga of Matsyendranath. Th magnetic aura, the spiritual vibration, and the powerful currents o developed adepts produce a tremendous influence on the mind Satsanga elevates the mind to magnanimous heights. As flame i enkindled by flame, so also heart catches fire from heart.

In the East, students are always advised to seek the company o holy men and listen to their conversation, thus fanning into flame little spark of love and earnestness. Only a strong soul can kee itself glowing in isolation, and the beginner will do well to take th opportunity that comes in his way to strengthen his own aspiration by communion with others who share them.

The Power of Satsanga

Satsanga helps a long way in the attainment of Moksha. Satsang with a sage even for a minute is much better than rulership of kingdom. It gives all that is desirable and good. It overhaul worldly Samskaras and vicious thoughts, and gives a new spiritua turn of mind to the worldly man. It destroys Moha. It instil dispassion. It leads one to the right path and causes the sun o wisdom to shine upon one's mind. If you can have Satsanga, yo need not go to any Tirtha. It is the Tirtha of Tirthas. Wherever there is Satsanga, the sacred Triveni is already there.

There is nothing so inspiring, elevating, solacing, and delightful as Satsanga. Satsanga is the greatest of all purifiers and illuminators of man. Faith in God, in scriptures, attachment and devotion to God, slowly develop in those who are regular in Satsanga. Satsanga is unfailing in its results. The effect of saintly contact is unerring or infallible.

First comes keeping company with the righteous and good men, and serving them. By such company and service, there dawns the knowledge of the essential nature of one's own self, and of the Divine or Supreme Self. Then comes Vairagya or a total disgust for everything of this world and of the next, with a yearning for the Lord. This is Bhakti. When Bhakti becomes strong, the man becomes the beloved of the Lord, and because of such dearness to Him, he is chosen by Him. Then comes the direct vision of the Lord.

Those who hear the life-giving words of good men have their hearts that are tainted with evil, purified. They ultimately reach the lotus feet of the Lord. Rogues Jagai and Madai, dacoit Ratnakara, were all transformed into saints by Satsanga.

How Should Householders Behave towards Sannyasins?

As Satsanga is the only safe boat to take you to the other shore of Bliss or Moksha, you should all try as best as is in your power, never to miss it. Householders should approach Sannyasins with fruits in hand, wet with genuine Bhakti. As soon as they meet Sannyasins and get their Darshana, they should do Sashtanga Namaskara with Bhava and Prema. Householders should remember one thing above all other things, when they go to enjoy the company of Sannyasins. It is this: they should never, never try to enquire anything about the Sannyasin's life in his Purvashram, about his birthplace, his previous vocation in life, about his age, qualification, etc. Why? Because, all these matters are dead things for the Sannyasins as they live in the Atman.

Householders should not talk anything that is worldly in the presence of Sannyasins. If they have any question to ask, they should always keep ready their question, and should always take care to see that it pertains to spirituality and God. They should not try to invent some foolish questions, just for fun's sake, as soon as they enter the Ashrams of Sannyasins or their Kutirs. They should not also waste much time.

Householders should take with them clothes and Kowpeens, coloured in Gerua in their house itself, and present them to the Sannyasins for their daily use. They should ask with true Bhava and Prema if they could do any service to them by way of meeting their wants, if any, and should be ready to execute their wishes. Mere lip-sympathy or lip-service is deplorable. It is crookedness only. Sannyasins are visible gods on earth. There is no Yajna or sacrifice greater than service of Sannyasins. It is the most potent purifier.

Availability of Satsanga

There is a complaint by householders nowadays that there are no good Mahatmas. This is a lame excuse. The company of Sadhus is a question of supply and demand. If there is a sincere demand, the supply will come at once. This is the inexorable law of nature. If you are really thirsty, you will find your Master at your very threshold. You lead a happy-go-lucky life. Your mind is full of passion and unholy Vasanas. You do not care a bit for higher, divine life. You waste your time in idle gossiping and vain worldly talks. You have become a hopeless slave of passion, greed, and name and fame. And yet you complain: "I cannot get Satsanga". Blame yourself first. Admit your faults. Repent sincerely for your mistakes. Do Prayaschitta. Fast. Pray. Cry bitterly in solitude. Make yourself a deserving Adhikari first. The high souls are waiting to get hold of the right type of aspirants. Mahatmas are in plenty. Real seekers are few. If you bring a charge, "There are no good Mahatmas", the Mahatmas also will bring a serious charge, "here are no real seekers after Truth".

You may not be able to recognise a really worthy spiritual preceptor even after coming into contact with him, because great souls generally hide their greatness. An aspirant who has earned great merits by his strenuous endeavour in the present life or previous ones will be able to recognise the greatness of a Mahatma and obtain his grace. The lazy and indolent have no chance of obtaining the grace of a great soul.

Negative Satsanga

If you cannot get the Satsanga of living Mahatmas; you can take recourse to the study of books written by great souls. Books written by realised persons constitute negative Satsanga. When you study them, you are in holy communion with the authors. If you study Vivekachudamani, you are really having the Satsanga of Sankaracharya for the time being. If you read Yogavasishtha, you are really having Satsanga with sage Vasishtha.

In the evening, four or five people can assemble together in a temple or a quiet room and can study for one or two hours either the Gita or the Upanishads or the Ramayana or the Yogavasishtha or the Bhagavata. Slowly your mind will be purified. You will get real taste in the spiritual path. Women also should follow this method.

Resort to constant Satsanga. Then gradually, you will realise the incalculable benefits of Satsanga. Life is short.

Time is fleeting. Death is waiting to devour you all at any moment. That 'tomorrow' will never come. It is very difficult to get again this human birth. Utilise it profitably in the realisation of your Self through Satsanga. Realise the Sat-chit-ananda Atman through Satsanga. Then alone you can be free.

65. SCIENCE

Some scientists, and some so-called educated persons, believe that science can explain everything and can solve the riddle of the universe and all problems of life. They also think that the scientific method is the only method of finding out the truth, and that the scientific training and discipline alone can build very efficiently the character of man. They have ignored ethical discipline, morality, and religion altogether, and given religion an inferior position.

One scientist came to me and said, "The Upanishads and the Brahma Sutras have not been written scientifically. I am trying to give a scientific approach to this vital subject". I laughed, and said: "My dear scientist-friend! Upanishads are revelations. Brahma-vidya is transcendental. Atman is transcendental. You cannot take your test-tubes and spirit-lamps near Him. The scientists' conclusions cannot approach His region. Their observations are one-sided, as they concern the waking state alone. Their experiences are relative experiences". The scientist kept quiet, put down his head in shame, and walked away quietly.

Three blind people touched the different parts of an elephant. One touched the foot, and said: "The elephant is like a pillar". Another touched the ear, and said: "The elephant is like a fan". A third touched the belly, and said: "The elephant is like a pot". Even so, a scientist explores the physical plane, and speaks of atom, energy, and physical laws. He is also like a blind man. He has knowledge of one dimension alone. He has ignored the dreaming and deep sleep states. He has no all-comprehensive knowledge. A Vedantin alone has full knowledge of everything.

The Ease-loving Nature of Man

As life has been made physically comfortable and comparatively effortless by modern inventions, the ease-loving man is prone to disregard the place of religion in his life and exalt the values of a materialistic civilisation. But, events have always disclosed the unreliability of the purely objective views and methods of physical science, the experience of man that he is not really happier, and the world is not in fact better, even after his arduous attempts at extracting out of the external nature its latent resources in order to utilise the same for his own purposes. Where is satisfaction, where is happiness, and where is peace then?

Some of the wise scientists are fully conscious now of the limitations of science, and of its methods, in the investigation of phenomena in planes of subtler states of matter. The reality of the spiritual world is a closed book to them. They are equally conscious of the limitations of science in the regeneration of unregenerate human nature, and in the attainment of the Supreme Good or Eternal Bliss, the *summum bonum* of life.

What Has Science Done to Us?

Can scientific inventions make us really happy? That is the question of questions now. What has science done to us?

Science has now removed time and space. You can go to London even within thirty-six hours. What a great marvel! This earth has become very, very small now. But, has science really contributed to human happiness? The answer is an emphatic no, no. It has multiplied human wants and luxuries. A luxury of today becomes a necessity of tomorrow. It has made man a beggar.

Science has invented many marvellous things. Scientists are labouring day and night in their laboratories to invent many more things. But, science has made life very complex, and rendered very keen the struggle for existence. It has increased the restlessness of the mind. It has not contributed to the peace of man. Everybody admits this solid fact.

The scientists have made tremendous progress in the twentieth century. The atomic bombs can devastate a large country in the twinkling of an eye. Radios, telephones, telepathy, television, aeroplanes without pilots, mines, tanks, pocket radios, bombs in fountain-pens and cigarettes, underground palaces, shafts, V-bombs, fighters, bombers, anti-aircraft guns, gas bombs, torpedoes, submarines are all astounding marvels. But, the scientists have not improved the ethical condition of the people. They have not solved the problem of unemployment, poverty, war, starvation, disunity among communities, nations, and governments.

Science has analysed man. He is supposed to be a creature composed of various physical and chemical substances. Yet, no scientist has yet been able to assemble these constituent chemical elements of a man's body into one homogeneous creature which lives, talks, and acts like a man.

The scientist bombards the atoms, watches the movement of the electrons in his laboratory, spends his whole life in understanding the nature and secret of matter and energy, invents many things, studies the laws of nature; and yet, he is not able to comprehend the mystery of creation and of the Creator, and the meaning of life.

Science Is Defective

Scientists are very, very busy in studying the external world. They have entirely forgotten to study the internal world. Science gives you knowledge only of the phenomenal appearances, and not of the Reality behind them. Science has not been able to solve the ultimate questions: What is the ultimate stuff of the world? Who am I? What is the ultimate truth?

Science tells us that the ultimate goal of everything is unknown, and unknowable. But, Vedanta teaches that the ultimate goal is Brahman or the Infinite, and that It can be realised through hearing, reflection, and meditation.

The knowledge of the scientists is limited. It is only superficial. It is not real knowledge of the Truth. Scientists are immersed in transitory phenomena. They rely on external instruments, lenses, etc., for their knowledge. Their old theories are exploded by new theories. Their knowledge is not as infallible and true as the knowledge of the Self of the sages and Yogins.

Matter and Spirit

Science has got its limitations. Science does not have an instrument by which they could just collect the super-sensual or spiritual data, or those divine facts which exist in a subtle form but which we cannot see. True experiences include the experiences of the three states, viz., the waking, dreaming, and deep sleep states. The Vedantin studies the three states. He gains more real knowledge from the deep sleep state. He gets a clue for the existence of the fourth state or the state of Turiya from the deep sleep state.

The soul is beyond the realm of physical science. The soul is beyond the reach of material science. Man is a soul, wearing a physical body. The soul is extremely subtle. It is subtler than ether, mind, and energy. Consciousness and intelligence are of the soul, and not of the body. Consciousness is evidence of the existence of the soul. The soul is the immortal part in man.

Science is a systematic study of facts. It tries to reduce observations or observed facts into a system. In order that the fact may be valid for science, it must be perceptible to the senses. Sensing is false knowledge. Intuition is right knowledge. Intuitive knowledge alone is the highest knowledge. It is the imperishable, infinite knowledge of Truth.

A scientist is an extrovert. He bombards the atoms. He cannot find Pure Consciousness there. He will have to withdraw the senses and rest in his own Inner Self. He must dive deep into the ocean of Brahmic Consciousness.

Science and Religion

Science is not the enemy of religion, but a preparation for it.

Science is not an enemy of religion. Science is an enemy to superstitions alone. Both science and religion are engaged in the search for Truth. Their attitudes are essentially the same. But, the fields of application vary. Raja Yoga is an exact *science.* Its methods are very scientific. A scientist is an external Raja Yogin. Hindu Rishis, seers, and sages have recognised the harmonious relation between science and religion. The divorce of science from religion is the cause of confusion and conflict. Science is religion as applied to the investigation of Truth in the finite nature outside—the object. Religion is science as applied to the realisation of the Infinite, the Bhuma, the Truth that underlies all objects—the Subject.

Science interprets on the phenomenal plane the One as energy. Religion interprets the One as the Self, "the Atman". Science analyses, classifies, and explains phenomena. But. Brahma-vidya teaches you to transcend phenomena and attain immortality.

The scientific and the religious approaches to Truth are really complementary, and not contradictory. Religion and science are the twin-brothers. They should help mutually and harmoniously to search Truth and live the life of Truth here.

Science has to do with facts; religion with values. Where science ends, religion begins. A close study of the observations and revelations of science brings a man nearer to God. Who gave power to electrons? What is at the bottom of these electrons? What is that power that has combined four parts of nitrogen and one part of oxygen? Who has framed the laws of nature? Nature is blind. What is that intelligence which moves nature? Who is the primum mobile? A study of the physical forces and the physical laws, an understanding of the mental forces and the mental laws, are not sufficient to make us perfect. We should have a thorough knowledge and realisation of the substratum that lies hidden behind these names and forms and all physical and mental phenomena. Then only we will become perfect masters or full-blown adepts or Arhatas or Buddhas.

Mind and intellect are finite instruments. They cannot Realise the infinite Reality. But, they are a means. When the intellect has passed through the various stages of reasoning, and when it has been completely purified, then revelation dawns. True religion begins where the intellect ends.

Let it not be thought that religion is dogmatic, otherworldly, a pet tradition of blind believers or irrational emotionalists. Religion is the most rational science, the science of life itself, the science of man as he essentially is, not merely as he presumes himself to be. The basis for all the secular sciences is Brahma-vidya or the Adhyatmic science. Brahma-vidya is the foremost among all sciences, because by it one attains immortality. Secular experiences are partial, while spiritual experience is the experience-whole. If you know this supreme science of Brahma-vidya through direct intuition, you will have knowledge of all other worldly sciences; just as you will have knowledge of all articles made of clay, if you have the knowledge of clay itself. You cannot learn this Science of sciences in any university. You will have to learn this from a Brahma-srotri, Brahma-nishtha Guru, after controlling your senses and the mind.

Matter cannot be totally ignored; but, matter should be subordinated to spirit. Science should be subordinate to Brahma-vidya. Science cannot be the be-all and end-all. If you end your life in the laboratory alone, you cannot enjoy the eternal bliss of the Soul. You cannot attain immortality and perfection. You cannot attain the supreme wisdom which can free you from births and deaths. Science cannot give you salvation.

SCIENCE

Seek within. Stand not as a beggar before the door of science-power that kills, more than heals. Do not surrender yourself to the scientists. They are not able to explain anything. Science knows nothing of the origin of life, the origin of thought, and the origin and destiny of human nature and the universe. There are many questions to which religion alone can give answers—and not science.

66. SERVICE

God's plan for man's evolution is work.

Love of God and service of man is the secret of true life. The meaning of true life is service and sacrifice.

Life is meant for service, and not for self-seeking Sacrifice! Do your duties well, sincerely. Your privileges will follow unasked.

Hold your life for the service of others. The more the energy you spend in elevating and serving others, the more the divine energy which will flow to you.

Serve. You will rule. Serve humanity with divine Bhava. The cancer of individuality will be dissolved.

Selfless Service Purifies

What is the object in Seva or service? Why do you serve poor people and the suffering humanity at large? Why do you serve the society and the country? By doing service, you purify your heart. Egoism, hatred, jealousy, idea of superiority vanish. Humility, pure love, sympathy, tolerance, and mercy are developed. Sense of separateness is annihilated. Selfishness is eradicated. You get a broad outlook of life. You begin to feel oneness or unity of life. You develop a broad heart with broad, generous views. Eventually, you get Knowledge of the Self. You realise the 'One-in-all' and 'all-in-One'. You feel unbounded joy.

The first step in the spiritual path is selfless service of humanity. Selfless service is the watchword along the road to salvation. Selfless service of humanity prepares the aspirant for the attainment of cosmic consciousness, or the life of oneness or unity with God. Aspirants should direct their whole attention in the beginning towards removal of selfishness by protracted selfless service.

Through selfless service and charity, develop the heart and cleanse the lower mind. Purify your heart by selfless and humble service of the poor and the afflicted, and make it a fit abode for God to dwell. Selfless service alone can purify your heart and fill it with divine virtues. Only the pure in heart will have the vision of God.

Grow in love, purity, and self-sacrifice. Live for others. You will attain the state of blessedness. Selfless service and cosmic love are the Ganga and the Yamuna that irrigate the field of the human heart and enable the rich harvest of peace, joy, prosperity, immortality, and Atma-jnana to be reaped.

Opportunities for Selfless Service

The world is yourself. Therefore love all, serve all, be kind to all, embrace all. Behold the Lord in the poor, the down-trodden, the oppressed and lowly ones.

Become a servant of humanity. This is the secret of attaining God-realisation. Seek out the lowly and the miserable; cheer up and bring a ray of comfort to them by serving them unstintingly. Console the disconsolate. Comfort the distressed. You will be blessed.

Serve your parents, elders, teachers, and guests with divine Bhava. Wash the clothes of your parents, elders, the sick, and the Mahatmas.

Feed the hungry, nurse the sick, comfort the afflicted, and lighten the sorrow of the sorrowful. God will bless you. Clothe the naked. Educate the illiterate. Feed the poor. Raise the down-trodden. The world is burning with misery and suffering. Wake up, O man! Serve! Serve with love. Serve untiringly. Attain the peace of the Eternal.

Have a knowledge of homoeopathy or Dr. Schussler's Twelve Tissue Remedies. Now serve the sick and the needy. And with first-aid knowledge, always give first help in all cases of emergency. Get medicine from the hospital or the dispensary for the helpless and deserving neighbours. Visit a hospital daily, if you can, or weekly, and give your best attention to the non-paying wards. Distribute oranges, if you can. Sit by the side of the patient and speak a few encouraging words. Smile awhile. Repeat, if you can, the Sahasranama of the Lord or the like. Tell him that you will meet him 'tomorrow'; and meet him.

Collect some old clothes and distribute them to the needy.

Distribute a few pies to the lame, the blind, and to the hungry mouths as you walk along the street.

Serve any social institution for one hour daily without any remuneration.

Meet your friends and the members of your society in a common place once a week or a fortnight for Satsanga and Kirtana. Develop an understanding heart. Help your younger brothers in the spiritual path. Lift them up. Throw light on their path. Do not expect perfection from them. Be kind to them. They are doing their best, as you are yourself doing yours. You will grow by helping them.

Finally, think for yourself, how best you can utilise your energy, your intellect, your education, your wealth, your strength, or anything you possess, for the betterment of others who are low-placed in life, and for society in general.

No Service Is Inferior

There is no superior or inferior service in Karma Yoga. There is no superiority or inferiority among Karma Yogins. In a machine, the smallest bolt or spring is as essential to its smooth running as the mighty wheel. Similarly, in an organised effort, the man who does even the least work, or attends to an insignificant detail, contributes as much to the success of the endeavour as the chief organiser himself; for, if there is some defect in even a small detail, perfect success cannot be achieved.

A raw, untrained aspirant feels: "My preceptor is treating me like a servant or a peon. He is using me for petty jobs". He who has understood the right significance of Karma Yoga will take every work as Yogic activity or worship of the Lord. There is no menial work in his vision. Every work is Puja of Narayana. In the light of Karma Yoga, all actions are sacred. That aspirant who always takes immense delight in doing works which are considered by the worldly man as menial services, and who always does willingly such acts, will become a dynamic Yogin. He will be absolutely free from conceit and egoism. He will have no downfall. The canker of pride cannot touch him.

Study the autobiography of Mahatma Gandhiji. He never made any difference between menial service and dignified work. Scavengering and cleaning of the latrine was the highest Yoga for him. This was the highest Puja for him. He himself had done cleansing of latrines. He had annihilated this illusory little 'I' through service of various sorts.

Many highly educated persons joined his Ashram for learning Yoga under him. They thought that Gandhiji would teach them Yoga in some mysterious manner in a private room, and would give lessons in Pranayama, meditation, abstraction, awakening of

Kundalini, etc. They were disappointed when they were asked to clean the latrine at first. They left the Ashram immediately.

Gandhiji himself did the repairing of his shoes. He himself used to grind flour and would take upon his shoulders the grinding work of others also when they were unable to do their allotted portion of work for the day in the Ashram. When an educated person, a new Ashramite, felt shy to do grinding work, Gandhiji himself would do his work in front of him, and then the man would do the work himself from the next day willingly.

How to Serve

Do not lose a single opportunity in helping and serving others. Serve cheerfully and willingly. Never show sunday-face or castor-oil face.

Utilise every minute in serving others in the best possible manner. Do not expect anything when you serve a man or when you give a gift. Thank him for giving you a good opportunity to serve him.

Service of man is service of God. Service of humanity must not be mere mechanical acts. It must be done with Atma Bhava. Service is Yoga for the purification of heart, and the consequent descent of light. All the workers must drill and hammer the mind with this Bhava.

Do service of others with the feeling that God dwells in all and receives your service as worship. The world is nothing but a manifestation of God. Service of humanity is service of God only. Service is worship of God. Never forget this. God can be best served or worshipped through the service of His creatures.

When you serve, remember that you work for God. Do every act as Isvararpana, an offering unto God. You will soon grow spiritually. You will soon be transmuted into Divinity. Always scrutinise your motives. Slay selfish motives.

Remember God is the inner prompter who impels you to action. You are only His instrument. On account of egoism, one thinks that one does everything, and so one is bound. Work in the awareness of being pulled by the Cosmic Will. You will have more strength, less vanity. Work will not bind you.

It is through the light provided by the self-effulgent Lord within you that you are able to work. Feel this every moment of your life. Act as a trustee, not as an owner or proprietor. You will not be bound, as there will be no 'mine-ness'.

Ora et labora. Pray and work. This is the formula of a Karma Yogin for God-realisation.

Help and serve, but do not fight. Create harmony, peace, but not dissension, discord, and split. Pocket insults when offered. Blame and praise are sheer vibrations in the air. Soar above them.

Do every work perfectly well with concentration and devotion. Be absorbed in work. Give your full heart, mind, and soul. Do not care for results. Do not think of success or failure. Do not think of the past. Have complete confidence. Practise self-reliance. Be cheerful always. Keep a cool, balanced mind. Work for work's sake. Be bold and courageous. You are bound to succeed in any undertaking. This is the secret of success.

Work in a systematic and methodical manner. Be fiery in service. Also be intent on service. Take a little rest, and sleep only for some time. No pains, no gains.

Work without Attachment

It is extremely difficult to perform real selfless service. Many people ascend the public platform under the garb of selfless workers, but they only serve themselves. Even some Sannyasins do the same. Is this not very sad?

Actions should be performed without attachment, without the feeling of doing them for one's own personal purity. Perform works merely for God's sake, abandoning even such attachment as 'May God be pleased'. You must be prepared to abandon the work at any time, however much interesting the work may be, however much you like the work. Whenever the inner voice of the soul commands you to give up the work, you must at once relinquish it. Attachment to any work will bind you. Understand well these subtle secrets of Karma Yoga and march boldly in the path of Karma Yoga.

May your ideals be to serve the poor, the sick and the saints, and the country; to raise the fallen; to lead the blind; to share what you have with others; to bring solace to the afflicted; to cheer up the suffering! May your watchword be to have perfect faith in God; to love your neighbour as your own Self; to love God with all your heart, mind, and soul; to protect cows, animals, children, and women! May your goal be God-realisation! May you all shine as glorious Jivanmuktas and dynamic Yogins in this very birth!

67. SEX

There is the great illusion in front of man. It troubles him in the form of woman. There is the great illusion in front of woman. It troubles her in the form of man.

Go wherever you like—Amsterdam, London, or New York. Analyse this world of phenomenal experience. You will find only two things—sex and ego.

This world is nothing but sex and ego. Ego is the chief thing. It is the basis. The sex is hanging on the ego. Sex and ego are the products of Avidya or nescience. Man—master of his destiny—has lost his divine glory and has become a slave, a tool in the hands of sex and ego, on account of ignorance.

The World Is All Sexy

Passion is reigning supreme in all parts of the world. The minds of people are filled with sexual thoughts. The world is all sexy. The whole world is under a tremendous sexual intoxication. All are deluded and move in the world with perverted intellects. No thought of God. No talk of God. It is all fashion, restaurants, hotels, dinners, dances, races, and cinemas. Their life ends in eating, drinking, and procreating. That is all.

Young men of the present day indiscriminately imitate the West for their own ruin. Men are swayed by lust. They lose their sense of righteousness, and of time and place. They never discriminate between right and wrong. They lose all sense of shame.

Read the history of the crimes—robbery, rape, kidnapping, assaults, murders—that come up for trial before the Sessions Courts. Lust is at the root of all this. It may be lust for money or lust for carnal pleasure. Lust ruins life, lustre, strength, vitality, memory, wealth, fame, holiness, Peace, wisdom, and devotion.

The Pathetic Plight of Young Boys and Girls

What do we find in these days? Men and women, boys and girls drowned in the ocean of impure thoughts, lustful desires, and little sensual pleasures. It is highly deplorable, indeed. It is really shocking to hear the stories of some boys. Many college students have personally come to me and narrated their pitiable lives of gloom and depression, brought about by heavy loss of semen by unnatural means. Their power of discrimination has been lost owing to sexual excitement and lustful intoxication.

Boys and girls suffer in silence on account of ignorance, on account of misuse of bodily parts which constitute a definite drain upon the vitality; and this retards normal mental and physical progress. When the human system is deprived of its natural secretions, there must be a corresponding decline in nervous energy. This is the reason why functional disorders develop. The number of wrecks is increasing.

Young boys suffer from anaemia, bad memory, and debility. They have to discontinue their studies. Diseases are increasing. Thousands of injections have come into the pharmacy, hospitals, and dispensaries. Thousands of doctors have opened their clinics and shops. Yet, misery is increasing day by day. People do not get success in their enterprises and business. What is the reason for this? The reason is not far to seek. It is because of wastage of the vital force or semen through evil habits and immoderate sexual intercourse. It is because of an unclean mind and an unclean body.

Responsibility of Teachers and Parents

Teachers and parents should give proper instructions to boys and girls as to how they should lead a clean life of Brahmacharya. They should get rid of a false sense of modesty and shame. They are a good deal responsible for the ignorance of the boys and girls. There has been more suffering caused by ignorance of these matters than anything else. You are paying the price of ignorance, the false modesty that matters of sex and sexual physiology should not be discussed. The teachers and parents should diligently watch the conduct of children. They should clearly impress on their minds the vital importance of a clean life, and the dangers of an unclean life.

Sex in Men and Animals

Man, with his boasted intellect, has to learn lessons from birds and animals. At the heat of sexual excitement, man repeats the same ignoble act again and again. He has not a bit of self-control. He is an absolute slave to passion. He is a puppet in the hands of passion. Like rabbits, he procreates and brings forth numberless children to swell up the number of beggars in the world. Lions, elephants, and other powerful animals have better self-control than men. Lions cohabit only once in a year. After conception, the female animals will never allow the male animals to approach them till the young ones are weaned and they themselves become healthy and strong. Man only violates the laws of nature, and consequently suffers from innumerable diseases. He has degenerated himself to a far lower level than animals in this respect. Food, sleep, fear, and copulation are common to both animals and men. That which differentiates man from animals is Vichara Sakti. If he does not possess the higher faculties, he is also an animal only.

Power of the Sex Urge

The sex instinct is the greatest urge in human life. Sex energy or lust is the most deep-rooted instinct in man. Sex energy has entirely filled the mind, intellect, Prana, senses, and the whole body. It is the oldest of factors that have gone into the constitution of the human being.

A man has a thousand and one desires. But, the central, strong desire is sexual desire. The fundamental desire is the urge for a mate. All hang on this central basic desire. Desire for money, desire for son, desire for property, desire for houses, desire for cattle, etc., come later on.

Because the whole creation of this universe is to be kept up, God has made the sexual desire very, very powerful. Otherwise, many Jivanmuktas would have cropped up quite easily, just as graduates from universities. It is easy to get university qualifications. It demands a little money, memory, intelligence, and a little strain. But, it is an uphill climb to obliterate the sexual impulse. He who has completely eradicated lust and is established in mental Brahmacharya is Brahman or God Himself.

The sex instinct is most powerful. The sex urge is formidable. It will attack you with redoubled force. It may conceal itself in underground compartments in the mind and assail you when you are not vigilant. Visvamitra fell a victim to Menaka. Another great Rishi became a prey to Rambha. Jaimini got excited by a false woman Masa. A powerful Rishi was excited by the sight of the mating of a fish. A householder aspirant carried away even his Guru's wife. Many aspirants are not aware of this secret urge, a treacherous enemy. They think they are quite safe and pure. When they are put to test, they become hopeless victims. Always remain alone, meditate, and slay this urge.

In a Jnani, the sexual craving is entirely eradicated. In a Sadhaka, it remains well-controlled. In a householder, when not controlled, it does havoc. It exists in him in its fully expanded state. He cannot resist it. He yields to it helplessly on account of his weak will and lack of firm resolution.

Enjoyment and Repression

Enjoyment cannot bring in satisfaction. It is a mistake to think so. Enjoyment fans the desire. It is like pouring ghee in fire. Enjoyment strengthens, increases, and aggravates a desire. See the case of Raja Yayati of yore. He borrowed the youthful state from his son to have sexual enjoyment for thousands of years. At last, he cries out in his old age with bitterness, "Alas! What a fool I am! Still my sexual desires are waxing. There is no end of desires, I have wasted my life. Oh God! Have mercy on me. Lift me up from this mire of Samsara".

Repression or suppression of the sexual desire will not help very much. It will again manifest with redoubled force when the suitable opportunity arises, when your will becomes weak, when Vairagya or dispassion wanes, when there is a slackening in meditation or Yogic Sadhana, when you become weak owing to an attack of any disease.

Suppression of the sex urge is not eradication. You can never be free of that which is suppressed. The suppressed sex desire will attack you again and again and will produce wet dreams, irritability, and restlessness of the mind.

The sexual energy must be transmuted into spiritual energy or Ojas-sakti by the practice of Japa, prayer, meditation, study of religious books, Pranayama, Asanas, etc. Then only the sexual desire will be annihilated.

The Process of Sex-sublimation

If the sexual energy is transmuted into spiritual energy by pure thought, it is called sex-sublimation in Western psychology. Just as a chemical substance is sublimated or purified by raising it by heat into vapour which again becomes solid, so also, the sexual energy is purified and changed into divine energy by spiritual Sadhana, by entertaining sublime, soul-elevating thoughts of Self or Atman.

Sublimation is not a matter of suppression or repression, but is a positive, dynamic, convertive process. The material energy is changed into spiritual energy, just as heat is changed into light and electricity. If the reproductive energy is controlled, transmuted, and sublimated, you will get Ojas or tremendous brain-power. Ojas is spiritual energy that is stored up in the brain. By sublime thoughts, meditation, Japa, worship and Pranayama, the sexual energy can be transmuted into Ojas-sakti. Just as the oil comes up in a wick and burns with glowing light, so also, the Virya or semen flows up by the practice of Yoga Sadhana and is converted into Tejas or Ojas. This Ojas helps you much to meditate deeply for a long time. It is stored up in the brain. It helps contemplation. Even in advanced old age, it is serviceable. You will have good memory. You can write books and turn out tremendous brain work.

An Oordhvareto-Yogin is one in whom the seminal energy flows upwards to the brain and is stored up as Ojas-sakti, which is used for contemplative purposes in the practice of Dhyana. He not only converts the semen into Ojas, but checks through his Yogic power, through purity in thought, word, and deed, the very formation of gross semen by the secretory cells of the testes or seeds. This is a great secret.

Allopaths believe that even in an Oordhvareto-Yogin the formation of semen goes on incessantly and that the fluid is reabsorbed in the blood. That is a mistake. They do not understand the inner Yogic secrets and mysteries. They are in the dark. Their vision is concerned with the gross things of the universe. The Yogin penetrates into the subtle, hidden nature of things through Yogic vision and inner vision of wisdom. The Yogin gets control over the astral nature of semen, and thereby prevents the formation of the very fluid itself.

The body of a man who is truly an Oordhvaretas has the scent of a lotus. A man who is not a Brahmacharin, in whom gross semen is formed, may, on the other hand, smell like a buck goat.

The process of sex-sublimation is very difficult, and yet, is most necessary for the aspirant in the spiritual path. It is the most important qualification for the Sadhaka either in the path of Karma

Yoga, Upasana, Raja Yoga, or Vedanta. You must achieve this at any cost. That man in whom the sex-idea is deep-rooted, can never dream of understanding Vedanta and realising Brahman even within one hundred crores of births. Truth cannot dwell where passion lives.

The Epicureans

Some ignorant people say: "It is not right to check passion. We must not go against nature. Why has God created young, beautiful women? There must be some sense in His creation. We should enjoy them and procreate as many as possible. We should keep up the progeny of the line. If we check passion, we will get disease. We must get plenty of children". This is their crude philosophy. They are the direct descendants of Charvaka and Virochana. They are life-members of the Epicurean school of thought. They have a very large following. They are friends of Satan. Admirable is their philosophy! When they lose their property, wife, and children, when they suffer from an incurable disease, they will say, "O God, relieve me from this horrible disease. Forgive me my sins. I am a great sinner".

Passion should be checked at all costs. Not a single disease comes by checking passion. Sexual abstinence has never yet hurt any man. It has, on the other hand, increased his vigour, energy, and lengthened his life. By checking passion, you will get immense power, joy, and peace.

There are also effective methods to control passion. One should reach Atman which is beyond nature, by going against nature. Just as a fish swims upstream, going against the current in a river, so also, you will have to move against the worldly currents of evil forces. Then alone you can have Self-realisation. Passion is an evil force, and it should be checked if you want to enjoy undecaying Atmic bliss.

Sexual Pleasure Is No Pleasure

Sex-pleasure is the most devitalising and demoralising of pleasures. Sexual pleasure is no pleasure at all. It is a mental delusion. It is false, utterly worthless, and extremely harmful. It is full of pain. It is attended with dangers, fear, exertion, and disgust. Passion is not power, but weakness and slavery. These beautiful women and wealth are the instruments of Maya to delude you and entrap you into the nets.

You must understand the psychological working of the sex-impulse. When there are itches on the body, mere scratching of it is a pleasure. The sex-impulse is only a nervous itching. The satisfaction of this impulse begets a delusive pleasure, but it has a disastrous effect on the spiritual well-being of the person.

Sex Is Illusory

The sex-affair is a mere idea. It is mere imagination. It is a mental Kalpana. The body is composed of five elements. There is no sex in the elements. If you ponder over this point well, you can slowly eliminate sex-ideas.

For a scientist, a man or a woman is a mass of electrons only. For a tiger, he or she is an object of prey. For a man of discrimination, he or she is a combination of flesh, bone, urine, faecal matter, pus, perspiration, blood, phlegm etc. It is only for a passionate man or woman, she or he is an object of enjoyment.

There is neither sex nor sexual Vasana in the Atman. The Atman is Nitya-suddha, eternally pure. Thou art that Nitya-suddha Atman. See Atman in all men and women. By constant thinking on that sexless Atman, you will be established in Brahmacharya. This is the most powerful and effective method

Sex and Spiritual Life

Sexual indulgence is a great obstacle in the spiritual path. The lure of the flesh is your invulnerable foe. It bars the spiritual practices definitely. The sexual urge must be controlled by entertaining sublime, divine thoughts, and regular meditation. There must be complete sublimation of the sexual energy. Then only is the aspirant safe.

The total annihilation of the sexual desire is the ultimate spiritual ideal. Therefore, entertain always sublime divine thoughts. The old, evil sexual thoughts will gradually vanish, just as the old nail in a plank is driven away by inserting over it a new nail. The Yogic student should be pure in thought, word and deed. Perfect sublimation can hardly be achieved within a day or two. It demands continuous struggle with patience and perseverance for some time. Even the householders should keep the above ideal before them and should try to realise it gradually. If the state of perfect sublimation is attained, there will be purity in thought, word and deed. No sexual thought will enter at any time.

Sex urge is a creative force. Direct the sex-energy to the higher spiritual channel. It will be sublimated. It will be transformed into divine energy. Unless you are inspired by spiritual ideals, it is difficult to keep the sexual instinct in check.

68. SHAT-SAMPAT

A student who treads the path of Truth must equip himself with the four means of salvation or Sadhana-Chatushtaya, viz., Viveka, Vairagya, Shat-Sampat and Mumukshutva. Then only he can march quite fearlessly on the path. Not an iota of spiritual progress is ever possible unless one is really endowed with this fourfold qualification. These four means are as old as the Vedas or this world itself. Every religion prescribes these four essential requisites for the aspirant. Names only differ. This is really immaterial. Only ignorant people raise lingual warfare and unnecessary questions. The Brahma-Vidya or the Science of the Self is not a subject that can be understood and realised by mere intellectual study, reasoning or ratiocination or even by discussions or arguments. It is the most difficult of all sciences. Mere scholarly erudition and vast study with a high degree of intelligence alone cannot help one in the practical realisation of the Truth inculcated by this science. It demands perfect discipline, a discipline that is not to be found in our modern universities and colleges, and solid Sadhana for the achievement of the goal that is indicated by this Para-Vidya or Highest Science.

Viveka is discrimination between the real and the unreal (Sat and Asat), permanent and impermanent (Nitya and Anitya), Self and the not-Self (Atman and Anatman). Viveka should not be an ephemeral or occasional mood in an aspirant. A Viveki (man of discrimination) is always on the alert and never gets entangled in anything. Viveka gives inner strength and mental peace. From Viveka is born Vairagya.

Vairagya is dispassion but does not mean abandoning social duties and responsibilities of life. A Vairagi (dispassionate man) has no Raga-Dvesha (attraction and repulsion). A worldly man is a slave of these two mighty currents. A dispassionate man has a different training. He has a different experience altogether. He is a pastmaster in the art or science of separating himself from the impermanent, perishable objects. A dispassionate person is the most powerful, the happiest, and the richest person in the world.

The third requisite is Shat-Sampat or sixfold virtue which consists of Sama, Dama, Uparati, Titiksha, Sraddha, and Samadhana. The six equipments are taken as one because they are all calculated to bring about mental control and discipline. Concentration and meditation can never be possible without mental control and mental discipline.

Sama

Sama is serenity or tranquillity of mind that is brought about by eradication of Vasanas (mental impressions). The mind is kept in the chambers of the heart. It is not allowed to join with the Indriyas (senses) and to move outside into sensual objects or grooves. The mind is fixed in the source. Serenity of mind is the most important qualification for an aspirant. This is difficult of attainment. But the aspirant must have this qualification at any cost. It demands incessant and protracted practice. The mind is the commander of the ten Indriyas,—five organs of perception, and five organs of action. If the commander is subjugated first of all, the soldiers, viz., the Indriyas are already conquered. Control of the Indriyas cannot become perfect unless their head, viz., the mind is controlled first. If one is established in Sama, Dama or control of the Indriyas comes by itself. No Indriya can work independently without the help or co-operation of the mind.

Dama

Dama is control of the Indriyas. This is rational control. This is not blunting or deadening of the senses by foolish austerities. This body is the moving temple of God. It should be kept healthy and strong. It is a vessel to take you to the other shore of fearlessness and immortality. It is a horse to take you to the goal. Many foolish aspirants amputate the organ of reproduction. They think that lust can be eradicated completely by such a procedure. Some swallow tons of nux vomica to kill this organ. What a great foolish act! Lust is in the mind. If the mind is subdued, what can this external fleshy organ do? They fail in their attempts to be centred in Brahmacharya. The state of their minds is the same, though they become impotent by taking nux vomica. Remember it is only the abuse or misuse of the organs that brings misery and untoward results. What is wanted is judicious control of Indriyas. They should not be allowed to run riot into sensual grooves. They should not be allowed to throw us ruthlessly into the deep pit of worldliness just as the turbulent horse carries away the rider wherever it likes. The Indriyas should be consecrated at the Lotus-Feet of the Lord for His services. If the Indriyas are disciplined properly, if they are kept under control, they become your useful servants. People ask: "Where is the necessity for the practice of Dama, when one practises Sama?". Dama or control of the Indriyas, I say, is also necessary. Then only one will get supreme control of mind and the Indriyas. Though the Indriyas cannot independently do any havoc when the mind is under control, yet their control ensures perfect safety and supreme peace of mind.

Uparati

Uparati comes next. It is satiety. It is turning the mind resolutely away from desire for sensual enjoyment. This state of mind naturally comes when one has practised Viveka, Vairagya, Sama, and Dama. Sri Sankara defines Uparati in his Vivekachudamani as follows: "The best Uparati or self-withdrawal consists in the mind-function ceasing to act by means of external objects". According to the Atma-Anatma-Viveka, Uparati is the abstaining on principle from engaging in any of the acts and ceremonies enjoined by the Sastras. Otherwise it is the state of the mind which is always engaged in Sravana, Manana, and Nididhyasana, without ever diverging from them. Some take Uparati as taking up Sannyasa by renouncing all works.

Titiksha

Titiksha is power of endurance. The aspirant should patiently bear the pairs of opposites such as heat and cold, pleasure and pain and the rest. Sri Sankara defines it in Vivekachudamani as follows: "The bearing of all afflictions without caring to redress them, being free at the same time from anxiety or lament on their score is called Titiksha or forbearance. According to Atma-Anatma-Viveka Titiksha is the showing of forbearance by a person who is capable of punishing another for some wrong doing.

Some perform Panchagni Tapas (five-fire austerity). They sit amidst four fires on all the four sides with the blazing sun overhead as the fifth. But foolish austerities of a rigorous kind are condemned by Lord Krishna in the Bhagavadgita: "Those men who practise terrific austerities not enjoined by the scriptures, given to hypocrisy and egoism, impelled by the force of lust and attachment, senseless, torturing all the elements in the body and Me also, who dwells in the body,—know thou these to be of demoniacal resolves" (Ch.

XXII-5-6). Some make Titiksha as the end. Titiksha is only a means. Wherever there is movement, wherever there is manifestation of life, the two opposed forces, the pairs of opposites, do exist. Some ignorant men desire to get rid of the unpleasant experiences and to keep only the pleasant ones. This is the height of folly. Can there be light alone without darkness, roses alone without thorns, gain alone without loss, success alone without failure, victory alone without defeat, pleasure alone without pain? A wise man who rightly understands them and moves in close co-operation with them can be happy, not others. A wise man never grumbles. He tries to fix himself up in that unchanging, permanent, witnessing Consciousness which is hidden in his heart, which is beyond all the pairs of opposites and then watches the movements and the phenomena of this universe with an unruffled mind. He sees intelligence in every inch of creation. He has a very comprehensive understanding of the eternal laws of nature and the pairs of opposites. This is true Titiksha based on knowledge. He is superior to physical Titikshus (who practise only physical endurance), who have trained themselves by physical torture, because the latter ones will show signs of failure when confronted by serious disasters. A Titikshu who has developed his Titiksha through knowledge is the king of all Titikshus.

Sraddha

Sraddha is intense faith in the words of the Guru and in the sayings of the Vedantic scriptures and, above all, in one's own self. This is not blind faith. It is based on accurate reasoning, evidence, and experience. Then only it can be lasting faith. Then only it can be perfect, unshakable faith. Superstitious beliefs, beliefs in mere religious traditions or social customs cannot help a man in his spiritual advancement. The mind will be ever restless. Various doubts will be cropping up every now and then. Sectarians force their beliefs on others, try to convert them and take them in their fold to strengthen their numbers. The new convert does not find the real solace in the newly-embraced cult. He then embraces yet another cult or Sampradaya. Sraddha is a most important qualification. No spiritual progress is possible without Sraddha. From Sraddha comes Nishtha or one-pointed devotion and from

Nishtha comes Self-realisation. If the faith is flickering, it will die soon and the aspirant will be drifted aimlessly hither and thither.

Samadhana

Samadhana is mental balance by attention. This is the fruit of the practices of Sama, Dama, Uparati, Titiksha, and Sraddha There is perfect concentration now. It is fixing the mind on the Atman without allowing it to turn towards objects and have its own way. It is self-settledness. Sri Sankaracharya defines it in his Atma-Anatma-Viveka: "Whenever a mind engaged in Sravana, Manana, and Nididhyasana wanders to any worldly object or desire, and finding it worthless, returns to the performance of the three exercises—such returning is called Samadhana". The mind is free from anxiety amid pains. There is indifference amid pleasures. There is stability of mind or mental poise. The aspirant or practitioner is on every side without attachment. He neither likes nor dislikes. He has great deal of strength of mind and internal peace. He has unruffled supreme peace of mind.

Some aspirants have peace of mind when they live in seclusion and when there are no distracting elements or factors. They complain of great tossing of mind or Vikshepa when they come to a city, and mix with people. They are completely upset. They cannot do any meditation in a crowded place. This is a weakness. This is not achievement in Samadhana. There is no balance of mind or equanimity in these persons. Only when a student can keep his balance of mind even in a battlefield when there is a shower of bullets all round, as he does in a solitary cave in the Himalayas, can he be really said to be fully established in Samadhana. Lord Krishna says in the Gita: "Perform all actions, O Dhananjaya, dwelling in union with the Divine, renouncing attachments, and balanced evenly in success and failure". This is Samadhana. Again you will find in the Gita: "The disciplined self, moving among sense-objects with senses free from attraction and repulsion mastered by the Self, goeth to Peace". This is also Samadhana.

Lastly, we come to the fourth of the main qualifications, viz., Mumukshutva. It is intense desire for liberation or deliverance from the wheel of birth and death with its concomitant evils of old age, disease, delusion, and sorrow. If one is equipped with the previous three qualifications, viz., Viveka, Vairagya, and Shat-Sampat,

Mumukshutva will come by itself. The aspirant should practise all the four means to the maximum degree. There is a definite significance in the sequence of the four Sadhanas. That aspirant who is in possession of the four means is a blessed divinity on the surface of this earth.

69. SHINTOISM

Shinto is an all-pervading indefinable way which is quite universal. Shinto or Kaminomichi or the way of the Kami or the gods is the name of the religion observed by the Japanese from time immemorial. Kami means God or deity or sometimes soul. Shinto implies spontaneous following of the "Way of the gods". Shinto is not really any 'ism'. It is only a teaching. It is not a set of verbal theories or concepts. It is the all-pervading way.

Shinto is divided into two classes, viz., the Sectarian Shinto, which is subdivided into 13 sects, and the Shinto of the national faith of the Japanese, or the state Shinto Religion. The patriotic spirit of the Japanese is unique. The loyalty of the Japanese to the Mikado or the Sovereign is unprecedented.

There is neither much grand philosophy nor complicated ritual in Shintoism. Shinto is not a religion adopted by the State. It is a religion of the heart. Shinto is a natural and real spiritual force which pervades the life of the Japanese. Shinto is a creative or formative principle of life. The Shinto principle is the background of Japanese culture, code of ethics, fine arts, family, and national structure.

Shinto is the chief agent which has rejuvenated, vitalised, and reinforced the social and religious life of Japan.

The system of Shinto resembles more the system of Hinduism than that of Confucianism or Buddhism. It is a kind of personal religion. It ascribes divine attributes to every being. It is a kind of pantheism.

For the Japanese, nation means a harmonious complex of individuals, Kuni-hito. Salvation, for the Japanese, means the salvation of the whole nation instead of salvation of a few individuals.

Shinto Theology

According to Shinto theology Ame-no-mi-nakanushi is the Absolute Universal Self. This corresponds to Hiranyagarbha or the Sutratman of the Hindus. The visible universe (Ken Kai) and the invisible world (Yu Kai) have come into being from Ame-no-mi-nakanushi through the activities of the three deities of Musubi, Principle of Creation, Completion and the Controlling

Bond between the spiritual and the material, the invisible and the visible, the real and the ideal. These contradictory attributes are functional only. The Absolute Universal Self is not affected by these contradictory attributes. It is beyond these attributes. It corresponds to the Nirguna Brahman of Hinduism. The idea of time has come into existence from the attributes.

Absolute loyalty to the Sovereign Emperor, who is regarded as a direct descendant and representative of the higher God, respect for ancestors, profound feeling towards the parents, and love for children form the fundamental structure of the Great Universal Way.

The mirror, the sword, and the jewel have a figurative meaning in the course of the development of Shinto. They symbolise wisdom, courage, and benevolence, or intelligence, will, and love in Shinto theology. These three are the holy ensigns of royalty of the Sovereign Emperor. They are supposed to symbolise the dynamic working of the Great Way and so they are found in the forefront of every Shinto Shrine, popularly known as Mistu-tomo-e or the three big commas.

There are many gods in Shinto, but the ancestral Sun-God, Anaterasu-omi Kami, stands supreme above them. Susano-o-no-Mikoto is the impetuous divine brother of the Sun-God. He is the God of rain-storm. Tsukiyomi-no-Mikoto is the Moon-God. These three constitute a divine triad. They preside respectively over the plane of Higher Heaven, the vast ocean, and the realm of Night.

Shinto Ethics

Purity is one of the fundamental virtues of Shinto ethics. There are two significations of purity. One is outer purity or bodily purity, and the other inner purity or purity of heart. If a man is endowed with true inner purity of the heart, he will surely attain God-realisation or communion with the Divine. Sincerity is also the guiding ethical principle of Shinto.

Ten Precepts of Shinto

(i) Do not transgress the will of the gods.

(ii) Do not forget your obligations to ancestors.

(iii) Do not offend by violating the decrees of the State.

(iv) Do not forget the profound goodness of the gods through which calamities and misfortunes are averted and sickness is healed.

(v) Do not forget that the world is one great family.

(vi) Do not forget the limitations of your own person.

(vii) Do not become angry even though others become angry.

(viii) Do not be sluggish in your work.

(ix) Do not bring blame to the teaching.

(x) Do not be carried away by foreign teachings.

The most important sayings of Shinto are: "A single sincere prayer moves heaven. You will surely realise the divine presence through sincere prayer.

"Where you have sincerity there also is virtue. Sincerity is a witness to truth. Sincerity is the mother of knowledge. Sincerity is a single virtue that binds Divinity and man in one.

"The first and surest means to enter into communion with the Divine is sincerity: If you pray to a deity with sincerity, you will surely feel the divine presence".

Common Shinto Prayer

Our eyes may see some uncleanliness, but let not our mind see things that are not clean. Our ears may hear some uncleanliness, but let not our mind hear things that are not clean.

Conclusion

Shinto is the 'Way to God'. 'Tao' of Lao-Tzu is also the 'Way to God'. Lord Jesus says: "I am the Truth, the Way, and the Life". Lord Krishna says: "Howsoever men approach Me, even so, do I welcome them, for the path men take from every side is Mine, O Partha!".

The Way to God is as much important as the end or destination or God Himself. The Way to God is righteousness or Dharma. He who shows the Way is Guru or the spiritual preceptor. Guru and God are one. If you stick to the Way you will soon reach God. If you stick to Guru, you will surely attain God-realisation. The Way, Truth, and Life-everlasting are one.

Glory to the Way, Shinto or Tao! Glory to Guru! Glory, glory to God, the destination or Goal of all religions! May Shinto or Tao guide you, rejuvenate, vitalise, and reinforce you all! Be true to Shinto or Tao.

70. SILENCE

Once the disciple Bhaskali approached his Guru, Bhava, and asked him where that Eternal, the Supreme Infinite, the Brahman of the Upanishads, was. The master spoke not. The disciple asked him again and again, but the master did not open his mouth. He kept perfect silence. At last the teacher said: "I have been telling you again and again, but you do not understand me. What am I to do? That Brahman, the Infinite, the Eternal, cannot be explained. But, by deep silence, know It. There is no other place for Him to dwell in, but the one eternal deep silence! *Ayam Atma Santah.* This Atman is Silence".

God or Brahman is Supreme Silence. Soul is Silence. Peace is Silence. Atman is Silence. Silence is the language of Brahman. Silence is the language of the heart. Silence is the language of the sage. Silence is immense strength. Silence is great eloquence.

Silence is God. Silence is the substratum for this body, mind, Prana, and senses. Silence is the background for this sense-universe. Silence is power. Silence is a living force. Silence is the only reality. The peace that passeth all understanding is Silence. The goal of your life is Silence. The aim of life is Silence. The purpose of your existence is Silence. Behind all noises and sounds is Silence—thy innermost Soul. Silence is thy real name. Silence is intuitive experience. Silence helps the intuitional Self to express Itself. To go into Silence is to become God.

The message of the desert Sahara is silence. The message of the Himalayas is silence. The message of the Avadhoota who lives stark naked at the icy Gangotri or Kailas is silence. The message of Lord Dakshinamurti to His four disciples Sanaka, Sanatana, Sanandana, and Sanatkumara was silence. When the heart is full, when you get overjoy, there is silence. Who can describe the glory of this silence?

There is no healing balm better than silence for those persons who have a wounded heart from failures, disappointments, and losses. There is no soothing panacea better than silence for those who have wounded nerves from the turmoil of life, from friction, rupture, and frequent domestic quarrels.

In deep sleep, you are in close touch with this stupendous Silence, but there is the veil of Avidya or primal nescience. The silence that you enjoy during deep sleep and the silence that you experience at dead of night give the clue to the existence of that Ocean of Silence or Brahman.

Physical Silence and Silence of the Mind

In common parlance, to sit quiet without talking to anybody is silence. If your friend does not write to you for a long time, you will say, "My friend is keeping icy silence. I don't know why". If anybody does not talk in a big lecture hall for some time when there is a thrilling lecture, you say, "There was pindrop silence last evening when the philosopher delivered a lecture". When the boys make much noise in the class, the teacher says to the boys: "Silence, please". When you come across two Sadhus, one Sadhu tells: "The other Sadhu is a Mauni. He is my friend. He is observing the vow of silence for the last six years". This is all physical silence.

If you do not allow the eyes to see objects, and if you withdraw them from objects through the practice of Pratyahara or Dama, this is silence of that particular sense, eye. If you do not allow the ears to hear any sound, it is silence of that particular Indriya. If you observe complete fast on Ekadasi days without taking even a drop of water, it is silence of the Indriya tongue. If you do not perform any work and if you sit on Padmasana for three hours, it is silence of the feet and hands.

What is really wanted is silence of the bubbling mind. You can observe the vow of silence, but the mind will be building images. Sankalpa will be cropping up. Chitta will be developing memories. Imagination, reasoning, reflection, and various other functionings of the mind will be going on continuously. How can you have real peace or silence now? Intellect should cease functioning. The inner astral sense should be at perfect rest. All the waves of the mind should completely subside. The mind should rest in the Ocean of Silence or Brahman. Then only you can enjoy real, everlasting silence.

Mauna or the Vow of Silence

Mauna means a vow of silence. There are different kinds of Mauna. The control of speech is Vang-Mauna. If you keep the Vag-Indriya quiet, it is Vang-Mauna.

The complete cessation of one's physical actions is Kashtha

Mauna. In Kashtha Mauna, you should not nod your head. You should not show any signs. You should not write anything on a paper or slate to express your ideas. In Vang-Mauna and Kashtha Mauna, the mental modifications are not destroyed.

Equality of vision over all, and quiescence of mind with the idea that all are no other than Brahman, is Sushupti Mauna. The expurgation from the mind of all doubts, after realising firmly the illusory character of this world, is Sushupti Mauna. The settled conclusion that the universe is no other than the all-full Brahman is Sushupti Mauna.

Brahman is called Maha Mauna, because He is an embodiment of silence. Maha Mauna is true Mauna.

Vang-Mauna is only a help in the attainment of Maha Mauna. Mauna of the mind is far superior to Mauna of Vak or speech.

The Organ of Speech

The Vag-indriya or the organ of speech is a strong weapon o Maya to delude the Jivas and to distract the mind. Talkative peopl cannot enjoy peace of mind. Miscellaneous talking is a very ba habit. It distracts the mind. It keeps the mind always outgoing an makes a man unspiritual.

Quarrels, disputes, etc., occur through the play or mischief of thi turbulent Vag-Indriya. There is a sword in the tongue. Words ar like arrows. They injure the feelings of others.

Ladies of the house are very talkative. They always create som kind of noise in the house. Mothers-in-law and daughters-in-la cannot keep quiet even for a second. Some kind of smoke o friction will be coming out of the house.

The study of Sanskrit makes some persons very talkative an forces them to enter into unnecessary discussions with others t show their scholarly erudition. Pedantry or vain display of learnin is a special attribute of some Sanskrit scholars.

The Vag-Indriya is very mischievous, troublesome, turbulent, an impetuous. It must be steadily and gradually controlled. When yo begin to check it, it will try to rebound on you. You must be bol and courageous.

Do not allow anything to come out from the mind through th Vag-Indriya. Observe Mauna. This will help you. Now you hav shut out a big source of disturbance. If the Vag-Indriya is checked, the eyes and ears also can come easily under control. If you control the Vag-Indriya, you have already controlled half the mind.

Benefits of the Practice of Mauna

Energy is wasted in idle talking and gossiping. Worldly people do not realise this. Mauna conserves the energy and you can turn out more mental and physical work. You can do a lot of meditation. It has a marvellous soothing influence on the brain and nerves. By the practice of Mauna, the energy of speech is slowly transmuted or sublimated into Ojas-Sakti or spiritual energy.

Mauna develops will-force, checks the force of Sankalpa, curbs the impulse of speech, and gives peace of mind. You will get the power of endurance. You will not tell lies. You will have control over speech.

Mauna is a great help in the observance of truth and control of anger. Emotions are controlled and irritability vanishes. When one is ailing, observance of Mauna will give great peace of mind.

He who observes silence possesses a peace, a strength, a happiness unknown to worldly people. He has abundant energy. He is ever serene and calm. In silence, there is strength, wisdom, peace, poise, joy, and bliss. In silence, there is freedom, perfection, and independence.

How to Observe Mauna

Busy people should observe Mauna for at least one hour daily. If you can do for two hours daily, it is all the better. On Sundays, observe Mauna for six hours, or the whole day. People will not disturb you at that time. They will come to know that you observe Mauna at such and such hours. Your friends will not worry you. Your family members also will not trouble you. Utilise this period of Mauna in Japa and meditation. You must observe Mauna at a time in the afternoon when you will expect many visitors. If the place is not suitable for observing Mauna, go to a solitary place where your friends will not visit you.

If you wish to observe Mauna, you should keep yourself perfectly occupied in Japa, meditation, and Mantra-writing. You should not mix with others. You should not come out of your room frequently. The energy of speech should be sublimated into spiritual energy and utilised for meditation. Then only you will enjoy serenity, calmness, peace, and inner spiritual strength.

During the period of Mauna, you should not read newspapers. Reading newspapers will bring in revival of worldly Samskaras and will disturb your peace of mind. Though you live in the Himalayas, you will be in the plains throughout the day. You will not be benefited much by observing Mauna. Your meditation will be seriously disturbed.

During Mauna, you should not write too many slips, or write on a slate, or write on the forearm with your finger to express your thoughts to your neighbours. You should not laugh. These are all breaks in Mauna. These are all worse than talking.

Reduce your wants. You should previously arrange with those who attend on you for your menu or regimen of diet, and the time at which the food should be served. You should not frequently make changes in diet and think always of the different items of diet. You should yourself attend to the cleaning of your room and other ordinary daily duties. Do not bother much about your shaving, polishing the shoes, and washing of the linen by the washerman. All these will interfere with the continuity of divine thoughts. Do not think much of body, bread, and beard. Think more of God or Atman.

Some Special Hints

When you take a vow of silence, never assert from within very often, "I won't talk". This will produce a little heat in the brain, because the mind wants to revenge on you. Simply, once make a determination and then remain quiet. Attend to other affairs. Do not be thinking always, "I won't talk. I won't talk".

In the beginning, when you observe Mauna, you will find some difficulty. There will be a severe attack of Vrittis. Various kinds of thoughts will arise and force you to break the silence. These are all vain imaginations and deceptions of the mind. Be bold. Concentrate all energies on God. Make the mind fully occupied. The desire for talk and company will die. You will get peace.

The practice of Mauna should be gradual or you will not be able to observe all of a sudden Mauna for ten or fifteen days. Those who are in the habit of observing Mauna daily for two or three hours, or twenty-four hours on holidays, will be able to observe Mauna for a week or fifteen days. You should clearly understand the value of Mauna. Observe Mauna for two hours daily. Gradually increase it to six hours, twenty-four hours, two days, one week, and so on.

If you find it difficult to observe Mauna for a long time and if you do not utilise the time in Japa and meditation, break it at once. When the energy of speech is not controlled and utilised properly in spiritual pursuit, when it is not perfectly sublimated, it runs riot and manifests or bursts out in the form of *hu-hu-hu* sounds, showing various sorts of gestures, and producing various sounds. There is more loss of energy by exhibition of these gestures, etc., than by ordinary talking.

You should feel that you would derive much benefit from observing Mauna and experience much peace, inner strength, and joy. Then only you will take pleasure in observing Mauna. Then only you will not attempt to speak a word even. Forced Mauna simply to imitate, or from compulsion, will make you restless and gloomy. Forced Mauna is only wrestling with the mind. It is an effort. Mauna should come of itself. It must be natural. If you live in Truth, Mauna will come of itself. Then only will there be absolute peace.

Long Mauna and Kashtha Mauna for a long period are not necessary. Mouna for a protracted period in an unregenerate and undeveloped aspirant does harm.

Discipline of Speech

Try to become a man of measured words. Strictly avoid long talk, big talk, tall talk, all unnecessary talk, all sorts of vain debates and discussions, etc., and withdraw yourself from society as much as possible. This itself is Mauna. To talk profusely for six months and to observe Mauna for the rest of the year are of no avail.

Watch every word. This is the greatest discipline. Words are great forces. Use them carefully. Control your speech. Do not allow the tongue to run riot. Control the words before they pass over to your lips. Speak little. Learn to be silent.

High-sounding words cause exhaustion of the tongue. It is mere weariness of speech. Use simple words and conserve energy. Conserve speech for the praise of God. Devote more and more of your time for an inward life of meditation, reflection, and Atma-Chintana.

Purify the mind and meditate. Be still, and know that you are God. Calm the mind. Silence the bubbling thoughts and surging emotions. Plunge deep into the innermost recess of your heart and enjoy the magnanimous Silence. Mysterious is this Silence. Enter into Silence. Know that Silence. Become Silence Itself. Become a Maha Mauni. Realise God now and here.

71. SIN

In the din and noise of the world, in the midst of sensual pleasures, the mind is led astray.

Temptation forms the groundwork of all sins. Ignorant men yield to temptations and commit sins.

Those who put on the appearance of righteous men are more sinful than the unrighteous. They will have to undergo great miseries.

Sinning and evil have become so much a habit with man that he never feels that he is committing them, even though day and night he is doing so constantly.

Think not lightly of sin. Just as a pot is filled with water by the constant falling of drops of water, even so, the ignorant man fills himself with evil and sin little by little.

How Sin Originates

Sin is an evil deed. Sin is wilful violation of the laws of morality and religion. It is transgression of the Law of God.

Vice issues as sins and crimes. Vice is a stain of character. It is a flaw of character. It is a blemish or fault. Vice issues in evil deeds which are called sins.

Anger, lust, sorrow, loss of judgment, an inclination to injure others, jealousy, malice, pride, envy, slander, incapacity to see the good of others, unkindness, and fear are very powerful enemies of all creatures. These approach men and tempt them from all sides. They goad and afflict a careless or a foolish man. They attack him powerfully, like a tiger jumping upon its prey. From these originate all sorts of grief and sin.

It is selfishness that prompts a man to do evil acts. A selfish man injures others, robs their property, and does many sinful actions to satisfy his selfishness. Selfishness is the devil incarnate in every man.

It is a sin to be pleased with oneself. By shutting out the possibility of progress, self-inquiry, and introspection, the process of degeneration sets in.

Egoism is the greatest sin. The wrong notion, "I am the body", is the real, original sin. This one thought—the 'I' thought—has wrought all mischiefs. This one thought has multiplied into thousandfold thoughts. This one thought separated man from God. This self-arrogating ego is the real, hereditary sin of human nature. All evil Vrittis are hanging on this little ego.

What Is Virtue? What Is Sin?

Papa is sin. Punya is virtue. Remember the motto always: "Do unto others as you wish others do unto you". This is the Kasoti or test for virtue and sin. You do not wish to be hurt by another person. So do not hurt another person. You wish to be helped by others. So help others. You do not wish to be robbed by others. So do not rob others' property. When you enter the compartment in a train, you wish that others should give you a seat. They should not drive you to another compartment. So, when anyone enters your compartment, give him a seat. Do not drive him away. Hurting another is sin; non-hurting is virtue. Selfishness is sin; helping others is virtue. Robbing others' property is sin; doing charity is virtue. Driving a man from the compartment is sin; giving a seat to a man in your compartment is virtue.

That which elevates you is virtue; that which pulls you down is vice or sin. That which takes you to the Goal is virtue; that which makes you a worldly man is sin. That which helps you to attain Godhead is virtue; that which hurls you down in the dark abyss of ignorance is sin. That which gives you illumination is virtue; that which causes intoxication is sin. That which purifies your heart is virtue; that which taints your heart is sin. That which gives you peace, joy, satisfaction, exhilaration, expansion of heart, is virtue; that which brings restlessness, dissatisfaction, depression, and contraction of heart, is vice.

Service of humanity and Guru is virtue; mischief-mongering is sin. Faith in God, in the scriptures, in the words of the spiritual preceptor, is virtue; doubting is sin. Loving all is virtue; hating others is sin. Unity is virtue; separation is sin. Independence is virtue; dependence is sin. Brahmacharya is virtue; lust is sin. Truthfulness is virtue; falsehood is sin. Generosity is virtue; miserliness is sin. Oneness is virtue; duality is sin. Knowledge is virtue; ignorance is sin. Strength is virtue; weakness is sin. Courage is virtue; cowardice is sin. To behold the One Immortal Self everywhere is virtue; to see diversity is sin.

That which you are ashamed to do in public is a sin. That which you dare not admit before your Guru is a sin.

Learn to discriminate between virtue and sin, and become wise. The Antaryamin will guide you rightly; hear Him.

Atonement

Sin is expiated by self-punishment such as fasting, Japa, penance, meditation, and repentance with a contrite heart. Even a wicked man can have communion with God through repentance, prayer, and meditation.

The confession of evil deeds is the first beginning of good deeds. Be not ashamed to confess that you have been in the wrong. If you confess your evil actions, you now have more sense than you had before, to see your error. If you confess your sins, you begin your journey towards emancipation. He who is sorry for having done evil actions mends himself and improves quickly.

Repentance is a divine streamlet for sinners to wash their sins. Repent with a contrite heart. God will forgive you.

If you commit a wrong on a certain occasion, you should not commit it again. There should be no wrong over wrong. You may claim forgiveness, if you are resolute to do the evil thing no more.

A woman was charged with adultery. The Pharisees wanted Jesus to pronounce the Mosaic verdict of stoning her until death. Lord Jesus quietly said, "Let him that is without sin among you, cast the first stone on her". This powerful utterance of the Lord at once turned the gaze of each one there within himself. Who could be without sin? Introspection revealed their own defects. One by one, the people hung their heads down and left the place. "Where are they?". Lord Jesus asked the woman, "Did no man condemn thee?". "No, my Lord", said she. "Neither do I condemn thee. Go thy way, and sin no more", said the Lord, summing up in this beautiful incident the very essence of His divine message.

Contrition, change of heart, is the only condition for God's forgiveness of human sin. Confess your sin. Repent for your sin. Turn away from sin. Do not repeat it again. Pray. Do Japa. Meditate. Practise Pranayama. Do expiatory acts. All your sins will be washed away. You will shine with lustre and brilliance.

Hear the words of assurance of Lord Krishna in the Gita: "Even if the most sinful worshipeth Me with undivided heart, he too must be accounted righteous, for he hath rightly resolved". There is great hope even for a cut-throat, if he makes a strong determination and takes up the spiritual path.

Sin is a mistake committed by the ignorant Jiva during his journey towards the Sat-Chit-Ananda abode. Every mistake is your best teacher. One has to evolve through sins or mistakes. Mistakes are inevitable. Some people become a prey to thoughts of sin. They ever brood: "We are great sinners. We have committed great sins". This is a great blunder. Do not brood too much on the past events. Learn the lesson and forget the past. Once you make up your mind to tread the path of Truth, all sins will be destroyed.

Eternal Damnation—An Ungodly Doctrine

There is no such thing as eternal damnation or eternal hell-fire for the sinners. It cannot be. It is a theory that has long since been exploded. Eternal damnation is an ungodly doctrine, a terror and nightmare for ages. To make people desist from doing wicked actions, a terrifying description of hell is given. It is a Bhayanaka Sabda.

God has not created men to become everlasting fuel to feed the flame of hell. This is not certainly His purpose in His creation. If God be such, no one will pay homage to Him. Who then can be saved? How many spotless men are there in this world? Who is of such untainted character as to receive a direct passport to heaven?

Everybody has his secret sins. Few are born saints. No person is found on earth who shines with all the excellent qualities. No one is wise at all times, and no one is a fool always. The sinner of today is the saint of tomorrow. Hate the sin, but not the sinner.

A rogue is not an eternal rogue. A prostitute is not an eternal prostitute. Put these people in the company of saints. They will be newly moulded, and will be transmuted into saints with virtuous qualities. The transformation of Ratnakar into Valmiki is an epic example of this truth.

Purification

It is never too late to mend. A good, resolute start in virtuous life will give you peace and happiness. Do it now. Leave off evil ways. Follow the good. Be pure in life. You will attain God-realisation.

Steadily resist the promptings of your lower nature. Gradually, it will lose its power over you. You will gain strength. The spirit may pull in one direction and the flesh in the opposite direction. Be firm and courageous. Yield not to flesh. Be strong. Be positive always. Think and feel: "I can do everything if I will. There is nothing that I cannot do". Never give up the hope of realising God.

Watch every action. Allow not any impure action to stain your body. When anything pricks thy conscience, abandon it. Fight against the tempting power of self-gratification and self-aggrandisement. Overcome anger by love, lust by purity, greed by generosity, pride by humility, falsehood by truth.

Lose the sense of I-ness and mine-ness. Control the mind. Repeat the Lord's Name. Purify every part of yourself.

Paropakarah Punyaya; Papaya Parapidanam: Service of others brings on virtue; harming others is sin. Therefore, serve others. Purify your heart by selfless and humble service of the poor and the afflicted, and make it a fit abode for God to dwell.

Every day is a fresh beginning. Forget your past mistakes and failures. Enter a new life of victory. March on and on. Exert. Purify. Approach the saints. Abandon all anxiety, fear, and worry. Rest in your Centre. Sing Om. Meditate on Om. Realise the Self.

72. SVADHYAYA

What Is Svadhyaya?

Svadhyaya is daily study of religious scriptures and books written by realised sages. It is the daily Patha or Parayana of sacred books. It is the fourth Anga or limb of Raja Yogic Niyama. Svadhyaya is also enquiry of the nature of Atman or "Who am I?". It is recitation of Mantras also. Svadhyaya forms a sort of negative Satsanga when you cannot get positive Satsanga of Mahatmas.

Svadhyaya is the study of scriptures such as Bhagavadgita, Upanishads, Ramayana, Bhagavata, etc. The study should be done with concentration. You should understand what you have studied and try to put in your everyday life all that you have learnt. There will be no benefit in your study, if you do not exert to live up to the teachings of the scriptures. Svadhyaya includes also Japa, the repetition of Mantras. Constant study and its practice in daily life will lead one to have communion with God

Why Svadhyaya?

Svadhyaya means 'Self-study'. Brahman is to be learnt through the Srutis, and independent thinking and reasoning have nothing to do with it. Badarayana (Vyasa) seeks shelter always in the letter of the Vedas. Srutis are infallible and authoritative. Sruti Pramana is superior to perception. Perception leads to errors. Perception of a jar is really perception of jar minus the rest of the world. The jar and the rest of the world are directly presented before the mind. Then only perception is possible. How can the atomic mind see the rest of the world? It is impossible. Therefore, perception is not so authoritative and reliable as 'Srutis'. You see a blue colour in Akasa. It is a false attribution or Adhyasa. You cannot depend on the Pramana of perception. Srutis are revelations. They are the direct superintuitive experiences of Rishis, sages. Srutis give an accurate knowledge of Brahman. Srutis remove your Pramanagata Sandeha, doubt about the validity of the Vedantic text. God or Brahman is Atindriya, beyond the reach of the senses; is Avang-Mano-Gochara, beyond the reach of mind and speech. Sruti is the basis of Nididhyasana or deep meditation. The Brahmakara-Vritti is generated from the hearing of the Mahavakyas, "Tat Tvam Asi", "Aham Brahma Asmi", of the Srutis.

SVADHYAYA

Jnana Yoga is impossible without Sravana, Manana of the Srutis. Some learned fools, big wise fools who pose to possess reason, whereas they really mistake their fancies and preferences for reason declare that they will accept that portion of the Srutis which appeals to reason. They will never get out of this Samsara Chakra. They are doomed for destruction.

If, for a moment, the aspirant relaxes his vigilance and falls into a spiritual or ethical slumber then the lower pull asserts itself and, immediately the allegiance shifts from the higher to the lower self. If, at that time, he comes into contact with sensual objects, there takes place a setback in his spiritual life. Therefore, this alert vigilance and spiritual awareness, the state of being always awakened, has necessarily to be kept up at this stage.

One of the ways of doing this is Svadhyaya, study of scriptures. One of the most powerful methods of keeping the mind fully alive to the Ideal, is reading of scriptures and the lives of saints daily. For, when you read the lives of saints and spiritual books, a host of powerful and positive ideas rush to your mind and, at once, your mental powers are sharpened. They at once inspire the man and lift him and enable him to conquer the lower forces in his everyday life. Therefore, Svadhyaya should not be given up even for a single day in the life of a Sadhaka.

Benefits of Svadhyaya

Svadhyaya inspires and elevates the mind to high spiritual altitude. It clears doubts. It weeds out unholy ideas. It cuts new spiritual grooves for the mind to move on. It reduces wandering of the mind or Vikshepa. It helps concentration. It forms a kind of lower Savikalpa Samadhi. It serves pasture for the mind to graze upon. When you study the sacred books, you are in tune with the authors who are realised souls. You draw inspiration and become ecstatic.

When you cannot get positive Satsanga of Mahatmas, Svadhyaya clears doubts. It strengthens the flickering faith. It induces strong yearning for liberation or aspiration. It gives encouragement and illumination. It places before you a list of saints who trod the path, encountered and removed difficulties and thus cheers you up with hope and vigour. It fills the mind with Sattva or purity; it inspires and elevates the mind. It helps concentration and meditation. It cuts new Sattvic grooves and makes the mind run in these new grooves.

To translate the precepts contained in the books of the sages and saints into action is to have your afflicted body soothed, to have your bruised soul healed and to save yourselves from all kinds of ills of life which are due to ignorance. Spiritual books act as consoling companions under all vexing circumstances, ideal teachers in all difficulties, as guiding lights in the nights of nescience and folly, as panacea for evils, and as shapers of destiny.

Scriptures contain the wisdom of sages and saints, philosophers and mystics. By Svadhyaya, master the secrets of all scriptures, know the exact nature of things, and tune your localised being or individualised personality with the workings of the Divine Nature of the Laws of Truth. Wisdom is the key to the Plenitude of Power and Joy. Wisdom annuls countless sufferings, innumerable sins, cuts the root of ignorance, and confers upon you the Peaceful Harmony and Absolute Perfection.

Be regular in the study of religious books, Ramayana, Bhagavata, Yoga-Vasishtha, and other good books. If you reflect on the ideas of the Bhagavadgita and fix the mind on these ideas this itself is a form of lower Samadhi. Gita is a unique book for Svadhyaya. It contains the essence of all the Yogas and the cream of the Vedas. You can devote half an hour to three hours daily for this purpose according to the time at your disposal. Study of scriptures is Kriya Yoga or Niyama. It purifies the heart and fills the mind with sublime and elevating thoughts.

Therefore, study of scriptures, bearing the sacred truths propounded by men of wisdom, listening to the Lilas of the Lord are never to be given up by sincere Sadhakas, at whatever stage of spiritual evolution they may be. Are you more advanced than Sri Sukadeva who was a born sage and Parivrajaka? Are you more advanced than the great sages who assembled at Naimisharanya to listen to Srimad Bhagavata being narrated by Sri Suta? Learn a lesson from these illustrious examples of great sages. Be for ever a Sadhaka. Be for ever a thirsting aspirant after spiritual knowledge. Be for ever a student. He and he alone is an old man who feels that he has learnt enough and has need for no more knowledge. He is a man dead while alive who does not feel a compelling eagerness to listen to the stories of the Lord's Lilas or to spiritual discourses. You can stave off old age and even death itself by preserving within you the youthful zeal and a devout eagerness to learn more, to practise more and to realise more deeply, the great spiritual Truth, which is inexhaustible, in spite of having been extolled and expounded by millions of saints, sages, and seers from times immemorial.

Svadhyaya Prevents 'Back-Sliding'

Moreover, forget not that on all sides you are surrounded by materialistic influences. If you are slack even for a day, the evil forces around you would find their opportunity and play havoc. The ball dropped on the top of the staircase takes less than a split-second to reach the ground, whereas it took much longer to take it up. In a moment of heedlessness, much could be lost. Life is short, time is fleeting; you cannot afford to lose an inch of the ground that you have gained with so much effort, in your battle against this formidable foe--Satan, Maya, Mara, or the evil mind.

Do not let this monkey mind have a minute's respite. It is here that Satsanga and spiritual literature come to your great aid. They are your saviours. How many sublime thoughts are brought to your very doors by the scriptures? Study the pages of the scriptures carefully. Underline the sentences that strike you as having a direct bearing on your life. Reflect over then in your leisure moments. Thus would you find that you are able to surmount many obstacles and jump over many pitfalls. Is the mind disinclined to read these passages over and over again? That is Maya's potent weapon to put you to sleep. Beware! Are you not taking the same food over and over again? You will have to go on reading and rereading the selfsame spiritual sentences over and over again till they are indelibly engraved on the tablet of your heart, till they become part and parcel of your inner nature.

Repetition Augments Inner Strength

Then will a fortress of Nirodha Samskaras be erected within you. Repetition gives strength. Repetition pushes the ideas into the innermost chambers of your heart and mind. Then the ideas will percolate your subconscious mind. The evil thoughts lurking there will be scorched and annihilated. You may not even know what wonders have been effected within you. Such is the salutary influence of repeatedly studying the same spiritual text. That is why our ancestors insisted on our ceremoniously reading a text like the Gita, Ramayana, Bhagavata, etc., daily regularly, with faith and devotion. They will augment your inner strength. Your will will grow stronger. When thus the entire inner nature is transformed into divine, then a single effort to meditate will lead you to Nirvikalpa Samadhi and superconsciousness. You will then realise God in the twinkling of an eye.

Scriptures that Develop Devotion

A devotee should study books which place before him the ideals of devotion; the glory, the sweetness, and the Lilas of the Lord; the stories of saints; and the practices which help him to cultivate devotion. Devotion develops by the study of such devotional scriptures.

The most important books are Ramayana, Srimad Bhagavata, Narayaniyam, Gita, Vishnupurana, Adhyatma Ramayana, Tulasi Ramayana (Ramacharitamanas), Vishnu Sahasranama, Sandilya Sutras, Siva Purana, Devi Bhagavata, the Narada Pancharatram, Practice of Bhakti Yoga, Essence of Bhakti Yoga, Bhakti and Sankirtan, Bhakti-Rasamritam, songs of Alvars and Nayanars, Tevaram, Tiruvachakam, Dasabodha, Tukaram's Abhangas, Jnanesvari, Bhakti Rasayana, Bhakti Rasamritasindhu, etc.

Scriptures that Develop Knowledge

A student of Jnana Yoga or a seeker of Truth should study the following books regularly, reflect and meditate on their meaning with proper personal guidance of a Guru. The important books for Svadhyaya are: Atma-Bodha, Vivekachudamani. The Ten Classical Upanishads, Bhagavadgita, Panchadasi, Jivanmukti Viveka, Yoga-Vasishtha, Advaita Siddhi, Brahma-Sutras, Karikas of Gaudapada, The Realisation of the Absolute, Atma-Purana, Sanat Sujatiya, Avadhuta Gita, Ashtavakra Gita, Adhyatma Ramayana, etc.

73. TANTRA (AGAMA)

Sanskrit literature can be classified under six orthodox heads and four secular heads. They are: (i) Sruti, (ii) Smriti, (iii) Itihasa, (iv) Purana, (v) Agama, and (vi) Darsana; and (i) Subhashita, (ii) Kavya, (iii) Nataka and, (iv) Alankara.

The Agamas are theological treatises and practical manuals of divine worship. The Agamas include Tantras, Mantras, and Yantras. These are treatises explaining the external worship of God, in idols, temples, etc. All the Agamas treat of (i) Jnana or Knowledge, (ii) Yoga or concentration, (iii) Kriya or making, and (iv) Charya or doing. They also give elaborate details about the ontology, cosmology, liberation, devotion, meditation, philosophy of Mantras, mystic diagrams, charms and spells, temple-building, image-making, domestic observances, social rules, and public festivals.

The Agamas are divided into three sections: the Vaishnava, the Saiva, and the Sakta. The three chief sects of Hinduism, viz., Vaishnavism, Saivism, and Saktism, base their doctrines and dogmas on their respective Agamas. The Vaishnava Agamas or Pancharatra Agamas glorify God as Vishnu. The Saiva Agamas glorify God as Siva and have given rise to an important school of philosophy known as Saiva Siddhanta. The Sakta Agamas or Tantras glorify God as the Mother of the world under one of the many names of Devi. The Agamas do not derive their authority from the Vedas, but they are not antagonistic to them. They are all Vedic in spirit and character. That is the reason why they are regarded as authoritative.

The Tantra Agamas belong to the Sakta cult. They glorify Sakti as the World-Mother. They dwell on the Sakti (energy) aspect of God and prescribe numerous courses of ritualistic worship of Divine Mother in various forms. There are seventy-seven Agamas. These are very much like the Puranas in some respects. The texts are usually in the form of dialogues between Siva and Parvati. In some of these, Siva answers the questions put by Parvati and in others, Parvati answers, Siva questioning. Mahanirvana, Kularnava, Kulasara, Prapanchasara, Tantraraja, Rudra Yamala, Brahma Yamala, Vishnu Yamala, and Todala Tantra are the important works. The Agamas teach several occult practices, some of which confer powers, while the others bestow knowledge and freedom. Among the existing books the Mahanirvana Tantra is the most famous.

Tantra Yoga

Tantra Yoga had been one of the potent powers for the spiritual regeneration of the Hindus. When practised by the ignorant unenlightened, and unqualified persons, it has led to certain abuses and there is no denying that some degraded forms of Saktism have sought nothing but magic, immorality, and occult powers. An example of the perverted expression of the truth, a travesty of the original practices, is the theory of the five Makaras (Pancha Makaras);—Madya or wine, Mamsa or flesh, Matsya or fish, Mudra or symbolical acts, and Maithuna or coition. The esoteric meaning of these five Makaras is: "Kill egoism, control flesh, drink the wine of God-intoxication, and have union with Lord Siva".

Tantra explains (Tanoti) in great detail the knowledge concerning Tattva (Truth or Brahman) and Mantra (mystic syllables). It saves (Trayate). Hence it is called Tantra.

The Tantras are not books of sorcery, witchcraft, magic spells, and mysterious formulae. They are wonderful scriptures. All persons without the distinctions of caste, creed, or colour may draw inspiration from them and attain spiritual strength, wisdom, and eternal bliss. Mahanirvana and Kularnava Tantras are the important books in Tantra Sastra. Yoga Kundalini Upanishad of Krishna Yajurveda, Jabala Darsana, Trisikha Brahmana, and Varaha Upanishad are useful for getting knowledge of Kundalini Sakti and the methods to awaken it and take it to Sahasrara Chakra at the crown of the head.

The Tantra is, in some of its aspects, a secret doctrine. It is a Gupta Vidya. You cannot learn it from the study of books. You will have to get the knowledge and practice from the practical Tantrikas, the Tantric Acharyas and Gurus who hold the key to it. The Tantric student must be endowed with purity, faith, devotion, dedication to Guru, dispassion, humility, courage, cosmic love, truthfulness, non-covetousness, and contentment. Absence of these qualities in the practitioner means a gross abuse of Saktism.

The Sakti Tantra is Advaita Vada. It proclaims that Paramatman (Supreme Soul) and Jivatman (individual soul) are one. The Saktas accept the Vedas as the basic scriptures. They recognise the

Sakta-Tantras as texts expounding the means to attain the goal set forth in the Vedas.

Tantra Yoga lays special emphasis on the development of the powers latent in the six Chakras, from Muladhara to Ajna. Kundalini Yoga actually belongs to Tantric Sadhana which gives a detailed description about this serpent-power and the Chakras (plexus). Entire Tantric Sadhana aims at awakening Kundalini, and making her to unite with Lord Sadasiva, in the Sahasrara Chakra. Methods adopted to achieve this end in Tantric Sadhana are Japa of the Name of the Mother, prayer, and various rituals.

Guru and Diksha (Initiation)

Yoga should be learnt from a Guru (spiritual preceptor). And this is true all the more in the case of Tantra Yoga. It is the Guru who will recognise the class to which the aspirant belongs and prescribe suitable Sadhana.

The Guru is none other than the Supreme Divine Mother Herself, descended into the world in order to elevate the aspirant. As one lamp is lit at the flame of another, so the divine Sakti consisting of Mantra is communicated from Guru to the disciple. The disciple fasts, observes Brahmacharya, and gets the Mantra from the Guru.

Initiation tears the veil of mystery and enables the disciple to grasp the hidden truth behind scriptures texts. These are generally veiled in mystic language. You cannot understand them by self-study. Self-study will only lead you to greater ignorance. The Guru only will give you, by Diksha (initiation), the right perspective in which to study the scriptures and practise Yoga.

Qualifications of a Disciple

The qualifications of the disciple are purity, faith, devotion, dispassion, truthfulness, and control of the senses. He should be intelligent and a believer in Vedas. He must abstain from injury to all beings. He must be vigilant, diligent, patient, and persevering. He must be ever doing good to all. All Sadhana should be done under the personal direction of a Guru or spiritual teacher.

Tantra Sadhana

Bhuta Suddhi is an important Tantric rite. It means purification of the five elements of which the body is composed. The Sadhaka (aspirant) dissolves the sinful body and makes a new divine body. He infuses into the body the life of the Devi.

Nyasa is a very important and powerful Tantric rite. It is placing of the tips of the fingers of the right hand on various parts of the body, accompanied by Mantra.

In Kavacha the one Brahman is invoked by different names in order to protect different parts of the body. For example, Parabrahman is thought of as in the Sahasrara Padma in the head. The Supreme Lord is meditated upon in the heart. Protector of the world, Vishnu is invoked to protect the throat, so that the aspirant may utter the Mantras of his Ishta Devata.

Mudra is ritual of manual gestures. Mudra gives pleasure to the Devatas. There are 108 Mudras. In welcoming (Avahana) the Devata an appropriate gesture is made. In making offering (Arghya) Matsya Mudra is made. The right hand is placed on the back of the left and the two thumbs are extended finlike on each side of the hands. Similarly, there are Mudras for the various acts done during the worship.

Yantra takes the place of the image. It is an object of worship. Yantra is a diagram, drawn on paper. It is engraved on a metal sheet also. A Yantra is appropriated to a specific Devata only. Various Yantras are peculiar to each Devata. They are various designs according to the object of worship. Yantra is the body of the Devata. All the Yantras have a common edging called Bhupura. They have a quadrangular figure with four doors, which encloses and separates the Yantra from the external world.

The Sadhaka first meditates upon the Devata or Deity and then arouses the Devata in himself. He then communicates the Divine presence thus aroused to the Yantra. When the Devata has been invoked into the Yantra by the appropriate Mantra, the vital airs (Prana) of the Devata are infused therein by the Pranapratishtha ceremony. The Devata is thereby installed in the Yantra. The materials used or acts done in Puja are called Upachara. They are sixteen in number, viz., (1) Asana (seating of the Devata); (2) Svagata (welcoming of the Devata); (3) Padya (water for washing the feet); (4) Arghya (water for ablution); (5) Achamana (water for sipping); (6) Madhuparka (honey, ghee, milk, and curd); (7) Snana (bath); (8) Vastra (cloth); (9) Abharana (jewels); (10) Gandha (perfume); (11) Pushpa (flowers); (12) Dhupa (incense); (13) Dipa (light); (14) Naivedya (food) and Tambulam (betel); (15) Nirajana (Arati); and (16) Vandana (prostration and prayer).

Sadhakas are of three kinds, viz., Pasu (animalistic), Vira (valorous), and Divya (divine).

Tantra Yoga is the saving wisdom. It is the marvellous boat which takes man safely to the other shore of fearlessness, immortality, freedom, and perfection, when practised with understanding under personal guidance of well-established Tantric Guru.

74. TAOISM

The Founder of Taoism was Lao-Tze. Lao-Tze was born in 604 B.C. in the village Chu-Jhren, in Li country, belonging to the Ku province of the State Chu. He was born under the plum tree (in Chinese 'Li'). He adopted it as his surname. The hair of the head was white when he was born. Hence he was called Lao-Tze (old boy) or philosopher, one who is childlike even when old.

He was popularly called Lao-Tze. His name was Er (ear). He was called Tan after his death. 'Tan' means 'long lobe'. He had peculiar long ears. His appellation was 'Po Yang' or 'count of positive principle'. He was a keeper or recorder of the secret Archives in the Royal court of Chore. He was a State Historian.

'Tao' is a Chinese word meaning 'way', 'way of Heaven', 'Path' or 'road' or 'method'. It indicates a line or principle of conduct. There is no proper English term for 'Tao'. It means the 'Eternal Being'.

Tao

Lao-Tze says: Tao is one. It was in the beginning. It will remain for ever. It is impersonal, eternal, immutable, omnipresent, bodiless, immaterial. It cannot be perceived by the senses. It is nameless. It is indescribable.

It is the first cause from which all substances take their origin and all phenomena flow. The great Tao is all-pervading. All things depend on it for life. It is the mother of all phenomena, of heaven and earth. It existed before the Personal God. It is the father of God. It is the producer of God. It is the originator of heaven and earth. It is the mother of all things.

You will find that there is an aroma of Indian Vedantic philosophy in the teachings of Lao-Tze.

Tao is everywhere. It is in the ant. It is in the grass. It is in the earthenware vessel. It is in excrement. It is in the highest place, but is not high. It is in the lowest place, but is not low. It is in ancient times, but itself is not ancient. It is in old age but itself is not old. It is everywhere and yet it is nothing, as it were.

Tao is the sanctuary where all things find refuge. It is the good man's priceless treasure. It is the guardian and saviour of him who is not good. Tao overspreads and sustains all things.

The Tao which can be expressed in words is not the Eternal Tao. The name which can be uttered is not its Eternal Name. Whatever is contrary to the Tao soon ends. When the great Tao prevails, the outer doors need not be closed. All will be virtuous. There will be no theft.

If Tao perishes, then virtue will perish. If virtue perishes, then charity will perish. If charity perishes, then righteousness will perish. If righteousness perishes, then ceremonies will perish.

The man who achieves harmony with Tao enters into close union with external objects. No object has the power to harm or hinder him.

Tao does nothing. It has no bodily form. It cannot be seen. It has its root in itself. From Tao came the mysterious existence of God. It produced heaven and earth. It was before the primordial ether. Tao produces all things and nourishes them. It presides over all. Tao is the fundamental principle of the philosophy and religion of Lao-Tze.

The way of the Tao is to act without thinking of acting, to taste without discerning any flavour, to consider what is small as great and a few as many, and react to injury by kindness.

The Means for Attaining the Tao

Purity, humility, contentment, compassion, kindness towards all living creatures, higher knowledge, and self-control are the means to attain the Tao. Concentration and Pranayama (breathing exercises) are helpful in the path of Tao.

Sayings of Lao-Tze

Tao Te Ching (Canons of Tao and Its Manifestation) contains the sayings and teachings of Lao-Tze. Lao-Tze himself wrote this book in the sixth century B.C. This title was given by Emperor Ching. He issued an imperial decree that Lao-Tze's work on Tao should be respected as a canonical book. Some of the sayings are:—

Without going out of doors, one may know the entire universe; without looking out of the window, one may see the way of heaven. The further one travels, the less one may know. Thus it is that without moving you shall know; without looking you shall see; without doing you shall attain.

To the good I would be good. To the not good also, I would be good in order to make them good.

He who humbles himself shall be preserved entire. He who bends shall be made straight. He who is empty shall be filled. He who is worn out shall be renewed. He who has little shall succeed. He who has much shall go astray.

Those who know, do not speak; those who speak, do not know. To know when one does not know is best. To think one knows when one does not know is a dire disease. Only he who recognises this disease as a disease can cure himself of the disease.

I have three precious things which I hold fast and prize. The first is gentleness, the second is frugality, and the third is humility which keeps me from putting myself before others. Be gentle, and you can be bold; be frugal, and you can be liberal. Avoid putting yourself before others and you can become a leader among men.

There is no greater sin than yielding to desire; no greater misery than discontentment; no greater calamity than the propensity to acquire.

Hold fast to that which will endure.

He who overcomes others is strong, but he who overcomes himself is mighty.

Conclusion

Taoism has its monks and nuns. They wear yellow caps. They retire from the world and live in caves, forests, and secluded retreats in mountains.

Emancipation is attained through the realisation of Tao through self-conquest.

There is the idea of purgatory in Taoism, of the reward and punishment after death. There is also rebirth. Lao-Tze believed in the immortality of the soul. He advocated the doctrine of reincarnation of the soul after death.

Sincerity is the first step towards the knowledge of the Tao. That knowledge is maintained by silence. Tao is employed with gentleness.

When the aspirant is serene and tranquil, his wisdom becomes complete. When his wisdom becomes complete, the light of intelligence grows around him. When the light of intelligence grows around him, he is one with the Tao. This is true forgetfulness, a forgetting which does not forget, a forgetting of what cannot be forgotten. That which cannot be forgotten is the true Tao.

Glory to Lao-Tze, the founder of Taoism, that old boy who was born under the plum tree with peculiar long earlobes, with white hair, the reputed Sage of China. Glory, glory to Tao, the Eternal Great one, the Brahman of the Upanishads.

75. THOUGHT

Thought is a vital, living force, the most vital, subtle and irresistible force that exists in the universe.

Thought is a great force. Thought is a dynamic force. It is caused by the vibrations of psychic Prana or Sukshma Prana on the mental substance. It is a force like gravitation, cohesion or repulsion.

You are surrounded by an ocean of thought. You are floating in the ocean of thought. You are absorbing certain thoughts and repelling some in the thought-world. The thought-world is relatively more real than this physical universe.

Thoughts are living things. Every change in thought is accompanied by vibration of its mental matter.

Every thought has a certain name and a certain form. Form is the grosser and name the finer state of a single manifestating power called thought.

Thought Is Subtle Matter

Thought is subtle matter. Thought is as much a thing as the yonder piece of stone. Thought has form, size, shape, colour, quality, substance, power and weight. A spiritual thought has yellow colour; a thought charged with anger and hatred is of a dark red colour; a selfish thought has a brown colour; and so on.

You may die, but your thoughts can never die. The powerful thoughts of great sages and Rishis of yore are still in the Akasic records. Yogins who have clairvoyant vision can perceive those thought-images. They can read them.

Thought is supplied to us by food. If the food is pure, thought also becomes pure. He who has pure thoughts speaks very powerfully and produces a deep impression on the minds of the hearers. He influences thousands of persons through his pure thoughts. A pure thought is sharper than the edge of a razor. Entertain always pure, sublime thoughts.

Thought Builds Character

Every thought of yours has literal value to you in every possible way. The strength of your body, the strength of your mind, your success in life, and the pleasures you give to others by your company—all depend on the nature and quality of your thoughts.

You must know thought-culture. Thought-culture is an exact science.

Man is created by thought. What a man thinks upon, that he becomes. Think you are strong; strong you become. Think you are weak; weak you become. Think you are a fool; fool you become. Think you are God; God you become. A man forms his own character, becoming that which he thinks. If you meditate on courage, you shall work courage into your character. So with purity, patience, unselfishness and self-control. If you think nobly, you shall gradually make for yourself a noble character. But if you think basely, a base character will be formed. You can build your character as surely as a mason can build a wall, working with and through the law.

The mind has got a 'drawing power'. You are continually attracting towards you, from both the seen and the unseen side of life-forces, thoughts, influences and conditions most akin to those of your own thoughts and lines. Carry any kind of thought you please about with you, and so long as you retain it, no matter how you roam over land or sea, you will unceasingly attract to yourself, knowingly or inadvertently, exactly and only what corresponds to your own dominant quality of thought.

The Progeny of Thoughts

A good thought is thrice blessed. First, it benefits the thinker by improving his mental body. Secondly, it benefits the person about whom it is entertained. Lastly, it benefits all mankind by improving the general mental atmosphere.

An evil thought, on the contrary, in thrice cursed. First, it harms the thinker by doing injury to his mental body. Secondly, it harms the person who is its object. Lastly, it harms all mankind by vitiating the whole mental atmosphere.

Thoughts are your own real children. Be careful of your progeny of thoughts. A good son brings happiness, name and fame, to the father. An evil son brings infamy, discredit to his father. Even so, a noble thought will bring happiness and joy to you. An evil thought will bring misery and trouble to you. Just as you rear up your children with great care, so also, you will have to rear up good, sublime thoughts with great care.

Thoughts lead to action. Evil thoughts produce evil actions.

Good thoughts generate good actions. Thoughts are the sources of all actions. Thought is the real Karma. Thinking is the real action. If you can root out all evil thoughts in the beginning, you will not do any evil action. If you can nip them in the bud, you will be free from the miseries and tribulations of this world. Watch your thoughts with vigilance and introspection.

Eradication of Evil Thoughts

At first, an evil thought enters the mind. Then you entertain a strong imagination. You take delight in dwelling on that evil thought. You give consent to its stay in the mind. Gradually, the evil thought, when it is not resisted, takes a strong hold in your mind. Then it becomes very difficult to drive it off.

Thoughts gain strength by repetition. If you entertain an evil thought or good thought once, this evil thought or good thought has a tendency to recur again. Similar thoughts crowd together just as birds of the same feather flock together. If you entertain one evil thought, all sorts of evil thoughts join together and pull you down. If you entertain any good thought, all good thoughts join together and raise you up.

Control your thoughts. Just as you retain only the good fruits from the basket and discard the bad ones, so also, keep good thoughts in your mind and reject the evil ones. Wipe out lust, greed and egoism. Entertain only pure holy thoughts. Though this is a difficult task, you will have to practise this. No pains, no gains.

Just as you close your door or gate when a dog or an ass tries to come in, so also, close your mind before any evil thought can enter and produce an impression on your physical brain. You will become wise soon and attain eternal, infinite peace and bliss.

Thoughts are like the waves of the ocean. They are countless. You may become desperate in the beginning. Some thoughts will subside, while some other thoughts will gush out like a stream. The same old thoughts that were once suppressed may again show their faces after some time. Never become despondent at any stage of practice. Inner spiritual strength will gradually manifest in you. You can feel this. You are bound to succeed in the end. All the Yogins of yore had to encounter the same difficulties that you are experiencing now.

Fully realise for yourself the grave and ruinous consequences of evil thoughts. This will set you on your guard when the evil thoughts would come. The moment they come, exert yourself or divert the mind to some other object of divine thoughts, prayer, or Japa. A real earnestness to drive away the evil thoughts will keep you on the alert so much so that even if they appear in dream you will at once wake up.

Keep the mind fully occupied. Then evil thoughts will not enter. An idle brain is the devil's workshop. Watch the mind every minute. Always engage yourself in some work. Avoid loose talk and gossip. Fill the mind with sublime thoughts, such as those contained in the Gita, the Upanishads, the Yoga-Vasishtha.

Conservation and Utilisation of Thought-energy

Just as energy is wasted in idle talk and gossiping, so also, energy is wasted in entertaining useless thoughts. Therefore you should not waste even a single thought. Do not waste even an iota of energy in useless thinking. Conserve all mental energy and utilise it for meditation and helpful service to humanity.

Do not store in your brain useless information. Learn to unmind the mind. Unlearn whatever you have learnt. They are now useless for you. Then only you can fill your mind with divine thoughts. You will gain new mental strength as all the dissipated mental rays are collected now.

Drive away from your mind all unnecessary, useless and obnoxious thoughts. Useless thoughts impede your spiritual growth; obnoxious thoughts are stumbling blocks to spiritual advancement. You are away from God when you entertain useless thoughts. Substitute thoughts of God. Entertain only thoughts that are helpful and useful. Useful thoughts are the stepping-stones to spiritual growth and progress. Do not allow the mind to run into the old grooves and to have its own ways and habits. Be on the careful watch.

You must eradicate through introspection all sorts of mean thoughts, useless thoughts, unworthy thoughts, impure thoughts, all sexual thoughts, thoughts of jealousy, hatred and selfishness. You must annihilate all destructive thoughts of disharmony and discord. You must develop good, loving, sublime thoughts, divine thoughts. Every thought must be of a constructive nature. It must be strong, positive and definite. The mental image must be of a clear-cut and well-defined nature. You must develop right thinking. Every thought must bring peace and solace to others. It should not bring even the least pain and unhappiness to anyone. Then you are a blessed soul on the earth. You are a mighty power on the earth. You can help many, heal thousands, spiritualise and elevate a large number of persons as did Jesus and Buddha.

Thought-transference or Telepathy

Thought is very contagious, nay, more contagious than the Spanish Flu. Thought moves. It actually leaves the brain and hovers about. It enters the brains of others also.

The medium through which thoughts travel from one mind to another is Manas. Manas or mind-substance fills all space like ether and it serves as the vehicle for thoughts as Prana is the vehicle for feelings, ether is the vehicle for heat, light and electricity, and air is the vehicle for sound. Mind is all-pervading like Akasa. Hence, thought-transference is possible. Thought-transference is telepathy.

If we throw a piece of stone in a tank or a pool of water, it will produce a succession of concentric waves travelling all around from the affected place. The light of a candle will similarly give rise to waves of ethereal vibrations travelling in all directions from the candle. In the same manner, when a thought, whether good or evil, crosses the mind of a person, it gives rise to vibrations in the mental atmosphere, which travel far and wide in all directions.

The velocity of thought is unimaginable. While electricity travels at the rate of 1,86,000 miles per second, thoughts travel virtually in no time, their speed being as much faster than electricity as their vehicle Manas is finer than ether, the medium of electricity.

When you send out a useful thought to help others, it must have a definite, positive purpose and aim. Then only it will bring out the desired effect.

The stronger the thoughts, the earlier the fructification. Thought is focussed and given a particular direction, and in the degree that thought is thus focussed and given direction, it is effective in the work it is sent out to accomplish.

You should learn the method of sending out helping, loving thoughts to others and the whole world at large. You should know how to remove distraction and collect all thoughts and send them out as a battalion of helpful forces to do good to the suffering humanity.

Clear Thinking

The common man does not know what deep thinking is. His thoughts run riot. There is a great deal of confusion in the mind sometimes. His mental images are very distorted. It is only thinkers, philosophers and Yogins who have well-defined, clear-cut mental images.

Thinkers are very few in this world. Thinking is very shallow in the vast majority of persons. Deep thinking needs intense Sadhana or practice. It takes innumerable births for the proper evolution of the mind. Then only it can think deeply and properly. A man who speaks the truth and has moral purity has always powerful thoughts. One who has controlled anger by long practice has tremendous thought-power.

The Waveless Jnanin

The fewer the thoughts, the greater the peace. The fewer the desires, the lesser the thoughts. Remember this always.

A wealthy man who is engaged in speculation in a big city and who has a large number of thoughts has a restless mind in spite of his comforts; whereas, a Sadhu who lives in a cave of the Himalayas and who is practising thought-control is very happy in spite of his poverty.

Every thought that is reduced adds strength and peace to the mind. Reduction of even one thought will give mental strength and peace of mind. You may not be able to feel this in the beginning as you do not possess a subtle intellect; but there is a spiritual thermometer inside to register the reduction of even a single thought. If you reduce one thought, the mental strength that you have gained by this reduction will help you to reduce the second thought easily.

Through constant and intense practice, you can become waveless and thought-free. The waveless Yogin helps the world more than the man on the platform. Ordinary people can hardly grasp this point. When you are waveless, you actually permeate and pervade every atom of the universe, purify and elevate the whole world. The names of waveless Jnanins such as Jada Bharata and Vamadeva are even now remembered. They never built Ashrams. They never lectured. They never published books. They never made disciples. Yet, what a tremendous influence these waveless Jnanins had produced on the minds of the people! Glory to such waveless Jnanins!

76. TIME

The serpent has the frog in its mouth. Only the head of the frog is projecting outside. It will be devoured within a few minutes. But the poor frog projects its tongue outside to catch one or two insects. Even so, O ignorant man, you are already in the mouth of Kala or time. You will be nowhere in a few minutes. Yet you think of the sensual objects again and again. You have become a slave of Moha or delusion, and attachment

You do not realise the value of time. When one is in the dying condition, you will ask the doctor who is standing by the side of the patient: "My dear doctor! Just do something for this patient. Give a powerful injection. Let the breath continue for some hours at least. My brother is coming from Bombay to see the patient". The doctor will give a reply: "My dear friend, I cannot do anything. The case is perfectly hopeless. He will pass away within five minutes". Now you will realise the value of time. You will repent for the days, months and years you have wasted in idle gossiping and sensual pleasures.

Time and the Timeless Eternity

Time is more precious than money. Time is more precious than the most valuable thing in the world. It is the richest treasure. Time is the soul of the world. Time is life. Utilise time profitably in spiritual pursuits. Waste not even a second.

Time is formless. But, it devours everything. Time digests everything. Time does not spare anybody. Time is relentless. Time is Lord Yama. Time is Kala.

Time is the rat that cuts off the thread of life in this universe. There is nothing in this world which the all-devouring time will spare. It obliterates even what apparently looks to be very enduring. Time spares not even the greatest person for a moment. Time pervades and controls all things. Time dances about with a long chain of the bones of the dead hanging from its neck to its feet. It assumes the formidable form of a burning fire during the dissolution and reduces the whole world to ashes. Nothing can stop its course. Only the sages, seers, and saints of God-realisation have defied its might.

The Eternal is timeless. Brahman transcends time. Brahman is eternal. It is a timeless reality.

Kings and lords will pass away. This world will pass away with all its occupants. The sun, moon, and stars will pass away. All joys and sorrows will pass away. Wife, children, wealth, property will pass away. The five elements, the earth, and heaven will pass away. Only Brahman, the pure Satchidananda, will shine eternally. Attain Brahman and conquer time. Transcend time and become one with the Eternity.

The Fleeting Nature of Sensual Life

This world is a play of colours and sounds. This sense-universe is a play of nerves. It is a false show kept up by the jugglery of Maya, mind, and senses. You enjoy the sensual pleasures for a period of twenty years, when the senses are young and strong. What is this short, evanescent period of twenty years in eternity? What is this despicable, jarring, monotonous, sensual life when compared with the eternal and peaceful life in the Immortal Self within?

Being much hemmed in on all sides and whirling in different conditions in this ever-fluctuating world, you are ever whirling with delusion and afflicted with pains, like dust of sand floating in the midst of a large stone. Now, reflecting upon 'time' which is eternal in its true nature, you cannot but term the hundred years of your life as a moment. While being so, how is it that you estimate your life so greatly, and fall into all sorts of despondencies through the insatiable desires? Who is there so debased in life as you who are spoiled through the gross mind? Fie on your uneven life which cannot be considered as of any moment.

You have spent eight hours in sleep, and the rest of the day in idle gossiping, telling lies, deceiving others, in selfish activities in amassing wealth. How can you expect spiritual good, how can you expect immortality and peace, if you do not spend even half an hour in the service of the Lord, in singing His Names and in divine contemplation?

You may waste two hours in tying your turban. You may waste much time in self-shaving, in combing the hair; but, if a devotee calls you to attend the Sankirtan, you will say, "Babuji! I have no time at all. I have to go to the doctor to get medicine. I must go to the market for shopping"; and you will give a thousand and one lame excuses.

There are people who waste days and nights in idle talk, in playing card and chess. There are people who waste weeks in drinking and chitchatting. There are people who waste months in the company of sisters of evil repute, and in gambling. There are people who waste years and years in wandering, idle gossiping, attending cinemas, smoking, chewing betels, and various other licentious deeds.

You do not know even a single Sloka of the Gita or the Upanishads. You do not know how to sit on Padmasana. You do not know the efficacy of Mantra, Kirtan. You do not know anything about self-analysis, mind-control, self-restraint, concentration, and introspection. You have lived in vain! You have wasted this precious life. Hotels, restaurants, cinema houses, are your abodes of immortality or Vaikuntha Dhama. Really you are leading a miserable life. If you can talk something on dry politics, you think you are a great hero!

The Purpose of Human Life

What a great pity! Man has come here with a definite purpose. Life is not meant for eating, drinking, dressing, and procreating. There is something grand and sublime behind. There is an eternal life of bliss beyond. Every second must be well utilised for the achievement of this goal of life.

Half of your life is spent in sleep. A great portion goes away in sickness. Some portion is spent in eating, drinking, and talking. You are enveloped in ignorance and play in childhood. You are caught up in the net of women in adolescence. In old age, you pine under anxiety and the burden of family affairs. When will you, my dear friends, find time in doing virtuous deeds and worship of God? Be serious. Think and reflect now.

Life is short. Time is fleeting. Obstacles are many. Cut this knot of Avidya and drink the Nirvanic bliss. Life is short. Time is fleeting. The world is full of miseries. Apply yourself diligently to Yogic Sadhana. The world is a Mela for two days. This life is a bubble for two seconds. You came alone. You will go alone. No one will follow you. You came naked. You will go naked. No one will follow you. Do Bhajan, do Kirtan; for, this alone will follow you.

People have risen to greatness and prominence by utilising every second profitably. Keep daily diary. Reduce your sleep. Give up all the idle talk. Enough, enough! observe Mauna. Understand the value of time. Draw up a daily routine and stick to it tenaciously. Grow. Evolve. Expand. Get success in life. Realise God. Shut yourself in a room. Reflect. Meditate. Unfold the hidden spiritual consciousness.

Days, months, and years are rolling away. Hairs have become grey. Teeth have fallen. You are attached to perishable objects through Moha. Tell me, friends, how long will you be slaves to the fleeting things of the world? How long are you going to repeat the same sensual enjoyments? How long do you wish to worship Mammmon and woman. When will you find time to meditate on the Lord, and to do virtuous deeds? Think and reflect.

Uncertainty of Earthly Life

The leaves of life are falling off. Youth is fading. The days are rolling on. Time, the destroyer, lays his icy hands on the whole world. Existence in this world is as momentary as a bubble or lightning!

A doctor speaks on the telephone and ascends the stair-case to take his breakfast, and is found dead on the stair-case itself on account of cardiac failure. A princess drives a car along with her husband and loses her life on the way, through some accident. A Zamindar comes outside to sit on the chair for getting good breeze at night; a cobra bites him and he passes away. Such is the uncertainty or evanescent nature of life here; and yet, man foolishly wastes his time.

A man loses his father. On the following day, he loses his son also. Yet, he is foolish enough to think that he will live for ever—when the persons who came before and after him have died—and postpones Sadhana.

How to Utilise Time

Mr. Rockefeller and Mr. Austin know the value of time. They get millions of pounds as interest every day. A second is most precious for them. In an hour, they earn a lot. Time is all money. Just as worldly people who are engaged in business are very careful about their time, so also, spiritual aspirants are very careful about their time, and they use it in contemplation of God. They will not speak even a single word unnecessarily. They want to spend every second in the service of God. That is the reason why they observe Mauna and hide themselves in the Himalayan caves. If you take care of the seconds, the hours will take care of themselves.

Time is, indeed, most precious. It can never come back. It is rolling on with a tremendous speed. When the bells ring, remember you are approaching death. When the clock strikes, bear in mind that one hour is cut off from the span of your life. You must tremble with fear and say, "Death is drawing near. I am wasting my time. When shall I realise the goal of life? When shall I have Darsana of my Ishta-Devata, Sri Krishna? When shall I meet Him? When shall I be free from this wheel of Samsara?".

Your birthday reminds you that your life is shortened by a year. On this day, make a firm resolve to make your future life more fruitful and useful.

Do not postpone doing good deeds; for, there is no certainty of life. What you propose to do tomorrow, do that today. What you propose to do today, do this very instant.

Do in the daytime that by which you will live happily in the night. Do in the early part of your life that by which you will live happily in old age. Do all throughout your life that by which you will live happily after death.

O man! Sit down before retiring to bed, and count the acts that you have done. If you have wiped out the tears of even one man, by a single word of comfort and cheer, by a single good deed, then you may count that day well spent. You have done an act that is pleasing to the Lord. But, if you have not done any act that has brought solace to any man, if you have not spoken one word that eased the heart of a man in agony, you have lived in vain on that day. Then count you have wasted that day.

Life is a link in the chain of time. If you waste time, you waste life. Know the value of time. You cannot salvage a second spent in worthless ways. Time is most precious. Trifle not with time. Make the utmost use of it. Utilise every second in spiritual pursuits and service.

The Nature of Time

Time is a mode of the mind. It is mental creation. It depends on the nature of the event.

When your mind is deeply concentrated, a period of two hours passes like five minutes. If the mind is distracted and wandering, half an hour hangs on as two hours. This is everybody's experience. In dream also, many events that represent a period of fifty years take place within ten minutes. Through the play of the mind, a Kalpa is considered by it as a moment and *vice versa.* Time is but a mode of the mind. It is Kala Sakti. It is also illusory like the objects.

Time is a concept of mind. Without mind, there is no concept of time. Annihilate the mind. You will go beyond time. You will enter the realm of the Timeless. You will live in the Eternal.

In the Absolute, there is no time. Time is a measure or duration of experiences. You sit for taking food at 1 p.m. and get up at 2 p.m. You have spent one hour for taking food. There is interval between two experiences. Then you go to bed from 3 p.m. to 4 p.m. This is another experience. You have spent one hour in sleep. Where there is only one homogeneous Experience of Self, how can time be there?

Yesterday, Today, and Tomorrow

Time is formless, but it makes an appearance when some motion occurs in nature. The wheels of time are mysterious.

Past, present, and future are all relative. Present becomes past. Future becomes present. Present alone is real. Live always in the present.

Today becomes yesterday. Yesterday is today's memory. It is a remembrance only. Tomorrow is today's dream. It is a longing only. Live in the solid present alone. Wipe off yesterday and tomorrow. In God, there is neither past nor future. It is all eternity. It is all solid present alone. Present only is the solid reality.

You cannot remedy the past. You are not sure of tomorrow. The only best thing is to make today as useful as can be.

Yesterday is gone. Forget it. Tomorrow is not here. Worry not. Today is present. Use it well. Today is your own. Tomorrow perchance may never come.

Yesterday is but a dream. Tomorrow is but a vision. Do not worry about dead yesterday or unborn tomorrow, but concentrate on today, the eternal present. Live well every day as if it is the last. Every moment is vitally important; every day is like the turning of a new leaf; and every year, the beginning of a new hope.

Do not love leisure. Do not waste even half a second. Be bold. Plunge yourself in Japa, Kirtan, and service of saints and the poor. Meditate. Realise the Truth here and now! Go beyond time and become a Kalatita.

77. TRUTH

Truth is the seat of God. Truth is God. Truth alone triumphs.

Truth is the basic law of life. Truth is the means and the goal ultimate.

Truth is the law of freedom, falsehood the law of slavery and death.

Truth is Justice, fair play, adherence to the fundamental laws of ethics. Purity and truth are the twin factors that unfold and awaken the divinity that lies dormant within you and lead you to perfection.

Truthfulness is the first pillar in the Temple of God-realisation. Truth is the gateway to the Kingdom of God.

Truth is like a ladder. It leads you to the Kingdom of Immortal Bliss.

The All-inclusive Virtue

Speaking truth is the most important qualification of a Yogin. Truth is the queen of virtues. Truth is the supreme virtue.

Truth constitutes the essence of the Vedas. Control over passions constitutes the essence of truth. Self-denial or refraining from the worldly enjoyments forms the essence of self-control. These attributes are always present in a virtuous man.

Truth is righteousness. Righteousness is light, and light is bliss. Ahimsa, Brahmacharya, purity, justice, harmony, forgiveness, peace are forms of truth.

Impartiality, self-control, modesty, endurance, goodness, renunciation, meditation, dignity, fortitude, compassion, and abstention from injury are the various forms of truth.

All the above virtues, though seemingly different, have but one and the same form, namely, truth. All these hold up truth and strengthen it.

When the path of truth is trodden, everything else also is done. When the root is watered, all the branches are automatically watered.

The Supreme Commandment

Be truthful. All righteousness is contained in this one commandment.

Whatever you do, be true to yourself and to the world. Hide not your thoughts. Be frank. Be sincere. Be candid. Be straightforward. Be courageous to express your views.

Be faithful to your trust. Deceive not the man who relies upon you. Keep up your promise even at the cost of your life. Your life may go, but not the given word.

Do not hastily give your assent to anybody, to anything. Think deeply. Cogitate. Reflect. Say, "I shall think over the matter and talk to you later on". Thus you will not be entangled.

Do not make promises, but say, "I shall try. I shall think over the matter". You are saved. You will not be caught in the whirlpool of troubles, repentance, and sorrow.

To tell a lie is a great sin. He who utters falsehood loses the faith of other persons. People will not believe him even if he speaks the truth. The habit of telling lies becomes deep-rooted by repetition of lies. Man tells several lies to cover up one lie.

A lie concealed by another lie leads to more lies. A sin concealed by another sin leads to more sins.

A liar is a coward. Uttering falsehood is a certain mark of cowardice. Speak truth. You will become courageous.

Truth Is Fearless and Strong

Truth is complete in itself. Truth has a strong foundation in itself. It is bold, it has no fears. It has no limit of space or time. It is a fearless, free bird in the sky. It does not care for status. It is wealth in itself. Truth stands even when there is no public support.

Truth can be compared to a road of pasture, while falsehood can be compared to a bush of thorns. In a man who indulges in false thoughts, there is a lurking fear at every moment, an uneasiness, a fear of the self, a want of confidence and a feeling that something wrong may happen. Truth, on the other hand, is the path of righteousness which certainly leads to success in the long run. It is a straight road with no doubtful crossroads.

In the day-to-day world, it seems as though it is impracticable to strictly follow the path of truth, but if it is practised as your ideal and goal in life, you have your way. All the stumbling blocks on your road to Truth will melt away as you proceed along the direct road.

Certain Fallacies

There are certain fallacies that arise in following the straight path of truth. It is absolutely no harm for a mother who fondly nurses the child in just diverting the attention of the child by saying that the small piece of sweetmeat has been carried away by the crow a short while back, and when she shows to be extremely sorry for it and brings round the ideas of the child by saying, "Papa, do not mind it, I shall bring a bigger cake for you in the evening". It is absolutely no untruth if you do not interfere with others, wound their feelings, harm others or spoil others. If you refuse a small loan, certainly with something for you to fall back upon, if you refuse to lend your pen or any object that you would like not to lend, these cannot be counted as untruths.

Varying Conceptions of Truth

A worldly man, a moralist, and a spiritual man have different conceptions of truth. A moralist cares for the result of truth. If a man can save the lives of many innocent persons by telling a lie, it is truth for a moralist, because an untruth has brought greatest good. If the uttering of a truth brings greater harm to many persons, it is an untruth according to a moralist. According to a spiritual man, Brahman is truth; this world is unreal.

Brahman: The Only Truth

The world is untruth and the Absolute is Truth. The world is represented by sex and ego; the Absolute is represented by the noumenal, gnostic Being.

Truth is not expressed even by Existence-Consciousness- Joy! It is only the nearest relative of Truth. Truth is even greater, grander, mightier, truer!

Truth is; untruth is not. Hence, it is not absolutely correct even to say that Truth is one, for Truth is Existence itself, and is neither one, nor not-one. Truth is undivided.

Truth is utterly public. It cannot be hidden even if one would try to do so. Truth persists and is expressed even in the extreme of untruth. The extreme of truth is the Absolute. Untruth is a shadow of Truth.

Everything that changes itself is untruth. Hence, Truth is infinite. Truth alone endures, while everything else perishes.

Everyone, right from Brahma down to a blade of grass, moves towards Truth, some consciously, some unconsciously. They differ only in the degree of consciousness or to the extent of mental purification or subtlety of condition. Every leaf that flies in the air, every breath that flows from us, in other words, every act of universal life, is a step taken nearer the Truth; for, Truth is the eternal home of all beings. Into it they all enter and find permanent satisfaction and peace. It is Truth that triumphs over falsehood, not falsehood over Truth, whatever the apparent and immediate experience may be.

The Practice of Truth

Scriptures emphatically declare: "Speak the truth. Truth alone triumphs, falsehood never". God is Truth and Truth must be realised by speaking truth. A truthful man is absolutely free from worries and anxieties. He has a calm mind. If one observes speaking truth for twelve years, one will get 'Perfection of Speech'. Then, whatever one speaks will come to pass. There will be power in the speech of such a person.

Your thoughts should agree with your words, and the words should agree with your actions. In the world, people think of one thing, say another thing, and do another thing. This is horrible. This is nothing but crookedness. You must carefully watch your thoughts, words, and actions. The little gain that you get by telling lies is no gain at all. You pollute your conscience and infect your subconscious mind. The habit of telling lies is carried to your next birth also and you undergo suffering from birth to birth.

Meditate on truth. Derive inspiration from the lives of those who have sacrificed their all for the sake of truth. Write in bold types the words "SPEAK TRUTH" on cardboards and hang them in different places in your house. This will caution you when you are about to speak a lie. You will then check yourself at once. A time will come when you will be established in the habit of speaking truth. Punish yourself by fasting if you tell a lie and record the lies in a diary. Gradually the number of lies will decrease and you will become a truthful man.

Stick to the path of truth at all costs. Truth has a lustre of its own. It shines for itself and sheds its light on others. When you stick to truth as your only religion, when you strictly adhere to truth alone at all times, at all places, and on all occasions, you cannot afford to harm any one. Perfect peace and real happiness will be yours.

Have ceaseless devotion to truth. Be ready to sacrifice your all for it. You will develop a strong will. You will become fearless. You will draw immense strength and courage from the Atman or the Supreme Self within. You will attain Self-realisation.

Truth: The First and the Last Thing

Should you ask me "What is the first thing in Realisation?", I should reply "The first, second, and third thing therein, nay, all—is truthfulness".

Let truth and purity light up your career, guide your conduct, and mould your character.

If the mind is impure, Self-realisation cannot be attained even if you meditate for twenty hours daily. Even Yudhishthira had to see the hell as he once told a lie—a modified, twisted truth, in a dexterous manner.

In truth, there is no deceit. That which is simulated is untruth.

Truth can never contradict non-injury. When it does, it is no more a truth, but the selfishness of the man which is on the fore.

When truth-speaking leads another to dishonour, injury and pain, it is no longer a virtue. Then it becomes a deadly sin.

Speak what is true. Speak what is pleasant. Speak no disagreeable truth, speak no agreeable falsehood.

Truth always exists in a pure and unmixed state. Truth includes Self-restraint, absence of jealousy, forgiveness, patience, endurance, kindness, love.

Peace is truth. Truth is peace. If you want to attain peace, be truthful at all times.

Mind is exalted by truthfulness. Intellect is refined by sublime, divine ideas.

By the practice of speaking the truth, the Antahkarana is purified of its dirt. It shines like a clean mirror and reflects the divine form of the Lord with great effulgence.

All is well with him whose heart is turned towards the True. No disease, physical or mental, can assault him.

The mover towards the Truth is mighty, lives long, knows everything, and is ever delighted; for he is nearing the Almighty.

The path of Truth is a precipitous one. It is slippery and as sharp as the razor's edge. Hard it is to tread, difficult a path it is. Giants among spiritual men walk over it to the City of Perfection.

Keep company with evolved souls who tread the path of Truth. Always mark carefully what is going on in the inner mental factory. Give up all sorts of mean actions. Become a noble, magnanimous soul. Nobility is good. Magnanimity is truth. If people mock at you, keep quiet. Never retort. Excuse them. Give a Vedantic smile. Stand adamantine as that yonder rock. Will you, my dear Niranjan?

78. UPANISHADS

The Upanishads are metaphysical treatises which are replete with sublime conceptions of Vedanta and with intuitions of universal truth. The Indian Rishis (seers of yore) endeavoured to grasp the fundamental truths of Being. They tried to solve the problems of the origin, the nature, and the destiny of man and of the universe. They attempted to grasp the meaning and value of *knowing* and *being*. They endeavoured to find a solution for the problems of the means of life and the world, and of the relation of the individual to the 'Unseen' or the Supreme Soul. They sought earnestly for a satisfactory solution of these profound questions: "Who am I? What is this universe or Samsara? Whence are we born? On what do we rest? Where do we go? Is there any such thing as Immortality, Freedom, Perfection, Eternal Bliss, Everlasting Peace, Atman, or Brahman (the Self or the Supreme Soul which is birthless, deathless, changeless, self-existent)? How to attain Brahman or Immortality?"

There is no book in the whole world that is so thrilling, soul-stirring, and inspiring as the Upanishad. The philosophy taught by the Upanishads has been the source of solace for many both in the East and the West. The human intellect has not been able to conceive of anything more noble and sublime in the history of the world than the teachings of the Upanishads.

They are rich in profound philosophical thought. They are regarded as the very acme of philosophical thought. Their intrinsic value is very great. There is depth of meaning in the verses. The language is beautiful. The Upanishads have undoubtedly exercised and will continue to exercise a considerable influence on the religions and philosophies of the world. They present a view of Reality which would certainly satisfy the scientific, the philosophic, as well as the religious aspirations of man.

Origin of the Upanishads

The Rishis and seers of yore practised right living, Tapas, introspection, self-analysis, enquiry, and meditation on the pure, inner Self, and attained Self-realisation. Their intuitions of deep truths are subtle and direct. Their inner experiences which are direct, first-hand, intuitive, and mystical, which no science can impeach, and which all philosophies declare as the ultimate goal of their endeavours, are embodied in the sublime books called the Upanishads.

Knowledge of the Upanishads destroys ignorance, the seed of Samsara. Knowledge of Brahman is called Upanishad, because it leads to Brahman and helps the aspirants to attain Brahman. The term Upanishad is applied to the book also in a secondary sense by courtesy.

The Upanishads are the knowledge portion or Jnana Kanda of the Vedas. They are eternal. They came out of the mouth of Hiranyagarbha or Brahma. They existed even before the creation of this world.

Upanishads are a source of deep mystic divine knowledge which serves as the means of escape from this formidable Samsara. They are world-scriptures. They appeal to the lovers of religion and truth in all races, and at all times. They contain profound secrets of Vedanta and Jnana Yoga, and practical hints and clues which throw much light on the pathway to Self-realisation. The glory or grandeur of the Upanishads cannot be adequately described in words because words are finite and language is imperfect. The Upanishads have indeed greatly contributed to the peace and solace of mankind. They are highly elevating and soul-stirring. Millions of aspirants have drawn inspiration and guidance from the Upanishads. They are the cream of the Vedas. They are treasures of incalculable value.

Significance and Ideal

There are four Vedas, viz., Rik, Yajus, Saman, and Atharva. There are as many Upanishads to each Veda as there are Sakhas or branches (subdivisions). There are 21, 109, 1000, and 50 subdivisions to Rik, Yajus, Saman, and Atharva Vedas respectively. Thus there are one thousand one hundred and eighty (1,180) Upanishads.

In Muktikopanishad of Sukla-Yajurveda, Sri Rama says to Hanuman: "The only means by which one can attain liberation is by understanding and meditation on the teachings of Mandukya-Upanishad alone, which is enough for the salvation of all aspirants. If wisdom is not attained thereby, study the Ten Upanishads and if thy Jnana is not made firm, read and meditate well on the teachings of the Thirty-two Upanishads. Thou shalt get embodied liberation. If thou longest after disembodied salvation study the One Hundred and Eight Upanishads".

The following two ideas dominate the teachings of all the Upanishads: (1) Final emancipation can be attained only by knowledge of the Ultimate Reality or Brahman (Brahma-Jnana), (2) He who is equipped with the four means of Salvation, viz., discrimination, dispassion, sixfold virtues, and yearning for liberation, can attain Brahman. The Upanishads teach the philosophy of Absolute Unity.

The goal of man according to the Upanishads is realisation of Brahman. Self-realisation alone can dispel ignorance and give immortality, eternal bliss, and everlasting peace. Knowledge of Brahman alone can remove all sorrows, delusion, and pain.

Anubandha Chatushtaya

The subject matter (Vishaya) of the Upanishads is the highest Brahman or Supreme Soul. The fruit (Prayojana) of this knowledge is the attainment of Immortality or Moksha and the consequent freedom from the bondage of Samsara (Atyanta Samsara Nivritti and Brahmaprapti). The connection (Sambandha) has also been stated as the achievement of this result through the Upanishads. The person (Adhikari) entitled to study the Upanishads, to practise the enquiry of Brahman, and meditation on the Self is one who is equipped with the four means of salvation. This is Anubandha Chatushtaya.

Vidyas in Upanishads

The Vidyas or mystic meditations on Brahman are described in the Upanishads, mainly the Chhandogya and the Brihadaranyaka. In the Chhandogya Upanishad we have Sat Vidya, Bhuma Vidya, Sandilya Vidya, Dahara Vidya, Vaisvanara Vidya, Panchagni Vidya, Udgita Vidya, Purusha Vidya, Samvarga Vidya, Madhu Vidya, Prana Vidya, Upakosala Vidya, Akshi Vidya, Aditya Vidya, Satyakama Vidya, Akasa Vidya, Svetaketu Vidya, etc. In Brihadaranyaka Upanishad Maitreyi Vidya, Akshara Vidya, Antaraditya Vidya, Ushasta-Kahola Vidya, Uddalaka-Aruni Vidya, and Jyotisham Jyotir-Vidya are important ones. Bhrigu-Varuni Vidya, Anandamaya Vidya, and Satya-Jnana-Ananta Vidya of

Taittiriyopanishad, and Shodasakala Vidya of Prasnopanishad are also important ones.

All these Vidyas lead one from the unreal to the Real, from darkness to Light, from mortality to Immortality. They lead the soul from the Mula-Ajnana to the Highest Brahman either through Krama-Mukti or Sadyo-Mukti. These Vidyas are helpful in meditation both on the Saguna Brahman and on the Nirguna Brahman. There are, according to the Brahma-Sutras, three kinds of meditation: Nirguna, Saguna, and Pratika,—unconditioned or attributeless, conditioned or qualified, and symbolical or idolatrous. Many of the Vidyas abound in qualitative and relative conceptions of the Highest Self. But, in spite of this limitation, these Vidyas can be utilised even for Nirguna meditation, provided the meditator conceives of the absolute aspect of the descriptions given therein and avoids all dual and gradatory differentiations. Even then, some Vidyas like the Brahma Vidya, the Maitreyi Vidya, etc., are highly useful even for Ahamgraha Upasana and Nirguna Dhyana of the Vedantins. Meditation must be practised only on one Vidya suitable to the temperament of the meditator. The fruit of these meditations is Atyantika Sukha or absolute happiness, free from the pains of birth, life, and death in Samsara. These Vidyas cannot be meditated upon without being directly initiated by a Guru (spiritually qualified preceptor). They are very complex and hard to understand for oneself without a guide.

79. VAIRAGYA

There is a way to the immortal abode. There is a way to supreme happiness. There is a way to the fourth dimension. That way is Vairagya. Follow the way. Follow the way.

Vairagya is dispassion, desirelessness, or non-attachment. It is indifference to sensual objects herein and hereafter. It is born of and sustained by right discrimination or Sad-viveka.

Vairagya is the opposite of Raga or attachment. Raga binds a man to Samsara; Vairagya liberates a man from bondage.

Vairagya thins out the fatty sensual mind. It turns the mind inward. Vairagya is the most important qualification for a spiritual aspirant. Without it, no spiritual life is possible.

The Pull of Raga-Dvesha

The two currents of the mind—attraction and repulsion—really constitute the world of Samsara. A worldly man is a slave of these two mighty currents. He is tossed about hither and thither like a piece of straw. He smiles when he gets pleasure; he weeps when he gets pain. He clings to pleasant objects; he runs away from objects that cause pain.

Wherever there is sensation of pleasure, the mind gets glued, as it were, to the object that gives pleasure. This is what is called attachment. This only brings bondage and pain. When the object is either withdrawn or when it perishes, the mind gets unspeakable pain. Attraction is the root cause for human sufferings.

A dispassionate man has a different training. He has a different experience altogether. He is a pastmaster in the art or science of separating himself from the impermanent, perishable objects. He has absolutely no attraction for them. He constantly dwells in the Eternal. He stands adamantine as a peak amidst a turbulent storm, as a spectator of this wonderful world-show.

A dispassionate man has no attraction for pleasant objects and no repulsion for painful ones. Nor is he afraid of pain. He knows well that pain helps quite a lot in his progress and evolution, in his journey towards the goal. He stands convinced that pain is the best teacher in the world.

How to Cultivate Vairagya

Vairagya comes through looking into the defects of sensual life. Look into the defects of sensual life or sensual pleasure. You will develop dispassion.

When you are not impressed with rich living, rich style of living cannot attract you. When you are impressed with the idea that meat and wine are not at all pleasurable, meat and wine cannot tempt you. When you are impressed that a woman is nothing but a leather-bag of pus, urine, bones, and flesh, woman cannot tempt you. In that case, if you fail to get meat or wine or woman, or to have a rich living, you will not be agonised at all in your mind.

Aspirants should study Bhartrihari's *Vairagya Satakam* and other works on Vairagya. These will increase your desire for liberation and your conviction in spiritual life. Sri Rama describes the disastrous effects of lust, wealth, the miseries of birth, and infancy. A beautiful description is given in the Vairagya Prakarana of the Yoga-Vasishtha. Everyone should read it. This will induce Vairagya in the mind.

Degrees in Vairagya

There are different degrees in Vairagya. Supreme dispassion or Para Vairagya comes after one attains Self-realisation. The whole world then looks like a straw. The Vairagya becomes perfectly habitual. That is intense spiritual strength. That is Para Vairagya.

Temporary fleeting dispassion is not Vairagya. It will not help the aspirant in the attainment of Self-realisation. It is common to have dispassion for some particular objects, by some cause or the other. But, it is only by having dispassion for all objects at all times that one will get Knowledge of the Self.

Intense Vairagya only will help the aspirant to stick to the spiritual path. Karana Vairagya born of disappointment, loss, death of relatives, will leave you at any moment. It will be waiting for chances to seize again the objects that were once renounced. It will evaporate quickly like ether, chloroform, or ammonia.

But the Vairagya that is born of Viveka is enduring and everlasting. It will not fail the aspirant at any time like the Vairagya that comes temporarily when a lady gives birth to a child or when a man attends a funeral in the crematorium.

Real Vairagya should come from enquiry, Vichara. All these objects do not give us lasting happiness. They lead us into pain and sorrow. Such deep enquiry, again and again persisted in for a very long time, produces lasting Vairagya. It is the real wealth for an aspirant. It helps him to do real Sadhana. It makes the mind introvert. This Vairagya puts a break to the extrovert tendency of the mind. Even if the mind runs towards objects, at once it will point out that there is pain there, that sensual enjoyment is the cause for rebirth and intense suffering. So the mind is terribly afraid, and gradually, through intense practice, it is established in real, lasting, sustained, intense Vairagya.

The mind should gradually be weaned off its old habits and cravings. If you cut off all at once its pleasure-centres, it will get puzzled. You should slowly train the mind in meditation and make it taste the inner bliss. Gradually, it will leave off its old habits and old cravings, and you can get yourself established in true Vairagya

Vairagya—A Mental State

Vairagya does not mean abandoning social duties and the responsibilities of life. It does not mean detachment from the world. It does not mean a life in the solitary caves of the Himalayas or in the crematorium. It does not mean living on neem-leaves, cow's urine and dung. It does not mean wearing of matted hair and a Kamandalu made of gourd or coconut-shell in the hand. It does not mean shaving of head and throwing off clothes. Vairagya is mental detachment from all connections of the world.

A man may remain in the world, and discharge all the duties of his order and stage of life with detachment. He may be a householder. What if? He may live with family and children. But at the same time, he may have perfect mental detachment from everything. He can do his spiritual Sadhana. That man who has perfect mental detachment while remaining in the world is a hero, indeed. He is much better than the Sadhu living in the cave of the Himalayas, because the former has to face innumerable temptations at every moment of his life.

Wherever a man may go, he carries with him his fickle, restless mind, his Vasanas and Samskaras. Even if he lives in solitude in the Himalayas, still he is the same worldly man if he is engaged in building castles in the air and in thinking of the objects of the world. In that case, even the cave becomes a big city for him. If the mind remains quiet, if it is free from attachments, one can be a perfect Vairagi even while living in a mansion in the busiest part of a city like Calcutta. Such a mansion will be converted into a dense forest by him. Vairagya is purely a mental state.

Generally, aspirants say, "I have given up shirt"; "I have given up sweater"; "I have given up shoes"; "I live only on bread and Dhal". Their whole Sadhana consists in 'giving up'—give up this, give up that. Real spiritual life does not involve any giving up or taking. The only thing is you should not give leniency to the mind. If you are very hungry in the morning, take one or two *Iddlies* and a small cup of milk. But do not give leniency to the mind. It will hurl you down. Always be watchful. Be eternally vigilant.

Some Sannyasins practise Vairagya in order to get Pratishtha or fame and respect. Some Sannyasins, working for the public good, make resolves: "We will not travel in trains. We will walk only. We will not take milk, fruits, etc. We will not use fountain-pens or watch". These are not desirable resolves. This is not the real nature of Vairagya. This is another kind of defect.

Attachment to Vairagya is as much an evil as attachment itself. These Sannyasins want to do service. If they move in cars or trains, if they keep the body strong and healthy, they can do more service in a short space of time. Those who do much writing work can turn out much work they use a fountain-pen. Foolishness assumes various forms. This is one kind. It does not leave even educated persons or cultured Sannyasins.

You should have extreme or Teevra Vairagya internally, and at the same time, follow the middle path externally.

Vairagya is a means for attaining Wisdom of the Self. It is not the goal Itself. A Jivanmukta or realised sage has neither Raga nor Vairagya. If you give him a little dry bread alone, he is quite satisfied. He will not grumble. If you give him the best sweetmeats, milk and fruits, he will not refuse, but he will not be elated by good food. He has equanimity of mind. He is above likes and dislikes. He always takes delight in his own Self only, but not in external objects.

Maha-Tyagi and Maha-Bhogi

He who is endowed with equanimity of mind towards objects is called a Maha-Tyagi and Maha-Bhogi in the Yoga-Vasishtha. It is easy to practise Vairagya, but it is extremely difficult to keep the evenness of mind.

Sukadeva was tested by Raja Janaka. He was made to remain without food at the gate for some days. He was quite peaceful. Then he was taken to the harem. Ranis served him and gave him best food. He remained unaffected. This is wisdom.

Young aspirants should be very careful and cautious. They should not take advantage of the liberty of a Maha-Tyagi and Maha-Bhogi. This can be practised only by an advanced Yogin who has got equal vision over all beings. Beginners should stick to their resolves of truth, Ahimsa, Brahmacharya, and Vairagya to the very letter and spirit.

Do not imitate Jivanmuktas. You are still a Sadhaka, Vasishtha had a wife, but he was a born Siddha. Janaka ruled a kingdom after severe Tapas and realisation of the Truth. Krishna lived a princely life, but He was one with the Infinite. You are not expected to behave like them. You must do Sadhana. You must have Abhyasa and Vairagya.

80. VEDANTA

Vedanta is Brahma-Vidya. It is the Moksha-Sastra or the Science of Emancipation.

Absolutism is the pivot of the Vedanta philosophy. The Upanishads form the basis of Vedanta.

Vedanta reveals the majesty of man in his essential nature. The oneness of all existence is the message which Vedanta teaches.

Vedanta upholds the reality of the indivisible, immanent, and transcendent Spirit. It does not exclude matter. It does not exclude anything.

Vedanta is the basic culture of India. It is the national philosophy of India. It is the summit or peak or acme of Indian philosophy. It has kept Hindu society alive for the past eight thousand years.

The Gospel of the Vedanta

Vedanta is the only bold philosophy which dares call man God, not merely the son of God, or His servant. It proclaims with emphasis that you are the immortal, all-pervading Atman, the Universal Soul or Supreme Brahman in essence, in reality.

Boldness is the keynote of Vedanta. The message of Vedanta is fearlessness, soul-force, and unity of consciousness.

Vedanta does not ask for converts or proselytes, but a deeper reassessment of the divine-human equation, a return to the fundamental question of every being: "What am I really? What is my real Self?".

Vedanta proclaims: "Man, in essence, is identical with the Supreme Being". Vedanta reminds you of your true, essential, divine nature. Vedanta says: "O little man! Do not identify yourself with this perishable body. Give up 'I-ness' and 'mine-ness'. Do not hate your neighbour or brother. Do not try to exploit him. He is your own Self. There is a common Self or common Consciousness in all. This is the same in a king and a peasant, an ant and a dog, a man and a woman, a cobbler and a scavenger. This is the real, immortal entity. Mind is the dividing principle. It tempts, deludes. Kill this mischievous mind. Control the senses which drag you out to the external objects. Fix the mind in the source. Rise above body and mind. Eradicate desires. Learn to discriminate the Real from the unreal. Identify yourself with this immortal, non-dual, self-existent, self-luminous Essence. Behold the one Self in all. See the One in many. All miseries will come to an end".

The student of Vedanta puts the Neti-Neti doctrine into daily practice. He says: "I am not this perishable body. I am not this mind. I am not this Prana. I am not the Indriya". 'Neti, Neti' means 'not this, not this'. This is the path of negation. But he tries to identify himself with the all-pervading Atman or Self. This practice culminates in the attainment of Self-realisation. It leads to the immediate intuition of the all-filling Brahman.

Who Is Qualified to Study Vedanta?

The path of Vedanta is not so easy as it is generally supposed to be. It is a sharp and razor-edge path. It is certainly not meant for all.

It is very, very easy to say, "Soham. Sivoham. Aham Brahmasmi. I am He. I am Siva. I am Brahman"—like a parrot. But to live in the very spirit of Vedanta, to feel the oneness or unity of consciousness, to become 'That' in reality and to radiate the Brahmic bliss, joy and peace, is an extremely difficult affair. While repeating 'Soham', if the man's mind is easily upset when another utters a single harsh word, and if he begins to fight with that other man vehemently, there is no use at all in that repetition. It is mere hypocrisy. He will not be able to influence others. People will take him for a cheat.

Vedanta can be practised only by those who are endowed with real, lasting, deep Vairagya or dispassion, and who lead the path of renunciation. Vedanta is for a select few who are equipped with the Four means of salvation and who have removed the impurities of their minds and mental oscillation through constant practice of Nishkamya Karma Yoga and Upasana.

Wholesale preaching of Vedanta to the masses is not advisable. It will result in chaos, bewilderment, and stagnation. Grasping of Vedantic principles and a right understanding of the philosophy and Sadhana are very difficult.

Universality of the Vedanta Philosophy

Vedanta denotes one's identity with the rest of humanity. According to Vedanta, there is no stranger in this world. Everyone is related to one another in the kinship of the Spirit In Vedanta, there is no 'mine' and 'for me'; but 'ours' and 'for us'; and ultimately, 'His' and 'for Him'. If the Vedanta philosophy is rightly understood and acted up to, then it will obliterate all evils that emanate from factional and racial prejudices.

Vedanta is no creed, no ceremony or form of worship. It is the science of right living. It is not the sole monopoly of the Hindus or the recluses. It is for all.

Vedanta is the property of all. It has no quarrel with any religion whatsoever. It preaches universal principles. Vedanta is the only universal, eternal religion. It is a great leveller. It unites all. It gives room to all.

Vedanta encloses within its sphere all the religions of the world and is strong enough to make them all useful and enduring. Vedanta never interferes with forms. It concerns itself solely with the life of religions. The Christian need not renounce his Christianity, the Buddhist may stick to his Noble Eightfold Path, the Mohammedan may stick to his Koran, and yet all these may follow the Vedanta and realise in practice all its high ideals and truths. Their love to their respective prophets and bibles will become more sober, more enlightened, and more enduring. Religious animosity will vanish and the world will move on to its great end without any friction, with greater dignity and more goodwill among its denizens.

Vedanta means no slavery. It gives freedom to all. It embraces one and all. It includes one and all. It is the religion of the Upanishads. It is the religion of Paramahamsa Sannyasins.

Vedanta never condemns any man as beyond hope, never looks upon anyone as accursed, but takes all mankind within its fold. Vedanta is extremely catholic and liberal in its outlook.

Vedanta can offer to the modern society a common faith, a common body of principles, and a common moral discipline. It is highly scientific in outlook and has a real appeal to men and women of today.

There is no philosophy so bold and sublime as the philosophy of the Vedanta. It is Vedanta alone that can eradicate totally human sufferings and can bring everlasting peace and happiness. Even a little understanding and a little practice of Vedanta can raise a man to magnanimous heights of Brahmanhood or God-consciousness and remove all sorts of fears, worries, and anxieties of this mundane life.

A Misunderstanding

Some ignorant people only say that Vedanta preaches immorality, hatred, and pessimism. This is a very sad mistake.

Vedanta does not preach either immorality or even indifference to morality. Vedanta wants you to destroy Moha or selfish love and passion for the body, and develop pure, disinterested cosmic love or the magnanimous divine Prem. The realisation of Brahman is not possible for the immoral.

Vedanta never preaches pessimism, but it preaches the pinnacle of optimism. It preaches, "Give up this little illusory pleasure. You will get eternal and infinite Bliss. Kill this little 'I'. You will become one with the Infinite. You will become immortal. Give up this illusory world. You will get the vast domain of supreme peace or Kingdom of God". Is this pessimism? Certainly not. It is wonderful optimism.

Vedanta and Socialism

Some say that the socialist movement is an offshoot of Vedanta only which speaks of equal vision and equal treatment. They say, "We are Vedantins".

Socialists say, "We do not want capitalists, Rajas, and emperors. The state will look after the education of all children. We will give food to all from the common kitchen. We will issue tickets to the cinema. We will take care of all people. Let all work according to their capacity, temperament, ability. The public will have ample leisure, study, amusement, fun, and frolic. They will be very happy. They will have no cares and worries. They will have plenty of bread and jam".

This philosophy is nice. But it is Virochana's philosophy. It is only the philosophy of flesh. Their goal is comfortable living. Comfortable living is the enemy of peace and divine wisdom. Bread and jam cannot make one perfect and immortal. It cannot confer salvation. It will not lead to the attainment of the knowledge of the Eternal.

The foundation of society, the substratum or background for the whole universe, body, mind, and the senses, is the Absolute or the Atman, the Immortal Soul. An 'ism which denies the existence of such a source and support, which has not Self-realisation as the goal of life or *summum bonum,* will soon dwindle into an airy nothing.

Common kitchen is not Vedanta. Socialism is not Vedanta. Socialism cannot remove all social evils. It cannot contribute to perfect peace and bliss of men. That philosophy, that discipline alone can lead to perfect bliss, everlasting happiness, and immortality which can help to control the mind and the senses, remove ignorance, and attain knowledge of the Imperishable.

Pseudo-Vedantins

Vedanta is today a much abused term. All sorts of vanity, hypocrisy, and self-conceit have been masquerading in its name. It has become the fashion of the day to pass for a Vedantin.

Man feels ashamed to call himself a Bhakta, but he takes great pride in calling himself a Yogin or a Vedantin, because he foolishly imagines he will be respected by the public.

Licentiousness is mistaken for a life of expansion. If a man can eat anything in any hotel in any part of the world, if he can move socially with any man or woman, that does not mean he is a Vedantin. There is much tall talk of Vedanta nowadays. There is idle Vedantic gossiping. But, there is no real, practical Vedanta. Nobody wants to do any real, solid Vedantic Sadhana. People talk of unity, oneness, and equality, but fight out for little useless things. They are full of jealousy and hatred. I cannot imagine. I am simply stunned.

Practice of Vedanta

I believe in practical Vedanta. I believe in solid spiritual practices. I believe in thorough overhauling of worldly nature, worldliness of various sorts.

You must put Vedanta in daily practice, in every action of yours. Vedanta teaches oneness or unity of Self. You must radiate love to one and all. The spirit of Vedanta must be ingrained in your cells, tissues, veins, nerves, and bones. It must become part and parcel of your nature. You must think of unity, speak of unity, and act in unity.

You must be a practical Vedantin. You should live in the spirit of Vedanta. Mere theorising and lecturing is only intellectual gymnastics and lingual warfare. This will not suffice. What is the use of reading too many books on Vedanta, Chit-Sukhi, Khandana Khanda Khadyam, etc.? They will intoxicate you and lead you astray.

The sun, the flowers, the Ganga, the sandal trees, the fruit-bearing trees, the cows—all teach practical Vedanta to the world. They live for serving the humanity in a disinterested spirit. The sun radiates its light alike over a cottage of a peasant and a palace of a Maharaja. The flowers waft their fragrance to all without expecting anything. The cool refreshing waters of the Ganga are drunk by all. The sandal tree wafts its aroma even to the man who cuts it with an axe. All fruit-bearing trees behave in the same manner. They please the gardener who nourished them as well as the man who cuts them. The cows live to nourish the babies, the children, the invalids, and the convalescents. Imagine for a moment that the world is devoid of cows for six months or the race of cows has become extinct. How miserable and weak you will become! The world will abound with anaemic patients. O selfish, ignorant man! Learn lessons from these practical Vedantins and become wise.

Vedanta or the Knowledge of the Self is not the sole property of Sannyasins or recluses. Study the Upanishads and you will find that many Kshatriya kings who were very busy in the affairs of life were in possession of Brahma-Jnana. They gave instructions to Brahmana priests even.

Vedanta does not require colouring of cloth. Vedanta does not want you to retire to Himalayan caves. It can be practised at home. It can be practised in all circumstances of life.

Vedanta does not preach a doctrine of negation of human effort. It wants you to have a changed mental attitude. It demands a changed angle of vision. Till now, the world was everything. Hereafter, the Reality alone is everything.

Learn to discriminate between the permanent and the impermanent. Behold the Self in all beings, in all objects. Names and forms are illusory. Therefore sublate them. Feel that there is nothing but the Self. Share what you have, physical, mental, moral or spiritual, with all. Serve the Self in all. Feel when you serve others, that you are serving your own self. Love thy neighbour as thyself. Melt all illusory differences. Remove all barriers that separate man from man. Mix with all. Embrace all. Destroy the sex-idea and body-idea by constantly thinking on the Self or the sexless, bodiless Atman. Fix the mind on the Self when you work. This is practical Vedanta. This is the essence of the teachings of the Upanishads and sages of yore. This is real, eternal life in Atman. Put these things in practice in the daily battle of life. You will shine as a dynamic Yogin or a Jivanmukta. There is no doubt of this.

81. VEDAS

The term 'Veda' comes from the root 'Vid', to know. The word 'Veda' means knowledge. When it is applied to scripture, it signifies a book of knowledge. The Vedas are the foundational scriptures of the Hindus. The Veda is the source of the other five sets of scriptures, viz., Smritis, Itihasas, Puranas, Agamas, and Darsanas, why, even of the secular and the materialistic knowledge. The Veda is the storehouse of Indian wisdom and is a memorable glory which man can never forget till eternity.

Revealed Truths Without Beginning or End

The Vedas are the eternal truths revealed by God to the great ancient Rishis of India. The word Rishi means a seer, and is derived from *Dris,* to see. He is the Mantra-Drashta, a seer of Mantra or thought. The thought was not his own. The Rishis saw the truths or heard them. Therefore, the Vedas are what are heard—'Sruti'. The Rishi did not write. He did not create it out of his mind. He was the seer of thought which existed already. He was only the spiritual discoverer of the thought. He is not the inventor of the Vedas. The Srutis are called the Vedas or the Amnaya. The Hindus have received their religion through revelation, the Vedas. These are direct intuitional revelations and are held to be *Apaurusheya* or entirely superhuman, without any author in particular. In that sense the Vedas are eternal. Vedas are eternal spiritual truths. Vedas are an embodiment of divine knowledge. The books may be destroyed, but the knowledge cannot be destroyed. Knowledge is eternal. Vedas came out of the breath of the Lord. They are without beginning and end.

The Vedas represent the spiritual experiences of the Rishis of yore. All the other religions of the world claim their authority as being delivered by special messengers of God to certain persons, but the Vedas do not owe their authority to anyone. They are themselves the authority as they are eternal, as they are the Knowledge of the Lord.

Lord Brahma, the Creator, imparted the divine knowledge to the Rishis or seers. The Rishis disseminated the knowledge. The Vedic Rishis were great realised persons who had direct intuitive perception of Brahman or the Truth. They were inspired writers.

They built a simple, grand, and perfect system of religion and philosophy, from which the founders and teachers of all other religions have drawn their inspiration.

The Vedas are the oldest books in the library of man. The truths contained in all religions are derived from the Vedas, and are ultimately traceable to the Vedas. The Vedas are the fountainhead of religion. The Vedas are the ultimate source to which all religious knowledge can be traced. Religion is of divine origin. It was revealed by God to man in the earliest times. It is embodied in the Vedas.

The Four Vedas and Their Subdivisions

The Veda is divided into four great books: the Rig-Veda, the Yajur-Veda, the Sama-Veda, and the Atharva-Veda. The Yajur-Veda is again divided into two parts, the Sukla and the Krishna. The Krishna or the Taittiriya is the older book, and the Sukla or the Vajasaneya is a latter revelation to sage Yajnavalkya from the resplendent Sun-god.

The Rig-Veda is divided into twenty-one sections, the Yajur-Veda into one hundred and nine sections, the Sama-Veda into one thousand sections, and the Atharva-Veda into fifty sections. In all, the whole Veda is thus divided into one thousand one hundred and eighty parts.

Each Veda consists of four parts: the Mantra-Samhitas, the Brahmanas, the Aranyakas, and the Upanishads. The division of the Vedas into four parts is to suit the four stages in a man's life.

The Mantra-Samhitas are hymns in praise of the Vedic God for attaining material prosperity here and happiness hereafter. They are metrical poems comprising prayers, hymns, and incantations addressed to various deities, both subjective and objective. The Mantra portion of the Vedas is useful for the Brahmacharins.

The Brahmanas guide people to perform sacrificial rites. They are prose explanations of the method of using the Mantras in the Yajna or the sacrifice. The Brahmana portion is suitable for the householders.

The Aranyakas are the forest books, the mystical sylvan texts which give philosophical interpretations of the rituals. The

Aranyakas are intended for the Vanaprasthas or hermits, who prepare themselves for taking Sannyasa.

The Upanishads are the most important portion of the Vedas. The Upanishads contain the essence or the knowledge portion of the Vedas. The philosophy of the Upanishads is sublime, profound, lofty, and soul-stirring. The Upanishads speak of the identity of the individual soul and the Supreme Soul. They reveal the most subtle and deep spiritual truths. The Upanishads are useful for the Sannyasins.

The subject matter of the whole Veda is divided into Karma-Kanda Upasana-Kanda, and Jnana-Kanda. The Karma-Kanda or ritualistic section deals with various sacrifices and rituals. The Upasana-Kanda or worship section deals with various kinds of worship or meditation. The Jnana-Kanda or knowledge section deals with the highest knowledge of Nirguna Brahman. The Mantras and the Brahmanas constitute Karma-Kanda; the Aranyakas, Upasana-Kanda; and the Upanishads, Jnana-Kanda.

The Mantra-Samhitas

The Rig-Veda Samhita is the grandest book of the Hindus, the oldest and the best. It is the great Indian Bible, which no Hindu would forget to adore from the core of his heart. Its style, the language, and the tone are most beautiful and mysterious. Its immortal Mantras embody the greatest truths of existence and it is perhaps the greatest treasure in all the scriptural literature of the world. Its priest is called the Hota.

The Yajur-Veda Samhita is mostly in prose and is meant to be used by the Adhvaryu, the Yajur-Vedic priest, for superfluous explanations of the rites in sacrifices, supplementing the Rig-Vedic Mantras.

The Sama-Veda Samhita is vastly borrowed from the Rig-Veda Samhita, and is meant to be sung by the Udgata, the Sama-Vedic priest, in sacrifice.

The Atharva-Veda Samhita is meant to be used by the Brahma, the Atharva-Vedic priest, to correct the mispronunciations and wrong performances that may accidentally be committed by the other three priests of the sacrifice.

The Brahmanas and the Aranyakas

There are two Brahmanas to the Rig-Veda—the Aitareya and the Sankhayana. "The Rig-Veda", says Max Muller, "is the most ancient book of the world. The sacred hymns of the Brahmanas stand unparalleled in the literature of the whole world; and their preservation might well be called miraculous" (History of Ancient Sanskrit Literature).

The Satapatha Brahmana belongs to the Sukla Yajur-Veda. The Krishna Yajur-Veda has the Taittiriya and the Maitrayana Brahmanas. The Tandya or Panchavimsa, the Shadvimsa, the Chhandogya, the Adbhuta, the Arsheya, and the Upanishad Brahmanas belong to the Sama-Veda. The Brahmana of the Atharva-Veda is called the Gopatha. Each of the Brahmanas has got an Aranyaka.

The Upanishads

The Upanishads are the concluding portions of the Vedas, or the end of the Vedas. The teaching based on them is called Vedanta. The Upanishads are the gist and the goal of the Vedas. They form the very foundation of Hinduism.

There are as many Upanishads to each Veda as there are Sakhas or branches (subdivisions), i.e., 21, 109, 1000, and 50 respectively to the Rik, Yajus, Saman, and Atharva Vedas.

The different philosophers of India belonging to different schools such as Non-dualism or Monism, Qualified Monism, Dualism, Pure Monism, etc., have acknowledged the supreme authority of the Upanishads. They have given their own interpretations, but they have obeyed their authority. They have built their philosophy on the foundation of the Upanishads.

Even the Western scholars have paid their tribute to the seers of the Upanishads. At a time when the Westerners were clad in barks and were sunk in deep ignorance, the Upanishadic seers were enjoying the eternal bliss of the Absolute and had the highest culture and civilisation.

The most important Upanishads are Isa, Kena, Katha, Prasna, Mundaka, Mandukya, Aitareya, Taittiriya, Chhandogya, Brihadaranyaka, Kausitaki, and Svetasvatara. These are supremely authoritative.

May the fundamental truths of the Vedas be revealed unto you all like the Amalaka fruit in the palm of your hand. May Gayatri, the blessed Mother of the Vedas, impart to you the milk of knowledge, the ancient wisdom of the Upanishads.

82. VEGETARIANISM

Sage Uddalaka instructs his son Svetaketu: "Food when consumed, becomes threefold. The gross particles become the excrement, the middling ones flesh, and the fine ones the mind. My child, when curd is churned, its fine particles which rise upwards form butter. Thus, my child, when food is consumed, the fine particles which rise upwards form the mind. Hence, verily, the mind is food".

Mind is formed of the subtlest portion of food. If the food is impure, the mind also becomes impure in its workings. This is the dictum, both of the ancient sages of India and of the modern psychologists.

That food does wield a tremendous influence on the mind can be seen in everyday life around us. After a heavy sumptuous, indigestible meal, it is very difficult to control the mind; it runs, wanders, and jumps like an ape, all the time. Alcohol causes great excitement in the mind.

Three Kinds of Diet

Diet is of three kinds, viz., Sattvic diet, Rajasic diet, and Tamasic diet. In the Bhagavad-Gita, Lord Krishna says to Arjuna: "The food which is dear to each is threefold. The foods which increase vitality, energy, vigour, health, and joy and which are delicious, bland, substantial, and agreeable are dear to the pure. The passionate persons desire foods that are bitter, sour, saline, excessively hot, pungent, dry, and burning, and which produce pain, grief, and disease. The food which is stale, tasteless, putrid, rotten, and impure, is dear to the Tamasic".

Milk, barley, wheat, cereals, butter, cheese, tomatoes, honey, dates, fruits, almonds, and sugar-candy are all Sattvic foodstuffs. They render the mind pure and calm and play a very important part in the practices of spiritual aspirants, in the mental development of the student, and in the personality-power of the leaders of mankind. Fish, eggs, meat, salt, chillies, and asafoetida are Rajasic foodstuffs; they excite passion and make the mind restless, unsteady, and uncontrollable. Beef, wine, garlic, onions, and tobacco are Tamasic foodstuffs. They exercise a very unwholesome influence on the human mind and fill it with emotions of anger, darkness, and inertia.

Stress on Moral and Spiritual Values

No doubt, animal diet may produce a strong Sandow, or a dauntless soldier, or a keen, brainy scientist. But, in the Hindu view of life, the real value is placed upon the moral and spiritual worth of the man.

Man is more than just body and mind; he is essentially an ever-perfect, ever-pure, and ever-free spirit in his true inner nature. Human birth is given as an opportunity and a means to attain this sublime knowledge of his inner spiritual nature and to regain his divinity. In this process, all grossness and animalistic tendencies have to be totally eliminated from the human personality. Non-vegetarian diet, which is gross and animal by its very nature, is a great hindrance to this process. Whereas, pure Sattvic diet is a great help to the refinement of the human nature.

The chemical components of different foods vibrate at varying rate. Each particle of food is a mass of energy. The intake of certain foodstuffs sets up discordant vibrations in the physical body which throw the mind into a state of oscillation and disequilibrium. Concentration of mind is rendered difficult and high thinking is disturbed, because elevating thoughts imply fine vibrations.

Meat Diet Generates Diseases

Meat generates diseases, excites passions, and produces restlessness of mind. Scientists are coming to the conclusion that there are, in meat, certain things which are absolutely poisonous. A very large number of medical men who have studied the subject of diet in relation to health are forbidding their patients to eat animal flesh, not only as a means of cure for such diseases as gout, rheumatism, etc., but also as a preventive against uric-acid ailments and diseases of many kinds, including consumption, cancer, and appendicitis.

Meat is not at all necessary for the keeping up of perfect health, vigour, and vitality. On the contrary, it is highly deleterious to health; it brings in its train a host of ailments such as tapeworm, albuminuria, and other diseases of the kidneys. In large meat-eating countries, cancer mortality is admittedly very high.

Flesh-eating Involves Cruelty

Moreover, flesh-eating involves the exercise of cruelty which is not an elevating virtue. It is a bestial quality which degrades man. Cruelty is condemned by all great men. Pythagoras condemned meat diet as sinful food. The cruel slaughter of animals and the taking of innocent lives which flesh-eating entails makes it abhorrent to all right thinking men and women all over the world.

Butchery and bloodshed is a great disgrace to civilisation and culture. Killing of animals for food is a great blunder; and the mentality it engenders is fraught with potential dangers for the life of humanity, a recognition of which made George Bernard Shaw say that as long as men torture and slay animals and eat their flesh, we shall have war.

Abolish Slaughter-houses

If you want to stop taking mutton, fish, etc., just see with your own eyes the pitiable, struggling condition of the animals at the time of killing. Now mercy and sympathy will arise in your heart. You will determine to give up flesh-eating. If you fail in this attempt, just change your environments and live in a vegetarian hotel where you cannot get mutton and fish, and move in that society where there is only vegetable diet. Always think of the evils of flesh-eating and the benefits of a vegetable diet. If this also cannot give you sufficient strength to stop this habit, go to the slaughter-house and the butcher's shop and personally see the disgusting, rotten muscles, intestines, kidneys and other nasty parts of the animals which emit bad smell. This will induce Vairagya in you and a strong disgust and hatred for meat-eating.

All slaughter-houses should be abolished, and the use of animal flesh as food should be absolutely given up. Flesh-eating is unnecessary, unnatural, and unwholesome. The countless instances of reputed philosophers, authors, scholars, athletes, saints, Yogins, Rishis who lived on vegetable diet conclusively prove that vegetarian diet produces supreme powers both of mind and body, and is highly conducive for divine contemplation and practice of Yoga.

Man is created a frugivorous or fruit-eating creature. This scientific fact is evident on a comparison with the carnivorous animals from whom he differs completely in respect of his internal organs, teeth, and external appearances, whereas, anatomically, he is most intimately allied to the anthropoid apes whose diet consists of fruits, cereals, and nuts.

When man abandons flesh foods and takes his nutriment direct from nature's hand, of well-ripe and healthy fruits and grains, nuts and vegetables with the addition of honey, cheese and milk, we shall find a large number of diseases disappearing. People will have more power of endurance and attain longevity.

What is needed is a well-balanced diet, not a rich diet. A rich diet produces diseases of the liver, kidneys, and pancreas. A well-balanced diet helps a man to grow, to turn out more work, increases his body-weight, and keeps up efficiency, stamina, and a high standard of vim and vigour.

People who are slaves to the flesh-eating habit cannot give up animal diet, because they have become confirmed and inveterate meat-eaters, and hence they try to justify their habit by various arguments and statistics. One cannot change their ways merely by argumentation and disputation. Ultimately, it is only the force of personal example that has a strong effect upon the people around you.

83. WOMAN

Woman is the mighty work of God, the wonder of nature, the marvel of marvels, the abridgement and epitome of the world, the queen of the house, the real governor, the sweet companion and helpmate of man.

Woman is Chaitanya Maya. She is the energy-aspect of the Lord. She is the child of Adi Sakti. She holds the key of this world. She controls the destiny of children. She is the mother of Sankaras, Buddhas, and Janakas.

Woman is a mysterious mixture of softness, gentleness, and gracefulness. She is a compound of service, patience, and love. She is an emblem of beauty. She is full of sweetness. She is Maya's tempting charm and magic. She comforts and cheers up her husband, children, and guests. Even Brahma, the Creator, failed to describe her fully. She is some mysterious something that gives charm to this world. Without her, the house is a void. Without her, man is helpless. Without her, this world loses all charm. Without her, there is no creation.

Woman, the Mother

Woman is a cheering companion for you in distress. She bears all difficulties and sorrows patiently. She wipes your tears when you are smitten with grief. How patient and enduring she is! She spends sleepless nights in nursing the children. What a lot of pain she undergoes in child-bearing and care for the child, and by submission to her husband? Have you ever thought of this seriously, friends? Without woman, the beginning of your life is helpless, the middle destitute of happiness, and the end would be without consolation.

The beginning of your life was in the mother's breath. Your first small words are taught from her lips. She is your first teacher and Guru. It is she who wiped your first tears. It is she who watches your last breath and last sighs, when men have shrunk from attending on you.

In the West, the woman is wife. In India, the woman is the mother. The mother is worshipped. In the West, the wife governs the home. In an Indian home, the mother rules. In the West, the mother has to be subordinate to the wife. In India, the wife has to be subordinate to the mother.

India recognises the ideal of motherhood as the highest for a woman. It is not for nothing that we worship the Motherhood of God in Kali and other goddesses, and our own country we call as Matrubhumi.

The idea that man and woman are equals is a purely Western concept. The Indian or Hindu concept is that man and woman, Purusha and Sakti, are one and indivisible. Wife is Ardhangini. She ever dwells in her husband. She occupies half the body of her Lord. Sita did not think herself a separate entity. She was in and of Rama. The Indian woman always identifies herself completely with her husband in all domestic, religious, and social life. No religious ceremony can be performed by the husband without his wife. The Vedic hymns chant of her: "Be an empress to your father-in-law. Be an empress to your mother-in-law. Be an empress to your husband's brothers and sisters". She is the queen of the house. She illumines the home through the glory of motherhood.

Pativrata-Dharma

The chief duty of a woman is to maintain her Pativrata-Dharma. Pati means husband. Vrata means a vow. Pativratyam is a Mahavratam or great vow for a woman. A Pativrata is a chaste woman who has taken the vow of Pativratyam, who sticks to her Pativrata-Dharma even at the risk of her life, who is faithfully devoted to her husband, who worships her husband as the Lord, and who serves him with heart, mind, and soul. For a Pativrata, her husband is all in all. He is her sole refuge, protector, saviour, and God. She deifies him as the Lord, and adores him day and night. An evil thought can never enter her mind even in her dream. Anasuya, Savitri, Nalayani are examples of true Pativratas. A woman who practises Pativrata-Dharma need not go even to temples for worship. The Lord of the temple is in her husband.

Ladies, by their Pativrata-Dharma, can do anything. Savitri brought back life to her dead husband Satyavan. She fought with the God of Death actually. You are all aware of the chastity of Anasuya, wife of Atri, mother of Sri Dattatreya. She turned the Trimurtis as her children by her power of chastity.

The wife should not look to the defects of her husband. Even if the husband is blind and deaf, even if the husband is extremely poor and illiterate, even if he is suffering from an incurable chronic disease, even if he is easily irritable and mean, the wife should serve him whole-heartedly. She must love him with a full heart. She should speak to him with warm affection. This is difficult; but, gradually she will gain strength of mind, power of endurance, through the grace of the Lord.

Even if the husband is unrighteous, the wife should be faithful to him. She should pray to God to put him in the path of righteousness, to infuse in his heart faith and devotion, and to make him realise God-consciousness. A chaste wife who is sticking tenaciously to her Dharma can change the life of her husband to the path of righteousness even if he is leading a wicked life. Many have done so.

Sacred Ideals of Indian Womanhood

If a woman be pure, she can save and purify man. Woman can purify the race. Woman can make a home a sacred temple. The Hindu women have been the custodians of the Hindu race. The Hindu religion, the Hindu culture and civilisation, still survives in spite of the many foreign invasions, when other civilisations have come and gone, on account of the purity of Hindu women. The women are taught to regard chastity as their most priceless possession, and the loss of it as equal to the eternal damnation of their souls. Religion is ingrained in the Hindu women from her very childhood. Hindu women illumine and enliven the house through the glory of their purity.

The eternal fidelity of a Hindu woman to her husband makes her an ideal of the feminine world. From time immemorial, Sita, Savitri, Damayanti, Nalayani, Anasuya, and Draupadi have been regarded as sacred Ideals of Indian womanhood. They are sublime and exemplary characters who have exalted womanhood to the height of divine perfection. All of them were subjected to very severe tests in which their purity, courage, patience, and other virtues were severely tried, and nobly did they come out through those tests.

Ladies of modern times should draw inspiration from them. They should try to lead the life they led. There is no use in becoming a star in the glittering cinema firmament which is set with dark, dense clouds. This is a very poor ambition of ignorant persons. They should not come under the poisonous, materialistic influence. They have no idea of real independence. To move freely here and there, to do everything, to eat and drink anything, to imitate others, to drive a car, to go to the courts and do the work of a barrister is not independence.

Woman in the West

Woman in the West has opened a new chapter in her life. She is dazzled by the glamorous rush and speed of the modern age. She does not like to do her household duties. You can find her now in the House of Parliament, or at the typewriter. She is a telephone operator, she is a pilot, a film-star, a shop-girl. She is proud of the work she does. She compliments herself that she is sharing and lessening the work of man. Gradually, she has got into his trousers. She vies with man in his field, and tries to oust and replace him.

She has asserted her rights and has broken the four walls of her home. She works in the war zones and industries. She thinks that she lives a glorious life. But, it is not so. She is not really peaceful and happy.

Home—The Proper Sphere for Woman

Women of India should not try to imitate the ladies of the West. India is India. It is a spiritual country. It is a country of sages, Rishis, Yogins and Yoginis, and philosophers. It is an unprecedented country in matters that relate to the soul or the Adhyatmic science. The ladies will have to play a very important part in the religious field, and in training of children.

Women can no more do men's work in the world than men can do women's. By taking part in politics, by exercising political power, by becoming voters or law-makers, women cannot attain enlightenment and refinement. If women become salaried workers, if they withdraw from their home, the result will be disastrous. There will be subversion of domestic discipline and family order, and family-social decay. Children grow up uneducated and neglected.

The finer affections and sentiments get blunted. Woman is no more the gentle wife, partner of man. She becomes his fellow-labourer or fellow-worker.

The performance of domestic duties, the management of her household, the rearing of children, the economising of the family means—these are the woman's proper office. Woman is already endowed with divine power. She already governs the whole world by her power of love and affection. To make noble citizens by training their children, and to form the character of the whole human race, is undoubtedly a power far greater than that which women could hope to exercise as voters, or law-makers, or presidents, or ministers, or judges.

One Sachi rocked the cradle of her son with the Dhvani of Hari's Name, infused in him the honey of devotion, and brought forth to the world a Gauranga who changed the mentality of the people of Bengal. Shivaji imbibed from his mother the spirit that worked in him; her true blood ran through his veins and made him what he turned out to be. Addison's mother—and not his ignorant teachers—answered his obstinate questions.

Women should become good mothers only. This is the function they will have to perform in the grand plan of God. This was meant in the divine plan. This is the will of God. Women have their own psychological traits, temperament, capacities, virtues, instincts, and impulses. They have got their own disadvantages in society. They cannot, and should not, compete with men. They should not do the work of men.

Education of Women

Women should certainly be educated. I do not oppose giving them education and freedom. I have the highest veneration for women. I adore them as Devis. But, I am not in favour of such freedom for women as will ruin them. I am in favour of such education and culture as will make them ideal women.

Women should have a knowledge of Sanskrit. It is the duty of parents to give their daughters Sanskrit education. This is indispensable. Women should have a knowledge of the Gita, the Bhagavata, the Ramayana, and other holy scriptures. They should know something of hygiene, domestic medicine, nursing of the sick, training of children, dietetics, gynaecology, etc.

A woman can have knowledge of medicine, law, biology, and science for her own enlightenment, but not for the sake of getting a job. She can be a doctor to serve the poor and her family members.

She can be a teacher to teach her own children and the poor children in the vicinity.

Educated ladies can do any useful service to society according to their capacity, taste, temperament, aptitude, nature and standard of education, in a manner that is consistent or in perfect agreement with established principles or Dharmas of their mode of life. They should not do anything that can bring dishonour or infamy on them and their family, and a blot on their character. Without character, a man or woman is considered as dead while living.

The ideal woman is one who manages the house efficiently, who looks after the comforts of the husband and serves him as God, who trains the children to become good citizens, who leads a chaste and virtuous life, and who plays the noble and important part of a good wife and a good mother. Women should become ideal wives and mothers. This is nature's scheme in the grand plan. O Devis! Fulfil this and be happy for ever.

84. YOGA

To live in God, to commune with God, is Yoga. Life in God brings eternal bliss.

Yoga shows you the way. Yoga unites you with God. Yoga makes you immortal.

Yoga is complete life. It is a method which overhauls all the sides of the human personality.

Yoga is a system of integral education, education not only of the body and the mind or the intellect, but also of the inner spirit.

Yoga shows you the marvellous method of rising from badness to goodness, and from goodness to godliness, and then to eternal divine splendour.

Yoga is the art of right living. The Yogin who has learnt the art of right living is happy, harmonious, and peaceful. He is free from tension.

Yoga is a science perfected by ancient seers of India, not of India merely, but of humanity as a whole. It is an exact science. It is a perfect, practical system of self-culture.

A Way of Life

Yoga does not want a turning away from life. It demands spiritualisation of life.

Yoga is primarily a way of life, not something which is divorced from life. Yoga is not forsaking of action, but is efficient performance in the right spirit. Yoga is not running away from home and human habitation, but a process of moulding one's attitude to home and society with a new understanding.

Yoga Is Universal

Yoga is for all. Yoga is universal. It is not a sectarian affair. It is a way to God and not a creed.

The practice of Yoga is not opposed to any religion or any sacred Church. It is purely spiritual and universal. It does not contradict any one's sincere faith.

Yoga is not a religion, but an aid to the practice of the basic spiritual truths in all religions. Yoga can be practised by a Christian or a Buddhist, a Parsee, a Mohammedan, a Sufi or an atheist.

To be a Yogin means to abide continuously in God and to live at peace with men. Yoga is union with God. Yoga is union with all. God dwells in all.

Yoga Is not Physical Exercise

The idea of the novice that Yoga constitutes physical exercises or mere Asanas and Pranayama, etc., is a terrible error. Yogasanas, Pranayama, Bandhas, Mudras, and Kriyas have nothing to do with real Yoga. They are considered to be aids in Yoga practice.

Most people do not have access to Yoga beyond its physical level, because true Yoga needs intense personal discipline coupled with intense thinking under the guidance of an able teacher. Yoga promises superphysical and spiritual blessing. It becomes unattractive to a common man who clamours for immediate fruits and worldly prosperity.

Prerequisites for Yoga Life

Moral purity and spiritual aspiration are the first steps in the path of Yoga. One who has a calm mind, who has faith in the words of his Guru and Shastras, who is moderate in eating and sleeping, and who has the intense longing for deliverance from the Samsara-Chakra is a qualified person for the practice of Yoga.

An aspirant in the path of Yoga should have faith, energy, cheerfulness, courage, patience, perseverance, sincerity, purity, lack of despondency of mind, dispassion, aspiration, concentration, serenity, self-restraint, truthfulness, non-violence, non-covetousness, etc.

An austere and simple life is indispensable for Yoga. The foundation of Yoga is self-control. Discipline is the essence of Yoga, discipline of the body as well as discipline of the mind.

In the practice of Yoga, there is a reversal of the normal outgoing activity of the mind. Steadiness of mind is very essential for a reversal of the normal outgoing activity of the mind. Unless the mind is first made steady and brought under complete control, it will not be possible to change its course to the opposite direction.

The Four Paths

The four main spiritual paths for God-realisation are Karma Yoga, Bhakti Yoga, Raja Yoga, and Jnana Yoga. Karma Yoga is suitable for a man of active temperament, Bhakti Yoga for a man of devotional temperament, Raja Yoga for a man of mystic temperament, and Jnana Yoga for a man of rational and philosophical temperament.

Karma Yoga is the way of selfless service. Bhakti Yoga is the path of exclusive devotion to the Lord. Raja Yoga is the way of self-restraint. Jnana Yoga is the path of wisdom.

Karma Yoga is the exercise of the will. Jnana Yoga is the exercise of the intellect and reason. Bhakti Yoga is the exercise of the emotion. Will consecrates all activities through complete surrender to God. The intellect realises the glory and majesty of the Lord. The emotion experiences the bliss of divine ecstasy.

The three eternal truths are: Jnana, Karma, and Bhakti. God is love, goodness, and truth. God is experienced by the devotee as love. God is experienced by the Karma Yogin as goodness. God is experienced by the Jnani as truth.

Some maintain that the practice of Karma Yoga alone is the means to salvation. Some others hold that devotion to the Lord is the only way to God-realisation. Some believe that the path of wisdom is the sole way to attain the final beatitude. There are still others who hold that all the three paths are equally efficacious to bring about perfection and freedom.

The Yoga of Synthesis

One-sided development is not commendable. Religion must educate and develop the whole man—his heart, intellect, and hand. Then only he will reach perfection.

Man is a strange, complex mixture of will, feeling, and thought. He wills to possess the objects of his desires. He has emotion; and so he feels. He has reason and so he thinks and ratiocinates. In some the emotional element may preponderate, while in some others the rational element may dominate. Just as will, feeling and thought are not distinct and separate, so also, work, devotion, and knowledge are not exclusive of one another.

In the mind, there are three defects, viz., Mala or impurity, Vikshepa or tossing, and Avarana or veil. The impurity should be removed by the practice of Karma Yoga. The tossing should be removed by worship or Upasana. The veil should be torn down by the practice of Jnana Yoga. Only then Self-realisation is possible.

If you want to see your face clearly in a mirror, you must remove the dirt in the mirror, keep it steady, and remove the covering also. You can see your face clearly on the surface of a lake only if the turbidity is removed, if the water that is agitated by the wind is rendered still, and if the moss that is lying on the surface is removed. Even so is the case with Self-realisation.

Action, emotion and intelligence are the three horses that are linked to this body-chariot. They should work in perfect harmony or unison. Then only the chariot will run smoothly. There must be integral development. You must have the head of Sankara, the heart of Buddha and the hand of Janaka.

The Yoga of Synthesis alone will bring about integral development. The Yoga of Synthesis alone will develop the head, heart, and hand, and lead one to perfection. To become harmoniously balanced in all directions is the ideal of religion. This can be achieved by the practice of the Yoga of Synthesis.

To behold the one Self in all beings is Jnana, wisdom; to love the Self is Bhakti, devotion; to serve the Self is Karma, action. When the Jnana Yogin attains wisdom, he is endowed with devotion and selfless activity. Karma Yoga is for him a spontaneous expression of his spiritual nature, as he sees the one Self in all. When the devotee attains perfection in devotion, he is possessed of wisdom and activity. For him also, Karma Yoga is a spontaneous expression of his divine nature, as he beholds the one Lord everywhere. The Karma Yogin attains wisdom and devotion when his actions are wholly selfless. The three paths are, in fact, one in which the three different temperaments emphasise one or the other of its inseparable constituents. Yoga supplies the method by which the Self can be seen, loved, and served.

Benefits of Yoga Practice

Life today is full of stress and strain, of tension and nervous irritability, of passion and hurry. If man puts into practice a few of the elementary principles of Yoga, he would be far better equipped to cope with his complex existence.

Yoga brings in perfection, peace, and lasting happiness. You can have calmness of mind at all times by the practice of Yoga. You can have restful sleep. You can have increased energy, vigour, vitality, longevity, and a high standard of health. You can turn out efficient work within a short span of time. You can have success in every walk of life. Yoga will infuse in you new strength, confidence, and self-reliance. The body and mind will be at your beck and call.

Yoga brings your emotions under control. It increases your power of concentration at work. Yoga discipline gives poise and tranquillity and miraculously rebuilds one's life. The Yoga way of life deepens man's understanding and enables him to know God and his relationship with Him.

Yoga leads from ignorance to wisdom, from weakness to strength, from disharmony to harmony, from hatred to love, from want to fullness, from limitation to infinitude, from diversity to unity, and from imperfection to perfection. Yoga gives hope to the sad and forlorn, strength to the weak, health to the sick, and wisdom to the ignorant.

Through Yogic discipline, mind, body and the organ of speech work together harmoniously. For a Yoga practitioner, a new outlook, a new health, a new awareness and a new philosophy rush in and vividly transform his life.

Lust for power, material greed, sensual excitement, selfishness, passion for wealth, and lower appetites have drawn man from his true life in the spirit into the materialistic life. He can regain his lost divine glory if he practises, in right earnest, the principles of Yoga. Yoga transmutes animal nature into divine nature and raises him to the pinnacle of divine glory and splendour.

Spiritual Growth Is Gradual

It is within the power of everybody to attain success in Yoga. What is wanted is sincere devotion, constant and steady Abhyasa.

Spiritual growth is gradual. There is progressive evolution. You should not be in a feverish hurry to accomplish great Yogic feats or enter into Nirvikalpa Samadhi, in two or three months.

The senses have to be thoroughly subjugated. Divine virtues have to be cultivated. Evil qualities have to be eradicated. The mind has to be controlled thoroughly. The task is a stupendous one. It is an uphill work. You will have to practise rigorous Tapas and meditation and wait patiently for the results. You will have to ascend the ladder of Yoga step by step. You will have to march in the spiritual path stage by stage.

A Note of Caution

After attaining perfection in Yoga, one can enter the world if he is not affected even a bit by the unfavourable, hostile currents of the world. Many persons enter the world before perfection in Yoga to demonstrate their minor powers in the name of Loka-Sangraha and for fame. They have been reduced to a level worse than that of a worldly man.

If a Yogin is not careful, if a Yogin is not well-established in the preliminary practices of Yama, Niyama, he is unconsciously swept away from his ideal by temptation—Mara or Satan. He uses his powers for selfish ends and suffers a hopeless downfall. His intellect becomes blind, perverted, and intoxicated. His understanding gets clouded. He is no longer a divine Yogin. He becomes a black-magician or Yogic charlatan. He is a black sheep within the fold of Yogins. He is a menace to the society at large.

Many people are attracted to the practice of Pranayama and other Yogic exercises, as it is through Yoga that psychic healing, telepathy, thought-transference, and other great Siddhis are obtained. If they attain success, they should not remain there alone. The goal of life is not 'healing' and 'Siddhis'. They should utilise their energy in attaining the highest.

Yoga is not for attaining Siddhis or powers. If a Yogic student is tempted to attain Siddhis, his further progress is seriously retarded. He has lost the way.

The Yogin who is bent upon getting the highest Samadhi must reject Siddhis whenever they come. Siddhis are invitations from Devatas. Only by rejecting these Siddhis can one attain success in Yoga.

Do not stop Sadhana when you get a few glimpses and experiences. Continue the practice till you attain perfection. Do not stop the practice and move about in the world. Examples are not lacking. Numerous persons have been ruined. A glimpse cannot give you safety.

85. YOGASANAS

Yogic culture is divided into eight Angas or limbs or steps, viz., Yama, Niyama, Asana, Pranayama, Pratyahara, Dharana, Dhyana, and Samadhi. The first two accessories of Yoga are Yama and Niyama. Asana is the third Anga of Ashtanga-Yoga, while Pranayama is the fourth Anga.

If the foundation of a building is not properly laid, the superstructure will fall down in no time. Even so, if you want to enjoy the full spiritual benefits of Asanas, you must first practise well the first two steps, Yama and Niyama.

Similarly, if a Yogic student has not gained mastery over the Asanas, he cannot successfully proceed in his higher courses of Yogic practices. When you are established in Asana, then only you will derive the benefits of Pranayama.

Kinds of Asanas

The Asanas or postures are as many in number as there are species of living creatures in this universe. There are eighty-four lakhs of Asanas, corresponding to the eighty-four lakhs of bodies. The Asanas correspond to the different modes of sitting found in the different types of creation.

Among the eighty-four lakhs of Asanas, eighty-four are the best; and among these eighty-four, thirty-two have been found very useful for mankind.

Asanas can be divided into two broad divisions, viz., meditative poses, and poses for health and strength. According to Yoga Sastras, there are four excellent meditative poses: Padmasana, Siddhasana, Svastikasana, and Sukhasana.

The Meditative Poses

The meditative poses are highly suitable for Japa and contemplative purposes. They detach the mind from the cares and worries of everyday life. They soothe the nerves, relax the body, steady the mind, and give poise. The meditative poses increase the digestive fire and give good appetite, health, and happiness. They remove rheumatism. They keep the wind, bile, and phlegm in proper proportions. They purify and strengthen the nerves of the legs and thighs. They are suitable for keeping up Brahmacharya.

'*Sthira Sukham Asanam*—Posture is that which is firm and comfortable'. It should not cause any painful sensation or trouble. If the Asanas are not firm, the mind will be disturbed quickly. You will not have concentration of mind. The body must be firm as a rock. There must not be the least shaking of the body. You must become as a living statue when you sit for Dhyana. If the seat becomes firm, you will have progress in your meditation. You will have no consciousness of the body.

When you sit in the posture, think: "I am as firm as rock. Nothing can shake me". Give these suggestions to the mind a dozen times. Then the Asana will become steady soon.

You must be able to sit in any one of the four meditative poses at a stretch for full three hours without shaking the body. Then only will you get Asana Jaya or mastery over the Asana. If you can be steady in the posture even for one hour, you will be able to acquire one-pointed mind and feel thereby infinite peace and Atmic Ananda inside.

In one year, by regular practice, you will have success; and you will be able to sit for three hours at a stretch. Start with half an hour and gradually increase the period.

If there is severe pain in the legs after some time, unlock the legs and then shampoo them for five minutes and sit again in the Asana. When you advance, you will not experience any pain. You will experience, on the other hand, immense joy. Practise the Asana both morning and evening.

Stick to one Asana, either Padma, Siddha, Svastika or Sukha; and make it quite steady and perfect by repeated attempts. Never change the Asana. Adhere to one tenaciously. Cling to it like a leech. Realise the full benefits of one Asana for meditation.

The Cultural Poses

Among the cultural poses, there are some Asanas which can be practised while standing. They are Tadasana, Trikonasana, Garudasana, etc. There are some which can be practised sitting. They are Paschimottanasana, Janusirshasana, Padmasana, Lolasana, etc. Some are practised while lying down. These are Uttanapadasana, Pavanamuktasana. Weak and delicate persons can do Asanas while lying down. Some Asanas such as Sirshasana,

Vrikshasana, Sarvangasana, Viparitakarani Mudra, etc., are done with head downwards and legs upwards.

Yogasanas and Physical Exercises

Ordinary physical exercises develop the superficial muscles of the body only. One can become a Sandow with a beautiful physique. But, Asanas are intended for the thorough exercise of the internal organs, viz., the liver, spleen, pancreas, intestines, heart, lungs, brain, and the important ductless glands of the body. Asanas tone the internal organs and vitalise the thyroid and other endocrine glands which play a very important part in maintaining health.

Physical exercise draw the Prana out. Asanas send the Prana in and distribute it quite evenly throughout the body and different systems.

Asanas are not mere physical exercise alone. They are something more than that. They bestow mental poise. They help you in controlling the emotions. They confer spiritual benefits.

Asanas awaken the Serpent-Power or Kundalini that is sleeping in the Muladhara Chakra. This gives bliss, power, and Yogic Samadhi to the aspirant. If you do Dand and Baithaks five hundred times a day or pumping marches on the parallel bars fifty times a day for five years, they will not in any way help in the awakening of this mysterious power, Kundalini. Do you see the difference now?

No expense is needed for the practice of Asanas. You do not need bar-bells, springs, weights, and parallel bars for constructing the Yogin's gymnasium. At the most, what you need is a simple, soft blanket to practise Asanas over.

Who Can Practise Asanas?

Generally, after the age of ten or twelve, these Asanas can be practised. People of twenty or thirty years of age perform all Asanas nicely. Practice for a month or two will render all rigid tendons, muscles, and bones very elastic. Even old persons can practise all Asanas. They can give up Sirshasana if they are not physically fit. There are persons of advanced age who practise Sirshasana also.

Ladies also should practise Asanas. If ladies practise a course of Asanas systematically with interest and attention, they will have wonderful health and vitality. If mothers are healthy and strong, children also will be healthy and strong. Regeneration of the young ladies means the regeneration of the whole world.

Therapeutic Value of Yogic Exercises

Asanas keep the muscles supple and the spine elastic, develop mental faculties and lung capacity, strengthen the internal organs, and bestow longevity. By the practice of Yogasanas, the blood is charged with abundant oxygen; the accumulation of veinous blood is stopped. The body is filled with abundant energy. The brain centres and the spinal cord are strengthened and renovated. Memory is improved. Intellect is sharpened. Intuition is developed.

The practice of Asanas establishes physiological balance in the body and secures mental poise also. Yogic exercises help to relax the body so as to dispel nervous tension.

Practice of Asanas removes diseases and makes the body light, firm, and steady. A particular Asana removes a particular disease. Mark this wonderful power of Asana.

Sirshasana is useful in foggy brain. It bestows brain-power and develops the intellect and the memory. It helps the storage of Ojas-Sakti in the brain. It is useful in maintaining Brahmacharya. It cures many diseases. It improves eyesight and hearing capacity through extra circulation of blood in the brain box.

Sarvangasana develops the thyroid gland, strengthens the lungs and the heart, and makes the spine elastic.

Sirshasana and Sarvangasana increase the vitality and prevent old age. They give elasticity to the spine. They revitalise and rejuvenate the entire system. The pituitary glands are toned and energised.

Matsyasana is good for the development of the lungs, the brain, and the eyes; it also strengthens the upper part of the spine.

Paschimottana and Mayura Asanas increase the digestive fire and improve digestion. Paschimottanasana reduces fat in the belly.

Bhujangasana, Salabhasana, and Dhanurasana, increase the peristaltic movement of the bowels, remove constipation, and cure the diseases of the abdomen. Rolling from side to side in Dhanurasana gives very good abdominal massage.

Agnisara Kriya, Uddiyana Bandha, and Mayurasana also help

digestion and give good appetite. Ardhamatsyendrasana is good for the liver and the spleen.

Tadasana, Trikonasana, and Garudasana increase the height of the body.

Savasana relaxes the body and the mind, and gives perfect poise and rest.

You are not practising Asanas and Pranayama in order to gain big muscles. Muscles do not mean health. The healthy, and harmonious functioning of the endocrine glands and the internal viscera, and more so, of the nervous system and the mind—this is what you need and what the regular practice of Yoga Asanas and Pranayama will bestow upon you.

86. ZOROASTRIANISM

Zoroastrianism is the religion of the Parsees. The correct name for the religion established by Zoroaster is Mazdayasnism which means the worship of Mazda or the Lord.

Mazdayasnism was first revealed by Homa to king Jamshid. Afterwards it was revealed to king Fiedoon. Then it was revealed to Thirta. Lastly it was revealed to Zoroaster.

After the death of Zoroaster his son-in-law Jamaspa became his successor. Jamaspa wrote down the teachings of Zoroaster which are known as Zend Avesta, the scriptures of the Zoroastrians. Frashaoshtra, the father-in-law of Zoroaster was the first apostle of this faith. He expounded the tenets of this religion. Zoroastrianism became the state religion of Persia.

After the time of Zoroaster, Zoroastrianism underwent many changes at the hands of the priests who were called Magi. The priests reintroduced ritualism and the worship of the old nature-deities in a new garb by making them archangels of Ahura Mazda.

Zoroaster was not a philosopher or a metaphysician. He was only a prophet who had the divine revelation. Zoroastrianism is not a system of philosophy. It is a revealed religion of faith and devotion. During the days of Zoroaster there was an urgent need for ethics and virtuous life. The need for philosophy did not arise. At all times the need to lead a virtuous, divine life, is far more imperative for the vast majority than the need to understand the various philosophical problems. If one leads the divine life according to the instructions of the sages and scriptures, one will find a solution for all the philosophical problems from within through the voice of the Indweller.

The principal truths taught by Zoroaster were based on and derived from the Vedas. Zoroastrianism is based on the Vedic religion. The doctrines and ceremonials of the Zoroastrians have a mostly remarkable similarity to those of the Vedas.

Zoroastrian Scriptures

The Yasna and the Visparad are the Vedas of Zoroastrianism. The first part of Yasna consists of Gathas or hymns which came from the mouth of the prophet. The Gathas are five in number. The

Gathas are written in metres which correspond to the metres of the Sama-Veda. The second part of Yasna contains prayers addressed to the Supreme Lord and other deities who form the spiritual hierarchy.

Visparad is a collection of invocations or litanies which are recited before other prayers and scriptures. The twenty-one Nasks deal with all kinds of sciences, viz., medicine, astronomy, agriculture, botany, etc. They correspond to the Vedangas of Hinduism. Then there is the Khordah Avesta or little Avesta which contains Yashts (invocations) and prayers for the use of lay persons. The modern Parsees recite these prayers daily.

Zoroastrian scriptures are called Zend Avesta. They contain three parts. The first is Vendidad. This contains religious laws and ancient mythical tales. The second is Visparad. The third is Yasna. The Avesta contains direct conversations between Zoroaster and Ahura Mazda, the Supreme Lord.

Ethics of Zoroaster

The following are the ethical teachings of Zoroaster: To do good actions; to be pure in thought, word, and deed; to have a clean heart; to wish others' good; to speak the truth; to do charity; to be kind; to be humble; to attain knowledge; to control anger; to be pious; to respect parents, the teachers, and the old and the young; to utter sweet and pleasant words; to be patient; to be friendly towards all; to be contented; to feel shame for doing forbidden actions.

Teachings

Zoroastrianism teaches that Ahura Mazda created man and gave him his body and mind. Ahura Mazda is the protector and nourisher of all. Man is responsible for his thoughts, speeches, and actions. Individual will and individual intellect are connected with the cosmic will and cosmic-intellect.

Ahura Mazda created this world in six periods. Mashya and Mashyana are the first man and woman created by God. During the deluge an underground palace 'Vara of Yima' was built for the protection of all creatures.

Zoroastrianism is a religion of absolute faith and unswerving devotion to Ahura Mazda. A devotee bows, prays, and sacrifices.

He makes offerings unto the Lord. He prays and Ahura Mazda grants all his wishes. He prays to remove his sins by repentance.

Zoroastrianism teaches that the goal of life is to attain perfect eternal happiness through companionship with Ahura Mazda. The means for attaining the everlasting bliss is Asha or holiness. Holiness or purity is the soul of Zoroastrianism.

Pure thoughts, pure words, pure deeds—this is the famous axiom of Zoroastrian religion. This is the constantly reiterated rule of the Zoroastrian life. Pure thoughts, pure words, pure actions can be practised only through faith in the Ahura Mazda, the Lord of righteousness. The word Asha includes all the principles of morality. The word Asha comes in almost every chapter of the Zend Avesta. Zoroastrianism teaches that holiness is happiness, and that is the most precious gift of Ahura Mazda and that is the best offering to be presented to the Lord by the virtuous.

A Zoroastrian must act in harmony with the will of God. He should study the scriptures and perform his duty to God and his fellowmen. He should strictly observe the divine laws. Then only he will attain holiness and happiness.

General

Just as the Jews place their hope in Messiah, the Hindus on the coming Kalki Avatara, so also the Parsees have been looking forward to the birth of Saoshyant who will establish on earth righteousness and happiness.

There is no Tapas or austerity in Zoroastrianism in order that the body may not be weakened and rendered unfit for work.

Reincarnation is not found in the scriptures as accepted by orthodox Parsees, but it is taught in the fragments preserved by the Greeks and in the Desatir.

Parsees perform prayers for the dead at stated fixed periods. They perform ancestor-worship and do anniversaries for the dead in an elaborate manner.

GLOSSARY

of Indian Terms

NOTE

1. All Indian terms used in this book, excepting those whose meaning in English is available in the text itself (simultaneously or almost simultaneously with the occurrence of the Indian terms), have been included in this glossary.

2. The meaning of compound words, where such words have not been specifically included in the glossary, may be made out by referring to the separate meanings of their component terms in the glossary.

A

Abhanga—a devotional poetic composition

Abhimana—ego-centred attachment

Abhyasa—spiritual practice

Acharya—preceptor

Adhara Suddhi—purification of the Muladhara, centre of spiritual energy located at the base of the spinal column

Adhara—support

Adharma—non-righteous conduct

Adhikari—a qualified person

Adhyatmic—spiritual

Adi Sakti—the Primeval Power

Advaita—non-duality

Agami—current action, Karma now produced to be enjoyed in the hereafter

Agni—fire

Aham Brahma asmi (Aham Brahmasmi)—a Vedantic assertion meaning "I am Brahman"

Ahamta—I-ness

Ahankara—egoism

Ahimsa—non-violence
Aisvarya—divine powers
Ajati-Vada—the theory of non-evolution
Ajna Chakra—centre of spiritual energy between the two eye-brows
Akasa—ether
Akasavani—ethereal voice
Akshara—the imperishable Brahman; the sacred monosyllable OM
Amalaka—the Indian gooseberry
Amara-Purusha—immortal being
Amnaya—the Vedas
Amsa-Avatara—part-incarnation
Anahata—mystic sounds heard by Yogis
Analhaq—a Sufistic assertion meaning "I am He"
Ananda Kutir—abode of bliss
Ananda Svarupa—of the form of bliss
Ananda—bliss
Anatma—not-Self
Anga—a limb, a part
Anna-Dana—charity of food
Antahkarana—the inner instrument; the enternal organ
Antaratma—the Inner Self
Antaryami (n)—the Inner Witness
Anubhava—experience
Anusandhana—enquiry into the nature of Brahman
Anushthana—performance of certain religious rites in accordance with definite scriptural injunctions
Apara Bhakti—devotion of a lower grade
Apara Brahman—the sound Omkara, the first manifestation of the transcendent Brahman
Aparoksha—direct
Apsara—a celestial nymph
Archana—devout offering
Ardhangini—consort, the female half
Arhata—a perfected soul
Aryavarta—India, the land of the Aryans

Asamprajnata Samadhi—superconscious state where the mind is totally annihilated
Asana—pose
Asanti—restlessness
Ashram—a hermitage
Ashtakshara Mantra—the eight-lettered Mantra of Lord Narayana
Ashtakshari—same as above
Ashtanga Yoga—the eight-limbed Raja Yoga of Maharshi Patanjali
Asrama-Bheda—distinction between the different orders of life
Asrama—order of life
Asura—a demon
Asuric—demoniac
Atma(n)—the Self
Atma-Bhava—seeing everything as the Self
Atma-Chintana—contemplation on the Self
Atma-Jnana—Knowledge of the Self
Atma-Nivedana—devout offering to the Self
Atma-Sakshatkara—Self-realisation
Atma-Samarpana—same as Atma-Nivedana
Atma-Sankalpa—the will of the Atman
Atma-Svarajya—freedom of the Self
Atma-Vichara—enquiry into the nature of the Self
Avadhuta—a naked Sadhu
Avatara—incarnation
Avidya—nescience
Ayah—a maid-servant
Ayudha Puja—worship of weapons and instruments performed on the ninth day of the Navaratri festival
Ayurveda—the ancient Indian science of medicine

B

Babu—a gentleman
Badam—almond
Badmash—a rogue
Badshah—emperor
Bahurupi—an actor who appears in many roles
Bandha—bondage; a Hatha Yogic Kriya

Bania—trader
Banki-Behari—Krishna, wanderer in the woods
Bansiwala—Krishna, the flute-bearer
Bhagavan—the Lord
Bhagavathar—one who discourses on the glories of the Lord
Bhaitak—an exercise involving alternate sitting and standing
Bhajan(a)—singing the glories of the Lord
Bhakta—a devotee
Bhakti—devotion
Bharatavarsha—India, the land of Bharata
Bhasma—sacred ash
Bhava(na)—attitudinal feeling
Bhayanak Sabda—a fear-inducing sound
Bhedabheda—a system of Indian philosophy
Bhiksha—alms collected by the mendicant
Bhogi—enjoyer
Bhuma—the Unconditioned, the Great Infinite, Brahman
Bhuta—element
Bhuta Siddhi—a psychic power by which mastery is gained over the elements
Brahma—the Creator, the first of the Hindu trinity
Brahma-Bhavana—feeling that all, indeed, is Brahman
Brahmabhyasa—constant practice of the above feeling
Brahmachari (n)—a celibate
Brahmacharya—celibacy
Brahma-Chintana—constant thinking of Brahman
Brahma-Jnana—Direct Knowledge of Brahman
Brahma-Loka—the celestial sphere of Brahma, the Creator
Brahma-Muhurta—the early morning hours most conducive to spiritual practice
Brahman—the Absolute Reality
Brahmana—a member belonging to the priestly Hindu caste
Brahma-Nishtha—one who is established in the Knowledge of Brahman
Brahma-Parayana—one whose faith and sole refuge is in Brahman
Brahmarandhra—opening of the skull, head fontanelle

Brahma-Rishi—the highest category of Hindu Rishis or seers
Brahma-Srotri—one who has knowledge of the Vedas and the Upanishads
Brahma-Tejas—spiritual halo
Brahma-Vidya—the science of Brahman
Brahmin—same as Brahmana
Brij Raj—Krishna, the Lord of the land of Brij
Buddhi—intellect

C

Chaitanya—pure consciousness
Chakra—a centre of spiritual energy
Chandala—an outcaste
Chandana—sandal paste
Charana—a class of astral beings
Charvaka—a leader of the Hindu school of epicureanism
Chinmaya—full of consciousness
Chiranjivi—one who has gained eternal life
Chit—consciousness
Chitta—subconscious mind
Chyavanaprash—an Ayurvedic tonic
Croropati—a billionaire

D

Daivic—divine
Daivi Sakti—divine power
Dama—restraint of the sense-organs
Dana—charity
Dand—a kind of physical exercise
Danda—a stick
Darsan (a)—vision
Dasya—service
Dasya Bhava—attitude of a servant
Daya—compassion
Deva—a celestial being
Devata—a deity; also, the Lord
Devi—Divinity in its female aspect

Dhal—pulse
Dharana—concentration
Dharma—righteous conduct
Dharma-Sankata—quandaries in Dharma
Dharma Sastra—scriptures dealing with righteous conduct
Dhvani—sound
Dhyana—meditation
Diksha Guru—the Guru by whom initiation has been given
Dirgha—elongated, long
Divya Drishti—divine perception
Divya Gandha—divine scent
Dusserah—the nine-day Hindu festival of Goddess-worship
Dvadasakshara—the twelve-lettered Mantra of Lord Krishna
Dvaita—dualism
Dvapara Yuga—the third of the four Hindu time-cycles
Dvesha—hatred

E

Ekagrata—one-pointedness of mind
Ekakshara—the monosyllable OM
Ekoham Bahu Syam—"One am I. May I be many."
Ektar Tambura—a single-stringed musical instrument

G

Gandharva—a class of celestial beings
Gandharva Vidya—the celestial science of music
Garbhadhanam—the sacred act of procreation
Gerua—ochre
Giridhar Nagar—Sri Krishna
Gopas—cowherds
Gopi Bhava—the attitude of a Gopi towards Sri Krishna, the attitude of a lover towards her beloved
Gopis—the maidens of the land of Brij
Grihastha—a householder
Grihasthasrama (Grihastha Asram)—the second of the four orders of life, the life of the householder
Guna—quality

Guru—preceptor
Gurukula—the preceptor's hermitage
Guru Mantra—the Mantra into which initiation has been given by the Guru
Guru-Parampara—the Guru-disciple-lineage
Guru-Seva—service to the Guru

H

Hatha Yogi(n)—one who practises the science of Hatha Yoga, one who has mastered the science
Havan—sacred oblations
Himavan—the legendary king of the Himalayas
Himsa—violence, injury

I

Ichha—will
Iddily—a South Indian cake made of rice and blackgram
Indra—the Lord of the celestials
Indrajala—magic
Indriya—sense-organ
Ishta Devata—favourite deity
Ishtam—same as above
Ishta Mantra—favourite Mantra, Mantra of one's chosen deity
Isvara—the Lord
Itihasas—the Hindu epics

J

Jada—insentient
Jagrat—the waking state
Jai Ramji Ki—a Hindu greeting meaning "Victory to Sri Rama"
Jai Sri Krishna—a Hindu greeting meaning "Victory to Sri Krishna"
Japa—repetition of the Lord's Name
Jiva(tman)—the individual soul
Jivanmukta—one who has realised the Self even while living
Jivanmukti—Self-realisation even while living
Jnana—Self-knowledge
Jnanabhyasa—same as Brahmabhyasa

Jnana Chakshus—divine vision
Jnana Indriyas—organs of knowledge or perception
Jnana Nishtha—same as Brahma-nishtha
Jnani(n)—a sage of wisdom
Jyotis—light

K

Kaivalya—isolated freedom, state of absolute independence
Kaivalya-Moksha—same as above
Kala—ray, digit of manifestation
Kalamas—sacred chantings of the Muslims
Kala Sakti—Divine Mother manifesting as Time
Kalatita—beyond time
Kali Yuga—the last of the four Hindu time-cycles, the present iron age
Kalpa—a period of 432,00,00,000 years
Kalpana—imagination
Kama—desire
Kamandal(u)—the water-pot of the Hindu monk
Kanta Bhava—the attitude of lover and beloved
Karana Vairagya—temporary dispassion arising out of some calamity
Karika—commentary
Karma—action operating through the Law of Cause and Effect
Karma Indriyas—organs of action
Karma-Kandi—one who observes strictly the duties ordained in the scriptures
Karma-Marga—the path of action
Karmasraya—receptacle of actions
Karma Yoga—the Yoga of selfless service
Karma Yogi(n)—one who practises Karma Yoga
Kashtha Mauna—observing silence in which thoughts are not communicated to others even in writing or by signs
Katha—a religious discourse interspersed with stories from the Hindu epics
Kaupina—loin-cloth
Kevala-Advaita—pure non-dualism

Kevala-Advaita-Jnani—one who is established in the wisdom of pure non-dualism
Kevala-Jnani—same as above
Khir—a sweet milk-pudding
Khol—a musical instrument
Kinnara—a class of celestial beings
Kirtan(a)—singing the Lord's Name
Kosha—sheath
Krishna-Prema-Rasa—the nectar of the love of Krishna
Kriya—a Hatha-Yogic exercise
Kriya-Advaita—a non-dualist in life and action
Kriyamana—current action; action performed in the current birth
Kshatriya—a member belonging to the ruling caste
Kumbhak(a)—retention of breath
Kumkum—sacred red powder worn on the forehead by Goddess-worshippers
Kundalini—the primordial cosmic energy located in the individual
Kunja—a street in Brindavan associated with Sri Krishna
Kusa-Grass—a variety of grass sacred to the Hindus
Kutir—cottage

L

Lakshya—goal
Laya—absorption
Loka—world
Loka-Sangraha—work for the uplift of the world
Likhita Japa—repetitive writing of the Lord's Name
Lila—divine sport
Lila-Avatara—incarnation for the play of divine sport
Lila-Vilasa—the splendour of divine sport
Linga Sarira—the subtle body, the astral body

M

Madhurya Bhava—same as Kanta Bhava
Maha-Bhogi—a great enjoyer
Maha Mauni—one who observes absolute silence
Maha Mudra—a Hatha Yogic exercise

Mahapurusha—a great soul
Maharaja—an emperor
Maharshi—a great seer
Mahasamadhi—final emancipation from the body and absorption in the Lord
Mahatma—a great soul
Maha-Tyagi—a great renunciate
Mahavakya—a great sentence of the Upanishads
Makesvari—the Supreme Goddess, the Consort of Lord Siva
Maitri—friendliness
Makaradhvaja—an Ayurvedic tonic
Mala—impurity
Mamata—mine-ness
Manah Kalpitam Jagat—the world is a mental creation
Manas—mind
Mandalesvar—a Hindu spiritual head
Mandali—group
Mandir—temple
Manomatram Jagat—the world appears because of the mind
Manonasa—annihilation of the mind
Mantra—an incantation
Mantra-Diksha—initiation into Mantra
Marga—path
Masjid—a Muslim shrine
Massoor-Ki-Dal—Bengal gram
Matra—unit; alone
Matrubhumi—motherland
Mauja—sweet will
Maya—the illusory power of Brahman
Mela—festival
Moha—delusion
Mohalla—locality
Moksha—liberation
Moksha-Dvara—door to liberation
Moksha-Mantra—Mantra which leads to liberation
Moksha-Samrajya-Lakshmi—the wealth of liberation

Moong-Ki-Dal—green gram
Mouna—silence
Mouni—one who observes silence
Mridanga—a musical instrument of the percussion type
Mudra—a type of exercise in Hatha Yoga
Mukta—liberated
Mukti—liberation
Muladhara Chakra—the centre of spinal energy located at the base of the spinal column
Muni—an ascetic
Murti—an idol; god
Mutt—a hermitage
Muzub—a silent sage of the highest category

N

Nada—a mystic sound
Nadi—an astral nerve
Naishthika Brahmacharin—a life-long celibate
Namasmarana—remembrance of the Lord's Name
Narayana Bhava—the attitude that Lord Narayana pervades all
Navaratri—the nine-day Hindu festival of Goddess-worship, same as Dusserah
Nayanars—a group of sixty-three South Indian saints devoted to Lord Siva
Neti-Neti—not this, not this
Nididhyasana—deep meditation
Nirakara—formless
Niranjana—spotless, immaculate
Nirguna—without attributes
Nirvana—liberation
Nirvikalpa Avastha—superconscious state where mental modifications cease to exist
Nirvikalpa Samadhi—same as above
Nirvishaya—without object
Nishkama-Bhava—mental attitude wherein there is no desire for the fruits of one's actions
Nishkama-Karma Yoga—the Yoga of selfless service

Nishtha—meditation, establishment (in a certain state)
Nitya-Mukta—one who is eternally free
Nitya-Siddha—a liberated soul of marvellous powers who is ever present on the astral plane
Nivritti—renunciation
Niyama—observances

O

Ojas—spiritual energy
Omkara—the sacred monosyllable OM which symbolises Brahman
Om Namah Sivaya—Salutations unto Lord Siva
Om Santi—Om peace
Om Tat Sat—a benediction; a solemn invocation of the divine blessing
Oordhvaretas—a Yogi who has stored up the seminal energy in the brain after sublimating the same into spiritual energy

P

Pada—word
Paise—the smallest Indian coins
Pakoda—a fried Indian dish
Panchagni Tapas—practice of austerity in the midst of five blazing fires
Pancha Kosas—the five sheaths encasing the individual soul
Panchakshara Mantra—the five-lettered Mantra of Lord Siva
Panchakshari—same as above
Para Bhakti—supreme devotion
Para Brahman—the Supreme Brahman
Paramahamsa—a sage; a category of Hindu Sannyasins
Paramatma(n)—the Supreme Soul
Parampara—lineage
Parasakti—the Supreme Goddess
Para Vairagya—supreme dispassion
Pasu-Svabhava—animal nature; bestial nature
Pativrata—a chaste lady
Pativrata-Dharma—duties of a chaste woman

Pativratyam—Chastity
Prajapati—the Creator
Prakasa—luminosity
Prakriti—Mother Nature
Pralaya—deluge
Prana—the vital air
Pranamaya Kosha—the vital sheath
Pranava—the monosyllable OM
Pranava-Nada—sound produced by the chanting of OM
Pranayama—the science of breath-control
Prarabdha—destiny
Prasthanatraya—the three authoritative scriptural books of the Hindus
Pratima—image
Pratipaksha-Bhavana—a method of mind-conquest adopted by the Raja Yogins wherein the positive forces are made to overcome the negative forces
Pratyahara—abstraction of the senses
Pratyaksha Devata—a deity whose powers are tangibly felt and experienced by the devotee
Pravritti Marga—the mundane path
Prayaschitta—atonement
Prem—love
Preyas—enjoyment
Prithivi—earth
Puja—worship
Pundit—learned man
Punya-Bhumi—holy land
Puraka—inhalation
Purana—Hindu myths and legends
Purascharana—an observance in which Japa of a Mantra is done as many lakhs of times as there are letters in the Mantra
Purna-Avatara—full incarnation
Purna-Jnani—a full-blown sage
Purna-Yogi—a full-blown Yogi
Purohit—priest
Purusha—male; the male principle in Godhead

Purvashram—the previous order of life
Pushti—nourishment

R

Raga—tune (masculine); attachment
Raga-Dvesha—attachment and repulsion, likes and dislikes
Ragini—tune (feminine)
Raja—king
Rajas—activity
Rajasuya Yajna—a kind of sacrifice performed by Hindu kings of yore
Raja Yoga—the kingly science, the eight-limbed Yoga of Maharshi Patanjali
Raja Yogi(n)—one who practises Raja Yoga, one who has attained mastery in Raja Yoga
Rama-Nama—the Name of Lord Rama
Rani—queen
Rasa-Lila—the divine sport of Lord Krishna with the maidens of Vraja
Rasogolla—a Bengali sweet
Rechaka—exhalation
Rig-Veda—one of the four Vedas
Rishi—a seer
Rudraksha—a special kind of bead threaded into a rosary, the bead symbolising the third eye of Lord Siva

S

Sadachara—righteous conduct
Sadhaka—a spiritual aspirant, a seeker
Sadhana—spiritual practice
Sadhana Chatushtaya—the fourfold qualification required of a student of Vedanta
Sadhu—a spiritual person
Sad-Viveka—righteous discrimination
Saguna—with attributes
Saguna-Mantra—a Mantra pertaining to a deity with form
Sahaja-Advaita-Nishtha—by nature established in the non-dual state of superconsciousness

Sahaja Samadhi—same as above
Sahasranama—the thousand Names of the Lord
Saivism—the cult of Siva-worship
Saivite—a person belonging to the cult of Saivism
Sakara—with form
Sakhi Bhava—the attitude of a companion
Sakhya Bhava—same as above
Sakti—power; the feminine aspect of Divinity
Sakti-Sanchar(a)—transference of power by a developed Yogi
Saktism—the cult of Goddess-worship
Sala—a term of abuse
Sama—tranquillity
Samadhi—superconsciousness
Samadhi Jnani—a sage who is ever immersed in a state of superconsciousness
Sama-Drishti—equal vision
Samata—mental balance
Samhara-Sakti—power of destruction
Sammohana-Vidya—the science of black magic
Samsara—the round of births and deaths
Samsara-Chakra—the birth-and-death cycle
Samskara—an impression in the subconscious mind
Samyama—the simultaneous occurrence of concentration, meditation and Samadhi in a developed Yogi
Sanatana Dharma—the eternal religion, Hinduism
Sanchita—the accumulated storehouse of Karma in each individual soul
Sangita—music
Sankalpa—thought, imagination
Sankalpa-Vikalpa—thought and counter-thought
Sankhya—a system of Hindu philosophy founded by Kapila
Sankirtan(a)—divine music
Sannyasa—renunciation
Sannyasin—a renunciate, a monk
Santa—peaceful
Santa Bhava—peaceful attitude

Santi—peace
Sapta-Rishi—the seven Rishis or seers of Hindu mythology
Sarangi—a stringed musical instrument
Sashtanga Namaskar(a)—flat prostration in which eight limbs of thc body touch the ground
Sastra—scripture
Sat—Existence Absolute
Satchidananda—Existence Absolute, Knowledge Absolute, Bliss Absolute
Satee-Dharma—duties of a wife
Satguru—the true preceptor
Satsanga—company of the holy
Sattva—purity
Sattvic—pure
Satya(m)—truth
Satyam Jnanam Anantam—Truth-Knowledge-Infinity
Satya Yuga—the Age of Truth, the first of the four Hindu time-cycles
Sesha—balance, remainder, what is left
Seva Kunja—a place in Brindavan associated with Sri Krishna
Saucha—cleanliness
Siddha—one who possesses Siddhis or psychic powers
Siddhi—psychic power
Siksha Guru—the preceptor who teaches the scriptures
Siva—the destructive aspect of Godhead, the third of the Hindu Trinity; also, the Supreme Lord
Sivanandam—the Bliss of Siva
Sivoham—a Vedantic assertion meaning "I am Siva"
Sloka—scriptural verse
Smarana—remembrance
Smriti—that which has been remembered; works of law-givers like Manu which are inferior to the Sruti or revealed scriptures in point of religious authority
Soham—a Vedantic assertion meaning "I am He"
Sraddha—faith
Sreyas—religious merit
Srishti-Krama—the order of creation

Srishti-Sakti—the power of creation
Srivatsa—an ornament adorning the body of Lord Vishnu
Sruti—revealed scripture
Sthiti-Sakti—the power of maintenance
Stotra—hymn
Suddha—pure
Suddha-Bhavana—pure attitude
Suddha Manas—pure mind
Sudra—the servant class, the lowest of the Hindu castes
Surya Mantra—the Mantra of the Sun-god
Sushumna Nadi—the chief among the astral tubes in the human body running inside the spinal column
Sushupti—deep sleep
Svabhava—nature
Svapna—dream
Svarajya—freedom
Svarga—heaven
Svarupa—essence; the essential nature of Brahman
Svarupa Sthiti—the natural state, the state of being established in Brahman

T

Tamas—inertia
Tamasic—dull, lazy, inert
Tambur(a)—a musical instrument
Tantrik(a)—pertaining to an esoteric cult among the Hindus
Tapas—austerity
Tapascharya—Performance of austerity
Tapasvi(n)—an ascetic
Tapasya—same as Tapas
Tattva—principle; the Supreme Principle or Brahman
Tattva-Jnana—Knowledge of the Supreme Principle or Brahman
Tat Tvam Asi—a Vedantic assertion meaning 'That Thou Art'
Tirtha—a sacred place
Tivra Vairagya—extreme dispassion
Tratak(a)—an eye exercise to improve mental concentration and eyesight

Treta Yuga—the second of the four Hindu ages or time-cycles
Trimurtis—the Hindu trinity, viz., Brahma, Vishnu and Siva
Tulasi Mala—a rosary whose beads are made of the stalks of the holy Basil
Turiya—the state of superconsciousness, the fourth state transcending the waking, dreaming and deep sleep states
Turiya Avastha—same as above
Tushti—contentment
Tyaga—sacrifice, renunciation
Tyaga-Abhimana—attachment to renunciation
Tyagi—a renunciate

U

Udara Vritti—generous nature
Uddharsha—excessive merriment
Udgitha—sonorous prayer prescribed in the Chhandogya Upanishad to be sung aloud
Upades(a)—spiritual advice
Upa-Gurus—secondary preceptors
Upasana—worship

V

Vaidika Dharma—duties as prescribed in the Vedas
Vaidya—a doctor
Vaidya Sastra—the medical science
Vaikuntha (Dhama)—the abode of Lord Vishnu
Vairagya—dispassion
Vairagi—a sect of renunciates who are worshippers of Rama and found mostly around Ayodhya
Vaishnavism—the cult of worshipping Lord Vishnu
Vaishnavite—a devotee of Lord Vishnu
Vak Indriya—the sense-organ of speech
Vanaprastha—the third of the four Hindu orders of life
Varnashrama—the classification of castes and stages of life in orthodox Hinduism
Vartamana—pertaining to the present
Varuna—the deity presiding over the water-element

Varuna-Astra—water-missile
Vasana—latent, subtle impression
Vasana-Kshaya—the destruction of subtle desires
Vasudevah Sarvam Iti—All this, indeed, is Vasudeva or the Lord
Vatsalya Bhava—a mother's attitude towards her child
Veda—the revealed scripture of the Hindus containing the Upanishads
Vedanta—(lit.) the end of the Vedas; the school of thought based primarily on the Vedic Upanishads
Vedantin—a follower of the Vedanta philosophy
Vedic—pertaining to the Veda
Vibhuti—sacred white ash worn on the forehead by devotees of Siva
Vichara—right enquiry
Vidya—knowledge, science, art
Vidya-Dana—charity of knowledge
Vidyadhara—a class of celestial beings
Vijaya Muhurta—the hour of victory
Vikshepa—tossing of mind
Vina—a stringed musical instrument
Vinaya—humility or sense of propriety
Virakta—a man of detachment
Virat Svarup(a)—the macrocosm, the cosmic form of the Lord
Virochana—a leader of the Hindu school of epicurean philosophy
Virya—seminal energy
Vishaya—object of perception, sense-object
Vishayasakta—clinging to sense-objects
Vishnu-Sahasranama—the thousand Names of Lord Vishnu
Vishta—faeces
Visishtadvaita—qualified monism
Visva-Prem—cosmic love
Visvarupa Darsan(a)—vision of the Lord in His cosmic form
Viveka—discrimination
Vraja—the land around Mathura and Brindavan
Vrata—religious observance
Vritti—a wave in the mind-lake

Vyabhicharini Bhakti—the devotion of a prostitute, changing loyalty
Vyavahara—worldly activity
Vyavahara Jnani—a sage who takes part in worldly activity
Vyavaharic Buddhi—worldly intellect

Y

Yadava—a member belonging to the Yadava dynasty
Yajna—sacrifice
Yama—the third limb of Maharshi Patanjali's Raja Yoga pertaining to ethical perfection; the Lord of Death
Yamala Arjuna—a species of trees
Yoga—(lit.) union; union of the individual soul with the Supreme Soul; any course which makes for such union
Yogasana—a Yoga posture
Yogesvar(a)—the Lord of the Yogis
Yogi(n)—one who practises Yoga; one who is established in Yoga
Yogini—feminine form of Yogi
Yoni—source, womb

Z

Zamindar—a rich landlord